THEORIES OF
PERSONALITY

THIRD EDITION

THEORIES OF
PERSONALITY

THIRD EDITION

DUANE SCHULTZ
UNIVERSITY OF SOUTH FLORIDA

Brooks/Cole Publishing Company

Monterey, California

Brooks/Cole Publishing Company
A Division of Wadsworth, Inc.

Printed in the United States of America

10   9   8   7   6   5   4   3   2   1

Library of Congress Cataloging-in-Publication Data

Schultz, Duane P. [date]
    Theories of personality

    Bibliography: p.
    Includes index.
    1. Personality. I. Title.
BF698.S36   1985   155.2   85-21361
ISBN 0-534-05544-3

Sponsoring Editor: Claire Verduin
Production Editors: C. Diane Brown, S. M. Bailey
Manuscript Editor: Peggy Hoover
Permissions Editor: Carline Haga
Interior Design: Vicki Van Deventer
Cover Design and Illustration: Ron Grauer
Art Coordinator: Michele Judge
Interior Illustration: Ron Grauer, Maggie Stevens
Photo Editor: Judy Blamer
Photo Researcher: Suzi Shepherd
Typesetting: G & S Typesetters, Inc., Austin, TX
Cover Printing: Phoenix Color Corporation, Long Island City, NY
Printing and Binding: The Maple-Vail Book Manufacturing Group, Manchester, PA

(Credits continue on p. 478.)

To Sydney Ellen

Preface

This text is written expressly for the undergraduate student who has had no previous exposure to personality theories. My purpose is to inform and interest people who know little about the topic and to make their difficult task of learning about personality theories easier. I have not written for instructors or researchers in the field. Rather, I offer the general outline and flavor of various theories, a clear map or picture of the forest, not an exhaustive analysis of every tree.

The theories are discussed as objectively and fairly as possible. The book is not an indoctrination to any one point of view but an introduction to diverse points of view. The students may well form their own biases, but they should not feel compelled to accept mine.

Because the beginning undergraduate student must be aware of the diversity of approaches to the understanding of personality, I have included theorists representing psychoanalytic, neopsychoanalytic, trait, life-span, humanistic, cognitive, and behavioral approaches, as well as both clinical and laboratory work. The last chapter deals with theorists who treat personality in limited-domain fashion by focusing on only one personality construct rather than attempting to account for the total personality.

Where biographical data are sufficient, I have speculated on how the development of various theories might have been influenced by specific events and experiences in the theorists' personal and professional lives. Students are often surprised and fascinated by how closely a theoretical position may reflect early experiences in the life of a theorist. This apparent correspondence suggests that the development of science through theory construction is not always objective but rather can be influenced by personal experiences that are refined and extended by more rational processes.

Each theory is discussed as a unity. Although I recognize the value of an "issues" or "problems" approach that compares a number of theories on specific points, its usefulness is greater with more advanced students. The issues-oriented book may not permit the beginning student to synthesize the many facets of a theory and to gain an understanding of its essence. In this book, each theory is organized and presented in the way that seems clearest for that theory; I have not attempted to force the divergent points of view into a standard format. However, the last four sections in the discussion of each theory are the image of human nature, assessment, research, and a final comment.

Except for placing Freud first, in recognition of his chronological priority, I have not arranged the theories in any order of perceived importance. They are, however, arranged in eight categories. This approach allows for a more meaningful presentation of the individual systems. The organization places a theory in the perspective of competing viewpoints, each with its own assumptions, definitions, and methods for studying personality. Each group of theories is introduced by a brief description of its major themes.

The changes in this third edition reflect comments from instructors and students who used the previous editions, reviews obtained from psychologists teaching in the area of personality, and my own continuing growth as a student of the field.

A major change is the addition of material on assessment and research in personality. An overview of assessment and research methods is provided in Chapter 1, along with specific examples from some of the theories we will be discussing.

In the new assessment section for each chapter, the specific techniques developed by the theorist are described, and in the new research section, a representative coverage of the relevant research is offered. The intent is not to be exhaustive but to show the student the kind and extent of empirical support that is available, as well as the approach to research chosen by the theorist.

In the final commentary section of each chapter, material has been added on the criticisms and contributions of each theory, to provide a more comprehensive evaluation of the weaknesses and strengths of each position.

An afterword has been added to the book, in which I attempt to put in perspective the diversity, controversies, and contributions to be found among the personality theorists.

This edition also offers expanded coverage of the following topics: Jung's psychological types, Horney's feminine psychology, Erikson's epigenetic principle of maturation, Rogers' organismic valuing process, Maslow's metamotivation and metapathology, Bandura's concept of self-efficacy, Rotter's notion of interpersonal trust, McClelland's achievement motivation as it applies to women, and the behavioral and cultural correlates of Witkin's concept of psychological differentiation. By popular demand, the theories of Sullivan and Festinger have been deleted.

A number of pedagogical aids have been added to each chapter: outlines, glossaries,* summaries, suggested readings, review questions, and illustrations. A complete reference list appears at the back of the book, and a test item booklet is available for instructors.

I would like to thank the many students and colleagues who have written to me about the book and have offered suggestions for this new edition, especially Steve Dawes of Clemson University, Kathleen McCormick of Ocean County College (New Jersey), Donna Raymer of the College of Lake County (Illinois), Thomas Rocklin of Texas Christian University, and Kathryn M. Ryan of Lycoming College. I am also grateful to the following reviewers of this newest edition: Gordon Henley of St. John's University, Kathleen McCormick, Cheryl Newberg of Lycoming College, and Brian Yates of American University.

My wife, Sydney Ellen, deserves my greatest thanks, not only for her research skills, but also for providing both criticism and encouragement when needed.

Duane Schultz

---

*Important terms in each chapter are boldfaced in the text and defined in the end-of-chapter glossary.

Contents

CHAPTER 1   **The Study of Personality: Assessment, Research, and Theory   1**

The diversity of personality theories   2
Why study theories of personality?   3
The place of personality in psychology   5
The definition of personality   8
The role of assessment in the study of personality   9
The role of research in the study of personality   15
The role of theory in the study of personality   22
Images of human nature: Issues in personality theory   25
Summary   28
Glossary   30
Review questions   30
Suggested reading   31

PART 1   **The Psychoanalytic Approach   33**

CHAPTER 2   **Sigmund Freud   35**

The life of Freud (1856–1939)   36
Instincts: The propelling force of personality   39
The structure of personality: Id, ego, and superego   42

Anxiety: A threat to the ego   45
Defenses against anxiety   47
The psychosexual stages of personality development   50
Freud's image of human nature   56
Assessment in Freud's theory   57
Research in Freud's theory   60
A final commentary   63
Summary   *65*
Glossary   *67*
Review questions   *69*
Suggested reading   *70*

PART 2   The Neopsychoanalytic Approach   71

CHAPTER 3   Carl Jung   73

The life of Jung (1875–1961)   74
Psychic energy   77
The systems of personality   78
The development of the personality   85
Interaction among parts of the personality   89
Jung's image of human nature   89
Assessment in Jung's theory   90
Research in Jung's theory   92
A final commentary   94
Summary   *96*
Glossary   *98*
Review questions   *99*
Suggested reading   *99*

CHAPTER 4   Alfred Adler   100

The life of Adler (1870–1937)   101
Inferiority feelings: The source of human striving   103
Striving for superiority: The ultimate goal   106
The development of a lifestyle   107
Social interest   109
The influence of birth order   111
Adler's image of human nature   113
Assessment in Adler's theory   114
Research in Adler's theory   117
A final commentary   119
Summary   *121*
Glossary   *123*

Review questions *123*
Suggested reading *124*

CHAPTER 5   Karen Horney   125

The life of Horney (1885–1952)   126
Safety and satisfaction: The needs of childhood   128
Basic anxiety: The foundation of neurosis   130
Neurotic needs   131
Neurotic trends   132
The idealized self-image   135
The flight from womanhood: Feminine psychology   136
Horney's image of human nature   138
Assessment in Horney's theory   139
Research in Horney's theory   140
A final commentary   141
Summary   *142*
Glossary   *143*
Review questions   *144*
Suggested reading   *144*

CHAPTER 6   Erich Fromm   145

The life of Fromm (1900–1980)   146
Freedom versus security: The basic human dilemma   148
The development of the personality in childhood   151
Psychological needs   153
Productive and nonproductive character types   155
The influence of the society   157
Fromm's image of human nature   157
Assessment in Fromm's theory   158
Research in Fromm's theory   159
A final commentary   161
Summary   *162*
Glossary   *164*
Review questions   *165*
Suggested reading   *165*

CHAPTER 7   Henry Murray   166

The life of Murray (1893–   )   168
The basic principles of personology   170
The divisions of personality: Id, superego, and ego   171
Needs: The motivation of behavior   172
Complexes: The development of the personality   176
Murray's image of human nature   178

Assessment in Murray's theory   179
Research in Murray's theory   181
A final commentary   183
Summary   185
Glossary   187
Review questions   188
Suggested reading   189

PART 3   The Trait Approach   191

CHAPTER 8   Gordon Allport   193

The life of Allport (1897–1967)   195
The nature of personality: Consciousness, growth, and uniqueness   197
Personality traits   199
Personality and motivation   201
The proprium: The unique self   205
Personality in childhood   207
Personality in adulthood   207
Allport's image of human nature   208
Assessment in Allport's theory   209
Research in Allport's theory   212
A final commentary   214
Summary   215
Glossary   217
Review questions   218
Suggested reading   218

CHAPTER 9   Raymond Cattell   219

The life of Cattell (1905–   )   221
The trait approach to personality   223
Source traits: The Sixteen Personality Factor Questionnaire   225
The dynamic organization of the personality   227
Chronic anxiety   229
The influences of heredity and environment   230
The stages of personality development   231
Cattell's image of human nature   232
Assessment in Cattell's theory   233
Research in Cattell's theory   236
A final commentary   238
Summary   240
Glossary   242
Review questions   243
Suggested reading   243

PART 4   The Life-Span Approach   245

CHAPTER 10   **Erik Erikson**   247

The life of Erikson (1902–   )   248
Psychosocial development: Ways of coping with conflicts   251
Basic strengths   258
Erikson's image of human nature   259
Assessment in Erikson's theory   260
Research in Erikson's theory   261
A final commentary   265
Summary   266
Glossary   268
Review questions   268
Suggested reading   269

PART 5   The Humanistic Approach   271

CHAPTER 11   **Carl Rogers**   273

The life of Rogers (1902–   )   275
Actualization: The basic human tendency   277
The experiential world   278
The development of the self   279
Characteristics of the fully functioning person   282
Rogers' image of human nature   283
Assessment in Rogers' theory   285
Research in Rogers' theory   286
A final commentary   290
Summary   292
Glossary   294
Review questions   294
Suggested reading   295

CHAPTER 12   **Abraham Maslow**   296

The life of Maslow (1908–1970)   297
Motivation and personality: The hierarchy of needs   300
Metamotivation: The development of the self-actualizing person   305
Characteristics of the self-actualizing person   307
The failure to self-actualize   310
Maslow's image of human nature   311
Assessment in Maslow's theory   312
Research in Maslow's theory   314
A final commentary   316

Summary   317
Glossary   318
Review questions   319
Suggested reading   319

PART 6   The Cognitive Approach   321

CHAPTER 13   George Kelly   323

The life of Kelly (1905–1967)   325
Personal constructs: Ways of anticipating and interpreting life events   327
Kelly's image of human nature   335
Assessment in Kelly's theory   336
Research in Kelly's theory   339
A final commentary   341
Summary   343
Glossary   345
Review questions   345
Suggested reading   346

PART 7   The Behavioral Approach   347

CHAPTER 14   B. F. Skinner   349

The life of Skinner (1904–   )   353
Reinforcement: The basis of behavior   355
Schedules of reinforcement   359
Successive aproximation: The shaping of behavior   361
Superstitious behavior   362
The self-control of behavior   363
Applications of operant conditioning   363
Skinner's image of human nature   366
Assessment in Skinner's theory   368
Research in Skinner's theory   370
A final commentary   372
Summary   373
Glossary   376
Review questions   376
Suggested reading   377

CHAPTER 15   Albert Bandura   378

The life of Bandura (1925–   )   380
Modeling: The basis of observational learning   380

The processes of observational learning 384
The self 387
The developmental stages of modeling 390
Modifying learned behavior 390
Ethical issues in behavior modification 394
Bandura's image of human nature 395
Assessment in Bandura's theory 396
Research in Bandura's theory 396
A final commentary 397
Summary 398
Glossary 400
Review questions 401
Suggested reading 401

CHAPTER 16 Julian Rotter 402

The life of Rotter (1916–) 404
Social learning theory 404
The motivation of behavior 409
Internal versus external locus of control 411
Interpersonal trust 412
Rotter's image of human nature 412
Assessment in Rotter's theory 413
Research in Rotter's theory 415
A final commentary 416
Summary 417
Glossary 419
Review questions 419
Suggested reading 420

PART 8 The Limited-Domain Approach 421

CHAPTER 17 Limited-Domain Theories 425

David McClelland: The need for achievement 426
Herman Witkin: Psychological differentiation 436
Arnold Buss and Robert Plomin: A temperament theory 444
Summary 449
Glossary 452
Review questions 452
Suggested reading 453

The Study of Personality: An Afterword 455

References 459
Index 469

CHAPTER 1

The Study of Personality: Assessment, Research, and Theory

The diversity of personality theories
Why study theories of personality?
The place of personality in psychology
The definition of personality
The role of assessment in the study of personality
  Self-report assessment techniques
  Projective techniques
  Other techniques of personality assessment
The role of research in the study of personality
  The clinical approach
  The experimental approach
  The correlational approach
The role of theory in the study of personality
  Formal versus personal theories
Images of human nature: Issues in personality theory
Summary
Glossary
Review questions
Suggested reading

The diversity of personality theories

Many students take their first course in psychology excited at the prospect of learning all about personality—their own or someone else's. They are often surprised and sometimes disappointed to discover that personality is only one part of psychology, and a small part at that.

In the standard thick and heavy introductory psychology textbook, perhaps only two or three chapters out of 20 or so are devoted to the topic that may have first sparked students' interest in the field. They find themselves reading instead about the nervous system, drives, perception, learning, thinking, and statistics. If my own experience in teaching the first course in psychology is any indication, many students feel almost cheated, as though they had signed up for one course and were given something else instead.

That will not be a problem with the course you are now beginning or with this textbook. Both are devoted to theories that have been devised to explain the nature of personality. However, before you experience a different kind of disappointment, there is one point on which you should be warned. Reflected in the title of this book, *Theories of Personality*, is the fact that there is a plurality of ways of looking at the topic. There is not one single theory, not even the best known (Freud's), that you can turn to with absolute assurance of finding the ultimate answer to the riddle of personality.

You will find, in the pages to follow, a lack of consensus among psychologists regarding the nature of personality. There is no single conception of the subject on which all, or even most, psychologists agree. Indeed, it is even difficult to find agreement on the definition of personality, much less on its nature and characteristics. Instead, many definitions and theories of personality are developed, expounded, and defended with equal passion and conviction.

We will discuss 18 theories of personality, each with a different view of what personality is all about. Lest you be overwhelmed by what may seem to be a bewildering array of theories and a lack of agreement among them, we should note that there are some common themes.

It is possible to organize these theories into eight categories, each with its own assumptions, methods, and definitions of personality. Although there are differences among the theories within each group, they share enough characteristics to distinguish them from other approaches.

The eight approaches to the personality theories described in this book are: psychoanalytic, neopsychoanalytic, trait, life-span, humanistic, cognitive, behavioral, and limited-domain. No doubt you are familiar with most of these terms from other courses in psychology. In some cases, these viewpoints represent major forces active throughout psychology, not just in the area of personality.

Although this organization of theories will allow for a more meaningful presentation of individual systems of personality, it will not supply you with a single answer to the question "What is personality?" There is no neat or simple answer—at least not yet. The complexity of the subject matter is evident in the diversity of the attempts to come to grips with it. What you will find in this book is a discussion of some of the better answers thus far offered. As to which, if any, of these theories or approaches is the best or ultimate answer, who is to say? Only those persons already committed, intellectually and emotionally, to one position, and thus perhaps no longer able to take an objective view, can answer that question with certainty.

This is not to suggest that one of these theories may turn out to be correct and all the others wrong. It is not so simple as that. That the theories conflict with one another does not necessarily indicate that they are misguided and destined to fall into disrepute. Any one theory may be partly correct or all of them may be partly correct, and the final answer may involve the combination of part-truths into yet another theory. Thus, although it may eventually transpire that none of these theories will suffice as the complete explanation, for now they represent the highest level of development of the part of psychology that attempts to understand the human personality.

Why study theories of personality?

Because psychology is not yet in a position to agree on a common definition and theory of the nature of personality, why, you may ask, should you spend the effort and time demanded by this course? Of what value is the study of personality theories to you?

The lack of agreement among theorists does not necessarily imply that the various theories are not useful. Psychologists do not agree on a single definition of intelligence, but that has not prevented them from using the concept of intelligence, through various means of assessing it, to understand and predict human behavior. So it is with personality, as we shall see in a later section on personality assessment.

Each of the personality theories offers tantalizing insights into human nature—conclusions based, for the most part, on years of probing, questioning, and listening to what people have to say, or observing their behavior under the rigorous conditions of the experimental laboratory. These theories are the work of highly perceptive and intelligent individuals, each of whom has looked closely at humankind through the uniquely ground lens of his or her theoretical viewpoint.

All of the theorists have something important, impressive, and provocative to say about the nature of human beings. If they do not always agree, we must look to three factors to explain the dissension: (1) the complexity of the subject matter, (2) the differing historical and personal contexts in which each theory was formulated, and (3) the fact that psychology is such a young discipline, a recent entry in the catalog of sciences. The study of personality is an even more recent entry, having begun in the 1930s. In the history of science, a span of 50 years is a very short time.

Indeed, the very facts of its newness and complexity make personality a fascinating subject for study. It is not a closed or finished subject in which one simply learns the rules and definitions and then moves on to something else. On the contrary, the study of personality is still evolving, and, for those who like the challenge and excitement of exploring areas not yet fully mapped, there could be no more appropriate or useful study than personality.

Interest in personality theories today is strong. An article in the 1984 *Annual Review of Psychology* states that in the 1980s "there has been an increase in both the amount and the vigor of theorizing about personality, as well as an increasingly positive attitude toward the utility of this endeavor" (Lanyon, 1984, p. 669). Personality theories remain a fundamental part of psychology's continuing effort to understand human nature.

There is also a personal reason for this course of study: natural curiosity about our own behavior. Why do we act and think and feel as we do? Why do you respond to a certain event in one way and your friend in another way?

Why is one person aggressive and another inhibited, one courageous and another fearful, one sociable and another shy? What makes us the way we are and our brother or sister—reared in the same house—totally different? Why do some people seem so successful at life in terms of their friendships, careers, and marriages, while others, perhaps with equal potential, move from one failure to another?

Surely the need to understand ourselves, the curiosity about our motives and fears, is strong in most of us. In examining the various approaches to personality, you may achieve at least a modest beginning to the difficult and usually lifelong task of knowing yourself.

Another reason for studying personality theories is a practical one. No matter what kind of career you undertake when you leave college, you will be working with and for other people. Some understanding of the nature of the human personality will enhance the interpersonal relationships that are so important to your success. The ability to get along well with others may be as vital to your advancement as your technical skills and managerial abilities.

Research in the field of industrial/organizational psychology has demonstrated the importance of this idea. In a study of several thousand white-collar workers to determine why people were fired from their jobs, it was found that only 10 percent were dismissed because they were unable to perform their job duties. The rest, a staggering 90 percent, were fired because they could not get along with co-workers and supervisors. Another study showed that 14 percent of the executives who lost their jobs had been fired for inadequate job performance, whereas 76 percent had been fired because of problems in getting along with others (Schultz & Schultz, 1986).

This is not to suggest that this course or this textbook will make you an expert on personality, give you the ability to succeed in any job, or make you the life of the party. What the study of personality theories can do is provide an awareness and an understanding of the forces and factors that constitute personality in yourself and in other people.

Should you be considering a career in psychology, especially in clinical or counseling psychology, this course will have even greater practical value. A survey of universities that award the Master of Arts or Master of Science degree in clinical psychology revealed that 74 percent of these schools consider a course in personality theories to be a crucial part of the training. The study of personality theories is also rated as of major importance by 70 percent of the hospitals, clinics, and mental-health centers surveyed (Annis, Tucker & Baker, 1984).

There is one additional reason for the study of personality—perhaps the most vital and compelling reason of all. When we examine the multitude of crises and problems confronting us in the final years of the 20th century, we see one root cause: human beings themselves.

Consider some of the problems that we face today: threat of nuclear war, environmental decay, overpopulation, crime, terrorism, starvation, emotional sickness. The human misery these problems provoke and reflect is evident all around us.

Perhaps these conditions can be ameliorated through a more fully developed understanding of human nature. Abraham Maslow, whose theory we will describe in Chapter 12, wrote: "If we improve human nature we improve all, for we remove the principal causes of world disorder" (Maslow, 1957, p. 32). Only through a truer understanding of ourselves and those around us can we better cope with the problems of modern life. This may be more important than achieving a higher standard of living and certainly more vital than producing new weapons or technological breakthroughs. History has shown repeatedly that advances in technology have disastrous consequences when put to use by greedy, selfish, fearful, or hate-filled people. Thus, because humanity's greatest hope may lie in an improved understanding of itself, the study of personality may well be psychology's most important endeavor.

The place of personality in psychology

Because of the importance of the study of personality, and of its primary role in the understanding of behavior, it seems quite natural to assume that the field of personality has occupied a prominent position in psychology throughout the history of the field. Indeed, it might reasonably be assumed that personality is what psychology is all about. This is not the case. Personality is not the dominant emphasis in psychology today. For more than half of psychology's history as a science, it paid relatively little attention to personality.

Psychology emerged as an independent and primarily experimental science out of an amalgamation of certain trends in philosophy and physiology. The birth of the new discipline took place more than a century ago in Germany and was primarily the work of Wilhelm Wundt, who began psychology's first laboratory in 1879.

The new science of psychology was directed toward the analysis of conscious experience into its elemental components, and its method was strongly modeled after the approach taken by the natural sciences. Physics and chemistry were, so it seemed, unlocking all the secrets of the physical universe by reducing the material world to its basic elements and studying each of those elements. If, it was argued, the material world could be understood by the method of reduction—breaking it down into elements—why couldn't the mental universe, the mind, be studied in the same way?

The method by which physics and chemistry pursue their work is the experimental method. So convinced was Wundt of the efficacy of this approach that he studied only those psychological processes that could be investigated by the experimental method—for example, reaction time, the time taken for various conscious processes to occur. Thus, Wundt and others of his time who were concerned with studying human nature were greatly affected by the example of the natural-science approach.

In this way, researchers proceeded to study the mind. Because they believed they could use only the experimental method, they were limited to the study of those mental processes that could be affected by some external stimulus capable of being manipulated and controlled by the experimenter. In practice, that constraint restricted them to the study of sensory-perceptual processes and of other experience of quite limited dimensions. There was little room in this approach for consideration of a multidimensional construct such as personality. The topic, complex and vague, was not compatible with either the subject matter or the methodology of the new science of psychology.

In the early decades of the 20th century a revolution occurred in American psychology, directed against the work of Wilhelm Wundt. The new movement, *behaviorism*—led by the psychologist John B. Watson—opposed Wundt's focus on conscious experience. (At approximately the same time, a German movement, Gestalt psychology, was also revolting against the Wundtian approach. Our focus, however, is on behaviorism and the uniquely American form of psychology that it shaped.) Even more devoted to a natural-science approach than Wundt, Watson argued that psychology, if it was to become a science, must focus only on the tangible aspects of human beings: that which can be seen, heard, recorded, and measured. In short, only overt behavior could be the legitimate topic of psychology. Watson's revolution was highly successful; his definition of psychology as the "science of behavior" became the standard for many decades.

Consciousness, Watson said, cannot be seen or experimented upon, and so, like the older concept of soul, it is meaningless for science. The psychologist must deal only with what he or she can see and manipulate and measure, and that means only the external stimulus and the subject's response to it. According to Watson, whatever happens inside the organism after the stimulus is presented and before the response is made cannot be seen or experimented upon and is, as a result, sheer speculation of no scientific interest.

Behaviorism presents a mechanistic image of human beings, who are seen as well-ordered machines responding automatically to external stimuli. It has been said that behaviorists depict a person as a vending machine. Stimuli are fed in and appropriate conditioned responses (learned from past experiences) spill out. Personality, in this view, is nothing more than the accumulation of learned responses, or "habit systems," a view developed by B. F. Skinner (Chapter 14). Personality is reduced to what can be seen and observed objectively, and there is no place in such a system for consciousness or for the unconscious. However, we shall see in Part 7, "The Behavioral Approach," that consciousness has returned to psychology in contemporary derivatives of Watsonian behaviorism.

Where, in this early behavioral approach, were all those notions, feelings, and confusions that come to mind when you use the word *personality*? Where was the consciousness that you experience every moment you are awake? Where were those unconscious forces that sometimes seem to move you in mysterious ways and over which you feel no sense of control?

These aspects of human nature were dealt with in another area of inquiry, one that began independently of Wundt and experimental psychology. They were investigated by Sigmund Freud and what he called *psychoanalysis*. There seems no doubt that much of contemporary personality theory has been influenced more by Freud than by any psychologist. Notice that I did not say any *other* psychologist.

Psychoanalysis and psychology are not synonymous or interchangeable terms. Freud was not a psychologist by training. He was a physician in private practice, working with persons suffering emotional disturbances. Though trained as a scientist, he did not use psychology's method of experimentation in his work. Instead, he developed his theory of personality on the basis of *clinical observation* of his patients. That is, through a lengthy series of psychoanalytic sessions, Freud applied his creative interpretation to what the patients told him of their feelings and past experiences, both actual and fantasized. While his work can certainly be considered scientific (in the broad sense of the term), it was far removed from the rigorous experimental laboratory investigation of the elements of behavior, whether defined in Wundtian or in behavioral terms.

Under the impetus of Freud's psychoanalytic approach, the first small group of personality theorists developed unique conceptions of human nature outside the mainstream of academic experimental psychology. These theorists, following the neopsychoanalytic approach, focused on the whole person as he or she functions (or tries to function) in the real world, rather than on elements of behavior (stimulus-response units) as studied in the laboratory. Further, these early personality theorists assumed or accepted the existence of both conscious and unconscious forces. Such assumptions were anathema to the behaviorists, who accepted the existence of nothing they could not see. As a result of their emphases and methods, these initial personality theorists had to be speculative in their work, relying more on inference based on observations of patients' behavior than on the quantitative and experimental operations dictated by experimental psychology.

Thus, we see that psychology and the study of personality began in two entirely separate traditions, using different methods and pursuing different aims.

This is not to suggest that experimental psychology in its early years totally ignored personality. Aspects of personality were being studied (primarily in the area of the measurement of individual differences), but there did not exist a psychology of personality as an area of specialization. Personality did not have a separate identity, as did child psychology or social psychology.

It was not until the mid-1930s that the study of personality became formalized and systematized in American psychology. Professional books appeared, universities offered courses, research was begun, and there was a growing recognition that psychoanalysis—or at least some aspects of it—could be incorporated into psychology to form the basis of a scientific study of personality.

Experimental psychology has made increasing use of certain concepts from Freudian theory and its derivatives, and psychoanalysis is more and more aware of the benefits of the experimental method, but there has not been a full merging of or agreement between the two approaches. They began as separate traditions and so, for the most part, they remain. We shall see examples of both approaches, and others, in the theories to follow. Each approach offers advantages, and one of the basic issues in psychology today is the question of which approach may ultimately prove to be of greater value. Each has a definite contribution to make, and all must be given an open and impartial hearing.

The definition of personality

The lack of agreement about the nature of personality and which approach to studying it is most effective is reflected by an equal amount of disagreement with regard to the word itself. In his classic study of personality, Gordon Allport (Chapter 8) discussed some 50 definitions of **personality** (Allport, 1937). Rather than describing these and the many definitions offered since his work, let us try to relate "personality" to our own, everyday usage of the term. It is a word that we all use, however loosely or inaccurately, and that we all feel we know the meaning of. And perhaps we do.

One psychologist suggested that we can get a fairly good idea of the meaning of the word *personality* if we closely examine what we intend and encompass every time we use the word *I* (Adams, 1954). When you say *I*, you are, in effect, summing up everything about yourself—your likes and dislikes, preferences and penchants, fears and loathings, virtues and weaknesses. The word *I* is what defines you as an individual, as a person separate and apart from all the other individuals in the world.

We could, in our effort to define the word more precisely, look to its source. *Personality* derives from the Latin word *persona*, which refers to the masks used by actors in the Greek theater. It is easy to see how the word *persona* came to refer to an outward appearance, a public face that individuals display to those around them.

Based on its derivation, then, we might conclude that personality refers to those external and visible aspects of a person that other people can see. Thus, a person's personality would be defined in terms of the impression that he or she makes on others—that is, what the person appears to be. The first definition of personality in a standard college dictionary is in accord with that derivation: the visible aspect of one's character as it impresses others.

But is that all we mean when we use the word *personality*? Are we talking only about what we can actually see, what a person displays to us? Does personality refer solely to the facade, the mask, the role that we play for other people? Most of us, I think, mean more than that when we use the term. We are usually referring to many attributes of an individual—a sum total or constellation of various characteristics including more than just surface appearances. We refer to a host of subjective or internal characteristics or traits as well, ones that we may not be able to see directly or that a person may try to hide from us—and that we may try to hide from others.

We may also, in our use of the word *personality*, refer to enduring characteristics. We assume a degree of stability and predictability in a person's personality. However, while we recognize that a friend may be calm much of the time, we know that he or she can also be excited, nervous, or even on the verge of panic at other times. Personality, therefore, is not necessarily rigid and unchanging. It can vary with the situation. This idea has led personality theorists to recognize that they must consider not only the individual's internal characteristics, but also the situation and the interaction between them to adequately account for behavior.

We may also feel that personality is unique to each of us. While we recognize similarities among people, we sense that individuals possess special properties or combinations of properties that distinguish them from one another. Thus, in everyday life, we tend to think of personality as an enduring and unique cluster of characteristics that nevertheless may change in response to different situations.

But this is not a definition on which all psychologists would agree. To achieve any degree of precision in defining the concept, we will have to understand what each theorist means by his or her own use of the term. Each theorist offers a unique version—a personal vision of the nature of personality—and that view becomes a definition of the term. And that is what this course is all about: to reach an understanding of these different versions of the concept of personality and to examine the various ways of defining *I*.

Psychologists do much more than formulate theories in their attempts to define the nature of personality. They also devote considerable time and effort to assessing personality and to conducting research on it. Although the role of theory remains the focus of this book, let us briefly consider the roles of assessment and research.

The role of assessment in the study of personality

To assess something means to evaluate it. The assessment of personality is one of the major areas of the application of psychology to real-world concerns. Consider a few examples. The work of clinical psychologists involves assessing personality—attempting to differentiate the normal from the abnormal and trying to evaluate the nature of the patient's personality to understand his or her symptoms and feelings. Only through an adequate assessment of personality can the clinician decide on the best course of therapy.

School psychologists assess personality to determine the cause of a child's adjustment or learning difficulties. Industrial/organizational psychologists assess personality to help find the best person for a particular job, and counseling psychologists measure personality to find the best job for a particular person, matching the requirements of the position with the individual's needs and interests. Research psychologists assess the personalities of their laboratory subjects to try to account for their behavior in an experiment or to correlate their personality characteristics with other measurements.

It is likely that most people will have their personality assessed in some way, whether formally, through the personality tests used for counseling and employee selection, or informally, in a job interview or by friends and acquaintances.

Some techniques of assessment are more objective than others. Indeed, some are wholly subjective and hence prone to personal bias. Their results may be distorted by the personality characteristics of the person who is making the assessment. The best techniques of personality assessment satisfy three requirements: standardization, reliability, and validity.

Standardization involves the consistency or uniformity of the conditions and procedures for administering a test or other assessment device. If we want to compare the performance of different people on the same test, then it is vital that they all take that test under identical conditions. Everyone taking the test must be exposed to the same instructions, be allowed the same amount of time in which to respond, and be situated in an identical, or at least highly similar, environment.

Reliability involves the consistency of the response to an assessment device. If you took the same test on two different occasions and received two widely different scores, the test would be considered unreliable because its results were inconsistent.

Validity is concerned with whether an assessment technique actually measures what it intends to measure. Does an intelligence test truly measure intelligence? Does a test of anxiety actually evaluate anxiety? If a test does not measure what it claims to, then it is not valid and its results cannot be used to predict behavior. An invalid intelligence test, for example, cannot predict how well you will perform in a situation, such as graduate or professional school, that requires a high level of intelligence.

We shall see that the various personality theorists discussed in this book have devised unique ways of assessing personality, methods that suit their theories. It is from the application of these techniques of assessment that the theorists derived the data on which their theories were based. These techniques vary in their objectivity, reliability, and validity, and they range from the interpretation of dreams and childhood memories to elaborately constructed paper-and-pencil tests. As we discuss the theorists, we will identify their specific techniques of personality assessment.

In the practice of psychology today, the major approaches to measuring personality are self-report inventories, projective techniques, and various questionnaire, interview, and observational techniques.

Self-report assessment techniques

The **self-report inventory** approach involves asking people to report on themselves by answering questions about their behavior and feelings in a variety of situations. These paper-and-pencil tests are composed of items dealing with specific symptoms, attitudes, interests, fears, and values. People taking the test must indicate how closely each item describes their own characteristics or how much they agree with each item.

Two frequently used self-report inventories are the Minnesota Multiphasic Personality Inventory (MMPI) and the California Psychological Inventory (CPI). The MMPI consists of 550 statements to which a person responds "true," "false," or "cannot say." These items cover physical and psychological health; sexual, religious, political, and social attitudes; educational, occupational, familial, and marital factors; and neurotic and psychotic behavioral tendencies. Statements similar to those contained in the MMPI are shown in Table 1.1.

The test contains three scales that can be scored to determine if the person taking the test was faking, was careless, or had misunderstood the instructions. Ten clinical scores from the test measure the following personality traits: hypochondriasis, depression, hysteria, psychopathic deviate, masculinity-femininity, paranoia, psychasthenia, schizophrenia, hypomania, and social introversion.

The MMPI is a highly valid and reliable technique of personality assessment and has generated considerable research. It is used as a clinical diagnostic tool for persons age 16 and older to enable psychologists to assess personality problems. It is also used in vocational and personal counseling and in research on the nature of personality.

The CPI, used with normal people age 13 and older, consists of 480 items calling for a "true" or "false" response. It has three scales to measure test-taking attitudes and provides scores on 15 dimensions of personality, including sociability, self-acceptance, and responsibility. The CPI has been successful in profiling potential delinquents and high school dropouts and in predicting success in various occupations. Along with the MMPI, the CPI is one of the better personality inventories in use today (Anastasi, 1982).

Other self-report inventories measure a variety of traits or focus on specific personality dimensions such as introversion-extraversion, sociability, ascendance-submission, emotional maturity, and emotional security. In addition, some personality theorists have devised their own self-report inventories, and some theories have inspired other psychologists to develop specific tests, as we shall see.

TABLE 1.1   Simulated items from the Minnesota Multiphasic Personality Inventory (MMPI). (Answer *true*, *false*, or *cannot say*)

At times I get strong cramps in my intestines.
I am often very tense on the job.
Sometimes there is a feeling like something is pressing in on my head.
I wish I could do over some of the things I have done.
I used to like to do the dances in gym class.
It distresses me that people have the wrong ideas about me.
The things that run through my head sometimes are horrible.
There are those out there who want to get me.
Sometimes I think so fast I can't keep up.
I give up too easily when discussing things with others.

One characteristic common to self-report inventories is objectivity of scoring. Virtually anyone with the proper scoring key can evaluate these tests accurately. The results do not depend on the scorer's personal or theoretical biases. This objectivity in scoring, combined with the widespread use of computers, has led to automated personality assessment computer programs. Instead of a psychologist interpreting a test, a computer does it, even to the point of issuing sets of programmed interpretive statements.

The MMPI is, to date, the most fully automated test, but programs have also been developed for other self-report inventories, and computer assessment of personality is becoming a popular and lucrative business (Lanyon, 1984).

Projective techniques

Projective tests of personality were developed primarily for use by clinical psychologists in their work with emotionally disturbed individuals. Inspired by Freud's emphasis on the importance of the unconscious mind, these tests attempt to probe that invisible aspect of personality. The theory behind the **projective technique** is that when a person is presented with an ambiguous stimulus, such as an inkblot or a picture that can be interpreted in more than one way, he or she will project personal needs, fears, and values onto that stimulus when asked to describe it.

Projective techniques are not high in reliability and validity, partly because their interpretation is such a subjective process. It is not unusual for different examiners to form different impressions of the same person, based on the results of a projective test. Nevertheless, they remain popular clinical tools. Two widely used projective techniques are the Rorschach Inkblot Test and the Thematic Apperception Test.

The Rorschach was developed in the 1930s by the Swiss psychiatrist Hermann Rorschach. He constructed a series of symmetrical designs by dropping blobs of ink on blank paper and then folding the paper in half. After trying out a large number of patterns, he settled on ten blots that are still in use today. Figure 1.1 shows an inkblot similar to those of the Rorschach Inkblot Test.

Subjects are shown the inkblots one at a time and asked to describe what they see. Then the inkblot cards are shown a second time and the subjects are asked specific questions about their earlier answers. The examiner also observes the person's behavior during the testing session, noting specific gestures, reactions to particular inkblots, and general attitude.

Responses can be interpreted in several ways, depending on whether the subject reported seeing movement, human or animal figures, animate or inanimate objects, and whole or partial figures.

Because the scoring is subjective, the interpretation of the responses depends on the training, skill, experience, and personality of the examiner. As a result, the reliability and validity of this instrument remain low. Attempts have been made to standardize the process of administering, scoring, and interpreting the Rorschach. The most successful of these, called the Comprehensive System, claims, on the basis of much research, to lead to increased levels of reliability and validity (Exner, 1974, 1978).

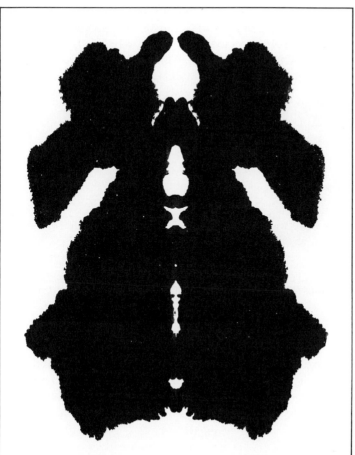

FIGURE 1.1   An inkblot similar to a Rorschach inkblot.

The Thematic Apperception Test (TAT) was developed in the 1930s by Henry Murray (Chapter 7). The test consists of 20 ambiguous pictures showing one or more persons. Figure 1.2 shows a typical TAT picture. This picture, like the others in the TAT series, is vague as to the events portrayed. Therefore, it is subject to interpretation in more than one way.

People taking this test are asked to construct a story describing in detail what is happening to the people in the picture. They are to describe what led up to the depicted situation, what emotions the people are feeling, and what the outcome will be.

In clinical work, psychologists consider several factors in interpreting these stories, including the kinds of personal relationships involved, the motivations of the characters, and the degree of contact with reality exhibited by those in the stories.

FIGURE 1.2 Picture contained in the Thematic Apperception Test (TAT). In describing a TAT picture, people may reveal their own feelings, needs, and values. *(Reprinted by permission of the publishers from Henry A. Murray, THEMATIC APPERCEPTION TEST, © 1971 by Henry A. Murray.)*

There are no objective scoring systems for the TAT, and its reliability and validity are low. For research purposes, however, special scoring systems have been devised to measure specific aspects of personality, such as the needs for achievement, affiliation, and power. In Chapter 17 we will deal with some of the research on the need for achievement.

Other techniques of personality assessment

Psychologists use other techniques to assess personality. Verbal methods such as word association or sentence completion are projective techniques. In the word-association test, the subject is given a series of words and is told to respond with the first word that comes to mind. Responses are analyzed for their commonplace or unusual nature, for their possible indication of emotional tension, and for their relationship to sexual conflicts. The speed of response is also considered.

The sentence-completion test also assesses personality in terms of verbal responses. Subjects are asked to finish such sentences as "My ambition . . ." or "What worries me. . . ." The interpretation of the responses with both these approaches is highly subjective.

A more objective technique involves the observation of behavior. One example is the Personality Inventory for Children, consisting of 600 items to be answered "true" or "false" (Wirt & Lachar, 1981). The responses are not given by the subject (the child), but rather by an adult, usually the mother, who is knowledgeable about the child's behavior. The inventory, developed from 20 years of research, includes 12 clinical scales that provide measures of emotional and social conditions such as depression, anxiety, and hyperactivity.

The role of research in the study of personality

One of the criteria for a useful personality theory is that it must stimulate research. In other words, the theory must be testable. Psychologists must be able to conduct research to determine which of its propositions should be accepted or rejected. Ideally, a theory will be reshaped, modified, and elaborated or discarded on the basis of the research it has generated.

Not only should a theory generate research, but it may also result from research. That is, a theory may be formed initially on the basis of empirical data. Thus, theories both incorporate research data and lead to the search for new data.

Research psychologists study personality in different ways. The method used depends on the specific aspect of personality under investigation. Some psychologists are interested only in overt behavior, in what we do and say in response to certain stimuli. Other psychologists are concerned with our feelings and our conscious experiences. Still others try to understand the deep, powerful, unconscious forces that may motivate us. A method that allows the psychologist to examine one type of subject matter may be inappropriate for another. Throughout this book, we shall describe examples of all these aspects of personality—behavior, conscious processes, and unconscious processes—and the different techniques used to study them.

In general, three research approaches are taken in the study of personality: the clinical approach, the experimental approach, and the correlational approach. Although different in their specifics, these methodologies rely on the fundamental defining characteristic of scientific research in any discipline: objective observation. Researchers must base their conclusions only on the objective evidence at hand and must consider that evidence dispassionately, without any preconceived ideas or biases.

Let us examine the nature of these research approaches to personality.

The clinical approach

The primary method in the clinical approach to personality is the **case study** or case history, in which psychologists search for clues in the patients' past and present lives that might point to the source of their emotional problems. Undertaking a case study is not unlike writing a miniature biography of a person's emotional life, from the early years up to current feelings, fears, and experiences.

Such an approach can provide a great deal of information, and the primary purpose and value of the case study is in diagnosing and treating emotional disorders. As such, case histories usually deal with abnormal or troubled individuals. Case studies can also provide the primary data for constructing a theory of personality and for testing its various propositions, though its use for the latter purpose is questionable because the data of the case study (the patient's recollections) are not obtained in controlled or systematic fashion.

Case studies were used extensively by Sigmund Freud in his development of psychoanalysis (Chapter 2). He probed deeply into his patients' early lives, particularly their childhood years, seeking those experiences and conflicts that may have caused their present neuroses. Consider the case of Katharina, an 18-year-old girl suffering from anxiety attacks and shortness of breath. By reconstructing what he considered to be the relevant experiences in her childhood, Freud was able to trace her symptoms to a number of unfortunate sexual experiences, including a seduction attempt by her father when she was 14.

With another patient, Lucy, Freud linked the hallucinations she was experiencing to earlier events in her life when she had first encountered those particular sensations. Both of these incidents were related to her love for her employer, which had been severely rebuffed (Sulloway, 1979).

It was through a number of such case studies, all of which revealed to Freud that neuroses could be traced to early sexual traumas, that he developed his theory of personality with its emphasis upon sex as a causal factor in neurosis. Freud and later theorists who used the case-study method searched for consistencies in the lives of their patients. On the basis of these perceived congruities, the theorists generalized their findings to all human beings.

Psychologists employ a variety of clinical methods in addition to case studies to investigate, diagnose, and treat their patients and to formulate theories of personality. These methods include tests, interviews, and dream analysis. We noted in the previous section that these are also methods of assessment. A sharp distinction between research and assessment techniques cannot always be made in clinical and counseling psychology. In part, the distinction lies in the uses to which the data are put, for example, to test a theory or to treat a patient. Some theorists, such as Freud, used the same techniques for both purposes.

Although the clinical methods attempt, in general, to be scientific, they do not offer the precision and control that characterize the experimental and correlational approaches to the study of personality. The data obtained by the clinical approach are more subjective, dealing with mental and largely unconscious events and with early life experiences. Such data are open to an interpretation that may reflect the personal biases of the therapist, more so than data obtained by other methods. Further, our memories of childhood events may be distorted by time, and their accuracy cannot easily be verified.

The clinical approach does provide us with a window through which to view the depths of the personality, and we shall see many examples of its use, particularly by Freud and other psychoanalytically oriented theorists.

The experimental approach

We said that the fundamental defining characteristic of research in any scientific discipline is objective observation. The clinical methods do not meet that requirement very well. Two other requirements of scientific research are even more difficult to fulfill by use of the clinical approach but are satisfied by the experimental approach to personality.

One of these requirements is that observations be well controlled and systematic. The conditions under which objective observations are made must be determined in advance so that every factor that could possibly influence the responses of the subjects is known to the researcher. Such control is impossible when dealing with a person's past life events or unconscious phenomena.

The other requirement involves duplication and verification. With careful control of conditions, a psychologist working at another time and in a different setting can duplicate the conditions under which the earlier research was conducted. Events in a person's life history cannot be repeated or duplicated. Researchers can have greater confidence in research findings that have been verified by an independent investigator, and this verification is possible only under objective and controlled experimental conditions.

The essence of the experimental method is straightforward. Conducting an experiment is a little like saying, "Let's try it and see what happens." Keep in mind, however, that in an experiment, "trying something" must be done in a well-controlled and systematic manner, and "seeing what happens" must be recorded objectively and without bias.

We can define an experiment as a technique for determining the effect of a single variable or event on behavior. People are constantly exposed to stimuli in the everyday world—lights, sounds, sights, odors, instructions, demands, trivial conversations, and so on. If a psychologist wants to determine the effect of just one of these stimuli or variables, an experimental situation must be arranged in which only that single variable is allowed to operate.

All the other variables must be eliminated or held at a constant level during the experiment. Then, if the subjects' behavior changes while only that stimulus variable is in operation, we can be certain that it alone is responsible for the change in behavior. The change could not have been caused by any other variable because no other variable was allowed to operate during the experiment.

Scientists distinguish two kinds of variables in an experiment. One is the independent or stimulus variable, which is manipulated by the experimenter. The other is the dependent variable, which is the subjects' behavior or response to that manipulation.

There is more to an experiment than defining these two variables. To be sure that no variable other than the independent variable can affect the results, it is necessary to study two groups of subjects: the experimental group and the control group. Both are chosen at random from the same population of subjects.

The experimental group includes those subjects to whom the experimental treatment is given. This is the group exposed to the stimulus or independent variable. The control group is not exposed to the independent variable. Measures of the behavior in question are taken from both groups before and after the experiment. In this way, researchers can determine if any additional variables have influenced the subjects' behavior. If some other variable was operating, then both groups would show the same changes in behavior. But if no other variable was in operation—if only the independent variable influenced the subjects—then only the behavior of the experimental group would change. The behavior of the control group would remain the same.

Let us demonstrate the experimental approach in action, using data on which a social-learning theory of personality was based (Chapter 15). The psychologist Albert Bandura wanted to determine if children would copy or imitate the aggressive behavior they observed in adults (Bandura, Ross & Ross, 1973). What was the best way to study such a phenomenon? Bandura could have observed children on the neighborhood streets or at a playground, hoping to catch their reactions if they happened to witness a violent incident. He could have watched and waited to learn if the children imitated the aggressive behavior they had seen.

This approach is decidedly unsystematic and uncontrolled and certainly would not allow for duplication and verifiability; it would be highly unlikely for the same conditions to recur. Also, observing the children who happened to be present at a particular time and place would not necessarily provide an appropriate sample of subjects. Some of the children might already possess the tendency to behave in an aggressive manner, regardless of the adult behavior they observe. It would be impossible to decide whether their behavior resulted from witnessing violent actions or from some factor that had long been part of their personality.

Also, observing children at random does not allow for control of the type of aggressive act to which they might be exposed. Children see many different kinds of violence—television actors in a gun battle, teenagers in a fistfight, or parents slapping each other. Each form of aggressive behavior would have to be studied individually before its effects on behavior could be reliably determined. For Bandura to study the phenomenon, it was vital that all the children in his research be exposed to the same instance of violent behavior.

Bandura approached the problem systematically by designing an experiment in which children, whose preexperiment levels of aggression had been measured, were exposed to an identical display of adult aggression. Control groups witnessed nonaggressive adults in the same setting. Both groups of children were observed to see how they would behave.

Those children who watched the aggressive model behaved aggressively themselves, whereas the children in the control group exhibited no change in aggressiveness. Bandura concluded that aggressiveness, one aspect of personality, can be learned through the imitation of other people. We will discuss the results of this study and Bandura's subsequent research in Chapter 15 and see how the data enabled him to formulate his personality theory.

The experimental method is the most precise method of psychological research, but it does have limitations and there are situations to which it cannot be applied. Some aspects of behavior cannot be studied under the rigorously controlled conditions of the experimental method because of safety and ethical considerations. Psychologists cannot deliberately create conditions that are likely to induce riot or panic, for example, such as assembling people in a theater and observing their reactions when the building is set afire. Even though the findings might prove valuable for our understanding of human nature, there is a limit to what may be undertaken in the name of science.

In another instance, psychologists might be better able to treat emotional problems if they had data from controlled experiments in which children were exposed from birth to different child-rearing techniques. Obviously, however, ethical considerations preclude this kind of experimental manipulation of people's lives.

Another difficulty with the experimental method is that the subjects' behavior may change not because of the manipulation of the independent variable but because the subjects know they are being observed. They might behave quite differently if they thought no one was watching them. In addition, when people know they are participating in an experiment, they may try to guess its purpose and behave accordingly, either to please or to frustrate the experimenter. This defeats the purpose of the experiment because the resulting behavior is influenced by the subjects' attitudes toward the experiment, a variable quite different from the one the psychologist is studying.

Thus, objective experimental research has its limitations, but when it is well controlled and systematic it provides excellent data. We shall see throughout this book examples of the successful application of the experimental method to various aspects of personality.

The correlational approach

There are situations in which the experimental approach is not used by psychologists because the manipulation of the independent variable would be too difficult or expensive. In these cases, the correlational approach offers an alternative.

In the correlational approach, psychologists investigate the relationships that already exist among variables. Rather than manipulating an independent variable, the research deals with attributes of that variable. For example, instead of experimentally creating a certain level of stress in subjects in the laboratory—something that can be complicated, expensive, and questionable on ethical grounds—the researcher can study people who are already in acknowledged stress-producing situations, such as police officers on the job or race car drivers at the track.

Another way in which the correlational approach differs from the experimental approach is that subjects are not assigned to experimental and control groups. Instead, subjects who differ on an independent variable, such as level of aggressiveness, sex, age, order of birth, or level of neuroticism, are compared with their own performance on some dependent variable, such as their response on a personality test or performance on the job.

In the correlational approach, psychologists are interested in the relationship between two variables, in how behavior on one variable changes or differs as a function of the other variable. For example, do people who score high on an IQ test perform well in college, on the job, or in pilot training? Does the oldest child in a family differ in anxiety level or aggressiveness from the youngest child? Do girls score higher than boys on a test of assertiveness?

The answers to such questions are useful not only in research but also in applied situations where predictions must be made about a person's chances of success. The college entrance examinations you took are based on correlational studies that have demonstrated the strength of the relationship between standardized test scores and success in the classroom.

In the study of personality, a great deal of correlational research has been conducted on the need for achievement, a concept formulated by Henry Murray (Chapter 7) and subsequently studied by David McClelland and others (Chapter 17). Much of that research compared a person's measured level of the need for achievement with performance on a number of other variables. For example, researchers wanted to determine if people high in the need for achievement earned higher grades in college than persons low in the need for achievement.

The psychologists might have designed an experiment in which some children would be reared by adults who had been trained in techniques known to increase a child's need for achievement. Years later, when some of these children attended college, the grades of those high in achievement could be compared with the grades of those low in that need. Such an experiment is, of course, ridiculous to contemplate. Using the correlational method, however, a researcher measures the achievement-need levels of college students and compares them with their grades. The independent variable (the different levels of the need for achievement, from high to low) is not manipulated or changed. Rather, the researcher works with the existing data. In this particular study to correlate the need for achievement with college performance, the researchers found that students high in the need for achievement made higher grades than students low in the need for achievement. The correlational research also showed that those high in the need for achievement were more likely to be involved in extracurricular activities (Atkinson, Lens & O'Malley, 1976).

We shall describe several examples of the correlational approach to personality research in the following chapters, particularly when discussing the development and application of assessment techniques. The reliability and validity of such assessment devices are normally determined through the correlational approach. In addition, many facets of personality have been studied by correlating them with other variables.

You are no doubt familiar with the primary statistical measure of **correlation**—the correlation coefficient—which provides information about the direction and intensity of the relationship between two variables.

The direction of the relationship may be positive or negative. If high scores on one variable are accompanied by high scores on the other variable, the direction is positive (see Figure 1.3). As the hypothetical test scores increase, so do the ratings. We can predict that a test score of 20 will be accompanied by a rating of 1, a test score of 100 by a rating of 5.

If high scores on one variable are accompanied by low scores on the other variable, the direction is negative (see Figure 1.4). As the test scores increase, ratings decrease. In both of these examples, knowledge of a person's test score will enable us to make a sound prediction about the rating he or she will receive.

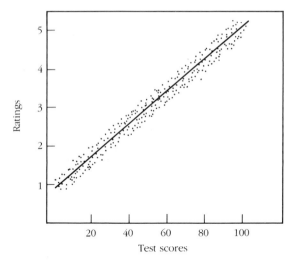

FIGURE 1.3   Example of hypothetical positive correlation between test scores and ratings of college achievement.

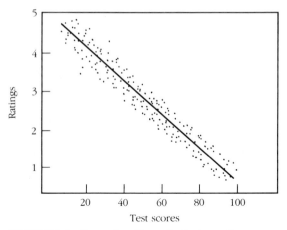

FIGURE 1.4   Example of hypothetical negative correlation between test scores and ratings of college achievement.

Correlation coefficients range from −1.00 (a perfect negative correlation) to +1.00 (a perfect positive correlation). Thus, the closer the correlation coefficient is to −1.00 or +1.00, the more confidently we can make predictions about one variable from another.

Data obtained by the correlational approach may be analyzed by other procedures. We will discuss the technique of factor analysis, used by personality theorist Raymond Cattell, in Chapter 9.

The primary limitation on the use of the correlational approach relates to the postulation of a cause-and-effect relationship between the variables under study. Just because two variables show a high correlation, it does not necessarily follow that one has caused the other; correlation does not imply causation. This does not mean that there is no cause-and-effect relationship, but rather that researchers cannot automatically conclude that one exists, as they can in a well-controlled and systematic experiment.

Consider the thoroughly documented positive correlation between smoking and lung cancer. We cannot conclude, however, on the basis of this correlation, that lung cancer is caused by smoking; there may be some other variable as yet unidentified. We do know that the variables are strongly and positively related; when smoking increases, the rate of lung cancer increases. Still, we cannot conclude that one has caused the other.

This presents a problem for researchers, whose goal is to identify specific causes of behavior, but not for practitioners, whose goal is to predict behavior in the real world. To be able to predict, for example, success in college on the basis of the need for achievement, we need only establish that the two variables are highly and positively correlated. If a college applicant scores high on the need-achievement test, we can predict that he or she will earn good grades in college. In this situation, we are not concerned with the question of whether one's level of the need for achievement causes good academic performance. We are concerned only that the two variables are related and that one can be predicted from the other.

We have reviewed several ways in which psychologists study and assess personality. Let us now see how personality theorists make use of the data they obtain.

The role of theory in the study of personality

Despite the fact that all sciences use theories, they are often described in contemptuous or derogatory terms, as exemplified by the comment "Well, it's only a theory." Many people feel that a theory is always vague, abstract, speculative—really no more than a hunch or a guess and quite the opposite of a fact.

It is true that a theory without evidence to support it is speculation. It seems equally true, however, that a mass of research data can be meaningless unless it is organized into some sort of explanatory framework or context. A theory provides this framework for simplifying and describing empirical data in a meaningful way. A theory can be considered a kind of map that represents the data in their relationships with one another. It attempts to bring data into some kind of order, to fit them into an overall structure in which each datum is an integral part.

Theories are hypotheses or propositions used to explain a particular class of phenomena, in this case, behaviors and feelings relating to personality. If theories about personality are to be useful, they must fulfill several purposes. They must be testable, capable of stimulating research into their own postulates. Researchers must be able to conduct experiments on aspects of the theory to determine if they should be accepted or rejected. Personality theories must be able to clarify and explain the data of personality by organizing those data into a coherent framework. Theories should also help us understand and predict why people behave as they do. Those theories that can be tested and can explain, understand, and predict behavior may then be used to help people change behaviors, feelings, and emotions from harmful to helpful, from undesirable to desirable.

Formal versus personal theories

Theories are not restricted to science, nor are all theories of the formal variety, which we have been discussing. We all use implicit personal theories in our everyday interactions with others. As discussed earlier, we all have some idea of the concept of personality, and we all make certain suppositions about the personalities of those with whom we interact. Further, many of us speculate about human nature in general. We may believe, for example, that "all people are basically decent" or that "people care only about themselves."

These suppositions are theories. They are frameworks within which we place the data of our commonplace observations of other people. We usually form these personal theories on the basis of data derived from our perception of the behavior of those around us. In that respect—the fact that our theories derive from our observations—personal theories are similar to formal theories in psychology.

However, formal theories in psychology, and in the other sciences, have certain characteristics that set them apart from our personal theories. Formal theories are based on data from observations of large numbers of people of diverse natures. Personal theories, on the other hand, are derived from our observations of a limited number of persons, usually our small circle of relatives, friends, and acquaintances as well as ourselves. Because formal theories are supported by a broader range of data, they are more comprehensive, and we can generalize more effectively from them to explain and predict the behavior of more kinds of people.

A second difference is that formal theories are likely to be more objective because scientists' observations are, ideally, unbiased by their own needs, fears, desires, and values. Our personal theories are based as much on observations of ourselves as of others. We tend to interpret the actions of other people in terms of our own thoughts and feelings, evaluating their reactions to a situation on the basis of what *we* would do or how *we* would feel. We view others in subjective, personal terms, whereas scientists try to observe more objectively and dispassionately.

Another difference is that formal theories are repeatedly tested against reality, often by a scientist other than the one who proposed the theory. A formal theory may be subjected to many objective, experimental tests and, as a consequence, be supported, modified, or rejected in the light of the results. Our personal theories are not so tested by ourselves or by a neutral party. Once we develop a personal theory about people in general, or about one person in particular, we tend to cling to it, perceiving only those behaviors that confirm our theory and failing to attend to those that contradict it.

In principle, scientists can see and accept data that do not support their theories. Unfortunately, in reality, this is not always the case. There are many examples in the history of science and the history of psychology of individuals who were so prejudiced by their theory, so emotionally committed to it, that their objectivity was compromised. However, the ideal of objectivity remains the goal toward which scientists strive.

Thus, the intent of formal theories is greater objectivity. Personal theories, as we have noted, tend to be more subjective. We might think, then, that personality theories, because they belong to a discipline that calls itself a science, are all of the formal, objective variety. That conclusion is incorrect. In recent years, psychologists have developed an awareness and acceptance of the subjectivity of personality theories, the notion that "all personality theory is disguised autobiography" (Page, 1983).

This realization seems to have been relatively sudden, becoming widespread in the psychological literature in the late 1970s. George Atwood and Silvan Tomkins noted in 1976 that personality theories "are inevitably colored by subjective factors. The visions or images of man underlying the different theories of personality are determined not only by certain empirical facts which can be agreed upon by everyone, but also by a whole range of idiosyncratic factors and motivations affecting each theorist as an individual" (Atwood & Tomkins, 1976).

In 1977, Raymond Corsini wrote that "personality theorists project their own personalities into their views about human nature. . . . Personality theories often seem to be a reflection of the theorist's own personality" (Corsini, 1977). He suggested that no matter how hard theorists try to be impartial and objective, some kind of personal bias will probably distort their perception.

In a 1978 review of developments in the field of personality, Ravenna Helson and Valory Mitchell spoke of the growing awareness that "theorists rely on their own lives as a primary source of empirical material" (Helson & Mitchell, 1978). This recognition of subjectivity in personality theory is also exemplified in a 1979 book by R. D. Stolorow and George Atwood, *Faces in a Cloud: Subjectivity in Personality Theory*, in which the authors attempt to relate the lives of four individuals—Sigmund Freud, Carl Jung, Wilhelm Reich, and Otto Rank—to their theories (Stolorow & Atwood, 1979).

Such findings should not be surprising. Personality theorists are, after all, human beings. Thus, they may find it "hard to accept conclusions about personality that appear strongly at variance with their own personal experience" (Elms, 1981).

The distinction between formal and personal theories may not be as notable in the field of personality as in other disciplines or other areas of psychology. This does not mean that all personality theories are personal theories. Personality theories do have some of the characteristics of formal theories. Some personality theories are based on the observation of a large number of and diverse kinds of people. The theories are tested against reality, either by the theorist who proposed the idea or by others, and the scientists try to be objective in their observations and analyses of data, which may or may not support the theory. Ultimately, the theories are as objective as the subject matter—the complex human personality—permits, but their principles owe much to the personalities and life experiences of the originators.

Salvatore Maddi suggested that the first stage of theory construction is based primarily on intuition, which he defined as "an inarticulate, private, emotional, though vivid, immediate, and compelling sense of the meaning of what is happening" (Maddi, 1980). In later stages of the development of a theory, the intuitively-based ideas may be modified and refined by two other kinds of knowledge used by personality theorists: rational knowledge and empirical knowledge. Through the use of reason and data, what started out as a personal theory takes on more of the characteristics of a formal theory, "but this does not change that fact that it is largely intuitive knowledge with which the theorist begins."

Thus, whatever the level of objectivity to be found in personality theories—and we shall see that some are more objective than others—there is no denying that they are also partially subjective, reflecting the experiences, needs, fears, intuitions, and motivations of each theorist.

It follows that to understand a theory properly, we should also try to learn about the person who proposed it. It is important to demonstrate, or to speculate on, how the development of the various theories may have been influenced by specific events in the theorists' lives. Where sufficient biographical information is available, we shall often see that the theory seems to reflect the theorist's own life; the theorist may, at least initially, be describing himself or herself, and then seeking appropriate data to support generalization of that view from self to others.

A note of caution must be introduced into this intriguing relationship between a personality theory and the theorist's life experiences. Suppose that it is not the life experiences that influence the development of the theory, but rather that the theory has influenced what the theorists remember about their own life experiences (Pervin, 1984a; Steele, 1982).

Most of our information about a theorist's life comes from recollections expressed in autobiographies. These autobiographies are usually written late in life, after the person has already proposed, strengthened, and defended his or her theory of personality. Perhaps the years spent developing the theory and affirming a commitment to it distort the theorist's memory of his or her early life experiences. Are only those events that support the theory recalled? Are those that do not fit the theory conveniently forgotten? Are experiences invented to enhance the credibility of the theory? We cannot know the answers to these questions, but it is important to keep them in mind as we explore the notion that personality theory may be at least partially autobiographical.

Images of human nature: Issues in personality theory

One important aspect of personality theories is the image of human nature expressed by a theorist. Albert Bandura noted that "interest in the basic conceptions of human nature underlying different psychological theories" is increasing (Bandura, 1978). The range of views on the meaning of being human is rooted in personal experience and reflected in one's outlook on life. Each theorist has an image of human nature that addresses a number of fundamental questions that people have asked, and are still asking, about their own nature—questions that go to the very core of what it means to be a human being (see Table 1.2). Poets, philosophers, and artists continually rephrase these questions, and we see their widely

TABLE 1.2   Questions about human nature

1. *Free Will–Determinism*
   Do we consciously direct our own actions, or are they governed by other forces?
2. *Nature–Nurture*
   Are we influenced more by heredity or by our environment?
3. *Childhood Experiences–Later Experiences*
   Is our personality fixed by early events in our lives, or can it be affected by experiences in adulthood?
4. *Uniqueness–Universality*
   Is the personality of each human being unique, or are there broad personality patterns that fit large numbers of people?
5. *Goals*
   Are we motivated simply to satisfy our physiological needs, or do higher aspirations shape our behavior?
6. *Optimism–Pessimism*
   Are people basically good or evil?

varying attempts at answers in our great books and paintings. Personality theorists too have addressed themselves to these thorny questions and have reached no greater consensus than have painters or writers.

The different images of human nature offered by the theorists allow for a meaningful comparison of their views. These conceptions are not unlike personal theories; they are the frameworks within which the theorists perceive other people and themselves, and within which they construct their theories. Wilbert McKeachie noted that "just as one's behavior is influenced by one's personal theory of human nature, the course of *psychology* is influenced by *psychologists'* concepts of human nature" (McKeachie, 1976).

The issues in personality theory that define a theorist's image of human nature are described below. As we discuss each theory, we shall return to these issues to consider how the theorist deals with them and what the image of human nature is like. Not all of these issues are dealt with explicitly by each theorist, but each viewpoint attempts to grapple with at least some of them.

The first of these basic issues that define an image of human nature concerns the perennial controversy between *free will* and *determinism*. Do we consciously direct the course of our own actions? Can we spontaneously choose the direction of our thoughts and behavior, rationally selecting from among alternatives? Do we, in other words, have a conscious awareness and control of ourselves? Are we free to choose, to be masters of our own fates, or are we victims of past experiences, biological factors, unconscious forces, or external stimuli—forces over which we have no conscious control? Have these events so firmly shaped our personalities that we are capable only of behaving in accordance with these dictates?

We will see personality theorists taking both extremes on this issue, and some, taking more moderate positions, arguing that some behavior is determined by past events while other actions can be spontaneously chosen and directed.

The second issue has to do with the *nature–nurture* controversy. Which is the more important influence on behavior: inherited attributes or the features of the individual's environment? Is our nature—our personality—determined solely by the abilities, temperaments, or predispositions that we may inherit, or are we shaped more strongly by the environments in which we live? Controversy rages on the topic of intelligence: is it influenced more by genetic endowment or by the quality and amount of stimulation available in the home and school? The same question is asked about personality.

As is the case with the first issue, the alternatives are not limited to extreme positions. A number of theorists assume that personality is shaped by both sets of forces. To some, one type of influence is predominant and the other is of minor importance, although both are believed to be determinants of personality.

A third issue involves the relative importance of one's early *childhood experiences* as compared with experiences that occur later in life. Which set of experiences is the more powerful in shaping personality? If we assume, as some theorists do, that what happens to us in infancy and childhood is critical to personality formation, we must consequently believe that the later development of the individual is little more than an elaboration of basic themes laid down in the early years of life. Our personalities, so this line of thought goes, are rather firmly fixed by the age of 5 or so and subject to little change over the rest of our lives. The personality of the adult, then, is determined by the nature of these early experiences.

The opposite position on this issue considers personality to be more independent of the past, capable of being influenced by events and experiences in the person's present and even by his or her future aspirations and goals. Of course, an intermediate position is also available. One could assume that early experiences do indeed shape personality, but not rigidly or permanently. In this view, later experience may function to reinforce or alter earlier personality growth.

Is human nature *unique or universal?* This is another issue that often divides personality theorists. A person's personality may be viewed as being so individual that each act, each utterance, has no counterpart or equivalent in any other person. This obviously makes comparison of one person with another absolutely meaningless. Other positions allow for uniqueness but interpret this characteristic within overall patterns of behavior accepted as more or less universal, at least within a given culture.

A fifth issue revolves around what might be called the *ultimate and necessary goals* of human beings. Theorists differ in opinion on what constitutes a person's major motivation. Are we each simply a sort of self-regulating mechanism, content as long as our basic physiological requirements are satisfied? Do we function solely to obtain pleasure and avoid pain? Is our happiness dependent only on keeping tensions at a minimum?

Some theorists view humans as more than tension-reducing, pleasure-grabbing animals. They consider individuals to be motivated primarily by the need to actualize or realize their full potentials, to stretch themselves, to reach for ever-higher levels of self-expression and development.

There is one additional issue that reflects a theorist's outlook on life. We may call it *optimism versus pessimism.* Are human beings basically good or evil, kind or cruel, compassionate or merciless? Here we are dealing with a question of morality, a value judgment, which supposedly has no place in the objective and dispassionate world of science. The question, however, has been dealt with, at least implicitly, by some of our theorists. Some views of personality are clearly more optimistic and hopeful than others, depicting people as humanitarian, altruistic, and socially conscious. Others see few, if any, of these qualities in humans—individually or collectively.

The important point about these issues is that there are diverse ways of looking at the development and growth of the human personality. Perhaps one or more of these theories (or parts of all of them) will be congenial to you, or perhaps they will clash with your personal views, your own image of human nature. It is a study few of us can approach with an absence of preconceptions, for it is the study of ourselves.

Summary

Eight approaches to personality will be discussed in this book: psychoanalytic, neo-psychoanalytic, trait, life-span, humanistic, cognitive, behavioral, and limited domain. Differences among personality theories may be attributable to the complexity of the subject matter, to the differing historical and personal contexts in which the theories were developed, and to the relative newness of psychology as a science. Knowledge of the various theories of personality can satisfy our curiosity about our own behavior and the behavior of our friends and acquaintances and also serve the practical purpose of helping in our career.

Psychology was formally founded in 1879 by Wilhelm Wundt, who used the methods of the natural sciences to analyze conscious experience. In the early decades of the 20th century, John B. Watson developed the behavioral approach to psychology as a protest against Wundt's focus on conscious experience. Watson argued that psychology must study only overt behavior. Psychoanalysis, developed by Sigmund Freud, used the method of clinical observation to probe the unconscious. The study of personality began in American psychology in the 1930s.

Personality can be defined as an enduring and unique cluster of characteristics that may change in different situations. Techniques for the assessment of personality should satisfy three requirements: standardization, the consistency of conditions and procedures for administering a test; reliability, the consistency of response on a test; and validity, the determination of whether a test measures what it intends to measure. The major approaches to personality assessment are self-report inventories, projective techniques, and other questionnaire, interview, and observation methods.

Self-report inventories, in which people report on their own behavior and feelings in a variety of situations, are objective in that the scores are not influenced by personal or theoretical biases. Two widely used self-report inventories that are standardized and high in reliability and validity are the Minnesota Multiphasic Personality Inventory (MMPI) and the California Psychological Inventory (CPI).

Projective techniques attempt to probe the unconscious by having people project their needs, fears, and values into their interpretation of ambiguous figures. These techniques are subjective, weak in reliability and validity, and poorly standardized. Two popular projective techniques are the Rorschach Inkblot Test and the Thematic Apperception Test (TAT).

An objective technique involving the observation of behavior is the Personality Inventory for Children, in which an adult knowledgeable about the child responds to questions about the child's behavior.

Research approaches in psychology depend on objective observation. Three approaches to research in the study of personality are the clinical approach, the experimental approach, and the correlational approach.

The primary method in the clinical approach is the case study, in which psychologists reconstruct patients' backgrounds and present lives to find clues to their emotional problems. Other clinical methods are tests, interviews, and dream analysis. The clinical methods do not offer the precision and control of the experimental and correlational approaches. The data obtained by the clinical methods are subjective and may reflect personal biases. Also, patients' memories of childhood events may be distorted and it is difficult to verify their accuracy. The primary purpose of the clinical methods is diagnosis and treatment of emotional disturbance.

Two other requirements of scientific research, in addition to objective observation, are controlled and systematic conditions and duplication and verifiability. None of these requirements is as well satisfied by the clinical approach as by the experimental and correlational approaches.

An experiment is a technique for determining the effect of a single variable or stimulus event on behavior. All other possible influencing variables are eliminated or held constant during an experiment. The variable being studied (the stimulus to which the subjects are exposed) is the independent variable. The subjects' response or behavior is the dependent variable. The experimental group is exposed to the experimental treatment (the independent variable). The control group is not exposed to the independent variable. If the behavior of the experimental group changes, while that of the control group does not, we can conclude that only the independent variable influenced the subjects' behavior. The experimental approach is the most precise method of research in psychology, but it cannot be used to study all behavior. Ethical and safety considerations may preclude its use. Another limitation is that behavior may change because the subjects know they are being observed or because they are trying to outwit the experimenter.

In the correlational approach, psychologists study the relationship between two variables to determine how behavior on one variable changes as a function of the other. The correlational approach is useful in predicting behavior in applied situations. The correlation coefficient, the primary statistical measure of correlation, indicates the direction and intensity of the relationship. Correlation coefficients range from -1.00 (a perfect negative relationship) to $+1.00$ (a perfect positive relationship). The most important limitation of the correlational approach is the difficulty in concluding that one variable caused the other, even if the two variables are highly correlated; correlation does not imply causation.

A theory provides a framework for simplifying and describing data in a meaningful way. Theories of personality must be testable, able to clarify and explain the data of personality, and useful in understanding and predicting behavior.

Formal theories are based on data from observation of large numbers of people of diverse natures, are objective, and are repeatedly tested against reality. Some personality theories tend to be autobiographical, reflecting a theorist's life experiences and personality. It is possible, however, that it is the theory that influences the theorist's recollections of his or her life experiences. The first stage in theory construction is based primarily on intuition. In later stages, intuitively based ideas are modified by rational and empirical knowledge.

Personality theories differ in their viewpoints on basic questions about human nature. These questions or issues include free will versus determinism, nature versus nurture, childhood experiences versus later experiences, uniqueness versus universality, life goals, and optimism versus pessimism.

Glossary

case study   The detailed history of an individual containing data from a variety of sources.

correlation   A measure of the degree to which two variables are related.

personality   The unique and relatively enduring internal and external aspects of an individual's character that influence behavior in different situations.

projective technique   A method of personality assessment in which a subject is presented with an ambiguous stimulus, onto which he or she is presumed to project personal needs, fears, and values when asked to describe it.

reliability   The consistency of the response to a psychological assessment device.

self-report inventory   A technique of personality assessment in which a subject answers a series of questions about his or her behavior and feelings.

standardization   The consistency or uniformity of conditions and procedures for administering an assessment device.

validity   The extent to which an assessment device measures what it is intended to measure.

Review questions

1. List three factors that may explain the diversity and disagreement among personality theorists.
2. What was the fundamental point of difference between the approaches of Wundt and Watson?
3. Give examples of some everyday situations that involve the assessment of personality.
4. Distinguish between self-report and projective techniques of personality assessment.
5. What are the advantages and disadvantages of the case-study approach?

6. Describe three requirements of scientific research that are met by the experimental method.
7. Give an example of personality research using the correlational method.
8. What is the relationship between data and theory? Distinguish between formal and personal theories.
9. In Table 1.2, we ask six questions about human nature. Answer these questions now and then again after you have read this book, to see how your views might have changed.

Suggested reading

Kleinmuntz, B. *Personality and psychological assessment.* New York: St. Martin's Press, 1982.

Lanyon, R. I. Personality assessment. *Annual Review of Psychology*, 1984, 35, 667–701.

Lanyon, R. I. & Goodstein, L. D. *Personality assessment*, 2nd ed. New York: Wiley, 1982.

Loevinger, J. & Knoll, E. Personality: Stages, traits, and the self. *Annual Review of Psychology*, 1983, 34, 195–222.

Parke, R. D. & Asher, S. R. Social and personality development. *Annual Review of Psychology*, 1983, 34, 465–509.

Pervin, L. A. *Current controversies and issues in personality*, 2nd ed. New York: Wiley, 1984.

Pervin, L. A. Personality: Current controversies, issues, and directions. *Annual Review of Psychology*, 1985, 36, 83–114.

Rorer, L. G. & Widiger, T. A. Personality structure and assessment. *Annual Review of Psychology*, 1983, 34, 431–463.

Stolorow, R. D. & Atwood, G. E. *Faces in a cloud: Subjectivity in personality theory*. New York: Aronson, 1979.

White, K. M. & Speisman, J. C. *Research approaches to personality*. Monterey, CA: Brooks/Cole, 1982.

PART 1

The Psychoanalytic Approach

The first approach to the study of personality was psychoanalysis, the work of Sigmund Freud. The systematic study of personality began with psychoanalysis in the closing years of the 19th century. So important and far-reaching were Freud's formulations that much of his theory of personality and his unique approach to psychotherapy are still accepted today. Nearly every theory of personality developed in the years since Freud's work owes a debt to his position. Freud's theories have inspired other viewpoints that extended and refined his ideas or that deliberately opposed them.

Psychoanalysis reflects a deterministic and pessimistic image of human nature. It emphasizes unconscious forces, biologically based urges of sex and aggression, and conflicts in early childhood as the rulers and shapers of personality.

Freud's views have been influential not only in psychology but also in the general culture. He revolutionized our ways of thinking about ourselves and our definition of the human personality.

CHAPTER 2

Sigmund Freud

The life of Freud (1856–1939)
Instincts: The propelling force of personality
The structure of personality: Id, ego, and superego
Anxiety: A threat to the ego
Defenses against anxiety
The psychosexual stages of personality development
  The oral stage
  The anal stage
  The phallic stage: Resolving the Oedipus complex
  The latency period
  The genital stage
Freud's image of human nature
Assessment in Freud's theory
  Free association
  Dream analysis
Research in Freud's theory
  Scientific validation of Freudian concepts
A final commentary
Summary
Glossary
Review questions
Suggested reading

Man's chief enemy and danger is his own unruly nature and the dark forces pent up within him.

ERNEST JONES

Contemporary personality theory in general has been influenced more by Sigmund Freud than by any other single individual. His system of psychoanalysis was the first formal theory of personality and to this day remains the best known of any personality theory. Indeed, the term **psychoanalysis** has become virtually a household word, known and recognized by most of the literate peoples of the world. Not only did Freud greatly influence psychological and psychiatric work on personality, but his work also had a tremendous effect on our view of ourselves and our world. It can be argued that few ideas in the history of civilization have had such a broad and profound influence.

Many of the subsequently developed personality theories are, as we shall see, derivatives of or elaborations on Freud's basic work; others owe their impetus and direction in great part to their opposition to psychoanalysis. It would be extremely difficult to comprehend and assess the development of the field of personality without first understanding Freud's system.

Psychoanalysis was *his* system, and his alone. On that point he was most adamant. "Psychoanalysis is my creation," he wrote. "No one can know better than I do what psychoanalysis is" (Freud, 1966, p. 7). Those who disagreed with his views were excommunicated from the official psychoanalytic community, as we shall see in later chapters.

An understanding of Freud is essential not only for the historical reasons discussed, but also because of his continuing influence. Though his loyal followers have revised and modified the system since his death in 1939, it remains in widespread use in both academic and mental-health settings. "Freud continues to provide employment for personality theorists as well as clinicians; rereading Freud is a growth industry" (Loevinger & Knoll, 1983, p. 197). Thus it would be difficult to justify any other starting point for a discussion of contemporary theories of personality.

The life of Freud (1856—1939)

Freud was born in 1856 in what is now Czechoslovakia and moved with his family to Vienna four years later. His father was a never-too-successful wool merchant, and Freud's youth and adolescence could hardly be described as affluent.

When Freud was born, his father was 40 years old. His mother (the elder Freud's second wife) was only 20. The father was somewhat strict and authoritarian. Freud recalled, as an adult, his childhood hostility toward his father; he had felt superior to his father as early as the age of 2. Freud's mother, on the other hand, was slender and attractive, and very protective and loving. Freud felt a passionate, sexual attachment to her, a situation that set the stage for the development of the concept of the Oedipus complex. This complex is an important part of Freud's system, as it was an integral part of his own childhood.

His mother took great pride in her firstborn, convinced that an old woman's prophecy—that he would be a great man in the world—would come true. Among Freud's lifelong characteristics were his high degree of self-confidence, his intense ambition to succeed, and his dreams of glory and fame. Again reflecting the impact of early experiences, Freud wrote: "A man who has been the indisputable favorite of his mother keeps for life the feeling of a conqueror, that confidence of success that often induces real success" (Jones, 1953, p. 5).

There were eight children in the family, two of them grown half-brothers with children of their own. Freud's closest companion in childhood was his nephew, who was only a year older. So strong an influence did this nephew have on Freud that he later described him as the source of all his (Freud's) friendships and hatreds. The young Freud evidently experienced much rivalry with and resentment toward all the children in his family and was jealous and angry when new rivals for his mother's affection were born. Perhaps as a result, he became highly competitive.

We can see preludes to Freud's theory of the nature of human beings in the experiences and insecurities of his own childhood. "The child," the poet Wordsworth wrote, "is father of the man," and perhaps too the father of the theory of mankind one formulates in adulthood.

From a very early age, Freud evidenced an extremely high intelligence, which his parents helped to foster in every way possible. His sisters, for example, were not allowed to study the piano lest the noise disturb Freud's studies. He was given a tiny room to himself—so small it was called a cabinet—containing little more than a narrow bed, a desk, and chairs. Here he spent most of his time; he even took his meals there so as not to waste time. The room was the only one in the apartment to contain a prized oil lamp; the rest of the family had to use candles.

Freud entered high school a year earlier than was usual and was at the head of his class most of the time. In addition to Hebrew and German, the young Freud mastered Latin, Greek, French, and English and taught himself Italian and Spanish. He particularly enjoyed English; he had been reading Shakespeare since the age of 8.

Freud had many interests, including military history, but, when it came time to choose a career (from among the few professions open to a Jew at that time in Vienna), he settled on medicine. It was not that he had a desire to practice medicine, but he thought that medical study could lead to a career in scientific research, which was then his goal. While completing his medical degree at the University of Vienna, he conducted intensive physiological research into such areas as the spinal cord of fish and the testes of the eel, making very respectable contributions to the field.

While he was in medical school, Freud began to experiment with cocaine. He took it himself and insisted that his fiancée, sisters, and friends try it as well. He became enthusiastic about the substance, calling it a "miracle drug" and a "magical substance" that would cure many ills. He earned much notoriety as a result of his endorsement of cocaine in articles and lectures, but he later regretted his involvement when cocaine came to be recognized as addictive. For many years it was believed that by 1887, Freud had stopped using cocaine himself. However, recently published letters from Freud to his friend Wilhelm Fliess reveal that Freud used the drug at least 10 years longer, well into middle-age (Masson, 1985).

Freud was discouraged from his intended career in scientific research by a professor who convinced him that it would be many years before he could support himself financially in the university system of the day. Since he lacked an independent income, Freud decided to enter private practice upon completing his training. A further impetus toward private practice was his engagement to Martha Bernays, which lasted four years before he could afford to marry. (Even then, he had to borrow money and pawn his watch.) Thus, Freud established a practice as a clinical neurologist in 1881 and began his exploration into the personalities of those suffering emotional disturbances.

He studied for a time in Paris with the psychiatrist Jean Charcot, from whom he learned a great deal about the use of hypnosis. Charcot also alerted him to the possible sexual basis of neurosis. Another significant influence on Freud and the system he was to develop was his friendship with Josef Breuer, a Viennese physician who had achieved some success in working with disturbed patients by encouraging them to talk freely about their symptoms. Freud, who grew dissatisfied with hypnosis (he was not a good hypnotist), turned to Breuer's "talking-cure" method and found it most effective. It was to form the basis of Freud's chief method of inquiring into the unconscious. Breuer was later to disappear from the arena of the development of psychoanalysis because of his disagreement with Freud's view of the central role of sex in emotional disturbance.

In 1897, when Freud was 41 years old, he underwent a severe neurotic episode and was troubled by a variety of physical symptoms including migraine headaches, urinary problems, and spastic colon. He worried about dying, feared for his heart, and became anxious about open spaces and travel. For the next three years, he engaged in the difficult task of psychoanalyzing himself through the study of his dreams.

It was during this period that he conducted his most creative work, developing the core of his theory of personality. Through the exploration of his dreams he realized, for the first time, how much hostility he felt toward his father. He also recalled his childhood sexual longings for his mother and dreamed of his sex wish toward his eldest daughter.

Thus, Freud's theory was formulated initially on an intuitive basis, drawn from his own experiences and memories. It was then constructed along more rational and empirical lines through his work with patients, examining their childhood experiences and memories through case studies and analysis of their dreams. From all this material he fashioned a coherent picture, as he saw it, of the development of the individual personality and its processes and functions.

As his work became known through books and papers, Freud attracted a group of young student-disciples (most of whom were physicians) who met with him weekly to learn about his new psychoanalysis. Some of them (several of whom will be discussed in the chapters to follow) later broke away from Freud and developed their own theories.

Freud's private practice grew as more and more people began to pay respectful attention to his work. In 1909 he received his first recognition on an international scale: he was invited to the United States to give a series of lectures at Clark University in Massachusetts, where he was awarded an honorary doctoral degree.

During the 1920s and 1930s, Freud reached the pinnacle of his success, but, unfortunately, at the same time his health began to deteriorate. From 1923 until his death 16 years later, he underwent 33 operations for cancer of the mouth. (He smoked 20 large cigars every day.) Portions of his palate and upper jaw were removed, and he suffered almost continuous pain, for which he refused medication.

When the Nazis came to power in Germany in 1933, they expressed their feelings about Freud by publicly burning all of his books, along with those of other "enemies of the state," including Einstein and many other Jewish intellectuals. In 1938 the Nazis occupied Austria, but despite the urgings of his friends Freud refused to leave Vienna. Finally, after his home was repeatedly invaded by gangs of Nazis and his daughter Anna was arrested, Freud left for London. He was in very poor health by this time, yet he was alert mentally and continued to work almost to the last day of his life. Finally he said to his physician, Max Schur, "Now it's nothing but torture and makes no sense any more" (Schur, 1972, p. 529). The doctor had promised Freud that he would not let him suffer needlessly. He administered two injections of morphine, and Freud's long years of pain came to an end.

Instincts: The propelling force of personality

Freud interpreted the functioning of the human organism in physiological terms. From his medical training he knew that the human body operates by creating and expending a kind of physical energy. Food is transformed in the body into a form of energy that is used to fuel such functions as breathing, blood circulation, and muscular and glandular activity.

The mind also performs certain functions. It perceives the external world; it thinks, imagines, remembers. Using the analogy with the body, Freud assumed that the mind also carries out its functions through the use of energy—psychic energy—which differs in form but not kind from the body's physical energy. He further assumed, based on the principle of the conservation of energy, that the body energy could be transformed into psychic energy, and vice versa. The energy of the body therefore influences the mind. The link between these two forms of energy, the frontier between the psychic and the somatic, lies in Freud's concept of *instinct*.

Briefly defined, an **instinct** is the representation in the mind of stimuli that originate within the body. The instinct became Freud's basic element or unit of the personality. It is the motivating, propelling force of personality that not only drives behavior but also determines its direction. Freud's term in German for this concept is *Trieb*, which is best translated as a *driving force* or an impulse (Bettelheim, 1984). Instincts are a form of energy—transformed physiological energy—that serves to connect or bridge the body's needs to the mind's wishes.

The stimuli for instincts are internal, such as the tissue deficit of hunger. These instinctual stimuli arise within the body and can best be described as *needs*. When a need such as hunger is aroused, it generates a state of physiological excitation in the body—a physiological energy. This somatic energy, or need, is transformed in the mind into a *wish*. It is the wish—the mental representation of the body need—that is the instinct or driving force that motivates the person to behave so as to satisfy the body need; for example, the person may look for food. Thus, the instinct is not the body state—the tissue deficit of hunger—but rather the transformation of that body need into a mental representation, a wish.

We can see that, to Freud, the processes and functions of the mind—such as perception, thinking, remembering—depend upon activities of the body; indeed, they are manifestations of body processes.

When the body is in a state of need, the person experiences a condition of tension or pressure. The aim of an instinct in every case is to satisfy the need and thereby reduce the state of tension. Thus, Freud's theory is essentially a homeostatic approach. We are motivated continually to restore and maintain the equilibrium of the body, to eliminate the tension and keep the body tension-free.

Freud believed that there is always a certain amount of instinctual tension or pressure that we must constantly operate to reduce. It is not possible to escape these bodily needs, as one might escape an annoying external stimulus; they are always present. This means that instincts influence our behavior as long as we live, in a continuing cycle of bodily need leading to reduction of need.

While the goal of every instinct remains constant, the individual may take different paths to achieve the goal. For example, the sexual drive or need may be satisfied in a variety of ways—heterosexually, homosexually, autosexually—or the need may be channeled into some other form of activity.

Freud thought that psychic energy may be displaced to substitute objects, and this energy displacement he considered of prime importance in determining an individual's personality. While instincts remain the exclusive source of energy for behavior, the energy can be displaced in a variety of ways. And it is this variation that explains the diversity we see in human behavior. All of the assorted interests, preferences, and attitudes that we display as adults were seen by Freud to be displacements of energy from the original objects that satisfied the instinctual needs. Instincts, then, as noted earlier, are the basic motivating forces of all human behavior.

Having determined what instincts are, the next question we must ask is: How many of them exist? Freud said there are as many instincts as there are bodily needs to give rise to them. How many bodily needs are there? This question Freud did not answer. He felt that we did not yet know enough about bodily states and that their investigation was within the province of physiology, not psychology.

However, Freud said that an exact knowledge of these body needs was not necessary; the important point is how they affect behavior, and that effect can be observed in the aims of the instincts. So, to Freud, it was not important to know how many instincts there are. Regardless of their number, the instincts can be grouped into two categories: the life instincts and the death instincts.

The **life instincts** serve the purpose of survival of both the individual and the species by seeking to satisfy the needs for food, water, air, and sex. The life instincts are oriented toward growth and development. The form of psychic energy manifested by the life instincts is the **libido**. The libido can be attached to or invested in objects, a concept that Freud called **cathexis**. For example, if you like a particular person, Freud would say that your libido is cathected to that person.

The life instinct that Freud considered the most important to personality is sex, which he defined in very broad terms. He did not refer solely to the erotic but included almost all pleasurable behaviors and thoughts. Freud stressed sex as our primary motivation. Regarding the erotic component, Freud was quite specific. Erotic wishes arise from the erogenous zones of the body: the mouth, anus, and sex organs.

Freud viewed human beings as predominantly pleasure-seeking, and much of his personality theory revolves around the necessity for inhibiting or suppressing our sexual longings. In another example of how personal experiences and feelings influenced his theory of personality, Freud's own attitude toward sex was negative. Reflecting this view, he consistently warned in his writings of the dangers of sex— that "common animal need," he called it—and argued that the sex act was degrading. It contaminated the mind as well as the body. At the very time he began to formulate a theory that stressed the role of sex as a force in personality development, he gave up sex in his own life. In 1897, when Freud was 41, he wrote to a friend, "Sexual excitation is of no more use to a person like me" (Freud, 1954, p. 227).

Freud postulated, in opposition to the life instincts, the destructive or **death instincts**. Drawing from biology, Freud stated the obvious fact that all living things decay and die, returning to their original inanimate state. In line with this, he assumed that people have an unconscious wish to die. The death instincts were not developed as fully by Freud as were the life instincts, for Freud felt they were difficult to study; they operate internally and silently. Neither did Freud discuss a separate energy by which the death instincts operate.

A vitally important component of the death instincts is the *aggressive drive*, which is the wish to die turned against objects other than the self. The aggressive drive compels us to destroy, conquer, and kill. Eventually, Freud came to consider aggression to be as important a part of human nature as sex.

It is interesting that Freud did not develop the notion of the death instincts until late in life, when such a concern became personal. As the physiological and psychological debilitations of age began to affect him, as his cancer worsened, and as he witnessed the carnage of World War I, death and aggression became major themes in his theory. Not so incidentally, Freud in his later years greatly dreaded his own death and exhibited hostility and aggression toward colleagues and disciples who broke away from his theoretical viewpoint. He has been described as a good hater (Roazen, 1975).

The concept of the death instincts achieved only a limited acceptance, even among Freud's most dedicated followers. A contemporary psychoanalyst noted in 1973 that the idea could "now securely be relegated to the dust bin of history" (Sulloway, 1979, p. 394).

There is one important point to reiterate about instincts: all the psychic energy needed by the personality is derived directly from them. They provide energy, motivation, and direction for all facets of the individual's personality.

The structure of personality: Id, ego, and superego

Freud's original conception divided personality into three levels: the conscious, the preconscious, and the unconscious.

The *conscious*, as Freud defined and used the term, corresponds closely to its ordinary everyday meaning. It includes all the sensations and experiences of which we are aware at any given moment. As I write these words, for example, I am conscious of the feel of my pen, the sight of the page, the idea that I'm trying to express, and a dog barking in the distance.

Freud considered the conscious to be a small and limited aspect of our personality, because only a small proportion of our thoughts, sensations, and memories exists in conscious awareness at any one time. Freud likened the mind to an iceberg. The conscious is the portion above the surface of the water—merely the tip of the iceberg.

What is much more important, according to Freud, is the larger, invisible portion below the surface: the *unconscious*. This is the focus of psychoanalytic theory. Its vast, dark depths contain the instincts, wishes, and desires that direct and determine our behavior. The unconscious, then, contains the major driving power behind our behavior and is the repository of forces we cannot see or control.

Between these two levels of consciousness, Freud posited the *preconscious* (or foreconscious). This is the storehouse of all memories, perceptions, thoughts, and the like of which we are not consciously aware at the moment but which we can easily bring into consciousness.

For example, in the unlikely event that your mind strayed from this page, and you began to think about someone else or what you did last night, you would be summoning material up from your preconscious into your conscious. There is a great deal of two-way traffic between these two levels, and we often find our attention shifting back and forth suddenly from experiences of the moment—this page or a lecture or a television program—to events from the preconscious.

In later years, Freud revised this notion and introduced three basic structures in the anatomy of the personality: the id, the ego, and the superego.

The **id**, the original or oldest system of the personality, corresponds closely to Freud's earlier notion of the unconscious (though there are unconscious aspects of the ego and superego as well). The id is the storehouse or reservoir for all the instincts. It also contains the total psychic energy—libido. The id is thus a powerful structure in the personality; indeed, it supplies all the power for the other two structures.

Because the id is the reservoir of the instincts, it is vitally and directly related to the satisfaction of bodily needs. As we discussed earlier, a tension or pressure is produced when the body is in a state of need, and the organism then acts to reduce this tension by satisfying the need.

The id operates in accordance with what Freud called the **pleasure principle**; that is, it functions to avoid pain and increase pleasure, through its concern with tension reduction. There is one important point about the id's tension-reduction function: it strives for immediate satisfaction of its needs. It does not tolerate delay or postponement of satisfaction for any reason, be it manners or morals or some other dictate of everyday reality. The id—that "cauldron full of seething excitations"—knows only one thing: instant satisfaction. The id drives people to want what they want when they want it, without regard to what anyone else may want or need. It is a purely selfish, pleasure-seeking structure—primitive, amoral, insistent, and rash.

Further, the id has no perception of reality. If we may oversimplify a bit, we might compare the id to a newborn infant. It screams and claws frantically when its needs are not satisfied, but it has no knowledge of how to bring about such satisfaction. The hungry infant cannot find food for itself. The only ways the id is able even to attempt to satisfy these needs are through *reflex action* and through wish-fulfilling hallucinatory or fantasy experience—what Freud called **primary-process thought**. Left to its own devices, the newborn would die, since it knows nothing of the external world. As the infant grows, it learns about objects in the environment that can satisfy its needs—where these objects are, which behaviors are appropriate to obtain them, and so on.

For example, most children learn that they cannot take food from other people unless they are willing to face certain consequences, that they must postpone the pleasure obtained from relieving anal tensions until they get to a bathroom, and that they cannot indiscriminately give vent to sexual and aggressive longings. In short, the growing child must learn to deal intelligently and rationally with the outside world and must develop the powers of perception, recognition, judgment, and memory that an adult uses to satisfy his or her needs. Freud called these processes **secondary-process thought**.

These abilities, perhaps best known simply as reason or rationality, are subsumed under Freud's second structure of personality, the **ego**. The ego possesses an awareness of reality. It is capable of perceiving and manipulating the individual's environment in a practical manner and operates according to what Freud called the **reality principle**.

We might refer to the ego as the rational master of the personality. Its purpose is not to thwart the impulses of the id but rather to help the id in obtaining its necessary tension reduction. The ego, since it is aware of reality, decides when and in what manner the instincts can best be satisfied. It determines appropriate and socially acceptable times, places, and objects that will satisfy the id impulses. While the ego does not prevent id satisfaction, it does try to postpone or delay or redirect it in accordance with the demands of reality. Thus, it tries to control the id impulses.

Freud compared the relation of the ego to the id with that of a rider to a horse. The raw brute power of the horse must be guided, checked, and reined in by the rider, otherwise the horse may bolt and run, throwing the rider to the ground.

The ego serves two masters—the id and reality—and it is constantly mediating and striking compromises between their often conflicting demands. (It serves a third master as well, as we shall see shortly.) Also, the ego is, in a sense, never independent of the id. It is always responsive to the demands of the id and derives all its power or energy from it.

It is the ego, this rational master, that keeps you working at a job you may dislike (if the alternative is an inability to provide food and shelter for your family) or tolerating people you may not care for, because reality demands such behavior as an appropriate way of satisfying the incessant demands of the id. The controlling, postponing function of the ego must be continuously exercised, or the impulses of the id would dominate and overthrow the rational ego. Individuals must constantly protect themselves from being controlled by the id, and Freud postulated a variety of mechanisms (to be discussed later) by which people may defend their egos.

Thus far we have a picture of the individual in battle, trying to restrain the id while at the same time serving it, perceiving and manipulating reality so as to relieve the tensions of the id impulses. Human beings are driven by their biological instinctual forces, which they are continually trying to guide—walking the tightrope between the demands of reality and those of the id, both of which require constant attention.

But that is not Freud's complete picture of human nature. There is a third set of forces—a powerful and largely unconscious set of dictates or beliefs—which the individual learns in childhood: his or her ideas of right and wrong. In everyday language we call this internal morality a "conscience." Freud called it the **superego**. This moral side of the personality is learned, usually by the age of 5 or 6, and consists initially of the rules of conduct set down by the parents. Through punishment, praise, and example, the child learns which behaviors the parents consider wrong or bad. Those behaviors for which the child is admonished or punished become part of the *conscience*, which is one part of the superego. The other part is the **ego-ideal** and consists of good or correct behaviors, for which the child is praised.

The child thus learns a series of rules—"Thou shalts" and "Thou shalt nots"— that earn acceptance or rejection from the parents. In time, the child internalizes these teachings, and the rewards and punishments are then self-administered. Parental control is replaced by self-control. The parents' rules and commands have influenced the child, who lives in at least partial conformity with these now largely unconscious moral guidelines. As a result of this internalization, the child (and later the adult) experiences guilt whenever he or she performs—or even thinks of performing—some action that is contrary to this moral code.

The superego, as the arbiter of morality, is relentless—even cruel—in its constant quest for moral perfection. In terms of its intensity, irrationality, and blind, determined insistence on obedience, it is not unlike the id. Its purpose is not to postpone the pleasure-seeking demands of the id but rather to inhibit them— particularly, in Western society, those concerned with sex and aggression. The superego strives neither for pleasure (as does the id) nor for the attainment of realistic goals (as does the ego). It strives solely for moral perfection. The id is pressing for satisfaction, the ego is trying to delay it, and the superego urges morality above all. Like the id, the superego admits no compromise with its demands.

As you can see, the ego is very much caught in the middle, pressured by these insistent opposing forces. The superego, then, is the ego's third master. To paraphrase Freud, the poor ego has a hard time of it, pressured on three sides, threatened by three different dangers—the id, reality, and the superego.

Thus, we see continual conflict within the human personality. The British psychologist Donald Bannister describes Freud's human being as "basically a battlefield. He is a dark cellar in which a well-bred spinster lady [the superego] and a sex-crazed monkey [the id] are forever engaged in mortal combat, the struggle being refereed by a rather nervous bank clerk [the ego]" (Bannister, 1966). The inevitable result of this friction, when the ego is too severely pressed, is the development of anxiety.

Anxiety: A threat to the ego

We all have a general idea of what the word **anxiety** means and of how we feel when we say we are anxious. We can agree to some extent on the internal experiences associated with such feelings. We know that anxiety is a feeling not unlike fear. We feel frightened, but we do not know of what. Anxiety has been defined by Freud as an objectless fear; we cannot point to its source, to an object that induces it.

Freud made anxiety an important part of his system of personality, asserting that it is fundamental and central to the development of neurotic and psychotic behavior. He suggested that the prototype of all anxiety is the trauma of birth (a notion elaborated upon by a disciple, Otto Rank).

The fetus in its mother's womb is in the most stable and secure of worlds, where every need is satisfied without delay. Suddenly, at birth, the organism finds itself thrust into a hostile environment. It must at once begin to adapt to reality, since its instinctual demands may not always be immediately met. The newborn's nervous system, immature and ill-prepared, is suddenly bombarded with intense and diverse sensory stimuli. Consequently, the infant engages in massive motor movements, heightened breathing, and increased heart rate.

The birth trauma, then, with its tension and fear that the id instincts won't be satisfied, is the individual's first experience with fear and anxiety. Out of this experience is created the pattern of reactions and feeling states that will occur whenever the individual is exposed to danger in the future.

When an individual is unable to cope with his or her anxiety, when he or she is in danger of being overwhelmed by it, the anxiety is said to be *traumatic*. What Freud meant by this is that the person, regardless of age, is reduced to a state of total helplessness, like that experienced in infancy. In adult life, infantile helplessness is reenacted, to some degree, whenever the ego is threatened.

Freud posited three types of anxiety, which vary as a function of the kind of situation that produces them. The types of anxiety differ in terms of their seriousness or potential harm to the individual.

The first type of anxiety, from which the other two are derived, is *reality* or *objective anxiety*. As the name indicates, it involves a fear of tangible dangers in the real world. Most of us fear—justifiably—fires, tornadoes, earthquakes, and similar dangers. We run from a wild animal, get out of the way of a speeding car, flee a burning building. Reality anxiety, then, serves the very positive purpose of guiding our behavior with regard to actual dangers. Our fear subsides when the threat is no longer present.

These reality-based fears can be carried to an extreme, however, and can become harmful. The person who won't leave home for fear of being hit by a car, or won't light a match for fear of fire, is carrying reality-based fears beyond the point of normality.

The other two kinds of anxiety are much more consistently troublesome to an individual's mental health.

Neurotic anxiety has its basis in childhood, in a conflict between instinctual gratification and reality. Most children suffer at least some punishment from parents for impulsively satisfying the demands of the id, particularly those of a sexual or aggressive nature.

The child is often punished for overtly expressing sexual or aggressive impulses. Anxiety or fear is therefore generated by the wish to gratify certain id impulses. This anxiety is at first conscious but is later transformed into an unconscious threat—a province of the ego. The neurotic anxiety that emerges is a fear of being punished for impulsively displaying id-dominated behavior. Notice that the fear is not of the instincts themselves but rather of what may happen as a result of gratifying the instincts. The conflict becomes one between the id and the ego, and its origin, as noted, has some basis in reality.

Moral anxiety is the third type, and it results from a conflict between the id and the superego. Basically, it is a fear of one's own conscience. When you are motivated to express an instinctual impulse that is contrary to your moral code, your superego retaliates by causing you to feel shame or guilt. In everyday terms, you might describe yourself as "conscience stricken."

Moral anxiety is obviously a function of how well developed the superego is. A person with a strong, puritanical, inhibiting conscience will experience much greater conflict than someone with a less virtuous set of moral guidelines. Like neurotic anxiety, moral anxiety has some basis in reality. Children are punished for violating their parents' moral codes, and adults are punished for violating society's moral code. The shame and guilt feelings in moral anxiety are, however, from within. It is the person's own conscience that causes the fear and the anxiety, and Freud believed that the superego can exact a terrible retribution for violation of its tenets.

Whatever the type, anxiety serves as a warning signal to the person that all is not as it should be. It induces tension in the organism and so becomes a drive— much like hunger or thirst—that the individual is motivated to satisfy. The tension must be reduced.

Anxiety alerts the individual that the ego is being threatened and that, unless action is taken, the ego might be overthrown altogether. What can be done? How can the ego protect or defend itself? There are a number of options: the person may try to run away from the threatening situation, may try to inhibit the impulsive need that is the source of danger, or may try to follow the dictates of the conscience. But if none of these rational techniques works, the person may resort to nonrational mechanisms to defend the ego.

Defenses against anxiety

Anxiety functions as a signal that impending danger, a threat to the ego, must be counteracted or avoided. The ego must reduce the conflict between the demands of the id and the strictures of society or of the superego. This conflict is ever present in the "dark cellar" that is human nature, according to Freud, because the instincts are always pressing for some degree of satisfaction, and the taboos and mores of society tend to limit such satisfaction. Freud felt, therefore, that the *defenses* must always be in operation to some extent. Just as all behavior is motivated by instincts, so too all behavior is defensive in nature, in the sense of defending against anxiety. The intensity of the battle within the personality may fluctuate, but it invariably continues.

Freud postulated a number of specific **defense mechanisms** but noted that an individual rarely uses just one. We typically defend ourselves against anxiety by using a variety of the mechanisms at the same time. Also, there is quite a bit of overlap in these mechanisms. Although varying in their specifics, the defense mechanisms share two very important characteristics. First, they are denials or *distortions of reality*—necessary ones, but distortions nonetheless. Second, the defense mechanisms operate *unconsciously*. Individuals are unaware of them, which means they have distorted or unreal images of themselves and their environments on the conscious level. After we discuss several specific mechanisms, we will return to this important point.

Repression is a word we use quite frequently in everyday conversation. When we say "I've repressed that," we usually mean we have put it out of our conscious awareness, deliberately and consciously suppressed something we no longer wanted to think about. This is not the sense in which Freud used the term. Repression, as explained by Freud, is an *involuntary* removal of something from consciousness. It is, in essence, an unconscious denial of the existence of something that brings us discomfort or pain.

At first glance, there might seem to be a contradiction here. The defense mechanisms are operated by the ego, which, as we have seen, functions in accordance with the reality principle. Is it not unrealistic to omit or deny segments of reality, as happens with repression?

To answer that, we must recall the primary function of the ego: to aid the id in bringing about pleasure and avoiding pain. Of course, the pressing of certain id impulses for satisfaction leads to anxiety when these impulses are contrary to one's moral teachings or to the demands of reality. By repressing the source of the anxiety, the organism relieves the tension the anxiety induces. It does so by denying the existence of the original wish. The immediate danger to the ego of being overpowered by the id is thus reduced. Of course, anxiety remains in the unconscious, where it may wreak all sorts of havoc, but the conscious conflict is no longer present. In a sense, a false reality (although true as the individual perceives it) within which the individual can function is established.

Repression can operate on memories of situations or people, on our perception of the present (so that we may fail to comprehend some disturbing event that is in open view), and even on the physiological functioning of the body. For example, sexual drives can be so strongly inhibited that the person becomes impotent.

Once a repression is in use, it is extremely difficult to get rid of. After all, we are using it to protect ourselves from some danger, and we would have to know that the idea or memory is no longer dangerous in order to remove the repression. But how can we find out that the danger no longer exists unless we release the repression?

The concept of repression is basic to much of Freud's system of personality and is involved in all neurotic behavior.

One defense against a disturbing impulse is to actively express the opposite impulse. This is known as **reaction formation**. A person who is strongly driven by, let us say, sexual impulses that are threatening may repress those impulses and replace them with more socially acceptable behavior. For example, a person who is threatened by his or her sexual longings may reverse them and become an active crusader against pornography. Another person, disturbed by extreme aggressive impulses, may become overly solicitous and friendly. Thus, lust becomes virtue, and hatred becomes love.

This does not mean that everyone who is especially considerate, or concerned about X-rated movies, is masking deep feelings of hostility or sexual longings. What distinguishes behavior arising from true convictions from that which results from reaction formation is the intensity and extremity of the behavior. A person who crusades against "loose morals," "free love," "dirty movies," and the like, to a degree out of proportion to their actual incidence, may well be reflecting reaction formation.

Another way of defending oneself against disturbing impulses is to attribute them to someone else. This type of defense mechanism is called **projection**. Thus, lustful, aggressive, or other unacceptable impulses are seen as being possessed by others, not by oneself.

The person says, in effect, "I don't hate him—he hates me." A middle-aged mother may ascribe her troublesome sexual drive to her adolescent daughter. The impulse is still being manifested, but in a way that is more acceptable to the individual.

In **regression**, another mode of defense, the individual retreats or regresses to an earlier period in life that was more pleasant and free of the frustration and anxiety he or she now faces. Regression usually involves a return to one of the psychosexual stages of development (discussed later in this chapter). The person returns to this more secure time of life by manifesting behaviors that he or she displayed at that time, such as childish and dependent behavior.

Rationalization is a defense mechanism that many of us use from time to time. It involves a reinterpretation of our own behavior to make it seem more rational and acceptable to us. We excuse or justify a thought or act that is threatening to us by convincing ourselves that there is a rational explanation for that thought or act.

The person who is fired from his or her job may rationalize by saying that the job wasn't a good one anyway. The loved one who turns you down suddenly has many faults. If you miss a ball in tennis, you may glare at the racket or throw it to the ground. There is something wrong with the racket, you are saying, and not with your playing.

It is less threatening to blame someone or something else for our failures instead of ourselves. It is perhaps a point to remember when you next blame your instructor for your failing an exam (unless, of course, your instructor is disguising his or her aggression by projecting it onto you, but it is probably not a good idea to ask if that is the case).

If, for some reason, an object that satisfies an id impulse is not available, the person may shift the impulse to another object. This is known as **displacement**. For example, if a child hates his or her father or an adult hates his or her boss, but is afraid to express this hostility toward the father or boss for fear of punishment, he or she may displace the aggression onto someone else. The child may hit a younger brother, or the adult may shout at his or her children.

In these examples, the original object of the impulse has been replaced by one that is not a threat. Of course, the substitute object will not be as good a source of tension reduction as the original object. If the person is involved in a number of displacements, a reservoir of undischarged tension accumulates. As a result, the person is increasingly driven to find new ways of reducing the tension.

While displacement involves finding a substitute object to satisfy id impulses, **sublimation** involves an altering or displacing of the id impulses themselves. The instinctual energy is diverted into other channels of expression—ones that society considers not only acceptable but admirable. Sexual energy, for example, is diverted or sublimated into artistically creative behaviors. Freud believed that a great variety of human activities, particularly those of an artistic nature, are manifestations of id impulses that have been redirected into socially acceptable outlets.

As with displacement (of which sublimation is a form), sublimation is a compromise. As such, it does not bring total satisfaction but leads to a buildup of undischarged tension.

As we noted earlier, Freud said that all defenses are denials or distortions of reality. Further, all the defenses are unconscious. We are, in essence, lying to ourselves when we use these defenses but are not aware of doing so. Indeed, if we knew we were lying to ourselves, the defenses would not be effective. If they are working well, defenses keep threatening material out of our conscious awareness. As a result, we do not know the truth about ourselves. We have a distorted picture of our needs, fears, longings, and so on.

It follows that such rational processes as problem solving, decision making, and logical thinking are not based on an accurate picture of the individual. In short, according to Freud, we are driven and controlled by internal and external forces of which we are unaware and over which we can exercise little rational control.

There are, however, certain situations in which the truth about ourselves does emerge—that is, when the defenses break down and fail to protect us. This can happen in times of great stress and when a person is under psychoanalysis. When the defenses fail, we are stricken with overwhelming guilt or anxiety. We feel worthless, dismal, and depressed—a situation we cannot long endure.

Unless the defenses are put back into operation, or new ones are formed to take their place, the individual is very likely to become neurotic or psychotic. The defense mechanisms, then, are vital and necessary. We could not survive long without them.

The psychosexual stages of personality development

We have seen that all behavior is defensive but that not everyone uses the same defenses in the same way. We are all driven by the same id impulses, but there is not the same universality in the nature of the ego and the superego. While they perform the same functions for everyone, their specific content or nature varies from one person to the next. They differ because they are formed through experience, and no two people have precisely the same experiences, not even siblings raised in the same home. Thus, a part of our personality is formed on the basis of the unique set of relationships we each have as children with a variety of people and objects. We develop a personal set of character attributes, a consistent pattern of behavior that defines us as individuals.

Freud felt that a person's unique character type develops in childhood from the nature of the parent–child interaction. The child tries to maximize its pleasure by satisfying the id demands, while its parents (as representatives of society) try to impose the demands of reality and the strictures of morality. So important did Freud consider childhood experience that he believed the adult personality was shaped and crystallized by the fifth year of life. What convinced him of the importance of these early years were his own childhood memories and the memories revealed by his adult patients. Invariably, as they lay on Freud's psychoanalytic couch, they reached far back into childhood. Increasingly he saw that the adult neurosis had been formed in the early years of life.

Freud sensed strong conflicts of a sexual nature in the infant and young child—conflicts that seemed to revolve around specific regions of the body. Further, he believed that each body region assumes a greater importance (is the center of conflict) at a different age. And so he formulated the theory of **psychosexual development**, in which the infant passes through a series of stages, each defined by an erogenous zone of the body. (An erogenous zone is a body region that is sensitive to stimulation. It feels good when rubbed or massaged or stimulated in certain ways.) In each stage of development there is a conflict that must be satisfactorily resolved before the infant or child can move on to the next stage.

Sometimes an individual is reluctant or unable to move from one stage to the next because the conflict has not been resolved or because the needs have been so supremely satisfied that he or she doesn't want to move on. In either case, the individual is said to be *fixated* at this stage of development. In **fixation**, a portion of libido (psychic energy) remains invested in that stage of development, leaving less energy for the next stages.

Central to these psychosexual stages of development is the infant's sex drive. Freud shocked colleagues and the public alike when he argued that babies are motivated by sexual impulses. However, as we have noted, Freud did not define sex solely in the narrow sense in which we usually think of it. The infant is driven to obtain a very diffuse form of bodily pleasure, which Freud said derived from the mouth, the anus, and the genitals—the erogenous zones that define the stages of development during the first five years of life.

The oral stage

The first stage of psychosexual development lasts from birth to some time in the second year of life. During this period, the principal source of pleasure for the infant is the mouth. Pleasure is derived from sucking, biting, and swallowing, with the attendant sensations of the lips, tongue, and cheeks. Obviously, the mouth is used for sheer survival—for food and water—but Freud placed a much greater emphasis on the erotic and sexual (broadly defined) satisfactions derived from oral activity.

The infant, at this time, is in a state of complete dependence on the mother, who becomes the primary object of the child's libido. In more familiar terms, we might say that the infant is learning, in a very primitive way (because it is functioning at a primitive level), to love the mother. How the mother responds to the infant's demands, which are totally id demands at this time, determines the nature of the baby's small world. The infant learns from the mother, during the oral stage, to perceive the world as good or bad, satisfying or frustrating, safe or perilous.

In the oral stage of psychosexual development, pleasure is derived from sucking, biting, and swallowing.

There are two modes of activity during this stage: oral incorporative behavior (taking in) and oral aggressive or sadistic behavior (spitting out).

The *oral incorporative* mode occurs first and involves the pleasurable stimulation of the mouth by other people and by food. An adult fixated at the oral incorporative stage is excessively concerned with oral activities—eating, drinking, smoking, kissing, and the like. If, as an infant, the person was excessively gratified, his or her adult oral personality will be predisposed to excessive optimism and dependency. Because they have been overindulged in infancy, these persons continue to depend upon other people for gratification of their needs. As a result, they are overly gullible, will swallow anything they are told, and trust other people inordinately. Such people are referred to as oral passive personality types.

The second oral phase—*oral aggressive*—occurs during the painful and frustrating eruption of teeth. As a result of this experience, the infant for the first time views the mother with hatred as well as love. Persons fixated at this phase are prone to excessive pessimism, hostility, and aggression. They are likely to be argumentative and sarcastic, making "biting" remarks and exhibiting sadistic tendencies toward others. These people tend to be envious of others and try continuously to exploit and manipulate them in an effort to dominate. This personality type is also called *oral sadistic*.

The oral stage ends at the time of weaning, although some libido may remain if fixation has occurred, and then the infant's focus shifts to the other end.

The anal stage

For the most part, society, in the form of parents, has deferred to the infant's needs during the first year, adjusting to its demands and expecting relatively little adjustment in return. This state of affairs changes around age 2, when a new demand is made on the child—namely, toilet training. Freud saw the experience of toilet training as crucial to personality development.

Elimination of feces produces pleasure for the child, but, with the onset of toilet training, he or she must learn to postpone or delay this pleasure. For the first time, the gratification of an instinctual impulse is interfered with as parents attempt to regulate the time and place of defecation.

As any parent can attest, this is a time of trauma and conflict for all parties. The child learns that he or she has (or is) a weapon that can be used against the parents. For the first time, the child has control over something and can choose to comply or not with the parents' demands.

If the toilet training is not going well—if the child has difficulty learning or the parents are excessively harsh and demanding—the child reacts in one of two ways to this frustration. One way is to defecate when and where it is forbidden by the parents to do so, thus defying the parents' attempts at regulation. If the child finds this a satisfactory technique for reducing frustration and uses it frequently, he or she is on the way to developing what Freud called an *anal aggressive* personality. This is the basis for all forms of hostile and sadistic behaviors in adult life, including cruelty, destructiveness, and temper tantrums. Such a person is likely to be disorderly and to view other people as objects to be possessed.

A second way the child may react to these parental demands is to hold back or retain the feces. This also produces a feeling of pleasure (derived from a full lower intestine) and can be another successful technique for manipulating the parents. They may become overly concerned if the child doesn't defecate for long periods of time. Thus, the child has discovered a new method of securing attention and affection from them.

This behavior is the basis for the development of an *anal retentive* personality, described as being stubborn and stingy. Such a person hoards or retains because his or her security depends on what is saved and possessed and on the careful order in which possessions and life are maintained. The person is likely to be rigid, compulsively neat, obstinate, and overly conscientious.

The phallic stage: Resolving the Oedipus complex

Assuming the parents and child have survived the combats and conflicts of the child's first two stages of development, they face a new set of problems around the fourth to fifth year. The focus of pleasure shifts at this time from the anus to the genitals. Again the child faces a battle between an id impulse and the demands of society as reflected in the parents' expectations.

Children at this age seem to spend a good deal of time exploring and manipulating the genitals—their own and others'. Pleasure is derived from the genital region, not only through behaviors such as masturbation but also through fantasies. The child becomes curious about birth, and about why a sister or brother is different in the genital area; he or she talks about marrying the parent of the opposite sex.

Phallic conflicts constitute the last of the so-called pregenital or childhood stages of development and are the most complex ones to resolve. In addition, they are difficult for people to accept because they involve the notion of incest, a strict taboo in the Western world. Between incestuous desires and masturbation we can see the seeds of potential shock, anger, and suppression being sown in the parents of the 4-year-old. Reality and morality come to grips with the evil id once again.

The basic conflict of the phallic stage centers around the unconscious incestuous desire of the child for the parent of the opposite sex. Accompanying this desire is the unconscious desire of the child to replace, or even destroy, the parent of the same sex. (Small wonder that people at the turn of the century considered Freud a pervert and a pornographer.)

Out of this conflict appears one of Freud's best-known concepts: the **Oedipus complex**. Its name is taken from the Greek myth described in the play *Oedipus Rex* (written by Sophocles in the 5th century B.C.). In this story, young Oedipus kills his father and marries his mother, not knowing who they are at the time.

The Oedipus complex operates differently for the boy than for the girl; the male part is the more fully developed of the two concepts.

As we have stated, the mother becomes a love object for the boy. Through both fantasy and overt behavior, he exhibits his sexual longings for her. However, the boy sees an obstacle in his path—the father—whom he comes to look upon as a rival and a threat. He perceives that the father has a special kind of relationship with the mother in which he, the boy, is not allowed to participate. As a result, he becomes jealous and hostile toward his father. Along with the desire to replace his father is the fear that his father will retaliate and harm him. At the same time, his mother may be reacting to his sexual "advances" with punishment and threats of withholding her love. Freud saw this as a time of great anxiety for the young boy.

To make matters worse, the boy develops a specific fear about his penis. He interprets his fear of his father in genital terms; in other words, he fears that his father will cut off the offending organ—the source of his pleasure and sexual long-ings. And so **castration anxiety**, as Freud called it, comes to play a significant role in the boy's life. So great is his fear of castration that he is forced to repress his sexual desire for his mother. This is what Freud termed the resolution of the Oedipal conflict. It involves replacing the sexual longing for the mother with a more acceptable affection and developing a strong identification with the father.

By identifying with his father, the boy is able to experience a degree of vicarious sexual satisfaction. To further the identification, he attempts to become more like his father, adopting many of his mannerisms, behaviors, and attitudes. One of the results of the resolution of the Oedipus complex is the development of the super-ego. The boy adopts his father's superego standards, which prompted Freud to say that the superego is the "heir to the Oedipus complex" (Freud, 1949, p. 62).

Freud was less clear about the **Electra complex**, the female version of these phallic conflicts. In Greek mythology, Electra cajoled her brother into killing their mother and the mother's lover, both of whom had earlier killed Electra's father—another warm and happy mythical family.

The girl's first object of love, like the boy's, is her mother, for she is the primary source of food, affection, and security in infancy. During the phallic stage, however, the father becomes the girl's new love object.

Why does this shift from mother to father take place? Freud explained it in terms of the girl's reaction to her discovery that boys have a protruding sex organ and girls do not. The girl blames her mother for her castrated and therefore in-ferior condition and therefore loves her mother less. Indeed, she may even hate her mother for what she imagines the mother did to her. She transfers her love to her father because he possesses the highly valued organ. However, as much as she loves her father for this possession, she also envies him. And so what Freud called **penis envy** develops in the girl as the counterpart to the boy's castration anxiety. She feels she has lost her penis; he is afraid he is going to lose his.

Freud was not specific about the resolution of the Electra complex, although he did believe it could never be totally resolved. This, Freud believed, led to poorly developed superegos in women. He thought that an adult woman's love of men was always tinged with some degree of penis envy, which he believed could be partially compensated for by having a male child. Of course, there is less need for the girl to resolve her phallic conflict than for the boy; she is not threatened with castration. As a means of resolving the complex, the girl does come to identify with her mother and to repress her love for her father.

The Oedipus complex (using the term now to include both sexes) and the degree of its resolution are paramount in determining adult relations with and atti-tudes toward the opposite sex. Poorly or insufficiently resolved Oedipal conflicts may cause lingering forms of castration anxiety and penis envy in the adult. The so-called *phallic* character or personality evidences strong narcissism and, although continually trying to attract the opposite sex, has difficulty establishing mature heterosexual relationships. Such persons need continual recognition and appreciation of their attractive and unique qualities. As long as they receive such support, they seem to function well, but when it is lacking they are gripped by feelings of inadequacy and inferiority.

The male phallic personality is seen to be brash, vain, self-assured, and displaying a kind of "devil-may-care" attitude. Such men constantly have to assert or express their masculinity, for example, through repeated sexual conquests. The female phallic personality exaggerates the woman's femininity and uses her talents and charms to overwhelm and conquer men. These so-called "castrating women" continue to be motivated by penis envy.

The tense drama that marks the phallic period is repressed in all of us. Its effects operate in the adult at the unconscious level, but we recall little, if any, of the conflict.

The latency period

The storms and stresses of the oral, anal, and phallic stages of psychosexual development are the amalgam out of which most of the adult personality is shaped. The three major structures of personality—the id, ego, and superego—have now largely been formed, and the important relationships among them are being crystallized.

Fortunately—for the child certainly could use some rest—the next five or six years represent a quiet period. This period is not a psychosexual stage of development; the sex instinct is largely dormant during this time, apparently temporarily sublimated in school activities, hobbies, and sports and in developing friendships with members of the same sex. Freud has been criticized for his lack of interest in this time of life. Other personality theorists consider this period to have its own problems and conflicts, which involve getting along with peers and learning to adjust to an ever-widening world.

The genital stage

The fourth and final psychosexual stage of development begins at the time of puberty. The body is becoming physiologically mature, and, if there have been no major fixations at any of the earlier stages of development, the individual may be able to lead a nonneurotic life with normal heterosexual relationships.

There is conflict during this period but less than in the earlier stages. There are still many societal sanctions and taboos concerning sexual expression to which the adolescent must conform, but conflict is minimized through the use of sublimation. The sexual energy pressing for expression in adolescence can be at least partly satisfied through the pursuit of socially acceptable substitute outlets, and then more fully through a committed relationship in adulthood with a person of the opposite sex. In such normal development, this genital type is able to find satisfaction in love and in work, the latter being a socially acceptable activity for sublimation of the id impulses.

Freud strongly emphasized the importance of the early years of childhood in determining the adult personality. The first five years are the crucial ones. Later childhood and adolescence received less attention in his personality theory, and he was little concerned with personality formation in adulthood. What we are as adults, how we behave and think and feel, is determined by the complex of conflicts to which we are exposed and with which we must cope before many of us have even learned to read.

Freud's image of human nature

Freud's position is clear on those issues in personality that define one's image of human nature (see Chapter 1). Freud did not present us with a flattering or optimistic picture of human nature—indeed, quite the opposite. The individual is a dark cellar in which conflict continually rages. We are depicted in pessimistic terms, condemned to this struggle with our own inner forces—a struggle we are almost always doomed to lose. All people are doomed to anxiety, to the thwarting of at least some of the constantly driving impulses. Tension and conflict are always present, and we are endlessly defending ourselves against the forces of the id, which stand ever alert to topple us.

In Freud's system, there is only one ultimate and necessary goal in life—that of tension reduction. We must try to remain as free of tension as possible. On the nature-nurture issue, Freud adopted a middle ground. He believed that much, but not all, of human nature is inherited. The id, the most powerful part of the personality, is an inherited, physiologically based structure, as are the stages that constitute our psychosexual development. However, part of our personality is learned in early childhood, from parent–child interactions.

Although Freud recognized a universality in human nature, in that we all pass through the stages of psychosexual development and are motivated by the same id forces, he also asserted that part of the personality is unique to each person. The ego and the superego perform the same functions for everyone, but the content or nature of the ego and superego varies from one person to another, because they are formed through experience. Also, as we saw, different character or personality types can emerge during the psychosexual stages of development.

On the issue of free will versus determinism, Freud held a deterministic view of human beings. Everything we do and think (and even dream) has been predetermined by inaccessible and invisible forces within us. We are perpetually in the grip of the life-and-death instincts. Our adult personality is fully determined by interactions that took place before we were 5, at a time when we had only limited control over our lives. We are doomed by these early experiences, which forever cast a pall over us, determining our every move.

And what of human intellect and the powers of reason and logic—the abilities that supposedly raise us above the level of the lower animals? Cannot these powers of thought and reason release us from the dark cellar? No, not according to Freud. The idea of a rational person in control of his or her destiny, spontaneously acting on the basis of reason and logic, crumbles under the heavy weight of the id. It is the id, not the intellect, that is our master. Thought and reason are mere servants, operating only to serve our primal desires—a full-time job in itself.

In performing this task, the ego, operating through the defense mechanisms, must often distort or conceal the truth. How, then, in the absence of a realistic and accurate self-perception, can logical thinking or other forms of rationality be of any value?

Freud's picture of human nature, painted in these dark hues, reflected his personal view. Toward individuals he sometimes expressed a benevolent and optimistic attitude (unless they disagreed with his point of view), but for people in general his judgment was harsh. He believed that most people were worthless. "I have found little that is 'good' about human beings on the whole," he wrote. "In my experience most of them are trash" (Meng & Freud, 1963, pp. 61–62). This stern judgment was clearly reflected in his theory.

Assessment in Freud's theory

As you now know, Freud considered the unconscious to be the major motivating force in our lives. All our childhood conflicts are repressed out of conscious awareness. Freud believed that the goal of psychoanalysis was to bring these repressed memories, fears, and thoughts back to the level of conscious awareness.

But how can one evaluate or assess this invisible portion of the mind, this dark arena that is not even accessible to ourselves? Over the course of his work with many patients, Freud developed two basic methods of assessment: *free association* and *dream analysis.*

Free association

Freud developed the technique of **free association**, the "fundamental rule of psychoanalysis," over a number of years of working with his patients. Its origin owes a great deal to Josef Breuer, the Viennese physician mentioned earlier, who befriended Freud during Freud's early years in private practice. Breuer found, in treating a young female hysteric, that placing her under hypnosis enabled her to recall repressed experiences and events. Recalling the events—reliving the experience, in a sense—brought relief of the disturbing symptom.

Freud used this technique himself with some success and applied the term **catharsis** (from the Greek word meaning "purification") to the process. After a while he gave up hypnosis, in part because of his difficulty in hypnotizing some people, and he developed a new method for helping patients to recall repressed material. In this method, the patient lies on a couch while the therapist sits behind it, out of sight. Freud may have chosen this position because he could not bear being stared at (Roazen, 1975). The patient is encouraged to relax as much as possible and to concentrate on events in the past. The patient engages in a kind of daydreaming out loud, saying whatever comes to mind. He or she is instructed to express spontaneously every idea and image exactly as it occurs, no matter how trivial, embarrassing, or even painful the thought or memory might be. There must not be any omitting, rearranging, or restructuring of the memories.

Freud believed that there was nothing random about the information uncovered during free association, and that it was not subject to a patient's conscious choice. The material revealed by patients in free association was predetermined, forced upon them by the nature of their conflict.

Freud found, in the course of using free association, that it sometimes did not operate very freely. Some experiences or memories were evidently too painful to talk about, and the patient would refuse to disclose them. Freud called these moments **resistances**, and he felt that they were of great significance, indicating proximity to the source of the patient's problems. Resistance is a sign that the treatment is going in the right direction and that it should continue to probe more deeply in that area. Part of the task of psychoanalysis is to break down or overcome resistances so that the patient can face the repressed experience.

Freud found that a patient's memories inevitably were of childhood experiences, either real or fantasied, which were most often of a sexual nature. It was due, for the most part, to his patients' fascination with and concentration on childhood experiences, as well as the memories of his own early years, that Freud came to emphasize this period as the source of all later neuroses.

Dream analysis

The other basic technique of assessment that Freud developed is **dream analysis**. Some patients, in the course of free association, told Freud their dreams, and he began to use these dreams as a basis for further associations, asking the patient to free-associate to specific features or events that appeared in a dream. He found that dreams often revealed important repressed memories.

Freud also used this technique to conduct his own analysis. On awakening each morning, he would write down his dreams of the previous night and then free-associate to them. So necessary did Freud consider this method that he continued it for self-analysis all his life.

Freud believed that dreams represent, in disguised or symbolic form, repressed desires, fears, and conflicts. So strongly have these feelings been repressed that they can surface only in disguised fashion during sleep. Thus, Freud distinguished two aspects of the content of dreams: the actual events in the dream (the *manifest content*) and the hidden symbolic meaning of those events (the *latent content*).

Over the course of his work with many patients, Freud found consistent symbols in dreams—events that signified the same thing for nearly every patient. For example, he said that steps, ladders, and staircases represented sexual intercourse; candles, snakes, and tree trunks stood for the penis; and boxes, balconies, and doors signified the female body. Table 2.1 shows additional Freudian dream symbols. However, Freud warned that, in spite of this apparent universality of certain symbols, they still have to be interpreted within the context of the individual con-

TABLE 2.1 Dream symbols or events and their latent psychoanalytic meaning

Symbol	*Interpretation*
Smooth-fronted house	Male body
House with ledges, balconies	Female body
King and queen	Parents
Small animals	Children
Children	Genital organs
Playing with children	Masturbation
Baldness, tooth extraction	Castration
Elongated objects (e.g., tree trunks, umbrellas, neckties, snakes, candles)	Male genitals
Enclosed spaces (e.g., boxes, ovens, closets, caves, pockets)	Female genitals
Climbing stairs or ladders; driving cars; riding horses; crossing bridges	Sexual intercourse
Bathing	Birth
Beginning a journey	Dying
Being naked in a crowd	Desiring to be noticed
Flying	Desiring to be admired
Falling	Desiring to return to a state such as childhood, where one is satisfied and protected

flict. Further, many symbols are specific to the patient at hand and could have a vastly different meaning for another patient.

An additional characteristic of dreams is that they reveal conflicts only in a condensed and intensified form. Further, Freud felt that any single event in a dream has many sources, that dream events rarely result from a single cause.

It is important to note that Freud believed dreams could also have mundane origins, that they are not all necessarily caused by conflicts. Physical stimuli, such as the temperature of the room or contact with one's partner, can cause dreams of a particular nature. Dreams can also be caused by an internal stimulus, such as an upset stomach.

Both techniques of assessment—free association and dream analysis—reveal to the therapist a great deal of repressed material, but all of it is in disguised or symbolic form. The therapist then has the difficult task of interpreting or translating the material for the patient. Freud compared this process with the task of an archeologist in reconstructing a building or community that has been destroyed and buried under the accumulation of more recent years. Just as the archeologist reconstructs a building from the broken fragments, so a psychoanalyst reconstructs an experience from fragmented, buried memories. Thus, much depends on the skill, training, and experience of the psychoanalyst.

Freud's methods of assessment have two points in common: they deal with what is called *depth psychology* and they are indirect measures of personality. Thus, they differ from more objective self-report inventory approaches to personality assessment.

We know that Freud conceived of personality in terms of levels, from the high-

est and most visible (consciousness) to the deepest and most invisible (the unconscious). Both free association and dream analysis are capable of probing the
unconscious. Because the focus of psychoanalysis is on the unconscious, which
cannot be measured directly, indirect approaches were necessary. Psychoanalysts
believe that techniques such as self-report inventories cannot reveal information
about the unconscious.

Other indirect measures of depth psychology are the projective techniques,
which grew out of Freud's attempts to assess the nature of unconscious forces in the
personality.

Research in Freud's theory

Freud's basic research method was the case study, which, as we noted in Chapter 1,
has several limitations. The case study does not rely on objective observation, the
data are not gathered in controlled and systematic fashion, and the situation (the
case study itself) is not amenable to duplication and verification. For example, we
cannot systematically control and vary the conditions of childhood in which patients are reared, nor can a person's environment be duplicated in the laboratory
for further study. In general, then, clinical observations cannot be repeated in controlled experiments.

A more fundamental criticism of Freud's case studies has to do with the nature
of his data. Because he did not keep verbatim records of the therapy sessions, but
rather made notes several hours after seeing each patient, the data may be incomplete, consisting only of what Freud remembered. It is possible that his recollection
was selective, that he recorded only what would support his theory. On the other
hand, Freud's notes may have been highly accurate, but it is impossible to be certain. We are unable to compare his case reports with what his patients actually said.

Further, even if a record of the therapy sessions had been kept, we cannot determine the validity of the patients' comments. Freud made few attempts to verify
the accuracy of his patients' stories, which he could have done, for example, by
questioning friends and relatives of his patients about the events they described.
Therefore, the first step in Freud's research—collection of data—may be characterized as incomplete and inaccurate.

Another criticism of Freud's research is that it was based on a small and unrepresentative sample, restricted to himself and those who chose to undergo analysis
with him. Only a dozen or so cases have been included in any detail in Freud's
writings, and most of these were of middle-class women of good education. It is
difficult to generalize from such a limited sample to the population at large.

Freud's analysis of his data, the process of drawing generalizations and inferences, has been criticized as being subjective and, hence, unreliable. Freud
never explained his procedures adequately, and because the data were not amenable to quantification, their statistical significance cannot be determined.

The same criticisms have been leveled against most of the personality theorists
who followed a neopsychoanalytic approach, as we shall see. They, too, chose the
case study as their primary research method and based their theories mainly on

their patients' reports. This does not mean, however, that their work should be condemned. Freud and the others who took an analytic approach have offered us a wealth of material about the human personality. The problem lies in testing their data by the experimental method. That has proven to be extremely difficult, so those who accept Freud's views, or the views of the neopsychoanalysts, do so on some basis other than experimental verification. The psychologist Edna Heidbreder wrote more than 50 years ago:

> Anyone who accepts or rejects psychoanalytic theories does so by means of the same kind of reasoning that gives him the thousand and one judgments he is forced to make in everyday life on the basis of insufficient or inadequate evidence—the kind of judgments, in fact, that he is forced to live by, but which have no standing in science. Such estimates, growing out of a multitude of impressions and interpretations, guesses and insights, often result in unshakable convictions, convictions which may be right or wrong but which, from the standpoint of science, cannot be recognized as either proved or disproved (Heidbreder, 1933, pp. 403–404).

As far as Freud himself was concerned, his work was scientific, and he believed that he had ample proof for his conclusions. He also thought that only psychoanalysts, using the same techniques he had used, were qualified to judge the scientific worth of his work. In 1938, he wrote that psychoanalysis was based "on an incalculable number of observations and experiences, and only someone who has repeated those observations on himself and on others is in a position to arrive at a judgment of his own upon it" (Freud, 1938, p. 144). As we pointed out, however, the difficulty arises because Freud's observations cannot be repeated; we do not know exactly what he did in collecting his data and in translating his observations into hypotheses and generalizations.

Scientific validation of Freudian concepts

In the years since Freud's death, some of his ideas have been tested scientifically, if the term *science* is broadened sufficiently to include techniques other than the experimental method. There have been many attempts to empirically validate certain aspects of psychoanalysis, although few of them can be described as well-controlled experiments (Silverman, 1976). In an exhaustive analysis of some 2,000 studies in psychology, psychiatry, anthropology, and other disciplines, Seymour Fisher and Roger Greenberg evaluated the scientific credibility of some of Freud's ideas. Case histories were not considered. The data used were those that had been "secured through procedures that are repeatable and involve techniques that make it possible to check on the objectivity of the reporting observer" (Fisher & Greenberg, 1977, p. 15). Thus, every effort was made to restrict the investigation to data considered to have a high degree of objectivity.

The first point to note about this large-scale analysis is that some Freudian concepts continue to resist efforts at scientific validation. For example, there are no conclusions about such major aspects of Freud's theory as the id, ego, superego, death wish, libido, or anxiety. Concepts that are amenable to scientific validation and that appear to be supported by the available evidence include aspects of the oral and anal personality types, the idea that dreams serve as an outlet for tension, and some aspects of the Oedipus complex in males (rivalry with the father, sexual fantasies about the mother, and castration anxiety).

Concepts not supported by the data include the notion that dreams are disguised expressions of repressed wishes and desires, that boys resolve the Oedipus complex by identifying with their fathers and accepting their superego standards out of fear, and that women have inadequately developed superegos and inferior conceptions of their bodies because of penis envy.

Those Freudian concepts that were amenable to validation fared reasonably well, although the evidence supporting some propositions was not overwhelming. More important was the demonstration that the concepts could be reduced to propositions that were testable by the experimental method. However, it must be remembered that the major aspects of Freud's theory defy testing by the methods of science.

Let us consider a few examples, beginning with dreams. You are probably familiar with the research that has established distinct stages of sleep, from very light to very deep. In the stage known as REM (rapid eye movement) sleep, the stage during which most dreaming occurs, the eyes move or dart about as though they were watching the events of the dream (Aserinsky & Kleitman, 1953). If the dream involves a tennis match, for example, the eyes move as though they were following the ball back and forth across the net (Dement & Kleitman, 1957).

In research to test Freud's ideas about the content of dreams, subjects were awakened during the REM phase of sleep and questioned about their dreams. These studies confirmed Freud's notion that dreams can reflect a person's current emotional concerns, expressed in some disguised or symbolic fashion (Breger, Hunter & Lane, 1971). Research did not show that dreams represented a fulfillment of wishes or desires, as Freud had proposed (Dement & Wolpert, 1958).

Dreams were also used in research on the Oedipus complex. The researchers wanted to determine if men reported more dreams about castration anxiety and if women reported more dreams about penis envy and castration wishes (Hall & Van de Castle, 1965). Dreams of normal college student subjects were analyzed by trained raters using objective criteria for detecting the presence of castration anxiety, castration wishes, or penis envy. For example, dream content involving the acquisition of a phallic-like object, or envy of male physical characteristics, was interpreted as an indication of penis envy. Pain, loss, or injury to some part of the body was seen as indicative of castration anxiety. The raters agreed with one another in almost 90 percent of their judgments, reflecting a high degree of reliability and objectivity in their ratings.

The results supported Freud's ideas in that significantly more males had dreams reflecting castration anxiety and significantly more females had dreams reflecting castration wishes or penis envy. The research also shows an imaginative approach to an elusive and subjective topic.

Investigations were also made of Freud's oral and anal personality types. Oral types, it was predicted from Freud's theory, should eat more and hence weigh more than non-oral types. One study reported a strong relationship between obesity and persons who were identified by the Rorschach as being orally oriented (Masling, Rabie & Blondheim, 1967).

Another study compared oral and anal personalities in terms of their degree of conformity to the suggestions of an authority figure (Tribich & Messer, 1974). According to Freud, oral personalities tend to be dependent upon and submissive to other people. Thus, they should conform much more than anal personalities. Anal types tend to be hostile and should actively resist conformity. This hypothesis was supported. Oral and anal types were determined on the basis of a projective technique. The subjects were then given a laboratory task—to report on how many inches a spot of light had moved. Before stating their answer, the subjects heard the judgment of a psychiatrist (presumed to be an authority figure) as to how far he thought the light had moved. The answers of the oral personalities were much closer to that of the authority figure than were the answers of the anal personalities. Thus, the oral types had shown greater conformity.

In general, the research evidence available to date is stronger in supporting Freud's notion of the anal personality type than it is for the oral type. The evidence is quite weak for the phallic personality type (Kline, 1972).

A final commentary

Freud's theory has had a phenomenal impact on psychology and psychiatry, on our image of human nature, and on the understanding of personality. Some consider Freud to be one of the great contributors to civilization, on a par with Albert Einstein and Jesus Christ. More than 40 years after his death, a popular American magazine stated that Freud's ideas "about dreams, religion, creativity and the unconscious motivations underlying all human behavior are so pervasive that it would be difficult to imagine twentieth-century thought without him" (*Newsweek*, November 30, 1981, p. 64).

Whether we agree or disagree with his theory, there is no denying Freud's importance. We see daily evidence of it in the fact that so many people know his name and something about his ideas. He is recognized the world over, and this alone makes him a candidate for that small roster of individuals who have been pivotal in human history.

Within psychology itself, Freud's importance also remains secure. Psychoanalysis contributed greatly to the growing interest of American psychologists in the study of personality, beginning in the 1930s. In the 1940s and 1950s, psychoanalysis influenced the emerging study of motivation. In addition, some of Freud's concepts have been absorbed into the mainstream of contemporary psychology. These include the role of the unconscious, the importance of childhood experiences in shaping adult behavior, and the operation of the defense mechanisms. Interest in these areas and others has, as we have seen, generated a great deal of research.

In the early 1980s, 679 members of the American Psychological Association, chosen at random, were asked to rank 286 prominent psychologists to determine their relative influence on contemporary American psychology (Gilgen, 1982). Freud was rated second in importance, following B. F. Skinner (Chapter 14). This is high praise for a theorist who began his investigation of the human personality nearly 100 years before the survey was undertaken and who was being compared with many psychologists whose impact was much more recent.

An eminent historian of psychology, E. G. Boring, wrote, "It is not likely that the history of psychology can be written in the next three centuries without mention of Freud's name and still claim to be a general history of psychology. And there you have the best criterion of greatness: posthumous fame" (Boring, 1950, pp. 706–707).

We shall see further evidence of Freud's importance as we discuss other personality theorists. A great many psychologists and psychiatrists continue to use Freud's work, either as a starting point or as a base of opposition against which to develop their own theories. Great ideas inspire, not only by being perceived as valid and true, but also by being perceived as incorrect and thus stimulating the development of another viewpoint.

There is no need to expound further on Freud's greatness. What is important before we leave Sigmund Freud is placing his work within the context of legitimate criticism.

We have already discussed criticisms directed against the case study, Freud's primary method of research. In addition to these criticisms, which come mainly from experimental psychology, there are substantial questions raised by other personality theorists, many of which we will discuss in the following chapters. Other individuals have developed their own theories of personality to counteract what they perceive to be weaknesses and errors in Freud's formulations.

Some personality theorists argue that Freud placed too great an emphasis on biological forces as shapers of personality. Some critics take issue with Freud's focus on sex and aggression as major motivating forces and believe that we are shaped more by social experiences than by sexual ones. Other critics disagree with Freud's deterministic picture of us as passive victims of our instincts and conflicts. They believe that we have more free will than Freud granted and that we can choose to act and grow spontaneously, having at least partial control of our fate.

Another criticism has focused on Freud's stress on past behavior to the exclusion of future aspirations. These critics argue that we are shaped as much by the future as by the past, by what we hope for and plan to do as much or more than by what we experienced before the age of 5. Still other personality theorists feel that Freud placed too much emphasis on the emotionally crippled, the immature, and the disturbed, to the exclusion of the healthy and mature individual. If we are interested in developing a theory of human personality, these critics argue, we should study the best and the healthiest individuals, not the disturbed ones—the positive human emotions rather than only the negative ones.

Many critics take exception to what they see as Freud's degrading views on women. The concept of penis envy and the notions that women have poorly developed superegos and a sense of inferiority about their own bodies are specific targets of criticism. One personality theorist, Karen Horney (Chapter 5), broke with Freud over the issue of feminine psychology.

The ambiguous definitions of certain of Freud's concepts have been questioned. Critics point to what they see as confusion, and even contradiction, in such terms as id, ego, and superego. Are they physical structures or levels in the brain?

Are they fluid processes and functions? Are they even sharply separated from one another? It is interesting to note that in his later writings Freud himself spoke of difficulties and ambiguities in these and other concepts.

Evidence from anthropological studies of various cultures seems to contradict Freud's basic assumption that the biological basis of personality is universal. So much diversity in human behavior has been found across cultures that the assumption of an instinctual commonality is subject to question. The evidence suggests that child-rearing practices are more important in personality formation than are inborn biological forces. For example, cultures exist in which there is no taboo against incestuous sexual relations and in which no evidence of Oedipal conflict— castration anxiety or penis envy—can be found.

There are theorists who remain faithful, in large part, to Freud's basic assumptions and overall point of view, although they too challenge certain of his premises. A major change introduced into psychoanalysis by these loyalists is an expanded emphasis on the ego (Hartmann, 1964). Rather than being the servant of the id, the ego, in this new conception, is seen as being more independent of the id, possessing its own energy not derived from the id, and having its own functions separate from the id. Another change introduced by the loyalists is the deemphasis of biological forces as influences on personality in favor of social and psychological forces.

From this brief overview of the criticisms, questions, and contemporary modifications of Freud's system, we can see that some of his original formulations may not be as appropriate in the final years of the 20th century as they might have been when the century began. As times change, we must continually seek new and better ways of looking at ourselves.

This book is a history of modern insights into human nature. We are, in our personal and social growth, never free of the past, nor should we want to be. It offers the foundation on which to build, as later personality theorists have done on Freud's work.

If Freud's theory has served no other purpose than that—an inspiration for others, a framework within which to develop new insights—then his importance to the world of ideas is secure. Every structure is dependent upon the soundness and integrity of its foundation. Freud gave personality theory a solid and challenging base on which to build, and his position retains a great deal of contemporary influence.

Summary

Freud's hostility toward his father and attachment to his mother set the stage for his formulation of the concept of the Oedipus complex. During Freud's neurotic mid-life crisis he undertook his self-analysis and developed the core of his personality theory.

Instincts are mental representations of stimuli that originate within the body. Instincts give rise to needs which generate physiological energy that is transformed in the mind into wishes. Needs induce tension that must be reduced. Life instincts serve the purpose of survival and are manifested in a form of psychic energy called libido. Death instincts and their component aggressive drive compel us to destroy, conquer, and kill.

Freud originally divided personality into three levels: the conscious, the preconscious, and the unconscious. Later he introduced three structures of the personality: the id, the ego, and the superego.

The id, the biological component of personality, is the storehouse of the instincts and the libido. It operates in accordance with the pleasure principle. The ego, the rational component of personality, includes the powers of perception, judgment, and memory, and operates in accordance with the reality principle. The superego, the moral side of personality, consists of the conscience (behaviors for which the child is punished) and the ego-ideal (behaviors for which the child is praised). The ego constantly mediates between the demands of the id, the pressures of reality, and the dictates of the superego.

Anxiety develops when the ego is pressured too greatly. Reality anxiety is a fear of real dangers in the real world. Neurotic anxiety is a conflict between instinctual gratification and reality. Moral anxiety is a conflict between the id and the superego.

Defense mechanisms protect us from these threats to the ego. They distort reality and operate unconsciously. Defense mechanisms include: (1) repression, involuntarily removing disturbing ideas from conscious awareness; (2) reaction formation, expressing an impulse opposite to the one that disturbs us; (3) projection, attributing disturbing impulses to someone else; (4) regression, retreating to an earlier, more pleasant, period of life; (5) rationalization, reinterpreting behavior to make it seem more rational and acceptable; (6) displacement, displacing an impulse to an object other than the one intended to satisfy it; and (7) sublimation, altering the troublesome id impulse.

Everyone is driven by the same id impulses, but the contents of the ego and the superego differ from person to person because they are formed through experience. A person's character type develops in childhood from the nature of the parent-child interaction. Children pass through psychosexual stages of development, each defined by a different erogenous zone of the body. The oral stage involves two modes of activity: oral incorporative behavior and oral aggressive behavior. Adults fixated at the incorporative stage are concerned with oral activities and are dependent and optimistic. Adults fixated at the oral aggressive stage are pessimistic and hostile, and attempt to manipulate others. The anal stage involves the first interference with the gratification of an instinctual impulse. Anal aggressive personalities tend to be hostile, destructive, and sadistic. Anal retentive personalities tend to be stingy, rigid, and compulsively neat.

The phallic stage involves the child's unconscious sexual longings for the parent of the opposite sex and feelings of rivalry and fear toward the parent of the same sex. In males, this is the Oedipus complex; in females, the Electra complex. Males develop castration anxiety; females develop penis envy. Boys resolve the Oedipus complex by identifying with their fathers, adopting their superego standards, and repressing their sexual longing for their mothers. Girls are less successful in resolving the Electra complex, which, according to Freud, leaves them with poorly developed superegos. Male phallic personalities are brash, vain, and self-assured. Female phallic personalities exaggerate their femininity to conquer men.

The latency period is not a psychosexual stage of development. During this period, the sex instinct is sublimated in school activities, sports, and friendships with persons of the same sex. The genital stage, at the time of puberty, marks the beginning of heterosexual relationships.

Freud's image of human nature is pessimistic. People are doomed to anxiety, to the thwarting of impulses, and to tensions and conflicts. The goal of life is tension reduction. Much of human nature is inherited, but part is learned through parent–child interactions. Freud recognized some degree of universality in human nature, but he also believed that part of personality is unique to each person. His view was deterministic in that personality is irrevocably shaped by biological forces and childhood experiences.

Freud's two methods of personality assessment are free association and dream analysis. In free association, resistances develop in which a patient resists talking about particularly disturbing memories or experiences. Dreams have both a manifest content (the actual events in the dream) and a latent content (the symbolic meaning of those events). These methods deal with depth psychology, that is, the unconscious, and are indirect measures of personality.

Freud's research method is the case study, which does not rely on objective observation. It is not controlled and systematic, nor is it amenable to duplication and verification. His data are not quantifiable, may be incomplete and inaccurate, and were based on a small and unrepresentative sample of people. His analysis of the data has been criticized for being subjective.

Some of Freud's concepts have been supported by research. These include some characteristics of the oral and anal personality types, the idea that dreams serve as an outlet for tension and reflect emotional concerns, and certain aspects of the Oedipus complex. Major portions of the theory (such as the id, ego, superego, death wish, libido, and anxiety) resist efforts at scientific validation.

Freud has had an enormous impact on 20th-century thought and is considered to be one of the most important influences on postwar psychology in the United States. Some personality theorists criticize Freud for placing too much emphasis on biological forces, sex, aggression, emotional disturbance, and childhood; for his deterministic image of human nature and his negative views of women; and for the ambiguous definitions of some of his concepts. It is partly in reaction to these problems that competing theories have been offered.

Glossary

anxiety A feeling of fear and dread without an obvious cause.

castration anxiety A boy's fear during the Oedipal period that his penis will be cut off.

catharsis The expression of emotions that is expected to lead to their reduction.

cathexis An investment of psychic energy in an object or person.

death instincts   The unconscious drive toward decay, destruction, and aggression.

defense mechanism   A strategy used by the ego to defend itself against the anxiety provoked by the conflicts of everyday life; involves denials or distortions of reality.

displacement   A defense mechanism that involves shifting id impulses from an object that is threatening or unavailable to one that is available—for example, replacing hostility toward one's boss with hostility toward one's child.

dream analysis   A technique involving the interpretation of dreams to uncover unconscious conflicts.

ego   The rational aspect of the personality responsible for directing and controlling the instincts according to the reality principle.

ego-ideal   The moral or ideal behaviors for which a person should strive.

fixation   State in which a portion of the libido remains invested in one of the psychosexual stages because of excessive frustration or gratification.

free association   A technique in which the patient says whatever comes to mind; a kind of daydreaming out loud.

id   The aspect of personality allied with the instincts that is the source of psychic energy; operates according to the pleasure principle.

instincts   Mental representations of internal stimuli, such as hunger, that drive the individual to take certain actions.

libido   The form of psychic energy

manifested by the life instincts that drives the individual toward pleasurable behaviors and thoughts.

life instincts   The drive for survival of the individual and the species by satisfying the needs for food, water, air, and sex.

Oedipus/Electra complex   The unconscious desire at about ages 4 and 5 (the phallic stage) for the parent of the opposite sex, accompanied by a desire to replace or destroy the parent of the same sex.

penis envy   The envy females feel toward males because they possess a penis, accompanied by a sense of loss because females do not have one.

pleasure principle   The principle by which the id functions to avoid pain and to maximize pleasure.

primary-process thought   Childlike thinking by which the id attempts to satisfy the instinctual drives.

projection   A defense mechanism that involves attributing one's disturbing impulses to someone else.

psychoanalysis   Freud's theory for understanding personality and his system of therapy for treating mental disorders.

psychosexual stages of development   The oral, anal, phallic, and genital stages through which children pass and in which instinctual gratification depends on the stimulation of corresponding areas of the body.

rationalization   A defense mechanism that involves reinterpreting our behavior to make it more acceptable and less threatening to us.

reaction formation A defense mechanism that involves the expression of an id impulse that is the opposite of the one that is truly driving the person.

reality principle The principle by which the ego functions to provide appropriate constraints on the expression of the id instincts.

regression A defense mechanism that involves retreating to an earlier, less frustrating period of life and manifesting the usually childish behaviors characteristic of that more secure time.

repression A defense mechanism that involves the unconscious denial of the existence of something that causes anxiety.

resistances In free association, a blockage or refusal to disclose painful memories.

secondary-process thought Mature thought processes needed to deal rationally with the external world.

sublimation A defense mechanism that involves altering or displacing id impulses, diverting instinctual energy into socially acceptable behaviors.

superego The moral aspect of personality; the internalization of parental and societal values and standards.

Review questions

1. What are the life and death instincts? How do they motivate behavior?
2. Describe the id, ego, and superego, the basic structures of the personality. How are they related?
3. Describe the three types of anxiety. According to Freud, what is the purpose of anxiety?
4. How do we defend ourselves against anxiety?
5. Describe the oral and anal stages of psychosexual development. What activities characterize the adult fixated at the oral incorporative phase? At the anal retentive phase?
6. How do boys and girls resolve the conflicts of the phallic stage?
7. What is Freud's position on the relative influences of heredity and environment? What is Freud's position on the issue of free will versus determinism?
8. What type of material may be uncovered by the technique of free association? What are resistances?
9. Describe the two aspects of dreams distinguished by Freud. Discuss the recent research to test Freud's ideas about dream content. Which of these ideas have received empirical support?
10. What criticisms have been made of Freud's case-study method?
11. What is the position of psychoanalysis within psychology today?

Suggested reading

Clark, R. W. *Freud: the man and the cause; a biography*. New York: Random House, 1980.

Ellenberger, H. F. *The discovery of the unconscious*. New York: Basic Books, 1970. (See Chapter 7, "Sigmund Freud and Psychoanalysis.")

Fisher, S. & Greenberg, R. P. *The scientific credibility of Freud's theories and therapy*. New York: Basic Books, 1977.

Freeman, L. & Strean, H. S. *Freud and women*. New York: Ungar, 1981.

Freud, S. *The standard edition of the complete psychological works of Sigmund Freud* (24 vols.). New York: Norton, 1953–1974. (This is the definitive reference source for Freud's writings. See especially Vol. 1, "On the origins of psychoanalysis"; Vols. 4 & 5, "The interpretation of dreams"; and Vol. 6, "The psychopathology of everyday life.")

Masson, J. M., Ed. *The complete letters of Sigmund Freud to Wilhelm Fliess, 1887–1904*. Cambridge, MA: Belknap Press of Harvard University Press, 1985.

McGuire, W., Ed. *The Freud/Jung letters*. Princeton, NJ: Princeton University Press, 1974.

Roazen, P. *Freud and his followers*. New York: Knopf, 1975.

Sulloway, F. J. *Freud, biologist of the mind: Beyond the psychoanalytic legend*. New York: Basic Books, 1979.

PART 2

The Neopsychoanalytic Approach

Nearly all personality theories owe their origin, in some degree, to the work of Freud, whether they elaborated upon or opposed his approach to personality. Some theories were developed in the years since Freud's death in 1939. Others were proposed during his lifetime, and thus may have been more directly influenced by his work. Some theorists, who initially were loyal to Freud's ideas and to the man himself, broke away because of growing opposition to certain aspects of his approach.

This is the case with several of the theorists in this section. Carl Jung and Alfred Adler were close personal associates of Freud before they rebelled and offered their own views of personality. Karen Horney and Erich Fromm, although they did not have a personal relationship with Freud, nevertheless were orthodox Freudians before seeking different paths. Henry Murray, the first American theorist discussed here, developed a view of personality that offers unique interpretations of some formal psychoanalytic concepts. The work of Erik Erikson (Chapter 10) is also derived from orthodox psychoanalysis.

The neopsychoanalytic theorists differ from one another on a number of points. They represent neo-Freudian approaches rather than a unified point of view. They have been grouped in a single section because of their opposition to Freud's emphasis on instincts as primary motivators and his deterministic view of personality. These theorists stress social influences more than Freud did, which is why (with the exception of Jung) they have been called social-psychological theorists. They also present a more hopeful and optimistic image of human nature, and their view that personality is more a product of environment than of inherited, physiological forces is highly compatible with American culture and thought. Their work shows how quickly the field of personality began to diversify, within little more than a decade after it began.

CHAPTER 3

Carl Jung

The life of Jung (1875–1961)
Psychic energy
The systems of personality
   The ego
   Psychological types
   The personal unconscious
   The collective unconscious
   Archetypes
The development of the personality
   Childhood to young adulthood
   Middle age to old age
Interaction among parts of the personality
Jung's image of human nature
Assessment in Jung's theory
   The word-association test
   Symptom analysis
   Dream analysis
Research in Jung's theory
   Studies of psychological types
A final commentary
Summary
Glossary
Review questions
Suggested readings

My life is a story of the self-realization of the unconscious. Everything in the unconscious seeks outward manifestation, and the personality too desires to evolve out of its unconscious conditions.

CARL JUNG

Originally an intimate of Freud's, who considered him his spiritual heir, Carl Jung went on to develop his own theory of personality, which differed dramatically from orthodox psychoanalysis. Jung fashioned a new and elaborate theory of personality quite unlike any other theory that had been developed. To this day, his **analytical psychology** stands apart from all other approaches to personality in its complexity and unique emphases.

The first point on which Jung came to disagree with Freud was the role of sexuality. In a sense, Jung broadened Freud's definition of libido by redefining it as a more generalized dynamic force of personality, a psychic energy that includes sex but is not restricted to it.

The second major difference is concerned with the direction of the forces that influence personality. While Freud viewed human beings as largely prisoners or victims of past events and processes, Jung argued that we are shaped by our future as well as by our past. A person is influenced not only by what happened to him or her as a child but also by what he or she aspires to do in the future.

The final major point of difference between Freud and Jung revolves around the unconscious. Rather than placing less emphasis than Freud did on the unconscious (as is the case with the other dissenters discussed), Jung placed a greater emphasis on the concept. He probed more deeply into the unconscious and added new dimensions to its composition: the inherited experiences of humans as a species and human beings' animal ancestry. While Freud had recognized this phylogenetic aspect of personality (the influence of inherited primal experiences), Jung made it the central point of his system of personality. As a result, history, mythology, primitive rituals and symbols, and religion all came to play a part in Jung's view of human nature.

The life of Jung (1875–1961)

Black-frocked clergymen, deaths and funerals, neurotic parents in a failing marriage, a sexual assault by an adult he had worshiped, religious doubts and conflicts, strange dreams and visions, and a wooden mannequin for a companion marked Jung's early-childhood years. Born in Switzerland into a family that included nine clergymen (eight uncles and his father), Jung was introduced at an early age not only to religion but to the classics as well. He was very close to his father, although he considered him weak and powerless. While generally kind and tolerant, his father often had periods of great moodiness and irritability and failed to be the strong authority figure his son needed.

His mother was the more powerful parent, although she had a number of emotional disorders that caused her behavior to be inconsistent. As a result, Jung came to distrust women, a suspicion that took many years to dispel. His mother was also fat and unattractive, which may explain why Jung later rejected Freud's notion that every boy has a sexual longing for his mother. To escape his parents and their continuing marital problems, Jung spent many hours alone in the attic of his home, playing with and confiding in a figure he had carved out of wood.

During his childhood years, Jung recalled, he attended many funerals for fishermen who had drowned in a nearby waterfall. When he was 6 and living near Basel, he discovered the corpse of a man who had been killed in a flood, and once he nearly fell from a very high bridge. The notion of death, then, was no secret to the young boy.

As a child, Jung was extremely lonely. Distrustful of his mother and disappointed in the weakness of his father, he came to feel cut off from the external world of conscious reality. As an escape, he turned inward, to the world of his unconscious—the world of dreams, visions, and fantasies—in which he felt more secure. This choice would guide him for the rest of his life.

Whenever Jung was faced with a problem, he found a solution in the form of his dreams and visions. The essence of his theory of personality was shaped in the same way. When he was 3 years old, he dreamed he was in a huge cavern. In another dream, later in life, he saw himself digging beneath the surface, unearthing the bones of prehistoric animals. To Jung, such dreams represented the direction his approach to the human personality should take; he should explore the unconscious that lies beneath the surface of behavior. So strongly was he guided by these manifestations of his unconscious that he called his autobiography *Memories, Dreams, Reflections*. In Jung's personal life, as in his theory of personality, the unconscious was paramount.

Introverted and solitary, Jung disliked school, resenting the time he had to devote to his formal studies rather than to topics that truly interested him. To his delight, however, he was forced to miss six months of school as a result of a series of fainting spells. When he overheard his father lament to a friend "What will become of the boy if he cannot earn his living?" (Jung, 1963, p. 31) his illness disappeared and he immediately returned to school to work harder than ever before.

He read a great deal, particularly on religious and philosophical topics, and was curious and confused about a great many of life's issues. In describing the loneliness that characterized his childhood, Jung wrote: "Thus the pattern of my relationship to the world was already prefigured; today as then I am a solitary" (Jung, 1963, pp. 41–42).

He studied medicine at the University of Basel and decided, to the disappointment of his professors, to specialize in psychiatry, a field then held in low repute. He believed that psychiatry would give him the opportunity to pursue his interest in fantasies, dreams, the supernatural, and the occult.

Beginning in 1900, he worked at a mental hospital in Zurich, under Eugen Bleuler, the famous psychiatrist who coined the term *schizophrenia*. During the following years, Jung lectured at the University of Zurich, developed a sizable private practice, and conducted research using a word-association test to investigate the emotional reactions of his patients.

Thus, when he became associated with Freud in 1907, it was as a professional with a well-established reputation, not as an unknown student. Freud and Jung began their relationship through correspondence, and when they met for the first time they were so congenial and had so much to share that they talked for 13 hours.

Jung remained in Zurich, but the two men met periodically, continued a voluminous correspondence, and journeyed together to the United States in 1909 to give a series of lectures at Clark University. Freud was grooming Jung to take over the presidency of the International Psychoanalytic Association. Concerned that psychoanalysis might come to be labeled a "Jewish science" (as it was called later, during the Nazi era), Freud wanted a non-Jew to assume titular leadership of the movement. Their relationship was an intimate one. "I formally adopted you as an eldest son," Freud once wrote to Jung, "and anointed you as my successor and crown prince" (McGuire, 1974, p. 218). Jung apparently considered Freud a father figure. "Let me enjoy your friendship not as one between equals," he wrote, "but as that of father and son" (McGuire, 1974, p. 122). Their relationship had many of the elements of the Oedipus complex about it (Alexander, 1982).

Contrary to what Freud had hoped, Jung was not a totally uncritical disciple. He had his own ideas, his own view of the human personality (which differed from Freud's view), and when he began to express these unorthodox notions it became inevitable that they would part company. They severed their relationship in 1913.

In that same year, when Jung was 38 years old, he experienced a severe neurotic crisis that lasted for three years. He felt in danger of losing contact with reality and was so disturbed that he resigned his lectureship at the University of Zurich. He was unable to continue with his scientific work, but he did persist in seeing his patients during that time.

Freud had suffered a neurotic episode at approximately the same time of life and resolved it by analyzing his dreams, thus formulating the core of his personality theory. Jung's situation is a remarkable parallel. He overcame his disturbance by confronting his unconscious through the exploration of his fantasies and dreams. Although Jung's self-analysis was less systematic than Freud's, his approach was similar.

Out of Jung's confrontation with his unconscious he fashioned an approach to personality. "The years when I was pursuing my inner images," he wrote, "were the most important in my life—in them everything essential was decided" (Jung, 1963, p. 199). He developed the conviction that the most crucial stage in personality growth was not childhood, as Freud had thought, but middle age—the time of Jung's own crisis.

We can see that Jung's theory was established on an intuitive base, derived from his own experiences, memories, and dreams. It was then refined, along more rational and empirical lines, by data provided by his patients, nearly two-thirds of whom were middle aged and suffering from the same difficulties Jung had faced. It is no surprise, then, that emotional changes at midlife became an important part of Jung's theory of personality.

The rest of his long life was fruitful, both personally and professionally. His analytical psychology was attracting increasing numbers of followers, his books were popular, and he explored diverse cultures in America, Africa (he even learned Swahili), Egypt, India, and Ceylon in order to broaden his understanding of human nature. In later years, the University of Basel established a special professorship for him, and a group of his students organized a Jungian training institute that is still active in Zurich today.

Psychic energy

One of the earliest and most important points on which Jung took issue with Freud concerned the nature of libido. Jung could not agree that libido was exclusively a sexual energy, and he argued instead that it was a broad and undifferentiated life energy.

Actually, Jung used the term **libido** in two different ways: first, as the diffuse, general life energy mentioned above and, second, as a narrower psychic energy that, in a sense, fuels the work of the **psyche**, his term for personality. It is through the psychic energy that psychological activities such as perceiving, thinking, feeling, and wishing are carried out. This view is not unlike Freud's.

When a great deal of psychic energy is invested in a particular idea or feeling, that idea is capable of strongly influencing a person. For example, if you are highly motivated to obtain power, then most of your psychic energy will be devoted to seeking power. The amount of energy so devoted or concentrated is called a *value* in Jung's system.

Psychic energy has its counterpart in the physical energy used by the body to carry out its physiological activities. Jung described a reciprocal relationship between these two forms of energy. The energy of the body can be transformed into the energy of the psyche, and the energy of the psyche can be transformed into the energy of the body. In other words, the body can affect the mind, and the mind can affect the body (as is the case, for example, with psychosomatic illness).

Jung drew heavily from physics to explain the functioning of psychic energy in his principles of opposites, equivalence, and entropy.

The **principle of opposites** is a major tenet of his theory of personality. "I see in all that happens the play of opposites," he wrote. He notes the existence of opposites or polarities in physical energy—heat versus cold, height versus depth, creation versus decay.

So it is with psychic energy; every wish or feeling has its opposite. There must be antithesis, Jung felt, or there would be no energy. Without polarities or extremes, there would be no process or tendency toward equalization, and that process of equalization is energy. The principle of opposites, this conflict between polarities, was considered by Jung to be the prime mover of behavior, the generator of all energy. Indeed, the sharper the conflict between polarities, the greater the energy produced.

The **principle of equivalence** is essentially the first law of thermodynamics in physics—the principle of conservation of energy—applied to psychic energy. It states that energy is not lost to the personality but rather is shifted from one part to another. If, for example, one's psychic value in a particular area weakens or disappears altogether, that energy is transferred elsewhere in the psyche. If we lose interest in a person or a hobby or a field of study, the psychic energy formerly invested in that area is shifted to a new area or to several different areas. Also, the psychic energy in use for conscious activities while we are awake is shifted to dreaming when we are asleep.

The word *equivalence* means that the new area to which energy has shifted must be of an equally strong psychic value—that is, equally desirable or compelling or fascinating. If that is not the case, the excess energy will flow into the unconscious. In whatever direction and manner energy flows, the principle of equivalence means that there is a continuing redistribution of energy within the personality.

The second law of thermodynamics is represented in Jung's system by his **principle of entropy**. In physics, this principle refers to the equalization of energy differences. For example, if a hot object and a cold object are placed in direct contact with each other, heat will flow from the hotter to the colder object until they are in equilibrium at the same temperature. It is, in effect, an exchange of energy resulting in a kind of homeostatic balance between the objects.

The same thing occurs, in principle, with psychic energy, according to Jung. There is always a tendency toward a balance or equilibrium in the personality. For example, if two desires or beliefs differ greatly in psychic value or intensity, energy will flow from the more strongly held to the weaker. Ideally, the personality would have an equal distribution of psychic energy over all its systems and aspects (a condition known as *self* or *selfhood*), but this state is never achieved totally. Indeed, if such a perfect balance or equilibrium were achieved, then no psychic energy would be produced, for, as we have seen, energy requires conflict between opposites. Thus, complete entropy remains a state to be striven for but never realized.

Psychic energy, then, through the principles of opposition, equivalence, and entropy, provides the dynamic mechanisms and power for the operation of the personality.

The systems of personality

The total personality or psyche was viewed by Jung as composed of a variety of separate structures or systems that, while quite different from one another, are nevertheless capable of influencing one another. The major systems are the ego, the personal unconscious, and the collective unconscious.

The ego

The **ego** is the conscious mind, that part of the psyche concerned with perceiving, thinking, feeling, and remembering. It is our awareness of ourselves and is responsible for carrying out the normal activities of waking life. The ego performs a selective function, admitting into conscious awareness only a portion of the stimuli to which we are constantly exposed. The ego also provides a sense of continuity, coherence, and identity—a stability in the way we perceive our world and ourselves.

Much of our conscious perception of and reaction to the world around us is determined by the *attitudes* of **extraversion** and **introversion**. Jung believed that the libido can be channeled externally, toward the outside world, or internally, toward the self. These two attitudes—extraversion and introversion—are probably the best-known parts of Jung's system; the terms and concepts have come into general prominence and have generated much research.

We all have a good idea of what these terms mean. When we say people are introverted, we mean that they are somewhat withdrawn, often shy, and focusing on self. Extraverts, on the other hand, are much more open, sociable, and socially aggressive. Everyone, according to Jung, has the capability for either attitude, but one becomes dominant (for reasons he did not make clear). Once an attitude has become the dominant one, the person's behavior and consciousness are largely ruled by it.

However, the nondominant attitude remains; it has not disappeared. It becomes part of the *personal unconscious*, where it is still capable of influencing behavior. For example, an introverted person may on occasion (or consistently in certain situations) display characteristics of extraversion, or he or she may wish to be more outgoing or may be very attracted to someone who is extraverted. The nondominant attitude, then, is ever present, so that a person is not exclusively or totally an extravert or an introvert. We all carry both attitudes within.

Shortly after he developed the concepts of extraversion and introversion, Jung came to realize that this pair of opposites did not, as he had thought for a time, fully explain all the differences found among people.

He began to see that there were different kinds of introverts and extraverts, and so he developed another level of categorization dealing with what he called the *psychological functions*. The functions refer to different ways in which we perceive or apprehend both the external world of reality and the inner world of subjectivity. Jung posited four functions of the psyche: thinking, feeling, sensing, and intuiting.

Thinking and *feeling* are grouped together as *rational* functions. They involve making judgments and evaluations about experiences. While feeling is a function totally different from thinking, Jung believed that both are concerned with the ability to organize and categorize experience. Nevertheless, he did say that they were opposite functions. The kind of evaluation made by the feeling function is in terms of liked or disliked, pleasant or unpleasant, stimulating or dull. The thinking function involves a conscious judgment of whether an experience is true or false.

The second pair of opposing functions—*sensing* and *intuiting*—are called *irrational* functions because they make no use of the process of reason. These functions do not evaluate experiences; they simply experience them. Sensing reproduces an experience accurately through the senses in the way that a photograph copies an object. Intuiting does not arise directly from a stimulus in the external world. A person who believes someone else is with him or her in a darkened room may not do so on the basis of actual sensory experience but rather on the basis of intuition or a hunch.

Just as everyone has the capacity for the attitudes of extraversion and introversion, so everyone has the capacity for all four of these functions. However, just as one attitude is dominant, so only one function is dominant. The other three are submerged in the personal unconscious. Only one of the two paired functions can be dominant—either the rational or the irrational. Their incompatibility prevents equal status or power. And within each pair only one of the functions can be dominant, for again they are contradictory. A person cannot have both thinking and feeling modes or both sensing and intuiting modes dominant.

However, Jung stated that one representative of each pair of functions (rational and irrational) can be observed in the dominant or superior mode. For example, sensing and thinking may both be represented, or feeling and intuiting. Nevertheless, only one function remains exclusively dominant. The other serves as an auxiliary function.

Psychological types

There is still more to Jung's approach to categorizing personalities. The two attitudes and four functions can interact to form eight **psychological types**. An introverted person can be of the thinking, feeling, sensing, or intuiting type. Similarly, an extravert can be of any of the four types. Let us briefly describe each of these psychological types.

The thinking extraverted type.   Such people live in accordance with rigid rules. They tend to repress feelings and emotions, to be objective in all aspects of their lives, and to be dogmatic in their thoughts and opinions.

The feeling extraverted type.   These people repress thinking and tend to be highly emotional. They cling and conform to the values, mores, and traditions they have been taught. They are unusually sensitive to the expectations and opinions of others.

The sensing extraverted type.   This personality type focuses on pleasure and happiness, on continually seeking new experiences and sensations. Such persons tend to be strongly oriented toward reality and highly adaptable to different people and situations.

The intuiting extraverted type.   Jung believed that these people are excellent in business and politics because of their keen ability to exploit opportunities. They are attracted by new ideas and tend to be creative and to be able to inspire others to accomplish and achieve.

The thinking introverted type.   These people do not get along well with others, have difficulty communicating their ideas, and appear to be cold and lacking in consideration for others. They focus on thought rather than feelings and have poor practical judgment.

The feeling introverted type.   In these people, thinking is repressed, as is the outward expression of emotion. They seem mysterious and inaccessible to others and tend to be quiet, modest, and childish, with little consideration for the feelings and thoughts of others.

The sensing introverted type.   Introverted, sensing people are irrational types, detached from the everyday world. They look upon most human activities with benevolence and amusement. They are highly sensitive aesthetically, focus on sensations, and repress intuition.

The intuiting introverted type.   These people may focus so intensely on intuition that they have little contact with reality. They are visionaries and daydreamers. They are poorly understood by others and may seem odd and eccentric.

To fully determine the nature of an individual's personality, one must know which of the functions and attitudes are dominant—that is, which express themselves in consciousness and which have been relegated to the personal unconscious. Jung pointed out that pure types represent extreme cases and that there is a wide range of variation in any one type. Also, no single type is better or more preferred than any other.

Obviously, such attitudes and functions are important to an individual, but Jung insisted that the ego—the conscious level of personality—is secondary in importance, in terms of its effect on thought and behavior, to the two unconscious levels. Consciousness forms only the uppermost level of the structure of the psyche. The unconscious, like the lower levels of a building, helps to provide support for the upper level. Thus, Jung is in basic agreement with Freud on the relatively greater role played by the unconscious. But the two men differed sharply in their views of its nature.

The personal unconscious

There are two levels to the unconscious in Jung's system—a higher, more superficial level and a deeper, more profoundly influencing level. The more superficial aspect is the **personal unconscious**, which is not unlike Freud's preconscious. The personal unconscious is, in essence, a reservoir of material that was once conscious but that has been forgotten or suppressed because it was either trivial or distressing.

As was the case with Freud's preconscious, there is a great deal of two-way traffic between the ego and the personal unconscious. Our attention can shift readily from this printed page to the memory of what we did last night. All manner of experience is stored in a sort of file cabinet of our personal unconscious, and little effort is required to take something out, examine it for a while, and then put it back, where it will remain until the next time we want it or are reminded of it.

As an individual files more and more experiences in the personal unconscious, he or she begins to categorize or group them into clusters that Jung called **complexes**. A complex is a core or pattern of emotions, memories, perceptions, and wishes clustering around a common theme. In everyday terms, we might say that a person has a complex about power or status, for example; he or she is preoccupied with that theme, and it influences his or her behavior. The person may try to become powerful personally or to identify or affiliate with power, perhaps driving a motorcycle or a powerful car. In a variety of ways, the power complex determines how the person perceives the world; it directs him or her. Jung noted: "A person does not have a complex; the complex has him."

Once a complex is formed, it is no longer under conscious control but can intrude upon and interfere with consciousness. The person with a complex is not aware of its guiding influence, although others may observe his or her constant focus on one theme.

While the majority of complexes with which Jung dealt are harmful—indeed, are at least partly responsible for the neurotic condition that drove the person to an analyst—complexes may also be extremely useful to a person. For example, a perfection or achievement complex may cause a person to work hard at developing a particular talent or skill.

As to the origin of complexes, Jung stated that they grow out of childhood, adult, or ancestral experiences, the last being the heritage of the species contained in the collective unconscious.

The collective unconscious

The deepest and most inaccessible level of the psyche—the **collective** or **transpersonal unconscious**—is the most unusual and controversial aspect of Jung's system; to some critics it is the most bizarre aspect.

Jung believed that, just as a person individually accumulates and files all of his or her past experiences, so does humankind collectively, as a species. In the personal unconscious, each of us stores our individually accumulated experiences. In the collective unconscious, humankind as a whole accumulates the experiences of the human and prehuman species and passes this wealth of experience on to each new generation. The collective unconscious, then, is a storehouse of all the experience of humankind transmitted to each of us. It contains the entire catalog of experiences that have marked human evolution, and it is repeated in the brain of every human being in every generation.

Whatever experiences are universal—that is, are repeated, relatively unchanged, by each generation—become a part of each individual's personality. Indeed, the primitive past of human beings becomes the primary base of a person's psyche, directing and influencing current behavior. To Jung, the collective unconscious was the "all-controlling deposit of ancestral experiences." There is, then, in Jung's view, a definite linking of a person's present personality with the past—with his or her own childhood and early years as well as with the history of the entire species.

It is important to note that we do not inherit these collective experiences directly. We do not, for example, inherit an actual fear of snakes. Rather, we inherit the potentiality or predisposition to fear snakes. We are predisposed to behave and feel in certain ways, the same ways in which people have always behaved and felt. Whether the predisposition becomes a reality depends on the specific experiences the individual encounters.

Jung believed that certain basic experiences have characterized every generation throughout the history of humanity. For example, people have always had a mother figure, experienced birth and death, faced unknown terrors in the dark, worshiped power or status or some sort of god-like figure, and feared an evil, Satan-like figure. The universality of these experiences over countless evolving generations leaves their imprint on each person at birth. Since all people face essentially the same experiences, these universal experiences determine how we will perceive and react to our own world. Jung said: "The form of the world into which [a person] is born is already inborn in him, as a virtual image" (Jung, 1953, p. 188).

Thus, a baby is born predisposed to perceive the mother in a certain manner. Assuming that she behaves as we have generally considered mothers should behave, then the baby's predisposition will correspond with its reality. Thus, the form of the infant's world "inborn in him" determines how it adapts and reacts to its world.

Because the collective unconscious is such an unorthodox concept, the reason Jung proposed it and the kind of evidence he thought supported it are important. In his voracious reading about ancient cultures, both mythical and real, Jung discovered that certain common themes and symbols appear in diverse parts of the world. As far as could be determined, these common themes had not been transmitted or communicated orally or in writing from one culture to another.

Further, Jung's patients, in their dreams and fantasies, recalled and described the same kinds of symbols he had found in ancient cultures. He could find no other explanation for these shared symbols and themes over such great geographical and temporal distances than that they were transmitted by and carried in each individual's collective unconscious.

It should be pointed out that Freud also believed that basic primal experiences are passed on to each individual as general tendencies. In 1911, two years before their split, Freud wrote in a letter to Jung that "phylogenetic memory . . . will soon prove to be so."

Archetypes

The ancient experiences contained in the collective unconscious are manifested or expressed in the form of images that Jung called **archetypes**. These images or pictures of universal experiences form a vital part of Jung's theory of personality, and he devoted much of the last half of his life to their study.

There are a great many of these universal experiences, Jung wrote—as many as there are common human experiences. By being repeated countless times in the lives of countless people and generations, they have become imprinted on our psyche.

Archetypes are not actual, fully developed memories. We cannot see an archetype as we can clearly see a picture of some past event or person in our own lives. Rather, an archetype is a predisposition that awaits an actual experience in a person's life before its content becomes clear. Archetypes are manifested or expressed in our dreams and fantasies.

Some of the archetypes with which Jung was concerned are: magic, the hero, the child, God, death, power, and the wise old man. Several archetypes are more fully developed than others and therefore influence the psyche more consistently. These are the persona, the anima and animus, the shadow, and the self.

The word *persona*, as we saw in Chapter 1, originally referred to a mask worn by an actor to display a different role or face to the audience. Jung used the term with basically the same meaning. The **persona** archetype is also a mask, a public face the person wears to present himself or herself as someone other than who he or she really is. The persona is necessary, Jung believed, because we are forced to play a variety of roles in life in order to succeed in our work and to get along with the diverse kinds of people with whom we are forced into contact.

While the persona can be very helpful to a person—and, indeed, necessary— it can also be quite harmful. A person may well come to believe that this persona really reflects his or her true nature and being. From playing a role, the person comes to be that role; as a result, other aspects of his or her personality are, in a sense, shunted aside and not allowed to develop. Jung described it this way: the ego comes to identify with the persona rather than with the person's true nature, and the resulting condition is known as *inflation of the persona*.

Both cases—simply playing a role and coming to believe the role—involve deception. In the former case, a person is deceiving others; in the latter, a person is deceiving himself or herself as well—obviously a dangerous situation.

The *anima* and *animus*, collectively, refer to Jung's recognition that humans are essentially bisexual animals. On the biological level, each sex secretes the hormones of the opposite sex as well as those of its own sex. On the psychological level, each sex manifests characteristics, temperaments, and attitudes of the other sex by virtue of centuries of living together. Thus, the psyche of a woman contains masculine aspects (the **animus** archetype), and the psyche of a man contains feminine aspects (the **anima** archetype).

These opposite sex characteristics aid in the adjustment and survival of humanity, for they better enable the person to understand the nature of the opposite sex. The archetypes predispose one to like certain characteristics of the other sex and guide one's behavior with reference to the opposite sex.

Jung was quite insistent that these archetypes must be expressed; that is, a man must exhibit his feminine as well as his masculine characteristics, and a woman must likewise express her masculine characteristics along with her feminine ones. Otherwise, these necessary characteristics will lie dormant and undeveloped, leading to a one-sidedness of personality. A person in this condition cannot become fully human, because one aspect of his or her nature has been suppressed.

There are potential dangers associated with all the archetypes discussed thus far, but the most dangerous and powerful archetype of all is the one with the sinister and mysterious label of the **shadow**. When Jung spoke of the collective unconscious as the repository of all past experiences, he included our animal (prehuman) ancestry. For that reason, the shadow has the deepest roots of all the archetypes; it contains the basic, primitive animal instincts.

That which society usually considers evil and immoral resides in the shadow, and this dark side of man must be tamed if people hope to live in harmony with one another. These primitive impulses must be suppressed, overcome, or defended against by the individual. If they are not, society will very likely punish him or her.

But there is a dilemma here. Not only is the shadow the source of that which society considers bad; it is also the source of vitality, spontaneity, and creativity. Thus, if the shadow is totally and absolutely suppressed, the psyche becomes rather dull and lifeless. Jung stated that it is the function of the ego to direct the forces of the shadow, to repress the animal instincts enough so that the person is considered civilized, while allowing enough expression of the instincts to provide creativity and vigor.

Jung's most important archetype is the *self*. It represents the unity, wholeness, and integration of the total personality—or at least the striving toward such wholeness. The symbol representing this archetype, one found in diverse cultures, is the *mandala*, or so-called magic circle.

We have mentioned Jung's principle of opposites and the importance of polarities to the psyche. The self is a point of equilibrium, midway between the polarities of the conscious and the unconscious, that forms the center of the psyche. The full realization of the self seems always to lie in the future. Jung spoke of it as a goal—something to be striven for but rarely achieved. As such, the self serves as a motivating force, one that pulls the individual from ahead rather than pushes from behind (as is the case with past experience).

The self archetype cannot begin to emerge until all the other systems of the psyche have become fully developed. This occurs, as we shall see, around the years of middle age, a crucial period of transition in Jung's view. The full actualization of the self involves a future orientation—plans, goals, a purpose—and an accurate perception and knowledge of one's self. Self-realization is impossible without a full knowledge of self. This makes the process the most difficult one we face, requiring persistence, perceptiveness, and great wisdom.

The development of the personality

We have seen that Jung's theory of personality is in part a forward-looking one. Achieving selfhood or self-actualization involves an orientation toward the future. Jung believed that an individual's present personality is determined both by what the person hopes to be and by what he or she has been. The system, then, is both *teleological*, in that it looks to the future, and *causal*, in that it looks to the past. Jung was highly critical of Freud for emphasizing only causal factors, or past events, as shapers of personality. Human beings, both individually and as a species, are constantly developing and growing, always moving toward a more complete or fully human level of development.

Personality development, therefore, is ideally marked by what Jung called *progression*. But he also pointed out that development can go backward as well as forward, and so he invoked the opposing principle of *regression* to help explain personality development.

In regression, the libido "flows backward," away from the external environment and inward to the unconscious. Regression does not necessarily mean a cessation of progression. Indeed, it may aid progression because, by delving into the past experiences of the personal and collective unconscious and by introspecting and reconciling these experiences, the person may be able to resolve the problem that led to the regression in the first place. Regression, then, can involve a quiet retreat into oneself in order to foster creative thought and revitalization. Jung also pointed out that dreaming is a regression into the unconscious.

Another principle in Jung's theory of development is **synchronicity**. The word derives from the adjective *synchronous*, which refers to events occurring together in time. Jung was concerned here with events bordering on the supernatural, such as clairvoyance. We have all read, for example, of someone having a vision or a dream in which a friend or relative has an accident or dies and, shortly thereafter, learning that the event in the dream actually occurred. Jung did not think that such coincidences are causal in nature; the death does not cause the dream, even though the events are synchronous. But he believed in the occurrence of such phenomena, and his principle of synchronicity is an attempt to account for them.

He explains such mystical events in mystical terms, saying that there is an unknown order or force in the world that is beyond causality. An archetype is able to synchronously manifest itself in someone's psyche and in the external world by a process not explained (and perhaps not capable of being explained). Jung, as we have seen, was very much concerned with spiritual phenomena, a concern not shared by most of psychology.

Childhood to young adulthood

Jung believed that the development of the personality never stops, regardless of age. Thus, Jung took a longer view of personality development than did Freud, who concentrated on the early years of life and foresaw little development after the age of 5 or so. Jung also differs from Freud's approach to development in not spelling out the sequential stages of growth in as much detail. Nevertheless, he did speak of specific levels or periods in the overall process of growth.

Jung had relatively little to say about childhood and considered the early years to be not very decisive in laying down a fixed personality pattern. Initially, the child is governed primarily by physical instincts, and the ego begins to form only when the child is able to distinguish between himself or herself and other objects. Consciousness begins to form when the child is able to say *I*.

It is not until the advent of puberty that the psyche begins to assume a definite form and content. This period, which Jung refers to as the *psychic birth* of an individual, is marked by a great many problems and the need to make a number of adaptations. Childhood fantasies must now end as the demands of reality confront the adolescent.

From the teenage years through young adulthood, the person is deeply concerned with preparatory activities—completing education, beginning a career, getting married, and starting a family. The primary attitude during these years is that of extraversion; the focus is external.

Middle age to old age

Major changes occur when the second half of life begins at middle age, between 35 and 40. As we noted earlier, this period was a time of intense crisis for Jung himself, and two-thirds of his patients were at the same stage of life. By middle age, the adaptational problems of life have usually been resolved. The 40-year-old is usually established in his or her job, community, and marriage. Why, when success has been achieved, are so many people gripped by feelings of despair, misery, and worthlessness? Jung's patients all told him essentially the same thing: adventure, excitement, and zest had gone, life had lost all meaning. They felt empty and deadened.

The more Jung analyzed this period of life, the more he came to believe that such drastic personality changes are inevitable and universal. Jung suggested that middle age is a natural time of transition in which the personality undergoes necessary and beneficial changes.

The reason for the changes, Jung thought, lies, ironically, in the fact that middle-aged persons have been successful in meeting life's demands. A great deal of energy has been invested in the preparatory activities of the first half of life, but by age 40 the preparation is finished, the challenges have been met. Yet while the person still possesses considerable energy, it has nowhere to go. It must be reinvested or rechanneled into a different facet of life.

In middle age, we may become bored with material success and need to shift our interest to the inner, subjective world of unconscious experience.

Jung noted that the first half of life focuses on the objective world of reality. The second half of life must be devoted to the inner, subjective world that heretofore had been neglected. The attitude of the personality must shift from extraversion to introversion. The previous focus on consciousness must be tempered by an awareness of unconscious experiences. The person's interests must shift from the physical and material to the religious, philosophical, and intuitive. Further, the earlier one-sidedness of the personality (the nearly exclusive focus on consciousness) must be replaced by a greater balance among all facets of the personality to begin the process of achieving self-realization.

Persons who are successful in achieving this balance, in integrating harmoniously the unconscious with the conscious and in experiencing their own inner beings, are in a position to achieve positive psychological health, the condition Jung called **individuation**.

Individuation involves, simply, becoming an individual. In infancy, the psyche is undifferentiated, a diffuse whole manifesting very little conscious activity. As the infant grows older, the structures of the psyche develop; that is, they become more sharply differentiated from one another, and within themselves. Each structure becomes more complex; the persona, the shadow, and the ego all develop and take on solid and unique form. They must individuate rather equally. All of the structures must grow. None must be stifled or suppressed, and none must be overdeveloped at the expense of others.

Individuation involves the fulfillment or realization of all one's capacities. The goal of individuation—a fully harmonious, integrated personality—is, of course, the self. Jung pointed out that the tendency toward individuation is an innate and therefore inevitable process. It will occur, but it can be helped or hindered by environmental factors such as the nature of the parent–child relationship and the individual's education.

Once all the psyche's structures are fully individuated, the next step in development, *transcendence*, occurs. Full individuation results in diversity within the psyche. Self-actualization requires that these diversities and opposites in the psyche be transcended or united and made whole. The tendency toward individuation and transcendence in each of us is natural and inevitable.

As with individuation, environmental factors such as a poor marriage or supremely frustrating work can inhibit the process of transcendence. Self, you remember, is a goal not reached by everyone, and any factor that stifles individuation and transcendence delays or may totally prevent the achievement of self.

The final stage of personality development is *old age*. Jung wrote little about old age, but he did note a similarity between the last years of life and the first. In both old age and childhood, the unconscious dominates the personality. Elderly persons must not look backward. They need a goal to orient themselves toward the future. In this regard, Jung believed that the decline of religious values has been harmful because fewer people can cling to the promise or goal of life after death. Yet the inevitability of death must somehow be viewed as a goal in itself, as something toward which to strive. To Jung, our psychological well-being depends on having such a goal.

Interaction among parts of the personality

As we have seen, the personality is made up of a number of separate structures or aspects. While these structures are truly distinct, they are nevertheless capable of influencing one another. The interactions take place through the mechanisms of opposition, unity, and compensation.

Opposition has been mentioned frequently in this chapter as a sort of cornerstone of Jung's approach to personality. It exists everywhere within the psyche and is the source of psychic energy. The tensions that are created by polarization of opposing forces, while potentially harmful, are nonetheless necessary for the development of the psyche. Without them, there would be no psyche. There is conflict between the unconscious and the conscious and between the personal unconscious and the collective unconscious. Extraversion opposes introversion, the rational functions oppose the irrational functions, the anima opposes the animus, sensing opposes intuiting, and so it goes. If the conflicts are too harsh or severe, they may shatter the psyche. The result is neurotic or psychotic behavior.

Alternatively, and much more desirably, opposites can *unite* to form a synthesis or wholeness in which they come to complement one another. It is through this kind of balancing of opposites, the leveling or reducing of the conflicts, that the personality becomes fully integrated in the state, now familiar to you, known as the self. The principle of transcendence, discussed earlier, brings about this integration and balancing of opposites.

The third mechanism of interaction among the structures of the psyche is **compensation**, by means of which one structure can act to overcome the weakness of another structure. For example, if you are highly extraverted, your unconscious will act to develop your suppressed introversion. Themes of introversion may appear in your dreams. If, for some reason, circumstances interfere with the expression of your extraversion, the attitude of introversion will then be expressed.

If it were not for compensation, there would be a dangerously lopsided quality to your personality—excessive extraversion, or sensing, or intuiting, for example. Such overemphasis on one function, attitude, or structure leads to maladjustment.

Through opposition, unity, and compensation, the systems of the psyche seek balance and equilibrium, striving toward the fullest, most complete stage of development—the self.

Jung's image of human nature

Jung's image of human nature is quite a bit different from Freud's. Jung did not hold such a deterministic view, but he did agree that personality may be partially determined by certain childhood experiences and by the archetypes. There is, however, more room in Jung's system for free will and spontaneity; the latter arises from the shadow archetype.

On the nature–nurture issue, Jung takes a moderate position. The drive or trend toward self-actualization is innate, but it can be either facilitated or thwarted by experience and by learning.

The ultimate and necessary goal of life was spelled out clearly in Jung's writings, and it differs sharply from Freud's goal of tension reduction. For Jung, the aim of the human personality is individuation, or the realization of the self. He noted that the goal is rarely achieved fully, but is always present, continually motivating us to strive for it.

Jung also differed from Freud on the importance of childhood experiences. Jung felt that they were influential but did not completely shape our personality. We are affected more by our experiences in midlife and by our hopes and expectations for the future.

Jung believed that each individual is unique, but only for the first half of life. When some level of individuation or selfhood is reached in middle age, we develop what he called a "universal personality," in which no single aspect of the personality continues to dominate. The uniqueness of individuals disappears at that time, and they can no longer be described as belonging to a particular psychological type.

While perhaps not so optimistic about human nature as the social-psychological theorists, Jung nevertheless presented us with a more positive and hopeful image than Freud's. Jung's air of optimism about human nature is apparent in his view of personality development. The individual is constantly trying to grow, to develop and expand, to improve and move forward. Human beings, individually and collectively, are forward-looking and forward-moving. Development, change, and progress do not stop in childhood, as Freud had assumed, but are never-ending processes. Thus, a person always has the hope of being better or more than he or she is at the moment.

The human species continues to improve, Jung argued. We 20th-century people, for all our faults, represent a significant step forward from our primitive ancestors. And Jung saw reason to hope that the 21st-century person would be an even more improved model. Jung's view is clearly forward, ahead, upward, and he applauds our psyche by calling it a "supreme realization," "an act of high courage," "the absolute affirmation of all that constitutes the individual."

Despite his basic optimism, Jung was concerned about a danger facing Western culture—the "sickness of dissociation" he called it. By placing too much emphasis on materialism, reason, and empirical science, we are losing sight of the unconscious. We must not abandon confidence and trust in the universal thought forms (archetypes) that form our heritage. We are, Jung feared, too one-sided. Thus, his hopefulness is of a watchful, warning kind. "The world," he cautioned, "hangs on a thin thread, and that thread is the psyche of man."

Assessment in Jung's theory

Jung's techniques for assessing the functioning of the psyche involve both science and what some call the supernatural—both an objective and a mystical approach. He investigated a variety of cultures and eras, noting their symbols, myths, religions, and rituals. Through the fantasies and dreams of his patients and through explorations ranging from Sanskrit to alchemy, clairvoyance to astrology, he formed the basis of his unique theory of personality. And yet, the work that first brought Jung to the attention of American psychology involved empirical and physiological assessments. His techniques were an unorthodox blend of opposites, perhaps appropriate for his polarity-based theory.

His sessions with patients were unusual, even chaotic at times. His patients did not lie on a couch, as Freud's did. "I don't want to put the patient to bed," he said (Brome, 1981, p. 177). Usually, he and the patient sat in comfortable chairs facing each other, although sometimes Jung faced a window so he could look at the lake while the patient talked. He had also treated patients aboard his sailboat, at least once during a high wind. As the boat raced across the lake, Jung was singing. Occasionally, when moved by ill-humor, Jung could be rude. "Oh no," he said when one patient appeared at the appointed time. "I can't stand the sight of another one. Just go home and cure yourself today" (Brome, 1981, p. 185).

Basically, Jung used three techniques: word association, symptom analysis, and dream analysis.

The word-association test

The **word-association test**, in which a subject responds to a stimulus word with whatever word comes immediately to mind, has become a standard laboratory and clinical tool in psychology. In the early 1900s, Jung first used this technique with a list of 100 words he selected that were capable of eliciting emotions. Jung measured the time it took for a patient to respond to each word. He also measured physiological reactions to each word, thus determining the emotional effects of the stimuli. Table 3.1 shows some normal and neurotic responses to Jung's stimulus words.

He used this technique to uncover complexes in his patients. A variety of response factors were indicative of complexes, according to Jung, including the physiological responses mentioned. For example, delays in responding to particular words, making the same response to widely differing words, slips of the tongue, stammering, responding with more than one word, using "made up" response words, or failing to respond to any words can all indicate the existence of a complex.

TABLE 3.1   Normal and neurotic responses to Jung's word-association test

Stimulus word	*Normal response*	*Neurotic response*
Blue	Pretty	Color
Tree	Green	Nature
Bread	Good	To eat
Lamp	Bright	To burn
Rich	Beautiful	Money–I don't know
To sin	Much	This idea is totally alien to me; I do not acknowledge it

Source: C. G. Jung, "The Association Method," 1909. In *The Collected Works of C. G. Jung*, Volume 2 (Princeton, NJ: Princeton University Press, 1973), pp. 442–443.

Jung also used the word-association test as a lie detector, finding suspects who were guilty of theft in at least two instances (Ellenberger, 1970).

Symptom analysis

The second technique, *symptom analysis*, focuses on the symptoms being experienced by the patient and is based on the person's free associations to a symptom. It is similar to Freud's cathartic method. Between the patient's associations to his or her symptoms and the analyst's interpretation of them, the symptoms will often be relieved and sometimes disappear altogether.

Dream analysis

The final technique involves the *analysis of dreams*, which Jung, agreeing with Freud, considered to be the "royal road" into the unconscious. Jung's approach to dream analysis differed from Freud's in that Jung was concerned with more than the causal factors of dreams. He believed that dreams were more than unconscious wishes and saw in them two functions or purposes. First, dreams are *prospective*; that is, they help an individual prepare himself or herself for the experiences and events he or she anticipates in the immediate future. Second, dreams serve a *compensatory* function, in that they help bring about a balance between opposites in the psyche by compensating for the overdevelopment of any single psychic structure.

A method of assessment closely related to Jung's approach to personality is the Myers-Briggs Type Indicator (MBTI), developed in the 1920s by Katharine Briggs and Isabel Briggs Myers. Katharine Briggs had become interested in the similarities and differences in the human personality and had pursued her own independent study of the topic. In 1923 she had read Jung's book, *Psychological Types*, and found that her view of personality was highly similar to Jung's. Without any research grant support, university affiliation, or graduate students to assist her, she and her daughter developed a test that remains widely used for both research and applied purposes (Yoe, 1984). As we shall see, the Myers-Briggs Type Indicator has since become the primary method for conducting research on Jung's psychological types. Another personality test, the Maudsley Personality Inventory, was developed by the English psychologist Hans Eysenck to measure Jung's attitudes of introversion-extraversion (Eysenck, 1947).

Research in Jung's theory

Jung, like Freud, used the case-study approach, which he called *life-history reconstruction*. This involved an extensive recollection of a person's past experiences in which Jung sought to identify the developmental patterns that may have led to the present neurotic condition.

The same criticisms we made of Freud's data and research methods can be made against Jung's. His data did not rely on objective observation, they were not gathered in controlled and systematic fashion, and the situations in which they were obtained were not amenable to duplication and verification.

Like Freud, Jung did not keep verbatim records of his patients' comments, nor did he attempt to verify the accuracy of their reports. Jung's case studies involved, as did Freud's, a small and unrepresentative sample of people, making it difficult to generalize to the population at large.

Jung's analysis of his data was subjective, unreliable, and not amenable to quantification. Again, as with Freud, we do not know how Jung analyzed his data; he never explained his procedures. Certainly the data were subjected to some of the most unusual interpretations to be found in any personality theory. As we have seen, Jung studied a variety of cultures and explored other approaches to understanding personality. It was on the basis of his knowledge of the ritualistic and symbolistic history of humankind, as well as his own dreams and fantasies, that he interpreted the data he collected from his patients.

He reported that he found striking similarities between his patients' fantasies and dreams (and his own) and the archetypes, those ancient, universal symbols and themes contained in the psyches of past and present generations. He believed he had demonstrated that the ritualistic and mythological history of the species is acted out in the life of every individual. Thus, to Jung, an inquiry into the psyche of one person is an inquiry into the psyche of all humanity for all time.

The problem is, as with Freud, that most of Jung's observations cannot be submitted to experimental test. Jung himself was indifferent to that criticism, however. He commented that anyone who "wishes to know about the human mind will learn nothing, or almost nothing, from experimental psychology" (Ellenberger, 1970, p. 694).

Studies of psychological types

Other researchers, more optimistic about the experimental and correlational approaches, have been able to submit certain limited aspects of Jungian theory to experimental test, with results that have supported some of Jung's propositions. Most of this research has focused on the attitudes of introversion and extraversion using the Myers-Briggs Type Indicator. The measurement of Jungian psychological types on the MBTI is so widespread that a formal organization has been established, the Center for Application of Psychological Types. This group claims 1,900 members, including university researchers in personality, career counselors, therapists, and management consultants.

One study of college students found that their job interests were closely related to Jung's psychological types. Introverts had strong interests in occupations that did not involve close interactions with other people, such as technical and scientific work. Extraverts were more interested in jobs that offered high levels of social interaction, such as sales and public relations (Stricker & Ross, 1962).

Another study using the MBTI revealed that different Jungian types are drawn to different professions. The test was administered to a large sample of police officers, schoolteachers, and social work and dental students. The teachers and social work students showed high levels of intuiting and feeling functions. Police officers and dental students, who deal with people quite differently from teachers and social workers, scored high in extraversion and in sensing and thinking (Hanewitz, 1978).

Jungian personality types also differ in their cognitive or mental functioning. Researchers concluded that introverted thinking types have better memories for neutral or impersonal stimuli, such as numbers, whereas extraverted feeling types have better memories for human stimuli with emotional overtones, such as various facial expressions (Carlson & Levy, 1973).

Research using Eysenck's test, the Maudsley Personality Inventory, also provides support for Jung's psychological types. (The test measures neuroticism and psychoticism in addition to introversion-extraversion.) In one study, persons scoring high on extraversion were more popular than those scoring high on introversion (Brown & Hendrick, 1971). Introverts were more sensitive to pain, more easily bored, and more careful in their work than were extraverts (Wilson, 1978).

Additional research using the Maudsley Personality Inventory revealed that extraverts are more suggestible, more sexually active, more likely to earn lower grades in school, and more strongly predisposed to jobs that will bring them in contact with other people than are introverts (Pervin, 1984b).

Another personality test, the Sixteen P. F. (Personality Factor) Test, developed by Raymond Cattell (Chapter 9), also measures introversion-extraversion. Research using this test has demonstrated the occupational differences between these two psychological types that are predictable from Jung's descriptions of them. Introversion was high among researchers and artists; extraversion was high among engineers and firefighters (Cattell, 1957).

It should be noted that not all research on Jung's psychological types has been supportive of his ideas. Some results have been negative or inconclusive (Wilson, 1977). But it is important to remember that the attitudes of introversion-extraversion and the four functions are amenable to experimental testing. However, as with Freud's work, the larger aspects of the theory—such as complexes, the collective unconscious, and archetypes—resist attempts at experimental validation.

A final commentary

Jung's highly complex, vastly unorthodox approach to the understanding of personality has had a considerable impact on such disciplines as psychiatry, cultural history, sociology, economics, political science, philosophy, and religion. As a result, Jung has been widely honored in the intellectual community at large. He received honorary degrees from Oxford and Harvard universities and has been acknowledged as a powerful influence on the work of many scholars, including the historian Arnold Toynbee.

Within psychology, Jung made several contributions that have been recognized. The word-association test is a standard projective technique and served to inspire the development of the Rorschach Inkblot Test and so-called lie-detection techniques. The concepts of complexes and of the introverted-extraverted psychological types are well accepted in psychology today, and the personality scales that measure introversion-extraversion are frequently used as diagnostic and selection devices.

Jung's notion of individuation or self-actualization anticipated the work of other personality theorists such as Abraham Maslow (Chapter 12). Jung was also the first theorist to emphasize the role of the future in determining behavior, an idea used by Alfred Adler (Chapter 4), among others. Jung's suggestion that middle age is a time of crucial personality change is a viewpoint later embraced by Maslow, Erik Erikson (Chapter 10), and Raymond Cattell (Chapter 9). The idea of a midlife crisis is now widely accepted in psychology as a stage of personality development. Jung's theory also influenced the work of Henry Murray (Chapter 7).

These are substantial contributions to the discipline of psychology. In the survey of 679 members of the American Psychological Association discussed in Chapter 2, in which 286 psychologists were ranked in terms of their importance in the last half of the 20th century, Jung was listed in 9th place. Of the 15 major personality theorists discussed in this book, Jung placed 5th, behind Skinner, Freud, Rogers, and Erikson (Gilgen, 1982).

Despite the impact of some of Jung's specific ideas, the bulk of his theory has not been endorsed or embraced by psychology. For the most part, his major concepts and approach have been ignored or rejected.

Perhaps one reason for psychology's ignoring Jung has to do with the sheer difficulty of reading and understanding his concepts. Freud, Adler, Fromm, and others wrote with clarity and smoothness of style that allow their books to be widely read. That is decidedly not the case with Jung, who did not write for the general public. It is often frustrating to read Jung, so beset are his books by apparent inconsistencies and contradictions. Jung once said of himself, "I can formulate my thoughts only as they break out of me. It is like a geyser. Those who come after me will have to put them in order" (Jaffé, 1971, p. 8).

Another criticism of Jung refers to the lack of systematization in his theory. It is difficult to focus on an overall and consistent system to evaluate. As mentioned, there are inconsistencies and contradictions in his work. Jung was quite clear on the matter of systematization; he was strongly against it and very distrustful of setting up an orthodoxy, an approved path to truth. "Thank God," he once wrote, "I am Jung and not a Jungian."

Jung's consistent appeal to the occult, the supernatural, mysticism, and religion is probably the source of most of the criticism directed at his theory. Evidence from mythology and alchemy is certainly not in favor in an era that argues that reason and science are the only legitimate approaches to knowledge and understanding. Critics charge that Jung accepted mythical and mystical occurrences in the reports of his patients as scientific evidence. Primarily for this reason, psychology has ignored his theory, rarely going beyond that charge to criticize his approach in more detail. Also, as we have seen, Jung's data and method of analysis are open to criticism, and his major concepts have resisted serious scientific attempts at validation.

Despite the mystical-religious content of Jung's theory (or perhaps because of it), Jungian analytical psychology has enjoyed a burst of growth, vitality, and acceptance in the United States in recent years. A number of new books about Jung and his system were published in the late 1970s, including four biographies. Many young people at that time found Jung highly congenial with their own interests in Eastern religions, existentialism, and mysticism and their growing disaffection with materialism. Since the 1960s, formal training in Jungian analysis has been available in New York, San Francisco, and Los Angeles, and the number of applicants to these centers increases every year. There are also Jungian training institutes in England, France, Germany, Israel, Italy, and Switzerland. Such interest is strong praise for a man who began his professional work almost nine decades ago.

Summary

Jung differed from Freud by broadening Freud's definition of libido, redefining it as a more generalized dynamic force. He argued that personality is shaped by the future as well as by the past, and he placed a greater emphasis on the unconscious. Jung's childhood was influenced by his dreams and fantasies, which led him to focus on the unconscious. He suffered a neurotic episode at midlife, during which time he analyzed himself and developed his theory of personality.

Jung used the term *libido* in two ways: a diffuse, generalized life energy and a narrower energy that fuels the psyche. The amount of energy invested in an idea or feeling is called a value. Psychic energy operates in accordance with the principles of opposites, equivalence, and entropy. The principle of opposites states that every aspect of the psyche has its opposite; this opposition is the generator of psychic energy. The principle of equivalence states that energy is never lost to the personality, but is shifted from one part to another. The principle of entropy states that there is a tendency toward an equilibrium in the personality.

The ego or conscious mind is concerned with perceiving, thinking, feeling, and remembering. Part of our conscious perception is determined by the attitudes of introversion and extraversion, in which the libido is channeled either internally or externally. The psychological functions include thinking, feeling, sensing, and intuiting. Thinking and feeling are rational functions. Sensing and intuiting are irrational functions. Only one attitude and function are dominant. The psychological types are formed of combinations of the two attitudes and four functions.

The personal unconscious is a reservoir of material that was once conscious but has been forgotten or suppressed. Complexes, which are part of the personal unconscious, are patterns of emotions, memories, perceptions, and wishes centering on common themes.

The collective unconscious is a storehouse of all the experiences of humankind transmitted to each individual. It becomes the primary basis of a person's psyche, directing and influencing behavior. Archetypes are images that express the ancient experiences contained in the collective unconscious. The most powerful archetypes are the persona, a public face or role a person plays; anima, the feminine aspects of a man's psyche; animus, the masculine aspects of a woman's psyche; the shadow, the repository of basic, primitive animal instincts and of spontaneity and creativity; and the self, the unity, wholeness, and integration of the total personality.

Jung's view of the development of personality is both teleological, in that it looks to the future, and causal, in that it looks to the past.

The principle of synchronicity refers to events that occur together in time, but without any cause-and-effect relationship between them.

The development of personality never stops. The ego forms when the infant can distinguish between self and other objects. The psychic birth of a person occurs at the time of puberty, when the psyche assumes definite form and content. Preparatory activities mark the period from adolescence through young adulthood. In middle age, when success has been achieved, changes take place in the personality; psychic energy must be rechanneled into the inner world of the unconscious, and the attitude must shift from extraversion to introversion. Individuation, the realization of one's capabilities, can occur only at middle age. Transcendence involves the unification of the personality. In old age, as in childhood, the unconscious is dominant.

The parts of the psyche interact through the mechanisms of opposition, unity, and compensation. Opposites within the personality can unite to form a synthesis in which they complement each other. The self results from this balancing or unity of opposites. Compensation means that one part of the psyche can act to overcome the weakness of another part.

Jung's image of human nature was more optimistic and less deterministic than Freud's. Part of personality is innate, part is learned. The ultimate goal of life is individuation. Childhood experiences are important, but personality is more affected by midlife experiences and by our hopes and expectations for the future. Personality is unique in the first half of life, but not in the second.

Jung's methods of assessment include the investigation of symbols, myths, and rituals in ancient cultures; the word-association test, used to uncover complexes; symptom analysis, in which patients free-associate to their symptoms; and dream analysis. Dreams are prospective, helping a person prepare for the future, as well as compensatory, bringing about a balance between opposites by compensating for the overdevelopment of any one structure.

Two methods of assessment deriving from Jung's approach are the Myers-Briggs Type Indicator and the Maudsley Personality Inventory.

Jung's case-study method, called life-history reconstruction, did not rely on objective observation, was not systematic and controlled, and was not amenable to duplication and verification. Jung's analyses of his data were subjective, unreliable, and unquantifiable.

Research using the Myers-Briggs Type Indicator, the Maudsley Personality Inventory, and the Sixteen P. F. Test has supported some of Jung's ideas on psychological attitudes and functions. Broader aspects of Jung's theory resist attempts at scientific validation.

Jung's work has exerted considerable influence on the intellectual community and within psychology. Concepts that have been well received include the word-association test, complexes, introversion-extraversion, self-actualization, and the notion that middle age is a time of crucial personality change. The bulk of Jung's work has not been accepted by psychologists because of the difficulty in understanding the concepts, the lack of systematization in the theory, and Jung's use of occult, supernatural, and mystical sources.

Glossary

analytical psychology   Jung's theory of personality.

anima/animus archetypes   Feminine aspects of the male psyche / masculine aspects of the female psyche.

archetypes   Images of universal experiences contained in the collective unconscious.

collective unconscious   Deepest level of the psyche containing the inherited, accumulated experiences of the human and prehuman species; also called transpersonal unconscious.

compensation   Mechanism by which the structures of the psyche interact to overcome the weakness of any one structure.

complexes   A core or pattern of emotions, memories, perceptions, and wishes in the personal unconscious organized around a common theme.

ego   The conscious aspect of personality.

entropy principle   A tendency toward balance or equilibrium within the personality, that is, the ideal equal distribution of psychic energy over all structures.

equivalence principle   The continuing redistribution of energy within the personality.

extraversion   An attitude of the psyche characterized by an orientation toward the external world and toward other people.

individuation   A condition of psy-

chological health resulting from the integration of all conscious and unconscious facets of the personality.

introversion   An attitude of the psyche characterized by an orientation toward an individual's own thoughts and feelings.

libido   A generalized form of psychic energy; a broader definition than Freud's concept of libido as sexual energy.

opposition principle   The idea that conflict between opposing processes or tendencies is necessary to generate psychic energy.

persona archetype   The public face or role an individual presents to others.

personal unconscious   The reservoir of material that was once conscious but has been forgotten or suppressed.

psyche   Jung's term for personality.

psychological types   Eight categories of personality based on interactions of the two attitudes (introversion and extraversion) and the four functions (thinking, feeling, sensing, and intuiting).

shadow   The archetype that contains the primitive animal instincts; the dark side of the personality.

synchronicity principle   An explanation for coincidental mystical events.

word-association test   A projective technique in which an individual responds to a stimulus word with whatever word comes to mind.

Review questions

1. Discuss three major points of difference between analytical psychology and psychoanalysis.
2. Describe the principles of opposites, equivalence, and entropy. How do they apply to the concept of psychic energy?
3. Describe how the principle of opposites applies to the attitudes and functions. Explain the derivation of the eight psychological types from the attitudes and functions.
4. What is the relationship between the ego and the personal unconscious? Distinguish between the personal unconscious and the collective unconscious.
5. What is a complex, in Jung's view? In what situations may a complex be helpful?
6. Distinguish between the persona and the self archetypes.
7. Describe any similarities between Jung's shadow archetype and Freud's concept of the id.
8. Discuss the development of the personality throughout the life span, especially the critical periods of adolescence and middle age.
9. What is the purpose of the word-association test? What are the two purposes of dreams, according to Jung?
10. Describe some of the recent research findings on the introverted and extraverted personality types.

Suggested reading

Brome, V. *Jung: Man and myth*. New York: Atheneum, 1978.

Ellenberger, H. F. *The discovery of the unconscious*. New York: Basic Books, 1970. (See Chapter 9, "Carl Gustav Jung and Analytical Psychology.")

Evans, R. I. *Conversations with Carl Jung and reactions from Ernest Jones*. Princeton, NJ: Van Nostrand, 1964.

Hannah, B. *Jung: His life and work*. New York: Putnam, 1976.

Jung, C. G. *Memories, dreams, reflections*. New York: Vintage Books, 1961.

Jung, C. G. *The essential Jung*. Princeton, NJ: Princeton University Press, 1983. (A selection of Jung's writings that provides a good introduction to his theory; selected and introduced by Anthony Storr.)

Mattoon, M. A. *Jungian psychology in perspective*. New York: Free Press, 1981.

McGuire, W. & Hull, R. F. C., Eds. *C. G. Jung speaking: Interviews and encounters*. Princeton, NJ: Princeton University Press, 1977.

Stern, P. J. *C. G. Jung: The haunted prophet*. New York: George Braziller, 1976.

CHAPTER 4

Alfred Adler

The life of Adler (1870–1937)
Inferiority feelings: The source of human striving
Striving for superiority: The ultimate goal
The development of a lifestyle
Social interest
The influence of birth order
   The first-born child
   The second-born child
   The youngest child
Adler's image of human nature
Assessment in Adler's theory
   Order of birth
   Early recollections
   Dream analysis
   Psychological tests
Research in Adler's theory
A final commentary
Summary
Glossary
Review questions
Suggested reading

Man is not bad by nature; whatever his faults have been, faults due to an erroneous conception of life, he must not be oppressed by them. He can change. The past is dead. He is free to be happy.

ALFRED ADLER

The work of Alfred Adler represented the other major early defection from the still-developing psychoanalysis. You can see quite readily from the opening quotation why Freud and Adler had to part company. Adler fashioned an understanding of human nature that did not depict us as victimized by instincts and conflict and doomed by biological forces and childhood experiences. He called his new approach **individual psychology** because it focused on the uniqueness of each person, denying the universality of biological motives and goals ascribed to us by Freud.

Each person, in Adler's opinion, is primarily a social, not a biological, being. Our personalities are shaped by our individual social environments and interactions, not by biological needs and our continual efforts to satisfy them. Sex, of primary importance to Freud, is greatly minimized by Adler as a determining factor in personality. Finally, the conscious rather than the unconscious is at the core of personality. Far from being driven by forces we cannot see and control, we actively direct and create our own growth, our own future.

We have, then, two vastly different theories created by two men raised in the same city in the same era and educated as physicians at the same university. There was only a 14-year difference in their ages. As we shall see, certain elements in Adler's childhood (which was quite different from Freud's) may have presaged his way of looking at human nature, yet he fashioned a theory holding that we are not bound by the past. Ironically, this notion may also have had its roots in childhood experiences.

The life of Adler (1870–1937)

The second of six children, Alfred Adler was born on February 7, 1870, and raised in a suburb of Vienna. Adler's father, like Freud's, was a merchant, though apparently a more successful one. While Freud was raised in a Jewish ghetto and was conscious of his minority-group status all his life, Adler knew only a few Jewish children and so was influenced more by Viennese culture than by Jewish culture. (At the age of 34, he converted from Judaism to Christianity.)

Adler's early childhood was not a happy one. It was marked by sickness, an awareness of death, unhappiness, and jealousy of his older brother. He suffered from rickets,[1] which kept him from running and playing with other children. At the age of 3, he witnessed the death of a younger brother in the next bed; at 4, Adler himself was close to death from pneumonia. It was then—when he heard the doctor tell his father "Your boy is lost"—that he decided to become a doctor himself (Orgler, 1963, p. 16).

A sickly child during the first two years of his life, he was pampered at first by his mother, only to be dethroned by the arrival of a new brother. There is some suggestion of rejection on the part of his mother, but Adler was clearly his father's

---

[1] Rickets is a childhood disease characterized by a softening of the bones. It develops as a result of a vitamin D deficiency.

favorite. His childhood relations with his parents were thus quite different from Freud's. Adler was much closer to his father than to his mother. Understandably, he later rejected Freud's Oedipus complex because it was so foreign to his own childhood experience.

Adler was jealous of his older brother, who was vigorous and healthy and could engage in the sorts of physical activities and games in which Alfred could not take part. He felt inferior to his brother and to the other children in the neighborhood, who all seemed healthier and more athletic than he was. To overcome these feelings, to compensate for his physical inferiority, the young Adler worked extremely hard. Despite his small stature, clumsiness, and unattractiveness—legacies of his illness—he forced himself to participate in games and to keep up with the other children. Gradually, he won his victory and was able to achieve a sense of acceptance and self-esteem. As a result, he developed a great fondness for the company of other people, a characteristic he retained all his life. In his personality theory, he emphasized the importance of a child's relations with his or her peer group. He saw the role of other children, both siblings and outsiders, as much more important to personality development than Freud did.

In school he was unhappy and was only a mediocre student. In fact, one of his teachers advised his father to apprentice him to a shoemaker; the teacher felt that the young Adler was unfit for anything else. He was particularly bad in mathematics, but through persistence and hard work he rose from a failing student to the best in the class.

In many ways, his childhood reads like a tragedy; it also reads like a textbook example of Adler's later theory of overcoming childhood weaknesses and inferiorities and shaping one's destiny instead of being shaped by it. The man who would give the world the notion of inferiority feelings certainly spoke from the depths of his own early experiences. He once admitted, "Those who are familiar with my life work will clearly see the accord existing between the facts of my childhood and the views I expressed" (Bottome, 1939, p. 9). And one of his biographers has given her book the subtitle "triumph over the inferiority complex" (Orgler, 1963).

Fulfilling his childhood ambition, Adler studied medicine at the University of Vienna. He entered private practice as an ophthalmologist but shifted after a few years to general medicine. He was particularly interested in incurable diseases but was so distressed at his helplessness in preventing death, particularly in younger patients, that he soon abandoned general medicine for neurology and psychiatry.

Adler's nine-year association with Freud began in 1902, when Freud invited him (and three others) to meet once a week at Freud's home to discuss his newly developing psychoanalysis. The two men worked closely together, although the relationship was never an intimate one. Freud once said that Adler bored him. It is important to note that Adler was never a student or disciple of Freud's and was never psychoanalyzed by him.

One of Freud's colleagues commented that Adler could not psychoanalyze people, that he found it difficult to probe the unconscious. Apparently, Adler did not possess whatever talents were required to conduct Freud's method of analysis. It is interesting to speculate on whether it was this temperamental lack that led

Adler to focus in his system on the surface level of consciousness and to minimize the role of the unconscious.

By 1910, although Adler was president of what was then called the Vienna Psychoanalytical Society and co-editor of its new journal, he was also an increasingly vocal critic of Freudian theory. "Adler is becoming a menace," Freud wrote at the time (McGuire, 1974, p. 401). In 1911, Adler severed all connection with psychoanalysis and went on to develop his own system. Freud remained hostile and bitter toward Adler for the rest of his life. He called Adler a pygmy, saying, "I have made a pygmy great"[2] (Wittels, 1924, p. 225). Adler remained equally bitter toward Freud. More than 20 years later Adler was describing Freud as a "swindler" and "schemer" and denouncing psychoanalysis as "filth" (Roazen, 1975, p. 210). In 1912, Adler founded his Society for Individual Psychology.

After serving in the Austrian army during World War I, Adler was asked to organize government-sponsored child-counseling clinics in Vienna. These clinics soon grew rapidly in number and popularity. In his work with the clinics, Adler introduced group training and guidance, a forerunner of modern group therapy. In 1926, Adler made the first of an increasingly frequent series of visits to the United States, where he taught and made highly successful lecture tours. Before long he was spending more time in the United States than in Vienna; by 1936 he no longer maintained a home there. In 1937, on a strenuous 56-lecture tour, he suffered a heart attack and died in Scotland.

Inferiority feelings: The source of human striving

Inferiority feelings is another of those many terms from psychology that have come into everyday use in the English language. It derives from Adler's approach to personality; indeed, it is at the core of his approach. A general feeling of inferiority, Adler believed, is ever-present and vital as a determining force in behavior. "To be a human being," he wrote, "means to feel oneself inferior" (Adler, 1964, p. 96). Thus, it is a condition common to all people and, as such, is not a sign of weakness or abnormality.

In fact, Adler believed the opposite: inferiority feelings are the source of all human striving. All individual progress, growth, and development result from the attempt to **compensate** for one's inferiorities, be they imagined or real. Throughout an individual's life, he or she is motivated by the need to overcome this sense of inferiority and to strive for ever-higher levels of development.

The process begins in infancy, according to Adler. The infant is small and helpless, totally dependent upon adults. Adler felt that the infant is aware of the relatively greater power and strength of its parents; it is aware of the hopelessness of trying to resist or challenge that power. As a result, the infant develops feelings of inferiority relative to the larger, stronger people in the environment.

This initial experience of inferiority happens to everyone in infancy but is not

[2] Adler was 5 feet 2 inches tall, 5 inches shorter than Freud.

genetically determined. Rather, it is a function of the environment, which, for the infant, is the same everywhere: helplessness and dependency relative to adults.

It is important to understand that inferiority feelings are inescapable, but—even more important—they are necessary. Again, they provide the major motivation to strive, to grow, to progress, to succeed. All forward and upward movement results from the attempt to compensate for these inferiority feelings. They are, therefore, beneficial and useful. They motivate us to solve the problems of adjustment and growth.

But suppose an individual does not grow and develop? What happens when a child is unable to compensate for his or her inferiority feelings? As you might imagine, an inability to overcome inferiority feelings heightens and intensifies these feelings and leads to the development of an **inferiority complex**. Adler defined this condition as "an inability to solve life's problems," and he found such a complex in the childhoods of many adults who came to him for treatment (Orgler, 1963, p. 63). An inferiority complex can originate in three ways in childhood: through organic inferiority, through spoiling, and through neglect.

The investigation of *organic inferiority* was Adler's first major effort, carried out while he was still associated with Freud (who, incidentally, approved of the notion). Adler stated that defective parts or organs of the body affected personality development through the person's efforts to compensate for the defect or weakness, just as Adler had compensated for rickets, his childhood organic inferiority.

For example, a child who is physically weak might concentrate on that weakness and work to develop superior athletic ability. History records many examples of such compensation: the stutterer Demosthenes became a great orator, and the weak and sickly Theodore Roosevelt became a specimen of physical fitness as an

Many people with physical disabilities strive to compensate for their weaknesses or defects.

adult. Thus, organic inferiority can lead to striking artistic, athletic, and social accomplishments. But it can also lead to an inferiority complex if the attempts at compensation are unsuccessful.

Here is another example of a personality concept developed initially along intuitive lines, drawn from the theorist's own experience, and later confirmed by data from patients. Adler's office in Vienna was near the Prater, an amusement park, and his patients included such entertainers as acrobats. They possessed extraordinary physical prowess and skills, some of which were developed, they told Adler, as a result of hard work to overcome (to compensate for) childhood weakness and illness.

Spoiling or pampering a child can also lead to an inferiority complex. The spoiled child is, of course, the center of attention in the home, where every need and whim is satisfied and little is denied. Under the circumstances the child quite naturally develops the idea that he or she is the most important person in any situation and that others should always defer to him or her. The first experience at school—where the child is no longer the center of all attention—comes as a rude shock for which the child is not equipped to cope.

Spoiled children have little, if any, social feeling and are exceedingly impatient with others. They have never learned to wait for what they want. Neither have such children learned to overcome difficulties or to adjust to others. When confronted with obstacles in the path to gratification, they come to believe that it is their own lack of ability that is thwarting them. Hence, an inferiority complex develops.

It is easy to understand how the *neglected* child—the one who is unwanted and rejected—can develop an inferiority complex. His or her infancy and childhood are characterized by a lack of love and security, because of indifferent or even hostile parents. As a result, the child may develop feelings of worthlessness—even anger—and look upon everyone with distrust.

Whatever the source of inferiority feelings, a person may tend to overcompensate and so develop what has been called a **superiority complex**. This involves, as you might guess, an exaggerated opinion of one's own abilities and accomplishments. A person may feel superior inwardly and not manifest a need to demonstrate it with accomplishments. Or, the person may feel such a need and so become extremely successful in some pursuit. In either case, the individual's behavior is characterized by boasting, extreme vanity and self-centeredness, and a tendency to denigrate others.

You can see, then, how vitally important inferiority feelings are to personality formation. A requisite for all positive growth and development, they can also cripple such development.

Inferiority feelings are what push us forward, but to what end? What is the ultimate goal for which we strive? Is it simply to be rid of inferiority feelings? No, Adler viewed humans as striving for something more.

His thinking with regard to our ultimate goal changed over the years. Initially he identified inferiority feelings with a general feeling of weakness or femininity and spoke of compensation for this weakness as "masculine protest." The goal of the compensation was a will to power in which aggression played a large part.

Later, he rejected the notion of equating inferiority feelings with femininity and the striving for power and developed instead a much broader viewpoint in which we strive for superiority, a condition quite different from the superiority complex.

Striving for superiority: The ultimate goal

The "fundamental fact of our life" was how Adler described his notion of striving for **superiority** (Adler, 1930, pp. 398–399). It is the ultimate goal toward which all people strive, but it does not mean superiority in the usual sense of the word.

By *striving for superiority*, Adler did not mean that each of us strives to be above everyone else in position or prestige. Nor does the phrase, in his usage, refer to an arrogant, domineering tendency. What he meant is best indicated by the word he often used synonymously with superiority: *perfection*. People strive for perfection, which is, as Adler variously described it, an overcoming, an upward striving, an increase, an urge from below to above, or the impetus from minus to plus. The word *perfection* derives from a Latin word meaning to complete or to make whole (Engler, 1979, p. 118). This is the sense in which Adler used the term.

This great upward drive, this completing or making whole, parallels physical growth and is a necessary part of life. Everything we do follows the impetus and direction of this striving, which is constantly in operation. We are never free of it because it is life itself. Everything is marked by this striving for superiority, for perfection. Drawing upon Darwin and the notion of evolution, Adler said that all life expresses itself as constant movement toward the goal of the preservation and improvement of the individual and the species. And this goal is attained by adapting to and mastering the environment.

The various species, including humans, have evolved to their present level through this continuing adaptation. The necessity for better and more complete adaptation always exists. It cannot end; the striving to adapt, the striving for perfection, is innate. It must be innate, Adler argued, or no form of life could survive.

This ultimate and overall goal—the great upward drive toward wholeness or completion—is, of course, oriented toward the future. Whereas Freud saw human behavior as rigidly determined by physiological forces (the instincts) and experiences of childhood, Adler saw our motivation in terms of expectations for the future. He argued that we cannot appeal to instincts or impulses as explanatory principles. Only the final goal of superiority or perfection can explain our motivation.

Thus, all psychological processes and phenomena can be explained by Adler's concept of *finalism*—the idea that we have an ultimate goal, a final state of being, and an ever-present tendency or necessity to move in that direction. There is an important aspect to this notion of finalism. The goals for which we as individuals reach do not exist as actualities, but rather as potentialities. We strive for ideals that exist in us subjectively.

Adler believed that our overall goals are fictional ideals that cannot be tested against reality. He added that we live our lives around such fictions. We may believe that all people are created equal or that all people are basically good, and such ideals influence the way we perceive and interact with those around us. The person who believes that he or she will be rewarded in heaven for a certain way of behaving lives in accordance with such a belief. Confidence in the existence of heaven is not a reality-based belief, yet it is quite real to the person who subscribes to the view.

Thus, we have Adler's concept of **fictional finalism**—the idea that fictional ideas guide our behavior. There are a great many such fictions by which we direct the course of our lives, but the most general one is the ideal of perfection. The best conception of this ideal so far developed by human beings is the concept of God, which represents what Adler described as "the concrete formulation of the goal of perfection."

There are two additional points about the striving for superiority. First, it functions to increase rather than lessen tension. In opposition to Freud, Adler did not see our sole motivation as the reduction of tension and the maintenance of a neutral or tension-free state. The striving for perfection, with its correlate notions of upward, forward, more, and increase, calls for great expenditures of energy and effort. Adler felt that human beings want quite the opposite of stability and quiet.

Second, the striving for superiority is manifested both by the individual and by society. Adler considered people very much social beings. We strive for superiority or perfection not only as individuals but also as members of a society; we strive for perfection of our culture. Adler viewed individuals and society as closely interrelated and interdependent, so that people must function constructively with others for the good of all. Contrary to Freud, Adler considered the individual not to be in conflict with his or her culture but rather to be totally compatible with it.

Thus, we have a picture of humanity perpetually striving for the fictional, ideal goal of perfection. How, in our daily lives, do we go about trying to attain this goal? This question Adler answered with his concept of style of life.

The development of a lifestyle

Human beings have only one ultimate goal—superiority or perfection—but there are a great many specific behaviors by which individuals strive for that goal. We each express our striving for superiority in a different way. Each of us develops a unique pattern of characteristics, behaviors, and habits by which we reach for the goal. In other words, every person develops a distinctive **lifestyle**.

To understand how the style of life develops we must return to the concepts of inferiority feelings and compensation, for they form the basis of our lifestyle. As we have seen, all infants are afflicted with inferiority feelings that motivate them to compensate in some way. In these attempts at compensation, the child acquires a set of characteristic ways of behaving. To repeat an earlier example, a sickly or weak boy may strive to increase his strength and physical prowess. This behavior becomes his style of life, or lifestyle—a set of behaviors designed to compensate for an inferiority.

Everything we do is shaped and defined by our unique lifestyle; it determines which aspects of our total environment we will attend to or ignore and what attitudes we will hold. The lifestyle is learned from social interactions that take place in the early years of life. According to Adler, the lifestyle is so firmly crystallized by the age of 4 or 5 that it is difficult to change thereafter.

The lifestyle so formed becomes the guiding framework for later behavior. The nature of the lifestyle will depend on the individual's order of birth (discussed later) and on the nature of the relationship between parent and child as the child works to find a way to compensate for his or her sense of inferiority. For example, a girl who has been neglected may feel inferior in coping with the demands of life. The neglect on the part of her parents may cause her to feel distrustful and hostile toward the world at large. Her style of life, then, may involve seeking revenge, resenting the success of others, and taking whatever she feels is due her. We might subsume all such behaviors under the term *character*, which is essentially what Adler meant by style of life.

You may have spotted the apparent inconsistency between this notion of lifestyle and our earlier comments about Adler's theory. We noted that Adler's approach was a more optimistic and less deterministic view than Freud's. People are in control of their fate, Adler said, not victims of it. But now we find that the style of life is fully fixed by the parent–child relationship in the first five years of life and subject to little change after that. This would seem to be almost as deterministic as Freud's view; both stressed the importance of the early years in the formation of the adult personality. The notion of lifestyle is not as deterministic as it may seem, however, as Adler later clarified with a concept known as the **creative power of the self**.

In his various writings, Adler used several terms as equivalents for style of life: *personality, individuality*, and *the self*. But whatever terms used, he expressed in his later writings the belief that the style of life (the self) is created by the individual. People create their selves rather than being passively shaped by childhood experiences. The experiences themselves are not so important as the person's attitude toward them. Adler wrote that the person "does not relate himself to the outside world in a predetermined manner. . . . He relates himself always according to his own interpretation of himself." He argued that neither heredity nor environment determines personality. Instead, the way we experience these influences ("the interpretation he makes of these experiences") provides the basis for the creative construction of our attitude toward life.

In other words, Adler is arguing for the existence of individual free will that allows each of us to create our own most appropriate lifestyle out of the abilities and experiences given us by heredity and environment. Although not very clear on precisely how this creative self operates, Adler insisted that our lifestyle is not determined for us; we are free to choose and create our own selves. Once created, the lifestyle remains constant throughout life and constitutes our basic character, which defines our attitudes and behavior toward outside problems.

Adler placed great importance on the problems in life that every individual must solve, and he grouped them into three categories: problems involving behavior toward others, problems of occupation, and problems of love. He posited the existence of four basic lifestyles adopted by people for dealing with these problems.

The first type shows a *dominant* or *ruling* attitude, with little, if any, social awareness or interest. Such a person is likely to behave without regard for others. The more virulent of this type directly attack others and become sadists, delinquents, and tyrants. The less virulent become alcoholics, drug addicts, and suicides. Adler argued that through such behavior they are indirectly attacking others. In other words, they see themselves as hurting others by attacking themselves.

The second type of lifestyle—the *getting* type—which Adler considered the most common, expects to get everything from other people and so becomes dependent on them.

The *avoiding* type, as the name suggests, makes no attempt to face or struggle with life's problems. By avoiding the problems, such a person avoids any possibility of defeat.

As you can see, these three types are not prepared to face or cope with the everyday problems of life. They are unable to cooperate with other people, and the clash between their lifestyles and the real world is sufficient to result in abnormal behavior as manifested in neuroses and psychoses. All three types lack what Adler called social interest.

The fourth type—the *socially useful* type—is able to cooperate with others and to act in accordance with their needs. Such a person copes with life's problems within a well-developed framework of social interest.

It should be noted that Adler was opposed to typing or classifying human beings in any manner. He proposed these four general types only, as he put it, "for teaching purposes." He noted that in clinical work one should never make the mistake of classifying people into mutually exclusive categories.

Social interest came to form a major part of Adler's system. He believed that getting along with others is the first task we encounter in life and that our subsequent social adjustment (part of our lifestyle) influences our approach to all of life's later problems.

Social interest

Adler viewed human beings as influenced much more strongly by social than by biological forces. However, he did consider the potential for **social interest** to be innate. In that sense, then, Adler's approach does have a biological element to it. But the extent to which the innate potential for social feeling is realized depends on the nature of the child's early social experiences. No person can detach himself or herself entirely from other people, Adler felt, or from obligations toward them. From earliest times, people have congregated with other people—in families, tribes, and nations. Such communities are indispensable to humans for protection and for the attainment of survival goals. Thus, it has always been necessary for people to cooperate, and this cooperation is what Adler meant by social interest. The individual must cooperate with and contribute to society in order to realize both his or her own and society's goals.

Beginning at birth, the newborn finds itself in a situation requiring cooperation from others—initially the mother, then other family members, and finally
those beyond the home. In infancy, we cannot function very well in isolation and
must develop social interest. Everything we do for the rest of our lives takes place
within a framework of other people. All aspects of our character or style of life reveal the extent of the development of our social feeling.

Adler noted the important influence of the mother as the first person with
whom the baby comes in contact. She can, through her behavior toward the infant,
foster and develop social interest, or she can distort or thwart its development. (Of
course, this influence depends, Adler noted, on how the child interprets the mother's
behavior. The creative self forms the baby's character on the basis of this interpretation.)

The mother must teach the child cooperation, comradeship, and courage, concepts Adler considered to be very closely related. Only if a person feels united with
all others, Adler said, can he or she act with courage in attempting to master life's
problems. The child (and later the adult) who looks upon others with hostility and
suspicion will approach life's problems with the same attitude. Those with no feeling of social interest will become socially undesirable people—neurotics, criminals, despots, and the like.

Obviously, there can be a wide latitude in social feelings. One could devote all
one's time and energy to others or live an entirely selfish existence and make no
sacrifice for the community. Of course, one could also sacrifice excessively for
some group and yet have no social interest on the individual level—for example,
for a member of one's own family. Adler was not arguing in favor of a blind subor-
dination of oneself to the wants and needs of others. Rather, he urged a coordina-
tion or cooperation in which the individual best develops his or her own abilities in
concert with efforts to improve society.

We saw, in the biographical sketch at the beginning of this chapter, that Adler
as a boy enjoyed the company of other children; he developed a high degree of
social interest, which characterized him all his life. It is interesting that early in his
career Adler viewed people as driven by a lust for power and a need to dominate.
This was during the time when Adler himself was struggling to establish his own
point of view within the Freudian circle. Later in life, after he broke with Freud,
achieved recognition on his own, and became aware of the human wreckage of
World War I, he came to feel that people are strongly motivated by social interest. It
is possible to attribute such changes in the theory to changes within the theorist;
Adler was almost 50 years old when the war ended—an age when many individuals
reassess themselves and their world.

Freud's biographer, Ernest Jones, commented that, when Adler was a part of
Freud's circle, he was cantankerous and contentious and seemed very ambitious as
he quarreled over the priority of some of his ideas. Years later, Jones observed,
Adler's "success had brought him a certain benignity" (Jones, 1955, p. 130). At any
rate, Adler's system changed, as perhaps he did, from emphasizing power and dominance as motivating forces to stressing the more benign force of social interest.

The influence of birth order

Adler posited birth order as one of the major social influences in childhood from which the individual creates a style of life. Even though siblings have the same parents and live in the same house, they do not have identical social environments. The facts of being older or younger than one's siblings and of being exposed to parental attitudes that have changed as a result of the arrival of more children create different conditions of childhood that greatly influence one's personality, as Adler knew from his own childhood. Adler would often amaze lecture audiences and dinner guests by telling accurately what a person's order of birth was on the basis of his or her behavior. He focused on three different positions: the first-born child, the second-born, and the youngest.

The first-born child

The first child finds itself in a unique and in many ways enviable situation. Usually the parents are extremely happy at the birth of their first child and devote a great deal of time and attention to the new baby. The first-born thus receives the full and undivided attention of the parents.

As a result, the first-born often has a happy, secure existence—until the second child appears. What a shock it must be. No longer the focus of instant and constant attention, no longer receiving the undivided love and care of its parents, the child is, in Adler's terms, "dethroned" at this time. Adler had experienced this himself; when he was 2 his younger brother was born. The constant love the first-born received for the period of its reign must now be shared. The child must often submit to the outrage of waiting until after the newborn has been attended to and must be quiet at times so as not to awaken the new baby.

No one could expect the first-born to suffer such a drastic displacement without putting up a fight. He or she must try to recapture his or her former position of power. All first-borns feel the shock of their changed position in the family, but those who have been excessively pampered will, of course, feel a greater loss. Also, the extent of the loss depends on the age of the first-born at the time the rival appears. In general, the older a first-born is when the next child appears, the less sense of dethronement he or she experiences. An 8-year-old, for example, will be less bothered by the birth of a sibling than will a 2-year-old.

The battle to retain his or her former supremacy is lost from the beginning; things will never be as they once were, no matter how hard the first-born tries. But the child tries anyway and becomes, for a time, a behavior problem, breaking rules and objects, being stubborn, or refusing to eat or to go to bed. He or she is striking out in anger. Of course, the parents will probably strike back, and their weapons are far more powerful. When the first-born is punished for the new, troublesome behavior, he or she interprets the punishment as more evidence of a changed position and may easily grow to hate the new child. The newborn is, after all, the cause of the problem.

How could such a situation not affect one's outlook on life? Adler found that oldest children are often oriented toward the past, locked in nostalgia, and pessimistic about the future. Having learned the advantages of power at one time, they remain concerned with it all their lives. To some degree, they can exercise power over the younger siblings. At the same time, however, they are usually more subject to the power of the parents than are the younger children; that is, more is expected of them.

As a result of all this, first-borns take an interest in the maintenance of order and authority. Adler found that they become very good organizers, conscientious and scrupulous as to detail and authoritarian and conservative in attitude. Incidentally—or perhaps not so incidentally—Freud was a first-born. In fact, Adler referred to him as a "typical eldest son." The first-born may also grow up to feel very insecure and hostile toward others. Adler found that perverts, criminals, and neurotics were often first-borns.

The second-born child

What lies in store for the second-born, the one who's caused such a commotion? This child too has a unique situation. For one thing, he or she never experiences the powerful and focal position once occupied by the first-born. Therefore even if a younger sibling should appear, the second-born does not experience the keen sense of dethronement felt by the first-born. Furthermore, the parents may have changed by the time the second child arrives. A second baby is not the novelty the first was, and the parents may be less concerned and anxious about their behavior in rearing the second one; they may take a more relaxed approach to the second child.

The second born has, from the very beginning, a pacesetter in the older sibling. The second child is not alone as a child but always has the example of the older sibling's behavior as a model or a threat to compete with. Adler was a second-born child who had a competitive relationship with his older brother all of his life. Even when he became a successful and famous analyst he still felt overshadowed by his brother, who was a wealthy businessman. For as long as he lived, Adler never overcame the rivalry with his older brother, whose name, incidentally, was Sigmund. Clearly, the concept of birth order was developed, initially, on the basis of personal experience.

Competition with the first-born child spurs the second-born on, often stimulating a faster development than the first-born exhibited. The second child is motivated to catch up to and surpass the older sibling, a goal that usually speeds language and motor development. For example, the second child usually begins speaking at an earlier age than the older child did. Not having experienced power, the second-born is not as concerned with it as the first-born is and is more optimistic about the future. The second child is likely to be highly competitive and ambitious, as Adler himself was.

However, there are a number of other outcomes that may arise from the relationship between the first-born and the second-born. Suppose, for example, the older sibling excels in sports or in scholarship—or in everything. The second-born may sense that he or she can never surpass the older one and so may give up trying.

In this case, competitiveness would not become part of his or her style of life. Of course, as they grow older, it might turn out that the younger child is smarter, better looking, or superior in some other way to the first, who then may again become a behavior problem.

The youngest child

The youngest or last-born child never faces the shock of dethronement by another child and often becomes the pet or baby of the whole family, particularly if the siblings are more than a few years older. Spurred on by the need to surpass older siblings, the youngest child often develops at a remarkably fast rate. As a result, last-borns are often high achievers in whatever work they undertake as adults.

But quite the opposite may take place if the youngest child is spoiled and pampered by the rest of the family to the point where he or she needn't learn to do anything for himself or herself. As the individual grows older, he or she may retain the helplessness and dependency that marked his or her childhood. Unaccustomed to striving and struggling, used to being cared for by others, the person will find it difficult to cope with the problems and adjustments of adulthood.

What about the only child? In essence, he or she is the first-born who never loses the position of primacy and power—at least not in childhood. The child continues to be the focus and center of family attention. Spending more time in the company of adults than a child with siblings does, the only child often matures very early and achieves adult-like behaviors and attitudes sooner.

The only child is likely to experience a severe shock as he or she grows older and finds that in areas of life outside the home (such as school) he or she is not the center of attention. The only child has learned neither to share nor to compete for the center stage. If the child's abilities do not bring sufficient recognition and attention, he or she is likely to feel keenly disappointed.

Adler was not laying down firm rules of development. As noted, a child will not automatically acquire one and only one kind of character as a result of order of birth. What he was suggesting was the likelihood of certain lifestyles developing as a function of one's position within the family. The individual must always be studied in his or her relationships with others, for these early social relationships are used by the creative self in constructing the lifestyle.

Adler's image of human nature

We noted in the beginning of this chapter how different Adler's image of human nature was from that of Freud. Adler's system provides a hopeful and flattering picture of human nature that many consider a welcome antidote to Freud's dreary picture. Certainly it is more satisfying to our sense of self-worth to consider ourselves capable of consciously shaping our own development and destiny rather than being dominated by sexual forces and childhood experiences. Adler's image of us is a very optimistic one. We are not driven by unconscious forces that we cannot see or control; we shape the forces ourselves and use them in our own creative way to construct a unique style of life. This uniqueness is another part of Adler's flattering picture. Many saw in Freud's system a depressing universality and sameness in human beings.

Adler's image of human nature is plain. Each person is unique and possesses the free will and choice to create his or her self. Although certain aspects of human nature are innate—social interest and striving for perfection, for example—it is experience that determines how well these inherited tendencies will be realized. Childhood influences are important, in Adler's view, particularly order of birth and relations with parents. We are not, however, unchangeable victims of these early experiences. We use them, consciously, to create our own style of life.

Not only did Adler see each person as unique and highly conscious, but he also viewed humanity as a whole in the same terms; he was optimistic about social progress. From childhood on, he was concerned with societal betterment. This persistent belief that we can change ourselves and our society was a hallmark of Adlerian theory. He was attracted to socialism and was very much involved in school guidance clinics and penal reform, illustrating his belief in the creative power of the individual.

His concept of social interest reflected the belief that people are capable of cooperating to bring about a morally desirable and healthy society. By portraying us as capable of feeling and expressing sympathy, affection, and identification with one another, Adler offered a picture of human nature that many feel is in keeping with the highest teachings of religion and ethics.

Assessment in Adler's theory

Like Freud, Adler developed his theory through observation of his patients—what they told him and how they behaved during treatment sessions. Adler's approach to his patients was more relaxed and informal than Freud's. Whereas Freud's patients lay on a couch while he sat behind them, Adler and his patients faced each other, seated in comfortable chairs. The sessions were more like chats between two friends than like the formal relationships maintained by Freud.

Adler assessed the personalities of his patients by observing everything about them: the way they walked and sat, their manner of shaking hands—even their choice of which chair to sit in. He believed that the manner in which we use our bodies indicates something of our lifestyle. Even the position in which we sleep was revealing to Adler. A person who sleeps flat on his or her back is seen as wanting to seem bigger than he or she is. Sleeping on one's stomach reveals a stubborn and negative personality.

Order of birth

Adler's primary methods of assessment, the "three entrance gates to mental life," as he called them, are order of birth, early recollections, and dreams. We have already discussed how one's position in the family, *order of birth*, influences personality in the Adlerian view.

Early recollections

A patient's **early recollections** provide, according to Adler, an excellent guide to uncovering his or her lifestyle. As we have seen, the lifestyle develops (is created) in the first four or five years, and Adler felt that the earliest memories from this period would indicate the lifestyle that continues to characterize the adult. Adler found that it made little difference whether these early recollections were of real events or were fantasies. In either case, the primary interest of the person's life revolves around the remembered incident.

As one test of his theory, Adler asked more than 100 physicians for their early memories. He found that a majority of these memories were concerned with either illness or a death in the family, which apparently led them into a career of combating sickness, as was the case with Adler himself.

Another early recollection of Adler's was also highly revealing. He recalled that when he was 5 years old and had just started school he was frightened because the path to school led through a cemetery (Adler, 1959). He became terrified every time he walked to school, but he was also disconcerted when he observed that the other children seemed not to notice the cemetery at all. He was the only one who was afraid, and this enhanced his sense of inferiority.

One day he decided to put an end to his fears. He placed his schoolbag on the ground and ran through the cemetery 12 times, until he felt that he had overcome his feelings. From that day on, he was able to attend school without being frightened by the cemetery.

Such a recollection tells us something about Adler's personality. It suggests that from a very young age he tried to overcome his fears, to compensate for them by deliberately acting bravely, to harden himself so that he would not feel inferior to others.

But there is more to this early recollection. Thirty years later Adler met one of his former schoolmates and, in the course of their conversation, asked if the old cemetery was still there. The man expressed surprise. He told Adler that there had never been a cemetery near the school.

Adler was shocked. His recollection had always been so vivid. He sought out other classmates and questioned them about the cemetery. They all said the same thing: there had been no cemetery. Finally, Adler realized that although his memory of the incident was faulty, it still symbolized the fear and inferiority, and his own efforts to overcome them, that distinguished his entire life. The early recollection revealed an important aspect of his lifestyle.

While Adler felt that each first memory must be interpreted within the context of the individual patient, he found some commonalities among them. For example, memories involving danger or punishment indicate a tendency toward hostility. Those concerning the birth of a sibling indicate a continued sense of dethronement. Memories that focus on only one parent show a preference for that parent. Memories of improper behavior indicate an attempt to avoid repeating the behavior.

Adler's other early memories revealed his physical weakness, rivalry with his older brother, a preference for his father over his mother, ambition, and the overcoming of his childhood fear of death.

Dream analysis

Adler agreed with Freud on the great value of *dreams* in understanding personality but disagreed on the manner in which dreams should be interpreted. Adler did not believe that dreams fulfill wishes or reveal deeply hidden conflicts. Rather, dreams involve a person's feelings about a current life problem and what he or she intends or would like to do about it.

Adler felt that dreams engender feeling tones. As proof of this, he pointed to the fact that we very often cannot recall the specific events of a dream, but we do remember its mood; we remember whether it was frightening or beautiful without being able to recall in any detail the story of the dream. The moods evoked by a dream deceive the person, weakening his or her common sense and logic. In the fantasies that are dreams (both night dreams and daydreams) we can surmount the most difficult obstacle, simplify the most complex problem. And that is the fundamental purpose of dreams: to help the individual solve present problems. Dreams are oriented toward the present and future—toward goals and not toward conflicts of the past.

Adler argued that dreams should never be interpreted by themselves—that is, without knowledge of the person and his or her situation. The dream is a manifestation of a person's lifestyle and so is unique to the individual.

However, as with early recollections, Adler did find common interpretations for some dreams. For example, he found, as did Freud, that many people have dreams of falling or flying. Freud interpreted such dreams in sexual terms. To Adler, a dream of falling indicates that one's emotional view is from above to below. The person might, for example, be afraid of losing self-esteem or prestige. The viewpoint in a flying dream is just the opposite and may indicate an upward striving, an ambitious lifestyle in which the person wants to be above others. Some dreams combine both flying and falling, which Adler interpreted as a fear of being too ambitious and then failing. A dream of being chased by someone (or something) suggests a feeling of weakness in relation to others. Dreaming that one is unclothed indicates a fear of giving oneself away.

By whatever technique, the purpose of assessing an individual's personality is to discover his or her lifestyle and to determine if it is the most appropriate one for that person.

Psychological tests

Adler was unenthusiastic about the use of psychological tests to assess personality. He argued that such tests were artificial situations that provided ambiguous results, and that therapists should develop their intuitions instead of relying on tests. Adler did believe, however, that tests of memory and intelligence could be useful. It was the tests of personality, whether objective (self-report) or subjective (projective techniques), that he argued against and refused to use (Rattner, 1983).

In recent years, two tests have been developed to assess Adler's concept of social interest. The Social Interest Scale (SIS) consists of pairs of adjectives (Crandall, 1981). Subjects choose the one in each pair that best describes the attribute they would like to possess. Some of these, such as "helpful," "sympathetic," and "considerate," are thought to indicate one's degree of social interest.

The Social Interest Index (SII) is a self-report inventory in which subjects judge the degree to which statements represent themselves or their personal characteristics (Greever, Tseng & Friedland, 1973). The items, such as "I don't mind helping out friends," were selected to reflect the ideas in Adler's writings and to indicate a person's ability to accept and cooperate with others.

Research in Adler's theory

Adler's primary research approach to personality was the case history. Unfortunately, little of Adler's data is available. Unlike Freud, Adler did not publish his case histories. The only published examples are two fragments: one a case history written by a patient, the other a case history written by a patient's physician. In neither case did Adler know the persons, but he analyzed their personalities by a careful examination of their writings (Ellenberger, 1970).

As you might predict, Adler's data and his research method are subject to the same criticisms we discussed for Freud and Jung. Adler's observations cannot be repeated and duplicated, nor were they conducted in controlled and systematic fashion. Adler did not attempt to verify the accuracy of his patients' reports and, like Freud and Jung, did not explain the procedures he used to analyze his data.

Most of Adler's propositions have resisted attempts at scientific validation, although several aspects of his theory have been the subject of research. These include dreams, social interest, and birth order.

Adler's belief that dreams help us solve current problems was investigated by exposing subjects to situations in which the failure to solve a puzzle was considered to be a threat to the ego. The subjects were then allowed to sleep. Some were permitted to dream; they were awakened only during non-rapid-eye-movement (REM) sleep. Others were awakened during REM sleep so that they could not dream. Those who dreamed recalled significantly more of the failed puzzle than those who did not dream. By dreaming (presumably about the puzzle), the subjects were able to reduce the ego threat of their failure. Therefore, they had less need to repress their memory of the situation and so could recall it better than those who did not dream and so did not have the opportunity to reduce the threat to the ego. The researchers concluded that dreaming enabled subjects to deal effectively with the ego-threatening situation (Grieser, Greenberg & Harrison, 1972).

Research on social interest has used the two assessment devices we mentioned in the previous section. Studies using the Social Interest Scale have attempted to test Adler's thesis that persons higher in social interest are better adjusted emotionally than persons scoring lower in social interest. Correlating test scores on the SIS with other data, including self-report measures, peer ratings, religious activities, and even food aversions, provided only a modest suggestion of support for Adler's view. The relationship between social-interest test scores and the measures of adjustment was not very high (Crandall, 1981).

Research using the Social Interest Index showed that women who scored high in social interest were significantly higher in self-actualization, a characteristic of the healthy personality described by Abraham Maslow (Hjelle, 1975).

Most of the research deriving from Adler's theory has been conducted on the effects of birth order. It should be noted, however, that many of these studies were not undertaken specifically to test Adler's ideas, but rather for other reasons. In addition, not all the studies that have attempted to test Adler's notions have produced supportive results. Nevertheless, Adler deserves credit for being the first personality theorist to propose that order of birth can affect behavior and personality.

According to Adler, first-borns are concerned with power and authority. One way for them to gain power and authority as adults is through a high level of achievement in their work. Thus, first-borns should score very high in achievement, an Adlerian proposal that has received much research support.

In virtually every field of endeavor, from college enrollment to serving as President of the United States, first-borns are overrepresented relative to their proportion in the population. More first-borns than later-borns become eminent. They tend to reach higher levels of intellectual achievement in academic settings, and higher levels of position and prestige in the world of work (Breland, 1974; Schachter, 1963).

Other studies have found first-borns to be more dependent on other people and more easily persuaded by them. They tend to be more anxious in stressful situations and to have a higher need to affiliate with other people during stress (Schachter, 1963, 1964). These findings could be predicted from Adler's views. He noted that first-borns are made anxious and fearful when they are dethroned and that they attempt to regain their earlier position partly by conforming to their parents' expectations.

Less research has been conducted on second-born children, and there seems to be no support for Adler's contention that they are more competitive and ambitious than their siblings. One study did find that second-borns were lower in self-esteem than first- or last-borns, particularly if there were about two years in age difference between them and the older and younger siblings (Kidwell, 1982).

Adler predicted that last-born children, if excessively pampered, may have difficulty as adults in coping with life's problems. It is often suggested that one reason some people become alcoholics is that they are unable to adjust to the needs of everyday life and, therefore, that more last-borns than early-borns are likely to become alcoholics. This prediction has been substantiated in the majority of studies dealing with alcoholism and birth order (Barry & Blane, 1977).

Adler viewed only-born adults as overly concerned with being the center of attention, as they were in childhood. Hence, they are considered to be more selfish than those who were reared with siblings. Research has not supported this prediction. Indeed, one study found that only-borns demonstrated more cooperative behavior than did first- and last-borns (Falbo, 1978).

A final commentary

Adler's theory of personality was warmly received by many people who had been repelled by Freud's dreary, doom-laden image of humanity. Adler's influence continues to be substantial within psychology. We shall see examples of that influence in the work of a number of personality theorists in this book.

Adler's ideas even reached into Freudian psychoanalysis itself. It was Adler who first proposed the existence of an aggressive drive, more than 12 years before Freud added aggression to sex as a primary motivating force. The works of the neo-Freudians, the so-called ego psychologists, who focused more on conscious, rational processes and less on the unconscious, were following Adler's lead (Ellenberger, 1970).

Adler's emphasis on social forces in personality can be seen in the works of Karen Horney (Chapter 5) and Erich Fromm (Chapter 6), who were more neo-Adlerian than neo-Freudian. Adler's focus on the unity of personality and the whole person is reflected in the later work of Gordon Allport (Chapter 8).

Adler's stress on the creative power of the individual in shaping his or her own life, and his insistence that future goals are more important than past events, influenced the work of Abraham Maslow (Chapter 12). Maslow commented, "Alfred Adler becomes more and more correct year by year. As the facts come in, they give stronger and stronger support to his image of man" (Maslow, 1970a, p. 13). Julian Rotter (Chapter 16), a contemporary social-learning theorist, was also influenced by Adler. "I was and continue to be impressed by his insights into human nature. . . . His contributions were indeed great" (Rotter, 1982, pp. 1–2).

These contributions and influences on the work of others, extending from the 1920s to the 1980s, make Adler's theory of personality one of the most enduring. Some psychologists have suggested that Adler was far ahead of his time, that his cognitive and social emphases are more compatible with trends in psychology today than with the psychology of his own day (Crandall, 1983).

This may help explain why Adler was ranked 9th among the theorists in this book and 21st out of 286 notable psychologists in the ratings made of the most important psychologists in the second half of the 20th century (Gilgen, 1982).

Some of Adler's specific concepts have also proved to be of lasting importance. These include his early work on organ inferiority, which has influenced the study of psychosomatic disorders; inferiority complex; compensation; and order of birth. He is also considered to be a forerunner of social psychology and of group therapy.

Curiously, although Adler's ideas are widely accepted and used, his personal recognition declined after his death in 1937, and he has received relatively little praise for his contributions. Many concepts have been borrowed from his system and used without acknowledgment of their source. Typical of this lack of recognition was Freud's obituary in the *Times*, London's leading newspaper, which gave Freud credit for the term "inferiority complex." When Jung died, the *New York Times* credited *Jung* with having coined the term (Kaufmann, 1980). Neither newspaper mentioned Adler, the originator of the concept. Adler did, however, receive one honor that is unique among personality theorists and is particularly appropriate since he was a lover of fine music. A British composer, Richard Stoher, named a string quartet for Adler (Hall, 1970).

As influential as Adler's work has been, it is not without its critics. One charge leveled by Freud was that Adler's psychology was oversimplified. Freud wrote that Adler's theory would be appealing to many people because it eliminated the complicated nature of the unconscious, introduced no difficult concepts, and ignored the problems of sex. Freud remarked that psychoanalysis could be taught for two years or even longer because it was so complex. But "Adler's ideas and technique can be easily learned in two weeks," Freud said, "because with Adler there is so little to know" (Sterba, 1982, p. 156).

Freud is not alone in making this charge. It is true that Adler's theory seems simpler than some others (certainly simpler than Freud's or Jung's), but that was Adler's deliberate intention. "I have taken forty years to make my psychology simple," he wrote. One point that may reinforce the charge of oversimplification is that his books are much easier to read than those of many other theorists, perhaps in part because he intended most of them for the lay public and also because some were compiled from popular lectures.

A related charge is that Adler's theories rely too heavily on common-sense observations from everyday life. Whether that is a valid criticism is debatable, since some of his observations appear to be insightful and useful.

Some critics allege that Adler was not always consistent or systematic in his thinking—that there are gaps and unanswered questions in his theory. Are inferiority feelings the only problem people have to cope with in life? Do all people strive solely, or even primarily, for superiority or perfection? Is it possible that some people might become reconciled to a certain degree of inferiority and no longer be concerned with attempts to compensate for it? How important, specifically, are heredity and environment in influencing one's lifestyle? These and many other questions have been asked, and they are not adequately answered in Adler's system. Of course, most theories leave us with a set of unanswered questions.

A problem that concerns many people—even some of Adler's followers—is the sticky question of determinism and free will. At the beginning of his career, Adler did not oppose the notion of determinism. It was, after all, strongly accepted in science at the time and certainly characterized Freud's position. Later, however, he felt the need to grant more autonomy to the self, and his final position was one that, as we have seen, rejected determinism. His doctrine of the creative self states that, before the age of 5, we each create our own lifestyle out of the materials provided by our heredity and environment. It is not clear, however, just how the child is able to make such momentous decisions.

We know that Adler came out strongly in favor of free will and against the idea that a person is merely a victim of heredity and past environment. The position is clear, but the specifics of the forming of a lifestyle are not.

Adler's loyal followers claim that individual psychology is becoming increasingly popular among psychologists, psychiatrists, social workers, and educators, and that more and more research is being performed on Adlerian concepts (Ansbacher, 1977). The *Journal of Individual Psychology* is quite active, and individual-psychology associations exist throughout the Western world. Adlerian training institutes have been established in New York, Chicago, and several other cities. The Alfred Adler Institute, originally under the direction of Adler's daughter Alexandra, is located in New York, a city that claims some 250 practicing Adlerian analysts. Thus, Alfred Adler's approach to personality is of far more than historical interest.

Summary

Adler's individual psychology differs from Freud's psychoanalysis in its focus on the uniqueness of each person, on consciousness, and on social rather than biological forces. It minimizes the role of sex. Adler's childhood was characterized by intense efforts to compensate for inferiorities and by jealousy of his older brother.

Inferiority feelings are the source of all human striving, which results from our attempts to compensate for those feelings. Inferiority feelings are universal and are determined by the infant's helplessness and dependency relative to adults.

An inferiority complex, an inability to solve life's problems, results from being unable to compensate for inferiority feelings. An inferiority complex can originate in three ways in childhood: through organic inferiority, a defective part or organ of the body; by spoiling the child; or by neglect of the child. A superiority complex, an exaggerated opinion of one's abilities and accomplishments, results from over-compensation.

The ultimate goal toward which people strive is superiority or perfection, the completing or making whole of the personality. The striving for perfection is innate and is oriented toward the future. Fictional finalism refers to fictional ideas that guide our behavior, the most general one of which is the idea of perfection. Striving for superiority serves to increase rather than decrease tension and is manifested by individuals and by society as a whole. Lifestyle or character refers to unique patterns of characteristics and behaviors by which people strive for perfection. Lifestyle behaviors were originally designed to compensate for an inferiority, are learned through childhood social interactions, and are established by age 4 or 5. The creative power of the self refers to our ability to create our selves from the abilities and experiences brought about by our heredity and environment. Thus, to Adler, there is considerable individual free will.

The three primary problems in life involve behavior toward others, occupation, and love. There are four basic lifestyles or types for dealing with these problems. The dominant or ruling type has no social interest, behaves with no regard for others, and may even attack others. The getting type is dependent on others, expecting to receive everything from them. The avoiding type avoids life's problems. The dominant, getting, and avoiding types lack social interest and are not prepared to cope with the everyday problems of life. The socially useful type copes with life's problems by cooperating with others.

The potential for social interest is innate; its realization depends on the child's early social experiences, particularly those with the mother. The mother must teach cooperation, comradeship, and courage.

Order of birth is a major social influence in childhood from which a lifestyle is created. The first-born child suffers the shock of being dethroned when the next child is born. First-borns are oriented toward the past, pessimistic about the future, and concerned with maintaining order and authority. The second-born has a pacesetter, the older sibling against whom to compete. As a result, second-borns, like Adler himself, are apt to be highly competitive and ambitious. The last-born may be the baby of the family. Spurred by the need to surpass older siblings, last-borns may become high achievers. The only child may mature early, but is apt to face a shock in school when he or she is no longer the center of attention, as was the case at home.

Adler's image of human nature is more hopeful and flattering than Freud's. In Adler's view, people are unique. They possess free will and the ability to consciously shape their own development. Certain aspects of human nature are innate, such as social interest and the striving for perfection, but experience determines how well these inherited tendencies are realized. Childhood experiences are important, but we are not victims of those experiences.

Adler's primary methods of assessment are order of birth, early recollections, and dreams. Early recollections can reveal a person's lifestyle, whether the recollections are of real or imagined events. Dreams reveal our feelings about a current problem and what we would like to do about it. Adler believed that personality tests were artificial situations that yielded ambiguous results. Two tests have been developed to measure social interest: the Social Interest Scale and the Social Interest Index.

Adler's primary method of research was the case study. Thus, his observations cannot be repeated, duplicated, or verified, and were not conducted in controlled and systematic fashion. Most of Adler's propositions have resisted attempts at scientific validation. Research has provided varying degrees of support for Adler's views on dreams; for his belief that social interest is related to emotional well-being; for his idea that first-borns are high in achievement, dependent on others, easily persuaded, and anxious in stressful situations; and for the suggestion that last-borns may become alcoholics.

Adler's views influenced Freud and the ego psychologists through his notion of the aggressive drive and his focus on conscious, rational processes. His emphasis on social factors in personality, the unity of personality, the creative power of the individual, the importance of goals, and cognitive factors has influenced many other personality theorists. His contributions also include the concepts of organ inferiority, the inferiority complex, compensation, and order of birth. His theory has been criticized for being oversimplified, inconsistent, and unsystematic; for relying too heavily on common sense; and for leaving unanswered questions.

Glossary

compensation   A motivation to overcome inferiority, to strive for higher levels of development.

creative power of the self   The ability of the individual to create an appropriate lifestyle.

early recollections   A personality assessment technique in which a person's earliest memories (whether of real events or fantasies) are assumed to reveal the individual's primary interest in life.

fictional finalism   The idea that there is an imagined or potential goal that guides an individual's behavior.

individual psychology   Adler's theory of personality.

inferiority complex   A condition that develops when an individual is unable to compensate for normal inferiority feelings.

inferiority feelings   The normal condition common to all people that is the source of human striving.

lifestyle   A unique character structure, or a pattern of personal behaviors and characteristics, by which an individual strives for perfection.

social interest   The innate potential of the individual to cooperate with other people to achieve personal and societal goals.

superiority   Perfection or completion, the ultimate goal toward which the individual strives.

superiority complex   A condition that develops when an individual overcompensates for normal inferiority feelings.

Review questions

1. Distinguish between inferiority feelings and the inferiority complex. How does each develop?
2. According to Adler, a striving for superiority motivates human behavior. How does this idea contradict Freud's view of motivation?
3. Distinguish between striving for superiority and the superiority complex.
4. How does the self develop? Do we take an active or a passive role in the development of the self?
5. Describe the four basic lifestyles.
6. What parental behaviors foster social interest in the child?
7. Which of the basic lifestyles is identified with social interest?
8. Describe the personality characteristics that may develop in the first-born, second-born, and youngest child as a result of their order of birth.
9. How well does empirical research support Adler's predictions about first-borns?
10. What is the importance of early recollections in the assessment of personality?
11. According to Adler, what is the purpose of dreams? Does contemporary sleep research support his views on dreams?

Suggested reading

Adler, A. Individual psychology. In C. Murchison, Ed., *Psychologies of 1930*. Worcester, MA: Clark University Press, 1930.

Adler, A. *Social interest*. New York: Putnam, 1939, 1964.

Ansbacher, H. L. *Alfred Adler revisited*. New York: Praeger, 1981.

Dreikurs, R. Adler's contribution to medicine, psychology, education. *American Journal of Individual Psychology*, 1952–1953, 10, 83–86.

Ellenberger, H. F. *The discovery of the unconscious*. New York: Basic Books, 1970. (See Chapter 8, "Alfred Adler and Individual Psychology.")

Manaster, G. J. & Corsini, R. J. *Individual psychology*. Itasca, IL: Peacock, 1982.

Orgler, H. *Alfred Adler: The man and his work*. New York: New American Library, 1963.

Rattner, J. *Alfred Adler*. New York: Ungar, 1983.

Sperber, M. *Masks of loneliness: Alfred Adler in perspective*. New York: Macmillan, 1974.

CHAPTER 5

Karen Horney

The life of Horney (1885–1952)
Safety and satisfaction: The needs of childhood
Basic anxiety: The foundation of neurosis
Neurotic needs
Neurotic trends
   The compliant personality: Moving toward people
   The aggressive personality: Moving against people
   The detached personality: Moving away from people
The idealized self-image
The flight from womanhood: Feminine psychology
Horney's image of human nature
Assessment in Horney's theory
Research in Horney's theory
A final commentary
Summary
Glossary
Review questions
Suggested reading

Man has the capacity as well as the desire to develop his potentialities and become a decent human being. . . . I believe that man can change and go on changing as long as he lives.

KAREN HORNEY

It is obvious from our opening quote that Karen Danielson Horney must be considered another defector from the orthodox Freudian point of view. While not a direct disciple or colleague of Freud's, Horney was nevertheless trained in the official psychoanalytic mode by one of Freud's most trusted students. She did not, however, remain long in the Freudian camp.

Horney began her divergence from Freud's doctrines by taking issue with his psychological portrayal of women. An early feminist, she argued that psychoanalysis focused more on the development of men than of women. Countering Freud's contention that women are driven by penis envy, Horney commented that, in her observation, men are envious of women for their ability to carry and give birth to children. "I know just as many men," she said, "with womb envy as women with penis envy" (Cherry & Cherry, 1973, p. 75). Although originally moved to depart from Freud on the issue of female psychology, Horney later broadened her attack on Freud and elaborated her own position, so that there came to be little in common between them.

Horney's theory was influenced, in part, by her sex but perhaps even more by the social and cultural forces to which she was exposed. She worked several decades after Freud's major developments appeared, and she formulated the essential lines of her theory in a culture radically different from Freud's—the United States. By the 1930s and 1940s, major changes had taken place in popular attitudes about sex and the roles of the sexes. These changes were noticeable in Europe but were even more visible in the United States. Social attitudes, too, were different in the United States.

Horney found that her American patients were so unlike her previous German patients, both in their neuroses and in their more normal personalities, that only the differences in social forces could adequately account for the differences in their personalities. Personality, she therefore argued, cannot depend wholly on invariant biological forces, as Freud had proposed. If it did, we would not see such important differences in personality from one culture to another.

Thus, Horney became, like Adler, a social-psychological theorist, placing heavy emphasis on social relationships rather than on physiological forces as pivotal factors in personality formation. She argued that sex is not the governing factor, as Freud had claimed, and also took issue with his concepts of the Oedipus complex, the libido, and the structure of personality.

The motivating force of personality, Horney theorized, is not sex or aggression but the need for and the efforts to obtain security. Like Adler, Horney's view of human nature is flattering and optimistic: we can overcome our anxieties and can grow and develop to the fullest use of our potential.

The life of Horney (1885–1952)

Karen Danielson was born in a small village not far from Hamburg, in northern Germany. Her father was a 50-year-old ship captain of Norwegian background, and her mother was Dutch. Mrs. Danielson was 17 years younger than her husband and differed sharply from him in temperament. While the father was a devout Bible reader, domineering, imperious, morose, and silent, the mother was attractive, vivacious, and a freethinker. The father was away at sea for long periods, and, when he was home, the opposing natures of the parents often led to arguments.

We can see the roots of Horney's theory of personality in her own childhood experiences. Her biographer, Jack Rubins, noted: "Her work comes through as a product of her personality and of her external milieu . . . filtered, as it were, through her personality" (Rubins, 1978, p. xiv). For most of her childhood and adolescence, she doubted that her parents, particularly her father, wanted her, and she believed that they loved her older brother much more than they loved her.

The young Horney admired her father and desired his love and attention, but she was intimidated by him. She long remembered "his frightening blue eyes" and his stern, demanding manner (Rubins, 1978, p. 12). Throughout her early years she felt completely rejected by him. He made frequent disparaging comments about her appearance and intelligence. She felt belittled and unattractive, even though she was actually very pretty. "It must be grand to have a father one can love and esteem," Horney confided to her diary. "I can't do it. I can't respect that man who makes us all unhappy" (Horney, 1980, p. 21).

She was close to her mother and became the adoring daughter as a way of getting affection. Until the age of 8 she was a model child, clinging and compliant, "like a little lamb," she wrote (Rubins, 1978, p. 13). In spite of these efforts, she still did not believe that she had the love and security she needed. Self-sacrifice and good behavior were not working, so she changed her tactics.

At age 9, Horney became ambitious and rebellious. She decided that if she could not have love and security, she would take revenge for her feelings of unattractiveness and inadequacy. Years later she wrote, "If I couldn't be beautiful, I decided I would be smart" (Rubins, 1978, p. 14). She vowed always to be the first in her class. As an adult she came to realize how much hostility she had developed as a child. Horney's personality theory describes how a lack of love in childhood helps to foster basic anxiety and hostility, providing another example of how a theory can be developed initially in intuitive, highly personal terms.

At the age of 12, after receiving very kind treatment from a doctor for an illness, she decided to pursue a medical career. In spite of spirited opposition from her father and her own strong feelings of worthlessness and despair, Horney worked hard in high school to prepare herself for medical school. So strongly did her father resist the idea that, when she began her studies at the University of Freiburg, her mother left him and moved nearby.

At the age of 24, in 1909, she married Oscar Horney, a Berlin lawyer, and in due course had three children and entered into psychoanalytic training. She received her own analysis from a devoted disciple of Freud's, who mentioned her in glowing terms to the master.

In 1926, she and her husband separated, and six years later she emigrated to the United States, working first in Chicago and then settling permanently in New York. There her friends included Erich Fromm and Harry Stack Sullivan. During these years she developed most of her theory. Toward the end of her life, she became interested in Zen Buddhism, and she visited a number of Zen monasteries in Japan the year before she died.

Safety and satisfaction: The needs of childhood

Horney agreed with Freud, in principle, about the vital importance of the early years of childhood in shaping the adult personality. However, the two differed on the specifics of how the personality is formed. Horney felt that it is social forces in childhood, not biological forces, that influence personality development. There are neither universal stages of development nor inevitable childhood conflicts. Rather, the social relationship between the child and the parents is the key factor.

Horney believed that childhood is characterized by two needs: the need for *safety* and the need for *satisfaction*. They are drives of a universal nature and are both extremely important. However, in Horney's theory safety assumes a much greater importance than satisfaction. The latter, simpler need includes certain of our basic physiological needs. Humans require certain amounts of food, water, sexual activity, sleep, and so on. Obviously, neither the infant nor the adult could survive very long without at least a minimal level of satisfaction of most of these requirements, but they are not of fundamental importance in shaping personality.

What is primary, according to Horney—what is decisive in determining personality—is the need for safety, by which term she meant security and freedom from fear. Whether or not the infant experiences a feeling of security and an absence of fear determines the extent of the normality of its later personality growth.

The child's security depends entirely on the treatment he or she receives from

The state of helplessness in infancy can lead to neurotic behavior.

the parents. In general, Horney felt, the major way in which parents can weaken or prevent security altogether is to display a lack of warmth and affection for the child, which was her own childhood situation. She believed that children can withstand much that is usually considered traumatic, such as occasional beatings, premature sexual experiences, or abrupt weaning, without ill effect, as long as they feel wanted and loved and are therefore secure.

Parents can, however, act in a variety of ways that undermine security and thereby induce hostility in the child. Some of these parental behaviors include: obvious preference for a sibling, unfair punishment, erratic behavior, unkept promises, ridicule, humiliation, and isolation of the child from others. Horney also believed that a child knows if the parents' love is genuine and is not easily fooled by false demonstrations and expressions of love.

For several reasons, hostility thus engendered in the child may be repressed. These reasons include a sense of helplessness, fear of the parents, the need for expressions of love, and guilt feelings.

Horney placed a heavy emphasis on the helplessness of the infant. Unlike Adler, however, she did not believe that each infant necessarily feels helpless, although when this feeling does arise, it fulfills a primary condition for the development of neurotic behavior. Whether or not the child feels helpless depends on how the parents treat him or her. If the child is excessively sheltered, babied, and kept in a state of dependency, then helplessness will be encouraged. The more helpless the child feels, the less he or she will dare to oppose or rebel against the parents in any way. This means that any feelings of hostility will be repressed. As Horney noted, the child in this situation says, in effect: "I have to repress my hostility because I need you" (Horney, 1937, p. 86).

A child can easily be made to feel fearful of his or her parents through punishment, threats, or beatings. More indirect means of intimidation may also be used. The child can be made apprehensive and fearful about germs, moving cars, dogs, strangers, or other children by observing what the parents say and do in regard to these things. The more fearful the child becomes of these dangers in the world and of his or her parents, the more he or she will repress the felt hostility toward the parents. It is as though the child were saying: "I have to repress my hostility because I am afraid of you" (Horney, 1937, p. 86).

Paradoxically, love can be another reason for the child's feeling the need to repress feelings of hostility toward the parents. In this case Horney was referring to the situation in which the parents continually tell the child how much they love him or her and how much they are sacrificing for the child but do not feel genuine warmth and love. The child recognizes that these verbal expressions are substitutes for a deeper love. Yet they are all that the child has, and so he or she represses the hostility for fear of losing them.

These three factors—helplessness, fear, and love—can cause the child to repress his or her hostility in order to avoid damaging the relationship he or she has with the parents. The child either needs them or is afraid of them or fears losing whatever love they offer.

There is one final reason for repression of hostility. In our culture, children are often made to feel guilty about any expression of hostility or rebellion made against parents. The child is made to feel unworthy, wicked, or sinful for expressing or even harboring feelings of resentment. The more guilt the child feels, the more deeply he or she will repress the hostility.

For one or more of these reasons, then, the child holds in his or her hostility. Eventually, this repressed resentment manifests itself in the condition Horney called *basic anxiety*.

Basic anxiety: The foundation of neurosis

Basic anxiety is the fundamental concept in Horney's theory of personality. She defined it as "an insidiously increasing, all-pervading feeling of being lonely and helpless in a hostile world" (Horney, 1937, p. 89). Basic anxiety is the foundation on which later neuroses develop, and it is inseparably tied to feelings of hostility.

As the definition indicates, basic anxiety is pervasive; it underlies all relationships the individual has or will have with other people. Horney drew an analogy between a person suffering basic anxiety and a nation undergoing political unrest. The anxiety and hostility within the individual are similar to the underground dissensions and protests against a government. In either case, the internal unrest may be manifested overtly—by strikes or riots in the nation or by neurotic symptoms in the individual.

Regardless of how the person manifests or expresses basic anxiety, Horney felt, the feeling state is more or less the same for everyone. The person feels "small, insignificant, helpless, deserted, endangered, in a world that is out to abuse, cheat, attack, humiliate, betray" (Horney, 1937, p. 92). Understandably, an individual, particularly in childhood, will try to protect himself or herself against these strong feelings of anxiety. Horney wrote that, in our culture, there are four such means of self-protection: gaining affection, being submissive, attaining power, and withdrawing.

By securing affection and love from other people, the person is saying, in effect: "If you love me, you will not hurt me" (Horney, 1937, p. 96). There are several ways in which the person may try to secure affection. He or she may, for example, try to do everything someone else wants or may try to bribe or even threaten others into giving the desired affection.

Submissiveness as a means of self-protection involves complying with the wishes of one particular person or of everybody. Such a person avoids doing anything that might antagonize others. The person dares not criticize or in any way give offense, must repress his or her own needs and desires, and cannot even defend himself or herself against abuse for fear that such defensive reactions might antagonize the abuser. Horney felt that most people who act in such a submissive manner believe that they are truly unselfish and self-sacrificing. Such a person seems to be saying: "If I give· in, I shall not be hurt" (Horney, 1937, p. 97). This could describe Horney's own behavior until the age of 9.

Achieving power over others is the third self-protective mechanism. In this way, the person can compensate for his or her sense of helplessness and gain security through the achievement of success or through a sense of superiority over others. Such a person seems to believe: "If I have power, no one can hurt me" (Horney, 1937, p. 98). Perhaps this describes Horney once she decided to strive for academic success.

These three self-protective devices have one aspect in common. By engaging in one of them, the person is attempting to cope with anxiety by interacting with other people. The final means of protecting oneself from basic anxiety is withdrawal from other people, not in a physical sense but in a psychological sense. The person attempts to become completely independent of others, not relying on anyone for the satisfaction of external or internal needs.

For example, if a person amasses a great many material possessions, then he or she can rely on them (and on personal effort) to satisfy external needs. Unfortunately, even when the person has accumulated such items, he or she may be bound by too much anxiety to enjoy them. Possessions must be guarded zealously because they are the only protection against the constant threat of anxiety.

Independence with regard to one's psychological needs is achieved by becoming aloof and detached from others, no longer depending on them for satisfaction of emotional needs. Actually, it involves more than that; it involves a blunting, a minimizing, of one's emotional needs. By withdrawing from emotional contact and renouncing one's emotional needs, one protects oneself from being hurt by other people.

These four self-protective mechanisms have one goal: defense against anxiety. They are oriented toward gaining security and reassurance, not happiness or pleasure. In other words, they are a defense against pain, not a positive pursuit of well-being.

Another common characteristic of these protective devices is their power and intensity. Horney believed they can be even stronger compelling forces than sexual or other physiological needs. And these devices can work. They can perform their mission of reducing anxiety, but the cost to the individual is usually an impoverished personality and conflict with his or her environment.

Very often, the neurotic will pursue his or her search for security using more than one of these devices, and their incompatibility can lay the groundwork for further conflicts. For example, a person may be driven at the same time by the needs to dominate others and also to be loved by them. Or he or she may want to be submissive to others while simultaneously desiring power over them. Such incompatibilities cannot be resolved. Thus, attempts to combat basic anxiety can form the basis of deep conflicts.

Neurotic needs

Horney believed that any of these protective mechanisms can become so permanent a part of the personality that it assumes the characteristics of a drive or need in determining the individual's behavior. At one time, Horney listed ten such needs, which she defined as neurotic because she thought them to be irrational solutions to the person's problems. The ten **neurotic needs** are the following (Horney, 1942, pp. 54–60).

1. Affection and approval
2. A dominant partner in life
3. Narrow and constricted limits to life
4. Power
5. Exploitation
6. Prestige
7. Personal admiration
8. Personal achievement or ambition
9. Self-sufficiency and independence
10. Perfection and unassailability

Horney noted that everyone has these needs to some degree. All of us are aware that at one time or another we have felt the need to exploit others or to be independent of them, the need for affection and approval, and so on. None of these needs is abnormal or neurotic in its everyday, transient appearance.

What makes them neurotic is the intensive and compulsive pursuit of their satisfaction as the only means of resolving basic anxiety. In this case, their satisfaction will not help the individual achieve security but will serve only to help him or her to escape from the pain of anxiety. Also, when pursuing gratification of these needs only to escape anxiety, the person tends to focus on only one need and to compulsively seek its satisfaction in any and all situations.

In her later work, Horney became dissatisfied with these ten needs, or at least with presenting them individually. She came to realize that they could be grouped into three clusters, each of which represents a person's attitudes toward himself or herself and others. Specifically, she said that each of the ten needs involves one of the following: movement toward other people, movement against other people, or movement away from other people. For example, Needs 1 and 2—for affection/approval and for a dominant partner—involve movement toward other people. Moving against other people includes the power, exploitation, prestige, admiration, and ambition needs. The needs for self-sufficiency, for perfection, and for narrow limits to life involve moving away from people. Horney called these three categories of directional movement neurotic trends.

Neurotic trends

Because these **neurotic trends** evolve from the protective mechanisms discussed above, we shall see similarities among them. In a sense, we can say that the neurotic trends are elaborations of the protective devices.

These behavioral and attitudinal trends are compulsive; that is, the neurotic individual is compelled to behave in accordance with at least one of them. They are also displayed indiscriminately. Each of these neurotic trends leads to a certain type of behavior. The types are: moving toward people (the compliant type), moving against people (the aggressive type), and moving away from people (the detached type).

The compliant personality: Moving toward people

The **compliant or self-effacing type of personality** is characterized by an intense and continuous need for affection and approval—a need to be loved, wanted, needed, and protected. These people display these needs toward all others, but they usually have a need for one person—a friend or a marriage partner, for instance—who will take charge of their lives and offer protection and guidance.

These people manipulate other people, particularly their one partner, in order to achieve their ends. In these manipulations they often behave in ways that others find attractive or endearing. For example, the compliant personality is often unusually sensitive and responsive to the needs of other people, particularly to their needs for sympathy and understanding. Since these people are so concerned with living up to the perceived ideals and expectations of others, they often behave in ways that others perceive as unselfish, including being considerate, appreciative, and generous to an exceptional degree.

In their dealings with others, compliant personalities are conciliatory, subordinating their own desires to those of other people. They are willing to take blame and to defer to others, never being assertive or critical or demanding of them. In short, they will do whatever the situation or another person requires (as they interpret it) to gain affection, approval, and love.

In addition to this consistent way of behaving toward others, compliant personalities display a consistent attitude toward themselves. Central to this attitude is a feeling of helplessness and weakness that they readily admit to themselves and to others, often in an appeal. They are saying, in effect: "Look at me. I am so weak and helpless that you must protect and love me."

As a result of this attitude toward themselves, they come to regard everyone else as better than they, superior in every way. Even in situations in which they are notably competent in comparison with others, they still regard themselves as vastly inferior to everyone else.

Because compliant people's security depends so totally on the attitudes and behavior of other people toward them, they become excessively dependent on others. They constantly need approval and love; any sign of rejection—actual or imagined—is terrifying, leading to increased efforts to regain the affection of the person they believe has rejected them.

Bear in mind that the source of this behavior is the person's own repressed hostility. Horney found that compliant people have repressed (in the Freudian sense) strong feelings of defiance and vindictiveness, have a desire to control, exploit, and manipulate others, and have a lack of interest in others—quite the opposite of what their behaviors and attitudes express. The repressed impulses must be kept in check, and so compliant people become submissive and subservient, doing whatever anyone asks, always trying to please, and asking nothing for themselves.

The aggressive personality: Moving against people

As the label clearly indicates, **aggressive personalities**, in their constant movement against people, are the opposite of the compliant type. These people live in a world in which, as they see it, everyone is hostile and only the fittest and most cunning survive. The world is seen as a jungle in which supremacy, strength, and ferocity are the paramount virtues.

Although their motivation is the same as that of the compliant type—the alleviation of basic anxiety—aggressive personalities never display the same evident fear of rejection. These people act in a tough, domineering manner with no regard for others. To achieve the control and superiority so vital to them, they must constantly perform at a very high level. In excelling and receiving recognition, such people find the satisfaction of having their strength and superiority affirmed by others.

They must surpass others, and therefore they judge every person in terms of what benefit can arise from the relationship. There is no appeasement of others for those with aggressive personalities; they argue, criticize, demand, and manipulate—whatever is necessary to achieve and retain the feeling of superiority and power.

Since they drive themselves so hard to become the best and most competent, they may actually become highly successful in their work, although they will not get any intrinsic satisfaction from the work itself. Their work, like everything else in their lives, is a means to an end, not an end in itself.

People with aggressive personalities may appear to be supremely uninhibited in asserting and defending themselves and confident of their abilities. However, like the compliant personalities, they are driven by insecurity, anxiety, and hostility.

The detached personality: Moving away from people

People characterized by **detached personalities** are driven to maintain an emotional distance from all other people. They must not become involved with others in any way. They must not love, hate, or even cooperate with people. In order to achieve this total detachment, they strive to become extremely self-sufficient and resourceful. After all, if they are to function completely aloof and detached from others, they must rely only on their own resources, which must therefore be well developed.

Detached personalities have an almost desperate need for privacy. They need to spend as much time as possible alone, and it disturbs them to share even such an experience as listening to music. The need for independence causes them to be overly sensitive to anything that might represent an attempt to influence, coerce, or obligate them. Persons or situations that constrain them must be avoided, including timetables and schedules, long-term obligations such as mortgages or marriages, or even the pressure of a belt or necktie.

Detached people also experience the need to feel superior, but not in the same sense as aggressive personalities do. The detached cannot actively compete with others for superiority, so they feel that their greatness should be recognized automatically, without any struggle or effort on their part. One manifestation of this sense of superiority is the feeling that one is a truly unique individual, different and apart from everyone else.

As you might imagine, since detached persons do not want to be involved in any way with other people, they suppress or deny all feelings toward others, particularly love and hate. To grow close to others brings one into conflict with them, and that must be avoided. Because of this necessary constriction of their emotions, detached personalities place great stress on the powers of reason, logic, and intelligence.

Horney found that, in the neurotic, one of these three trends is dominant, but the other two are also present in some degree. The person who is predominantly aggressive, for example, also has some need for compliance and for detachment. The dominant trend, of course, is the one that determines the person's behavior and his or her attitudes toward others. This is the mode of thinking and acting that best serves to keep the basic anxiety at bay, and any deviation from it is threatening to the neurotic. For that reason, the other two modes must be actively repressed. But this repression only serves to make matters worse; the strength of the repressed neurotic trends may be very great. Any indication that one of the nondominant modes is pushing for expression causes severe conflict within the individual.

Conflict is thus defined as the basic incompatibility of the three trends, and this conflict, according to Horney, is the core of neurosis. All people, Horney said, whether neurotic or normal, suffer the same kind of conflict among these basically incompatible modes. The difference between the normal person and the neurotic person is the intensity of the conflict; it is much more intense in the neurotic.

In the nonneurotic, all three modes are capable of being expressed. That is, a person may sometimes be aggressive, sometimes compliant, and sometimes detached, as circumstances require. The three trends are not mutually exclusive categories in the normal person; rather, they complement one another and are integrated harmoniously in the personality. The normal person is not fighting himself or herself as is the neurotic, who must battle to keep the nondominant modes repressed.

Another way to characterize the difference between the normal and the neurotic is in terms of flexibility in behavior and attitudes. The neurotic is rigid; he or she meets all situations with the same mode or trend regardless of its appropriateness. The normal person is more flexible, varying his or her behavior to adapt to various circumstances.

The idealized self-image

Horney argued that all of us—normal or neurotic—construct a self-image, an idealized picture of ourselves that may or may not be based on reality. In the normal person, this self-image is built on a realistic appraisal of one's abilities, potentials, weaknesses, goals, and relations with other people. This image supplies a sense of unity and integration to the whole personality and is the frame of reference from which we approach ourselves and others. In order for us to achieve the ultimate goal of self-realization—the maximum development and fulfillment of our potentialities—our self-image must clearly reflect our real self.

What of the neurotic, who experiences conflict between basically incompatible modes of behaving? By virtue of this conflict, the self, the personality, is in disunity and disharmony. How can the individual integrate and unite these disparate demands?

The neurotic constructs an **idealized self-image** for the same purpose as the normal person does: to unify his or her personality. This attempt at unification is doomed to failure, however, because the model of the self developed by the neurotic does not coincide with reality. The image is an illusion, not an ideal that can be attained.

Although the neurotic's self-picture is far removed from reality, it is nevertheless real and accurate to him or her. Others can easily see through this false picture, but the neurotic cannot. The neurotic believes that the incomplete and misleading self-picture he or she holds is real. The neurotic's idealized self-image is a model of what he or she feels that he or she is, can be, or should be.

A realistic self-image is flexible and dynamic, changing as the individual changes. It reflects new strengths, new growth and awareness, and new goals. The realistic image is always, in part, a goal, something to strive for. Thus, it both reflects and leads the person.

The neurotic self-image, however, is static, inflexible, and unyielding. It is not a goal but a fixed idea, not an inducement or goad to growth but a hindrance to it. It becomes a dictator, demanding rigid adherence to its proscriptions.

The self-image of the neurotic serves as an unsatisfactory substitute for a reality-based sense of self-worth and self-confidence. The neurotic has little enough self-confidence because of his or her insecurity and anxiety, and his or her false self-image does not allow him or her to correct that deficiency. It provides only an illusory sense of pride and worth.

This self-image serves to alienate the neurotic even further from his or her true self. Developed to reconcile incompatible modes of behavior, the neurotic's self-image becomes just one more element in the basic conflict. Far from resolving the conflict, it only adds to it and to a growing sense of futility. The slightest crack or flaw in the neurotic's idealized self-picture threatens the superiority and security that the whole edifice was constructed to provide. It is a weak structure at best, built on false premises, with a shaky foundation in reality. Little is needed to topple it. Horney wrote that the neurotic self-image is "a treasure house loaded with dynamite."

The flight from womanhood: Feminine psychology

We saw at the beginning of this chapter that Horney disagreed with Freud's views on female psychology. Indeed, that was her initial point of departure from Freudian psychoanalysis. She was especially critical of Freud's notion of penis envy, which she felt was derived from inadequate evidence—that is, from neurotic women—and was interpreted and described from a male standpoint in a place and time when women were second-class citizens.

Women were seen by Freud to be victims of their anatomy, forever envious and resentful of men for possessing a penis. Freud believed that women had poorly developed superegos (as a result of inadequately resolved Oedipal conflicts) and inferior images of and feelings about their own bodies; women viewed themselves as castrated men.

Horney countered by arguing that men, both as adults and as children, are envious of women because of their capacity for motherhood, which gives women a physiological superiority. Horney uncovered in her patients what she called **womb envy** among males. "When one begins, as I did, to analyze men only after a fairly long experience of analyzing women, one receives a most surprising impression of the intensity of this envy of pregnancy, childbirth, and motherhood, as well as of the breasts and the act of suckling" (Horney, 1967, pp. 60–61).

In the act of creating new life, Horney argued, men have such a small part to play that they must sublimate their womb envy, and possibly overcompensate for it, through achievement in their work. In addition, womb envy and the resentment that accompanies it are manifested unconsciously in behaviors designed to disparage and belittle women, to maintain their inferior status. By denying women equal rights, minimizing their opportunities to contribute to society, and downgrading their efforts to achieve, men attempt to retain their so-called "natural" superiority. Underlying such behavior, however, is the sense of inferiority deriving from their womb envy.

Horney was not denying that many women believed themselves to be inferior to men. What she was denying was a biological basis for such feelings, as Freud had claimed. Although women may view themselves as worthless and inadequate compared with men and may flee from their womanhood, they do so, she suggested, for social and cultural reasons. If women feel unworthy, it is because they have been treated that way for so long in male-dominated cultures, experiencing social, economic, and cultural discrimination. Thus, it seemed only natural that women would come to view themselves in this light.

The flight from womanhood can lead to an inhibition of femininity that results in frigidity, which Horney felt was a pervasive condition among many women. Part of the sexual fear associated with frigidity arises from childhood fantasies about the difference in size between the adult penis and the child's vagina. The fantasies focus on the imagined pain of forcible penetration and the fear of vaginal injury.

This produces conflict between the unconscious desire to have a child and the fear of intercourse. If this conflict is sufficiently strong, it can lead to emotional disturbances manifesting themselves in difficulties relating to men. Such women grow to distrust and resent men and will reject their sexual advances. The conflict may also lead these women to reject their own femininity and to wish, unconsciously, that they were men.

Horney also differed from Freud on the nature of the Oedipus complex. She did not deny that such conflicts between children and parents may exist, but she did not believe that they had a sexual origin. She interpreted the situation as a conflict between dependence on one's parents and hostility toward them.

We discussed earlier the parental behaviors that may undermine a child's security and lead to the development of hostility. At the same time, the child remains so dependent on the parents that expressing hostility is unacceptable; it could further undermine the child's security. As we noted, the child says, in effect, "I have to repress my hostility because I need you."

The hostile impulses remain, however, and so create anxiety. "The resulting picture," Horney wrote, "may look exactly like what Freud describes as the Oedipus complex: passionate clinging to one parent and jealousy toward the other" (Horney, 1939, p. 83). The reason for such feelings lies in neurotic conflicts that have nothing to do with sex.

In a sense, Horney de-sexed the Oedipus complex. She believed that it evolved from parent–child interactions, but that it was not biologically based or universal. It developed only in those situations in which parents acted to undermine their child's security.

Freud never responded to Horney's criticisms of his views on female psychology, and he did not change his theories about the Oedipus complex, penis envy, or women's self-image. Toward the end of his life, however, in what may have been a veiled allusion to Horney's work, he wrote, "We shall not be very greatly surprised if a woman analyst who has not been sufficiently convinced of the intensity of her own wish for a penis also fails to attach proper importance to that factor in her patients" (1949, p. 54).

Horney's image of human nature

As we saw in the beginning of this chapter, Horney's image of us, like Adler's, is considerably more optimistic than Freud's. Perhaps the most important reason for this optimism was her strong belief that we are not doomed by biological forces to conflict, anxiety, neurosis, or a universality in personality. To Horney, each person is unique. Neurotic behavior, of course, can and does appear, but, when it does, it is the result of social forces—the conditions that one faces in childhood. These conditions can either satisfy or frustrate the child's needs for safety and security. If they frustrate these needs, the result is neurotic behavior.

Thus, neuroses and conflict are not conditions that all people are fated to suffer. They can be avoided, Horney insisted, if the child is raised in a home offering security, trust, love, and genuine acceptance. Horney noted that the neurotic is "a stepchild of our culture."

Given the proper conditions of childhood, she believed, any child will grow and develop into a well-integrated and unified adult personality. Each person has the inborn potentiality for self-realization, the innate urge to grow, and this is our ultimate and necessary goal in life. These intrinsic potentialities will blossom as inevitably and naturally as an acorn grows into an oak tree. The only thing that can obstruct the individual's development is the frustration of the basic need for security in childhood.

Horney also believed, somewhat in agreement with Adler, that we have the capacity to consciously shape and change our personality; individuals and societies can change for the better. Neuroses can be prevented by proper conditions in childhood. Human nature or personality, because it is flexible, is not bent into immutable shapes in childhood. Each person possesses the capacity to change in basic ways. Later experiences, then, may be as important as those of childhood.

So confident was Horney of the self-growth capabilities of each individual that she emphasized self-analysis in her therapeutic work wherever possible. She wrote a book entitled *Self-Analysis*, which argues in favor of the individual's ability to help solve his or her own problems (Horney, 1942). Self-knowledge, she said, is a means of freeing our capability for spontaneous growth. The pursuit of self-knowledge is both a privilege and a responsibility. Each of us is capable of shaping our own life and achieving self-realization. Therefore, our behavior is not fully determined.

Assessment in Horney's theory

The methods that Horney used to inquire into the functioning of the human personality were essentially those favored by Freud—free association and dream analysis—although with certain modifications. Perhaps the most basic difference in technique between Freud and Horney was in the relationship between the analyst and the patient. Horney believed that Freud played too passive a role and was too distant and intellectual. She believed that analysis should be an "exquisitely cooperative enterprise" between patient and therapist, although the analyst quite deliberately conducts the proceedings (Cherry & Cherry, 1973, p. 84).

In her use of free association, Horney did not follow Freud's lead in trying to seek access to the patient's unconscious. She believed that patients could easily distort or hide aspects of their inner lives or falsify their feelings about events.

Horney focused instead on her patients' visible emotional reactions toward her, believing that these could explain their current attitudes toward other people. She then pursued these feelings and attitudes through free association. Her object was not to delve into presumed infantile sexual fantasies or experiences in the beginning of a course of analysis, but rather to inquire into those early events only after uncovering present attitudes, defenses, and conflicts.

She believed that each attitude or feeling resulted from a deeper, preexisting attitude which, in turn, had resulted from a still deeper one, and so on, until gradually early life experiences would be reached. Thus, to Horney, the personality was "somewhat like an onion, with each layer being peeled off until one arrived at the deepest core emotion" (Rubins, 1978, p. 183).

Horney even used free association on herself when trying to assess a patient's personality, responding to the material the patient had presented to her.

She also used dream analysis in her work, believing that dreams reveal a person's true self. They represent attempts to solve conflicts, either in a constructive way or in a neurotic way. They can indicate to a person a set of attitudes within that may be quite different from the illusory world of his or her self-image. Along with Freud, Horney believed that the real meaning of a dream must be interpreted by the analyst. However, she did not offer a list of universal symbols. Each dream, she thought, must be interpreted within the context of the patient's problem.

While she used free association and dream analysis as important techniques of assessment, Horney did not restrict herself to those methods. Believing that every person is unique and offers the analyst problems never before encountered, she was very flexible regarding how best to uncover the patient's problems. The analyst, she argued, must be adaptable enough to use whatever tools are best suited to each patient. Horney did not seem to use any personality tests as means of assessing personality, nor were any such tests developed later to attempt to measure any of her specific concepts.

Research in Horney's theory

Horney used the case-study method. Thus, her approach, data, and interpretations are subject to the same kinds of criticisms made of Freud, Jung, and Adler. The weaknesses inherent in the case-study method apply to her work no less than to theirs.

However, Horney tried to be as rigorous and scientific as possible in her clinical observations. On the basis of her data she formulated hypotheses, which were then tested in the therapeutic situation. She approached her work in the spirit of science, collecting data, testing them, and revising her theory on the basis of her findings. Throughout her career she continued to insist that her data were tested in the same way scientists in other fields tested theirs.

Ideally, using free association, a number of trained analysts would assess the personalities of a series of patients. If their findings were similar, then the approach and the conclusions would be considered scientifically valid. We know, of course, that such data cannot enjoy the degree of validity that can be obtained through the experimental or correlational approaches.

Virtually no research has been conducted on any of Horney's concepts, a fact some critics seize upon as a major limitation of her theory.

Some research, however, may be applied indirectly to her work on feminine psychology. In our discussion of research on the Oedipus complex (Chapter 2), we noted a study using dreams that provided some support for Freud's concept of penis envy (Hall & Van de Castle, 1965). This research fails to support Horney's minimization of penis envy.

We also saw that other research refuted Freud's notion that women have inadequately developed superegos and inferior conceptions of their bodies as a result of penis envy (Fisher & Greenberg, 1977). These findings can be taken to support certain of Horney's views.

A final commentary

Horney's contributions to psychology, while impressive, are not as well known and as recognized as those of Freud, Jung, or Adler. In the rankings of the relative importance of psychologists in the second half of the 20th century, Horney placed 55th out of 286. This is in the top 20 percent of all psychologists, but behind most of the other personality theorists discussed in this book (Gilgen, 1982). Professionally, Horney suffered one major disadvantage that served to limit the spread of her viewpoint. She never formed a loyal band of disciples to disseminate and elaborate upon her theory. In part for that reason, there has been little research on her theory. Unlike with Freud and Adler, there was no professional journal dedicated to examining and propounding her ideas.

On the other hand, her work drew a large public following. Her books are written for lay audiences, in a style readily understood by people without professional training. Her theory makes sense to many people and seems to be applicable to a person's own behavior (or that of an odd aunt or a weird friend). Primarily due to the heightened awareness of women's roles that began in the 1960s, Horney's books have enjoyed a recent renewed interest among members of both sexes.

Many feel that her ideas are more relevant to problems inherent to American culture than are those of Freud, Jung, or Adler. In addition, certain of her concepts are considered important contributions to the understanding of personality. For example, many see value in her concept of neurotic trends as a means of categorizing deviant behavior. Others accept Horney's emphasis on self-esteem, the need for security, the role of anxiety, and the idealized self-image.

Although Horney was trained in orthodox Freudian theory and paid tribute to Freud for providing the foundation and tools to work with, her work deviated from psychoanalysis in a number of important respects. Because of this deviation, she was subject to a great deal of criticism from those who continued to adhere to Freud's position. We have only to look at the major points of difference to see why she was criticized. Denying the importance of biological instincts and placing less emphasis on childhood development, sexuality, aggression, and the unconscious were weaknesses in her theory, as the Freudians saw it. They were also highly critical of her concept of self-realization and argued that no real evidence for this force or ability was presented. To the Freudians, there was a mystical quality about it; they considered it an outgrowth more of wishful thinking than of sound scientific evidence.

Freudians and others argued that Horney's theory of personality is not developed as completely or consistently as Freud's. These critics charge that, because Freud's model was constructed so elegantly and precisely, it would have been better to reject it completely and start anew rather than attempt to refashion it along different lines.

Another criticism leveled against Horney is that her theory, while emphasizing so heavily the impact of social and cultural forces, makes little direct use of the research data from sociology and anthropology. Thus, it is said, she has not worked out the details of how social forces shape personality as precisely as she might have.

A somewhat related charge is that her observations and interpretations are too greatly influenced by middle-class American culture. In her defense, it must be noted that all of us—including personality theorists—are products of the class, culture, and time in which we live.

That her position is still a viable one is evidenced by the establishment in 1955 of the Karen Horney Clinic in New York City. In more recent years, the clinic has expanded to become a training center for analysts. While it does not adhere rigidly to every aspect of Horney's system, the clinic operates under the philosophy of optimism that characterized her work—the idea that human beings "have the innate urge to grow, and are unhappy if they don't" (Cherry & Cherry, 1973, p. 84).

Summary

Horney differed from Freud in her views on feminine psychology and in her emphasis on social rather than physiological forces as the primary shapers of personality. Horney's childhood experiences involving a lack of parental love that fostered basic anxiety and hostility are reflected in her personality theory.

Childhood years are vital in shaping the adult personality. There are two needs in childhood: satisfaction and safety. Satisfaction involves the basic physiological needs. Safety refers to security and freedom from fear. Security depends on being loved and wanted as a child. When security is undermined, hostility is induced in the child. The child may repress this hostility for several reasons: a sense of helplessness, fear of the parents, the need to receive expressions of love from the parents, and guilt about expressing hostility. The repression of hostility leads to basic anxiety, defined as a feeling of being lonely and helpless in a hostile world. Basic anxiety is the foundation for neuroses.

There are four means of protecting oneself against strong feelings of anxiety: gaining affection, being submissive, attaining power, and withdrawing. The first three approaches involve attempting to cope with anxiety by interacting with other people. The fourth approach involves withdrawing from other people in a psychological sense and blunting one's emotional needs. These four devices are defenses; they are not a positive pursuit of well-being. They can be stronger compelling forces than sex or other physiological needs.

Any of these protective devices can become a neurotic need or drive. Horney postulated ten neurotic needs: affection and approval, a dominant partner, narrow and constricted limits, power, exploitation, prestige, personal admiration, personal achievement, self-sufficiency and independence, and unassailability.

Horney later grouped these needs into three categories or neurotic trends. They are: moving toward people (the compliant type of personality), moving against people (the aggressive type), and moving away from people (the detached type). Compliant types have a continual need for affection and approval and will always do what other people want. Aggressive types are hostile toward others and are out to achieve control and superiority. Detached types keep an emotional distance from others and have an almost desperate need for privacy.

In neurotic persons, all three trends are present, though only one is dominant.

When either of the nondominant trends pushes for expression, the result is internal conflict, the core of neurosis.

The idealized self-image in nonneurotic persons is built upon a realistic appraisal of one's abilities and goals. It helps one achieve self-realization, the maximum development and use of human potentialities. The idealized self-image of the neurotic is based on an unrealistic and misleading appraisal of one's abilities.

Horney argued against Freud's contention that women possess penis envy, poorly developed superegos, and inferior body images. She suggested that men were envious of women because of their capacity for motherhood. Men were seen to possess womb envy, which they sublimated through achievement. Resentment accompanying womb envy is manifested in behaviors designed to disparage and belittle women. Horney believed that women may feel inferior to men, but for social rather than biological reasons. The inferiority results from the discrimination practiced in male-dominated cultures.

The flight from womanhood can lead to an inhibition of femininity, resulting in frigidity. Part of the sexual fear in frigidity arises from childhood fantasies about vaginal injury during intercourse.

Horney did not think that the Oedipus complex had a sexual basis. Rather, it involves a conflict between dependence on the parents and hostility toward them. It arises only when parents undermine their child's security.

Horney's image of human nature is more optimistic than Freud's. Each person is seen as unique and not doomed to conflict and anxiety. Childhood influences are important, but later experiences also shape personality. The ultimate goal of life is self-realization, an innate urge to grow, which may be helped or hindered by environmental forces. We can consciously shape and change our personalities.

Horney's methods of assessment are free association and dream analysis. Her research method was the case study, in which she tried to be rigorous and scientific. Virtually no research has been performed on any of Horney's concepts, but research on Freud's theory provides support for some of Horney's views on women.

Some psychologists see value in Horney's concepts of neurotic trends, the need for security, the role of anxiety, and the idealized self-image. Her theory has been criticized for not being developed as consistently as Freud's, for not making use of research data from sociology and anthropology, and for being influenced too heavily by middle-class American culture.

Glossary

aggressive personality Behaviors and attitudes associated with the neurotic trend characterized by a moving against people, such as a domineering, controlling manner.

basic anxiety A pervasive feeling of loneliness and helplessness; the foundation of neurosis.

compliant personality Behaviors and attitudes associated with the neurotic trend characterized by a moving toward people, such as a need for affection and approval.

conflict The basic incompatibility of the neurotic trends.

detached personality Behaviors

and attitudes associated with the neurotic trend characterized by a moving away from people, such as a need for privacy.

idealized self-image   An idealized picture of oneself built on a flexible and realistic assessment of one's abilities; in neurotics, the idealized self-image is based on an inflexible and unrealistic self-appraisal.

neurotic needs   Ten irrational defenses against anxiety that become a permanent part of the personality and affect behavior.

neurotic trends   Three categories of behaviors and attitudes toward oneself and toward others that express an individual's needs; a revision of Horney's concept of neurotic needs.

womb envy   The envy males feel toward females because they can bear children; Horney's response to Freud's concept of penis envy in females.

Review questions

1. Describe the childhood needs for safety and satisfaction. What parental behaviors are necessary for the child's security?
2. What is the origin of basic anxiety? Describe four self-protective ways in which this anxiety may be expressed.
3. Define the three neurotic trends and the behaviors associated with each.
4. How are the neurotic trends related to the self-protective defenses against anxiety?
5. Explain the difference between normal and neurotic individuals in terms of the neurotic trends.
6. Compare the idealized self-image of the normal, realistic person with the idealized self-image of the neurotic person.
7. Horney rejected Freud's contention of a biological basis for female inferiority. How, then, did she account for women's feelings of inadequacy?
8. What was Horney's interpretation of the Oedipus complex?
9. How did Horney's use of the free-association technique differ from Freud's?

Suggested reading

Horney, K. *The neurotic personality of our time.* New York: Norton, 1937.

Horney, K. *Self-analysis.* New York: Norton, 1942.

Horney, K. *Feminine psychology.* New York: Norton, 1967.

Horney, K. The flight from womanhood: The masculinity-complex in women as viewed by men and by women. In H. Kelman, Ed., *Feminine psychology.* New York: Norton, 1967.

Horney, K. *The adolescent diaries of Karen Horney.* New York: Basic Books, 1980.

Martin, A. R. Karen Horney's theory in today's world. *American Journal of Psychoanalysis,* 1975, 35, 297–302.

Rubins, J. L. *Karen Horney: Gentle rebel of psychoanalysis.* New York: Dial Press, 1978.

CHAPTER 6

Erich Fromm

The life of Fromm (1900–1980)
Freedom versus security: The basic human dilemma
  Psychic mechanisms for regaining security
The development of the personality in childhood
Psychological needs
Productive and nonproductive character types
The influence of the society
Fromm's image of human nature
Assessment in Fromm's theory
Research in Fromm's theory
  Social character in a Mexican village
  Character types in American business
A final commentary
Summary
Glossary
Review questions
Suggested reading

The most beautiful as well as the most ugly inclinations of man are not part of a fixed and biologically given human nature, but result from the social processes which create man.

ERICH FROMM

With Erich Fromm we meet a theorist who, along with Adler and Horney, is often referred to as a social-psychological theorist. As the opening quote indicates, Fromm shares with the aforementioned theorists a basic disagreement with Freud. Humanity, Fromm argued, is not inexorably driven or inevitably shaped by biological forces of an instinctive nature. Fromm also took issue with Freud on the matter of sex; Fromm did not view it as a primary shaping force in either normal or neurotic behavior. Instead, Fromm saw our personality as influenced by social and cultural forces—both those that affect an individual within a culture and those universal forces that have influenced humanity throughout history. Thus, his stress on the social determinants of personality is broader than that of Adler or Horney. His goal is to develop "a theory of the various human passions as resulting from the conditions of the existence of man." Believing that an individual creates his or her own nature, Fromm felt that we must examine the history of humankind in order to understand that creation.

Note that Fromm said that people create their own natures. He rejected the notion that we are passively shaped by social forces, arguing that we shape the social forces ourselves. These forces act, in turn, to influence the personality.

We might say that Fromm takes a longer view of the development of the individual personality than other theorists do because of his concern with the history of humankind as well as the history of the individual. Because of our history, Fromm argued, modern people suffer from feelings of loneliness, isolation, and insignificance. Our basic needs, therefore, are to escape these feelings of isolation, to develop a sense of belonging, and to find meaning in life. Paradoxically, the increased freedom that people have achieved over the centuries—both from nature and from rigid social systems—has led to more intense feelings of loneliness and isolation. Too much freedom becomes a negative condition from which we attempt to flee.

Fromm believed that the kinds of conflicts that people suffer arise from the kind of society they have constructed. However, we are not irrevocably doomed to suffering. Quite the contrary is true; Fromm remained optimistic about our ability to solve our problems—problems that we ourselves have created.

While Fromm was a psychoanalyst (the first in our coverage without a medical degree), he was also a philosopher, a historian, and an anthropologist. He drew on data from many sources beyond the analytical couch, which makes it difficult to classify him neatly as a member of any single discipline.

The life of Fromm (1900–1980)

Fromm was born in Frankfurt, Germany, of a family deeply steeped in Orthodox Judaism. His father was a businessman, but his grandfather was a rabbi and his mother's uncle a well-known Talmudic scholar. As a child, Fromm was a devoted student of the Old Testament, the moral fervor of which influenced him greatly in his youth. Like Freud, the young Fromm was infused with the Jewish tradition of reason and intellectual activity and experienced the emotional impact of being a member of a minority group. In later life, Fromm severed all connection with organized religion and became what he described as an "atheistic mystic," but there is no denying the influence of his early religious experiences.

Fromm's homelife was not a happy one. He described his family situation as "tense." His father was moody, anxious, and morose, and his mother experienced frequent periods of intense depression. Thus, he had an early exposure to abnormal behavior.

At the age of 12, another example of senseless behavior shocked him. A young friend of his parents, a lovely female artist, spent all of her time with her widowed father. Fromm may simply have been jealous but he could not understand why the woman preferred the company of her old, unattractive father. Almost immediately after the father's death, the young woman killed herself. Her will stipulated that she be buried with her father—not alongside him, but with him. Fromm was deeply troubled by the suicide. He agonized over why she had taken her life when she had everything to live for, and why she had been so strongly attracted to her father. It is easy to see why Fromm later found meaning in the work of Freud, whose Oedipus complex seemed to offer an explanation of this tragedy.

When Fromm turned 14, another manifestation of irrationality—this time on a much larger scale—disturbed him. He observed the eruption of hysterical fanaticism on the part of the whole German nation during World War I. He was astonished by the hatred that swept the country as the people were whipped by propaganda into an orgy of maniacal thought and action. He saw the changes in his relatives, friends, and teachers, and wondered "why decent and reasonable people suddenly go crazy" (Evans, 1966, p. 57).

It was primarily from these baffling personal experiences—his homelife, the suicide, and the wartime behavior of an entire nation—that Fromm developed the need to understand the causes of irrationality. "My main interest was clearly mapped out," he wrote. "I wanted to understand the laws that govern the life of the individual man, and the laws of society" (Fromm, 1962, p. 9). He suspected that the human personality was profoundly affected by social, economic, political, and historic forces, and that a sick society produced sick people. Thus, his ultimate view of personality was shaped along intuitive lines, fashioned from his own experiences, and later refined and modified along empirical lines.

He began his search for the causes of abnormality in studies at the University of Heidelberg, where he pursued psychology, philosophy, and sociology. He read the works of leading economic and political theorists—Karl Marx, Herbert Spencer, and Max Weber. He received his Ph.D. from Heidelberg in 1922.

Still seeking the answer to the riddle of human motivation, Fromm underwent psychoanalytic training in Munich and at the Psychoanalytic Institute in Berlin, where he was trained along orthodox Freudian lines and came to know Karen Horney. Still troubled by the suicide in his childhood, he felt that Freud's view "seemed to be the answer to a puzzling and frightening experience" (Hausdorff, 1972, p. 16).

This answer, however, did not satisfy him for very long. In the 1930s, he began to write articles that were critical of Freud—particularly of Freud's refusal to admit the impact of socioeconomic forces on personality. In 1934, he emigrated to the United States to escape the Nazi menace and became associated with Karen Horney and Harry Stack Sullivan.

Fromm's theory has been presented in a number of books offered in a popular style, more for the public than for colleagues. Some of these books have been extremely popular, reaching best-seller status. Fromm lectured at several universities in the United States during his career and was a professor at the University of Mexico and director of the Mexican Psychoanalytic Institute. He died in Switzerland in 1980.

Freedom versus security: The basic human dilemma

The title of Fromm's first book, *Escape from Freedom*, provides us with an indication of his vision of the basic human condition. In the history of Western civilization, Fromm believed, as people have gained more freedom, they have come to feel more lonely, insignificant, and alienated from one another. Conversely, the less freedom people have had, the greater have been their feelings of belongingness and security. Thus, freedom would seem to be antithetical to our needs for security and identification. It is Fromm's contention that people at the present time, possessing greater freedom than has been available in any other era, feel more lonely, alienated, and insignificant than people of ages past.

To fully understand what Fromm means by this apparent paradox, we must examine briefly the history of Western civilization, as Fromm interpreted it. He began by discussing our evolution from the lower animals and noting the basic distinction between animal nature and human nature: people are free of the instinctive biological mechanisms that guide the animal's every move. The lower an animal is on the phylogenetic scale, the more firmly fixed the pattern and form of its behavior. The higher the animal, the more flexible its behaviors. Human beings, as the highest animals, have the greatest flexibility of all. Our actions are the least tied to instinctive mechanisms.

But there is more to us than greater flexibility of behavior. We *know*; we are conscious and aware of ourselves and the world around us. Through learning, we accumulate a knowledge of the past. Through imagination we can go far beyond the present. Because we know, because we master nature, we are no longer at one with nature, as are the lower animals. As Fromm put it, we have *transcended* nature. As a result, while still a part of nature, in that we are subject to its physical laws (and can't change them), we are separate from nature—homeless, as it were.

Unlike the other animals, we realize how powerless we are ultimately; we know that we will die. And we know how different we are from the other animals. Looked at in one way, this knowledge of being separate and apart from the rest of nature is a kind of freedom. Our minds give us infinite choice. But looked at in another way, this separateness spells alienation from the rest of nature. Human beings cannot revert to animal status; we cannot free ourselves of knowledge, of the mind. What, then, can we do? How can we escape the feelings of isolation and apartness?

Fromm said that early peoples tried to escape their state of alienation from nature by identifying fully with their tribes or clans. Sharing myths, religions, and tribal rites and customs, they obtained the security of belonging to a group. Membership in the group provided acceptance, affiliation, and a set of rules to follow. The religions that early peoples developed also helped them, to some degree, to reestablish their link with nature. The focus of worship was on objects in nature: sun, moon, fire, animals, and plants.

But this tenuous security could not last. Human beings are striving creatures who develop and grow, and postprimitive people revolted against this subservience to the group. Indeed, each period of history, according to Fromm, has been characterized by increasing individuality (a process Fromm called **individuation**) as people have struggled toward ever-greater independence and freedom to grow, to develop, and to use all of their uniquely human abilities. The process of individuation reached its peak somewhere between the period of the Reformation in the 16th century and the present day—a time during which great alienation and aloneness have been matched by a high degree of freedom. (Actually, we should say *caused* by a high degree of freedom.)

Fromm designated the Middle Ages, which ended at the close of the 15th century, as the last era of stability, security, and belongingness. It was a time of little individual freedom, since the feudal system rigidly defined every person's place in society. One remained in the role and status to which one was born; there was no mobility, either social or geographic. The individual had little choice of occupation, social customs, habits of dress, and the like. Everything was determined by the class into which one was born and by the rigid rules of the Catholic Church.

Yet, although people were decidedly not free, they were not isolated, not alienated from others. The rigid social structure meant that the individual's place in society was clearly delineated. There was no doubt or indecision on anyone's part as to where or to whom one belonged.

Fromm argued that the social upheavals brought on by the Renaissance and the Protestant Reformation destroyed this stability and security by considerably enlarging people's freedom. People began to have more choice and power over their own lives. Of course, they achieved this greater freedom at the expense of the ties that had provided security and a sense of belonging. As a result, they became beset by doubts about the meaning of life and by feelings of personal insignificance.

Fromm characterized the increasing freedom of Western people as a *freedom from* but not a *freedom to*. We have become *free from* slavery and bondage, but, because of the increased insecurity and alienation, we are not *free to* develop our full potentialities and enjoy this new freedom. Fromm has been especially critical of the American marketplace culture, in which we are quite free from many strictures but not free to develop the full essence of our selves. We find ourselves in quite a dilemma. How can we flee the sense of loneliness and insignificance? How can we escape from freedom?

Fromm told us that there are basically two approaches we can take in our attempts to find meaning and belongingness in life.

The first method, achieving *positive freedom*, involves the attempt to become reunited with other people without, at the same time, giving up one's freedom and integrity. In this optimistic and altruistic approach, Fromm saw us as relating to others through work and love—through the sincere and open expression of our emotional and intellectual abilities. In this kind of society, which Fromm called a *humanistic* one, no one would feel lonely and insignificant, because all people would be brothers and sisters.

The other way to regain security is by *renouncing freedom* and surrendering completely our individuality and integrity. Obviously, such a solution will not lead to self-expression and personal development. It does, however, remove the anxiety of loneliness and insignificance and explain, according to Fromm, why so many people are willing to accept a totalitarian system such as the Nazi regime in the 1930s.

Psychic mechanisms for regaining security

In addition to these general approaches to regaining lost security, Fromm posited three specific mechanisms of escape, or *psychic mechanisms*, which he thought were analogous to Horney's neurotic character traits. These psychic mechanisms are authoritarianism, destructiveness, and automation conformity.

The first mechanism, **authoritarianism**, manifests itself in either masochistic or sadistic strivings. Individuals described as *masochistic* believe themselves to be inferior and inadequate. While they may complain of these feelings and say that they would like to be rid of them, they actually feel a strong need for dependence, either on one person or on an institution. They willingly submit to the control of other people or of social forces and behave in a weak and helpless manner toward others. They gain security by these acts of submission and thus assuage their feelings of loneliness.

The *sadistic* striving, although the opposite of the masochistic, is found in the same kind of person, Fromm said. It represents, basically, a striving for power over others. There are three ways in which the sadistic striving may be expressed. In one way, the person makes others totally dependent on himself or herself so as to have absolute power over them. A second sadistic expression goes beyond ruling or dictating to others. It involves exploiting others by taking or using anything desirable that they possess—whether material things or intellectual or emotional qualities. The third form of sadistic expression involves the desire to see others suffer and to be the cause of that suffering. While the suffering may involve actual physical pain, it most often involves emotional suffering, such as humiliation or embarrassment.

The second escape mechanism Fromm called **destructiveness**, which is the opposite of authoritarianism. While the first mechanism, in either the sadistic or the masochistic expression, involves some form of continuing interaction with an object, destructiveness aims at the elimination of the object. A destructive person says to himself or herself, in effect: "I can escape the feeling of my own powerlessness in comparison with the world outside myself by destroying that world" (Fromm, 1941, p. 179). Fromm saw evidence of destructiveness, albeit disguised or rationalized, everywhere in the world. Indeed, he felt that virtually everything was used as a rationalization for destructiveness, including love, duty, conscience, and patriotism.

The third escape mechanism, described by Fromm as having the most important social significance, is **automation conformity**. Through this mechanism, a person eases his or her loneliness and isolation by erasing any and all differences between himself or herself and others. He or she accomplishes this by becoming just like everyone else, by conforming unconditionally to the rules that govern behavior. Fromm compared this mechanism with the protective coloring of certain animals. By being indistinguishable from their surroundings, the animals protect themselves. So it is with fully conforming human beings.

While such persons do temporarily gain the security and sense of belonging so desperately needed, it is at the price of the self. One who so totally conforms to others no longer has a self; there is no longer an *I*, as distinct from *them*. The person becomes *them*, and a false self takes the place of the genuine self. And this loss of self, the surrender of *I*, may leave the person in worse shape than he or she was in before. The individual is now beset by new insecurities and doubts. No longer having any identity of his or her own, no real self, the person is no more than a reflexive response to what others expect of him or her. The new identity, a false one, can be obtained and maintained only through constant conformity. There must be no relaxation, no slipups; approval and recognition from others would be lost if he or she did anything at variance with their norms and values.

We have seen so far the basic nature of human beings as viewed by Fromm. Historically and socially shaped, we must strike a balance between freedom and security so that we can form a self without experiencing loneliness and alienation. This ideal state has not yet been achieved.

But there is more to Fromm's personality theory than mechanisms of escape from freedom. There are additional aspects of personality that result from the social order in which we live and from our attempts to cope with it. To understand these factors, we must discuss the development of the individual, just as we discussed the historical development of humankind.

The development of the personality in childhood

Fromm believed that the development of the individual in childhood parallels the pattern of development of humankind. In a sense, the history of the species is repeated in the childhood of each individual, in that, as the child grows, he or she gains increasing independence and freedom. And the less dependent the child becomes on the primary ties with the mother, the less secure he or she feels. The infant knows virtually no freedom but is secure in its dependent relationship.

Fromm thought that some degree of isolation and helplessness always accompanies the maturation process and that the child will attempt to regain his or her former primary ties with security. In a very real sense, the child attempts to escape from his or her own growing freedom through several mechanisms similar to those described in the preceding section. Which mechanism the child uses is determined by the nature of the parent–child relationship. Fromm proposed three types of escape mechanisms: symbiotic relatedness, withdrawal–destructiveness, and love.

In **symbiotic relatedness**, the person never achieves a state of independence. Rather, he or she escapes aloneness and insecurity by becoming a part of someone else, either by "swallowing" or by being swallowed by that other person. Masochistic behavior arises from being swallowed. The child remains totally dependent on the parents and abnegates his or her self. Sadism arises from the reverse situation (swallowing) in which the parents give all authority to the child by submitting to his or her will on every issue. The child regains security by manipulating and exploiting the parents. Whether the child is doing the swallowing or being swallowed, the relationship is one of closeness and intimacy. The child really needs the parents for security.

The **withdrawal–destructiveness** interaction, in contrast, is characterized by a distance and separation from others. Fromm stated that withdrawal and destructiveness are simply the passive and active forms of the same type of relatedness with the parents. Which form the child's behavior takes depends on the behavior of the parents. For example, parents who act destructively toward the child, attempting to subordinate or subjugate him or her, cause the child to withdraw from them.

Love, the third form of interaction, is the most desirable form of parent–child relatedness. In this case, the parents provide the greatest opportunity for the child to develop his or her self by offering respect and a proper balance between security and responsibility. As a result, the child feels little need to escape his or her growing freedom and is able to love himself or herself and others.

Fromm agreed with Freud that the first five years of life are of extreme importance, but he did not believe that personality is firmly fixed by the age of 5. Later events, Fromm argued, can be just as effective in influencing personality as early events. He also agreed with Freud in viewing the family as the psychic agency or representative of society to the child. It is through interaction with the family that the child acquires his or her character and ways of adjusting to society. While there are differences in every family, Fromm felt that most people in a given culture have a common social character—a common set of mores and beliefs that define the proper way of behaving for that culture. The child develops this social character, as well as his or her own individual character, from the unique interactions with the parents plus his or her genetic endowment. This, Fromm said, explains why different people react to the same environment in different ways.

Overall, it is the complex of social-environmental experiences—especially how the child is treated by the parents—that determines the nature of the adult personality, although not irrevocably so.

Psychological needs

As living organisms, people have a number of basic physiological needs that must be satisfied in order to assure survival. These needs—for example, for food, water, and sex—are no different for us than for other animals in terms of their nature and origin. However, we differ from lower animals in two respects. In the first place, we do not satisfy these needs in instinctive fashion—that is, by following rigid innate behavior patterns. Our behavior is infinitely varied and flexible, since it is learned by each individual in his or her unique environment. The other difference is that we are motivated by a second set of needs—those of a psychological nature—which are socially created and vary greatly from one individual to another.

However, Fromm felt that the drive for security (to escape loneliness) and the conflicting drive for freedom (to create the self) are universal. The choice between regression to security on the one hand and progression to freedom on the other is inescapable. All human cravings are determined by this polarity. Fromm postulated the existence of six needs that result from this dichotomy: relatedness, transcendence, rootedness, identity, frame of orientation and an object of devotion, and excitation and stimulation.

The need for **relatedness** arises from the disruption of our primary ties with nature. By virtue of the powers of reason and imagination, the individual is aware of his or her separation from nature, his or her powerlessness, and the arbitrary nature of birth and death. Because people have lost their former instinctive relationship with nature, they must use reason and imagination to create a new relatedness with fellow human beings. The ideal way of achieving this relatedness is through what Fromm called *productive love*, which involves care, responsibility, respect, and knowledge. In loving, a person is concerned with another's growth and happiness, responds to the other's needs, and respects and knows the loved one as he or she really is.

Productive love can be directed toward the same sex (brotherly love), toward fusion and oneness with a member of the opposite sex (erotic love), or toward one's child (motherly love). In all three forms, the person's ultimate concern is with the development and growth of the other person's self.

Failure to satisfy the need for relatedness results in a condition of irrationality that Fromm called *narcissism*. People who are narcissistic are unable to perceive the world around them in objective terms. The only reality they have is the subjective world of their own thoughts, feelings, and needs. Because their focus is solely on themselves, they cannot relate to other persons or to the outside world. They perceive everything from their own subjective point of view, and thus ultimately have no objective contact with reality.

Transcendence refers to the need to rise above the passive-animal state, with which people cannot be satisfied because of their reason and imagination. People must become creative and productive individuals. In the act of creation, whether of life (as in having and rearing children), of material objects, of art, or of ideas, we surpass the animal state and enter into a state of freedom and purposiveness.

Fromm indicated clearly that, if the creative need is blocked for any reason, people become destructive; that is the only alternative to creativeness. Destructiveness, like creativeness, is in our nature. Both tendencies satisfy the need for transcendence. Creativity, however, is the primary tendency.

The human need for **rootedness** also arises from the loss of our primary ties with nature. As a result of that loss, we stand detached and alone. We must establish new roots in our relationships with others to replace our previous roots in nature. Feelings of brotherliness with others, according to Fromm, are the most satisfying kind of new roots we can develop.

The least satisfying or unhealthiest way of achieving rootedness is through the maintenance of the incestuous childhood ties with the mother, clinging to the security of those early maternal days. Such incestuous ties can generalize beyond the parent–child relationship to include the community and the nation. "Nationalism is our form of incest," Fromm wrote (1955, p. 58). It restricts our love and our feelings of solidarity to only some of the people, isolating us from humanity in general.

In addition to the needs for rootedness and relatedness, for a sense of belonging, people need a sense of **identity** as unique individuals. There are several ways of achieving this sense of identity. For example, a productive and creative person could develop his or her talents and abilities to the fullest, or he or she could identify with a group—a religion, a union, or a nation—perhaps to the point of conformity.

Conforming is an unhealthy way of achieving a sense of identity because one's identity is then defined only in reference to the qualities and characteristics of the group to which one is conforming, rather than to the qualities of the self. The self becomes a borrowed one and therefore not a genuine self.

The need for a **frame of orientation and an object of devotion** stems from our powers of reason and imagination, which require a framework for making sense of all the puzzling phenomena to which we are exposed. We must develop a consistent and coherent picture of the world by which we are able to perceive and understand all that is going on around us. This frame of orientation may be based on rational or irrational considerations. A rational frame of orientation provides for an objective perception of reality. An irrational frame of orientation involves a totally subjective view of the world, which eventually severs our contact with reality.

In addition to a frame of orientation, we need an overall goal or a god (an object to which we are devoted) through which we can find a consistent meaning in life. It is through such an object of devotion that we acquire a sense of direction for our future.

The need for **excitation and stimulation** refers to our continuing need for a stimulating external environment in which we may function at high levels of alertness and activity. The brain requires such constant external stimulation to maintain peak levels of performance. Without such excitation and stimulation, it would be difficult to maintain our involvement with the world around us.

The manner in which these needs are manifested or satisfied depends on social conditions and opportunities afforded by the culture. Thus, the way in which a person copes with or adjusts to his or her society is a sort of compromise that the individual works out between these needs and the social conditions in which he or she lives. As a result of this compromise or series of compromises, the person develops his or her personality structure—what Fromm called *orientations* or *character traits*.

Productive and nonproductive character types

Fromm proposed that the character traits underlie all behavior and are powerful forces by which a person relates or orients himself or herself to the world. He describes the traits in separate terms, but he is careful to note that the personality or character of an individual is a blend of some or all of these traits, although one usually plays a dominant role.

The traits are divided into nonproductive and productive types. Nonproductive traits include the receptive, exploitative, hoarding, and marketing orientations, all of which are unhealthy ways of relating to the world.

Individuals with **receptive orientations** expect to get whatever they want— be it love, knowledge, or pleasure—from some outside source: another person, an authority, or a system. They are receivers in their relations with others, needing to be loved rather than loving and taking rather than creating ideas or knowledge.

Obviously, such people are highly dependent on others and indeed feel quite paralyzed when left on their own; they feel incapable of doing anything without outside help. There is a similarity between this orientation and Freud's oral incorporative type, the receptive orientation also finding relief in eating and drinking. There is also a similarity with Horney's compliant type of personality, the one described as moving toward people. The kind of society that fosters this trait is one in which exploitation of one group by another (for example, slave by master) is practiced.

In the **exploitative orientation**, the person is also directed toward others for what he or she wants. However, instead of expecting to receive from others, these people take from them, either by force or by cunning. Indeed, if something is given to them, they see it as worthless. They want only what belongs to and is valued by others: wives or husbands, ideas, possessions, and so on. What has to be stolen or taken by force has much greater value than what is given freely. This trait is similar to Freud's oral aggressive type and Horney's aggressive type (moving against people) and can be seen in robber barons, fascist leaders, or domineering people in any setting.

As the name indicates, in the **hoarding orientation** the person derives his or her security from the amount he or she can hoard and save. This miserly behavior applies not only to money and material possessions but also to emotions and thoughts. In a sense, such people build walls around themselves and sit there, surrounded by all that they have hoarded, protecting it from outside intrusion and letting as little of it out as possible. There is an obvious parallel here with Freud's anal retentive type and Horney's detached type (moving away from people).

Fromm said that this kind of orientation was particularly common in the 18th and 19th centuries in those countries that had stable middle-class economies characterized by the Protestant ethic of thrift, conservatism, and sober business practices.

The **marketing orientation** is a 20th-century phenomenon characteristic of capitalist societies, particularly the United States. In a commodity-based marketplace culture, Fromm argued, people's success or failure depends on how well they sell themselves. The set of values is the same for personalities as for commodities; indeed, one's personality becomes a commodity to be sold. Thus, it is not so much one's personal qualities, skills, knowledge, or integrity that count but rather how nice a "package" one is. Superficial qualities, such as smiling, being agreeable, or laughing at the boss's jokes, become more important than the inner qualities one might possess.

Such an orientation cannot produce any feeling of security, because the person is left without genuine relatedness to others. Indeed, if the game is played long enough, there is no longer even a relatedness to or real awareness of one's self. The packaged role the individual is forced to play completely obscures his or her own genuine qualities and characteristics, not only from others but from the person himself or herself. As a result, such people find themselves in a state of total alienation, with no personal core or center and with no real relationship to those around them.

Fromm's fifth character type, the **productive orientation**, is the ideal and represents the ultimate goal in human development. Covering all aspects of human experience, this concept assumes our ability to use all of our capacities and to actualize or realize all of our potentials. Fromm did not define productivity as synonymous with creativity in an exclusively artistic sense. The productive orientation is an attitude that can be attained by every human being. It has as its most important object not the acquisition of material things but the development of our selves.

He believed that this orientation is the ideal condition for people, although it does not yet characterize any society. Actually, Fromm thought that it is not yet achieved totally by anyone. The best we can achieve—at least with our present social structure—is a combination of the productive and nonproductive orientations. The influence of the productive orientation can then transform the nonproductive traits. For example, guided by productivity, the aggressiveness of the exploitative type can become initiative, the miserliness of the hoarding type can become sound economy, and so on. Only through social change can the productive orientation become dominant in any culture.

Fromm later introduced another pair of orientations: necrophilious and biophilious. The **necrophilious** character type is attracted to death—to corpses, decay, feces, and dirt. Such a person seems most alive when he or she is talking about death, burials, or sickness. This person dwells on the past, is enamored of force and power, and is attracted more to machines than to people. Persons with a necrophilious orientation have a passion for technology and may surround themselves with appliances such as sophisticated stereo equipment, not for the joy of the music produced, but for the love of the machine itself. Fromm said that such a person "turns his interest away from life, persons, nature, ideas—in short from everything that is alive; he transforms all life into things, including himself" (1973, p. 350).

The opposite orientation, the **biophilious** type, is in love with life. He or she fights against death, darkness, and decay. This attitude is congruent with the productive orientation; such a person is concerned with growth and development of self and others.

As with the other orientations, pure forms of either of these traits are rare. Most personalities represent a blending of the two, with one orientation being dominant.

The influence of the society

We have seen, throughout our discussion of Fromm, the prominent role he ascribed to culture in shaping the personality. He also noted that, for any kind of society to function well, it is imperative that the personalities or characters of all the people be shaped to satisfy the demands of that society. In other words, individuals must be trained in childhood to behave in ways that will fit the needs of the society. A feudal or fascist society must shape its people to be passive and submissive, for example. Those in a commodity-oriented capitalist society must be shaped to consume—to buy the goods and gadgets the society produces and to replace them with newer ones shortly thereafter.

All societies, throughout history, have frustrated people by placing demands on them that are antithetical to human nature. Fromm thought that any society that does not satisfy people's basic needs is sick and should be replaced, and he remained optimistic about the possibility of shaping a society that would allow people to fulfill themselves.

Fromm called this ideal society **humanistic communitarian socialism** and described it as a world in which love, brotherliness, and solidarity characterize all human relationships, in which the productive orientation is able to develop to its fullest and in which all feelings of loneliness, insignificance, and alienation disappear. The future of civilization, Fromm pleaded, depends on how well and how quickly we can develop such a society.

Fromm's image of human nature

It should be clear by now that Fromm expressed a generally optimistic picture of human nature. Agreeing with Adler and Horney, he did not consider us doomed to conflict and anxiety by immutable biological forces.

It is true that he viewed us as shaped by social, political, and economic forces at work in the society in which we live. However, we are not infinitely malleable. A person is not simply a puppet reacting to the strings pulled by social forces, or "a blank sheet of paper on which culture can write its text." Thus, we are neither fixed by instincts or early childhood experiences nor totally commanded by social forces. On the contrary, we have an inherent nature, a set of psychological qualities by which we can shape our personalities and our societies. And this is where Fromm's optimism—or at least hope—enters the picture. He believed that we have an innate drive or tendency to grow, develop, and realize our potentialities. This, according to Fromm, is our major task in life and our ultimate and necessary goal—to become what we have the potential to become. The result of this inherent tendency in any individual is the personality. Fromm also believed that we possess an innate striving for justice and truth. Failure to realize all of our potentialities—failure to become productive—results in unhappiness and mental illness. Although Fromm saw a universality in personality—a common social character for those within a given culture—he also believed that each person is unique. One of the basic human needs, in his view, is for an identity as a unique individual.

Fromm continued to hope that humanity would reach the state of realization of its potential for full and harmonious growth and integration, although he was saddened by our failure thus far. He did not believe that we are inherently either good or evil but rather that we become evil if we fail to develop and grow fully. The only way in which we can be at one with one another and with ourselves is by making full, productive use of our abilities. There is no other way to achieve true harmony.

Neither outcome—goodness or evil, fulfillment or frustration, harmony or chaos—is predetermined, either by society or by human nature. Only the potential for goodness and fulfillment exists; the rest is up to us. And it is Fromm's optimism that permitted him to hope that we will make the right choice. At the age of 70 he wrote, "Who can give up hope as long as there is life?"

Assessment in Fromm's theory

Unfortunately, it is difficult to describe the methods Fromm used to develop and support his theories. The psychoanalysts we have discussed so far based their systems on the clinical data they obtained from their patients, and they were quite clear as to their precise methods of assessment. Relative to these earlier theorists, Fromm wrote very little about his techniques of assessment, and there seems to be no way of knowing on what data he based the theories. He occasionally referred to "psychoanalytic observations" but did not offer specific analytical findings or case studies. We do know that he used a form of free association and that he considered dream analysis to be one of the most important therapeutic tools, although he did not describe his use of the techniques in much detail.

On what basis, then, did Fromm develop his theories? For the most part, it seems that the theories are based on generalizations and speculations derived from his interpretations of historical changes and social-cultural forces. His data derived not only from such techniques as free association and dream analysis, but also from a consideration of all the social and cultural forces that can influence the human personality: religious, economic, historical, political, and anthropological.

Fromm did not use any self-report or projective techniques in his work with patients, nor were any such tests developed later to assess aspects of his theory. He did, however, use certain tests in a long-term research program, which we shall describe in the next section.

Research in Fromm's theory

The extent of Fromm's use of the case-study method is difficult to ascertain. We cannot say how closely it followed Freud's research approach or how extensive a case history Fromm developed on each patient.

However, the fact remains that Fromm was collecting data of a psychoanalytic nature on his patients. This means that the criticisms we have discussed in previous chapters on psychoanalytic theorists also apply to Fromm. As was the case with the other theorists, it is impossible to duplicate and verify Fromm's clinical observations or the conditions under which he made them.

Fromm was convinced, however, of the scientific worth and credibility of his primary psychoanalytic method of research, the case study. While admitting that his results could not be tested by the experimental or correlational research methods, he insisted that they could be tested by repeated analyses of different patients. Thus, he argued, a hypothesis generated from the observations of one or more patients could be tested by repeating the observations with other patients. The problem remains that no matter how carefully analysts make their observations, it is impossible for anyone else to repeat them or to establish identical conditions—which is a basic requirement of the scientific method.

Social character in a Mexican village

Little research has been conducted on Fromm's theory. Most of his concepts remain untested. Late in his career, however, Fromm and his colleagues undertook a cross-disciplinary study to test his notion of social character (Fromm & Maccoby, 1970). Over a period of several years, psychologists, anthropologists, physicians, statisticians, and other specialists analyzed an isolated village in Mexico in terms of its history, its economic and social structure, and the health, attitudes, and even dreams of its inhabitants.

The investigators lived among the villagers and came to be accepted and trusted as they made their observations. Through a combination of techniques, including an extensive questionnaire, detailed interviews, the Rorschach Inkblot Test, and the Thematic Apperception Test, the researchers found support for three of Fromm's character types: the receptive, hoarding, and exploitative orientations.

No evidence for the marketing orientation was found. This was not surprising, because Fromm had described it as being common only to 20th-century capitalist cultures, not to a primitive village. Some evidence was found to support the productive orientation.

The personal characteristics of those villagers possessing the receptive, hoarding, exploitative, and productive orientations matched the descriptions Fromm had offered in his earlier writings. Overall, this was an impressive piece of research providing substantial support for Fromm's views on character types.

Character types in American business

The co-author of the Mexican village study, Michael Maccoby, conducted two additional studies on Fromm's character types, this time in a radically different culture: the world of American business.

The first study involved extensive interviews with 250 managers in 12 large corporations (Maccoby, 1976). A character type somewhat analogous to the marketing orientation was identified and labeled as the "company man." "When they describe themselves, they seem to be trying to give the right impression, to sell themselves to the interviewers," Maccoby wrote. "It is as though they are constantly working on themselves in order to have the right kind of personality to fit the job" (Maccoby, 1976, p. 92).

Thus, like Fromm's marketing type, the company man focuses more on superficial, personal qualities to attain success rather than on actual job skills, knowledge, and abilities. The personality or packaging of this type of person is seen as all-important, and it can be changed to fit the perceived needs of superiors as readily as clothes are changed to fit different social situations.

The second study of American corporate leaders suggested the existence of a new character type, the *self orientation* (Maccoby, 1981). This type is described as a product of the turbulent American society of the 1960s, which was characterized by a questioning of traditional authority, of the Protestant ethic, and of the notion of commitment to corporate success. This is the generation of employees now in the early stages of their careers. The self orientation was found to be cynical, rebellious, detached, undisciplined, self-indulgent, lacking in loyalty, and generally unconcerned with the well-being of other people. In short, the orientation is highly narcissistic.

Although this research by Maccoby does not provide support for Fromm's basic character types, it does suggest a new one which, like the others, is a product of historical, social, and cultural forces. As these forces change, so will the character types associated with them, a view in keeping with Fromm's thesis on the sociocultural influences on personality and the crystallizing of personality into different orientations.

Finally, there is indirect research evidence to support Fromm's receptive, exploitative, and hoarding orientations. As we noted earlier, each of these orientations is similar to one of Freud's oral or anal personality types. To the degree that some empirical support exists for Freud's types, as described in Chapter 2, then, by extension, it also exists for Fromm's similar types.

To date, the remainder of Fromm's theory has not been submitted to experimental test.

A final commentary

Fromm's books have been tremendously popular, reaching audiences all over the world. He deliberately wrote for the lay audience because he wanted to reach the greatest number of people with his message about the kind of society we must develop to survive. Thus, his books are highly readable in style, with a minimum of technical jargon. This is not to say that the books are not challenging or provocative, but rather that the ideas are presented in an engaging and interesting form.

In the rankings of the most influential psychologists in the second half of the 20th century, Fromm was in 22nd place, following Alfred Adler. He ranked in 10th place among the personality theorists discussed in this book. His importance in psychology lies in his focus on broad social, historical, and cultural forces and their role in shaping personality. In later chapters we shall see similarities between Fromm's productive orientation and Allport's concept of the mature personality (Chapter 8) as well as Maslow's notion of the self-actualizing person (Chapter 12).

Fromm's approach to personality is wide ranging in its perspectives and propositions. He was not exclusively a psychoanalyst but drew on information from other disciplines—notably, history, sociology, and anthropology. One result of this diversity is that a critic must be well versed in these areas in order to be able to attack Fromm's total system. Few people can do so; therefore, criticisms have often been directed against only one part or another of his theory. For example, a major criticism, as we have noted, is that there is no strong empirical support for his theory. Fromm did not supply any specific, factual supporting data. The Mexican village study came considerably after the theory was proposed. One cannot find in his writings any data on which he based his theories (a criticism not unique to Fromm, however).

He has also been criticized for not keeping current with newer developments in psychoanalysis. His major reference has been the works of Freud, with occasional formulations from Jung and Horney. More recent works—for example, those of the humanistic psychologists, who have reached some conclusions that parallel his own—are not recognized in his publications. Many readers see this as a serious omission.

Some critics charge that Fromm's concepts are defined in imprecise and vague terms that are contradictory and confusing. In part because of this lack of precision, it has been difficult to attempt to test most of his propositions experimentally.

Those knowledgeable about the history and social conditions of the Middle Ages challenge Fromm's allegation that humanity had attained security, identity, and belongingness during that period. These critics charge that Fromm painted a highly idealized picture of that era and omitted the stark calamities that occurred—the religious persecutions, witch hunts, plagues, wars, and other physical and psychological hardships. If anything, they argue, the Middle Ages must have been a time of great insecurity and instability.

These criticisms notwithstanding, Fromm has presented us with a unique interpretation of the interaction between humanity and society. Perhaps more than any other theorist, he has made us aware of the continuing and interrelated impact of social, economic, and psychological factors on human nature. Whether or not his specific interpretations turn out to be valid, he has shown us that a human being is not the exclusive product of a single set of forces but the result of an interplay of forces and events. He has challenged us to think beyond the boundaries of any one discipline and has consistently goaded us to evolve a newer and more humane society, pointing out the consequences of not doing so. Thus, his contribution, whatever its impact, has extended beyond psychoanalysis or psychology to include the broad spectrum of social problems that concern us all.

Summary

Fromm, like Adler and Horney, is a social-psychological theorist who did not see sex or biological forces as the primary shapers of personality. Fromm argued that personality is influenced by historical, economic, political, and social forces. Fromm's childhood was marked by baffling personal experiences that led him to want to understand the causes of irrationality.

Fromm believed that as people throughout history have gained more freedom, they have come to feel more lonely and alienated from one another. The less freedom people have, the greater their sense of belonging and security. We are no longer in harmony with nature because of our conscious awareness, learning, and imagination. These powers give us infinite choice, but our separation from nature causes alienation.

The Middle Ages was the last era of security and belongingness. There was little individual freedom but much security, because everyone's place in society was clear. The social upheaval of the Renaissance and the Protestant Reformation enlarged human freedom and choice but reduced the sense of belonging and security.

People desire to escape from freedom, to flee the loneliness and insignificance that accompanies it. One way to escape from freedom is by achieving positive freedom, that is, by attempting to become reunited with others without giving up freedom and integrity. Another way to escape from freedom is to renounce freedom and accept totalitarianism.

Fromm's three psychic mechanisms of escape are (1) authoritarianism, in which people submit to others (masochistic striving) or gain power over others (sadistic striving), (2) destructiveness, and (3) automation conformity.

The development of the individual in childhood parallels the development of humankind throughout history. As children grow older they gain increasing independence and freedom, but at the expense of the security of the primary ties with the mother. Children attempt to escape from freedom through three mechanisms: (1) symbiotic relatedness, in which a person escapes aloneness and insecurity by becoming part of someone else; (2) withdrawal–destructiveness interaction, in which a person maintains a separation from others; and (3) love. The childhood years are important in shaping personality, but later events can also be influential.

All living organisms have physiological needs, but people differ from lower animals in that they do not satisfy those needs in instinctive fashion, but rather through behavior that has been learned. People also differ from lower animals in that they are motivated by psychological needs.

There are six psychological needs that result from the polarity between the drive for security and the drive for freedom. These needs are (1) relatedness, which involves achieving a feeling of connection with others, preferably through productive love, that is, concern for another person's growth and happiness (failure to satisfy this need results in narcissism); (2) transcendence, which involves the need to rise above the passive animal state and become creative and productive individuals; (3) rootedness, which refers to the need to establish new roots in our relationships with others, to replace our previous roots in nature; (4) identity, which involves developing our talents and abilities to the fullest, perhaps by identifying with a group; (5) a frame of orientation and an object of devotion, which requires building a frame of reference within which to order and understand the events in our lives, and finding an overall goal or a god to provide us with a consistent sense of meaning; and (6) excitation and stimulation, which involves providing the brain with sufficient external stimulation to maintain peak levels of alertness and activity.

Orientations or character traits evolve from the compromises we work out between our psychological needs and the social conditions under which we live. Traits are divided into nonproductive and productive types. Nonproductive types include the receptive, exploitative, hoarding, and marketing orientations.

Receptive types depend on others for satisfaction of their needs. Exploitative types take what they need from others. Hoarding types derive security from what can be hoarded or saved. Marketing types see themselves as commodities to be packaged and sold.

The productive type represents the ideal and ultimate goal of human development and involves the use of all of our capacities to achieve self-realization.

Fromm later introduced another pair of orientations: necrophilious, in love with death, force, and technology; and biophilious, in love with life, growth, and development.

Societies must shape personalities to satisfy societal demands. Fromm's ideal society, called humanistic communitarian socialism, allows the productive orientation to develop fully.

Fromm's image of human nature is optimistic. People have the ability to shape their own personalities and societies. Life's ultimate goal is the innate drive to realize our potentialities. Personality is shaped by both innate and learned forces, and by childhood experiences as well as those which occur later.

Fromm's methods of assessment include free association, dream analysis, and data from the social and cultural forces that influence personality. His method of research relies on psychoanalytic observations; these cannot be repeated and verified.

Fromm's research in a Mexican village provides support for the receptive, hoarding, exploitative, and productive orientations. Research in American corporations has identified one character type similar to the marketing orientation and another, the self orientation, that is a product of the 1960s.

Fromm's theory has been criticized for ignoring recent developments in psychoanalysis, for poorly defined terminology, and for presenting an idealized picture of the Middle Ages. His importance lies in his focus on broad social, historical, and cultural forces and their role in shaping personality.

Glossary

authoritarianism   A psychic mechanism for regaining security that is manifested in either masochistic or sadistic feelings.

automation conformity   A psychic mechanism for regaining security that is manifested in unconditional obedience to the prevailing rules governing behavior.

biophilious orientation   A character type congruent with the productive orientation, concerned with growth and development.

destructiveness   A psychic mechanism for regaining security that is manifested in a desire to eliminate threatening objects, persons, or institutions.

excitation need   The need for a stimulating external environment so that the brain will function at peak levels of alertness and activity.

exploitative orientation   A character type that takes from others by force or cunning.

frame of orientation need   The need for a consistent and coherent picture of the world within which to understand life events.

hoarding orientation   A character type that derives security from amassing and preserving both material possessions and personal feelings.

humanistic communitarian socialism   An ideal society characterized by positive human relationships and by the full development of the productive orientation.

identity need   The need to achieve an awareness of one's unique abilities and characteristics.

individuation   The process by which succeeding generations attain increasing individuality in their struggle for greater independence and freedom.

marketing orientation   A character type that values superficial qualities.

necrophilious orientation   A character type attracted by death and by inanimate objects.

productive orientation   A character type that is the ideal of self-development.

receptive orientation   A character type that is highly dependent on others.

relatedness need   The need to maintain contact with other people, ideally, through productive love.

rootedness need   The need to feel an attachment or sense of belonging to one's family, community, and society.

symbiotic relatedness   A childhood mechanism for regaining security in which the child remains close to and dependent upon the parents.

transcendence need   The need to rise above one's animal nature by becoming creative or destructive.

withdrawal–destructiveness   A childhood mechanism for regaining security in which the child distances himself or herself from the parents.

Review questions

1. Why, in Fromm's view, have people become less secure as they have achieved greater freedom?
2. Describe the three psychic mechanisms by which we can regain security and ease feelings of loneliness.
3. Describe the parental behaviors that can foster symbiotic relatedness, with-. drawal–destructiveness, and love.
4. Identify Fromm's six psychological needs. Describe how the satisfaction of each of these needs can contribute to the creation of the self.
5. Describe the productive and nonproductive character orientations.
6. Which orientation did Fromm consider to be typical of contemporary American society? Which orientations were supported by the Mexican village research?
7. What was Fromm's view of the relationship between personality and society?

Suggested reading

Evans, R. I. *Dialogue with Erich Fromm*. New York: Harper & Row, 1966.
Fromm, E. *Escape from freedom*. New York: Holt, Rinehart & Winston, 1941.
Fromm, E. *The sane society*. New York: Holt, Rinehart & Winston, 1955.
Fromm, E. *The anatomy of human destructiveness*. New York: Holt, Rinehart & Winston, 1973.
Hausdorff, D. *Erich Fromm*. Boston: Twayne, 1972.

CHAPTER 7

Henry Murray

The life of Murray (1893–   )
The basic principles of personology
**The divisions of personality: Id,
   superego, and ego**
Needs: The motivation of behavior
   Categories of needs
   Other characteristics of needs
**Complexes: The development of the
   personality**
Murray's image of human nature
Assessment in Murray's theory
   The OSS assessment program
   The Thematic Apperception Test
      and other personality tests
Research in Murray's theory
   The Harvard undergraduate assessment
      program
   Idiographic versus nomothetic research
   Studies of specific needs
A final commentary
Summary
Glossary
Review questions
Suggested reading

*For me, personality is an African jungle
without boundaries.*

HENRY MURRAY

Within the framework of what he called the *personological system*, Henry Murray has designed an approach to personality that is both eclectic and original. It contains partial and modified reflections of Freudian theory as well as highly original concepts and methods, drawn together effectively so as to be highly stimulating to others in the field of personality.

His formulations incorporate and develop his own diverse experiences in biochemistry and medicine, in psychoanalytic research and practice, and in his intensive study of literature, particularly of the writings of Herman Melville. As a result, his theory takes into account the unconscious as well as the conscious, one's past as well as present and future, and the influences of physiological as well as sociological forces.

The system places great emphasis on physiological functioning as it dictates to and directs the personality. As the center or seat of the personality, the brain functions to bring unity and coherence to behavior. Murray's interest in physiology is also evident in his concern (shared with Freud, among others) with tension reduction as a major force in behavior. On both the biological and psychological level, he invokes the concept of tension reduction as a primary law of human functioning, although he elaborates on this basic and much-used notion.

The influence of Freudian psychoanalysis is seen in Murray's system in his recognition of the importance of unconscious forces, the effect on adult behavior of experiences in infancy and childhood, and his incorporation of the notions of id, ego, and superego. However, while the imprint of Freud is clear, it is equally clear that Murray has given his unique interpretation to these psychological phenomena. Indeed, his deviations from classical psychoanalysis are so wide that his system must be classified with the neo-Freudians rather than with Freud.

Perhaps the two most distinctive features of Murray's system are the highly sophisticated approach to human needs and the source of the data on which he constructed his theory. His carefully determined list of human needs, highly specific and differentiated, has been put to large-scale use in research, in the assessment of personality, and in clinical treatment. As for the source of his data, Murray, unlike any of the theorists discussed so far, studied normal individuals (undergraduates at Harvard) rather than patients undergoing psychotherapy. Also, much of the data was derived from what could be considered the more empirically sound procedures of the laboratory rather than from case histories of people suffering from neuroses.

Because of his long affiliation with a major university instead of relative isolation in a clinic or private practice, and because of certain appealing qualities of the man and his system, Murray gathered and trained a large number of psychologists, many of whom have since gained prominence in their own right and who have carried on at least some of his teachings. This extension and follow-through of his work is a gratification often denied to other theorists.

The life of Murray (1893—   )

Neither poverty nor neurotic parents marked the childhood of Henry Murray. However, there were elements of Adlerian compensation for a physical defect, a supernormal sensitivity to the sufferings of other people, and a hint of rejection from his mother to ensure that his childhood would not be intolerably dull.

Despite these tantalizing aspects of his childhood and his personality, it is difficult to relate Murray's theory to the man himself. Either there is no relationship in this case, or Murray has not told enough about himself to allow us to speculate on the connection. As mentioned, Murray based his theory on research with normal subjects and not on the case histories of patients. Thus, it is possible that he approached the study of personality purely as a scientific enterprise, rather than as an attempt to understand his own emotional problems or needs. When Murray underwent psychoanalysis as an adult, as part of his training, his analyst could find nothing wrong with him.

At any rate, Murray was certainly born to great wealth. He spent his childhood in a house in New York City on what is now the site of Rockefeller Center. Summers were spent on a Long Island beach. While still a child, he accompanied his parents on four long trips to Europe.

For the Adlerians among you, Murray's first memory is an interesting one. He calls it "the marrow-of-my-being memory." At about 4 years of age, he was looking at a picture of a sad-faced queen sitting next to her equally sad-faced son. His mother told him that "it is the prospect of death that has made them sad." (It was the same kind of gloomy picture he later used in his famous Thematic Apperception Test.)

Murray interpreted the memory as indicating the severance of emotional ties between himself and his mother, because she had abruptly weaned him when he was 2 months old and because she spent more time with his sister and brother. Thus, Murray was left with what he called "a limited, third-best portion" of his mother's affection (Murray, 1967, p. 299).

Also at an early age, he became highly sensitized to the emotional problems and sufferings of others, due to his exposure to two neurotic aunts, one of whom was a hysteric while the other suffered intense bouts of depression.

As a child, Murray was afflicted with internal strabismus (crossed eyes). At the age of 9, in the dining room of his home, he was operated on to correct the condition. As a result, he no longer had internal strabismus; it was now external strabismus, the result of a slip by the surgeon, and Murray was left without stereoscopic vision. After his surgery, no matter how hard he tried he was never able to play well at tennis, baseball, or any such game, because he could not focus both eyes on the ball. It was at that time that he began to stutter. He remained unaware of the visual defect until he was in medical school, when a physician asked him if he had had trouble playing games as a child.

These two defects—stuttering and ineptness at sports—created a need to compensate. When he played football, it had to be as quarterback (and he never stuttered when giving signals). He also took up boxing in school, after being beaten in a schoolyard fight. He became so adept that he won the featherweight champion-ship. Murray noted about his participation in football and boxing that "an Adlerian factor was at work" in these compensations for his physical weaknesses (Murray, 1967, p. 302).

After Groton prep school, Murray went to Harvard. He majored in history and earned mediocre grades because he devoted so much time to athletics. His career then followed a devious route to the study of personality. In 1919, he graduated from Columbia University Medical School as the top-ranking member of his class. Following that, he received an M.A. in biology from Columbia, then taught physi-ology for a short time at Harvard.

After serving a two-year internship in surgery at a New York hospital, he con-ducted biochemical research in embryology at the Rockefeller Institute for another two years. Then he went to England for further study and in 1927 received his Ph.D. in biochemistry from Cambridge University.

How, you may well wonder, did this circuitous educational path ever lead to psychology, particularly since he disliked the few psychology courses he had taken in college and medical school? Indeed, by the second lecture in his first psychology course, he had begun "looking for the nearest exit."

Murray's sensitivity to the sufferings of others has been noted. This was re-inforced, during his internship, when he began to search for psychogenic factors in the backgrounds of his patients. Then, in 1923, he was greatly influenced by Jung's book *Psychological Types*. In 1927, he spent three weeks with Jung at his home in Switzerland. The two men spent every day together and, Murray wrote, "the great floodgates of the wonder-world swung open. . . . I had *experienced* the uncon-scious" (Murray, 1940, p. 153). He also spent an unforgettable evening with Sig-mund Freud and his daughter Anna at their home in Vienna.

After another year at the Rockefeller Institute, Murray, in 1927, was offered an appointment by psychologist Morton Prince as an assistant in founding the Harvard Psychological Clinic, which was set up expressly to study personality. As a part of his own training, Murray underwent psychoanalysis and reported that one of his ana-lysts became bored at the phlegmatic nature of his childhood and his lack of complexes.

In the 1930s, Murray and Christiana Morgan, who had also been influenced by Jung, developed the well-known Thematic Apperception Test (TAT), one of the most widely used projective measures of personality in both research and treat-ment settings (Morgan & Murray, 1935). During World War II, he joined the army and became director of assessment for the Office of Strategic Services, screening candidates for the dangerous assignments of that cloak-and-dagger organization. In addition, for some 25 years Murray investigated the work of author Herman Melville, and in 1951 he published an analysis of the psychological meaning of the novel *Moby Dick*.

Murray stayed at Harvard until his retirement in 1962, conducting research, formulating his theory of personality, and training a large number of psychologists, many of whom achieved fame themselves in the study of personality. Well re-spected and recognized in psychology today, Murray has been awarded the Gold

Medal Award of the American Psychological Foundation and the Distinguished Scientific Contribution Award from the American Psychological Association.

The basic principles of personology

Murray is careful to point out that his theory of **personology** (his term for the study of personality) is a tentative one, not intended to be a final, all-embracing formulation. Personology, he argues, is much too complex and new to allow for finality at this stage in our understanding. Rather, he views his theoretical and empirical work as "preparations for the scaffold of a comprehensive system" (Murray, 1959, p. 7). Nevertheless, there are certain basic principles that he apparently sees as solid foundation material for the scaffolding of his system.

The major principle in all of his work is the firm commitment to the notion that *psychological processes depend on physiological processes*. His pithy comment "No brain, no personality" sums up this viewpoint nicely (Murray, 1951, p. 267). Personality is rooted in the brain, for it is the individual's cerebral physiology that guides and governs the personality. For a simple example: a stroke or certain kinds of drugs can alter the functioning of the brain, and so the personality.

Everything on which the personality depends exists in the brain—feeling states, conscious and unconscious memories, and all of our beliefs, attitudes, fears, and values. The seat, therefore, of every aspect of personality is the brain. So important does Murray consider these controlling brain processes that he calls them *regnant* or ruling processes.

A second basic principle in Murray's system—he calls it an "all-embracing principle"—involves the importance to personality of altering the level of *need-induced tension* in the organism. Other theorists, as we have seen, also invoke the notion of tension reduction, but Murray goes a step beyond that in his formulation. It is true, he argues, that people try to reduce tension, whether of a physiological or psychological nature. However, Murray believes that it is not a completely tension-free state for which we strive. It is the process of reducing tension that is satisfying, rather than the condition of no tension.

Indeed, a tensionless state is a source of great distress, in Murray's view. Human beings have a constant need for excitement, activity, progress, movement, and zest—all of which involve increasing rather than decreasing tension. Thus, we generate tension in order to have the satisfaction of reducing it. Again, it is the act of reducing tensions that is most satisfying; Murray believes that a person's ideal state involves always having a certain level of tension to reduce.

A third general principle of Murray's system is the *longitudinal* nature of personality. The personality is always developing over time. Personality is, in a sense, constructed out of all the events occurring over the course of an individual's life. Therefore, the study of past events is of major importance in personality, and, in order to study those events, Murray introduced the notions of *serials* and *proceedings*. These are, in essence, the units of data used by the personologists and will be discussed later in this chapter in the section on research.

There are additional elements and principles in Murray's view of the nature of personality. Personality is ever changing and progressing, not static or fixed; therefore, it cannot really be described. Something in such a constant state of flux cannot be pinned down sufficiently for description.

Murray also focuses on the uniqueness of each individual personality, while nonetheless recognizing certain similarities among all personalities. As he sees it, an individual human being is like every other person, like some other people, and like no other person.

The divisions of personality: Id, superego, and ego

As noted earlier, Murray's system is drawn at least in part from Freud's. Murray's analytic training was conducted along Freudian lines, and his own analysis was conducted by orthodox Freudians. The imprint of Freud is, therefore, visible in Murray's formulations, but he changed some of the Freudian teachings in the act of incorporating them into his own point of view.

When dealing with the basic divisions (a term he uses in place of *structure*) of the personality, Murray uses the Freudian terms id, superego, and ego, but his concepts are not what Freud had in mind.

Like Freud, Murray believes that the **id** is the repository of all the innate impulsive tendencies. As such, the id provides both energy and direction to behavior. Thus, the id is basically concerned with the motivational forces of the personality.

Murray's conception of the id is that it contains all the primitive, amoral, and lustful impulses that Freud described but that it also contains innate impulses that society considers acceptable and even desirable. Here we can see the influence of Jung's view of the shadow, which has both good and bad aspects. For example, the id contains the tendencies to empathy, imitation and identification, forms of love other than lustful ones, and the tendency to master one's environment.

Virtually every aspect of the personality—what society considers good as well as what it considers evil—arises out of the id, which therefore provides all the energy, emotions, and needs to the individual. Murray also suggests that the strength or intensity of the id varies among individuals. Thus, one person can be seen to possess a much greater degree of zest and more intense appetites and emotions than someone else. Therefore, the problem of controlling and directing the id forces is not the same for all people; some have greater id energy to cope with.

Murray places great stress on the influencing force of the social environment, generally spoken of as culture, on personality. Agreeing with Freud, he defines the **superego** as the internalization of the culture's values, norms, and mores, by which rules the individual comes to evaluate and judge his or her own behavior and that of others. The form and substance of the superego are imposed on the child at an early age by parents and other authority figures, as Freud proposed.

However, Murray feels that other factors also shape the superego. He includes among them peer groups and the literature and mythology of the culture. He thus allows for influences beyond those of childhood experiences. The superego, therefore, is not rigidly crystallized by age 5 or so. Rather, it continues to develop throughout life, reflecting the greater complexity and sophistication of the experiences to which a person is exposed as he or she grows older.

Since, in Murray's conception, the id contains both good and bad forces—some that don't have to be suppressed—the superego is not constantly in conflict with the id, as is the case in Freud's view. It is true that the superego must try to thwart the bad (socially unacceptable) id impulses, but it also functions to determine when, where, and how an acceptable need should be expressed and which environmental objects may best satisfy it.

While the superego is developing, so is the *ego-ideal*. This ideal provides the individual with long-range goals for which to strive. The ego-ideal represents what the person could become at his or her best. This ideal self contains the individual's ambitions and aspirations. It may be congruent with the values of the superego or in conflict with them. In the latter case, the person may aspire to excellence in a kind of behavior that violates his or her internalized cultural norms, as exemplified by a person who aspires to be a master criminal.

The **ego** is the rational governor of the personality, which, as in Freud's view, tries to modify or delay the unacceptable impulses of the id. However, Murray considers the ego to do much more than police the personality. In its role as the central organizer of all behavior, the ego also consciously decides and wills the direction of positive behavior.

The ego thus assumes a much more active role in determining behavior than Freud had accorded it. Not merely the servant of the id, the ego directly and consciously plans courses of action; it seeks and makes opportunities for the gratifications that ensue from satisfying the positive id impulses. The ego is the spontaneously choosing *I* of the personality and includes the intellectual and perceptual abilities of the individual. The ego functions, then, not only to suppress id pleasure but also to foster and produce pleasure by organizing and directing the expression of the acceptable id impulses.

The ego is the arbiter between the id and the superego. As such, it may favor one over the other. For example, if the ego favors the id over the superego, it may direct the personality toward a life of crime. It can, of course, integrate both aspects of personality so that what a person wants to do (id) is in harmony with what society feels he or she should do (superego).

As you can see, there is opportunity in Murray's system for conflict between the id and superego. A strong ego can mediate effectively between the two, but a weak ego can leave the personality a battleground. The basic difference between Murray and Freud on this point is that Murray does not believe that this conflict is inevitable.

Needs: The motivation of behavior

Murray's most important contribution to both theory and research in personality is his concept of *need* to explain the motivation and direction of behavior. His extensive work in motivation, which forms the essence or core of his theory of personality, has provided the most elaborate and probably the most carefully determined categorization of needs to be found anywhere in psychology. It is important to note that this need concept is derived not from his own introspection or from case studies of patients undergoing treatment but from the intensive study of normal subjects.

A need, in Murray's view, is a hypothetical construct, "the occurrence of which is imagined in order to account for certain objective and subjective facts." It is physiologically based, in that it involves a physicochemical force in the brain that organizes and directs all the intellectual and perceptual abilities of the individual.

Needs may arise from internal activities or processes such as hunger or thirst or from events in the environment. From whatever source, the need arouses a tension level that the organism tries to reduce by satisfying the need. As noted, the need both energizes and directs behavior; it activates behavior in the proper direction to satisfy the need.

Murray's original, now classic, research led to a list of 20 needs. Since then, Murray and his colleagues and students have offered some modifications, but the original 20 still represent the major needs in his system (Murray, 1938).

Dominance (n Dom)   To control one's human environment. To influence or direct the behavior of others by suggestion, seduction, persuasion, or command. To dissuade, restrain, or prohibit.

Deference (n Def)   To admire or support a superior other. To praise, honor, or eulogize. To emulate an exemplar. To conform to custom.

Autonomy (n Auto)   To resist coercion and restriction. To be independent and free to act according to impulse. To defy conventions. To avoid or quit activities prescribed by domineering authorities.

Aggression (n Agg)   To overcome opposition forcefully. To fight. To revenge an injury. To oppose forcefully or punish. To deprecate and slander and to belittle or ridicule maliciously.

Abasement (n Aba)   To submit passively to external force. To accept injury, blame, criticism, punishment. To surrender and to admit inferiority, error, wrongdoing, or defeat. To seek and enjoy pain, punishment, illness, and misfortune.

Achievement (n Ach)   To accomplish something difficult, overcome obstacles, and attain a high standard. To rival and surpass others and to master, manipulate, or organize physical objects, human beings, or ideas.

Sentience (n Sen)   To seek and enjoy sensuous impressions.

Exhibition (n Exh)   To make an impression. To be seen and heard. To excite, amaze, fascinate, entertain, shock, intrigue, amuse, or entice.

Play (n Play)   To act for fun without further purpose. To laugh and make a joke of everything. To devote free time to sports, dancing, drinking, parties, cards.

Affiliation (n Aff)   To draw near and enjoyably cooperate with an allied other— one who resembles the subject or who likes the subject. To please and win affection of a cathected other. To adhere and remain loyal to a friend.

Rejection (n Rej)   To separate oneself from a negatively cathected other. To exclude, abandon, expel, or remain indifferent to an inferior other.

Succorance (n Suc)   To have one's needs gratified by the sympathetic aid of an

allied other. To always have a supporter. To be nursed, supported, sustained, surrounded, protected, indulged, forgiven, or consoled.

Nurturance (n Nur)   To give sympathy and gratify the needs of a helpless other—
an infant or any object that is weak, disabled, tired, inexperienced, infirm, de-
feated, humiliated, lonely, dejected, sick, or mentally confused. To feed, help,
support, console, protect, comfort, nurse, or heal.

Infavoidance (n Inf)   To avoid humiliation. To quit embarrassing situations or to
avoid conditions which may lead to belittlement. To refrain from action because
of the fear of failure.

Defendance (n Dfd)   To defend the self against assault, criticism, and blame. To
conceal or justify a misdeed, failure, or humiliation.

Counteraction (n Cnt)   To master or make up for a failure by restriving. To oblit-
erate a humiliation by resumed action. To overcome a weakness, to repress fear.
To maintain self-respect and pride on a high level.

Harmavoidance (n Harm)   To avoid pain, physical injury, illness, and death. To
escape from a dangerous situation. To take precautionary measures.

Order (n Ord)   To put things in order. To achieve cleanliness, arrangement, organization, balance, neatness, tidiness, and precision.

Understanding (n Und)   To ask or to answer general questions. To be interested
in theory, to analyze events and generalize.

Sex (n Sex)   To form and further an erotic relationship. To have sexual intercourse.

Murray does not suggest that all these needs exist in everyone. There are some
people who may experience all of them, at least over the course of a lifetime, but
there are other people who never experience some of the needs. Certain of these
needs are supportive of or congruent with others, while some are in opposition to
other needs. In recognition of this, Murray has pointed out that there are five ways
of categorizing needs.

Categories of needs

The first categorization of needs is the primary (or viscerogenic) and secondary (or psychogenic) dichotomy. **Primary needs** arise from internal body processes and include the needs for satisfactions vital to survival—air, water, food,
defecation, harmavoidance—as well as some needs that do not have to be satisfied
for an individual's survival, such as sex and sentience.

The **secondary or psychogenic needs** arise indirectly from primary needs
(in a way not made clear by Murray) but have no specifiable origins within the
body. They are called secondary not because they are less important to the organism but because they develop after the primary needs. They are concerned with
mental and emotional satisfactions and include most of the needs listed earlier,
such as achievement, dominance, affiliation, and so on.

Another way of categorizing needs is in terms of focal versus diffuse. This distinction has to do with the number of objects that can serve to satisfy the need. A
focal need can be satisfied by only one or at best a few goal objects, while a **diffuse need** can be satisfied by many objects.

The third categorization is into proactive and reactive types of needs. A **re-active need** involves a response to something specific in the environment, in that the need appears only when that object appears. Harmavoidance, for example, appears only when a threatening object is present. Ideally, it exists only when there is some harm to avoid.

Proactive needs, on the other hand, do not depend on the presence of any particular object in the environment. They are spontaneous needs that call forth appropriate behavior whenever they are aroused, independent of the environment. A person who is hungry, for example, looks for food. He or she does not simply wait to react when an appropriate stimulus, such as an ad for a hamburger, is presented.

Manifest and latent needs are the fourth type of classification. **Manifest needs** are expressed overtly because society approves of their expression and may even reward them. In our society, achievement is such a need; its expression brings social approval.

Other needs, however, can only be expressed covertly, in fantasies or dreams or through symbolism. These are **latent needs**. Aggression, for example, in a society that represses its expression, can be displayed only covertly and so remains latent.

The fifth categorization involves the effect, process, and modal types of needs. **Effect needs** lead to or cause an effect; that is, they lead directly and immediately to an object. The individual may derive a great deal of pleasure out of the various activities that go to make up the need-satisfying behavior. Murray calls this *sheer function pleasure* or **process activity** and defines it as the pleasure derived from doing something just for the sake of doing it.

Finally, there is often a need beyond sheer function pleasure. Not content with merely doing something, simply performing an act, there is pleasure to be derived from doing it extremely well. The behavior is now not satisfying when it is merely performed; it must be performed well. Murray calls this **modal** because pleasure derives from the mode of performance of some behavior.

Other characteristics of needs

Needs can differ greatly in terms of the urgency or insistence with which they impel behavior, a characteristic that Murray refers to as a need's *prepotency*. If, for example, the needs for air and water are not satisfied, they can become the most insistent of needs and totally dominate behavior. At other times, if the primary needs are satisfied, the need for aggression may be strongest.

Some needs, though not identical, may be complementary, so that they can be satisfied by one behavior or one set of behaviors. Murray calls this a *fusion* of needs. For example, by acquiring fame and wealth through one's work, the achievement, dominance, and autonomy needs may all be satisfied.

The concept of **subsidiation** refers to a situation in which one need is activated to aid in the satisfaction of another need. For example, to satisfy the affiliation need by joining and mixing with others, it may be necessary to act deferentially toward others (thus invoking the deference need). The deference need would thus be subsidiary to the affiliation need.

Murray recognized that environmental objects and events in childhood can strongly influence the development of specific needs and, later in life, can trigger or call forth'these needs. He called this influence **press**, because the object or event presses or pressures the individual in a certain way.

Of course, as you know, we often perceive the world around us in subjective terms; that is, our image of objects and events does not always coincide with reality. Thus, the environmental influence of press may be perceived subjectively or objectively. Objectively perceived pressure—that which directly reflects reality—is called *alpha press*, while subjectively perceived and interpreted pressure is called *beta press*.

Press also has the power to attract or repel an individual; it can be either positive or negative in its emotional tone. Murray used Freud's term *cathexis* to describe this characteristic of press. Thus, if a person is attracted to money, he or she is said to be positively cathected to it.

Because of the ever-present possibility of interaction between need and press, Murray introduced still another concept: thema. The **thema** is an amalgamation of both press and need, combining the nature of the environment and of the person. Largely unconscious, the thema relates needs and presses into a single pattern, the function of which is to give coherence to an individual's behavior. The pattern of the thema is formed through early childhood experience and comes to be a powerful force in an individual's personality. The pattern brings unity, order, and uniqueness to the individual's behavior and so is also called a *unity-thema*.

In his later work, Murray introduced another concept, **value-vector**, which is intended to substitute for his earlier concept of need. *Vector* refers to the direction shown by behavior and the intensity of the desire bringing about the behavior. Some of the vectors listed by Murray are acquisition, avoidance, construction, destruction, and expulsion.

Value refers to the ideals an individual holds, including intellectual, ideological, and aesthetic ideals. In working with an individual, Murray gathers information on what is worthwhile to that person (value) and how he or she behaves in relation to these values (vector) and plots them in the rows and columns of a matrix. The concept, still being developed, is intended to provide specific objective descriptions of behavior to replace the more vague theoretical descriptions arising from the use of the need and press concepts.

Complexes: The development of the personality

Murray takes a longitudinal approach to personality, emphasizing the developmental history of the individual. His approach to personality development draws upon the traditional Freudian view, which he elaborates and extends. Like Freud, he focuses on events and experiences of early childhood and the patterns of behavior that are formed during these crucial years. Murray divides childhood into five stages, each of which is characterized by a pleasurable condition that is inevitably terminated by the demands of society. Each of these stages leaves its mark on personality in the form of **complexes**, which are patterns, formed from the imprints of the various stages, which unconsciously direct the individual's later development.

Everyone develops these five complexes, according to Murray, because everyone passes through the same five stages of development. There is, therefore, nothing abnormal about them, except when they are carried to extreme. When they are manifested in the extreme, the person remains more or less fixated at one level of development. His or her personality then is unable to develop spontaneity and flexibility, and the formation of the ego and superego are interfered with.

The five pleasurable conditions or stages of childhood and their related complexes are:

1. The secure existence within the womb . . . .   claustral complex
2. The sensuous enjoyment of sucking nourishment while being held . . . .   oral complex
3. The pleasure resulting from defecation . . . .   anal complex
4. The pleasure accompanying urination . . . .   urethral complex
5. Genital pleasures . . . .   castration complex

Claustral complex.   Life within the womb is secure, serene, and highly dependent, a condition that we may occasionally wish to be able to reinstate. In its basic form, the *simple claustral complex* may be manifested by a desire to be in small, warm, dark places that are safe and secluded. It may mean remaining under the bedcovers in the morning, having a soundproof den or secret hiding place, living in a monastery or on an island, or enjoying a boat or a limousine. Such people tend to be highly dependent on others, passive, and oriented toward the safe, practiced behaviors of the past.

This wish to return to womb-like conditions is, however, only one of three forms the claustral complex may take. The complex can also center on the feeling of insecurity and helplessness and lack of support in the womb, which may cause the person to fear open spaces, falling, drowning, fires, earthquakes, or any situation of change and novelty. Murray calls this the *insupport complex.*

The third claustral complex is actually an anticlaustral complex centering around fear of suffocation and confinement. Murray calls it the *egression complex*; it manifests itself in a preference for wide open spaces and fresh air and for movement, change, and novelty. It may also manifest itself in claustrophobia.

Oral complex.   There are also three varieties of oral complex. The *oral succorance complex* is a combination of mouth activities, passive tendencies, and the need to be supported and protected. The behavioral manifestations of this complex include sucking, kissing, eating, drinking, and a hunger for affection, sympathy, protection, and love. The *oral aggression complex* combines oral and aggressive activities in the form of biting, spitting, or shouting, or in verbal aggression such as sarcasm. The behavior involved in the *oral rejection complex* includes vomiting, being picky about food, eating little, fearing oral contamination (as from kissing), needing seclusion, and avoiding dependence on others.

Anal complex. There are two anal complexes, involving rejecting or retaining. In the *anal rejection complex* there is a preoccupation with defecation, including anal humor, and an interest in feces or feces-like material (dirt, mud, plaster, or clay). Aggression often becomes a part of this complex and is manifested in dropping and throwing things, firing guns, or setting off explosives. This type of person is usually dirty and disorganized. The *anal retention complex* manifests itself in retentive kinds of behavior—accumulating, saving, and collecting things—and in cleanliness, neatness, and orderliness.

Urethral complex. This complex is unique to Murray's system and is associated with excessive ambition, a distorted sense of self-esteem, a history of bed-wetting, and a strong self-love. It is also called the Icarus complex, after the mythical Greek figure who flew so close to the sun that the wax holding his wings together melted. Like Icarus, the person with this complex aims too high, and his or her dreams are shattered by failure.

Castration complex. Murray disagrees with Freud's contention that fear of castration is the core of much adult anxiety. He interprets the complex in narrower and more literal fashion as simply "the fantasy that the penis might be cut off" (Murray, 1938, p. 385). Murray believes such a fear grows out of childhood masturbation and the parental punishment that may have accompanied it.

Murray's image of human nature

Although Murray's theory of personality agrees with Freud's on several points, his image of human nature is quite different. Even Murray's ultimate and necessary goal of life—which, like Freud's, is tension reduction—is considered from a different perspective. According to Murray, our goal is not a tension-free state, but rather the satisfaction derived from the process of reducing the tension.

On the free will–determinism controversy, Murray has argued that personality is partially determined by needs and by the environment. He accords us some degree of free will, however slight, in our capacity to change and grow. He sees each human being as unique, but he also recognizes similarities in the personalities of all people.

Murray believes that we are shaped both by inherited attributes and by our environment, and that each factor is of roughly equal influence. We cannot understand personality unless we accept the impact of physiological forces and of stimuli from the physical, social, and cultural environment.

Murray's view of human nature is fundamentally optimistic. He has been vocal in his criticism of those parts of psychology that project a negative and demeaning image of human beings. He argues that, with our vast powers of creativity, imagination, and reason, we are capable of solving any problem facing us. In line with these beliefs, Murray has been much involved in efforts to ameliorate social and personal problems. He has been concerned with both the intimate two-person level (as in marriage) and the broad cultural level, and he has advocated the abolition of war and the creation of a unified global state.

Humanity's orientation, in Murray's view, is largely toward the future. While he recognizes the imprint of childhood experiences on present behavior, he does not envision us as wholly captives of our past. The childhood complexes in his system may unconsciously affect our development, but personality is also influenced by events of the present and aspirations for the future. We have the continuing capability to grow and develop; indeed, such growth is a natural and inevitable concomitant of being a human being. We can change through our own rational and creative abilities, and if we as individuals can change, we collectively can change the social system in which we live.

Assessment in Murray's theory

Murray's techniques of assessing personality differ from those of the other personality theorists we have discussed. As we have seen, Murray was not assessing the personalities of emotionally disturbed persons, nor did he use such standard psychoanalytic techniques as dream analysis and free association.

Instead, in his intensive assessment of the normal personality, Murray used a variety of techniques and devices to collect huge amounts of data from 51 male Harvard undergraduates. These subjects were interviewed individually several times and were given projective tests, objective tests, and questionnaires covering, among other things, childhood memories, family relations, sexual development, sensorimotor learning, ethical standards, goals, social interactions, and mechanical and artistic abilities. This program of personality assessment was so comprehensive that it took Murray's staff of 28 investigators six months to complete. We shall discuss the analysis of these data in the research section.

The OSS assessment program

On the basis of the assessment of the Harvard undergraduates, Murray formulated the essence of his theory of personality. This was not the only program of personality assessment in which he was involved. We mentioned earlier that during World War II, Murray became director of assessment for the Office of Strategic Services (OSS), the forerunner of today's Central Intelligence Agency.

As with his evaluation of the Harvard undergraduates, Murray's wartime assessment effort involved the intensive investigation of the total personality (OSS Assessment Staff, 1948). Potential candidates for OSS positions submitted to the Rorschach and the TAT projective tests, questionnaires on a variety of topics, and several in-depth interviews. In addition, candidates participated in stressful real-life situations in which their behavior was closely observed.

These behavioral observations became known as *situational tests*. One such test required the candidate to build a bridge across a stream in a fixed period of time. No plans were provided, but the person was assigned a group of workers to help him. In this way, the man's ingenuity, ability to improvise, and leadership skills could be assessed in a realistic setting. Further, to determine the candidate's reaction to frustration, some of the so-called workers were stooges. They had been instructed to do everything possible to prevent the actual building of the bridge. Many candidates became enraged and were even reduced to tears when faced with the pressure of such maddening frustration.

The OSS program of personality assessment was not conducted to understand the nature of personality, as was the Harvard study. It had the highly practical purpose of selecting men to serve as spies and saboteurs, operating behind enemy lines in extremely dangerous situations.

This pioneering attempt at personnel selection through large-scale personality assessment has evolved into the popular and successful assessment-center approach widely used in industry and government today to select promising leaders and executives. It provides a striking example of the practical application of assessment techniques originally undertaken as pure research.

The Thematic Apperception Test and other personality tests

The assessment technique most often associated with Murray is the Thematic Apperception Test (TAT), which we described in Chapter 1. You will recall that the TAT consists of 20 ambiguous pictures showing one or more persons. The person taking the test is asked to make up a story describing the scene and the characters in each picture.

Murray derived the TAT, a projective technique, directly from Freud's defense mechanism of projection, in which a person projects or attributes disturbing impulses onto someone else. In the TAT, the person projects those impulses onto one of the characters in the picture and thereby reveals the nature of his or her own troubling thoughts.

The TAT is a device for assessing unconscious thoughts, feelings, and fears. It is highly subjective, a fact freely admitted by Murray in an interview when he referred to it as "a kind of booby trap which may catch more embryo psychologists than patients. The patient reveals parts of himself when he composes a story to explain the picture. Then the psychologist may reveal parts of himself when he composes a formulation to explain the patient's story" (Hall, 1968, p. 61).

Nevertheless, in the hands of a trained clinician, the TAT may reveal a great deal of useful information about a person. Because of its subjectivity, however, the information obtained should be used to supplement data from more objective methods rather than as the sole means of diagnosis.

A number of modifications and adaptations of the TAT have been developed for other purposes, such as executive assessment, career counseling, and measuring attitudes toward, for example, authority, labor unions, and minority groups (Harrison, 1965). In addition, the TAT has been used extensively for research purposes, including the study of some of Murray's postulated needs, particularly achievement and affiliation.

Three other assessment techniques have been developed from Murray's personality theory. The best known and most widely used of these is the Edwards Personal Preference Schedule (EPPS) (Edwards, 1953). Designed to measure 15 of Murray's needs, the EPPS consists of 210 pairs of statements. The persons taking the test choose one in each pair that best characterizes themselves. Although the validity data on the EPPS are meager and inconsistent, the test is used for both research and diagnostic purposes to assess a person's scores on Murray's needs and to correlate them with other measurements.

Another test derived from Murray's theory is the Jackson Personality Research Form (Jackson, 1967). This test measures 20 traits, including many of those measured by the EPPS, as well as others drawn primarily from Murray's list of needs. Twenty items are available for each scale. Persons taking the test indicate which items describe themselves. The Personality Research Form is used almost exclusively for research purposes. An applied version of the test, the Jackson Personality Inventory, measures 16 traits and is intended for selection and diagnosis (Jackson, 1978).

The third test deriving from Murray's theory is the Stern Activities Index, which consists of more than 300 statements describing different kinds of activities (Stern, 1958). Subjects indicate their preferences for these activities, which are designed to measure all of Murray's needs. The test is used primarily as a research instrument.

You can see that of all the theorists we have discussed thus far, Murray has developed or inspired more personality assessment programs and techniques.

Research in Murray's theory
The Harvard undergraduate assessment program

We noted that Murray's original research program involved the intensive study of the personalities of 51 normal male Harvard undergraduates. The subjects were tested, interviewed, and studied by a staff of scientists, including psychiatrists, psychologists, and anthropologists. Thus, each person was observed by specialists with different training and backgrounds using different techniques, in much the same way, in principle, that a medical diagnosis is conducted.

Each observer made his own diagnosis of a subject. This was then presented to a committee, which Murray called the Diagnostic Council, for a final evaluation. The council consisted of the five most experienced staff members. They met with each subject for 45 minutes, asking questions and having them perform certain tasks. Following that, each member of the council rated the subjects on several variables.

As new data were gathered on the subjects, the council met periodically to reassess the ratings on each person. It reviewed all the evidence on each subject to arrive at a final diagnosis by the standard committee procedure of discussion and vote. The final evaluation or diagnosis was reached by majority vote (though apparently Murray gave his own rating more weight).

So much data was collected on each subject's life that it was necessary to divide it into different time intervals or segments. The basic unit or temporal segment of behavior is the **proceeding**, a period of time in which an important pattern of behavior is carried through from beginning to end. A proceeding always involves some interaction between the person and other people or objects in the environment. However, this interaction may occur in fantasy as well as in reality. The imagined interaction is called an *internal proceeding*, while a real interaction is called an *external proceeding*.

Proceedings are often linked together, not necessarily in time but in function. For example, on Monday a man may meet a woman and ask her for a date (an external proceeding). He may daydream about her at varying periods through the week (an internal proceeding) and may get a haircut and wash his car (external proceedings) in preparation for the date. Each of those acts, including the imaginary one, is a proceeding, but taken together—as they should be, since they are related to the same function or purpose—they are called a **serial**. To be more precise, a serial is "a directionally organized intermittent succession of proceedings" (Murray, 1951, p. 272).

Idiographic versus nomothetic research

Murray's approach to personality research is **idiographic**, meaning that he favors the intensive study of a relatively small number of individuals using a variety of assessment techniques. This contrasts with the usual approach to personality research, the **nomothetic** approach, which deals with statistical differences among groups of subjects. Murray has been critical of the nomothetic approach for not gathering large enough amounts of data on the subjects studied. He argues that "the reason why the results of so many researches in personality have been misleading or trivial is that experimenters have failed to obtain enough pertinent information about their subjects" (Murray, 1938, p. ix).

Some of Murray's followers have been even more critical of standard laboratory research in personality, arguing that almost 50 years of research "has produced little in the way of illuminating insights into human behavior. . . . An increasing number of psychologists are finding that they cannot reproduce their own laboratory findings, let alone the findings of others" (Epstein, 1979, p. 650). Thus, they charge that the traditional experimental research approach to personality fails to meet the most fundamental requirements of duplication and verifiability.

The controversy about whether Murray's idiographic approach or the traditional nomothetic approach provides the more reliable and valid information about personality continues today. Murray's call for what he labels the "multiform assessment program," which would have all investigators studying the same group of subjects and meeting periodically to define each subject's personality, has not yet been put into practice beyond the circle of Murray's loyal followers.

Studies of specific needs

Considerable research has been conducted on specific needs, notably achievement and affiliation. The bulk of the work has been carried out on the need for achievement. We will discuss it in Chapter 17 as a limited-domain approach to the understanding of personality.

The need for affiliation has been found to be strong in many people, particularly in stressful situations. In one classic experiment, subjects who knew that they were going to receive electric shocks in an experiment were much more likely to wait in the company of others than were subjects who were not facing the stress of potential electric shocks (Schachter, 1959). Apparently, the presence of others helped allay the anxiety associated with the stress.

Another study found that people who had experienced severe effects of a thunderstorm, such as property damage, were much more likely to seek the company of others than those who had experienced no such harmful effects of the storm (Strümpfer, 1970).

Many people prefer the company of others even when not experiencing stress. Observations of college students in their everyday campus activities showed that 60 percent of them were in the company of at least one other person. Female students were much more likely to be with others than were male students (Latané & Bidwell, 1977).

The need for power is not one of Murray's specific needs, but several needs, such as dominance, deference, aggression, and abasement, have been subsumed under a category of needs that Murray calls the "response to power." The power need, defined as the motivation to be in control, to give orders, and to command obedience, has been studied in individuals through their responses to some of the TAT pictures. Further, the need for power has been correlated with other behaviors.

For example, the need for power has been related to excessive drinking (McClelland et al., 1972), to the coronary-prone personality known as Type A (McClelland, 1979), and to the possession of high-status objects such as expensive automobiles and stereo equipment (Winter, 1973). Male college students high in the need for power tend to serve as officers in campus organizations, to work at the school newspaper or radio station, to be quick to follow the latest trends in fashion, and to prefer to marry dependent women (Winter, 1973).

Although Murray's approach to personality has generated research on some of his needs, there has been no research evidence to support such other aspects of his theory as the divisions of personality or the stages of personality development.

A final commentary

Murray has exerted an impressive influence on the study of personality, an influence that is still being felt. Of particular importance is his list of needs, which has proven to be of great value for research, clinical diagnosis, and personnel selection, and his promising techniques for the assessment of personality. Murray stands in 12th place in the ratings of personality theorists we have discussed throughout this book and is 46th out of 286 psychologists in overall influence in the last half of the 20th century (Gilgen, 1982). This puts him in the top 16 percent of all the psychologists rated.

In 1978, the 40th anniversary of the publication of Murray's first book, *Explorations in Personality*, was celebrated by a symposium at the annual convention of the American Psychological Association. A special award was created in his name, and the Murray Research Center at Radcliffe College was dedicated.

In addition, a symposium on Murray's work was held at Michigan State University and the proceedings were published in a book entitled *Further Explorations in Personality* (Rabin et al., 1981). The fact that psychologists today are continuing with work begun before many of them were born is an impressive tribute. One personality researcher noted that the book "attests to the enduring significance of the bold, deep, and thoughtful approach that attracted us to personology in the first place" (Carlson, 1982, p. 7).

Murray is careful to note that he considers his personological system to be still in the embryonic and evolving stages. It is not, in his view, a finished or complete system by any means. This aspect of his system—its still-developing nature—must be kept in mind when we consider the criticisms directed against it. We cannot altogether condemn a building as ugly or useless, or praise it as beautiful and functional, when only the scaffolding is in place.

One problem in both the development and evaluation of Murray's position is that only some portions of it have been published. His ingenuity and full range of thought, therefore, are revealed only in limited amounts for careful study. His influence apparently has been most keenly felt by those who have worked with him— by those who have had access to his wide-ranging speculations, which he revealed in almost casual conversation. While some, perhaps many, of these ideas have been followed up by his students and colleagues, others have been lost to public scrutiny.

Murray's work has inspired much research, but that research has been conducted, for the most part, on limited aspects of the theory, such as the achievement and affiliation needs, the response to power, and techniques devised to assess personality. Thus, only certain aspects of his theory have been put to experimental test, not the theory as a whole. Of course, by now you will recognize that this criticism is not unique to Murray's theory.

Specific aspects of his work have been criticized, beginning with his method of research. It is argued that, while the Diagnostic Council is laudably democratic, it is hardly scientific. To reach a scientific conclusion by majority rule may not be the most objective procedure.

Other questions asked of his system relate to the concepts of proceedings and serials. It is argued that these temporal units are defined too vaguely to be identified or delimited precisely. Just what constitutes a significant pattern of behavior? What happens to those judged not significant? How long is a proceeding? These are some of the questions not yet satisfactorily answered.

It is argued by some that Murray's classification of needs is overly complex and that there is a great deal of overlap among the needs. It is also unclear how the needs relate to other aspects of the personality and how the needs develop within an individual. However complex his classification of needs may be, there is no denying the considerable impact the concept has had on personality research, particularly that devoted to the construction of psychological tests. In more theoretical terms, his concept of need and the importance he placed on motivation have influenced greatly the study of personality.

Overall, it is perhaps safe to say that Murray's innovations in technique (such as the TAT), his influence on methods of assessing personality, and the personal impact he made on at least two generations of personology researchers during their years at Harvard have had a more lasting effect than his theoretical system. Such points of influence are considerable, as evidenced by his awards, from both the American Psychological Association and the American Psychological Foundation, given in recognition of his important contributions to the study of personality.

Summary

Murray's approach to personology considers the unconscious as well as the conscious; the past, present, and future of the individual; and physiological and sociological forces. Murray sees the reduction of tension as a primary law of human functioning. The two most distinctive features of his system are his sophisticated approach to human needs and the gathering of data from extensive investigations of normal individuals. Murray's childhood experiences do not seem to be reflected in his theory. He did exhibit an Adlerian form of compensation for physical weakness and was strongly influenced by Freud and Jung.

The major principle of Murray's work is the dependence of psychological processes upon physiological processes. Personality is rooted in the brain, which is the regnant or ruling process. Altering the level of need-induced tension is vital to the personality. We generate tension to have the satisfaction of reducing it.

Murray focuses on the longitudinal nature of personality, arguing that the personality is always developing and changing over time and is unique to the individual. To study past events, Murray introduced units of data known as serials and proceedings.

The three basic divisions of personality are the id, superego, and ego. The id contains primitive, amoral impulses as well as tendencies to empathy, imitation, and identification. The superego is shaped by parents, peer groups, and the literature and mythology of the culture. It continues to develop throughout life. The ego consciously decides and wills the direction of behavior.

Needs are physiologically based hypothetical constructs that arise from internal processes or from events in the environment. Needs arouse a tension level that must be reduced and so energize and direct behavior. Murray's needs are dominance, deference, autonomy, aggression, abasement, achievement, sentience, exhibition, play, affiliation, rejection, succorance, nurturance, infavoidance, defendance, counteraction, harmavoidance, order, understanding, and sex.

Needs may be primary (viscerogenic), arising from internal bodily processes, or secondary (psychogenic), concerned with mental and emotional satisfactions. Focal needs can be satisfied by one or a few objects; diffuse needs can be satisfied by many objects. Proactive needs are spontaneous and do not depend on any environmental object; reactive needs involve a response to some specific environmental object. Manifest needs are expressed overtly because society approves of their expression; latent needs must be expressed covertly in fantasies or dreams. Effect needs lead to or cause an effect. Process activity or sheer function pleasure involves the pleasure derived from behaviors designed to satisfy needs. Modal activity refers to the pleasure derived from performing some behavior extremely well.

A need's prepotency is its urgency or insistence. The fusion of needs refers to needs that can be satisfied by one behavior or set of behaviors. Subsidiation involves a situation in which one need is activated to aid in the satisfaction of another need.

Press refers to the pressure, caused by an object in the environment or by events in childhood, to behave in a certain way. Alpha press involves objectively perceived pressure; beta press involves subjectively perceived pressure. Cathexis means the power of press to attract or repel an individual. Thema is an amalgamation of need and press. Unity-thema is the pattern of thema formed through childhood experience. Vector refers to the direction of behavior and the intensity of the desire bringing about the behavior. Value refers to an individual's ideals.

Complexes are patterns formed in each of the five childhood stages of development that unconsciously direct adult development. Everyone develops these five complexes. The claustral complex involves the secure existence within the womb. The simple claustral complex is manifested in a desire to be in small, dark safe places. The insupport complex causes a fear of open spaces, falling, or any situation of novelty and change. The egression complex is a preference for open spaces, change, and novelty.

The oral complex involves the sensuous enjoyment of sucking nourishment. The oral succorance complex is manifested in kissing, eating, and drinking; the oral aggression complex in biting, spitting, and verbal aggression; and the oral rejection complex in vomiting, being picky about food, and the need for seclusion.

The anal complex involves the pleasure resulting from defecation. The anal rejection complex involves a preoccupation with dirt and aggression; the anal retention complex involves saving, collecting, and being extremely orderly.

The urethral or Icarus complex involves the pleasure accompanying urination and is associated with excessive ambition and self-love. The castration complex involves genital pleasure and the fantasy that the penis might be cut off.

In Murray's theory, the ultimate goal in life is the reduction of tension. People have some free will, but much of personality is determined by needs and by the environment. Each person is unique yet shares certain similarities with other people, which are determined by both inherited and environmental forces. Murray holds an optimistic view of human nature, which is oriented toward the future and which grants people the ability to grow and develop.

Murray's assessment techniques include projective and objective tests, questionnaires, interviews, and ratings of behavior. In his assessment program for the

OSS, he also used situational tests, behavioral observations that led to the development of assessment centers, which are popular in industry today.

Murray and a colleague developed the Thematic Apperception Test based on Freud's concept of projection. Three other assessment techniques based on Murray's theory are the Edwards Personal Preference Schedule, the Jackson Personality Research Form, and the Stern Activities Index.

Murray's research involved the intensive analysis of 51 normal male undergraduate students by a staff of specialists with diverse training and backgrounds.

The proceeding, the basic unit of behavior in Murray's research, is a period of time in which an important pattern of behavior is carried through from beginning to end. A succession of proceedings is known as a serial.

Murray's approach is idiographic, involving the intensive study of a small number of people. The traditional approach to personality research is nomothetic, dealing with statistical differences among groups of subjects. Considerable research has been conducted on the needs for achievement and affiliation and the response to power.

Murray's primary influences are his proposed needs and his techniques for assessing personality. His system has been criticized on the following points: the diagnoses of the undergraduate students were not totally objective, proceedings and serials are defined in vague terms, and the classification of needs is overly complex.

Glossary

complexes   Normal patterns of childhood development that influence the adult personality; when manifested in the extreme at any stage, fixation occurs and the formation of the ego and superego is affected.

effect needs   Needs that lead directly to an object or cause an effect.

ego   The conscious organizer of all behavior; a broader definition than that offered by Freud.

focal versus diffuse needs   Focal needs can be satisfied by one or a few goal objects; diffuse needs can be satisfied by many objects.

id   In Murray's view, the id contains the primitive, amoral, and lustful impulses described by Freud, but it also contains desirable impulses

such as empathy and positive forms of love.

idiographic research   The intensive study of a relatively small number of individuals using a variety of assessment techniques; contrasts with nomothetic research.

manifest versus latent needs   Manifest needs, such as achievement, may be expressed overtly; latent needs must be expressed covertly or symbolically because their overt satisfaction may bring social disapproval.

modal needs   Needs that are satisfied when the mode or standard of performance of some behavior is extremely high.

nomothetic research   The study of the statistical differences among groups of subjects; contrasts with idiographic research.

personology   Murray's system of personality.

press   The influence of the environment and of past events on the current activation of a need.

primary versus secondary needs   Primary needs are survival and other needs arising from internal bodily processes; secondary needs are emotional and psychological needs such as achievement and affiliation.

proactive versus reactive needs   Proactive needs arise spontaneously; reactive needs involve a response to a specific object in the environment.

proceeding   The basic temporal segment of behavior; a period of time in which an important behavior pattern occurs from beginning to end.

process needs   Needs that can be satisfied by behaviors or actions that in themselves bring pleasure.

serial   A succession of proceedings.

subsidiation   A situation in which one need is activated to aid in the satisfaction of another need.

superego   In Murray's view, the superego is shaped not only by parents and other authority figures, as Freud proposed, but also by the peer group and the culture.

thema   An amalgamation of press (the environment) and need (the personality) that brings order to the individual's behavior.

value-vector   An amalgamation of the individual's ideals (value) and the direction of behavior, or the intensity of the need bringing about the behavior (vector); a later development of the concept of need.

Review questions

1. In Murray's view, what is the relationship between physiological processes and psychological processes?
2. What is the role of tension in the development of the personality? Is our ultimate goal a life free of tension? Why or why not?
3. How do Murray's views of the id, ego, and superego diverge from Freud's conceptions of these structures of personality?
4. From what sources do needs arise?
5. Describe five ways of classifying needs and give an example for each category.
6. Describe the five childhood stages in the development of the personality and the complexes associated with each stage.
7. How is the Thematic Apperception Test used to assess personality? What criticisms can be made of this type of assessment technique?
8. What is the difference between the idiographic and the nomothetic approaches to personality research? Which does Murray prefer?
9. What sort of data did Murray collect in his study of Harvard undergraduates?
10. Is Murray's view of human nature optimistic or pessimistic? Why?

Suggested reading

Epstein, S. Explorations in personality today and tomorrow: A tribute to Henry A. Murray. *American Psychologist*, 1979, 34, 649–653.

Hall, M. H. A conversation with Henry A. Murray. *Psychology Today*, September 1968, 56–63.

Maddi, S. R. & Costa, P. T. *Humanism in personology: Allport, Maslow, and Murray*. Chicago: Aldine-Atherton, 1972.

Murray, H. A. *Explorations in personality*. New York: Oxford University Press, 1938.

Murray, H. A. Autobiography. In E. G. Boring & G. Lindzey, Eds., *History of psychology in autobiography*, vol. 5. New York: Appleton-Century-Crofts, 1967.

Schneidman, E. S., Ed. *Endeavors in psychology: Selections from the personology of Henry A. Murray*. New York: Harper & Row, 1981.

PART 3

The Trait Approach

$\mathbf{A}$ dictionary definition of the word *trait* is "a distinguishing characteristic or quality of a person." This represents an approach we often take in our everyday lives when we try to describe the personality of someone we know. We tend to pick what we perceive is a person's outstanding characteristic, or set of characteristics, and use this to summarize what that person is like. We may say, for example, "John is a very uninhibited person" or "Debbie is very aggressive." This is an easy and quick way to categorize someone, and a potentially useful way too, although our personal judgments may often be wrong.

Because organizing people by their traits seems so simple and understandable, and because it has a common-sense appeal, the trait approach to the study of personality has been in use for a long time. This kind of classification dates back to the time of the Greek physician Hippocrates (around 460–377 B.C.), over 2000 years before the modern attempts to understand personality that are described in this book.

The works of Gordon Allport and of Raymond Cattell typify the trait approach to personality. These theorists differ from most of the other theorists we have discussed in one respect: they studied personality by observing normal, healthy people in an academic laboratory setting. Their insights are not based on work with disturbed individuals in a clinical setting, nor have they practiced any kind of psychotherapy.

Beyond that point of similarity, and the fact that they were trying to identify personality traits, Allport and Cattell approached their study in different ways. Also, Allport can be considered within the humanistic framework as well (see

Part 5), because he focused on the total human being and his or her innate potential for growth and self-realization.

You may be wondering about the differences between traits and types, which we have spoken about before. Consider some of the personality types we have discussed: Freud's oral, anal, and phallic types; Jung's introverted and extraverted types; Adler's dominant, getting, avoiding, and socially useful types. In these examples, people are grouped or classified in discrete categories. In other words, they are perceived as exclusively extraverts or introverts, or definitely anal types or oral types. A person either is or is not a particular type; he or she does not have some characteristics of one type and some of another.

Traits, on the other hand, involve classifying or categorizing people in terms of how much of some characteristic they possess. How aggressive is one person, how uninhibited another? Trait theorists believe that traits exist on a continuum ranging from a very low or small amount of the characteristic to a very high or large amount. Thus, everyone would possess some amount of the trait of aggression, for example, however small.

A person is or is not a particular type, but he or she will possess some degree of any and all traits.

CHAPTER 8

Gordon Allport

The life of Allport (1897–1967)
The nature of personality:
  Consciousness, growth, and
  uniqueness
Personality traits
  Habits and attitudes
Personality and motivation
  The functional autonomy of motives
The proprium: The unique self
Personality in childhood
Personality in adulthood
Allport's image of human nature
Assessment in Allport's theory
  Letters from Jenny
  The Study of Values
Research in Allport's theory
  Expressive behavior
A final commentary
Summary
Glossary
Review questions
Suggested reading

As the individual matures, the bond with the past is broken.

GORDON ALLPORT

Over the course of a productive career that lasted for more than four decades, Gordon Allport became one of the most stimulating and provocative psychologists to study personality. Indeed, it was Allport, more than anyone else, who made the study of personality an academically respectable part of psychology. We noted in Chapter 1 that the study of personality did not become formalized and systematized in psychology until the 1930s. Psychoanalysis and those theories that were derived from it were not considered to be in the mainstream of scientific psychology. Indeed, the area of personality as a whole was not a major part of psychology until Allport published an important book, *Personality: A Psychological Interpretation*, in 1937.

Allport, therefore, served two very important purposes in the study of personality; he helped to bring it into the mainstream of scientific psychology, and he formulated his own controversial and useful theory of personality, in which the concept of traits plays a prominent role. In addition to making many original contributions, he incorporated insights and ideas from other approaches to form a truly eclectic theory of personality that attempts to deal with the whole person as a unique and dynamic functioning individual.

Allport took issue with Freud on several crucial points. First, he argued that the role of the unconscious had been exaggerated. Allport did not believe that unconscious forces dominate or even play a major role in the personality of the normal, mature adult. Rather, he saw the healthy, normal individual as functioning in rational and conscious terms, aware of and controlling many of the forces that motivate him or her. The unconscious, according to Allport, is of importance in neurotic or disturbed functioning but not in the normal person.

A second point of disagreement with Freud was over the role of the past in controlling the present. In Allport's view, human beings are not prisoners of childhood conflicts and experiences. Rather, we are guided much more by the present—and our view toward the future—than by the past. His whole focus in the study of personality was on contemporary influences. For example, in his extensive work in the area of motivation, he looked not to the past but to the current self-image of a person. Similarly, he felt that a person's ego structure is based on current events and feelings, and upon anticipations and plans for the future. He wrote that people "are busy leading their lives into the future, whereas psychology, for the most part, is busy tracing them into the past" (Allport, 1955, p. 51).

Allport was much opposed to studying personality through data collected from pathological subjects. Unlike Freud, who posited a continuum between the normal and the abnormal, Allport saw a sharp break between the two, with the abnormal individual still functioning at the level of infantile complexes and experiences. He insisted that the only way to study personality is through healthy, normal, mature adults; other populations—neurotics, children, animals—cannot be compared to normal adults. There is no functional similarity in the area of personality between child and adult, abnormal and normal, or animal and human.

Perhaps the most distinctive feature of Allport's approach to personality is his insistence on the uniqueness of the individual personality as defined by the traits that characterize each of us. He was much opposed to the traditional scientific emphasis on forming general constructs or laws that can be applied to everyone. Personality, he argued, is not general or universal in nature. Rather, it is highly particular and specific to each individual.

In addition to formulating his theory, Allport, along with his students—many of whom became prominent themselves—performed important empirical research on a variety of aspects of personality. He also developed several tests for assessing personality that are still very much in use in both the clinic and the laboratory. Thus, Allport's influence has been keenly felt in psychology, and he has received nearly every honor the field has to offer.

The life of Allport (1897–1967)

Born in Montezuma, Indiana, Allport was the youngest of four sons. His father had been a businessman who turned to medicine rather late in life, opening a private practice when Allport was born. In fact, Allport believed that his own delivery was his father's first case. As the youngest child, Allport seemed to go very much his own way; he was too young to be a playmate to his brothers.

Allport was apparently isolated from children outside the family as well. "I fashioned my own circle of activities. It was a select circle, for I never fitted the general boy assembly." He described himself as an isolate who was skillful with words but not at sports or games and who worked hard at being the center of attention of the few friends he did have.

In spite of being "uninspired and uncurious," he stood in second place in his high school graduation class of 100. But he had no firm idea of what to do next. Finally, at the end of the summer of 1915, he applied to Harvard. Having barely passed the entrance exam, Allport entered Harvard, where, he wrote, "almost overnight my world was remade." The next four years were a time of great adventure and excitement, as whole new worlds of intellect and culture opened up to him. He was shocked by the low grades he received on his first exams, and so he doubled his efforts and finished the year with straight As.

Allport's interest in social ethics and social service, acquired initially from his parents, was reinforced at Harvard, where he engaged in extensive volunteer work with a boy's club, with factory workers, and with foreign students. He was also a volunteer probation officer for a time. He found these social-service activities extremely satisfying, in part because he genuinely liked to help people but also because "it gave me a feeling of competence (to offset a generalized inferiority feeling)." He felt that this kind of service to others reflected his search for a personal identity (Allport, 1967, pp. 4–7).

He took a number of undergraduate courses in psychology but did not intend a career in the field. When he graduated from Harvard, he had no definite idea of what he would do with his life. To see if he liked teaching, he accepted a position at Robert College in Istanbul, Turkey. He enjoyed the year very much, decided that he liked teaching, and so accepted a fellowship offered him by Harvard for graduate study in psychology.

Traveling back to the United States, he stopped in Vienna to visit with a brother. While there, he wrote to Freud and received an invitation to visit the great man. When Allport entered Freud's office, he found Freud sitting silently, waiting for the young American to tell him the purpose of his visit. The silence wore on, and suddenly Allport blurted out an incident that had taken place on the streetcar ride to Freud's office. He told of watching a small boy who had an obvious fear of dirt. Everything seemed dirty to the boy; he changed his seat and told his mother not to let a "dirty man" sit next to him.

When Allport finished the story, Freud looked at the prim and proper young man and said, "And was that little boy you?" Freud was expressing his belief that whatever people said or did betrayed their own inner conflicts and fears. Some psychologists believe that Freud's question to Allport was full of insight and much to the point. "Allport was indeed a person who was neat, meticulous, orderly and punctual—possessing many of the characteristics associated by Freud with the compulsive personality" (Pervin, 1984b, p. 267).

Allport was shaken by Freud's question and managed to change the subject, but the incident left a deep impression on him. He began to suspect that psychoanalysis explored the unconscious too deeply and to believe that it should pay more attention to visible or surface motives. This was the path he was to follow in his own theory of personality.

He completed his Ph.D. in 1922, after two years of graduate study, which, incidentally, he felt was "not nearly stiff enough" (Allport, 1967, p. 8). His thesis presaged his lifelong work on personality and was entitled "An Experimental Study of the Traits of Personality." The thesis was the first study in America on personality traits.

After receiving his degree, Allport spent two years traveling in Europe on a fellowship. When he returned to Harvard to teach, he offered a course on the psychological and social aspects of personality, which he said was probably the first course ever given in personality in the United States. He stayed at Harvard for two years, during which time he married, and then accepted a position at Dartmouth College, where he remained for the next four years.

He taught, studied, and worked in social psychology as well as in personality and produced a number of important papers, articles, and psychological tests, including the famous Allport-Vernon-Lindzey Study of Values and the A–S (ascendance–submission) Reaction Study. The rest of his career, from 1930 until his death in 1967, was spent at Harvard, where he influenced several generations of students through his popular undergraduate course and his graduate seminars.

He became an elder statesman in psychology, and his awards were many: the Gold Medal of the American Psychological Foundation, the Distinguished Scientific Contribution Award of the American Psychological Association, and the presidencies of the American Psychological Association, the regional Eastern Psychological Association, and the Society for the Psychological Study of Social Issues.

One of Allport's major propositions is that psychologically healthy people are divorced from and uninfluenced by the motivations and experiences of childhood. Perhaps reflecting this belief, Allport has told us relatively little about the first 18 years of his life. However, what he did reveal shows a parallel between his early experiences and his later theory.

Out of his childhood conditions of isolation and rejection, he developed a feeling of inferiority, which he attempted to compensate for by trying to be a star. He talked about the "self-seeking and vanity" that grew out of his inferiority feelings with respect to his older brothers and to other children. As he grew older, he began to identify more and more with his oldest brother, Floyd, perhaps out of envy of his brother's accomplishments. So strongly did he desire to be like Floyd that he followed in his footsteps, enrolling in the same university (Harvard), studying the same subject (psychology), and obtaining the same degree (Ph.D.). Floyd Allport also became a noted psychologist.

George Atwood and Silvan Tomkins suggested that because Allport was so strongly guided by his emulation of his brother, his own identity was endangered (Atwood & Tomkins, 1976). To assert his individuality, he had to negate his identification with his brother by declaring that his own motivations and interests were autonomous or independent of their childhood origins, an idea he formalized as functional autonomy, a concept that rules out any influence from childhood experiences. In his theory, as in his own life, Allport stressed the uniqueness of each person; it took Allport many years to find such an identity for himself.

The nature of personality: Consciousness, growth, and uniqueness

Allport reviewed some 50 different ways of defining personality before offering his own definition: "Personality is the dynamic organization within the individual of those psychophysical systems that determine his characteristic behavior and thought" (Allport, 1961, p. 28). We can best analyze his definition by elaborating upon certain key concepts within it.

By *dynamic organization*, he means that while personality is constantly changing and growing (dynamic), it is nevertheless an organized growth. Also, the form of the organization changes, as do specific aspects of the personality.

Psychophysical means that personality is composed of a mind and a body acting in concert and as a unit. Personality is neither all mental nor all biological, but a combination of the two. Allport believed that our knowledge of the mental side of personality was far advanced over our knowledge of its biological composition. As a result, a psychological approach to the study of personality may be much more fruitful than a biological approach, at least until such time as we know more about the functioning of the brain.

The third key term is *determine*, by which he meant that "personality *is* something and *does* something" (Allport, 1961, p. 29). All facets of personality, in other words, activate and/or direct highly specific behaviors and thoughts.

The phrase *characteristic behavior and thought* means that everything an individual does or thinks is characteristic of that person. Every person is thus unique and like no other.

A major point of support offered by Allport for his stress on uniqueness is that we are so much the product of the laws and form of our heredity and environment. Heredity provides the personality with its raw materials, which are then shaped (stretched or limited) by the conditions of the person's environment. These raw materials, according to Allport, consist of physique, intelligence, and temperament. Temperament involves one's general emotional tone, including how susceptible one is to stimulation and the fluctuation and intensity of one's moods.

It is this genetic background and the raw material of the personality that it provides that is responsible for the major part of a person's uniqueness. There are, after all, an infinity of possible gene combinations, and the chance that one's genetic endowment would be duplicated in someone else is, except in the case of identical twins, too small to warrant consideration. This individual combination of genes then interacts with one's environment—and no two people, even siblings in the same house, have precisely the same environment—to produce the inevitable result: a unique individual.

In studying personality, therefore, psychology must deal with the individual case—an approach Allport called *idiographic*. The opposite of the idiographic or individual approach is the *nomothetic* approach, which studies large numbers of subjects, describes them in terms of averages, and offers laws that explain the behavior of all people. (Murray also distinguished between the two approaches, but it was Allport who first introduced the approach to psychology.) Other areas of psychology, Allport said, may legitimately use the nomothetic approach, but the only way to study personality is idiographically, because each personality is unique and cannot be compared with any other.

But what of similarities? Surely there are certain broad similarities among those in the same culture or the same age-group or, on a larger scale, in the same species? Allport, of course, agreed with this point; it would be difficult not to. However, he insisted that a person can be effectively described independently of forces such as society or culture. Culture certainly influences behavior, in that it sets the limits or ranges of one's activities, but there remains a great deal of latitude for individuality within those limits.

A final point to be made about Allport's view is that he considered personality to be discrete or discontinuous. Not only is each person set apart from every other, but each person is also divorced from his or her own past. There is no continuum of personality between childhood and adulthood. The infant is driven by primitive drives and behaves primarily in terms of reflexes. The adult operates on an entirely different level, so that there are, in a sense, two different personalities. There is a world of childhood and a world of adulthood, one more biological in nature, the other more psychologically based. One does not grow out of the other. An adult's functioning is not constrained by his or her past.

We have, then, quite a distinctive picture of the nature of personality: an overall stress on the conscious as opposed to the unconscious, a stress on the present and the future rather than the past, a focus on the individual case rather than on generalities and similarities over all people, and a focus on the normal rather than the abnormal. Let us now examine other, more specific features of the "dynamic organization within the individual" that is personality, in the view of Gordon Allport.

Personality traits

The study of personality traits was of long and abiding interest to Allport. His Ph.D. dissertation dealt with traits and was the first such study done anywhere in the United States. Allport defined **traits** as predispositions to respond, in the same or similar manner, to different kinds of stimuli. Traits are consistent and enduring ways of reacting to the stimulus aspects of our environment. Allport summarized the characteristics of traits as follows:

1. Personality traits are real. They are not just theoretical constructs or labels conjured up to account for or explain certain behaviors. They exist inside each person.
2. Traits determine or cause behavior, guiding its course. Traits do not come into existence only in response to appropriate stimuli. They direct us to seek out certain stimuli.
3. Traits can be demonstrated empirically. Because traits are real, it should be possible to verify their existence and nature, even though the traits themselves cannot be seen. By observing a person's behavior over time, we can infer evidence of traits in the coherence and consistency of that person's responses.
4. Traits are not rigidly separated from one another, only relatively so. Traits may overlap; although they represent different characteristics, they often correlate highly with one another. For example, aggressiveness and hostility are separate traits, but they are also closely related. They are frequently observed to occur together in a person's behavior.

Early in his career, Allport spoke of two categories of traits: individual and common. As you might suspect, *individual traits* are unique to the person and define the nature of his or her individual character. *Common traits* are those shared by a number of people, such as the members of a culture.

Common traits are abstractions, in that they reflect social mores and values and result from social pressure to behave in a certain way. Allport did not consider them to be basic traits, belonging to the individual. Rather, they are surface manifestations only. The individual is not deeply committed to the common traits; they do not define specifically one person's personality as opposed to another. Allport noted, as evidence for the ephemeral nature of common traits, the fact that they can and often do change as social standards or mores change.

Because of the possible confusion that can result from calling both of these phenomena traits, Allport later revised his terminology and called common traits simply *traits* and individual traits **personal dispositions**. Both are still traits, of course. They are "neuropsychic structures," in Allport's words, and serve to initiate as well as guide behavior. The definitions he provided for traits and personal dispositions are almost identical, except that the phrase *peculiar to the individual* is added to the definition of personal dispositions.

Once an observer has inferred the existence of a trait, the label he or she attaches to it may be arbitrary, according to Allport, as long as it is not deliberately misleading. To help in the naming of traits, Allport presented a list of some 18,000 trait labels (for those at a loss for words). Some examples of Allport's traits are dominance, submission, neuroticism, authoritarianism, masculinity or femininity, and conformity.

Allport was careful to distinguish what he considered traits from other personal characteristics that are also capable of initiating and guiding behavior—specifically, habits and attitudes.

Habits and attitudes

Habits obviously have a determining influence on behavior. You have only to look at your own habits to see how they affect the way you behave. Habits, however, are much more narrow and limited influences than are traits. They are also inflexible, involving a specific response to a specific stimulus. A trait or personal disposition is much broader because it arises from the integration of a number of individual habits that have in common the performance of the same adaptive function for the person. A number of habits may thus blend or fuse to become a single trait.

Allport offered the example of a child learning to brush his or her teeth twice a day. After a while, the behavior becomes automatic (habitual). The child also learns to wash his or her hands after going to the toilet and before eating. These behaviors, and others serving the same function (cleanliness), become so many separate habits all directed toward the same purpose. All of them taken together form a trait of the person: cleanliness.

Allport noted that it is often more difficult to distinguish between a trait and an **attitude**. Consider, for example, patriotism. Is it a trait fostered by the mores of a culture, or is it an attitude directed toward one's country? Other terms, such as authoritarianism or extraversion, could also just as easily be called either traits or attitudes. Allport does not resolve the question, except by noting that in cases such as these it does not make any difference which label we apply to them; both are appropriate.

However, it is possible, in general, to distinguish between traits and attitudes in two ways. First, attitudes always have very specific objects of reference. A person has an attitude toward something: blond-haired people, or a particular teacher, or school, or pine trees. A trait is not so specifically directed to a single object or even to a class of objects. A person described as extremely shy (a personal disposition) would behave in the same way toward blonds, redheads, and brunettes. Traits, then, are much broader in scope.

The second point of distinction between traits and attitudes is that attitudes are either for or against something—positive or negative. They lead a person to like or hate, accept or reject, or approach or avoid the object. An attitude involves an evaluation, pro or con, which a trait does not.

Not all traits are of the same intensity or significance in an individual. Some are more masterful, meaningful, or powerful than others. Allport posited three types: cardinal, central, and secondary traits.

A **cardinal trait** is one that is so pervasive, general, and extremely influential that every aspect of a person's life is touched by it. A cardinal trait is so powerful that a person is truly dominated by it; every act is influenced by it. Allport called such a trait a "ruling passion," "a master sentiment," and gave as examples sadism and chauvinism. Not everyone, of course, has such ruling passions.

Less general and pervasive are the **central traits**, which everyone possesses in small numbers—between five and ten in the average individual, according to Allport. Central traits are the kinds of characteristics one would mention in writing a letter of recommendation; they are the handful of themes that describe a person's behavior, such as aggressive, self-pitying, sentimental, or cynical.

The least important and least general kind of trait is the **secondary trait**, which is displayed less conspicuously and less consistently than the other types. Secondary traits may be so seldom displayed or so slightly revealed that only a very close friend might notice them.

Personality and motivation

Allport believed that the central problem in any theory of personality is how it handles the concept of motivation. Indeed, he felt that a personality theory could stand or fall on the adequacy of its treatment of what motivates the individual. However, he acknowledged that no approach to motivation then available was fully adequate, even his own.

Allport began his analysis of motivation by laying down four requirements that a theory of motivation should meet. First, the theory must focus on the *contemporaneity* of motivation. As we have seen, Allport stressed the present in his approach to the understanding of personality, and this emphasis on immediacy is a central part of his theory of motivation. It is the present state of the individual—not what happened during toilet training or at the time of weaning—that is central. Whatever happened in the past is exactly that: past. It is no longer active. A person's past motivation explains nothing, unless it exists as a present or current motivating force.

The second requirement for a motivational theory is that it be *pluralistic*, recognizing the existence of many different types of motives. Human motivation is so vastly complex, Allport argued, that it is oversimplifying to reduce it to only a few drives, such as pleasure seeking, tension reduction, or needs for power or security. There is such a diversity of motivating forces that it is difficult to find a common thread among them, an overall drive that can include all the individual ones. Some motives are temporary, appearing once and never again, others recur from time to time, and still others are persistent and always at work. Some are conscious, others are unconscious, and so on. It is not possible, Allport insisted, to reduce this complexity to a simple model.

The third requirement of a motivational theory is that it consider the importance of *cognitive processes*—specifically, the individual's conscious plans and intentions. Allport was sharply critical of approaches to personality such as Freud's that stressed irrational and unconscious aspects of motivation at the expense of the rational and conscious. Deliberate, conscious intention, he believed, is an essential aspect of human personality. What a person wants and is striving to accomplish is the most important key we have to understanding the person's present behavior. Thus, Allport explained the present in terms of the future (intentions), rather than in terms of the past.

The final requirement for a motivational theory is that it recognize the *concrete uniqueness* of motivating forces. A motive must be defined concretely rather than abstractly. An abstract view of motives deals with personality or motivation in general, not with the individual case. Allport offered the following example to show the difference between a concrete motive and an abstract motive.

> *Concrete*: Mary has a strong desire to become a professional nurse.
> *Abstract*: She is cathecting an aim-inhibited sexual wish.

The concrete description is tied directly to the individual case. The abstract motive in the example could be applied by a Freudian to any number of cases to explain any number of behaviors.

Not surprisingly, the four characteristics Allport considered necessary to a motivational theory are accounted for by his own concept of motivation, known as functional autonomy.

The functional autonomy of motives

Allport was careful to point out that the concept of functional autonomy does not explain all human motivation. However, he believed that it recognizes the true nature of adult motivation more effectively than other approaches do.

Functional autonomy is really a simple concept. It says that a motive, in the normal, mature adult, is not functionally related to past experiences in which it may have originally appeared. The motive has become autonomous, independent of its original circumstances. Put another way, the means used to achieve an earlier goal become an end in themselves.

The same thing happens, in principle, with motives as happens with an individual as he or she becomes independent of the parents. The person becomes self-determining—historically related to the parents but no longer functionally related, in that they no longer control or guide his or her life. To give another example from Allport: it is obvious that the growth and development of a tree can be traced back to its seed. Yet, when the tree is fully grown, the seed is no longer necessary as a source of nourishment. The tree is now self-determining—no longer functionally related to its seed.

And so it is with motives. Consider a young man embarking on a career in business. He is poor, and so he works very hard, investing all of his energy in his work. Thirty years later, the hard work has paid off. He is financially secure and has enough money to live comfortably for the rest of his life without working anymore. Yet he continues to work just as hard at 50 as he did at 20. Such behavior can no longer be for the same goal; that goal has long ago been reached and surpassed.

The drive to work hard, once a means to a specific end (money), has now come to be an end in itself. The motivation is independent of its original source.

There are many other examples that could be given: a skilled craftswoman who insists on doing the best job possible, even when her extra concern brings in no additional money, or a miser who continues to live in a slum while he hoards his vast pile of money. In all such cases, the original motive is transformed into something else. A behavior that once satisfied some specific drive or need now serves only itself.

The adult motive, then, cannot be understood by exploring the childhood of the person. The only way to understand the motivation of the adult is to investigate why he or she now behaves in a certain way.

Some years after initially formulating the notion of functional autonomy, Allport elaborated upon his position somewhat and proposed two different levels of autonomy.

Allport called these two levels of autonomy perseverative functional autonomy and propriate functional autonomy. *Perseverative autonomy* is the more elementary and basic of the two types and is concerned with such behaviors as addictions and repeated physical movements—for instance, a child's performance of an act over and over again or an adult's routine and habitual way of performing everyday tasks. They are behaviors that once served a purpose but no longer do so and that are at too low a level to be considered an integral part of the personality itself.

Allport cited as supporting evidence for this kind of autonomy both human and animal examples. For instance, when a rat that is well trained to run a maze for food is given more than sufficient food, it may still run the maze, obviously for some purpose other than food. At the human level, he cited examples of our preference for the routine and the familiar. The behavior continues or perseveres on its own, without any external reinforcement.

Allport considered *propriate functional autonomy* to be by far the more important of the two and absolutely essential to the understanding of motivation in the mature adult. The word *propriate* derives from Allport's term for the ego or self: the *proprium* (to be discussed later in this chapter). Propriate autonomy, therefore, is directly and intimately related to the very core of the personality, and it describes the status of interests, sentiments, values, attitudes, intentions, and one's self-image and lifestyle.

Propriate motives are specific to the individual, unique and highly necessary to the ego, or proprium, which determines which motives are maintained and which are discarded. For example, those motives that enhance or enrich one's self-esteem or self-image are kept. Because of this, Allport noted, there is usually a direct relationship between a person's interests and his or her abilities; people enjoy doing what they do well.

He pointed out that the original motivation for learning a skill—say, playing the piano—may have nothing at all to do with the person's interests. As a child, a person may be forced, very much against his or her will, to practice. If, however, in spite of this initial resistance, the person becomes proficient at the piano, he or she may become totally committed to it. The original motive (perhaps fear of parental displeasure) has disappeared, and, once again, the means to an end has become an end in itself. Somehow, the behavior of playing the piano becomes necessary to the self-image, and so the behavior continues.

The propriate structure of a person—that is, our sense of ego or self—will determine how we perceive the world around us (what we will pick out to attend to), what we remember from our experience, and the tone and direction of our thought. In other words, all our perceptual and cognitive processes are highly selective, picking and choosing from the mass of stimulation available to us only that which is relevant to our interests and values. That we are perceptually selective is supported by a great deal of research in social psychology.

Propriate functional autonomy, then, is an organizing process that determines and maintains a person's sense of self. How it determines and organizes the personality is explained by Allport in three principles of propriate functional autonomy.

The first principle is that of *organizing the energy level*. While this principle does not explain how a motive develops (or, more correctly, how it is transformed from an earlier motive), it does try to account for the acquisition of new motives. New motives, or latent older motives, come to the surface out of necessity, to help consume excess energy that otherwise might be expressed in more destructive and harmful ways. For example, when a woman's children are grown and leave home for good, she may suddenly find herself with much extra time and energy, which must be channeled into new interests and motives.

The second principle, *mastery and competence*, refers to the high levels at which persons prefer to satisfy motives. It is not enough, Allport argued, to achieve at merely adequate levels. The normal, healthy adult is motivated to perform better and more efficiently—to increase his or her degree of competence and mastery.

The third principle of propriate autonomy is known as *propriate patterning*, which is basically a restatement of what was said earlier about propriate functional autonomy. Propriate motives are not all independent of one another; they are all dependent on the structure of the self, in which they are firmly anchored. Thus, as we noted, a person organizes or patterns his or her perceptual and cognitive processes around the self, keeping that which enhances the self and rejecting the rest. Propriate patterning is a striving for consistency and integration of the personality.

It was noted that Allport did not believe that absolutely every behavior or motive could be explained by his theory of functional autonomy. He listed eight kinds of behaviors or attributes that are not under the control of functionally autonomous motives.

1. Behavior arising from biological drives—for food, water, sleep, air, and so on
2. Reflex actions—blinking, knee jerk, digestive processes, and so on
3. Constitutional equipment—the fixed elements of body build, intelligence, temperament, and health
4. Habits, some of which are functionally autonomous, others of which have no motivational value at all
5. Behavior dependent upon primary reinforcement—behavior that is discon-

tinued in the absence of reinforcement (for example, when a child no longer goes to visit a neighbor after the neighbor has stopped giving the child cookies)
6. Infantilisms and fixations—when an adult continues to act out a childhood conflict
7. Some neuroses—those tied to a repressed incident in childhood, when the revealing of the incident leads to a cessation of the behavior
8. Sublimation—when the true motive is sublimated into another one

The proprium: The unique self

The **proprium** is Allport's term for the self or the ego, labels he rejected because of the diversity of meanings ascribed to them by other theorists. The word *proprium* can best be understood by considering its adjective form *propriate*, as in the word *appropriate*. The proprium includes all those aspects of personality that are distinctive and vital to the emotional life of an individual. The aspects encompassed by the proprium are unique to a person, setting the person apart from everybody else, and they unite his or her attitudes, perceptions, and intentions into a unified whole.

Allport discussed the nature and development of the proprium in terms of seven aspects or functions that develop gradually in stages until maturity is reached, at which time the proprium is fully developed (see Table 8.1).

Before the proprium begins to emerge, there is no sense or awareness of self. In very early infancy, there is not yet a separation of "me" from everything else—no

TABLE 8.1   The development of the proprium

Stage	*Development*
1. Bodily self	Stages 1–3 emerge during the first three years. In this stage, infants become aware of their own existence and distinguish their own bodies from objects in the environment.
2. Self-identity	Children realize that their identity remains intact despite the many changes that are taking place.
3. Self-esteem	Children learn to take pride in their accomplishments.
4. Extension of self	Stages 4 and 5 emerge during the fourth through sixth year. In this stage, children come to recognize the objects and people that are part of their own world.
5. Self-image	Children develop actual and idealized images of themselves and their behavior and become aware of satisfying (or failing to satisfy) parental expectations.
6. Self as a rational coper	Stage 6 develops during ages 6–12. Children begin to apply reason and logic to the solution of everyday problems.
7. Propriate striving	Stage 7 develops during adolescence. Young people begin to formulate long-range goals and plans.
Adulthood	Normal, mature adults are functionally autonomous, independent of childhood motives. They function rationally in the present and consciously create their own lifestyle.

sense of self-consciousness. The infant at this time simply receives sensory impressions from the external environment and reacts to them automatically and reflexively, with no sense of self to mediate between stimulation and response.

The first aspect of the proprium to develop is *bodily self*, when the infant begins to be aware of a "bodily me." For example, the infant begins to be able to distinguish between its fingers and an object it may be holding or manipulating.

Self-identity defines the second stage. It is marked by a sense of continuity of identity; that is, the child realizes that he or she remains the same person in spite of the great changes in growth and ability that are taking place. Greatly aiding the sense of self-identity is the child's learning his or her own name and gradually coming to see himself or herself as a distinct and continuous self.

Self-esteem refers to a growing sense of pride as the child learns that he or she is able to accomplish some things on his or her own. At this stage, the child wants to construct things and to explore and manipulate its environment, behaviors that can be destructive to the home. Allport viewed this stage as crucial. He noted that if parents frustrate this need to explore and manipulate, the emerging self-esteem can be thwarted and be replaced by feelings of humiliation and anger.

The fourth stage is *extension of self*, which involves the child's growing awareness of other objects and people in the world and the identification of some of them as belonging to him or her. For instance, the child begins to speak of "my house," "my parents," "my school," and so on.

A *self-image* develops next, and it incorporates how the child sees and would like to see himself or herself. These actual and ideal images develop from interaction with the parents, who make the child aware of their expectations and of the extent to which the child's behavior is satisfying (or failing to satisfy) these expectations.

The sixth stage is the *self as a rational coper*. This occurs when the child realizes that he or she has a rational ability that can be applied to the solving of problems. The child begins to see that he or she can handle problems in a rational and logical manner.

Propriate striving is the name of the final stage, which occurs when the person realizes the existence in himself or herself of long-range purposes, goals, and intentions. The individual's view is clearly toward the future, for which he or she now begins to plan. Allport believed that until a person begins to plan ahead to long-range goals, the sense of self cannot be complete.

The development of the proprium through these seven stages is gradual and lasts from infancy until sometime during adolescence. The stages occur at approximately the following ages: the first three stages (bodily self, self-identity, and self-esteem) take place during the first three years of life, self-extension and self-image occur from ages 4 to 6, rational coping from 6 to 12, and propriate striving during adolescence. All of these aspects are united under the term *proprium*.

As the proprium and its propriate functions become more and more fully developed, there gradually emerges a set of characteristic traits that distinguish the behavior of each person from that of every other individual.

Personality in childhood

In view of Allport's strong belief that there is a dichotomous rather than a functionally continuous relationship between the personality of the child and the adult—that the personality of the mature adult is more a function of the present and future than of the past—it is perhaps surprising to find any expression of interest on his part in childhood and the developmental aspects of personality. Yet, as we saw in the discussion of the proprium, Allport indicated recognizable changes in various aspects of personality as a function of the age of the individual. Further, one of his most important concepts—functional autonomy—involves a transformation of an original motive into an entirely new motive at a later time in life.

While Allport did discuss the development of personality, he did not do so in terms of a series of clear-cut steps in growth, except for the seven aspects of the proprium, which occur at well-defined ages. Rather, he presented us with a broadly stroked picture of the changes that take place from infancy through adolescence.

He described the infant as a purely pleasure-seeking, destructive, "unsocialized horror," totally selfish, impatient, and dependent. The genetic raw materials of physique, temperament, and intelligence—bases of an eventual personality—are present, but there exists in infancy little of what could be called a personality. The infant operates in accord with drives and reflexes concerned with reducing tensions and pain and maximizing pleasures.

Of vital importance during this period is the attainment of adequate affection and security, primarily from the mother. If the child is successful in having these needs met, then positive psychological growth will follow, along the lines noted in the discussion of the proprium. Motivations are free to be transformed into autonomous propriate strivings, selfhood and the ego begin to differentiate and grow, a network or pattern of personal dispositions is formed, and a mature, normal adult is the inevitable result.

Personality in adulthood

Under these conditions, the individual changes from a tension-reducing, biologically dominated organism to more of a psychological organism, in which motivations are divorced from those of childhood and become future-oriented and in which the characteristics of maturity develop. In this sense, then, the adult personality is discontinuous with that of the child. It grows out of childhood, to be sure, but is no longer dictated to or dominated by the nature of childhood drives.

That is what happens in the development of the normal personality—one whose needs for affection and security were well met in infancy. Quite a different picture emerges, however, in the case where those needs are thwarted and frustrated. In that situation, the child becomes insecure, aggressive, demanding, jealous, and totally self-centered. As a result, psychological growth is stunted and the person continues to function at the level of infantile drives and conflicts. Motives do not become functionally autonomous but continue to be tied to their original conditions. The proprium does not develop, nor do unique traits, and the personality as a whole remains undifferentiated, as it was in infancy.

Such a person, as an adult, is considered by Allport to be mentally ill. In this case, there is not a dichotomy between the personalities of adulthood and childhood. They remain one and the same in form. Allport was vague on the crucial question of whether such a person might be able to counteract or overcome unfortunate childhood experiences. He was much more interested in the positive growth of the normal, mature adult and had relatively little to say about the neurotic.

The final stage of normal development, the mature, healthy personality, is described in terms of six criteria.

1. Extension of the sense of self to persons and activities beyond the self
2. Warm relating of the self to others (intimacy, compassion, tolerance)
3. Emotional security (self-acceptance)
4. Realistic perception, the development of skills, and commitment to some form of work
5. Self-objectification (an understanding or insight into self and a sense of humor, which Allport considered the most striking correlate of insight)
6. A unifying philosophy of life, which directs all aspects of a person's life toward future goals

With the attainment of these criteria, the person has become autonomous of his or her infancy and childhood and is able to face the present and realistically plan for the future, without being victimized or imprisoned by the experiences of early years.

Allport's image of human nature

The quotation with which we opened this chapter—"As the individual matures, the bond with the past is broken"—tells us much about Allport's view of human beings. People (or at least normal, mature adults) are not inexorably tied to and irreversibly driven by the events of childhood. The neurotic, however, is very much a prisoner of early conflicts and experiences.

When we deal with the healthy adult, we find that Allport presented an optimistic picture, a view that depicts people as being in conscious control of their own lives. We are able to rationally attend to the present and plan for the future and to fashion our own identity. Allport stated that human beings are always in the process of *becoming*, by which he meant that each person can creatively design and implement a satisfactory style of life for himself or herself. The basic urge to become, to grow, to seek unity, and to find meaning is a given in human nature. Within the framework of this inherent need for autonomy, individuality, and selfhood, we each grow and develop through our own conscious, deliberate efforts. Growth is a fundamental law of life. We continually move forward, toward integrity and fulfillment. Thus, we are influenced much more by events of the present and our view of the future than we are by the past.

Allport took a moderate stance on the question of free will versus determinism. He granted us a great deal of free choice in our deliberate, conscious intentions for the future, but he also recognized that much of our behavior is determined by our traits. Once traits are formed, they are difficult (though not impossible) to change. On the nature–nurture issue, Allport believed that both heredity and environment influence the personality. Our genetic background is responsible for a significant portion of our personality because heredity provides the personality with its raw materials. However, these raw materials are then shaped by experience and by learning.

More than any theorist we have discussed, Allport saw each person as unique. Although common traits connote some degree of universality in our behavior, our individual traits or personal dispositions define our nature much more clearly.

The ultimate and necessary goal of life is not tension reduction, according to Allport, but rather the constant need for increases in tension, which impel us to seek new sensations and challenges. When one set of challenges has been met, we are motivated to seek another, in a never-ending process. What is rewarding to us is the achieving rather than the achievement itself, striving for the goal rather than reaching it. We always need new goals to pull us and to maintain a certain level of tension in the personality.

Allport's optimistic image of human nature was reflected in his personal liberal stance and his active campaign for social reform. The humanistic attitude expressed in his work was mirrored in his own nature. His colleagues and students tell us that he genuinely liked people and cared about them and that these feelings were reciprocated by those who knew him.

Assessment in Allport's theory

Allport wrote much more about the specific methods or techniques appropriate to the assessment of personality than have most other personality theorists. In one of his most popular books (*Pattern and Growth in Personality*, 1961), he devoted three long chapters to the topic. He noted that, despite the existence of so many techniques, there is no one best method. Personality is so complex that any and all legitimate methods must be employed.

To provide a general framework within which to assess personality, Allport described 11 different methods, all of which are subsumed under the basic method of all science: observation followed by interpretation. Allport used some of the 11 methods himself, suggesting that the others needed more careful study. The methods are:

1. Constitutional and physiological diagnosis
2. Sociocultural setting, membership, role
3. Personal documents and case studies

4. Self-appraisal
5. Conduct sampling
6. Ratings
7. Tests and scales
8. Projective techniques
9. Depth analysis
10. Expressive behavior
11. Synoptic procedures (combining information from a variety of sources in a synopsis)

Letters from Jenny

One of the techniques used by Allport was the **personal-document approach**. As the name suggests, this technique involves the study of diaries, autobiographies, letters, literary compositions—any written or spoken record of a person.

Allport considered such personal documents to be highly revealing records that "intentionally or unintentionally yield . . . information regarding the structure, dynamics, and functioning of the author's mental life" (Allport, 1942, p. xii). The most famous of these documents is a collection of 301 letters written by a middle-aged woman named Jenny over a period of 12 years (Allport, 1965). This kind of material is analyzed to determine the number and kinds of traits of the person in question.

The same sort of analysis can be performed with third-person material about an individual, such as that found in case histories and biographies. With both autobiographical and biographical material, it is a relatively simple procedure to have a group of judges read the material and note the number and kinds of traits they find in it. Given a reasonable degree of agreement among the judges, it is then possible to group individual judgments into a fairly small number of categories. Quite often in this approach, the agreement among judges is high, revealing a large element of consistency in their assessments. For example, in Allport's original research with the letters from Jenny, 36 judges yielded a total of almost 200 trait names. However, because so many of the trait terms given were synonymous, Allport was able to reduce that large number to eight categories: quarrelsome-suspicious, self-centered, independent-autonomous, dramatic-intense, aesthetic-artistic, aggressive, cynical-morbid, and sentimental (Allport, 1966, p. 7).

These categories, derived from analyses of Jenny's letters, describe the woman's personality in terms of the major traits she possessed. But how accurate is this list? Would another approach yield similar results?

One of Allport's students did a computer analysis in which each letter was searched to find categories of words that might indicate the existence of a particular trait (Paige, 1966). For example, all words expressing anger, rage, hostility, and aggression were coded together as comprising the trait of aggression. This approach is a more sophisticated, quantitative assessment technique, which, unlike Allport's analysis of the same letters, involves no subjective judgments.

The computer analysis yielded eight prominent traits in Jenny's personality: aggression, possessiveness, need for affiliation, need for autonomy, need for familial acceptance, sexuality, sentience, and martyrdom (Allport, 1966, p. 7).

Although there is a difference in terminology between these two lists—they do not duplicate each other exactly—Allport believed that there was a high degree of similarity between them. Because of that similarity, he contended that his subjective approach to personality assessment provided just as much information on traits as the more sophisticated and expensive computer analysis.

The Study of Values

Allport and two colleagues developed a psychological test, the Study of Values, to assess the values an individual holds (Allport, Vernon & Lindzey, 1960). Such personal values form the basis of a unifying philosophy of life, which we mentioned earlier as one of the six criteria for a mature, healthy personality. Values are traits, but they also represent a person's deeply held interests and motivations.

The values Allport proposed to assess were drawn from an earlier analysis of types of values undertaken by a European psychologist, Eduard Spranger, in the 1920s (Spranger, 1928). Allport subscribed to Spranger's belief that everyone possesses some degree of each of the values, but that one or two of them are dominant aspects of an individual's personality. These values are as follows.

1. *Theoretical*—concerned with the discovery of truth and characterized by an intellectual, empirical approach to life
2. *Economic*—concerned with what is practical, useful, and relevant
3. *Aesthetic*—concerned with artistic experiences and beauty
4. *Social*—concerned with human relationships and the love of others
5. *Political*–concerned with power and influence that is manifested in all activities, not just in politics
6. *Religious*—concerned with unity, harmony, and understanding of the world as a whole

The Study of Values is a self-report inventory containing 45 questions. Respondents indicate their degree of preference for or acceptability of the activity or point of view represented. The validity of the test has been established by comparing the performance of different occupational groups, all of which have scored in the expected directions. Business students, for example, scored highest on the economic scale, theological students on the religious scale, and art students on the aesthetic scale.

The test has proven to be a successful assessment device for research, guidance, counseling, and personnel selection purposes. Although it does not contribute to the empirical testing of Allport's theory of traits, it is nonetheless a useful outgrowth of that theory. Psychologist Jerome Bruner said of the test that it "really correlates with the things that matter in ordinary existence: the jobs you choose, the way you spend your free time, the friends you make, the stuff you read" (Bruner, 1983, p. 280).

Research in Allport's theory

Allport was openly critical of those who argued that the traditional techniques of science—the experimental and correlational methods—were the only legitimate research approaches to the study of personality. Not every aspect of personality, he argued, can be tested by these approaches. If we are to understand the nature of personality adequately, researchers must be more open and eclectic in their methodology.

Allport also opposed the application of methods used with disturbed individuals, such as the case-study and projective techniques, to the study of the normal personality. According to Allport, the case study, because it focuses intensively on one's past history, is of no value in understanding the normal individual whose personality is divorced from childhood influences.

Projective techniques such as the Thematic Apperception Test and the Rorschach Inkblot Test may present a highly distorted picture of the normal personality because they deal with the unconscious, with forces that play only a minor role in the normal person. More reliable information on inner processes can be obtained, Allport said, by simply asking people to describe themselves. In that way, they will reveal their major traits.

We noted that Allport favored the idiographic as opposed to the nomothetic approach to personality research. He argued that the nomothetic approach, in which means are compared among groups of subjects, reveals nothing about processes within an individual. Only idiographic research techniques can uncover information about the individual personality.

In general, the idiographic approach has not been in favor within psychology as a whole, even though two of the most influential experimental researchers in psychology's history, Ivan Pavlov and B. F. Skinner, favored the intensive study of a single subject. Both are noted for the rigor and precision of their research, yet neither used the group mean–comparison approach.

By this time you will have recognized that a number of personality theorists promoted the idiographic approach, including Freud, Jung, Adler, Horney, Fromm, and Murray. Erikson did to some extent, and so did the humanistic psychologists Carl Rogers and Abraham Maslow (see Chapters 11 and 12).

There is some indication that the idiographic approach has recently been gaining adherents. One personality researcher commented, "Over the past few years one has begun to see a reemergence of the term idiographic within personality" (Pervin, 1984a, p. 268).

Expressive behavior

Allport's most notable research was conducted on what he called **expressive behavior**, the behavior that expresses one's personality. He divided behavior into two types: coping and expressive. **Coping behavior** is oriented toward a specific purpose, consciously planned and formally carried out, determined by specific needs inspired by the situation, and ordinarily directed toward bringing about some change in the person's environment. Expressive behavior is quite the op-posite. It is more spontaneous, reflects basic aspects of the personality, is very diffi-cult to change, has no specific purpose, and is usually displayed without our being aware of it.

Allport offered the example of attending a lecture. The lecturer is actually communicating on two levels. The formal and planned level (coping behavior) in-cludes the content of his or her lecture. The informal and unplanned level consists of the lecturer's movements and tone of voice (expressive behaviors), which you observe while attending to the content of the lecture. Perhaps he or she is perspir-ing and flushed, speaks quickly in a shaky voice, repeats himself or herself, fidgets with a tie or earring, or walks back and forth. All of these are spontaneous behav-iors reflecting elements of the lecturer's personality.

By giving subjects a variety of tasks to perform, Allport was able to judge the consistency in their expressive movements over different situations (Allport & Ver-non, 1933). He found a high level of consistency in voice, handwriting, posture, and gestures and was able, on further analysis, to deduce the existence of certain traits, such as introversion–extraversion, from these expressive behaviors.

Other research on expressive behavior has shown that personality can be quite accurately judged on the basis of tape recordings and films of subjects and even, to some degree, handwriting. Our facial expressions, the tone of our voice, and our idiosyncratic gestures and mannerisms tend to give us away and communi-cate to a trained observer facets of our personality (Allport & Cantril, 1934; Estes, 1938).

Other than these studies on expressive behavior, Allport's theory has not stim-ulated research designed to test either the theory as a whole or any of its individual concepts.

Expressive behavior is a spontaneous reflection of our personality and is usually displayed without our being aware of it.

A final commentary

Allport's theory, so influential in psychology, is the first in our series not strongly influenced by or growing out of psychoanalysis. Allport is also our first theorist who was not himself psychoanalyzed and who did not provide therapy for the emotionally disturbed. His system, then, does not derive from long therapeutic sessions with neurotics. Because of the origins of his theory in an academic rather than an analytic setting, and because of the nature of the theory itself, it has been of great interest to academic psychologists concerned with the study of personality.

Psychologists rank Allport in 15th place in the ratings of the relative influence of 286 psychologists, and in 7th place among the personality theorists discussed in this book (Gilgen, 1982). His work is still frequently cited in the current literature on personality. He received many honors and awards from his peers and served as president of the APA.

In spite of this popularity, however, Allport's theory has not been very successful in stimulating research, for several reasons. His stress on idiographic research was generally against the main current of thought in contemporary psychology, which dictates that the only valid approach is to study large numbers of subjects and describe them in group terms through sophisticated statistical analyses. Allport's insistence on studying only healthy adult subjects is also at variance with the majority position in research in clinical psychology, which emphasizes the study of the neurotic and psychotic. Thus, there is virtually no research attempting to validate his theory.

Also, it must be said that it is difficult to translate some of Allport's concepts into specific terms and operations suitable for study by the more traditional research methods. How, for example, can one observe functional autonomy or propriate striving under laboratory conditions? How can one manipulate it in the laboratory in order to observe its effects or the effects of other variables on it?

Aside from the difficulties of experimentation, there are other criticisms of Allport's system, particularly of the concept of functional autonomy. Allport did not make clear exactly how an original motive is transformed into an autonomous one. By what process is an initial motive to work hard for money, for example, changed into a motive to work hard for its own sake when the person later becomes wealthy? Since the mechanism of transformation is not known, how, critics ask, can one predict which motives in childhood will turn out to be autonomous motives in adulthood?

Allport's conceptual focus on uniqueness is also criticized, the argument being that his position is focused so extremely on the individual that it is impossible to generalize from one person to another. The traditional approach in science is to seek uniformities and generalities. This is impossible, critics charge, when one focuses exclusively on the individual case.

Some critics argue that traits do not show the stability and consistency over time and in different situations that Allport claimed. They suggest that behavior changes too greatly from one situation to another to be attributable to such permanent behavioral dispositions as traits. This criticism is part of the continuing controversy cited in Chapter 1—whether personality in general is stable and consistent or whether it changes as a function of the situation.

Many psychologists also find it hard to accept Allport's statement of a discontinuity between child and adult, animal and human, and abnormal and normal. They point out that research on children, animals, and the abnormal has yielded much knowledge about the functioning of the normal adult.

Finally, we noted with earlier theorists the emphasis on social and cultural determinants of behavior. Not only in personality theory but in much of academic experimental psychology as well, there is a strong insistence on the role of the social environment in influencing behavior. Critics feel that this influence is not adequately recognized in Allport's theory.

In spite of these points of criticism, Allport's theory has been well recognized and received. His work has not been ignored by those studying and writing about personality, as has been the case with other theorists. Allport's approach to personality, his emphasis on the uniqueness of the individual, and his focus on the importance of plans and expectations for the future are clearly reflected in the work of the humanistic psychologists Rogers and Maslow.

Allport's books are written in a highly readable style, and the concepts are presented in a manner that has a common-sense feel and appeal for many readers. His approach to the definition and assessment of traits has found wide acceptance among psychologists; indeed, many feel it is his greatest contribution to the study of personality.

The major themes of Allport's theory, while criticized by some, are seen by others as positive contributions. It is argued that his emphasis on rational and conscious determinants of behavior is a useful alternative to the position that we are irrationally and unconsciously driven by uncontrollable forces. In the same vein, his view that we are shaped more by future events than by those of the past is looked upon with favor by those who see human nature in hopeful and humanistic terms.

Summary

Allport helped to bring the study of personality into the mainstream of scientific psychology. He disagreed with Freud on several points. Allport focused on the conscious instead of the unconscious; he believed that personality is guided more by the present and future than by the past; and he studied normal rather than pathological individuals. The most distinctive feature of Allport's approach is his emphasis on the uniqueness of the individual personality.

An embarrassing meeting with Freud influenced Allport and may have led him to minimize the importance of the unconscious. His concept of functional autonomy and his belief that adult motivations and interests were independent of their childhood origins may have derived from his need to negate his identification with his older brother.

Allport defined personality as the dynamic organization within the individual of those psychophysical systems that determine characteristic behavior and thought.

This means that personality is always changing, is composed of both mind and body, and determines all behavior and thought. Personality is a product of both heredity and environment and is divorced from childhood experiences. Allport's approach is idiographic (dealing with the individual case) rather than nomothetic (dealing with large numbers of subjects).

Traits are predispositions to respond in the same or similar manner to different stimuli. They are consistent and enduring ways of reacting. Traits are real, they cause behavior, and they can be demonstrated empirically. They are not rigidly separated from one another. Individual traits are unique to the person; common traits are shared by a number of people. Allport later labeled individual traits personal dispositions, neuropsychic structures that initiate and guide behavior.

Habits are narrower than traits and are inflexible, involving a specific response to a specific stimulus. Attitudes differ from traits in that they have specific objects of reference and are either for or against something.

Cardinal traits are all-powerful and pervasive. Central traits are less general and pervasive. Secondary traits are displayed less conspicuously and less consistently than the other two types.

A theory of motivation must meet four requirements: a focus on the contemporaneity of motivation, a pluralistic approach, a consideration of the importance of cognitive processes, and a recognition of the concrete uniqueness of motivating forces.

The concept of functional autonomy is that a motive in the normal adult is not functionally related to past experiences in which it originally appeared. Two levels of functional autonomy are perseverative functional autonomy (behaviors such as addictions and repeated physical movements) and propriate functional autonomy (interests, values, attitudes, intentions, lifestyle, and self-image related to the core of personality).

The three principles of propriate functional autonomy are (1) organizing the energy level, in which excess energy is channeled into new interests and motives; (2) mastery and competence, in which the adult is motivated to perform better and more efficiently; and (3) propriate patterning, in which the person strives for consistency and integration of the personality.

Behaviors not under the control of functionally autonomous motives include those arising from biological drives, reflex actions, constitutional equipment such as intelligence and temperament, habits, behaviors dependent upon primary reinforcement, infantilisms and fixations, some neuroses, and sublimations.

The proprium is the self or ego, and it develops in seven stages from infancy to adolescence. These stages are bodily self, self-identity, self-esteem, extension of self, self-image, self as a rational coper, and propriate striving.

An infant operates in accordance with drives and reflexes and has little, if any, personality. If the infant attains adequate affection and security, then positive psychological growth will follow and adult motivations will be divorced from those of childhood. If the infant fails to receive affection and security, psychological growth is stunted and the person continues to function at the level of infantile drives and conflicts.

The mature, healthy personality is characterized by an extension of the self to other people and to activities beyond the self, a warm relating of the self to others, emotional security, a realistic perception, the development of skills, a commitment to work, self-objectification, and a unifying philosophy of life.

Allport presented an optimistic image of human nature in which people are not driven by events of childhood, are in conscious control of their lives, creatively design a satisfactory style of life, and grow through an inherent need for autonomy, individuality, and selfhood.

Personality is partly determined by traits, genetic background, and childhood experiences, but these can be influenced by later experience and learning. The ultimate goal in life is the constant need for increases in tension that impel us to seek new sensations and challenges.

The personal-document approach to personality assessment involves the study of diaries, letters, and other personal records to uncover evidence of personality traits.

The Study of Values is a psychological test to assess six types of values: theoretical, economic, aesthetic, social, political, and religious.

Allport was critical of psychologists who used only the traditional methods of science and who applied techniques designed for disturbed individuals to the study of normal persons. The idiographic approach to personality, used by Pavlov, Skinner, and a number of personality theorists, seems to be gaining adherents.

Allport's research on expressive behavior revealed a consistency in expressive movements and showed that personality can be judged on the basis of such movements.

Allport's theory has been criticized for emphasizing idiographic research and the study of normal subjects only. There are difficulties in empirically testing such concepts as functional autonomy. Allport's focus on the uniqueness of personality, on the stability and consistency of traits over all situations, and on the discontinuity between the child and the adult has been questioned. Also, his lack of recognition of social influences on personality has been challenged.

Glossary

attitudes Similar to traits, except that attitudes have specific objects of reference and involve evaluations, that is, they are either positive or negative.

cardinal traits The most pervasive, general, and powerful category of traits.

central traits The handful of outstanding themes that describe an individual's behavior; less pervasive than cardinal traits.

coping behavior Consciously planned behavior, determined by the needs of the situation, designed for some specific purpose, usually to effect some change in the individual's environment.

expressive behavior Spontaneous, seemingly purposeless behavior, usually displayed without the individual's being aware of it.

functional autonomy of motives Motives in the normal,

mature adult that are independent of the childhood experiences in which they originally appeared.

habits   A specific, inflexible response to a specific stimulus; a number of habits may combine to form a trait.

personal dispositions   Traits that are peculiar to the individual, as distinguished from traits shared by a number of people.

personal-document technique   A method of personality assessment

that involves the study of a person's written or spoken records.

proprium   Allport's term for the self or ego.

secondary traits   The least important category of traits, inconspicuously and inconsistently displayed by an individual.

traits   Distinguishing characteristics or qualities of an individual that guide behavior and that can be measured on a continuum.

Review questions

1. Explain Allport's definition of personality. How does his view of personality differ from Freud's?
2. Describe four characteristics of traits. Distinguish between traits and attitudes.
3. In Allport's view, what is the relationship between personality and motivation?
4. What is the role of the cognitive processes in personality?
5. What is the relationship between adult motives and childhood experiences? What term does Allport use to describe this situation?
6. What is the proprium? Describe the seven stages in the development of the proprium.
7. What parental behaviors are necessary for positive psychological growth in childhood?
8. How does Allport's theory account for mental illness in adulthood?
9. What are the characteristics of the mature, healthy personality?
10. What is expressive behavior? Identify several behaviors that might express the personality traits of aggression and possessiveness.

Suggested reading

Allport, G. *Becoming: Basic considerations for a psychology of personality*. New Haven, CT: Yale University Press, 1955.

Allport, G. *Pattern and growth in personality*. New York: Holt, Rinehart & Winston, 1961.

Allport, G. Autobiography. In E. G. Boring & G. Lindzey, Eds., *History of psychology in autobiography*, vol. 5. New York: Appleton-Century-Crofts, 1967.

Allport, G. *The person in psychology: Selected essays*. Boston: Beacon Press, 1968.

Elms, A. C. Allport, Freud, and the clean little boy. *Psychoanalytic Review*, 1972–1973, 59, 627–632.

Evans, R. I., Ed. *Gordon Allport: The man and his ideas*. New York: Dutton, 1971.

Long, L. Alfred Adler & Gordon Allport: A comparison on certain topics in personality theory. *American Journal of Individual Psychology*, 1952–1953, 10, 43–53.

Maddi, S. R. & Costa, P. T. *Humanism in personology: Allport, Maslow, and Murray*. Chicago: Aldine-Atherton, 1972.

CHAPTER 9

Raymond Cattell

The life of Cattell (1905–)
The trait approach to personality
Source traits: The Sixteen Personality Factor Questionnaire
The dynamic organization of the personality
Chronic anxiety
The influences of heredity and environment
The stages of personality development
Cattell's image of human nature
Assessment in Cattell's theory
    Factor analysis
    Psychological tests
Research in Cattell's theory
A final commentary
Summary
Glossary
Review questions
Suggested reading

Personality is that which permits a prediction of what a person will do in a given situation.

RAYMOND CATTELL

$\mathbf{T}$he opening quote provides us with an indication of the general tone or theme of Cattell's view of the nature of personality and his approach to understanding it. His purpose or goal in studying personality is the prediction of behavior, of what a person will do in response to a particular stimulus situation. He expressed this view of personality mathematically, in the following equation:

$$R = f(P,S)$$

R stands for the response or reaction of the individual (what a person will do), S refers to a given situation or stimulus, and P stands for personality. Elements of the stimulus situation can be known and precisely defined. Indeed, in the laboratory, it is the experimenter who designs and sets up the stimulus situation. The unknown factor—or the one most difficult to know—is P, the structure and function of the personality.

In Cattell's approach to personality, there is no reference to changing or modifying behavior from undesirable to desirable or from abnormal to normal. That has been the aim of many of the previous theories discussed that were concerned with individuals in a clinical setting. The subjects or patients from which the more clinically oriented theories were derived had sought the services of a psychologist precisely because they were unhappy or disturbed by some aspect of their behavior, which they therefore wanted to change.

This is not the case with Cattell's subjects. They are normal individuals, whose personalities are studied, not treated. Cattell firmly believes that it is impossible (or at least very unwise) to attempt to change a personality before knowing in great detail what is being changed. A valid study of personality, then, must come first, and Cattell has been critical of clinicians who try to modify personality without knowing the exact nature of that which they are trying to modify.

Cattell's theory did not derive from a clinical frame of reference. Rather, his approach has been a rigorously scientific one, using extensive observations of behavior and collecting great masses of data on each individual. It is not unusual, in his studies, for more than 50 kinds of measurements to be made of each subject. Cattell's data come from questionnaires, objective tests and observations, and ratings of behavior as it occurs in real-life situations. The key aspect of Cattell's approach to studying behavior, and what makes it so totally different from all other approaches, is what he does with the huge amounts of data thus generated.

The data are subjected to the statistical process of **factor analysis**. In essence, this very complex procedure involves assessing the relationship between each possible pair of measurements taken from a group of subjects. Each pair of measurements (for example, scores on two different psychological tests or on two subscales of the same test) is analyzed to determine how highly the scores correlate with each other. In other words, a correlation coefficient is determined for each pair of measurements.

If two measures show a high correlation with each other, then it is assumed that they must be measuring related aspects of personality. To take a hypothetical case, if the guilt proneness and introversion subscales of a personality test yield a high correlation coefficient, then it is assumed that they both provide information on the same aspect or factor of personality. Thus, large amounts of data are statistically analyzed to determine these common factors (hence the term *factor analysis*).

Cattell calls these factors of personality **traits**, and this is the most important concept in his theory. He views traits as mental structures—the elements or component parts of personality. Only when we know which traits characterize an individual are we in a position to predict what he or she will do in a given situation. Cattell defines *trait* as a reaction tendency of a person that is a relatively permanent part of his or her personality. To fully understand a person, then, we must know in precise terms the entire pattern of traits that defines that person as an individual.

Cattell and his associates have devoted years of concentrated effort to isolating the factors or traits that underlie personality. It is difficult, detailed, tedious, and time-consuming work. In recent years, the use of computers has eliminated some of the drudgery but not the necessity for detailed attention.

Cattell's use of factor analysis is the strong point in his system as well as the reason that the theory has not received wider recognition in psychology. Psychologists not adequately trained in this highly sophisticated technique find it difficult to evaluate Cattell's approach. Further, this lack of adequate comprehension of factor analysis means that psychologists often neglect Cattell's theory in their teaching.

There is also the matter of the sheer volume of research data produced by Cattell and his associates. The amount is overwhelming, and considerable time and effort are required to pull from it an understanding of the findings. A mere glance at the lengthy list of Cattell's publications can easily instill a sense of the futility of trying to come to grips with it, however meaningful it might ultimately prove in the study of personality. And that is precisely the kind of attitude about which Cattell legitimately complains. Difficult though his system may be, it is much too important to ignore in any presentation of the variety of approaches available for understanding personality.

The life of Cattell (1905–   )

Cattell was born in England, where he had, by his own account, a happy childhood and youth, both at home and at school, an unusual situation for a personality theorist. His parents were exacting about the standards of performance they expected from their children but permissive regarding how the children spent their time. Cattell and his brothers and friends spent a great deal of time outdoors, sailing, swimming, exploring caves, and fighting mock battles over terrain in which they "occasionally drowned or fell over cliffs."

When Cattell was 9, England entered World War I, an event that profoundly influenced him. A mansion near his home was converted into a hospital, where Cattell saw trainloads of wounded men coming directly from the battlefields of France. As a result of this experience, he wrote, he became unusually serious for a young boy and aware of the "brevity of life and the need to accomplish while one might." His later amazing dedication to his work and the intensely long hours that he devoted to it may well have had their origins in these times (Cattell, 1974a, pp. 62–63).

And these characteristics of Cattell may also have been reinforced by his competition with his older brother. He wrote of the problems of trying to maintain his own freedom of development in the face of a brother three years his senior who could not be "overcome."

At the age of 16, Cattell entered London University to study what had interested him since boyhood—physics and chemistry. He graduated at 19 with high honors, but his years in London had intensified an already strong interest in social problems. He became increasingly concerned with social ills and realized that his training in the physical sciences did not equip him to deal with such problems. He concluded that the only recourse available to him was to study the human mind itself.

It was something of a courageous decision to make at that time in England (1924), because psychology was regarded as a discipline for "cranks" and there were few professional opportunities in the field. In all of England there were only six professorships in psychology. Against the advice of all his friends, Cattell began graduate studies at the University of London, under the eminent psychologist-statistician Charles E. Spearman, the man who developed the technique of factor analysis.

Awarded his Ph.D. in 1929, Cattell found that his friends had been correct—there were no jobs for psychologists—and so he took several fringe jobs, as he called them, in psychology. He lectured at Exeter University and set up a psychological service and clinic in the school system of the city of Leicester, all the while continuing to conduct research and to write. He had resolved to apply the method of factor analysis—which Spearman had used successfully to uncover the structure of human abilities—to the study of the structure of personality, a monumental task never before undertaken.

During the first year after receiving his Ph.D., Cattell became ill with a chronic stomach condition, the result of too much work, poor food, and poor living conditions. To compound his difficulties, there was the worldwide economic depression, and a few years later his wife left him because of their poverty-ridden circumstances and his total absorption in his work. Yet, through all this adversity, his single-minded devotion to the task of understanding the structure of personality never wavered.

He also derived, according to his own account, some positive benefits from that long period of hardship: "Those years made me as canny and distrustful as a squirrel who has known a long winter. It bred asceticism, and impatience with irrelevance, to the point of ruthlessness" (Cattell, 1974b, p. 90). The experience also caused him to focus on practical issues and problems, rather than on purely theoretical or experimental issues, which he said he might have pursued had he been in more comfortable and secure circumstances. Here we see another example of the effect of personal experience on one's approach to the study of personality.

Finally, in 1937, full-time work in psychology was made available by an invitation from the prominent American psychologist Edward L. Thorndike to spend a year in his laboratory at Columbia University. It was a marvelous opportunity, even though it was difficult for Cattell to leave his native country. He said that he was continually depressed during his year in New York.

In 1938, Cattell became Professor of Psychology at Clark University in Massachusetts and in 1941 moved to Harvard, where, as he put it, "the sap of creativity" rose (Cattell, 1974a, p. 71). Finally, in 1945, when he was 40 years of age, he was able to settle down and organize his life totally around his research. His second wife was a mathematician who shared his research interests, and he moved to the University of Illinois, where he was granted a research professorship.

In the absence of teaching or other responsibilities, Cattell could at last devote his every effort to research. He worked at the laboratory until at least 11:00 every night and was generally so involved in an ongoing research project that he joked that he could easily find his car at night because it was the last one remaining in the parking lot. Since 1945, he has continued to work at almost the same pace, never taking sabbatical leave or spending a significant amount of time away from the laboratory. He has published more than 400 articles and 35 books, a monumental accomplishment reflecting his obvious dedication and perseverance. In his seventies, Cattell joined the graduate faculty of the University of Hawaii, where he swims in the ocean every day and works "at least as hard as an assistant professor up for tenure and not sure that it will be granted" (Johnson, 1980, p. 300).

As the capstone to his life of research, Cattell established the Institute for Research on Morality and Self-Realization in Boulder, Colorado, in 1973. In this non-profit organization, Cattell hopes to integrate his interest in science with his interest in social and religious issues. He is definitely not turning away from science, despite the possible incongruence of the word *morality* in the institute's name. He feels that he has developed a reliable framework with which to measure personality and motivation—a technique of measurement that will allow psychology to proceed as a science.

The trait approach to personality

Although other psychologists, notably Gordon Allport, developed theories of personality around the concept of traits, only Cattell has given us such a detailed analysis and classification of traits. Traits are the factors of personality culled (by the method of factor analysis) out of the great masses of measurements taken of human subjects. Traits are relatively permanent reaction tendencies of a person, and they form the basic unit of structure of an individual's personality. Only through a thorough knowledge of an individual's traits is it possible to predict what that individual will do in any given situation. A person's personality, then, can be viewed as a pattern of traits.

Cattell does not believe, as Allport did, that traits have a real existence within each person. He considers them to be hypothetical or imaginary constructs inferred from the objective observation of overt behavior. This does not diminish the importance of traits in Cattell's system, however. Traits are the basic elements of personality and are vital to any attempt to predict behavior.

There are several ways of classifying or grouping traits. For instance, Cattell distinguishes between common traits and unique traits (a distinction shared by Allport). A **common trait** is one that is possessed by everyone, to some degree. General mental ability or intelligence is a common trait. Everyone possesses it, although some people have more of it than others. Introversion and gregariousness are other examples of common traits. The reason for the universal existence of common traits is that all people share a more or less similar background of hereditary potential and are subjected to similar patterns of social pressure, at least within the same culture.

People differ from one another, of course, in that they possess different amounts or degrees of these common traits. But they differ even more because of their **unique traits**—traits shared by few or perhaps no other people. According to Cattell, unique traits are particularly apparent in the areas of interests and attitudes: one person has a consuming interest in an obscure species of butterfly, while another is passionately in favor of banning bare feet in public. Very few people would share these interests and attitudes.

A second way of classifying traits is by dividing them into ability traits, temperament traits, and dynamic traits. The way that these three kinds of traits differ is in the modality through which they are manifested or expressed. **Ability traits** determine how efficiently a person will be able to work toward a goal. **Temperament traits** define the general style and tempo of behavior, while the **dynamic traits** are concerned with the motivations or driving forces of human behavior.

An example of an ability trait is intelligence. One's level of intelligence determines how effectively a goal—say, a college degree—is striven for. Temperament traits include how high-strung, bold, easygoing, or irritable a person is. These traits influence the way in which a person works or acts—the style of his or her behavior. Dynamic traits are concerned with motivations and interests, including factors such as ambition and interest in acquiring knowledge or material possessions. The dynamic traits are emphasized in Cattell's system, and we will discuss them in greater detail later.

A third way to classify traits is in terms of the difference between surface traits and source traits. A **surface trait** is a set of personality characteristics that show a correlation with one another but do not form a factor because they are not determined by a single source. In other words, various personality characteristics are seen to be complementary because of the overlap of several influences. In a normal individual, Cattell refers to this overlap of influences as a surface trait. In an abnormal personality, he calls it a *syndrome*.

For example, several elements of behavior—such as anxiety, indecision, and irrational fears—may cluster together to form the surface trait of neuroticism. Thus, the trait of neuroticism is due to a cluster of several elements; it does not derive from any single one. Because they are composed of several elements, surface traits are less stable and permanent in nature and are therefore considered by Cattell to be less important in the understanding of personality.

Of greater importance in Cattell's view, and much more stable and permanent, are the **source traits**, which are unitary or single factors, each of which is the sole source of some aspect of behavior. Source traits are the individual factors that derive from factor analysis and that, in combination, account for some surface trait. Source traits, therefore, are the basic elements of personality as we defined factors or traits in the beginning of this section. Examples of source traits will be seen in the list of Cattell's personality factors, to be discussed shortly.

Source traits can be divided into two types—constitutional traits and environmental-mold traits—according to their origins. The labels define the sources. **Constitutional traits** have their origin in the internal conditions of the organism. These traits are not necessarily innate (although they may be, in some cases) but do depend on the physiology of the organism. For example, the use of alcohol can yield a number of influences on human behavior, such as carelessness, talkativeness, and slurring of words—characteristics that factor analysis would indicate to be source traits.

Environmental-mold traits derive from influences in the social and physical environment. These traits are learned characteristics and ways of behaving, and they form a pattern that is imposed and imprinted on the personality by one's environment. For example, a person who grows up in an inner-city ghetto behaves differently from one raised in upper-class luxury; a career military officer shows a different pattern of behavior from a jazz musician.

Now that we have noted the ways in which traits can be classified, it is time to consider the traits themselves.

Source traits: The Sixteen Personality Factor Questionnaire

After more than two decades of intensive factor-analytic research, Cattell identified 16 basic factors, or source traits, that he was convinced constituted the building blocks of personality. These factors are perhaps best known in the form in which they are most often used—in an objective test of personality called The Sixteen P. F. Test (P. F. stands for Personality Factor) (Cattell, Eber, & Tatsuoka, 1970). This test, along with several others Cattell designed, has proved to be very useful and popular in both applied and research settings. The Sixteen P. F. Test has been used to profile such diverse personalities as the creative, the neurotic, and the psychosomatic, to predict the possibility of heart attacks in men, and to measure human sexual response to pornographic pictures. It is also used to predict accident proneness, scholastic performance, and occupational success in a number of kinds of jobs. Cattell's tests, while useful in psychology, are important to their author only as outgrowths of his factor-analytic studies. He makes it clear that he has little personal interest in psychological tests in general.

The traits listed below are in dichotomized, or bipolar, form. Thus, a low score on a particular factor indicates the presence of some characteristic, just as a high score does (Cattell, 1970).

A person with a low score on this factor is described as:

A person with a high score on this factor is described as:

Factor A
Reserved, detached, critical, aloof, stiff

Outgoing, warmhearted, easygoing, participating

Factor B
Less intelligent, concrete-thinking

More intelligent, abstract-thinking, bright

Factor C
Affected by feelings, emotionally less stable, easily upset, changeable

Emotionally stable, mature, faces reality, calm

Factor E
Humble, mild, easily led, docile, accommodating

Assertive, aggressive, stubborn, competitive

Factor F
Sober, taciturn, serious

Happy-go-lucky, enthusiastic

Factor G
Expedient, disregards rules

Conscientious, persistent, moralistic, staid

Factor H
Shy, timid, threat-sensitive

Venturesome, uninhibited, socially bold

Factor I
Tough-minded, self-reliant, realistic

Tender-minded, sensitive, clinging, overprotected

Factor L
Trusting, accepting conditions

Suspicious, hard to fool

Factor M
Practical, down-to-earth concerns

Imaginative, bohemian, absent-minded

Factor N
Forthright, unpretentious, genuine but socially clumsy

Astute, polished, socially aware

Factor O
Self-assured, placid, secure, complacent, serene

Apprehensive, self-reproaching, insecure, worrying, troubled

Factor Q_1
Conservative, respecting traditional ideas

Experimenting, liberal, freethinking

Factor Q_2

Group-dependent, a joiner and sound follower	Self-sufficient, resourceful, prefers own decisions

Factor Q_3

Undisciplined self-concept, lax, follows own urges, careless of social rules	Controlled, exacting will power, socially precise, compulsive

Factor Q_4

Relaxed, tranquil, unfrustrated, composed	Tense, frustrated, driven, overwrought

The four Q factors were derived from a factor analysis of other factors. Cattell has also developed second-, third-, and even fourth-order factoring, in which groups of factors or traits are factor analyzed. As a result, four composite second-order factors have been derived. The two principal second-order composites are *anxiety* and *extraversion–introversion*.

It is important to remember exactly what these factors or traits are in Cattell's system. They are the components, elements, or basic units of the personality, in the sense that atoms are the basic units of the material world. Cattell argues that we cannot generate laws about personality, nor can we fully understand it, without being able to define, in precise mathematical terms, the nature of these building blocks of the personality.

The dynamic organization of the personality

As noted earlier, the dynamic traits are directly concerned with motivation, a topic of central importance in almost every theory of personality. Cattell argues that a personality theory that does not take into account dynamic or motivating forces is incomplete and analogous to a description of an engine that does not take into account fuel.

There are two kinds of dynamic traits in Cattell's system—ergs and sentiments—both of which are manifested in attitudes. The word **erg** comes from the Greek *ergon*, which means work or energy, and is used by Cattell in place of the concepts of instinct or drive, which he feels are too vague. An erg is the energy source for all behavior; it is innate and therefore constitutionally derived. It is the basic unit of motivation and is directed toward specific goals. There are, of course, a wide range of behaviors that may lead to a goal, but the erg itself is primary and fundamental. Cattell's factor-analytic research has identified 11 ergs in humans, which are listed in Figure 9.1.

While an erg is a constitutional source trait, a **sentiment** is an environmental-mold source trait, which means that it derives from external social and physical influences. A sentiment is a pattern of attitudes one has learned; it is focused on important objects in one's life—for example, country, spouse, job, religion, hobby.

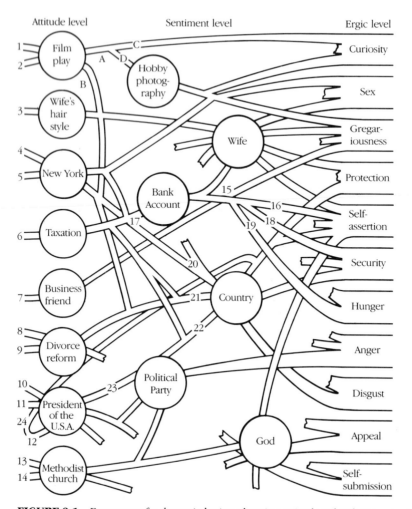

FIGURE 9.1   Fragment of a dynamic lattice, showing attitude subsidiation, sentiment structure, and ergic goals.   *Source: R. B. Cattell,* Personality *(New York: McGraw-Hill, 1950), p. 158. Copyright 1950 by Raymond B. Cattell. Reprinted by permission.*

Both ergs and sentiments serve to motivate behavior, but beyond that there is a vital difference between them. An erg, since it is constitutionally based, is a permanent structure, and while it can weaken or intensify, it cannot disappear altogether. Sentiments, which result from learning, can be unlearned and therefore can disappear, so that a particular sentiment may no longer be of any importance in a person's life.

An **attitude**, in Cattell's view, is a person's interest in some area, object, or person—an interest that will usually manifest itself in some form of overt behavior. As Cattell uses the term, it does not refer exclusively to an opinion for or against something, which is the traditional use of the word *attitude* in psychology. Cattell's definition of attitude is more inclusive, encompassing all of a person's emotions and actions toward an event or object.

Ergs, sentiments, and attitudes are related to one another through the concept of **subsidiation**, which simply means that some elements are subordinate to others in the system. Attitudes, for example, are subsidiary to sentiments, which, in turn, are subsidiary to ergs. And, at another level, one attitude can be subsidiary to a second (it *subsidiates* the other, to use Cattell's expression), which, in turn, subsidiates a third attitude. We may do one thing in order to do a second thing, with a view to accomplishing a third. Cattell gives the example of a young man who goes to college and studies accounting for the purpose of getting a job and earning a living so that he may have a wife and family.

The interrelationships of ergs, sentiments, and attitudes are expressed schematically in what Cattell calls the **dynamic lattice** (Figure 9.1.) The dynamic lattice is not really as forbidding as it might appear at first glance. The basic human motivations—the ergs—are listed at the right-hand side of the diagram. The large circles in the center are sentiments toward several aspects of this person's life. Note that each of the sentiments is subsidiary to one or more ergs. The sentiment toward bank account, for example, expresses two ergs: self-assertion and security. The sentiment toward wife expresses four ergs: sex, gregariousness, protection, and self-assertion. In other words, those four ergs energize this husband's sentiment toward his wife.

The smaller circles, on the left-hand side of Figure 9-1, are the attitudes—a person's emotions and actions toward an object. Each attitude is subsidiary to one or more sentiments; that is, one or more sentiments can be expressed in an attitude. For example, this man's attitude toward a business friend is linked to the sentiment toward bank account (perhaps the friend wants to borrow money or is trying to persuade him to invest in his business). Through the bank account sentiment, the attitude toward business friend expresses the ergs of self-assertion, security, and hunger. You can also see, by following the crisscrossing lines, that the attitude toward business friend directly expresses the erg of gregariousness.

Each person's set or pattern of sentiments is organized consistently through a master sentiment, which Cattell calls the self-sentiment. Perhaps the most important sentiment of them all, the **self-sentiment** refers to a person's conception of himself or herself, which is reflected in virtually all the attitudes he or she holds. It provides stability, coherence, and organization to all the source traits and is directly linked to the expression of the ergs and sentiments. If the self-sentiment were pictured in the dynamic lattice shown in Figure 9-1, it would appear to the far left of all the other sentiments, indicating that it is among the last of the sentiments to reach a full level of development. Because it contributes to the satisfaction of all the ergs and sentiments, the self-sentiment functions to control all the structures in the personality.

Chronic anxiety

Cattell places a strong emphasis on anxiety as an aspect of personality because of the harmful consequences it can exert on both mental and physical functioning. As he views it, anxiety is both a state of being and a trait of personality. That is, we may experience varying degrees of anxiety as a result of circumstances that we find threatening or stressful. In this case we would be in a state of anxiety. However, there are also people who are chronically anxious, in which case anxiety is a trait or factor of their personality.

While previous writings on the topic of anxiety have suggested its existence in a variety of forms, Cattell's factor-analytic research has identified anxiety as a unitary entity that encompasses five other factors. A person with chronic anxiety would be easily affected by feelings, be suspicious of others, be apprehensive and self-reproaching, have an inadequately formed self-concept, and be tense and excitable.

The influences of heredity and environment

Cattell has shown a much greater interest than most other personality theorists in the relative influences of heredity and environment in shaping personality. His method of investigating the importance of hereditary and environmental factors is known as Multiple Abstract Variance Analysis (MAVA), a technique that compares the extent of similarity found between twins raised in the same family, twins raised apart, non-twin siblings raised in the same family, and non-twin siblings raised apart. The result is an estimation of the extent to which differences in traits are due to genetic or to environmental differences.

On the basis of extensive research, Cattell has demonstrated a very important role for heredity, at least with some of the traits. For example, his data reveal that 80 percent of intelligence, 80 percent of venturesomeness versus shyness, and 30 percent of the dissatisfied emotionally traits can be accounted for by genetic rather than environmental influences. With some traits, heredity was found to be the dominant influence, a finding that led Cattell to argue strongly for the notion of selective breeding, which, at the very least, he contends, could lead to a more intelligent society. In general, Cattell believes that about one-third of personality is genetically determined and that about two-thirds is determined by environmental factors.

In his investigations of the influence of the environment on the individual, Cattell has studied not only a person's immediate environment but the larger social or cultural environment as well. In the same way that an individual can be described in terms of his or her traits, so a society can be described in terms of objective factors that compose it. The traits of a society, taken together, constitute what Cattell calls *syntality*, which refers to the relevant characteristics or attributes of a large social group. He argues that we must understand both the personality of the individual and the syntality of the groups that influence him or her (such as religion, peer group, school, and nation). Cattell described a number of factors that make up the syntality of small groups and also identified eight factors in the syntality of nations, including size, industriousness, enlightened affluence, and morale. No other personality theorist has made such a detailed objective analysis of the characteristics of a society and their effect on individuals.

The stages of personality development

Cattell divides the growth of the human personality into six stages, covering the full range of life, from birth through old age.

Infancy, lasting from birth until the age of 6, is the major formative period in the development of personality. During this stage, the individual is strongly influenced by parents and siblings and by the nature of his or her weaning and toilet-training experiences. As a result of these influences, primary social attitudes are formed, along with the stability and strength of the superego and the ego, the feeling of security or insecurity, the attitude toward authority, and the possible tendency to neuroticism. Cattell is certainly not a follower of Freud, but he did accept Freud's notion that the period of infancy is crucial in the formation of personality, and that oral and anal needs and conflicts may also affect personality.

Between ages 6 and 14, during the *childhood* stage, there are few psychological problems. Cattell calls it a time of consolidation after the more critical infancy period. There is the beginning of a trend toward independence from parents and a concomitant increase in identification with peers, but there are no major problems, compared with the next stage.

Cattell sees *adolescence* (which lasts, in his view, from 14 to 23) as the most troublesome and stressful stage of development. The incidence of mental disorders, neuroses, and delinquency rises sharply during the period, and a great deal of conflict is manifested around the drives for independence, self-assertion, and sex.

The fourth phase of development, *maturity*, lasts from ages 23 to 50. In general, it is, at least in its earlier years, a busy, happy, and productive time for most

Adolescence can be a stressful stage of development, with conflict manifested in the drives for independence, self-assertion, and sex.

people, as they prepare for and begin a career, marriage, and family. The personality tends to become less fluid and more set, as compared with earlier stages of growth, and emotional stability tends to increase. Indeed, Cattell found little change in interests and attitudes between 23 and 50.

The stage of *late maturity* involves shifts and adjustments in the personality in response to physical, social, and psychological changes. Health and vigor often dim at this time, along with attractiveness. Children leave home, and for the first time the end of one's life is in view. There is usually a reexamination of the values around which one has centered one's life, and a searching of (and for) oneself.

Old age, the final stage, involves adjustment to a number of losses—the deaths of relatives and friends, work lost in retirement, loss of status in a society that worships youth—and the accompanying loneliness and insecurity.

Cattell's image of human nature

Cattell does not present us with explicit views on the various questions about human nature. We can, however, get some indication of his image of us by reexamining his definition of personality: "Personality is that which permits a prediction of what a person will do in a given situation" (Cattell, 1950, p. 2). One would assume from this statement that Cattell views human behavior as capable of being predicted. Indeed, his formulation of the behavioral specification equation, to be discussed later, states just that quite directly. Once we know the traits of which personality is composed, we can predict how an individual will behave. And once we can predict that behavior, we are in a position to control it.

For behavior to be considered predictable, it must be assumed to be lawful and orderly: how would prediction be possible without regularity and consistency? Cattell notes that wives can predict with considerable accuracy what their husbands will do when placed in certain situations, because their past behavior has been consistent, lawful, and orderly. There would seem, therefore, to be no room in Cattell's view of human nature for irregularity and spontaneity, since such characteristics would preclude prediction. On the free will versus determinism issue, then, Cattell's view seems to fall on the side of determinism.

While the doctrine of free will, which accords spontaneity and randomness to behavior, cannot be part of a system that has as its goal the complete predictability of human behavior, it must be noted that Cattell does not totally rule out the possibility of free will. Psychology, he wrote, may someday find that its laws of behavior have misfired, but, until and unless that happens, "psychologists will continue to believe in orderly cause and effect."

Cattell's system does not posit any ultimate and necessary goal that dominates an individual's behavior. There is no self-actualization or other form of ultimate fulfillment constantly pulling us forward, nor are there universal instinctual psychosexual conflicts pushing from behind. He does note the determining influence of the period of infancy—"the great formation period." Basic social attitudes, the superego, a sense of security, and the tendency to neuroticism are formed by the time we are 6 years of age. Yet one does not get the impression from Cattell's writings that he views us as forever locked in or imprisoned by these childhood influences, unable to revise or modify them at a later stage of development.

On the nature–nurture issue, Cattell believes we are influenced by both. Constitutional traits, for example, may be innately determined, as are ergs, while environmental-mold traits are learned. Also, we noted that Cattell has undertaken considerable research to demonstrate the precise influence of heredity and environment on various traits. On the uniqueness–universality issue, Cattell takes a moderate position, noting that there are both common traits applicable to everyone in a culture and unique traits characteristic of each individual.

Although Cattell's professional views on human nature are not entirely clear on some issues, his personal view of human nature is. He has made direct, though brief, reference to it. The biographical sketch earlier in the chapter noted how Cattell became interested in social problems. He came to realize that the only way he, or anyone, might be able to ameliorate social ills was to study the workings of the human mind. This provided the basic motivation for his switch from the study of chemistry and physics to psychology. In his younger years he was optimistic about human nature and our ability to resolve social ills. People, he wrote, will gain greater knowledge and more control over their environment. Human intelligence will rise, he thought, and he expected to see within his lifetime "a more gracious community life of creatively occupied citizens" (Cattell, 1974b, p. 88).

Reality, of course, has not lived up to his expectations, and by 1974 Cattell wrote that he had lost some of his earlier optimism about humankind. Not only did people and their societies not progress and improve in line with Cattell's earlier hopes, but they have, he now sees, regressed in some respects.

Assessment in Cattell's theory
Factor analysis

The technique by which Cattell derived the traits of personality is the sophisticated statistical procedure of factor analysis. However, before the factor-analytic procedure can be applied, masses of data must be collected from a large number of human subjects. Believing that everything that exists is measurable, in some degree, Cattell has undertaken to assess personality objectively and precisely, using three techniques of assessment. The data provided by these techniques are called L-data, Q-data, and T-data.

The **L-data** technique (*L* stands for life record) involves ratings made by observers on specific kinds of behavior that occur in the people they are observing. The behavior being observed occurs in a real-life situation rather than in a laboratory. Some examples of L-data include: frequency of absence from work, grades in school, conscientiousness in performing duties, emotional stability on the playing field, sociability at work, conventionality, and considerateness. The two important points about this technique are that it involves actual behavior in a naturalistic setting and that it must involve behavior that can be observed by someone else.

The **Q-data** technique utilizes questionnaires that the subject answers personally. While the L-data technique had someone else rating the subject, the Q-data technique requires that the subject rate himself or herself. A variety of questionnaires are used: the standard self-report type of personality inventory, including Cattell's own Sixteen P. F. Test, as well as scales that measure attitudes, interests, and opinions. Even the interview can be used, as long as the essential ingredient of the technique is kept intact: the subject must introspect and rate himself or herself on whatever aspect of behavior is being examined.

Cattell recognizes that there are limitations in the use of introspection and self-report. First, some subjects may not know themselves very well, and so their answers might not reflect the true nature of their personality. Second, even if subjects do know themselves, they may not want others to know them and so may deliberately bias or falsify their answers. This stems from the fact that the Q-data technique involves tests or questionnaires that most subjects are usually able to see through to judge what aspect of their personality is being measured. For example, if you were asked whether you prefer to be by yourself or with other people, you might reasonably guess that the question relates to gregariousness or shyness and thus respond accordingly. If you were extremely shy, and sensitive about it, you might say that you preferred to be with other people, in order to conceal what you consider a disturbing aspect of your personality. Because of these limitations, Cattell warns that the investigator must not blindly accept Q-data reports as accurate.

The third technique, **T-data**, involves the use of objective tests, which Cattell defines as "miniature situations," in which a person responds without knowing what aspect of his or her performance is being evaluated. These tests circumvent the Q-data problems by making it impossible (or at least extremely difficult) for a subject to know what a test item, or a whole test, is measuring. And if you cannot see through the test, it follows that you cannot distort your responses to conceal something about yourself or to present yourself in a more favorable light. If, for example, you were shown an inkblot from the Rorschach Test, you could not predict the interpretation that would be given to your response. How could you know what your answer might be revealing about you? For the most part, you cannot know, and that is why Cattell calls the Rorschach, along with Murray's Thematic Apperception Test and Jung's word-association test, among others, *objective* tests. They are objective in that they are resistant to faking.

It is important to note that Cattell's choice of the word *objective* to describe such tests is unfortunate and may be misleading. As we saw in Chapter 1, these tests have traditionally been called *subjective* because of the subjectivity that can enter into their scoring and interpretation, as opposed to tests that can be scored by a key so that anyone who grades them will come up with the same score. It is the latter type of test that is usually called *objective*.

Psychological tests

Cattell has developed a number of specific tests to assess personality, the most notable being the Sixteen P. F. Test, based on his 16 major source traits. The test is intended for use with persons 16 years of age and older and yields scores on each of the 16 scales. There are two major forms of the test, each containing 187 items to which subjects respond by indicating "yes," "no," or "uncertain." The responses are scored objectively.

As we noted earlier, this test is widely used to assess personality for research purposes, for clinical diagnoses, and for predicting occupational success in a variety of jobs. In recent years, it has grown in popularity and may eventually surpass the MMPI as the most frequently used personality test (Fehr, 1983). It should be noted, however, that the reliability and validity of the Sixteen P. F. Test are such that some psychologists believe it should not be used in such an unqualified manner for any and all purposes (Lanyon, 1984).

The Sixteen P. F. Test is used primarily with normal subjects, though it does distinguish between normal and neurotic personalities. Cattell wanted to be able to assess the personalities of a wider range of neurotics and psychotics, and for this purpose he developed the Clinical Analysis Questionnaire (CAQ). The CAQ measures 28 source traits: the 16 traits from the Sixteen P. F. Test and 12 traits designed to assess abnormal personalities. The abnormal source traits include the following (Cattell & Kline, 1977; Krug, 1980).

1. *Hypochondriasis*—overconcern with health and bodily functioning
2. *Zestfulness*—contentment with life; no thoughts of suicide
3. *Brooding discontent*—concern with excitement and risk
4. *Anxious depression*—tense and easily upset
5. *Energy*—enthusiasm and alertness
6. *Guilt and resentment*—feelings of guilt and self-blame
7. *Bored depression*—uncomfortable with other people
8. *Paranoia*—feelings of persecution and threat from others
9. *Psychopathic deviation*—tendency toward antisocial behavior and illegal acts
10. *Schizophrenia*—uncontrollable impulses and lack of contact with reality
11. *Psychasthenia*—tendency toward obsessions and compulsions
12. *General psychosis*—feelings of inferiority and worthlessness

As with the Sixteen P. F. Test, each factor on the CAQ measures either a low or a high degree of each trait. For example, someone scoring low on paranoia is very trusting of others, experiences little envy or jealousy, and has no feelings of persecution. Someone scoring high on paranoia is bothered by feelings of persecution and of being spied upon by others and controlled by them.

Cattell developed several variations of the Sixteen P. F. Test. To assess the personalities of younger people, he compiled the High School Personality Questionnaire for ages 12 to 18, the Children's Personality Questionnaire for ages 8 to 12, and the Early School Personality Questionnaire for ages 6 to 8. Special versions have been prepared to measure specific areas of personality such as anxiety, depression, and neuroticism, and for specific purposes such as marriage counseling and the evaluation of executives (Anastasi, 1982).

Cattell also developed a test to assess intelligence or at least one particular kind of intelligence. He has distinguished between crystallized intelligence and fluid intelligence. *Crystallized intelligence* depends heavily on formal education and involves the kinds of abilities one learns in school. Cattell defined *fluid intelli-*

gence as an innate ability that can be applied to all kinds of material. Fluid intelligence affects crystallized intelligence because it influences how much we will benefit from formal schooling. Cattell's Culture Fair Intelligence Test is designed to measure fluid intelligence.

It is ironic that Cattell has developed so many psychological tests considering his self-professed lack of interest in them. "Appearances to the contrary," he wrote, "psychological tests *as such* are something for which I have not had much concern" (Cattell, 1974b, p. 99). His interest is not so much in measuring personality as in reducing it to concrete, quantifiable factors or traits, and this is what he has accomplished with his many assessment techniques.

Research in Cattell's theory

Cattell was more concerned with research than with theoretical approaches to the understanding of personality. He has been critical of most personality theories, arguing that they are too subjective and wordy, and lacking in quantitative data and attempts to validate them empirically. He also believes that too many psychologists overemphasize theories at the expense of rigorous methodology and the reliable data it can produce. "Theories are easier to talk about," he noted, "but glibness is no substitute for decisive experiment and the guts necessary to carry it out thoroughly in the face of practical difficulties" (Cattell, 1974b, p. 94).

In opposition to Allport, the other trait theorist we have discussed, as well as many other personality theorists, Cattell's research is decidedly nomothetic. His method of factor analysis involves the study of large groups of people and their average level of performance on various assessing instruments. Also, Cattell is more interested in finding broad, general principles that can be applied to many people than in understanding the personality of a single individual.

Although his approach is a nomothetic one, he sometimes used his data to understand the behavior of individuals. Thus, the data can be applied in idiographic fashion. For example, if you were to take the Sixteen P. F. Test, the traits that are unique to you as an individual would be revealed. Further, we shall see that one of Cattell's approaches to factor analysis is idiographic.

Cattell delineated three research methods by which personality might be studied: the bivariate, the clinical, and the multivariate. The bivariate or two-variable approach is the standard laboratory experimental method in psychology, which we described in Chapter 1. In this approach, the independent variable is manipulated to determine its effect on the dependent variable (the subjects' behavior). The approach could equally well be called a univariate one because only one variable is studied at a time.

Cattell agrees that this approach is laudably scientific, rigorous, and quantitative, but he argues that it can deal with only limited aspects of personality. In reality, personality is affected by many variables interacting simultaneously. The standard experimental method misses this complex and diverse assortment of influencing variables. Also, in the usually artificial situation of the laboratory, significant emotional experiences cannot be manipulated and duplicated. Thus, for Cattell, the bivariate approach is too restrictive to tell us much about the human personality. These are all familiar criticisms of the experimental method.

Other approaches to personality, notably the clinical and the multivariate, consider a broad range of variables simultaneously, allowing researchers to uncover the connections among all aspects of the personality as they exist in a real-life situation. Although these two approaches share that advantage, they differ in their scientific rigor and precision.

The clinical method, including the case history, dream analysis, free association, and similar techniques, is, as we saw with the psychoanalytic theorists, highly subjective. It does not produce verifiable and quantifiable data. The multivariate approach, on the other hand, involves the sophisticated statistical procedure of factor analysis and yields specific data.

Cattell's technique of factor analysis can also be said to represent the correlational method of research. Several approaches can be taken to factor analysis, but Cattell favors two specific forms, the R technique and the P technique.

The *R technique*, the most frequently used factor-analytic technique, involves the collection of large amounts of data from a large group of subjects. Correlations among all the scores are made to find factors or traits. The *P technique* involves the collection of large amounts of data from a single subject over a long period of time. Cattell typically measured as many as 40 different physiological and psychological variables every day for more than 100 days on the same person to uncover personality traits.

When the data are collected and traits uncovered by factor analysis, Cattell is in a position to accomplish his ultimate goal: to predict what a person will do in a given situation. For that purpose he uses a *behavioral specification equation*, given in the following formula:

$$R = s_1 T_1 + s_2 T_2 + s_3 T_3 + \ldots + s_n T_n$$

With this formula, it is possible to predict R (the response) from knowledge of a person's traits ($T_1 \ldots T_n$). Each trait is given a weight in accordance with how relevant it is in the present situation ($s_1 \ldots s_n$). A trait that is highly relevant to the situation is assigned a higher weight than one that is less relevant. For example, if, in a given situation, R stands for tennis-playing behavior, we could predict a person's ability by a knowledge of certain of his or her traits. The factor of general intelligence would be highly relevant because good tennis playing requires advance planning; in other words, intelligence is equal to ability to plan. That factor would therefore be assigned a high weight. Enthusiasm and high ergic tension might also be relevant, but somewhat less so than intelligence, and their assigned weights would thus be lower. In like manner, the analysis of all relevant traits proceeds until all the elements in the equation are known. Then it is possible to specify or predict how the person will behave in the situation of playing tennis.

Let us briefly consider a few of the factor-analytic studies conducted by Cattell and his associates. In Cattell's initial research, he compiled a list of 171 personality variables taken both from the published literature in psychology and from the dictionary. He asked friends and colleagues of 100 subjects to rate them on these variables. A second group of subjects was rated on an abbreviated list of variables. The ratings were analyzed, and the results identified the 16 source traits that make up the Sixteen P. F. Test (Cattell, 1946).

A later study by Cattell was concerned with the relative effects of heredity and environment on personality. A factor analysis of data from 3,000 male subjects ages 12 to 18 showed that three source traits were determined primarily by heredity. These are Factor F (sober versus happy-go-lucky), Factor I (tough-minded versus tender-minded), and Factor Q_3 (undisciplined self-concept versus controlled). Three other traits were found to be determined primarily by environmental influences. These are Factor E (humble versus assertive), Factor G (expedient versus conscientious), and Factor Q_4 (relaxed versus tense) (Cattell, 1982).

Another study used the Sixteen P. F. Test to determine the relationship between personality traits and marital stability. Married couples were identified as having either a stable or an unstable marriage; the criterion was whether a couple had ever taken steps toward dissolving the marriage. The results showed that the stability of a marriage could be predicted on the basis of test scores. Partners in stable marriages had highly similar personality traits. Partners in unstable marriages possessed highly different personality traits (Cattell & Nesselroade, 1967).

In a study using the P technique, a male college student was studied extensively for 40 days using the kinds of techniques we discussed in the section on assessment. The purpose of the study was to compare the factors derived from the factor analysis of this single subject with those derived from the factor analysis of a large group of subjects (the R technique). The results showed that while traits may indeed be unique to an individual, they are also similar, in general, to traits that are common to large groups of people (Cattell & Cross, 1952).

Additional research compared people who differed on one particular source trait, Q_1 (conservative versus experimenting or liberal). The subjects were asked for their preferences for a number of paintings that differed in complexity and degree of ambiguity. Some paintings were straightforward representations of people and objects. Others were highly abstract and nonrepresentational; it was not clear what these latter paintings were supposed to depict. As predicted, persons scoring on the low or conservative end of Factor Q_1 more strongly preferred the straightforward, representational works. Liberals more strongly preferred the abstract paintings (Wilson, Ausman & Mathews, 1973).

A final commentary

A man who has presented huge volumes of research, who has accumulated monumental amounts of experimental data in an area usually defined by subjective case histories and equally subjective intuitions and speculations, and who has developed new ways of assessing personality simply cannot be ignored. If for no other reason than the sheer quantity of his research, Cattell's system demands consideration.

However, as we pointed out, the amount of his research and the complex method of factor analysis are among the reasons for the general lack of acceptance of his point of view. Cattell wrote that he had "a sense of unquestionable failure" in convincing others of the ultimate wisdom of his approach, which he caustically defends as the only method that is of value in the study of personality (Cattell, 1974b, p. 122). His work has been described as being much respected but seldom read; this seems, unfortunately, all too accurate, particularly in the United States. Cattell reports that sales of his undergraduate textbook, *The Scientific Analysis of Personality*, are much higher in England, Germany, Australia, and Japan than in the United States. Also, he notes that his work is rated as being more relevant in Europe than in the United States.

In the ratings of 286 psychologists, Cattell ranked in 33rd place overall and in 11th place among the theorists discussed in this book (Gilgen, 1982). His theory is clearly not as popular among psychologists as some of the other personality theories, and it is virtually unknown among the general public (an audience with which Cattell has not attempted to communicate). While part of the reason is, as we have seen, its demanding and technical nature, there have also been specific criticisms directed against the substance of his approach.

Despite the legitimate claim that factor analysis is a highly objective and precise technique, there is still opportunity for subjectivity to creep into Cattell's overall research methodology. At several stages of the research process, decisions must be made, which, critics argue, may be influenced by personal opinions and preferences. For example, in the initial step of collecting data the psychologist must decide which specific tests to use and what aspects of behavior to measure. Next, the researcher must decide which specific technique of factor analysis to use, and there is not a unanimity of opinion on this question. If factor analysis is so objective, critics ask, why can't factor analysts agree on matters of technique? It must also be decided which level of statistical significance will be accepted as appropriate. Once the factors have been identified, the psychologist must decide what labels to apply to them. If a factor is given a name that may be ambiguously interpreted, it may not express the real meaning of the factor.

This is not to suggest that Cattell's theory is weak from the standpoint of these decisions, but the opportunity for subjective error can find its way into a factor-analytic approach. It is a point of possible vulnerability, not only in Cattell's approach but also in other techniques of research discussed in this book.

It is unfortunate that despite the tremendous efforts of Cattell and his small band of associates to convince the psychological world of the utility of his approach, they have not succeeded, at least not on a large scale. His theory is one of the most firmly grounded in data and one of the most systematically constructed, and it has taught us a great deal about the structure (if not the nature) of personality. His method and goal are in the best tradition of science—to measure the subject matter with utmost precision before attempting to theorize about it.

In spite of the lack of full recognition accorded his position, Cattell remains convinced that his approach will one day enable us to predict human behavior with the same degree of accuracy with which the movement of the planets can be predicted today.

Summary

Cattell's goal in studying personality is to predict behavior, as expressed in the equation $R = f(P, S)$. R stands for the person's response, S for the situation or stimulus, and P for personality. Cattell studied normal subjects using rigorous scientific methods to amass great amounts of data that were then subjected to the statistical procedure of factor analysis. This involves assessing the correlations between each possible pair of measurements taken from a group of subjects. When two measures show a high correlation, Cattell assumes they are measuring related aspects of personality. He calls these aspects factors or traits, described as the component parts of an individual's personality.

Cattell's childhood was marked by an awareness of the brevity of life, the need to accomplish while one can, and competition with his older brother. No childhood influences seem to be reflected in his theory of personality.

Traits are the basic structural units of the personality. They are hypothetical constructs inferred from the objective observation of behavior. A trait is defined as a reaction tendency that is a relatively permanent part of the personality. Common traits are possessed by everyone to some degree; unique traits are possessed by only one person or by a very few persons. Ability traits determine how efficiently a person will be able to work toward a goal. Temperament traits define a person's emotional style of behavior. Dynamic traits are concerned with the motivations or driving forces of behavior.

Surface traits are personality characteristics that correlate with one another but do not comprise a factor because they are not determined by a single source. In abnormal personalities they are called syndromes. Source traits are single factors, each of which is the sole source of some aspect of behavior.

Source traits are either constitutional traits, which originate in the internal conditions of the organism, or environmental-mold traits, which are derived from influences in the environment.

Cattell identified 16 source traits: Factor A (reserved vs. outgoing), Factor B (less intelligent vs. more intelligent), Factor C (affected by feelings vs. emotionally stable), Factor E (humble vs. assertive), Factor F (sober vs. happy-go-lucky), Factor G (expedient vs. conscientious), Factor H (shy vs. venturesome), Factor I (tough-minded vs. tender-minded), Factor L (trusting vs. suspicious), Factor M (practical vs. imaginative), Factor N (forthright vs. astute), Factor O (self-assured vs. apprehensive), Factor Q_1 (conservative vs. experimenting), Factor Q_2 (group-dependent vs. self-sufficient), Factor Q_3 (casual vs. controlled), Factor Q_4 (relaxed vs. tense).

The two kinds of dynamic traits are ergs (the energy source for all behavior) and sentiments (learned patterns of attitudes). Ergs and sentiments are manifested in attitudes, which are a person's interests in some area, object, or other person. Attitudes are subsidiary to sentiments; sentiments are subsidiary to ergs. The interrelationship of ergs, sentiments, and attitudes is expressed schematically in the dynamic lattice.

The self-sentiment is a person's self-concept, which provides stability and organization to all the source traits. Anxiety is both a state of being and a personality trait.

Cattell investigated the importance of heredity and environment by using Multiple Abstract Variance Analysis. His data revealed that 80 percent of intelligence and of venturesome vs. shyness and 30 percent of the dissatisfied emotionally traits resulted from genetic influences. In general, one-third of personality is genetically determined, and the rest is determined by environmental influences.

Syntality refers to the relevant characteristics of a large social group that can influence personality.

Infancy, from birth to the age of 6, is the major formative period of personality. Childhood, from 6 to 14, is a time of consolidation in which there are few psychological problems. Adolescence, from 14 to 23, is the most stressful stage of development. Maturity, from 23 to 50, is a happy and productive time in which the personality becomes more set. Late maturity involves personality adjustments in response to physical, social, and psychological changes. Old age involves adjustments to losses and the accompanying loneliness and insecurity.

Cattell holds a mostly deterministic view of personality and does not emphasize any ultimate goals of behavior. Childhood influences are important in personality development, as are heredity and environment. People have unique traits as well as common traits shared with others.

Cattell's three major techniques of personality assessment are L-data (ratings made by observers), Q-data (self-ratings made through questionnaires, personality inventories, and attitude scales), and T-data (data from tests that are resistant to faking).

Cattell has developed several specific tests, including the Sixteen P. F. Test, the Clinical Analysis Questionnaire for neurotics and psychotics, and modifications of the Sixteen P. F. Test for use with younger subjects and for specific purposes. The Culture Fair Intelligence Test is used to measure the innate ability Cattell calls fluid intelligence. Crystallized intelligence depends heavily on formal education.

Cattell's research is generally nomothetic, but he also used an idiographic approach. The bivariate research method is the standard experimental method in psychology in which one variable is manipulated to determine its effect on behavior. The clinical and the multivariate methods consider a broader range of variables simultaneously and can deal with all aspects of personality in real-life situations. Cattell uses the multivariate method because of its scientific rigor and precision.

Factor analysis represents the correlational method of research. Cattell uses two forms of factor analysis, the R technique, in which large amounts of data are gathered from large groups of subjects, and the P technique, in which large amounts of data are gathered from a single subject over a long period of time.

The behavioral specification equation is used to predict a person's behavior in a given situation. In the equation, each trait is weighted in accordance with its importance in the situation.

Cattell's work has not been widely recognized because of the technical nature of factor analysis and the overwhelming amount of data with which it deals. Factor analysis has been criticized for its potential subjectivity in that decisions at various stages can be influenced by personal opinions and preferences.

Glossary

ability traits   Traits that describe an individual's skills and how efficiently he or she will be able to work toward a goal.

attitudes   An individual's interests in and emotions and behavior toward a person, object, or event; by encompassing emotions and actions, in addition to opinions, Cattell offers a definition broader than that typically used in psychology.

common traits   Traits possessed, to some degree, by all persons.

constitutional traits   Source traits that depend on an individual's physiological characteristics.

dynamic lattice   The schematic representation of the interrelationships of ergs and sentiments (the dynamic traits) as well as attitudes.

dynamic traits   Traits that describe an individual's motivations and interests.

environmental-mold traits   Source traits that are learned from social and environmental experiences.

ergs   Permanent constitutional source traits that serve as the source of energy for all goal-directed behavior; the basic innate units of motivation.

factor analysis   A statistical procedure based on correlations between a number of measures, which may then be explained in terms of underlying factors.

L-data   Ratings made of specific behaviors observed in real-life situations, such as the classroom or office.

Q-data   Ratings made by an individual on self-report inventories of his or her personal characteristics, attitudes, and interests.

self-sentiment   The self-concept; the organizer of an individual's attitudes and motivations.

sentiments   Environmental-mold source traits, learned through interactions with the environment, that motivate behavior.

source traits   The basic elements of personality; stable, permanent factors deriving from factor analysis, measured by the Sixteen Personality Factor Questionnaire.

subsidiation   The interrelationships of ergs, sentiments, and attitudes in which some elements are subordinate or ancillary to others.

surface traits   Traits that show a correlation but that do not constitute a factor because they are not determined by a single source; they are less stable and permanent than source traits.

T-data   Data derived from various personality tests.

temperament traits   Traits that describe an individual's general style of behavior in responding to the environment.

trait   A reaction tendency of an individual that is a relatively permanent part of personality; derived by the method of factor analysis.

unique traits   Traits possessed by one or a few individuals.

Review questions

1. What is the goal of Cattell's work on personality? How does the behavioral specification equation relate to that goal?
2. How does Cattell's concept of personality traits differ from Allport's view of traits?
3. How does Cattell use the method of factor analysis to identify traits?
4. Describe three ways of categorizing traits.
5. What is the Sixteen Personality Factor Questionnaire?
6. According to Cattell's research, which source traits were found to be determined primarily by heredity?
7. How does the concept of subsidiation relate ergs, sentiments, and attitudes?
8. What is the self-sentiment? What is its role in personality?
9. Describe the six stages of personality development. During which stage does the personality tend to become less flexible?
10. Identify the three types of data collected by Cattell and give an example of each.
11. What is Cattell's position on the issue of free will versus determinism?

Suggested reading

Cattell, R. B. Personality pinned down. *Psychology Today*, July 1973, pp. 40–46.

Cattell, R. B. Autobiography. In G. Lindzey, Ed., *A history of psychology in autobiography*, vol. 6. Englewood Cliffs, NJ: Prentice-Hall, 1974.

Cattell, R. B. Travels in psychological hyperspace. In T. S. Krawiec, Ed., *The psychologists*, vol. 2. New York: Oxford University Press, 1974. (An autobiographical sketch.)

Cattell, R. B. & Kline, P. *The scientific analysis of personality and motivation.* New York: Academic Press, 1977.

Sells, S. B. Structured measurement of personality and motivation: A review of contributions of Raymond B. Cattell. *Journal of Clinical Psychology*, 1959, 15, 3–21.

PART 4

The Life-Span Approach

Most of the theorists we have discussed have paid some attention to the way in which personality develops over time. Some have described specific stages in the development of certain aspects of the personality; others have posited more general patterns of growth. The theorists have also differed in terms of the time period over which the personality continues to develop. Freud believed that personality evolved through a sequence of steps until the age of 5; it did not continue to develop after that time. Murray took a similar position. Allport held a longer view of personality development, believing that growth continued up to the time of adolescence. Jung argued that middle age was the most important time of change in the personality, and Cattell suggested that personality grew throughout the life span, though this was only a tangential aspect of his system.

The life-span approach to personality, represented here by the work of Erik Erikson, focuses on the evolution of the personality throughout a person's life. The theory attempts to explain human behavior in terms of eight stages from birth to death. All aspects of personality are accounted for by the turning points or crises that must be met and resolved at each stage of development.

CHAPTER 10

Erik Erikson

The life of Erikson (1902–)
Psychosocial development: Ways of coping with conflicts
  Trust vs. mistrust
  Autonomy vs. doubt and shame
  Initiative vs. guilt
  Industry vs. inferiority
  Identity vs. role confusion
  Intimacy vs. isolation
  Generativity vs. stagnation
  Ego integrity vs. despair
Basic strengths
Erikson's image of human nature
Assessment in Erikson's theory
Research in Erikson's theory
  Sex differences in personality
  Studies of the psychosocial stages
  Studies of ego identity
A final commentary
Summary
Glossary
Review questions
Suggested reading

The personality is engaged with the hazards of existence continuously, even as the body's metabolism copes with decay.

ERIK ERIKSON

The term *identity crisis* has come to be a widely used concept. The man who identified and refined the notion, and who built a personality theory at least partially around it, is considered by some to be among the most influential psychoanalysts today. His books sell hundreds of thousands of copies and in 1970 his picture appeared on the covers of both *Newsweek* and the *New York Times Magazine*—a most unusual sign of recognition for a personality theorist. In the same year, his book on the origins of militant nonviolence (*Gandhi's Truth*) was awarded a Pulitzer Prize. It is interesting that he has achieved such prominence and influence without an M.D. or a Ph.D. in psychology; indeed, he has no university degree at all.

Erik Erikson, trained in the Freudian tradition (by Freud's daughter, Anna), has developed an approach to personality that moves considerably beyond Freud while nevertheless maintaining much of the core of Freud's thought. Although he has offered significant innovations to psychoanalysis, his ties to the Freudian position remain strong. "I take Freud for granted," he once said. "Psychoanalysis is always the starting point" (Keniston, 1983, p. 29).

What Erikson has done in extending Freud's theory is basically threefold. First, he has elaborated extensively upon Freud's stages of development. Where Freud emphasized childhood and said that the personality is firmly shaped by the age of 5 or so, Erikson believes that personality continues to develop throughout the life span, moving through a series of eight crucial developmental stages.

Each of these stages, from infancy to old age, constitutes a crisis that must be resolved. At each stage there is a conflict, centering around an adaptive and a maladaptive means of dealing with the problems of that period. Failure at any one stage can lead to stress and anxiety and can retard development at a later stage.

The second change Erikson made in Freud's theory was to emphasize the ego much more than the id. (We noted in Chapter 2 that one of the basic modifications made in psychoanalysis since Freud's death was an expanded role for the ego.) The ego, in Erikson's view, is an independent part of the personality; it is not dependent upon or subservient to the id. The ego is influenced not only by one's parents, but also by one's social and historic environment. The ego continues to grow and develop long after childhood.

The third extension of Freudian doctrine is Erikson's recognition of the impact of culture, society, and history on the shaping of the total personality. People are not ruled entirely by biological forces at work in childhood. While these forces are important, they are far from being the whole explanation of the development of personality.

Erikson's is a life-span theory of personality, and the search for an ego identity is its central theme.

The life of Erikson (1902–   )

It is not surprising that the man who gave us the concept of identity crisis went through several such crises, each quite intense, in his early years. His theory definitely reflects his own experiences. Erikson was born in Frankfurt, Germany, to Danish parents. His father had abandoned his wife before the child was born, and the young Erikson moved with his mother to Karlsruhe, where, three years later, his mother married his pediatrician, Dr. Theodore Homburger. Erikson was given his stepfather's last name. He was not told for some years that Homburger was not really his father. Erikson later called this an act of "loving deceit." Thus, he was unsure not only of his psychological identity, but also of his actual identity in a fundamental sense—his name. He kept the name Homburger until he was 37 and changed it to Erikson in 1939, when he became an American citizen, retaining Homburger as a middle name.

Another crisis of identity began when he was old enough for school. He considered himself a German, despite his Danish parentage, but his German classmates rejected him because he was Jewish. At the same time, his Jewish peers rejected him because of his tall, blond, Aryan appearance. At the synagogue he was called "the goy." He later converted to Christianity.

He did not do well in school, achieving only mediocre grades. He did, however, evidence some talent for art, and when he graduated from high school he used that ability as a vehicle to try to find himself—that is, to establish an identity.

He became a dropout from society for a while and wandered throughout Germany and Italy, reading, recording his thoughts in a notebook, and observing the life around him. He described himself during that time as being morbidly sensitive and hovering on the vague borderline between psychosis and neurosis. He studied for brief periods at two art schools and had an exhibition in Munich, but each time he left formal training to resume his wandering, still searching for his own identity. Later, when discussing his concept of identity crisis, Erikson wrote, "No doubt, my best friends will insist that I needed to name this crisis and to see it in everybody else in order to really come to terms with it in myself" (Erikson, 1975, pp. 25–26). The statement provides another example of the subjective nature of personality theory and the impact of intuitive knowledge on its development.

In 1927, at the age of 25, he was invited to come to Vienna to teach at a small school established for the children of Sigmund Freud's patients and friends. (Many of Freud's patients came from other parts of the world and, being wealthy, settled in Vienna with their families for the duration of their analysis.) Erikson was drawn to Freud in part by his search for his own "mythical father," the father he had never known.

It was then that Erikson's professional career began. During the next years, he received his training in psychoanalysis; his own analysis was conducted by Anna Freud. She had a special interest in psychoanalysis of children, and this became Erikson's specialty. In 1933, when he finished his training, he became a member of the famed Vienna Psychoanalytic Institute. He continued to teach during his analysis and also studied the Montessori method of teaching, in which he was certified.

During his years in Vienna, he married a Canadian woman and, recognizing the new Nazi menace from neighboring Germany, in 1933 they emigrated, first to Denmark for a brief period and then to the United States. They settled in Boston, where Erikson set up a private practice specializing in the treatment of children.

The years in Boston were very productive. Erikson served on the staff of Henry Murray's clinic at Harvard (in the study of normal undergraduates discussed in Chapter 7) and also worked in a guidance center for emotionally disturbed delinquents and in Massachusetts General Hospital. During those years, he was fortunate in having contact with anthropologists Ruth Benedict and Margaret Mead and Gestalt psychologist Kurt Lewin, in addition to Henry Murray.

He began to study for a Ph.D. in psychology at Harvard but failed his first course, apparently because of dissatisfaction with a formal program of academic study. In 1936, he was invited to the Institute of Human Relations at Yale, where he continued his work with both normal and troubled children and also taught at the medical school. Two years later, Erikson and a Yale anthropologist studied methods of childrearing among the Sioux Indians of South Dakota. This study marked his initial focus on the influence of culture on the events of childhood, a concern that was to influence much of his later professional work.

He moved to San Francisco in 1939 to establish another private practice and to study the development of normal children at the Institute of Child Welfare at Berkeley. Unlike most psychoanalysts, Erikson was much concerned that his experience not be limited to the emotionally disturbed or to children of only one culture. In 1943, he investigated the life of another Indian tribe, the Yurok of Northern California.

In his contact with these two American Indian tribes, Erikson began to notice symptoms that could not be explained by orthodox Freudian theory. The symptoms revolved around a sense of uprootedness from one's cultural traditions and resulted in the lack of a clear self-image or identity. This phenomenon, which he initially called *identity confusion*, was observed also in the emotionally disturbed veterans with whom Erikson worked during and after World War II. He became convinced that the men were not suffering from repressed conflicts but rather from confusion as a result of traumatic war experiences and of being uprooted from their culture. Again, Erikson observed a confusion of identity—a confusion on the part of the veterans about just who and what they were.

Erikson left Berkeley in 1950 because he refused to sign a state loyalty oath and moved to Stockbridge, Massachusetts. There he worked at the Austen Riggs Center, a treatment center for disturbed adolescents. In 1960, he returned to Harvard, where he taught a graduate seminar and an extremely popular undergraduate course, entitled "The Human Life Cycle," until his retirement in 1970.

His strong interest in the role of history as it affects youth—that is, the impact of the times on youth—has resulted in a number of psychohistorical studies on such figures as Adolf Hitler, Maxim Gorky, and Martin Luther. His famous study of the great 20th-century leader of India, Mahatma Gandhi, dealing with nonviolence as a technique for bringing about social change, examined an identity crisis that occurred at a later stage in life.

At this writing, Erikson remains extremely productive. His primary activity now is continued psychohistorical analyses to demonstrate the role of identity confusion in the lives of influential people.

Psychosocial development: Ways of coping with conflicts

As noted earlier, Erikson has built upon and elaborated Freud's psychosexual stages of development and carried his own developmental theory through the entire life span of the individual. The growth of the personality is divided into eight **psycho-social stages** or "ages of man," as he calls them (Erikson, 1950, 1963). The first four are somewhat similar to Freud's oral, anal, phallic, and latency stages of growth, but Erikson focuses much more on the psychosocial correlates of these stages than on biological ones, as was the case with Freud.

Erikson argues that the process of development through the various stages is governed by what he calls the **epigenetic principle of maturation**. By this he means that the steps or stages of development are determined by inherited or genetic factors. The prefix *epi* means "upon." Thus, development depends upon these genetic factors. However, as we have seen, Erikson also emphasizes the role of environmental or social forces. It is these forces that influence the ways in which the biologically determined stages are realized. Overall, then, development is affected by both innate and learned factors.

Erikson sees human development in terms of a series of conflicts; the personality must cope with a particular conflict at each stage. Each conflict, existing potentially at birth as an innate predisposition, rises to prominence only at a definite stage in development, when the environment makes certain demands on the individual. Erikson calls this encounter or confrontation with the environment a **crisis**. The crisis involves a marked shift in perspective for the individual. It is a time of vulnerability as well as of new strengths, of a shifting of instinctual energy from one focus to another, and of new environmental demands.

Each stage of development, then, involves a turning point—a change in behavior and personality in which the individual is faced with a choice between two ways of coping: a maladaptive and negative way or an adaptive and positive way. Only as each crisis is positively resolved does the personality manifest a normal development with the strength to confront the next critical stage of development.

It is important to note that Erikson believes that both the maladaptive and the adaptive ways of coping at each stage must be incorporated into the ego identity. For example, consider the first stage in which the two ways of adapting involve the development of trust or mistrust. Obviously, trust is the more adaptive and desirable way of responding, the healthier psychological attitude to possess. Yet Erikson argued each person must also develop some sense of mistrust as a form of protection. If we are totally trusting and thus gullible, we would be vulnerable to attempts to deceive or mislead us. At every stage of development, the ego must consist primarily of the positive or adaptive attitude, but it must also contain a share of the negative attitude. Only then is the crisis associated with each stage resolved.

We shall discuss the nature of each of these eight ages of human beings, but, for the moment, let us take a brief overview of the entire developmental process. The left column below shows each stage, the middle column the approximate years in which it occurs, and the right column the contrasting ways of adapting. As you can see, the ages of the last three stages may vary considerably with the individual.

1. Oral-sensory . . . . Birth–1 year . . . . Trust vs. mistrust
2. Muscular-anal . . . . 1–3 years . . . . Autonomy vs. doubt, shame
3. Locomotor-genital . . . . 3–5 years . . . . Initiative vs. guilt
4. Latency . . . . 6–11 years . . . . Industry vs. inferiority
5. Adolescence . . . . 12–18 years . . . . Identity vs. role confusion
6. Young adulthood . . . . 18–35 years . . . . Intimacy vs. isolation
7. Adulthood . . . . 35–55 years . . . . Generativity vs. stagnation
8. Maturity . . . . 55+ years . . . . Ego integrity vs. despair

Since it is the ways of coping that are vital to the shaping of the personality, we shall use these as headings in discussing Erikson's developmental stages.

Trust vs. mistrust

The oral-sensory stage of development, paralleling Freud's oral stage, occurs at the time of greatest helplessness in the life of the individual. The infant is totally dependent on someone else for survival, security, and affection, and that someone else is usually the mother.

During this stage, the mouth is of vital importance. Erikson noted that the infant "lives through, and loves with, his mouth" (Erikson, 1959, p. 57). The relationship between the infant and its world is not, however, exclusively a biological one. It is also very much a social relationship—an interaction between mother and infant—which will determine the infant's later outlook on all the world. Specifically, it will determine whether the infant will view the world with an attitude of trust or mistrust.

If the mother is highly responsive to the baby's physical needs and is affectionate, providing ample love and security, then the infant will begin to trust the world around him or her. It has been, after all, good to the infant so far. The sense of basic trust that has thus arisen characterizes the baby's attitude toward himself or herself as well as toward others. As a result of the appropriate and affectionate responsiveness of the mother, the infant learns to expect a degree of "consistency, continuity, and sameness" from the world; this expectation provides at least the beginning of a sense of ego identity (Erikson, 1950, p. 247). Establishing lasting patterns for the solution of the basic trust versus mistrust conflict is the initial task of the ego. These patterns depend, as we have seen, on the quality (more than on the absolute quantity) of maternal care. From this beginning ego and sense of basic trust will later develop a sense of being all right—a contentment and security with being oneself and a trust of oneself and others.

If, on the other hand, the mother is rejecting, inattentive, or inconsistent in her behavior, the infant, quite understandably, develops an attitude of mistrust toward the world around him or her. The individual will be suspicious, fearful, and anxious in his or her later relations with everyone. Mistrust will also develop, according to Erikson, if mothers do not display an exclusive focus on the child. In his view, a mother who takes a full-time job shortly after her child is born, leaving it with a sitter or in a nursery, runs the risk of engendering mistrust in the child.

Thus, the pattern of trust or mistrust as a dimension of personality is set in infancy. However, the problem may appear again at a later stage in life. For example, an ideal mother–infant relationship may produce a high level of trust in a child, but this sense of trust may be destroyed if the mother suddenly leaves (through death or divorce). In that case, mistrust can develop, even though the earlier attitude was one of trust. Similarly, mistrust may be overcome later in life through the behavior of a very loving and patient teacher or friend.

You can see why this stage of development is called *psychosocial*: as with all the later stages, it depends on social relationships much more than on biological or instinctual drives.

Autonomy vs. doubt and shame

During the second and third years of life (Freud's anal stage), children rapidly develop a variety of physical and mental abilities. For the first time, they are able to do many things for themselves; they begin to walk, climb, push, pull, hold on to an object or let it go, and communicate more effectively. Children take great pride in these newly developing skills and abilities and want to do as many things for themselves as possible.

Of all these new abilities, Erikson places particular stress on those involving holding on and letting go; he considers these behaviors prototypes of later conflicting behavior and attitudes. For example, holding on can be done in a loving and benign fashion or in a hostile and destructive way. Similarly, letting go can become a venting of destructive rage or it can become a relaxed passivity, as exemplified by the phrase "let it pass." The important point here is that the child, for the first time, is able to exercise some degree of choice.

Thus, children experience their autonomous will. Although still dependent on their parents, they begin to see themselves as persons or forces in their own right. They want to exercise will, and the key question becomes this: to what extent will the world, in the form of the parents, allow them to do what they are now capable of doing at their own pace and time?

There is a clash of wills here between parent and child, and a major test is the matter of toilet training, the first instance of a societal regulation of an instinctive need (the child is taught to hold on and let go only at appropriate times and places). Do the parents let the child proceed at his or her own pace, or do they become annoyed and usurp the child's free will by forcing the training and showing impatience and anger when the child doesn't behave correctly? This situation is illustrative of a number of such clashes of will at this time.

When children are not allowed to exercise their will, Erikson believes, they develop a feeling of shame in their relations with others and a sense of doubt about themselves. The will to be oneself has been frustrated and thwarted. Thus, while the anal region may be a focus of this stage, the form and structure of the potential conflict is not so much biological as psychosocial.

Initiative vs. guilt

The third stage of development, occurring in ages 3 to 5, is analogous to the phallic stage in Freud's system. The child's motor and mental abilities have become more fully developed. He or she is able to do more things and strongly wants to do so; his or her initiative has grown strong.

Another development at this stage—an initiative in fantasy form—is the child's desire to possess the parent of the opposite sex, with an attendant feeling of rivalry with the parent of the same sex.

The key question is the same as at the earlier stages: how will the parents react to these new self-initiated activities and fantasies? If they punish the child and otherwise inhibit these initiatives, if they cause him or her to feel that the new initiatives are bad, the child will develop guilt feelings. The guilt will persist and color all self-initiated activities in later life.

With regard to the Oedipal relationship, the child must, of course, fail, but if the parents guide this particular failure in initiative in a loving and understanding manner, the child will be able to acquire a moral sense of what is permissible behavior and what is not. His or her initiative can be guided or channeled toward more realistic and societally sanctioned goals. The child is then on the way to developing an adult sense of responsibility and morality—in other words, a superego.

Industry vs. inferiority

The fourth stage, corresponding to Freud's latency stage (a time of relative quiet), begins when the child starts school and continues through about age 11. The child's world is considerably broadened at this time, as he or she is exposed to new influences and pressures outside the home. This does not mean, however, that parental influences are suddenly diminished; far from it. The child's experiences at home can greatly color the experiences in his or her new environment. At home and at school, the child begins to learn to work, to be industrious, primarily as a means of gaining recognition and obtaining the pleasure derived from the completion of a task.

In both the home and the school, the child's new powers of deductive reasoning and ability to play by rules (rather than at random), lead to the deliberate development and refinement of skills that are displayed in building things. Usually, the boy of this age makes tree houses or model airplanes and the girl cooks and sews—both serious efforts to complete a task through concentrated attention, diligence, and persistence. Erikson noted: "The basic skills of technology are developed, as the child becomes ready to handle the utensils, the tools, and the weapons used by the big people" (Erikson, 1959, p. 83).

How well children perceive themselves to be developing these new skills is determined in large part by the attitudes and behavior of their parents and teachers. If their efforts are ridiculed, scolded, or rejected, they are likely to develop feelings of inadequacy and inferiority with respect to their abilities and to themselves. Constructive and instructive praise and reinforcement, on the other hand, foster chil-

During the early school years when children begin to develop work-related skills, parents should offer constructive praise and reinforcement.

dren's feelings of competence in their industry, which encourages them to strive for further development.

These first four childhood stages are, as noted, psychosocial versions of Freud's psychosexual stages. There is another characteristic that these stages share. The outcome of each crisis is dependent more on other people than on oneself—a function more of what is done to the child than of what the child does. Although there certainly is increasing independence from birth to the age of 11, the nature of the child's development is still very much dependent upon the nature of parents and teachers. They are *significant others* over whom the child has no control or choice.

The last four stages of development differ from the previous stages in that the person is increasingly able to control his or her environment. The individual consciously chooses friends, career, a spouse, and so on. Of course, it must be remembered that these deliberate choices are strongly directed by the characteristics that have developed in the individual by the time he or she reaches adolescence. That is, whether the person is trusting, autonomous, industrious, and possessing initiative or mistrustful, doubting, guilt-ridden, and feeling inferior will influence the future course of his or her life, no matter how independent he or she may later become of the environment and of other people.

Identity vs. role confusion

The stage of adolescence, ages 12 to 18, is believed by Erikson to be particularly crucial, for it is at this time that the question of one's basic **ego identity** is met and must be resolved. It is a time of interpretation and consolidation, in which everything we feel and know about ourselves is fused into a whole. The person must form a self-image that makes sense and provides both a continuity with the past and an orientation toward the future. There is, then, an integration of our ideas of what others think of us and what we think of ourselves, which, ideally, should provide a consistent and congruent picture. This image—the picture of oneself—forms one's ego identity.

The shaping and acceptance of one's identity is, Erikson feels, an extremely difficult and anxiety-filled task, in which the adolescent must experiment with or try on different roles and ideologies to determine the best fit. Erikson looks upon adolescence as a hiatus between childhood and adulthood—a psychological moratorium that is absolutely necessary in order to allow time and energy to be devoted to role and image experimentation.

Those who emerge from this difficult stage with a strong sense of identity are equipped to face coming adulthood with an expanded sense of self-certainty and confidence. Those who fail to achieve an identity, who experience an **identity crisis**, show what Erikson calls role confusion. They do not know who or what they are, where they belong, or where they are going. As a result, they may drop out of the normal life sequence—education, job, marriage—as Erikson did for a time, and seek a negative identity, one opposite to that prescribed by society. Such an adolescent may become a delinquent or withdraw in isolation to a drugged state. This type of role is still an identification, and even a negative one (as society defines it) is preferable to no identification of any kind, although it is not as satisfactory as a positive identification.

Erikson stressed the impact that social groups with which the adolescent chooses to identify can have on the development of proper ego identity. Getting in with a bad crowd, as the saying goes, such as drug addicts or school dropouts, or identifying with cult figures such as rock stars or self-styled saviors, can restrict the budding ego.

Intimacy vs. isolation

The sixth stage of development, young adulthood, is much longer than any of the earlier ones, extending from the end of adolescence to the beginning of middle age. During what is usually quite an exciting time, a person finally establishes independence from his or her parents and from parent-like (protective) institutions such as school and begins to function as a mature, responsible adult.

Not only does the person perform some kind of productive work, but he or she also establishes intimate relationships with others in the form of close friendships and sexual unions. Thus, intimacy is not restricted to a sexual relationship. It also means a sense of caring and commitment, openly displayed, without the use of any self-protective devices and without fear of losing one's sense of self-identity in the relationship.

During young adulthood, we must be able to merge our identity with someone else's, without fear of losing something of ourselves in the process. Fusing one's identity in an intimate relationship is not the same as submerging it. One's ego identity must be blended but not lost. We must still know firmly who and what we are as individuals.

People unable to establish such intimacy function in a state of isolation; they avoid close contacts with others and may even come to reject or aggress against those whom they see as threatening to their own selves. Such people prefer being alone, because they fear intimacy.

Generativity vs. stagnation

The seventh stage of development finds the individual in middle age—roughly the years from 35 to 55. It is at this stage of maturity, Erikson argues, that people need more than intimacy with others. They need to be actively and directly involved in teaching and guiding the next generation.

This need extends beyond one's immediate family, although it can include one's own children, of course. The concern is broader and more long-range, however, extending to future generations and to the kind of society in which they will live. One need not be a parent to display generativity, nor does having children automatically guarantee satisfaction of this need.

Erikson feels that all human institutions—whether business, military, or academic—reinforce and safeguard the expression of generativity in that they all involve the establishment of a fund of knowledge and methods to provide guidance to each new generation. Thus, one can satisfy the need to guide the next generation in virtually any organization of which one is a part.

When such behavior is not displayed by the middle-aged individual, he or she is overwhelmed by a sense of "stagnation, boredom, and interpersonal impoverishment" (Erikson, 1968, p. 138). The person regresses to a stage of pseudointimacy, in which he or she indulges himself or herself in a childlike way. The person may become a physical or psychological invalid because of a total absorption (or obsession) with his or her own needs and comforts.

Ego integrity vs. despair

The final stage of life finds the individual in a state of either ego integrity or despair, which governs the way the person looks upon the whole of his or her life. At this time, a person's major endeavors are at or nearing completion. It is a time of reflection—of looking back and examining one's life and taking its final measure.

If a person looks back upon life with a sense of fulfillment and satisfaction, if he or she has adjusted to life's victories and failures, then he or she possesses what Erikson calls ego integrity. Simply stated, it involves the acceptance of one's place and one's past.

If, on the other hand, an individual views his or her life with a sense of frustration or rancor, angry at missed opportunities and regretful of mistakes that cannot now be rectified, then he or she is in a state of despair. He or she is disgusted with life, contemptuous of others, and bitter over what might have been, "if only. . . ."

Older persons who feel satisfied with life are said to possess ego integrity.

Basic strengths

Each of the eight stages of life has its own identity crisis, and each offers new opportunities for what Erikson calls **basic strengths** to develop. Originally he referred to these as "virtues," but then he realized that the word *virtue* derives from the Latin *virtus*, implying virility or manliness. "The linguistic implication could be that virtues are male qualities," he said, "so I had to change it to 'strengths'" (Hall, 1983, p. 27).

Erikson believes that these strengths are common over all generations and grow out of the positive, adaptive ways of handling each stage of growth. These basic human strengths are evolutionary in nature, developing over the course of the life of an individual and over the history of humanity as a whole. Each strength is a vital, animating force in life. The strengths are not innate but must be developed and then reaffirmed continuously throughout a person's life.

There are eight basic strengths, corresponding to the stages of development; each emerges (if it is going to) only when each crisis is met and resolved satisfactorily (see Table 10.1). The four strengths that may appear in childhood are hope, will, purpose, and competence. Fidelity arises in adolescence, and love, care, and wisdom come in adulthood. The strengths are very much interdependent; none can develop until the previous one is securely confirmed.

Hope, growing out of basic trust, is the persistent belief that desires can be satisfied. It is a sense of confidence that is maintained in spite of temporary setbacks or reverses. *Will*, developing out of autonomy, is an irrevocable determination to exercise both freedom of choice and self-restraint, and it forms the basis for

TABLE 10.1   Erikson's stages of psychosocial development

Stage	*Approximate Ages*	*Adaptive vs. Maladaptive Ways of Coping*	*Basic Strength*
Oral-sensory	Birth through first year	Trust vs. mistrust	Hope
Muscular-anal	Early child-hood, through third year	Autonomy vs. doubt, shame	Will
Locomotor-genital	3–5 years	Initiative vs. guilt	Purpose
Latency	6–11 years, to puberty	Industry vs. inferiority	Competence
Adolescence	12–18 years	Identity vs. role confusion	Fidelity
Young adulthood	18–35 years	Intimacy vs. isolation	Love
Adulthood	35–55 years	Generativity vs. stagnation	Care
Maturity and old age	55+ years	Ego integrity vs. despair	Wisdom

the necessary acceptance of law. *Purpose*, deriving from initiative, involves a sense of courage to envision and to pursue important goals. *Competence*, deriving from industry, might be called a sense of craftsmanship and involves the exertion of skill and intelligence in the pursuit and completion of tasks.

Fidelity, which grows out of ego identity, involves the maintenance of basic loyalties, a sense of duty, sincerity, and genuineness in relations with others. *Love*, deriving from intimacy, is considered by Erikson to be the greatest of the strengths— indeed, the dominant one. He defines it as a mutual devotion in a shared identity— the finding and fusing of oneself with another person. *Care*, emerging from gener-ativity, is a broad concern or solicitude toward others. It manifests itself in the need to teach and guide, not only for the sake of those being taught but also to fulfill one's own identity. The final strength, *wisdom*, arises out of ego integrity. It expresses itself in a detached concern with the whole of life and conveys to the next genera-tion an integration of experience perhaps best described by the word *heritage*.

Erikson's image of human nature

A personality theorist who speaks of basic strengths or virtues as being attainable and who writes of our "lofty moralism" must certainly be described as presenting an optimistic image of human nature. While it is true that not everyone is successful in attaining hope, will, purpose, wisdom, and the other strengths, everyone has the potential or the capability of reaching these goals. We are not, by our own nature, prevented from doing so. Nor must we inevitably suffer conflict, anxiety, and neu-rosis because of instinctive biological forces.

Erikson's theory allows for hope because each stage of growth, while stressful enough to be labeled a crisis, nevertheless holds the definite possibility of a positive outcome. A person may resolve each crisis in a way that is adaptive and strengthen-ing. Further, even if a person should fail at one stage and be left with a maladaptive character response (for example, isolation instead of intimacy), there is still hope for later stages. A failure at one stage can be corrected by success at a later stage. Thus, there is hope for the future at all stages of growth.

We are capable of consciously directing our own growth over the course of our lives. Therefore, we are not exclusively products of our childhood experiences. While we have little control over the first four stages of development, we have an increasing ability, beginning in adolescence, to chart our own course by choosing ways of responding to the crises of development we must face. Childhood influences are important, but influences at later stages of life can counteract unfortunate childhood experiences.

Erikson's theory seems to be partly deterministic. During the first four stages of development, the kinds of experiences to which the child is exposed—parents, teachers, peer groups, opportunities—are beyond his or her control. Some measure of free will enters into the last four stages of growth, though the choices made will be influenced by attitudes and strengths formed during the first four stages.

Erikson believes that we are influenced much more by learning and experience than by heredity. Psychosocial experiences, not biological forces, affect our personality development. In addition, he posits one ultimate and necessary goal: the development of a positive ego identity and of all eight basic strengths that make up the identity.

Assessment in Erikson's theory

As we have seen, Erikson followed Freud's lead in certain of his theoretical formulations. He deviated from Freud, however, in his methods of assessing personality. Erikson questioned the usefulness and even the safety of some of Freud's techniques, beginning with the psychoanalytic couch.

Having the patient lie on a couch, according to Erikson, can lead to "sadistic" and "faddish" exploitation of the patient. It also gives rise to the illusion of objectivity, an overemphasis on unconscious material, and an excess of impersonality and aloofness on the part of the therapist. To foster a more personal relationship between therapist and patient, and to ensure that they view each other as equals, Erikson preferred to sit facing his patients, with both of them in comfortable chairs in a relaxed atmosphere.

Erikson relied less on formal techniques of assessment than did Freud. He sometimes used free association, but it was not his primary method. He seldom used dream analysis, calling it a wasteful and harmful approach to therapy. He has been critical of Freud's methods of assessing personality, once commenting that they "may make some people sicker than they ever were" (Erikson, 1968, p. 164).

Erikson believes that no technique of assessment can be applied in the same way to every patient. Instead, the techniques must be selected, shaped, and modified to fit the unique requirements of the individual case. In the development of his theory, Erikson was guided by the data obtained through three techniques that have come to be associated with his approach to personality: play therapy, anthropological studies, and psychohistory.

In his work with emotionally disturbed children and in his research on normal children and adolescents, Erikson has used a variety of toys, observing how the subjects play with them. The form and intensity of acts of play can reveal aspects of the personality that might not be revealed verbally, particularly since children have limited powers of expression.

We have already mentioned Erikson's anthropological studies of Indian tribes. Living among the Indians as a participant–observer, Erikson watched behavior and interviewed the subjects at length, particularly with regard to child-rearing techniques.

Erikson's most unusual method of assessment is **psychohistorical analysis**. These are biographical studies in which Erikson has applied his theory of the life cycle and its crises to such people as Adolf Hitler, George Bernard Shaw, Mahatma Gandhi, Maxim Gorky, and Martin Luther. He invokes not only psychoanalytic principles but also his extensive knowledge of European literature and social and political history.

Erikson's analysis centers around a crisis in the person's development, an episode that crystallized and represented the major theme of his or her life, uniting past, present, and future activities. Using what he called *disciplined subjectivity*, Erikson attempts to take the person's viewpoint as his own and to consider events in that individual's life through his or her eyes.

Erikson did not use psychological tests as a means of assessment, although two tests based on his theory have been developed. The Ego-Identity Scale, consisting of 50 statements to be marked true or false, is designed to measure Erikson's notion of ego identity (Dignan, 1965). The Inventory of Psychosocial Development is a 60-item scale assessing both adaptive and maladaptive development for six of Erikson's eight stages, excluding adulthood and maturity (Constantinople, 1969). We shall describe research using these tests in the following section.

In general terms, Erikson's methods of assessment involve a combination of observation of normal and neurotic individuals, conducted within a framework of Freudian, historical, social, and anthropological insights and stirred by a fertile and creative imagination.

Research in Erikson's theory

Erikson used the case-study approach as his basic method of research. By now you are familiar with its weaknesses—the difficulty of duplicating and verifying case material—but you also know how much useful information can be obtained on a patient through this technique.

Erikson remains convinced of the worth of his approach, arguing that it yields many insights into a patient's problems and can lead to a resolution of those problems. He readily admits that the technique is not amenable to experimental verification, but suggests that if laboratory methods do not work with his theory, we should not automatically blame the theory. Perhaps the methods are at fault because they cannot be used with clinically derived data. Nevertheless, some research has been conducted on certain aspects of Erikson's theory.

Sex differences in personality

One controversial study used what Erikson calls **play constructions**, a derivative of his play therapy (Erikson, 1963). Erikson's subjects, 300 boys and girls ages 10 to 12, were asked to construct an exciting scene from an imaginary motion picture using toy figures of animals, automobiles, people, and wooden blocks (see Figure 10.1). The scenes built by the girls tended to be static and peaceful, containing low structures that were usually walled in. The focus was on interiors and enclosures. In many cases, intruders, who were always animals or males, never females, forced their way into the enclosures. The boys' creations tended to be action-oriented, with cars and people in motion and with tall towering structures. In these scenes, most of the people were outside the enclosures. The focus for the boys was on exteriors, action, and height.

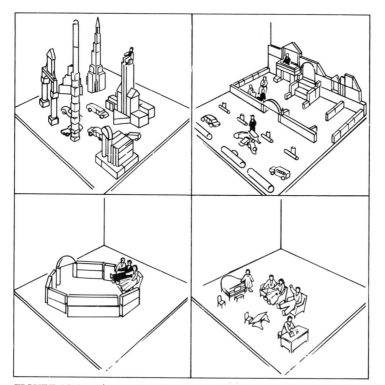

FIGURE 10.1.   Play constructions created by boys (top) and girls (bottom)   *Source: Erikson, 1963, pp. 100–105.*

You can imagine how Erikson, as a Freudian, interpreted these different kinds of play constructions. In his view, girls and boys were symbolically expressing their genitals. As he put it, "Sexual differences in the organization of a play space seem to parallel the morphology of genital differentiation itself: in the male, an external organ, erectable and intrusive in character . . . in the female, internal organs, with vestibular access, leading to a statically expectant ova" (Erikson, 1968, p. 271). Hence, girls would build low enclosures in which people are walled in and static; boys would build towers, and their people would be in motion and not enclosed.

We shall see that Erikson has been criticized for this interpretation, a view which suggests that he, like Freud, sees women as victims of their anatomy, whose personalities are shaped, at least in part, by the absence of a penis. Erikson did admit that such differences in play constructions could result not from anatomical differences but from sex-role training, in which boys may be oriented more toward aggression, action, and achievement than girls are.

Although this research was not conducted to test Erikson's notion of ego identity or the existence of various stages of development, it does demonstrate an imaginative way of studying children using their primary activity of play.

Studies of the psychosocial stages

Other studies have been more directly concerned with testing Erikson's stages of development. In one study, children ages 4, 8, and 11 were asked to make up stories based on several pictures. The stories were then analyzed by judges to determine the stage of development they reflected. Based on Erikson's theory, the stories at age 4 should reflect themes from Stage 2 (the stage just completed), the stories at age 8 should reflect themes from Stage 3, and the stories at age 11 the themes from Stage 4. The results supported these predictions (Ciaccio, 1971).

A study using the Inventory of Psychosocial Development found that there was a strong relationship between happiness and successful development at each of the first six stages (from infancy through young adulthood) (Constantinople, 1969). Another study showed a high correlation between unsuccessful development at each of Erikson's first six stages and anomie (a sense of uprootedness) (Reimanis, 1974). Both of these findings are supportive of Erikson's theory.

Studies of ego identity

Considerable research has been conducted on the concept of ego identity. Using the Ego-Identity Scale, one study tested Erikson's contention that too weak or too strong an identification with the parent of the same sex can harm an adolescent's ego identity (Dignan, 1965). Scores on the Ego-Identity Scale and on a test of maternal identification were correlated for a group of women college freshmen and sophomores. The results confirmed Erikson's prediction. Ego identity was positively related to the degree of maternal identification.

Another study dealt with Erikson's belief that positive outcomes in resolving the identity crisis are related to positive outcomes in each of the previous stages of development. Thus, adolescents who had developed trust, autonomy, initiative, and industry in the first four stages of development should display high levels of ego identity instead of role confusion. This was found to be the case. Conversely, adolescents who had not resolved their identity crises (who experienced role confusion) had not developed those positive characteristics in earlier stages (Waterman, Buebel & Waterman, 1970).

An intensive analysis of Erikson's adolescence stage of development identified five psychosocial criteria or statuses of the period of ego identity versus role confusion (Marcia, 1966). The first is *identity achievement*, which describes those who are committed to occupational and ideological choices and who have a strong sense of ego identity. Such adolescents are stable, concerned with realistic goals, and able to cope with changing environmental demands. In addition, they perform much better on difficult tasks, compared with adolescents who experience role confusion. The stable adolescents tend to major in more difficult subjects in college, particularly engineering and the physical sciences (Marcia & Friedman, 1970).

The second status of the adolescent stage of development is called *moratorium*, which describes those who are still undergoing their identity crises and whose occupational and ideological commitments are ill-formed and vague. These adolescents hold ambivalent views toward authority figures, alternately rebelling against them and needing guidance from them (Podd, Marcia & Rubin, 1968). Their behaviors range from indecisiveness to considerable activity and creativity.

The third status, *foreclosure*, describes adolescents who have not experienced any identity crisis and who are firmly committed to an occupation and an ideology. However, those commitments were determined by their parents and accepted as their own, rather than resulting from deliberate choice. These adolescents tend to be rigid, authoritarian, and unable to cope well with changing situations (Marcia, 1967).

The fourth status is *identity diffusion*, which characterizes adolescents who have no occupational or ideological commitments and who may or may not have undergone their identity crisis. Their lack of commitment may be expressed in a lifestyle that actively rejects a commitment to anything or in aimless drifting.

The fifth status is *alienated achievement*, which characterizes adolescents who have undergone identity crises, have no occupational commitment, and possess an ideology that is critical of the social and economic system. Thus, they have a consistent rationale, to which they are committed, that precludes their being committed to any occupation because that would bring them into the very system they oppose. As students, they tend to be highly cerebral and philosophical and cynically refuse to make any other commitments (Marcia & Friedman, 1970; Orlofsky, Marcia & Lesser, 1973).

Overall, there is a great deal of research support for Erikson's notion of ego identity and for the crisis of identity in the adolescent stage of development. There is also some support, though it is less decisive, for the earlier stages of development and for the positive effects of satisfactorily resolving the crises inherent in each of those stages.

A final commentary

Erikson's influence has been widely recognized in both professional and popular circles. In 1975, *Time* magazine referred to him as "probably the most influential living psychoanalyst" (March 17, 1975, p. 76). In 1983, *Psychology Today* described him as the "dean of American psychoanalysts—and an authentic intellectual hero" (Hall, 1983, p. 22). In the rankings of the relative importance of 286 psychologists in the last half of the 20th century, Erikson is in 5th place overall and in 4th place among the theorists discussed in this book (Gilgen, 1982).

In addition, his influence has spread to the fields of education, social work, and vocational and marriage counseling. In any endeavor in which people work with children and adolescents, Erikson's ideas have been put to use. Many children, both normal and emotionally disturbed, have been reared, taught, and cared for in ways directly affected by his concepts of the psychosocial stages of development and the identity crisis. His impact on childhood development has been honored by the establishment of the Erikson Institute for Early Childhood Education at Loyola University in Chicago.

The growing field of life-span developmental psychology, which has undergone a massive increase in research and theory in recent years, owes much of its impetus to Erikson's emphasis on the continuing growth of personality throughout life. The current interest in the developmental problems of middle-aged and older persons is also an outgrowth of Erikson's work.

Erikson also contributed to psychology through his method of play therapy, which has come to be a standard diagnostic and therapeutic device in work with emotionally disturbed children and with those who are victims of abuse. Children who cannot verbalize the details of a sexual attack, for example, are often able to express their feelings through play with dolls that represent themselves and their attackers. There has also been a renewed interest in psychohistory, a procedure pioneered and refined by Erikson.

Despite these impressive contributions to psychology, Erikson's system is not without its critics. Some point to what they see as poorly defined and ambiguous terms and concepts, to dogmatic pronouncements made in the absence of appropriate supporting data, and to a lack of precision in his writing.

Erikson has recognized the validity of such criticisms and blames them on his artistic temperament and his lack of formal training in science and logic, which has caused him to be less precise than he should. "I came to psychology from art," he wrote, "which may explain, if not justify, the fact that at times the reader will find me painting contexts and backgrounds where he would rather have me point to facts and concepts" (Erikson, 1950, p. 13).

A more specific criticism relates to the unsatisfactory and incomplete description of the last developmental stage. Erikson has had less to say about the stage of maturity than about any of the other stages. Also, some psychologists question whether personality development in old age is likely to be as positive as Erikson's concept of ego integrity suggests. They argue that there is much pain, loss, and depression in old age, even for those who possess Erikson's basic strength of wisdom.

Erikson's position on sex differences as revealed in his play-constructions research has come under attack. What he claims are biologically-based differences in personality originating in the possession or lack of a penis are seen by many as culturally-based differences instead. As we noted, Erikson has admitted this possibility. Further, he has said that he never claimed that personality was shaped solely by anatomy, but only partially.

Erikson's method of psychohistorical analysis can be faulted for its subjectivity, and he agrees that psychohistory may not provide an accurate representation of a person's life. Indeed, he has said that some of his analyses may be part legend, but he does not believe that this diminishes the value of his work. "If some of it is legend so be it; the making of legend is as much a part of the scholarly rewriting of history as it is part of the original facts used in the work of scholars." Thus, he sees nothing wrong in using such subjective material, provided that "a reported episode does not contradict other well-established facts; persists in having a ring of truth; and yields a meaning consistent with psychological theory" (Erikson, 1958, p. 37).

Overall, Erikson has shown little interest in responding to his critics (and the amount of criticism has not been all that large) or in defending his view of personality. He recognizes that there are many ways of looking at the same object or process, depending on one's perspective, and that no single perspective is the sole correct way. Therefore, one cannot accuse Erikson of being rigid and dogmatic about his work.

Erikson's influence continues to grow, through his books and through large numbers of primarily younger psychiatrists, psychologists, and teachers, who see in his work a useful way of viewing the development of the individual from infancy to old age.

Summary

Erikson built upon Freud's theory in three ways: by elaborating and extending the stages of development; by emphasizing the ego more than the id; and by recognizing the impact of culture, society, and history on the personality. Erikson underwent several identity crises in his youth, providing another example of the subjective nature of personality theories.

The growth of the personality is divided into eight stages. The first four are similar to Freud's oral, anal, phallic, and latency stages. Erikson focused more on psychosocial correlates of these stages than on biological ones. A conflict exists at each stage, in which the person is faced with both adaptive and maladaptive ways of coping. The ego must consist primarily of the adaptive way of coping at each stage, but it must also contain a share of the maladaptive way.

Development is governed by the epigenetic principle, that is, each stage is governed by genetic factors, but the environment influences whether these biologically determined stages are realized.

The oral-sensory stage, from birth to 1 year, results in trust or mistrust. The outcome depends on how responsive the mother is to the baby's physical needs.

The muscular-anal stage, from 1 to 3 years, results in autonomy or doubt and shame. The outcome depends on how well the parents allow the child to exercise his or her autonomous will. The locomotor-genital stage, from 3 to 5 years, results in initiative or guilt, depending on how the parents react to the child's initiatives, including the fantasies of the Oedipus complex. The latency stage, from 6 to 11 years, results in industry or inferiority, depending on how parents and teachers react to the child's attempts to learn how to work and to refine skills.

The outcomes of the crises for each of these four stages of development is dependent more on other people than on oneself. The outcomes of the crises for each of the next four stages is increasingly dependent on oneself.

The stage of adolescence, from 12 to 18 years, results in ego identity or role confusion. Adolescence involves a psychological moratorium that is necessary for role and image experimentation. The stage of young adulthood, from 18 to 35 years, results in intimacy or isolation. Intimacy means a sense of caring and commitment without fear of losing one's self-identity. The stage of adulthood, from 35 to 55 years, results in generativity or stagnation. Generativity refers to the need to be actively involved in teaching and guiding the next generation. The stage of maturity, from 55 until death, results in ego integrity or despair. Ego integrity involves accepting one's place and past, and viewing life with a sense of fulfillment and satisfaction.

Each of the eight stages of the life span allows opportunities for basic strengths to develop. These strengths emerge from the adaptive ways of handling each stage of growth. Hope, growing out of trust, is the persistent belief that desires can be satisfied. Will, deriving from autonomy, is a determination to exercise freedom of choice and self-restraint. Purpose, growing out of initiative, involves the courage to envision and pursue important goals. Competence, deriving from industry, involves the exertion of skill and intelligence in the pursuit and completion of tasks. Fidelity, arising from ego identity, involves the maintenance of basic loyalties and a sense of duty and genuineness in relations with others. Love, growing out of intimacy, is a mutual devotion in a shared identity. Care, emerging from generativity, is a broad concern for others. Wisdom, arising from ego integrity, expresses itself in a detached concern with the whole of life.

Erikson presents a flattering and optimistic image of human nature in which everyone has the ability to achieve basic strengths, to resolve each crisis in an adaptive way, and to consciously direct his or her own growth. People are not immutable victims of biological forces or childhood experiences. They are influenced more by learning than by heredity.

Erikson's primary methods of assessment are play therapy, anthropological studies, and psychohistory. His basic method of research is the case study. His research using play constructions persuaded him that male and female personalities are shaped in part by the presence or absence of a penis.

The research literature provides support for Erikson's first six stages of development and for the concept of ego identity. An analysis of the adolescence stage of development identified five psychosocial criteria of that period: identity achievement, moratorium, foreclosure, identity diffusion, and alienated achievement.

Erikson's ideas have had a great influence on work with children, on life-span developmental psychology, and on understanding the middle-aged and elderly.

Criticisms of his system include poorly defined terms, dogmatic pronouncements, lack of precision in his writing, incomplete description of the stage of maturity, poorly supported claims of personality differences based on the lack of a penis, and subjectivity in the method of psychohistorical analysis.

Glossary

basic strengths   Motivating characteristics and beliefs that derive from the satisfactory resolution of the crisis at each stage of development.

crisis   The turning point faced by the individual at each stage of development.

epigenetic principle of maturation   The idea that human development is governed by a sequence of stages that depend on genetic factors.

ego identity   The self-image formed during adolescence that integrates an individual's ideas of what he or she is and wants to be.

identity crisis   The failure to achieve ego identity during adolescence.

play constructions   A personality assessment technique for children in which structures assembled from dolls, blocks, and other toys are analyzed.

psychohistorical analysis   Erikson's application of his life-span theory as well as psychoanalytic principles to the study of historical figures.

psychosocial stages of development   Eight successive stages encompassing the entire life span during which the individual must cope, in an adaptive or maladaptive way, with a crisis.

Review questions

1. In what ways does Erikson's theory extend psychoanalytic theory?
2. What is the role of conflict in the stages of psychosocial development?
3. Describe the four childhood stages of psychosocial development and the influence of parental behaviors on the possible outcomes of each stage.
4. What is the major difference between the first four developmental stages and the last four developmental stages?
5. What factors affect the development of ego identity? Why do some people fail to achieve an identity at this stage?
6. What are the positive ways of resolving the conflicts of the adult stages of psychosocial development?
7. Describe the basic strengths. How do they develop?
8. What did the results of Erikson's play-construction research lead him to conclude about sex differences in personality? On what grounds have his conclusions been criticized?
9. Describe some recent research on the adolescent development of ego identity. Does the research support Erikson's theory?

Suggested reading

Erikson, E. H. *Childhood and society*, 2nd ed. New York: Norton, 1963.

Erikson, E. H. *Identity: Youth and crisis*. New York: Norton, 1968.

Erikson, E. H. Autobiographic notes on the identity crisis. *Daedalus*, 1970, 99, 730–759.

Erikson, E. H. *Life history and the historical moment*. New York: Norton, 1975.

Erikson, E. H. *The completed life cycle: A review*. New York: Norton, 1982.

Evans, R. I. *Dialogue with Erik Erikson*. New York: Harper & Row, 1967.

Roazen, P. *Erik H. Erikson: The power and limits of a vision*. New York: Free Press, 1976.

PART 5

The Humanistic Approach

The humanistic approach to personality is part of the larger-scale humanistic movement that attempted to reform all of psychology. Humanistic psychology objects to the two major forces in American psychology—the psychoanalytic approach and the behavioristic approach—arguing that both present too limited and demeaning an image of human nature.

The humanistic psychologists take issue with Freud and with those who follow his teachings (see Parts 1 and 2), on the grounds that they study only the sick side of human nature, concentrating on our neuroses and psychoses. The humanists ask, how can we ever know about positive human characteristics and qualities by focusing on mental illness? We must study human strengths and virtues; we must analyze the principles of mental health. We need to learn what people are like at their best, not just at their worst.

Behaviorism, with its disavowal of conscious and unconscious forces and its exclusive focus on the objective observation of overt behavior (see Part 7), is criticized by the humanistic psychologists as narrow and sterile. A psychology based only on conditioned responses presents an image of people as mechanical, robot-like organisms, reacting deterministically to physical stimuli in the environment. We are not big white rats or inefficient computers, the humanistic psychologists argue. Human beings are too complex to be understood fully by the methods of the behaviorists.

The humanistic approach to personality, represented here by the work of Carl Rogers and Abraham Maslow (and to some degree by Gordon Allport), stresses human virtues and aspirations, conscious free will, and the fulfillment of one's potentialities. It presents a flattering and optimistic image of human nature, depicting us as active, creative beings concerned with self-actualization, growth, and development.

271

CHAPTER 11

Carl Rogers

The life of Rogers (1902–   )
**Actualization: The basic human
    tendency**
The experiential world
The development of the self
  Positive regard
  Conditions of worth
  Anxiety
**Characteristics of the fully functioning
    person**
Rogers' image of human nature
Assessment in Rogers' theory
  The clinical approach: Person-centered
      therapy
  Psychological tests
Research in Rogers' theory
  Studies of the self-concept
A final commentary
Summary
Glossary
Review questions
Suggested reading

*The organism has one basic tendency and
striving—to actualize, maintain, and
enhance the experiencing organism.*

CARL ROGERS

Carl Rogers is no doubt well known to you already as the originator of an extremely popular approach to psychotherapy known initially as nondirective or client-centered therapy and more recently as **person-centered therapy**. This form of psychotherapy has generated an enormous amount of research and found wide application in the treatment of the disturbed. Indeed, Rogerian therapy seems to be almost as popular as Freud's psychoanalysis as a method of treatment.

As was the case with some other theorists, Rogers' theory of personality was developed from, and is continually being revised in the light of, his experiences in working with patients, or *clients*, as he prefers to call them. His formulations on the dynamics and structure of personality are tied directly to his approach to therapy. Therefore, his view of the therapeutic situation tells us a great deal about his view of the nature of personality. Consider the name of his approach: client- or person-centered therapy. It is intended to suggest that individuals have the ability as well as the responsibility in themselves to change and improve their personality, with the therapist acting to facilitate rather than to direct such change.

Rogers sees people primarily as conscious and rational beings ruled by the conscious perception of their own selves and of their experiential world. There is little influence of the Freudian position to be found in his theory. Rogers does not ascribe a dominant influence to unconscious forces of which an individual has neither awareness nor control.

Rogers also rejects the notion that past events exert a controlling influence on present behavior. While he does recognize that past experiences, particularly those of childhood, can influence the way in which people perceive their world and themselves, he insists that one's present feelings and emotions are of greater importance in the dynamics of personality. Rogers' ultimate concern, both in theory and therapy, is with the change and growth in present personality, not with unconscious or past experiences that might have led to the present state of the personality.

Because of the importance of the conscious and the present, Rogers believes, a personality can only be understood from an individual's own point of view—that is, on the basis of his or her inner, subjective experiences. Rogers, therefore, takes a *phenomenological* approach to personality—one that deals with reality as it is perceived by the individual. This perception may or may not always coincide with objective reality.

Rogers believes that people have one overriding motivation, with which we come equipped at birth: a tendency to actualize, to develop all of our abilities and potentialities, from the strictly biological to the most sophisticated psychological aspects of our being. The ultimate goal is the actualization of the self—a concept of central importance in Rogers' system. To maintain and enhance the self, to become a *fully functioning person*, is the goal toward which all of a person's being is directed.

Rogers' approach to both therapy and theory, and the optimistic and humanistic picture of human beings it provides, has met with an enthusiastic response and has been found to have wide relevance to psychology, education, and family-life research. He was also one of the more positive and sobering influences in the upsurge of interest in sensitivity training and encounter therapy that took place in the 1970s.

In addition, his work has been extended beyond the therapeutic situation and is being applied to conflicts between groups in a variety of situations, including international relations. He noted, "I am no longer talking simply about psychotherapy, but about a point of view, a philosophy, an approach to life, a way of being, which fits any situation in which *growth*—of a person, a group, or a community—is part of the goal" (Rogers, 1980, p. ix).

The life of Rogers (1902—   )

To relate Rogers' adult view of personality to his early life experiences, we would have to look not for insecurity or rejection, conflict or hostility, but rather for signs of an autonomous self, a reliance on his own experience, an emphasis on developing and actualizing potentialities, and a belief that people can consciously change and improve themselves. Not surprisingly, that is what we find.

Rogers was born in 1902 in suburb of Chicago, the fourth child in a family of six. His parents were strict in their fundamental religious views and emphasized moral behavior and the virtue of hard work. The religious teachings of his parents held Rogers in a vise throughout his boyhood and adolescence. They provided him with someone else's view of the world and later became a target to revolt against when he wanted to deal with himself and his world in his own way.

The parents were quite devoted to their children and also very controlling in their influence. As Rogers later did in his nondirective counseling, his parents promoted their influence in subtle and loving ways; he could not remember ever having been given a direct command. Yet it was clearly understood by all the children "that we did not dance, play cards, attend movies, smoke, drink, or show any sexual interest" (Rogers, 1967, p. 344).

The family was very close—so much so that Rogers had virtually no social life outside his home. The children teased each other a great deal—"unmercifully," as he described it—and Rogers felt that his parents favored an older brother over himself. As a result, there was "much rivalry and hard feeling" between the brothers, but at the same time there was a great deal of companionship (Rogers, 1967, p. 345).

Rogers describes himself as having been a solitary boy, dreamy and lost in fantasy much of the time. He read incessantly, any book he could find, even the dictionary and encyclopedia. As a result of this solitude, he came to rely on his own experience and his own view of the world, a characteristic that has stayed with him all his life and that forms a part of his personality theory. In his later years, he came to realize how strongly his early solitude and loneliness had influenced both his own personality and his approach to the formal study of personality. "As I look back," he wrote, "I realize that my interest in interviewing and in therapy certainly grew out of my early loneliness. Here was a socially approved way of getting really close to individuals and thus filling some of the hunger I had undoubtedly felt" (Rogers, 1980, p. 34).

When he was 12, the family moved to a farm 30 miles from Chicago, an experience that led to the awakening of Rogers' interest in science. This awakening came about in two ways. First, he became fascinated by a certain species of moth that he discovered in the woods. He did more than observe it; he captured some, bred and raised them over many months, and read everything he could find about moths. The second impetus to his interest in science was farming, which his father insisted be as scientific and modern as possible. He read the books his father brought home about scientific farming, learning about hundreds of experiments and coming to appreciate the scientific method of control groups, isolation of a single variable for study, and statistical analyses of the results. It was an unusual understanding for a boy of 15.

When it came time for college, Rogers chose to study agriculture at the University of Wisconsin, which his parents, two older brothers, and a sister had attended. After his second year, his goal in life changed. As a result of the religious influences in his home and student religious conferences in college, he shifted from the study of scientific agriculture to preparation for the ministry.

During his junior year at Wisconsin, in 1922, Rogers was selected to attend the World Student Christian Federation Conference in Peking, China. During the six months of travel, he wrote to his parents of his changing views, from fundamentalist to liberal, and of his own philosophy and goals. He finally freed himself of his parents' way of thinking, a departure that grieved his parents but that gave him an emotional and intellectual independence. He came to realize that he could, in his words, "think my own thoughts, come to my own conclusions, and take the stands I believed in" (Rogers, 1967, p. 351). This liberation, and the confidence and sense of direction it provided, led Rogers to the opinion that a person must come to rely only on his or her own experience. Reliance on and trust in one's experience became the core of his approach to personality. These events in Rogers' life provide another example of the impact of intuitive knowledge on personality theory, knowledge later verified along rational and empirical lines.

In 1924, Rogers graduated from the University of Wisconsin, married a woman he had known since childhood, and began formal study for the ministry at the Union Theological Seminary in New York City. He stayed there for two years, then transferred across the street to Columbia University Teachers College to study clinical and educational psychology, in which he had developed a greater interest than he had in the ministry.

He received his Ph.D. in 1931, having served an internship in child guidance and done his dissertation on the measurement of personality adjustment in children. For 12 years, from 1928 to 1940, Rogers served on the staff of the Child Study Department of the Society for the Prevention of Cruelty to Children in Rochester, New York. Most of that time was spent in the diagnosis and treatment of delinquent and underprivileged children, and, in 1939, when the agency was re-formed into the Rochester Guidance Center, he was made director.

In 1940, he moved from a clinical to an academic setting with an appointment as Professor of Psychology at Ohio State University. There, primarily in his work with bright graduate students, Rogers began to formulate and express his views on the counseling and treatment of the emotionally disturbed. He also became involved in professional affairs in psychology, helping to bring clinical psychology into the mainstream of contemporary psychological thought, as represented by the American Psychological Association.

He left Ohio for the University of Chicago in 1945, and went on to the University of Wisconsin in 1957. During these years he was very prolific, publishing a number of articles, papers, and books, which served to bring his method of therapy and view of personality before a wide and interested audience. In 1963, he moved to California, where he is now a Fellow at the Center for Studies of the Person in La Jolla.

In his eighties, Rogers is diligently pursuing the goal of reducing international tension. He is applying his person-centered philosophy to attempts to break down the barriers between such groups as Protestants and Catholics in Northern Ireland, Jews and Arabs in the Middle East, and Eastern bloc communist countries and Western democracies. "The problem of preventing a nuclear holocaust has top priority in my mind, my heart, and my work" (Rogers, 1984, p. 15).

Rogers was president of the American Psychological Association in 1946 and has received that organization's Distinguished Scientific Contribution Award and Distinguished Professional Contribution Award.

Actualization: The basic human tendency

As we saw in the opening quotation, Rogers views people as motivated by one overall basic tendency: the tendency to actualize, to maintain and enhance the experiencing organism, which is, of course, ourselves. This innate tendency is the one fundamental need of human beings, and it includes all the physiological and psychological needs; but it is, in reality, more oriented toward the biological than the psychological.

As our one fundamental need, the tendency toward actualization includes everything, even the simplest, most reflexive physiological needs, such as those for air, food, and water. It is by attending to these basic physiological needs and by defending the organism against attack that the actualization tendency serves to maintain the organism. That is, it provides for sustenance and for survival itself.

However, as we have seen, the actualization tendency does more than simply maintain the organism; it also facilitates and supports the growth and enhancement—the development—of the organism. It guides growth by providing for the development and differentiation of each and every organ and physiological function of the body. It is responsible for all those aspects of growth that are subsumed under the label *maturation*, which is the genetically determined development of the body's parts and processes, ranging from the growth of the fetus to the appearance of the secondary sex characteristics at the time of puberty.

All these changes, programmed in the person's genetic makeup, are brought to fruition and culmination, according to Rogers, by the actualizing tendency. Even though such changes are genetically determined (programmed in advance), the organism's progress toward full maturation is not an automatic and effortless progression of stages. Rather, Rogers describes the process as involving struggle and pain, such as when the child takes its first steps. The child falls and is hurt, and it would be less painful to remain in the crawling stage. But no, the child persists. He or she falls and cries again but still continues. The child persists in spite of the pain, Rogers says, because the tendency to actualize, to move forward, to develop and grow is much stronger than any urge to regress brought on by the pains of growth.

This actualizing tendency is seen not only in humans and animals but in all living things. In describing all life, Rogers uses such phrases as the "tenacity of life" and the "forward thrust of life," indicating his belief in the existence of virtually irresistible forces that cause an organism not only to survive, sometimes under extremely hostile conditions, but also to adapt and develop and grow.

There is, then, a strong biological core to the actualization tendency. We shall see shortly that as the individual matures, this tendency becomes more psychological in nature and reflects the impact of learning and experience more than of biology.

Rogers believes that throughout life people demonstrate what he calls the **organismic valuing process**. By that he means that all life experiences are evaluated in terms of how well they serve the actualization tendency. Those experiences that people perceive to be promoting or facilitating of actualization are seen as good and desirable and are thus assigned a positive value. Those experiences perceived as hindering actualization are seen as undesirable. These perceptions will influence behavior because experiences considered undesirable will be avoided, while those considered desirable will be sought out so that they can be repeated as often as possible.

The experiential world

Rogers was concerned with the environment in which a person operates—the frame of reference or context of the individual, which so strongly influences that person. We are exposed to countless sources of stimulation in the world around us—some trivial and some important, some threatening and some rewarding. How do we perceive and react to this multifaceted environment?

Rogers answers this question simply by saying that the reality of a person's environment is how he or she perceives that environment. And one's perception may not coincide with objective reality. We know that we may perceive some aspect of reality far differently from the way someone else does. You may look upon the behavior of another college student in a dramatically different light than does your 80-year-old grandmother or grandfather. Also, our perceptions can change with time and circumstances. Your own perception of a college student's behavior may have changed drastically by the time you are 80.

The notion that perception is highly subjective is an old one, certainly not unique or original with Rogers. The important aspect of it, in his view, is that the world of a person's reality is a strictly private affair. It can be known, in any complete sense, only to the individual.

A person's experiential world includes not only immediately present experiences of which the person is aware but also all the stimuli of which he or she is not aware (such as the pressure of the chair on your body as you read) and memories of past experiences, insofar as they are actively guiding the person's perceptions of the moment.

As the infant's actualizing tendency leads it on to ever-higher levels of development, its experiential world broadens. The baby is exposed to more and more sources of stimuli, and its behavior is always in reference to these stimuli as they are perceived.

Experiences combine to make up the experiential field, coalescing into one's own private view of the world. One's experiences, therefore, become of supreme importance. There is, after all, no other basis on which to make judgments and to behave. Rogers wrote: "Experience is, for me, the highest authority. The touchstone of validity is my own experience" (Rogers, 1961, p. 23). Higher levels of development sharpen and define one's experiential world, and they also lead to the formation of what is a central aspect of Rogers' view of personality—the *self.*

The development of the self

As an infant develops a more complex experiential field, as a result of more inter-actions with other people, one part of his or her experience becomes differentiated from the rest. This new and separate part is defined by the words *I, me,* and *myself.* It is the self or self-concept, and it involves distinguishing what is directly and immediately a part of oneself from what is external to oneself. The self-concept is the person's picture or image of what he or she is, should be, and might like to be.

There would seem to be room for inconsistencies here among these three facets of the self-concept. However, Rogers argues that the self, while fluid, is ideally a consistent pattern, an organized whole. Thus, all possible aspects of the self strive toward consistency. For example, someone who considers himself or herself to have absolutely no aggressive feelings toward others dares not express any need for aggression—at least not in any obvious and direct manner. All behavior must be similarly consistent with one's self-concept. (The consequences of inconsistency or incongruity will be discussed later.)

Positive regard

As the self emerges, the infant also develops a need for what Rogers calls **positive regard**. This need is probably learned, although Rogers believes that its source is irrelevant. Whether innate or learned, the need for positive regard is pervasive and persistent and is found in all human beings. As the name implies, positive regard includes acceptance, love, and approval from other people, notably the mother during infancy. It is satisfying to receive positive regard and frustrating not to receive it or to have it withdrawn. Indeed, it is critical to the infant, whose behavior is guided by the extent to which this affection and love are received.

If the mother does not bestow positive regard, the infant's tendency toward actualization and enhancement of the self is hampered. The baby perceives the mother's disapproval of his or her behavior as disapproval of all aspects of himself or herself. If this occurs very frequently, the infant ceases to strive to actualize the self and works instead to secure positive regard. Ideally, the infant feels sufficient acceptance, love, and approval overall, even though specific behaviors may be met

Ideally, a parent provides unconditional positive regard;
parental love, acceptance, and approval are granted freely
and are not conditional upon the child's behavior.

with disapproval. This state or condition is called **unconditional positive regard**, implying that the mother's love for the child is not conditional upon how the child behaves but is granted freely and fully to the child as a person.

An important aspect of the need for positive regard is its reciprocal nature. When people perceive themselves to be satisfying someone else's need for positive regard, they will, as a result, experience satisfaction of the need themselves. Thus, it is rewarding to satisfy someone else's need for positive regard.

Because of the importance of satisfying this need, particularly in infancy, people become highly sensitive to the attitudes and behaviors of others. In light of the feedback we receive from others (their approval or disapproval), we develop and refine our own self-concept. As a part of this self-concept, we begin to internalize the attitudes of others. As a result, the positive regard gradually comes more from within ourselves than from others, a condition Rogers calls **positive self-regard**. This becomes just as strong a need as was the need for positive regard from others, and what satisfies self-regard are the same conditions that brought regard from others. For example, infants who are rewarded by their mothers with affection, approval, and love when they are happy come to experience positive self-regard (on their own) whenever they are happy. They thus come to reward or punish themselves.

Conditions of worth

Out of this developmental sequence, from positive regard to positive self-regard, evolves the Rogerian version of Freud's superego—**conditions of worth**—which derives from *conditional positive regard*. We noted that unconditional positive regard involved love and acceptance for the infant without conditions—that is, independent of the baby's behavior. As you have probably guessed, conditional positive regard is quite the opposite.

Usually, and understandably, parents do not react to everything their baby does with positive regard. Some behaviors annoy or frighten or bore them, and for those behaviors they do not supply affection or approval. Indeed, they may supply just the opposite. And so the infant comes to learn that the affection and approval of the parents are dependent upon how he or she behaves. The baby comes to see that sometimes he or she is prized and sometimes not.

If the mother, for example, expresses disapproval every time an infant drops an object out of the crib, the infant eventually comes to disapprove of himself or herself for behaving in that way. External standards of judgment have become personalized, and the child, in a sense, punishes himself or herself as the mother did earlier. The child loves himself or herself only when he or she behaves in ways known to bring the mother's approval. Thus, the self comes to function as a mother-surrogate.

Out of this situation, infants develop conditions of worth, seeing themselves as worthy only under certain conditions. Having already internalized their parents' norms in their positive self-regard, infants now come to view themselves as worthy or unworthy, according to terms defined by the parents. Unless they abide by the terms of their conditions of worth, infants cannot look upon themselves in a positive manner.

Infants who have arrived at this point must begin to avoid certain behaviors and attitudes, regardless of how satisfying they might otherwise be. Therefore, they can no longer function in full freedom. They must judge and weigh their behavior closely, and so, according to Rogers, they are prevented from fully developing or actualizing their selves, because certain behaviors can no longer be expressed. In a sense, such children inhibit their own development by having to live within the confines of their conditions of worth.

Anxiety

Not only must the child inhibit certain behaviors, but he or she must also deny the awareness of certain perceptions in his or her experiential field, or at least distort them so they will not be perceived accurately. Thus, there develops what Rogers calls **incongruence** between the self-concept and some aspects of an individual's experience. Those experiences that are incongruent with the self serve as a source of threat and usually are experienced as a form of *anxiety*.

As a result of closing oneself off to certain experiences, one is not true to—and may even become estranged from—oneself. Experiences are evaluated and either accepted or rejected, not in terms of how they could contribute to the full actualization of self (the organismic valuing process), but rather in terms of the positive regard they will bring.

The anxiety accompanying the threat must be defended against, and the only way one can accomplish this is, as we have seen, to deny or distort aspects of the perceptual field, closing off a portion of it. The result is a rigidity in one's perceptions.

According to Rogers, the level of a person's psychological adjustment, the degree of a person's normality, is a function of how congruent or compatible the self is with experience. Psychologically healthy persons are able to perceive both themselves and their environments (including other people) much as they really are. They are freely open to all experience because none of it threatens their self-concept. No part of their experience has to be defended against by denial or distortion because they learned no conditions of worth in childhood. They had unconditional positive regard. Thus, they are free to utilize all experience, to develop all facets of the self, to fulfill all their potentialities. In other words, they are free to become self-actualizing—to proceed toward the goal of becoming fully functioning persons.

Characteristics of the fully functioning person

The fully functioning person is the desired end product of psychological development and of social evolution, according to Rogers. Perhaps the primary characteristic of this self-actualizing person is *awareness of all experiences*. No experience is cut off, distorted, or denied in any way; all of it filters through to the self. There is no defensiveness involved, for there is nothing to defend against; there are no threats to the individual's self-concept. The person is free and open to everything—both to positive feelings, such as courage and tenderness, and to negative ones, such as fear and pain. Such a person is more emotional in that he or she not only experiences a wider range of positive and negative emotions, but also experiences them more intensely than the defensive person.

A second characteristic of the fully functioning person is the tendency or ability to *live fully and richly in each and every moment*. Each moment, and the experience it can bring, is fresh and new, or at least has the potential to be fresh and new. Hence, each moment cannot be predicted or anticipated. It is lived in fully, participated in rather than observed.

There can be no rigidity, no tight organization or structure imposed on one's experience. The structure, a fluid, ever-changing organization, emerges from the experience. In the nonhealthy person, all experience is organized and distorted to fit one's structured preconceptions.

The third characteristic of the healthy personality is the *trusting of one's own organism*. By that Rogers means trusting the feel of one's reaction rather than being guided solely by the judgments of others, or by a social code, or even by intellectual judgments. Rogers wrote: "I have learned that my total organism's sensing of a situation is more trustworthy than my intellect" (Rogers, 1961, p. 22). Behaving in a way that feels right, he said, is a trustworthy guide to truly satisfying behavior.

This is not to suggest that the self-actualizing person completely ignores data from his or her intellect or from others. Rather, it means that all such data (such experiences) are congruent with the person's self-concept. They are not threatening and can be perceived accurately and evaluated and weighed accordingly. The final decision regarding how to behave in a particular situation, therefore, results from a consideration of all experiential data. However, the person is unaware of undertaking such considerations (because of the congruence between self and experience), and so the decision seems to be intuitive. It seems more emotionally than intellectually based; again, it feels right.

A fourth characteristic is a *sense of freedom*. Healthy, self-actualizing persons feel genuinely free to move in any direction they wish, to choose freely with a lack of constraint or inhibition. As a result, they experience a sense of personal power about their lives because they know that the future depends on their own actions and is not determined by circumstances, past events, or other people. The point is that they do not feel compelled—either by others or by themselves—to behave in one and only one way. They are not driven along a single path.

Rogers also believes that the healthy personality is a very *creative* individual, living constructively and adaptively even as his or her environmental conditions may change. Allied with this creativity—indeed, very much a part of it—is a sense of spontaneity. The person can flexibly adapt to—and seek out—new experiences and challenges. He or she does not need predictability, security, or a tension-free state. In fact, those conditions are anathema to the fully functioning person.

Rogers does not feel that adjectives such as *happy*, *blissful*, or *contented* are appropriate to describe the self-actualizing person, though such a person would certainly have those feelings at certain times. More appropriate descriptive labels to apply to the healthy person's experience are *enriching*, *exciting*, *rewarding*, *challenging*, and *meaningful*.

Admittedly, it is difficult to be a self-actualizing person, for it involves continually testing, growing, stretching, and using all of one's potentialities. Put simply, "it involves the courage to be," and there is much complexity, trial, and challenge in that prescription (Rogers, 1961, p. 196).

There is one final point to be made about the self-actualizing person, and it is implicit in the ending of the word *actualizing*. Rogers never uses the word *actualized*, for that would imply a finished and static personality. That is decidedly not the case; the development of such a person is always in process. Rogers describes it as "a direction, not a destination" (Rogers, 1961, p. 186). The self-actualizing person is continually changing and growing as he or she strives to actualize all of his or her potentialities. If such growth ceased, the person would lose the characteristics of spontaneity, flexibility, and openness to new experiences. The emphasis in Rogers' system is neatly captured in the title of one of his books: *On Becoming a Person* (Rogers, 1961).

Rogers' image of human nature

The humanistic approach to personality in general, and Rogers' approach in particular, provide an image of human nature different from that of many of the other theorists in this book. On the free will–determinism issue, Rogers' position is clear.

Human beings—at least those who are fully functioning—have free choice in creating their own selves. No aspect of their personality is determined for them.

On the nature–nurture issue, Rogers gives prominence to the role of the environment. Although the tendency to become self-actualizing is innate, the process of actualizing is influenced much more by social forces than by biological forces. Rogers views childhood influences as being of some importance in the development of personality, but he argues that later experiences are even more influential. It is our present feelings that are vital to personality, more than what happened to us in childhood.

He sees some degree of universality in personality in that people who are fully functioning share certain characteristics and qualities. Yet it is possible to infer from his system that there is opportunity for uniqueness in the ways in which these qualities are manifested or expressed. The ultimate and necessary goal of life, in Rogers' theory, is to become a fully functioning person.

A personality theory that credits human beings with the ability, motivation, and responsibility to understand and improve themselves obviously views people in an optimistic and positive light. Rogers sees us as having a basically healthy nature; we have an innate tendency to grow and actualize all aspects of our being—to become all that we are capable of becoming.

Human beings are not, in Rogers' view, doomed to conflict with themselves or with their society, are not ruled by instinctive biological forces, and are not dictated to by events that occurred in the first five years of life. Our view is always forward, progressive rather than regressive, and oriented toward growth rather than stagnation. We experience our world fully and freely, not defensively, and seek new challenges and stimulation instead of hiding behind the security of the familiar.

To be sure, emotional disturbances do occur; stagnation and regression do take place, but they are the exception, not the rule. Further, people are able to overcome these regressions and disturbances through person-centered therapy, using their own inner resources—their innate urge to grow and develop.

> I am quite aware that out of defensiveness and inner fear individuals can and do behave in ways which are incredibly cruel, horribly destructive, immature, regressive, antisocial, hurtful. Yet one of the most refreshing and invigorating parts of my experience is to work with such individuals and to discover the strongly positive directional tendencies which exist in them, as in all of us, at the deepest levels (Rogers, 1961, p. 27).

Since individuals are viewed in such positive terms, it follows that society is considered in the same light. After all, Rogers states, that which is compatible with enhancement and actualization of one individual is equally compatible with the growth of those with whom the individual interacts. The innate urge to fully develop one's potentialities, to become a fully functioning person, benefits not only the individual but society as well. Social enhancement follows the actualization of the individual members of a culture.

In summary, it is natural and inevitable for a human being to grow, to move forward, to be consciously aware of the self, and to facilitate and implement his or her own growth.

Assessment in Rogers' theory
The clinical approach: Person-centered therapy

Rogers believes that the only way to explore and assess personality is in terms of an individual's own subjective experiences—that is, through studying the individual's experiential field. The therapist, in Rogers' view, must see the client's world or experience (his or her reality) as much as possible through the client's own eyes. While Rogers considers this assessment of a person's experiential field as the only worthwhile approach to take, he is quick to point out that it is not infallible and that there are drawbacks to it.

For one thing, by focusing on subjective experiences, the psychologist gains information only about those aspects of the experiential field that the individual consciously experiences. Experience not represented in conscious awareness is lost to view. There is also a danger in trying to infer too much about these non-conscious experiences. The inference may come to represent more the projections of the therapist than the experiences of the client.

Rogers recognizes that the amount that can be learned about a person's internal frame of reference depends heavily on the fidelity of the communications from the client. Noting that all forms of communication in all settings are faulty and imperfect, Rogers argues that we see the client's world of experience imperfectly, not as a precise mirror image.

Within these limits, Rogers insists that his person-centered therapy provides the clearest view possible of a person's internal frame of reference. He maintains that other forms or approaches to therapy and assessment do not even attempt to explore the experiential field. One advantage he sees in his approach is that it does not deal with a person with a predetermined theoretical structure (Freudian or Adlerian, for instance) into which the patient must somehow be fit. The only predetermined belief of the nondirective therapist is in the inherent worth and value of the client with whom the therapist is working. Clients are accepted as they are and for what they are; in other words, they are given unconditional positive regard. No negative judgments are made of the clients' behavior, nor are clients given direction, guidance, or advice as to how they should behave or what they should do in their relations with themselves and others. As the name of the technique indicates, everything is centered in the person, including the responsibility and ability to change his or her own behavior.

Rogers is much opposed to the use of special assessment techniques, such as free association, dream analysis, psychological testing, and even the taking of case histories. He believes that the use of such techniques is more harmful than helpful because it puts the client in a position of dependency relative to the therapist, who assumes an aura of expertise and authority. These techniques take away any sense of responsibility the clients would otherwise assume, by giving them the impression that the therapist knows everything about them as a result of the case history, tests, and free associations. The clients may then come to feel that the therapist must also have the answers to everything and that all they have to do is sit back and follow the expert's directions and prescriptions.

Rogers uses no such techniques. His assessment of personality is characterized by the attitude that his clients have the ability to see to the roots of their own problems and to direct the future growth, enhancement, and actualization that was prevented by the incongruity that developed between themselves and their experience.

Thus, Rogers' only technique of assessment is the clinical interview, in which he explores a person's feelings and attitudes toward self and toward others. Rogers listens to the person in a naive fashion with no preconceptions, trying to understand the world of the person's own experience.

Psychological tests

As noted, Rogers does not use psychological tests in assessing personality, nor has he developed any tests. Other psychologists, however, have devised tests to measure aspects of a person's experiential world. The Experience Inventory (Coan, 1972) attempts to assess a person's openness or receptivity to experience. You will recall that one of the characteristics of the fully functioning person is an awareness of and openness to all experience. The Experience Inventory is an 83-item self-report questionnaire that measures seven factors thought to constitute openness to experience, including openness to unconventional ways of looking at reality and to hypothetical ideas, constructive uses of fantasy, and unusual perceptions and thoughts. The test has been used for research, but as yet there is no information on its reliability or validity.

Another test developed to assess a person's own experiences is the Experiencing Scale (Gendlin & Tomlinson, 1967; Klein et al., 1969). This also measures a characteristic of the fully functioning person, the trusting of one's own organism. The test is not a self-report inventory; indeed, the person being assessed does not respond to it directly. Instead, the subjects talk about anything they wish, and their tape-recorded comments are later rated for the degree of trust in their own organism that they seem to reveal. Ratings cover seven stages of experiencing, from the lowest, in which personal feelings are of no influence, to the highest, in which feelings are a trusted source of information and awareness.

The Experiencing Scale has been used with people undergoing person-centered therapy. Those who showed the most improvement during therapy revealed a much greater increase in organismic trusting, compared with their degree of organismic trust prior to therapy. Those who showed little or no improvement during therapy showed a smaller or no increase in organismic trusting. Also, those with less severe emotional disorders showed a higher level of organismic trust than those with more severe disorders (Klein et al., 1969).

Research in Rogers' theory

We noted at the beginning of the chapter that Rogers takes a phenomenological approach to personality, one that deals with reality as it is perceived by the individual. His focus on the subjective world of conscious experience is also an idiographic approach in that it involves the intensive study of the psychological world of the individual client.

Rogers remains convinced that his clinical methods, relying on self-reports, are of greater value than the methods of the experimental laboratory. The more orthodox scientific approach, he believes, has yielded much less information on the nature of personality than the clinical approach. "Generally," he wrote, "I never learned anything from research. . . . I'm not really a scientist. Most of my research has been to confirm what I already felt to be true" (Bergin & Strupp, 1972, p. 314).

He argues that there can be no such thing as scientific knowledge because each individual perceives his or her own reality or version of what constitutes scientific knowledge. Although there can be objective knowledge, as happens when one person's observations are verified by someone else, phenomenological knowledge, the understanding of a person's inner world of conscious experience through empathy with that person, is necessary for the study of personality.

Rogers may not use traditional research practices to gather information about personality, but he does use them extensively to attempt to verify his clinical observations, or to confirm what he already felt to be true. He has been particularly enthusiastic about research on the nature of the therapeutic encounter. He introduced a radical innovation into psychotherapy, one that enabled researchers for the first time to fully investigate the nature of the client-therapist interaction. He did this by the simple and now rather widely used method of tape recording therapy sessions and sometimes filming them as well. Prior to that, the only data that proceeded from a therapeutic situation were in the form of the therapist's written reconstruction of what had been said. In addition to the vagaries and distortions of memory (for the therapy notes were usually made after the session had ended), such a written record misses the postural and gestural data. A facial expression or tone of voice can sometimes convey or reveal more than a client's words.

With filmed and/or tape-recorded sessions, everything said and done during a session is available for study. Thus, much more data are available to Rogers than was the case for the early theorists, who developed their formulations in a clinical setting. It should be noted that Rogers always obtains the prior permission of a client to tape or film, and he has found that it does not seem to impede the course of therapy. In fact, clients quickly come to ignore the equipment and proceed as though it were not there.

While the bulk of the data from which Rogers' theory of personality is derived have come directly from therapy sessions, he and his associates have also conducted a large amount of research on the therapy process, the data from which have been used to further develop and support the theory. It is largely through Rogers' research that psychologists have been able to make at least a beginning in the understanding of the psychotherapeutic process.

Studies of the self-concept

In particular, Rogers' research focused on the self-concept and the various ways it may change during a course of therapy. Using both qualitative and quantitative techniques, Rogers and his associates analyzed various aspects of therapy sessions. Through the use of rating scales and content analysis of a client's verbalizations, it has been possible to investigate, in fairly precise terms, the nature of the changes in self-concept. Thus, despite Rogers' claim of not being a scientist, he is clearly behaving in a scientific way in his research attempts to quantify the changes that take place during therapy.

Rogers has also made great use of the **Q-sort** technique, a procedure developed by a colleague, William Stephenson (Stephenson, 1953). In this technique, a client sorts a large number of statements about his or her self-concept into categories that range from most descriptive of the person to least descriptive. Examples of these statements include "I enjoy being alone," "I feel helpless," and "I am emotionally mature." The technique is a way of empirically defining the client's image or picture of himself or herself. There are a variety of Q-sort procedures. For example, after sorting the statements in terms of the picture the person has of himself or herself, the person might be asked to sort the same statements in terms of his or her ideal self, that is, the kind of person he or she would like to be. Whatever specific procedure is used, the Q-sort technique allows for the quantification of various aspects of a client's self-concept.

The usual approach to such quantification is through the computation of correlation coefficients. Correlation, which we discussed in Chapter 1, is a measure of the strength or intensity of the relationship between two variables. Correlation coefficients range from -1.00 (a perfect negative correlation), through zero, to $+1.00$ (a perfect positive correlation). Using the correlational method, researchers can determine precisely how closely a person's self-image corresponds to his or her ideal self, or how a person's self-concept may have changed following therapy. The Q-sort technique has proven to be a valuable research tool for measuring how people feel about themselves.

Let us describe its use in the investigation of Rogers' theory of personality. Rogers himself asked some of his clients to complete the Q-sort so that he could compare their self-concept before therapy with their self-concept after therapy. With one client, the correlation coefficient between self-image and ideal self was $+.36$. A year after therapy had been completed, the correlation coefficient had increased to $+.79$, indicating that her self-image had come much closer to her ideal self. To Rogers, this dramatic change reflected a higher degree of positive emotional health (Rogers, 1954).

The client, whom Rogers called Mrs. Oak, used different terms to describe herself before and after therapy. Prior to her sessions with Rogers, she saw herself as a highly dependent and passive person who felt rejected by other people. Following therapy, she saw herself as much more like her ideal self, that is, more secure, less afraid, and better able to relate warmly to others. These changes in her perceived self are shown in Table 11.1, which indicates some of the statements she thought were the most characteristic of herself before and after therapy.

Remember that the primary advantage of the Q-sort technique (indeed, the reason for using it) is that it shows in precise, quantitative terms whether the person's image of self has changed as a result of therapy.

Another study measured the discrepancy between self and ideal self in 25 clients and found that the discrepancy decreased over time during and after therapy

TABLE 11.1. Mrs. Oak's perceived self before and after therapy in terms of Q-sort statements

Self before therapy	Self 12 months after therapy
I usually feel driven.	I express my emotions freely.
I am responsible for my troubles.	I feel emotionally mature.
I am really self-centered.	I am self-reliant.
I am disorganized.	I understand myself.
I feel insecure within myself.	I feel adequate.
I have to protect myself with excuses, with rationalizing.	I have a warm emotional relationship with others.

Source: C. R. Rogers, The case of Mrs. Oak: A research analysis. In C. R. Rogers & R. F. Dymond, Eds., Psychotherapy and personality change. Chicago: University of Chicago Press, 1954. p. 275.

(Butler & Haigh, 1954). Before therapy, the average correlation coefficient between self and ideal self was $-.01$. After therapy it increased to $+.31$.

Research using the Q-sort technique has provided impressive evidence for the effectiveness of Rogers' form of therapy in improving a person's self-image, but it tells us little about the validity of his theory of personality. Other studies, however, have attempted to verify aspects of his theory.

Rogers predicted, on the basis of his theory, that people will defend themselves against experiences that are incongruent with their self-image. They do this by denying or distorting the aspects of reality that are inconsistent with their self-image. This was tested in a study in which college students rated themselves on 100 socially desirable adjectives, indicating the degree to which each word described them (Suinn, Osborne & Winfree, 1962).

Five days later, each subject was given a rating scale and told that it represented the ratings made of them by two other students. These were faked ratings; they contained some adjectives that were consistent with the subjects' self-ratings and some that were inconsistent. Two days after that, the subjects were asked to complete the 100-item adjective rating scale again, but this time on the basis of the ratings allegedly made of them. Thus, they were being asked to recall the phony ratings. Their accuracy of recall was significantly higher for those adjectives that were consistent with their own self-image than it was for adjectives inconsistent with their self-concept. The researchers concluded that the subjects were defending themselves against the material that was incongruent with what they thought of themselves by being unable to recall it.

Another study relating to this defensiveness was designed to test Rogers' proposition that fully functioning persons are open to all experiences, whereas psychologically unhealthy persons erect defenses to protect themselves against experiences that threaten their self-image. A group of college students described themselves using the Q-sort technique (Chodorkoff, 1954). Another Q-sort description of the subjects was prepared by clinicians who based their reports on a variety of clinical material obtained from each person, including responses to the Thematic Apperception Test and the Rorschach Inkblot Test. On the basis of these measurements, the subjects were divided into good- and poor-adjustment groups.

Measures of perceptual defense (defense against perceiving threatening material) were obtained from the subjects' reactions to neutral words such as "table" and threatening words such as "penis" and "whore." The results showed that all subjects were slower to perceive threatening words than neutral words, but this was particularly characteristic of subjects rated poor in adjustment and hence believed to be defensive. Significantly less perceptual defense was displayed by subjects in the good-adjustment group, those considered to be psychologically healthier. An additional finding related to agreement between the subjects' self-descriptions and the descriptions made by others. The closer the two descriptions, the better adjusted the person was thought to be.

Another study explored the relationship between mothers who are self-accepting and the degree to which they accept their children (Medinnus & Curtis, 1963). This research was based on Rogers' notion that people who accept them-selves (whose self and ideal self-image are congruent) are much more likely to ac-cept others than people who do not accept themselves (whose self and ideal self-image are incongruent).

Measures of self-acceptance and child acceptance were taken from 56 mothers using an adjective checklist and a test of adjustment, both of which measured the discrepancy between self and ideal self. The results revealed significant differences between self-accepting and non-self-accepting mothers in terms of their acceptance of their children. The more self-accepting mothers were more accepting of their children. The findings also suggested that a child's degree of self-acceptance may depend on the mother's degree of self-acceptance.

Other studies also support Rogers' belief that parental behavior can affect the child's self-image. Children of parents who are high in acceptance of them and who display democratic child-rearing practices develop higher self-esteem and greater emotional security than children whose parents are not accepting of them and who display authoritarian child-rearing practices (Baldwin, 1949). Further, parents of children with high self-esteem are more loving and use reward more than punish-ment in guiding their children's behavior. Parents of low-self-esteem children were found to be more aloof, less loving, and more likely to use punishment (Coopersmith, 1967).

Several studies provide support for Rogers' proposal that incongruences be-tween self and ideal self are indicative of poor psychological adjustment. In gen-eral, the higher the incongruence or discrepancy, the higher the degree of anxiety, insecurity, social incompetence, and emotional disorder (Achenbach & Zigler, 1963; Turner & Vanderlippe, 1958). In addition, persons with a great discrepancy between self and ideal self-image are lower in self-actualization than are those with little or no discrepancy (Mahoney & Hartnett, 1973).

A final commentary

Rogers' person-centered approach to psychotherapy has been enormously popular among psychologists and has found wide application as a method of treating emo-tional disturbance. In the ratings of the relative importance of 286 psychologists in the last half of the 20th century, Rogers is in 4th place overall and in 3rd place among the personality theorists in this book. Only Skinner and Freud are considered to be more influential (Gilgen, 1982). Among psychotherapists and counselors, Rogers is considered to be the most influential psychologist of all (Smith, 1982). His theory of personality, while less influential than his form of psychotherapy, nevertheless has received recognition and acceptance, particularly for its emphasis on the importance of the self-concept. It must be noted, however, that most of his writings are concerned with his therapy. He has written relatively little in the way of a formal statement of the full dimensions of his personality theory.

Although Rogers readily admits to his influence in psychotherapy and counseling, he does not believe that he has "affected academic, or so-called scientific, psychology. . . . We have had very little influence on academic psychology, in the lecture hall, the textbook, or the laboratory" (Rogers, 1980, p. 51).

Nonetheless, Rogers' theory and his approach to therapy—and sometimes it becomes difficult to separate the two—have stimulated a wealth of research, performed by Rogers and his colleagues as well as by others moved by his formulations to take them into the laboratory. More than any theorist covered so far, he has been responsible for stimulating much valuable research on the nature of psychotherapy and the form and substance of the client-therapist interactions. Provoking even more research are his formulations on the self-concept. Probably no personality theorist has had a greater impact on both theoretical and empirical definitions of the self. If a theory is judged solely on the basis of its heuristic value—how much research it has provoked and generated—then the theory of Carl Rogers must be ranked very high indeed. And we have seen that much of the research is supportive of his theory.

Criticisms of his theory have been directed primarily at two aspects of it. First, Rogers has been criticized for failing to state, in precise terms, what constitutes the innate potentialities to enhancement and actualization that occupy such a central position in his theory. Critics ask whether this potential is primarily physiological or psychological and whether there are individual differences in it; that is, do some people have more of it than others? Nowhere in his writings does Rogers provide the answers to these and related questions about the exact nature of this potential. He describes it as a kind of genetic blueprint, in accordance with which the organism will develop. But the way this mechanism operates, critics charge, has yet to be clarified.

The second major criticism refers to Rogers' insistence that the only way to explore personality is through the examination of a person's subjective experiences. Since he does this by listening to the client's self-reports, he is missing, critics allege, those forces and factors of which the client is not conscious, yet which can influence his or her behavior. Psychoanalysts, in particular, argue that patients may consciously or unconsciously distort their own subjective experiences, repressing some and elaborating on (or inventing) others, so as to conceal their true nature, to present an idealized picture of themselves.

His background experience is a unique combination of clinic, lecture hall, and laboratory. Not confined either to clinic or to college, he has been able to draw on considerable experience in working with disturbed individuals as well as on the intellectual stimulation available to him during his years in academics. Further, he attracted large numbers of loyal Rogerian graduate students who continue to put his theory to the test in both the clinic and the laboratory.

Summary

Rogers' person-centered therapy holds that people are conscious, rational beings who are not controlled by unconscious forces or past experiences. Personality can be understood only from an individual's own point of view, on the basis of his or her inner, subjective experiences. This phenomenological approach to personality deals with reality as it is perceived by the individual. Our overall goal is self-actualization, the tendency toward which is innate. Rogers' theory reflects some of his childhood experiences, particularly those relating to an autonomous self, a reliance on one's own experience, an emphasis on actualizing potentialities, and a belief that people can consciously change and improve themselves.

The tendency to self-actualization includes physiological and psychological needs, but is oriented more toward the physiological. It facilitates the organism's growth and development and is responsible for maturation, the genetically determined development of bodily organs and processes. The actualizing tendency, present in all living things, involves struggle and pain.

The organismic valuing process evaluates life experiences in terms of how well they serve the actualizing tendency. Those experiences that promote actualization will be sought out; those that hinder it will be avoided.

The frame of reference for each person is his or her experiential field, which includes present experiences, stimuli of which we are unaware, and memories of past experiences. The self-concept is our picture of what we are, what we should be, and what we would like to be. Ideally, the self is a consistent pattern, an organized whole.

Positive regard is a need for acceptance, love, and approval from other people, particularly the mother during infancy. If the mother does not bestow positive regard, the infant's tendency toward self-actualization is hampered. Unconditional positive regard is a condition in which the mother's love and approval are granted fully and freely and are not made conditional upon the child's behavior. When love and approval are made conditional upon behavior, a state of conditional positive regard exists. The self-concept is developed in the light of the approval or disapproval we receive from others. Gradually, we internalize the attitudes of others, and positive regard will come from ourselves instead, a condition known as positive self-regard.

Conditions of worth, Rogers' version of Freud's superego, involves seeing ourselves as worthy only under certain conditions, according to the terms defined by our parents. People must avoid behaviors and perceptions that run counter to their conditions of worth. Thus, incongruence develops between the self-concept and behaviors and perceptions that are threatening. The anxiety accompanying the threat must be defended against. This is accomplished by denying or distorting certain aspects of the perceptual field.

Psychologically healthy persons are able to perceive themselves and their environment as they really are, and they are therefore free to become self-actualizing. The fully functioning person is the goal of psychological development. Such a person has an awareness of all experiences, in which there is nothing to defend against; the ability to live fully in each moment; trust in his or her own organism; a sense of freedom, including a sense of personal power over life; and creativity, allied with a sense of spontaneity. The self-actualizing process involves continual change and growth.

Rogers' image of human nature encompasses a belief in free will, in the prominence of environmental over innate forces, and in some degree of universality in personality. He holds an optimistic image of human nature in which individuals and societies are able to grow unhampered by past events.

Assessment of personality, for Rogers, is in terms of a person's own subjective experiences as revealed in self-reports during clinical interviews. In this approach, persons are given unconditional positive regard. He opposes such techniques as free association and dream analysis because they make the client dependent upon the therapist. Two psychological tests have been developed to measure aspects of a person's own experience: the Experience Inventory, which assesses a person's openness to experience, and the Experiencing Scale, which assesses a person's degree of organismic trust.

Rogers' phenomenological approach to personality is idiographic, involving the intensive study of the individual. Phenomenological knowledge, the understanding of a person's inner world of conscious experience, is seen by Rogers to be of greater value than scientific knowledge derived from the experimental method. By recording therapy sessions, Rogers has enabled researchers to investigate the nature of the client–therapist interaction. The Q-sort technique, in which a person sorts statements referring to self-concept into categories ranging from most to least descriptive, is a way of quantifying a person's self-image. Research using the Q-sort technique has demonstrated a greater correspondence between self and ideal self following therapy. It has also shown that people will defend themselves against material that is incongruent with their self-concept; that psychologically healthy people are more open to experience than are psychologically unhealthy people; and that the greater agreement there is between a person's self-description and descriptions made by others, the better adjusted the person is.

Other research has shown that mothers who are high in self-acceptance are more accepting of their children, that different child-rearing attitudes and practices influence the child's self-esteem, and that discrepancies between self and ideal self ratings indicate poor psychological adjustment.

Rogers' work has been immensely influential and has stimulated a great deal of research. It has been criticized for failing to define precisely the nature of self-actualization and for ignoring the impact of unconscious forces and the possible distortion of a client's subjective experiences in self-reports.

Glossary

conditions of worth   The individual's belief that he or she is worthy of affection and approval only if he or she expresses desirable behaviors and attitudes and refrains from expressing behaviors and attitudes that bring disapproval from others; similar to Freud's concept of the superego.

incongruence   Discrepancy between the self-concept and aspects of the individual's experience.

organismic valuing process   The process by which the individual judges experiences in terms of their value for facilitating or hindering his or her actualization and growth.

person-centered (client-centered) therapy   Rogers' approach to therapy in which the person (not the "patient") is assumed to be responsible for changing his or her personality.

positive regard   The pervasive need for acceptance, love, and approval from others.

positive self-regard   The condition in which acceptance and approval come from the individual himself or herself and form part of the self-concept.

Q-sort   A self-report technique to measure various aspects of the self-concept.

unconditional positive regard   The state in which approval is granted regardless of the individual's behavior; in person-centered therapy, the therapist offers unconditional positive regard.

Review questions

1. How does the need to actualize facilitate both the biological growth and the psychological growth of the individual?
2. What is the organismic valuing process? How is it related to the need to actualize?
3. What does Rogers mean by the term "experiential field"? How does a person's experiential field change with age?
4. What parental behaviors facilitate the development of positive self-regard?
5. Compare Rogers' concept of conditions of worth with Freud's concept of the superego.
6. Describe the characteristics of the fully functioning person.
7. How does Rogers' approach to the clinical interview differ from the psychoanalytic approach to the clinical interview? What does Rogers call his approach? Why?
8. How does the Q-sort technique measure self-image? What has Q-sort research revealed about a person's self-concept before and after therapy?
9. What is Rogers' view of the relative influences of childhood experiences and adult experiences on personality?

Suggested reading

Kirschenbaum, H. *On becoming Carl Rogers*. New York: Delacorte, 1979.

Rogers, C. R. *On becoming a person: A therapist's view of psychotherapy*. Boston: Houghton Mifflin, 1961.

Rogers, C. R. Autobiography. In E. G. Boring & G. Lindzey, Eds., *History of psychology in autobiography*, vol. 5. New York: Appleton-Century-Crofts, 1967.

Rogers, C. R. In retrospect: Forty-six years. *American Psychologist*, 1974, 29, 115–123.

Rogers, C. R. *A way of being*. Boston: Houghton Mifflin, 1980.

Rogers, C. R. & Dymond, R. F. *Psychotherapy and personality change*. Chicago: University of Chicago Press, 1954.

CHAPTER 12

Abraham Maslow

The life of Maslow (1908–1970)
**Motivation and personality: The
hierarchy of needs**
  Physiological needs
  Safety needs
  Belonging and love needs
  Esteem needs
  Self-actualization
  The needs to know and to understand: A
    second hierarchy
  Exceptions to the hierarchy of needs
**Metamotivation: The development of
  the self-actualizing person**
**Characteristics of the self-actualizing
  person**
The failure to self-actualize
Maslow's image of human nature
Assessment in Maslow's theory
  The Personal Orientation Inventory
Research in Maslow's theory
  Studies of self-actualization
A final commentary
Summary
Glossary
Review questions
Suggested reading

What a man can *be, he* must *be.*

ABRAHAM MASLOW

Maslow, perhaps even more than Rogers, has been a spokesperson for and leader of the humanistic movement in psychology. He has criticized both behaviorism and psychoanalysis, particularly Freud's approach to personality. By studying only the worst of humanity—that is, neurotics and psychotics—psychology ignores all the positive and beneficial human emotions, such as happiness, contentment, satisfaction, and peace of mind. One of Maslow's most frequently quoted statements is that "the study of crippled, stunted, immature, and unhealthy specimens can yield only a cripple psychology" (Maslow, 1970b, p. 180).

We have underestimated human nature, Maslow charged, by not studying the best examples of humanity—the most creative, the healthiest, and the most mature. And this approach—studying what he calls the growing tip of humankind, the best representatives of the species—is one of the most distinctive features of Maslow's theory of the human personality. As he noted, when you want to determine how fast humans can run, you study not the average runner but the fastest runner you can find. Only in this way is it possible to determine the heights of human potential.

Maslow's theory of personality, therefore, does not derive from the emotionally disturbed but from the healthiest personalities. As a result of years of study of such people, a theory of personality has evolved that could just as easily be called a theory of motivation, for motivation is the core and foundation of his approach.

Using primarily case histories, Maslow intensively studied a small group of the healthiest and best personalities, living and dead. For example, using biographical material, he studied Thomas Jefferson, Abraham Lincoln, and other historical figures. From these investigations and those of living persons, he concluded that each person is born with certain *instinctoid needs*, which cause the person to choose to grow, develop, and actualize himself or herself—to fulfill all his or her potentialities.

Maslow posited a hierarchy of needs, a ladder of motivations; those needs on the bottom rung must be satisfied before the next rung assumes prominence. When the second-level need is satisfied, then the third-level need takes precedence, and so on. At the bottom level, the physiological needs are prominent. When they are satisfied, safety needs become paramount, then the needs for belonging and love, followed by the need for esteem, and finally the need for self-actualization.

Maslow's theory was extremely popular in the 1960s and 1970s. It continues to be used today, particularly in applied settings such as the workplace, where many executives believe that the need for self-actualization is a useful motivating force and a potential source of job satisfaction.

The life of Maslow (1908–1970)

It is perhaps understandable that Maslow, who rose out of a childhood marked by poverty and hardship to a position of respect and prominence, would believe in the tendency of the self to grow, develop, and actualize. It is also understandable that, coming from a background where food and shelter were important everyday concerns, Maslow would develop a system in which those needs assume a position of primacy until they are satisfied. Since as a child he felt lonely and isolated, it is not surprising that needs for belonging, love, and esteem are important in his theory, once physiological and safety needs are satisfied.

Maslow was born in 1908 in Brooklyn, New York. His parents were immigrants with little education and little prospect of rising above the marginal conditions under which they lived. As with so many immigrant parents, their hopes were for the next generation; they hoped that their seven children, of whom Maslow was the eldest, would rise to a higher station in life. Maslow's father, at the age of 14, had walked and hitchhiked from Russia across all of western Europe, so great was his ambition to emigrate to America. This drive and motivation to succeed seems to have been instilled in the young Maslow.

Maslow's childhood was not an idyllic one. "With my childhood," he told an interviewer, "it's a wonder I'm not psychotic" (Hall, 1968, p. 37). As the only Jewish boy in his neighborhood, he was very aware of his minority-group status. By his own description, he was isolated and unhappy, growing up without friends or companions. He was not especially close to his parents. He described his father as a man who "neglected me no matter what I did" (Lowry, 1979, p. 53). He called his mother "absolutely selfish and narcissistic," someone who cast him off (Lowry, 1979, p. 387). As so many others have done in similar situations of isolation, Maslow turned to books for companionship. The library became the playground of his childhood, and books and education the road out of the ghetto of poverty and loneliness.

At his father's insistence, Maslow began the study of law, but he decided after two weeks that he did not like it. What he really wanted to do was study everything, a desire his father found difficult to understand. His passion for learning was accompanied by a passion, at age 16, for the girl he would one day marry—another desire his father found hard to accept. Maslow soon left home, going first to Cornell University and then to the University of Wisconsin, where his intended wife joined him.

They married—he at 20, she at 19—and it was a significant step for Maslow. The marriage seemed to provide him not only with a sense of belonging and love but also with a purpose and direction. He said that life did not really begin for him until he got married and began his studies at Wisconsin. In addition to his wife, he discovered and was enraptured by the behavioristic psychology of John B. Watson, the prime mover in the revolution to make psychology a science of behavior. Maslow looked upon behaviorism, as so many people did in the early 1930s, as a panacea for all the world's problems. At Wisconsin he received solid training in experimental psychology of the behaviorist mode, working with monkeys under psychologist Harry Harlow. In addition to his professional training, Maslow received personal help and advice from his professors.

It is a giant step from Maslow's graduate training and research in behaviorism to self-actualization, from monkeys to the growing tip of humankind. There were a number of influences that combined to bring about this profound shift—some intellectual and others highly personal and emotional. They ranged from exposure to the writings of Freud, Gestalt psychology, and the philosophies of Alfred North Whitehead and Henri Bergson to the birth of his first child. "That," he said, "was the thunderclap that settled things. . . . I was stunned by the mystery and by the sense of not really being in control. I felt small and weak and feeble before all this. I'd say anyone who had a baby couldn't be a behaviorist" (Hall, 1968, p. 56).

Maslow received his Ph.D. from Wisconsin in 1934 and returned to New York, first to Columbia University and then to Brooklyn College, where he remained until 1951. He was in New York at a most propitious time—the late 1930s and early 1940s—when the wave of emigrant intellectuals from Nazi Germany arrived. He eagerly met and learned from Erich Fromm, Karen Horney, Max Wertheimer (a leading Gestalt psychologist), and Alfred Adler. In addition, he was greatly influenced by the American anthropologist Ruth Benedict, whom he also met during this time. In fact, it was his awe of and admiration for Ruth Benedict and Max Wertheimer that led to his research on self-actualization and to the personality theory that derived from it.

During those early post-Ph.D. years, Maslow continued his Wisconsin research on sexual behavior, but shifted from monkeys to humans. The research lasted until 1941, when his interests changed at the start of World War II, an event that moved him deeply. The beginning of the war was an intensely emotional experience. Maslow told of watching, with tears streaming down his face, a ragtag parade, shortly after the attack on Pearl Harbor. "The moment changed my whole life," he wrote, "and determined what I have done ever since" (Hall, 1968, p. 54). He resolved to devote his life to the development of a psychology that would deal with the highest ideals and potentials of which we are capable. He wanted to improve the human personality and to demonstrate that human beings can display more noble behaviors than hatred, war, and prejudice. Thus, it was a personal experience that led to Maslow's theory of personality. The beginning of the war provided him with the compelling need to study the best of human nature. At the same time, his curiosity about Benedict and Wertheimer drove him, because they were living models for him of the best of human nature. The desire to humanize psychology and to understand humanity's loftiest potentials that emerged from those experiences never left him.

In 1951, he went to Brandeis University, where he later became chairman of the psychology department. He remained at Brandeis, developing and refining his theory, until 1969, when he moved to California (under a foundation grant) to undertake the large-scale effort of formulating a philosophy of politics, economics, and ethics generated by a humanistic brand of psychology.

Toward the end of his life, he became an immensely popular figure, not only in psychology but among many segments of the general population as well. He was much involved with the sensitivity-group movement and was a strong supporter of the Esalen Institute in California. After he suffered a heart attack, he threw himself into his work more vigorously than ever and gave up such favorite activities as plays, poetry reading, and long walks in the woods. In one of his last interviews, he said, "How can I piddle around at these things when work has to be done, and mankind has to be helped."

During his lifetime, Maslow received a great many awards and honors, including election to the presidency of the American Psychological Association in 1967.

Motivation and personality: The hierarchy of needs

Maslow's theory of motivation is very much at the heart of his approach to the understanding of personality. The basic idea of his motivational theory is straight-forward. There are, Maslow wrote, a number of innate needs that activate and direct the behavior of every individual. The needs themselves are instinctoid; we come equipped with them at birth. The behaviors that we use to satisfy the needs, how-ever, are not innate but learned and therefore subject to wide variation from one person to the next.

Another characteristic of these universal needs is their arrangement in a hier-archy of prepotency, as shown below and in Figure 12.1.

5. The need for self-actualization
4. The need for esteem
3. The needs for belonging and love
2. The need for safety
1. The physiological needs

In Maslow's **hierarchy of needs**, the needs that stand at the bottom rung of the motivational ladder must be satisfied before those at the top can be satisfied. Indeed, the needs at the top will not even appear until the lower-order ones have been at least partially satisfied. For example, a person who is hungry and fears for his or her safety will feel no need whatsoever for belonging or love. The individual is concerned (or perhaps obsessed) with bread, not love.

It is only when people have adequate food (and the rest of their physiological needs are satisfied) and when they feel safe that they come to feel the needs for belonging and love. And when those needs are satisfied, people long for esteem. When they achieve that, they desire self-actualization. The important point is that people are not driven by all these needs at the same time. Only one need is domi-

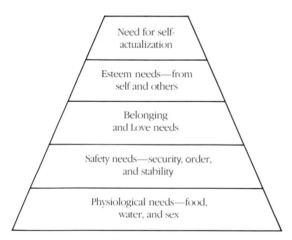

FIGURE 12.1   Maslow's hierarchy of needs

nant at a time; which one it will be depends on which of the others are satisfied or not satisfied.

A highly successful businesswoman is no longer driven by or even aware of the physiological needs; they are well taken care of. She may be driven now to seek esteem or self-actualization. However, the priority of the needs can be shifted or reversed. If a sudden economic recession grips the nation and the businesswoman loses her job and uses up all of her savings, then the physiological needs can re-assume priority, and she will forget all about esteem or self-actualization. A can of beans might then be more prized than an award from the Chamber of Commerce.

The lower the need is in the hierarchy, the greater its strength, potency, or priority. The higher needs are obviously weaker. Maslow made a number of other distinctions between higher- and lower-order needs:

1. The higher needs appeared later in the evolutionary development of man-kind. All living things need food and water, but only humans have a need to self-actualize and to know and understand. Therefore, the higher the need the more distinctly human it is.

2. Higher needs appear later in the development of the individual. The phys-iological and safety needs arise in infancy, the belonging and love and the esteem needs arise in adolescence, but the need for self-actualization usually does not ap-pear until midlife.

3. Higher needs are less necessary for sheer survival, hence their gratification can be postponed longer. Failure to satisfy a higher need does not produce as much of an immediate emergency or crisis reaction as failure to satisfy a lower need. Thus, the lower needs are also called **deficit** or **deficiency needs** because failure to satisfy them produces some kind of deficiency in the individual.

4. While they are less necessary for survival, the higher needs nevertheless can contribute to survival and growth. Higher-level need satisfaction produces better health, longer life, and a generally enhanced biological efficiency. For this reason, the higher needs are also called **growth** or **being needs**.

5. Higher-need satisfaction is productive or beneficial not only biologically but also psychologically, because it produces a deeper happiness, peace of mind, and fullness in one's inner life.

6. Higher-need gratification involves more preconditions and greater com-plexity than lower-need satisfaction. The search for self-actualization, for example, has the precondition that all the other needs have first been satisfied and involves more complicated and sophisticated behavior and goals than, say, the search for food.

7. Higher-need gratification requires better external conditions (social, eco-nomic, and political) than lower-need gratification. For example, greater freedom of expression and opportunity are required for self-actualization than for safety.

There is one additional point to be made before we discuss each of the spe-cific needs in more detail. A need does not have to be absolutely and fully satisfied before the next one in the hierarchy emerges. Maslow spoke instead of partial satis-faction, of a declining percentage of satisfaction in each need as we go up the hierarchy. Using strictly hypothetical figures, he described a person who has satisfied, in turn, 85 percent of the physiological needs, 70 percent of the safety needs, 50 percent of the love and belonging needs, 40 percent of the esteem needs, and 10 percent of the self-actualization need.

Physiological needs

The obvious needs for food, water, air, sleep, and sex are, of course, the most basic and powerful of all the needs. They are capable of totally blocking out every other need. If you have ever had the experience of struggling for air while under water or going for days without food, you realize how trivial the needs for love or esteem or anything else become when a physiological need is not satisfied.

Maslow noted that a starving person thinks, dreams, and wants only food. But once the need is satisfied, the person is no longer aware of it, no longer driven by it. It ceases to direct or control the person's behavior or assume any importance to him or her. Such is the case for most people in an affluent, industrialized Western culture; physiological needs are more important as motivating forces in people for whom sheer survival is an everyday concern. It is rare for middle-class Americans to be concerned with the satisfaction of survival needs. Because a need that is gratified is no longer a need, the physiological needs play a minimal role in our lives.

Safety needs

The need for safety is most important, Maslow believed, in infants and in neurotic adults. Healthy, normal adults generally have satisfied this need well. Its satisfaction requires security, stability, protection, structure, order, and freedom from fear and anxiety. In infants and young children, the safety needs can be seen most clearly, if for no other reason than that infants react more visibly and immediately to threats and fear than do adults, who have learned to inhibit their fear reactions to some degree.

Another visible indication of children's needs for safety is their preference for a structured routine—their need for a predictable and orderly world. Maslow felt that total permissiveness and freedom—a complete absence of structure and order—produces anxiety and insecurity in children because it is a threat to their security needs. Freedom must, of course, be granted to children, but only within the limits of what they can cope with. They must be given some guidance, for they are not yet capable of directing themselves.

A neurotic and insecure adult also needs a degree of structure and order in his or her environment because the safety need is still dominant. The neurotic compulsively avoids new, unexpected, or different experiences and orders his or her world so as to make it completely predictable. The person's entire life is constructed around a rigid set of routines—"At 9:00, I'll do this; at 10:00, I'll do that"—structuring every minute of the day and ordering every aspect of his or her world. Pencils must be kept in a certain place and clothes hung in a certain manner.

Maslow also pointed out that, although most normal adults have satisfied this need, they still require some degree of security. Most of us prefer predictability to the totally unknown, order to chaos, and so we save for the future, buy insurance, and remain in a safe job rather than take a chance on a new and unknown business venture. However, the need for this kind of security is not as compulsive or overwhelming in the normal adult as it is in the neurotic or the infant.

Belonging and love needs

Once an individual's physiological and safety needs have been reasonably well satisfied, he or she develops the needs for belonging and love. These needs can be manifested in a variety of ways: through affectionate relations with other people in general, or through a relationship with a particular friend, lover, or mate, or through finding a place or position in a particular group and/or in society at large.

The need to belong, Maslow thought, is difficult to satisfy in an increasingly mobile society. Few people stay in the same neighborhood and keep the same friends all their lives, or even for more than a few years at a time. We change jobs, schools, and towns too frequently to put down roots, to develop a secure sense of belonging, and so we must seek to satisfy the need in other ways. Maslow suggested that the eager acceptance of sensitivity groups, personal-growth encounter sessions, and communes, which began in the late 1960s and early 1970s, demonstrated efforts to satisfy the feelings of loneliness and alienation that derive from failure to satisfy the need to belong.

The need for love, which involves the need to give love as well as to receive it, can be satisfied in a warm relationship of intimacy with another person. Maslow did not equate love with sex (a purely physiological need) but recognized that sex is one way of expressing the love need. Failure to satisfy the need for love is, in Maslow's opinion, one of the fundamental causes of maladjustment in our culture. "Love hunger," he wrote, "is a deficiency disease" (Maslow, 1968, p. 42).

Esteem needs

Once people feel loved and have a sense of belonging, they then develop the need for esteem. They now need respect both from themselves, in the form of a feeling of self-worth, and from others, in the form of status, recognition, social success, fame, and the like. There are, then, two kinds of esteem needs: for self-esteem and for esteem granted by other people.

Satisfaction of the need for self-esteem allows a person to feel confident of his or her strength, worth, and adequacy. As a result of such feelings, the individual may become more competent and productive in all aspects of life. When there is a lack of self-esteem, on the other hand, the person feels inferior, helpless, and discouraged and lacks sufficient confidence to cope with problems. Maslow pointed out that self-esteem, if it is to be genuine, must be based on a realistic assessment of one's own abilities and competence and on truly deserved respect from others. It is vital that the status, prestige, and good reputation a person may be accorded by others not consist solely of unearned or undeserved praise but rather be earned recognition of real competence and adequacy.

Self-actualization

The person is now ready to move to the final stage of development, **self-actualization**, the realization and fulfillment of all his or her potentialities and capabilities. The person must become, and be, what he or she has the potential to be. Even though all four of the previous needs may be satisfied, the person who is not self-actualizing, not utilizing his or her potential, will be discontented and restless. The individual will be frustrated, as he or she would be at the failure to satisfy any other need.

Maslow wrote: "A musician must make music, an artist must paint, a poet must write, if he is to be ultimately at peace with himself" (Maslow, 1970b, p. 46). Self-actualizing can take many unique forms, not all of which result in some artistic product. Maslow pointed out that people in all walks of life—a woman raising children or driving a truck, or a man on an assembly line or employed as a cook—have the opportunity to fulfill their potential.

There are a number of preconditions necessary for self-actualization. One is freedom from restraints imposed either by the culture or by one's own self. Another is that the person not be distracted by concerns for food or safety, be secure in his or her self-image and with family and other groups, and love and be loved in return. Above all, the person must know himself or herself—have a realistic knowledge of his or her strengths and weaknesses, vices and virtues, and skills and abilities. After all, how can a self be actualized if it is not known and understood?

Maslow's personality theory grew out of his investigation of self-actualizing people, and, as we shall see, he had much to say about the psychological composition of these people.

The needs to know and to understand: A second hierarchy

Maslow was quite definite about another set of human needs—the needs to *know* and *understand*—which he did not place in the hierarchy that we have been discussing so far. He posited curiosity, and the needs to know and to understand, as innate drives that push for satisfaction. He noted a number of lines of evidence that converge to support the existence of these needs:

1. Laboratory studies with animals show that they actively explore and manipulate their environments for no other apparent reason than curiosity.
2. There is much historical evidence of people seeking knowledge at the risk of their lives, thus putting this need ahead of even the safety needs.
3. There are many studies suggesting that healthy, mature adults are strongly attracted to the unknown and mysterious, the unorganized and unexplained.
4. In his clinical practice, Maslow described otherwise healthy people who suffered from boredom and a lack of zest or excitement in their lives. He referred to them as intelligent people leading "stupid lives in stupid jobs" and found that they improved when they involved themselves in some challenging intellectual activity (Maslow, 1970b, p. 49).

Maslow believed that the needs to know and understand appear early in life—in late infancy and early childhood—and are expressed as a child's natural curiosity, which does not have to be taught, although schools and parents may teach a child to inhibit this spontaneous curiosity. Failure to satisfy these needs is harmful, as is failure to satisfy any of Maslow's needs, and can inhibit the development and full functioning of the personality.

There are several ways in which these needs are manifested. These include the need to analyze, to reduce things to their basic elemental parts; the need to experiment, to "see what will happen if I do this"; and the need to explain, to construct a system or personal theory that will make sense out of the events and conditions of one's world.

While these needs are not, as noted, a part of the basic hierarchy of needs, Maslow suggested that they form a small, separate hierarchy of their own. The need to know is more potent than the need to understand. This hierarchy operates in the same way as the larger one; that is, the first need must be at least partially satisfied before the next is able to emerge.

Finally, Maslow pointed out that there is an inevitable overlap or interaction between the two need hierarchies. Knowing and understanding, finding a meaning in one's world, is basic to interacting with that environment in order to function properly and so gain love, esteem, and self-fulfillment. Therefore, it is impossible to become self-actualizing if the needs to know and to understand are not satisfied.

Exceptions to the hierarchy of needs

While Maslow believed that the major need hierarchy is descriptive of most people, he pointed out that it does not apply to everyone. For example, throughout history, people especially dedicated to a cause or an ideal have willingly sacrificed everything, including their lives. People who fast until death, or set themselves on fire for a cause, are obviously denying their physiological and safety needs. Religious figures who abandon worldly goods to live a life of poverty and hardship may be expressing their fullest potential, in spite of the frustration of their deficiency or lower-order needs. The same may be said of artists who place their health and survival in danger for the sake of their work.

Maslow also pointed out a common reversal in the needs hierarchy: some people place a greater importance on self-esteem than on love. Such individuals feel that they can satisfy the love and belonging needs only if they feel very self-confident and worthy.

Metamotivation: The development of the self-actualizing person

As Maslow's work with self-actualizing persons progressed, he began to suspect that they differed from other people in terms of what motivates them. He proposed a radical, and sometimes less than clear, theory of motivation for self-actualizing persons called **metamotivation** (sometimes B-motivation or, simply, Being).

The prefix *meta* means "after" or "beyond." Maslow used it to indicate that metamotivation moves beyond our traditional idea of motivation. Paradoxically, it seems to mean a state in which motivation plays no role at all. "The highest motive,"

Maslow wrote, "is to be unmotivated and nonstriving" (Maslow, 1970b, p. 135). Self-actualizing persons do not strive; instead, they *develop*.

To understand Maslow's meaning, we must distinguish between the so-called motivation of self-actualizers (metamotivation) and the motivation of non-self-actualizers. Maslow labeled the latter Deficiency or D-motivation. As we noted in our discussion of deficiency needs, deficiency motivation involves making up for some lack within the organism.

Going without food, for example, produces a deficit in the body that is manifested in discomfort and a level of tension which the organism is motivated to reduce. A specific need (hunger) for a specific goal object (food) produces a kind of motivation designed to attain something we lack.

Apparently, although Maslow's writings are not precise on this point, deficiency motivation refers not only to the physiological needs but also to the needs for safety, belonging and love, and esteem. These are the lower needs and they motivate us to strive for something specific.

In contrast, self-actualizers are concerned with the higher needs, with fulfilling their potentialities and with knowing and understanding their world. In their situation, one of metamotivation, they are not seeking satisfaction for deficits or trying to reduce tension. Their goal is to enrich and enlarge their life and to increase tension through new, challenging, and diverse experiences.

If there are not specific goal objects for which to strive, what, then, is the motivating force for self-actualizers? Maslow said that they are not motivated in the usual sense (deficiency motivation). Instead, they are metamotivated to maximize their potential. Maslow described this state as "character growth, character expression, maturation, and development; in a word self-actualization" (Maslow, 1970b, p. 159).

Self-actualizers are beyond striving or wishing for something they need to correct a deficit. All of their deficits have been corrected through the satisfaction of the lower needs. Self-actualizers are no longer becoming, in the sense of satisfying the lower needs. Now they are in a state of *being*, spontaneously, naturally, joyously expressing their full humanness. In that sense, then, they are unmotivated.

Having explained all this, Maslow set forth a list of *metaneeds* or being-values, states of growth or being (perhaps goals) toward which self-actualizers move. He also referred to them as B-values and said that they are ends in themselves, not means of achieving other ends. Metaneeds represent states of being rather than the striving toward some specific goal object. These states, Maslow wrote, "behave like needs," and failure to satisfy them is harmful, as is failure to satisfy any of the lower needs. Frustration of the metaneeds produces *metapathology* (Maslow, 1967, p. 281).

The kind of illness produced by frustration of these growth needs is not experienced as explicitly as that produced by frustration of the lower needs. This does not mean that metapathologies are not felt as keenly as more ordinary illnesses, but the source or cause of the disturbance is less clear to the individual. When a deficit need such as hunger or love is frustrated, we are directly and immediately aware of feeling hungry or lonely. This is not true when the metaneeds are frustrated. Self-

TABLE 12.1   Maslow's metaneeds and metapathologies

Metaneeds	*Metapathologies*
Truth	Mistrust, cynicism, skepticism
Goodness	Hatred, repulsion, disgust, reliance only upon self and for self
Beauty	Vulgarity, restlessness, loss of taste, bleakness
Unity; wholeness	Disintegration
Dichotomy-transcendence	Black/white thinking, either/or thinking, simplistic view of life
Aliveness; process	Deadness, robotizing, feeling oneself to be totally determined, loss of emotion and zest in life, experiential emptiness
Uniqueness	Loss of feeling of self and individuality, feeling oneself to be interchangeable or anonymous
Perfection	Hopelessness, nothing to work for
Necessity	Chaos, unpredictability
Completion; finality	Incompleteness, hopelessness, cessation of striving and coping
Justice	Anger, cynicism, mistrust, lawlessness, total selfishness
Order	Insecurity, wariness, loss of safety and predictability, necessity for being on guard
Simplicity	Overcomplexity, confusion, bewilderment, loss of orientation
Richness, totality, comprehensiveness	Depression, uneasiness, loss of interest in the world
Effortlessness	Fatigue, strain, clumsiness, awkwardness, stiffness
Playfulness	Grimness, depression, paranoid humorlessness, loss of zest in life, cheerlessness
Self-sufficiency	Responsibility given to others
Meaningfulness	Meaninglessness, despair, senselessness of life

Source: Adapted from A. H. Maslow, *The Farther Reaches of Human Nature* (New York: Viking, 1971), pp. 318–319.

actualizers may know that something is wrong, but they do not know what they are lacking. Metapathology is thus a formless illness. They may feel alone, helpless, meaningless, depressed, and despairing, but cannot point to the source or to a goal that might alleviate the distress.

Table 12.1 shows Maslow's metaneeds and the metapathologies that result from metaneed frustration.

The metapathologies represent a diminution or thwarting of full human growth and development, preventing self-actualizers from fully expressing, utilizing, and fulfilling their potential.

Having described what metamotivates self-actualizing persons, let us now examine specific characteristics of these supremely healthy individuals.

Characteristics of the self-actualizing person

Maslow's research on the best and the healthiest people he could find—the growing tip of humankind—formed the basis for his personality theory. Although he did not find very many subjects who could be considered self-actualizing (he estimated that they constitute 1 percent or less of the population), he did study enough of them to show that they exhibit certain characteristics.

1. *A highly efficient perception of reality.* Self-actualizers are able to perceive the world around them, including other people, clearly and objectively. Their perception is not distorted by subjective factors such as fears and needs. They see reality exactly as it is, not as they might want or need it to be. Maslow called this highly objective, nonbiased kind of perception Being-cognition (or B-cognition). Self-actualizers are quite accurate in their judgments of other people and are able to see through the false and the phony. In sum, they see the world as it is, unbiased by any prejudgment or preconception.

2. *An acceptance of themselves, of other people, and of nature in general.* Self-actualizers can accept their own natures—their weaknesses as well as strengths—without trying to falsify or distort their image and without feeling excessive shame or guilt about any failings (and they do have imperfections). They take the same attitude of acceptance toward the weaknesses and evils of other people and of humankind in general.

3. *A spontaneity, simplicity, and naturalness.* The behavior of self-actualizers is quite open, direct, and natural, not based on the facade of a social role. Ordinarily, self-actualizers do not hide their feelings or emotions or pretend to be something they are not, although they may do so if it would prevent hurting someone else. They are highly individualistic in their ideas and ideals but not necessarily unconventional in their behavior. Such persons are essentially themselves, without being aggressively rebellious about it.

4. *A focusing on problems rather than on self.* Self-actualizers have a sense of mission in their lives—work outside of or beyond themselves to which they devote most of their energies. Dedication to some work or duty or vocation—a sense of commitment—is one of the outstanding requirements for self-actualization, in Maslow's view. He believed it was impossible to become self-actualizing without this sense of dedication. Because of this commitment, self-actualizers work very hard but find great pleasure and excitement in it.

Through this intense dedication to their work, self-actualizers are able to satisfy the metaneeds. A writer or a scientist may search for truth through his or her work, an artist may search for beauty, an attorney for justice. They do not engage in work primarily for money, fame, or power, but because it satisfies the metaneeds, challenges and develops their abilities, causes them to grow to their highest potential, and helps define their sense of self.

5. *A need for privacy and independence.* Not only are these extremely healthy people capable of withstanding isolation from others without harmful effects, but they also need solitude far more than the non-self-actualizing individual. They depend more upon themselves for their satisfactions and so do not need other people in the sense of being dependent upon them. Since they are so independent of others, even aloof, they are often considered unfriendly and cold, but this is not their intent or desire. They are simply more autonomous than most people and don't have to cling or to demand support or warmth from them.

6. *A continued freshness of appreciation.* Self-actualizers have the ability to continue to perceive and experience the world around them with freshness, wonder, and awe. While an experience may grow stale for the more average person, the supremely healthy one will enjoy a sunset, a flower, or a symphony as though it

were the first one ever experienced. Even mundane and trivial objects and experiences can be appreciated at a high level of delight, including possessions and accomplishments. Self-actualizers continue to freshly appreciate what they have, and they take nothing for granted.

7. *The mystical or peak experience.* Self-actualizers have moments of intense ecstasy, wonder, awe, and delight, not unlike deep religious experiences, during which the self is lost or transcended. During these **peak experiences**, the person feels all-powerful—extremely confident and decisive. Experience is intensified, becoming orgasmic in strength; this can occur in the context of virtually any activity. Maslow said that "any experience of real excellence, of real perfection, of any moving toward the perfect justice or toward perfect values, tends to produce a peak experience."

In his later work, he distinguished between two kinds of self-actualizers: peakers and nonpeakers. Both types are psychologically healthy, but they differ in terms of the quantity and quality of their peak experiences. Peakers have more peak experiences, and these tend to be more mystical and religious than those of nonpeakers. Peakers also tend to be more saintly and poetical, and less practical, than nonpeakers. Nonpeakers tend to be more down-to-earth, concerned with worldly affairs. Maslow also suggested that some non-self-actualizers can have peak experiences, although not as many as self-actualizers. Further, he insisted that peakers are not all mystics, artists, writers, or scientists. He identified peakers among business executives, educators, and politicians, although he noted that this finding was difficult for some of his colleagues to accept.

8. *Social interest.* Maslow borrowed Adler's concept of social interest to indicate the sympathy and empathy these extremely healthy people have for humanity in general. While they are often irritated or depressed by the behavior of individuals, they nevertheless feel a kinship with and an understanding of others and a desire to help humanity. Maslow described the self-actualizer as having the attitude of an older brother or sister toward other people.

9. *Interpersonal relations.* While their circle of close friends is not very large (there being so few other self-actualizing people), the friendships of self-actualizers are much more intense and profound than those of the average person. As you might imagine, they pick as close friends those who are healthier and more mature than most, just as we all choose friends whose characteristics are compatible with our own. Maslow also found that self-actualizers often attract admirers or disciples. Such relationships are usually one-sided, in that the admirer asks more of the self-actualizer than he or she is able (or willing) to give.

10. *Creativeness.* It is not surprising that those self-actualizing subjects in Maslow's research tended to be highly creative individuals, although they did not always produce artistic creations. That is, they were not all artists or writers, but they all exhibited inventiveness and originality in virtually every aspect of their lives.

In all their activities, self-actualizers are flexible, spontaneous, and willing to make mistakes. They are open and humble, in the same way that a child is before the world has taught it to be afraid of making mistakes or of doing something silly.

11. *A democratic character structure.* Self-actualizers, Maslow found, are very tolerant and accepting of everyone and display no racial, religious, or social preju-

dice. They are willing to listen to and learn from anyone who is able to teach them something. They do not act in a superior or condescending manner to those less educated or articulate than they but are able to relate to everyone openly and humbly.

12. *Resistance to enculturation.* These extremely healthy people are, as we have seen, autonomous, independent, and quite self-sufficient. As a result, they are free to resist social and cultural pressures to think and behave along certain lines. They do not openly rebel against cultural norms or deliberately flout social codes, but, on the other hand, they are governed by their own inner nature, not that of the culture.

This is truly an amazing set of characteristics. Self-actualizers seem almost saint-like; surely no one could be that perfect all the time. Rest easy. Self-actualizers do have imperfections and flaws. All is not constant goodness, truth, and beauty. After all, they are human. Maslow found that they could occasionally be rude and even extremely ruthless, displaying a surgical coldness toward others. They too have moments of doubt and fear, shame and guilt, and are sometimes gripped by conflict and tension. However, such incidents are definitely the exception rather than the rule in their behavior and are less frequent and usually of shorter duration and lesser intensity than those of the average person.

The failure to self-actualize

If, as Maslow suggested, the self-actualization need is innate (and so does not have to be learned), why isn't everyone self-actualizing? Why isn't the innate urge to actualize the self satisfied in all of us, just as the acorn naturally grows into an oak tree? Why has less than 1 percent of the population, according to Maslow, reached this state of being?

One excellent reason is that the higher the need in the hierarchy, the less potent it is. Self-actualization, as the highest need of all, is therefore the weakest. Because it is not very strong to begin with, it is easily interfered with or inhibited by a hostile or rejecting emotional environment that may make it difficult to satisfy love and esteem needs, by physical poverty that interferes with the satisfaction of the physiological and safety needs, and by inadequate education and poor child-rearing practices.

For instance, Maslow pointed to the sex-role training in our culture in which the little boy is taught to be manly, which usually means inhibiting such qualities as tenderness and sentimentality. One aspect of his nature is thus not allowed to develop fully. Also, if a child is overly protected, not allowed to explore new behaviors or ideas, excessively taken care of so that he or she is not able to develop new skills and abilities, then he or she will be inhibited in exploring and growing as an adult—activities that are vital to self-actualization.

Another reason for the failure to self-actualize is what Maslow called the **Jonah complex**. This refers to our fears and doubts about our own abilities and potentialities. We are afraid of our highest possibilities and at the same time thrilled by them, but all too often the fear takes precedence.

A third reason that self-actualization is so seldom reached is that it takes a great deal of courage. Even when all the lower-order needs have been satisfied, one simply cannot sit back and be passively swept along a royal road to self-actualization and fulfillment. Quite the contrary—it takes effort, discipline, self-control, and sheer hard work. Sometimes it is even painful. Therefore, it may well seem easier and safer to stay where one is (so to speak) than to grow, to deliberately seek out new challenges. The person who is self-actualizing is constantly testing and challenging himself or herself. It requires courage to give up safe, routine, well-practiced behaviors and attitudes.

It seems that childhood experiences are particularly crucial in allowing or inhibiting later growth toward self-actualization. As noted, excessive control and coddling may be harmful. Also, the opposite behavior—excessive permissiveness—may be equally harmful. Maslow warned that freedom in childhood can lead to anxiety and insecurity, which can prevent further growth. The right mixture of permissiveness and regulation (giving the child what Maslow called "freedom within limits") is required.

Maslow stressed that sufficient love in childhood is vitally important as a prerequisite for self-actualization. He noted also the importance of satisfying the basic needs within the first two years of life. If a person is made to feel secure and strong in these early years, he or she will tend to remain so when faced with the problems of adulthood. Without adequate love, security, and feelings of esteem in childhood, it is extremely difficult for the self to grow in adulthood to the point of actualization and fulfillment.

Maslow's image of human nature

We have already seen that Maslow's view of the human personality is a humanistic and optimistic one. His focus is on psychological health rather than malfunction, on growth and progress instead of stagnation, and on human virtues and potentials, not weaknesses and limitations. Basically, he had a strong sense of confidence, even trust, in our ability to shape our own positive and constructive growth and to shape a better society in the process. In fact, that trust remained the guiding credo for all of his work.

Maslow was a strong believer in free will. In his view, everyone can consciously choose how best to satisfy his or her needs and how to actualize potentialities. The choice is ours—to create a self that is actualizing or to hold back from that highest level of human development. People are responsible for the level of development they reach.

Maslow also felt that though the needs that compose his hierarchy are inherited, the behaviors through which we satisfy them are learned. Therefore, personality is affected by both nature and nurture, by heredity and environment.

It is not explicit in his writings, but Maslow's system seems to favor the idea of human uniqueness. It is true that our motivations and needs are universal, but the ways in which the needs are satisfied vary from person to person because these behaviors are learned. Therefore, not all self-actualizing persons are alike in their behavior, though they share certain qualities and attributes.

While he clearly stressed the importance of early childhood experiences in either facilitating or hampering later development, he did not believe that we are totally pawns or victims of these early experiences. People can take active roles in their own affairs. He believed that humanity has much more potential than it realizes and that we, as individuals and as societies, would be much more productive and happy if we could learn how to unleash that potential. His notion of self-actualization as the ultimate and necessary goal of life is a reflection of his belief that most people are capable of reaching a high level of functioning, given the proper conditions.

Maslow argued that our innate nature, the character with which we are born, is basically good, decent, and kind, but he did not deny the existence of evil in the world. Indeed, he believed that some people were evil beyond reclamation. With them, he confided to his diary, "nothing will work ultimately but shooting" (Lowry, 1979, p. 631). However, evil and wickedness are not an inherent part of human nature, but something thrust upon us by an inappropriate and inadequate environment. Self-actualization is, as we discussed, a relatively weak tendency or need. It always exists, but in the face of an inhibiting culture or repressive parents it has great difficulty being expressed.

Maslow cared deeply about people. His compassion is clear in his writings, and his hope for humanity is expressed in the firm belief that we can each fulfill our vast potential.

Assessment in Maslow's theory

Maslow's study of self-actualization did not begin as a formal program of assessment and research. It started simply as an effort to satisfy his own curiosity about something—in this case, about two people who impressed him greatly. They were, as we noted earlier, anthropologist Ruth Benedict and Gestalt psychologist Max Wertheimer. Maslow loved and admired them, and he wanted to understand what it was about them that made them so different from others.

He felt that his training and experience in psychology were not sufficient for the task of assessing the personalities of two such superior individuals. He observed them and made copious journal notes, finally concluding that they shared a common pattern of personal qualities. He found, to his great excitement, that they were the same kind of person, possessing characteristics that set them apart from the average individual.

Maslow then resolved to see if this same set of characteristics could be found in others. At first he turned to college students, but found only one subject out of 3,000 whom he considered self-actualizing. He concluded that the characteristics involved in self-actualization are not allowed the opportunity to develop in young people in our culture, and so he turned to the study of middle-aged and older

Self-actualization can be studied in historical figures by examining biographies and other written records; it is more difficult to study in living persons. (Shown are Thomas Jefferson and Margaret Thatcher.)

people. Even with these older subjects, however, only 1 percent of the population was capable of meeting his criteria for self-actualization.

The sample studied consisted of 49 probable, partial, and potential cases of self-actualization, including creative people drawn from among Maslow's friends and great figures drawn from history. The latter category included Thomas Jefferson, Albert Einstein, Aldous Huxley, Eleanor Roosevelt, Pablo Casals, and William James, among others.

It is difficult to describe the specific techniques he used to assess these people. As Maslow explained it, he used any technique that seemed appropriate to the problem at hand. In the case of the historical figures, he worked with biographical material, analyzing all the written records available on each person, searching for patterns of similarity among them.

With living subjects, Maslow relied on in-depth interviews, free association, the Rorschach Inkblot Test, and Henry Murray's Thematic Apperception Test. Maslow found that many of these subjects became self-conscious and, consequently, were difficult to probe. As a result, he said it became necessary to study them in an indirect and surreptitious manner, but he did not explain how that was carried out in practice.

The Personal Orientation Inventory

Maslow did not develop any assessment techniques, but the psychologist Everett Shostrom constructed a self-report questionnaire, the Personal Orientation Inventory (POI), to measure self-actualization (Shostrom, 1964, 1974). The test consists of 150 pairs of statements for which subjects indicate which of each pair is the most descriptive of them. Sample items from the POI are shown in Table 12.2.

The POI is scored for two major scales and ten subscales. The major scales are

TABLE 12.2   Sample items from the Personal Orientation Inventory

I do what others expect of me.
I feel free to not do what others expect of me.

I must justify my actions in the pursuit of my own interests.
I need not justify my actions in the pursuit of my own interests.

I live by the rules and standards of society.
I do not always need to live by the rules and standards of society.

Reasons are needed to justify my feelings.
Reasons are not needed to justify my feelings.

I only feel free to express warm feelings to my friends.
I feel free to express both warm and hostile feelings to my friends.

I will continue to grow only by setting my sights on a high-level, socially
   approved goal.
I will continue to grow best by being myself.

People should always control their anger.
People should express honestly felt anger.

Source: E. Shostrom, "An Inventory for the Measurement of Self-Actualization," *Educational and Psychological Measurement* 24 (1964): 207–218.

Time Competence, which measures the degree to which a person lives in the present; and Inner Directedness, which measures how much a person depends on self rather than on others for judgments and values. The subscales include self-actualizing values, spontaneity, self-regard, self-acceptance, acceptance of aggression, and capacity for intimate contact.

The POI, with a relatively high validity though somewhat questionable reliability, has become a widely used instrument for research on self-actualization.

Research in Maslow's theory

Maslow did not use traditional research techniques such as case studies or the experimental or correlational methods. His critics suggest that the way in which Maslow studied his self-actualizing subjects could not be characterized as research at all. Maslow agreed. He was the first to point out that his investigations leave much to be desired in the way of complying with the requirements for strict scientific research. "By ordinary standards of laboratory research, i.e., of rigorous and controlled research, this simply was not research at all" (Maslow, 1971, p. 42). However, he also noted that because the problem could not have been studied by rigorous scientific procedures, the alternative would have been to not study it at all, or to wait until appropriate procedures were developed. Maslow was too impatient for that, too committed to his conviction that humanity must be helped.

Five years before his death, he said that he did not have enough time to do careful experiments. "They take too long in view of the years I have left and the extent of what I want to do." He referred to his research as pilot studies, which, however inadequate, convinced him that the results were true and would one day be confirmed. He added that he needed fewer data than other psychologists "to come to correct conclusions" (Lowry, 1979, p. 694).

Studies of self-actualization

Although Maslow himself conducted no research on specific aspects of his theory, other psychologists did, particularly with the Personal Orientation Inventory. The bulk of the research is correlational, in which POI scores were correlated with other measures of behavior or personality. Scores indicating high self-actualization have been shown to be positively related to several characteristics, including emotional health and independent ratings of self-actualization (McClain, 1970; Shostrom, 1964); creativity (Braun & Asta, 1968); the well-being of patients following therapy, compared with their status at the beginning of therapy (Shostrom & Knapp, 1966); academic achievement (LeMay & Damm, 1968; Stewart, 1968); Q-sort ratings on emotional adjustment (Mattocks & Jew, 1974); and autonomy (Grossack, Armstrong & Lussieu, 1966).

Other studies report negative correlations between high self-actualization scores on the POI and alcoholism (Zaccaria & Weir, 1967); being institutionalized for symptoms of emotional disturbance (Fox, Knapp & Michael, 1968); high scores on a test of neuroticism (Eysenck & Eysenck, 1963; Knapp, 1965); and measures of depression and hypochondriasis (Shostrom & Knapp, 1966).

All of these results are in the expected direction, based on Maslow's descriptions of the characteristics of self-actualizers. We would expect self-actualizers to be high in emotional health, creativity, academic achievement, and autonomy, and low in alcoholism, neuroticism, depression, hypochondriasis, and other symptoms of emotional disturbance.

It is important to remember, however, that these are correlational studies and that there is as yet no independent, valid measure of self-actualization itself with which to correlate the scores obtained on the POI. It does not necessarily follow that the POI is actually measuring self-actualization, even though it correlates well with variables believed to be associated with self-actualization.

Additional research has been conducted on Maslow's theory, much of it in the field of industrial/organizational psychology where the theory, particularly the concept of self-actualization, has been well received. Some of this research appeared to be supportive of Maslow's views, prompting him to conclude that his ideas require a real-life situation, such as people on the job, for testing, rather than the artificial setting of the psychological laboratory.

Most of this industrial/organizational research has demonstrated that upper-level executives were more concerned than lower-level executives with the esteem and self-actualization needs (Porter, 1961, 1963). The findings suggested to the researchers that upper-level executives have satisfied their lower needs, allowing for the emergence of the higher needs.

Longitudinal research has not verified these findings. In this approach, behavior was studied as it changed over a long period of time, and the higher needs did not emerge once the lower needs were satisfied. Thus, this later research did not support Maslow's needs-hierarchy concept (Hall & Nougaim, 1968).

In general, despite the continued popularity of Maslow's concept of self-actualization among business executives, the theory has received little research support. One prominent industrial psychologist, upon examining the available evidence, concluded that Maslow's theory has a low degree of scientific validity and limited applicability to the world of work (Miner, 1984).

An elaborate test of Maslow's needs hierarchy, using a sample representative of the general population, did support Maslow's order of the five needs. It also demonstrated that the level of concern expressed about each need increased from lowest to highest (Graham & Balloun, 1973). For example, the physiological needs, presumably well satisfied in these subjects, were of low concern to them, whereas the self-actualization need was of great concern, presumably because it was not well satisfied.

A final commentary

Perhaps in part because of the optimism and compassion Maslow expressed, his theory became immensely popular in the 1960s and 1970s, particularly among the young. Arising from one of the prime movers of humanistic psychology, Maslow's work attracted admirers and disciples among students and professionals who had become disenchanted with the behavioristic and psychoanalytic approaches to personality and to psychology in general.

Although his theory may be waning in its appeal to the students and psychologists of the 1980s, Maslow's overall influence has been considerable. He was ranked in 12th place among 286 psychologists in importance in the last half of the 20th century, and in 6th place among the theorists discussed in this book (Gilgen, 1982).

There has been a good deal of criticism of Maslow's theory. The major target of this criticism is his research method and the data that support his theory. It is charged that the sample from which the data were derived was too small. How, critics ask, can such generalizations be made on the basis of 49 subjects, fewer than half of whom were personally interviewed and tested (the rest analyzed from biographical material)?

Also, Maslow selected as subjects people he admired, according to his own criteria of what constitutes a self-actualizing person. The criteria he used at the time were not specified. Further, his descriptions of the characteristics of self-actualizers derive from his own clinical interpretation of the data, and may have been influenced by his own moral values. Thus, his descriptions of their characteristics may have reflected his own ideals of a worthy and emotionally healthy individual.

The charge that Maslow's research methods are weak from the standpoint of scientific rigor is valid. And, as noted, Maslow readily agreed with this criticism, which must be familiar to you by now; few personality theorists are immune to it.

Other criticisms are directed at the definitions of many of Maslow's concepts, including metaneeds, metapathology, peak experiences, and, particularly, self-actualization. Critics point to inconsistencies or ambiguities in Maslow's use of these terms. Also, with reference to self-actualization, they ask on what basis this drive is assumed to be innate. Why, assuming such a need exists, could it not be learned behavior, the result of some unique combination of childhood experiences?

In Maslow's defense is his own estimate, shared by many others, that while his theory is not successful in the laboratory, it is highly successful in social, clinical, and personal terms. "It has fitted very well with the personal experience of most people, and has often given them a structured theory that has helped them to make better sense of their inner lives" (Maslow, 1970, p. xii).

Maslow issued a call to make psychology—at least humanistic psychology—relevant to the problems of modern society, arguing that the survival of civilization depends on our ability to develop our potential to the fullest, that is, to become self-actualizing.

Summary

Maslow argued that psychology must study the most creative and healthiest individuals to determine the heights of human potential. Each person is born with instinctoid needs that produce growth, development, and actualization.

Maslow's hierarchy of needs reflects his childhood experiences of poverty, isolation, and loneliness. The hierarchy of needs includes the physiological needs and the needs for safety, belonging and love, esteem, and self-actualization. The lower needs must be satisfied before the higher needs can emerge, although a need does not have to be fully and absolutely satisfied before the next one appears. Only one need is dominant at a time, depending on which of the others has been satisfied. The lower the need in the hierarchy, the stronger it is; the higher the need, the weaker it is. Higher needs appear later in the evolutionary development of the human species and in the development of the individual. Lower needs are called deficit or deficiency needs because failure to satisfy them produces a deficit in the individual. Higher needs are less necessary for survival but enhance physical and emotional well-being. Higher needs are called growth or being needs. Higher-need gratification requires more preconditions, greater complexity, and better social, economic, and political conditions.

The physiological needs include the needs for food, water, air, sleep, and sex. The safety needs, including security, stability, order, and freedom from fear and anxiety, are most important in infants and neurotic adults. The belonging and love needs can be satisfied through association with a group or through affectionate relations with one person or other people in general. The esteem needs include self-esteem and esteem from others. The self-actualization need involves the realization of a person's potentialities and capabilities and requires a realistic knowledge of strengths and weaknesses.

The needs to know and to understand form a second hierarchy of needs that emerges in late infancy and early childhood. The need to know must be satisfied before the need to understand can emerge, and both must be satisfied before self-actualization is possible.

There are exceptions to the needs hierarchy, as exemplified by religious figures who abandon worldly goods, people who fast until death for a cause, and artists who endanger their health for the sake of their work.

Motivation in self-actualizers is called metamotivation or B-motivation. It means a state in which self-actualizers develop rather than strive. The goal in metamotivation is not to make up for deficits or to reduce tension, but to enrich and enlarge life and to increase tension. Self-actualizers are no longer becoming, in the sense of satisfying the lower needs, but are in a state of being, in which they spontaneously and naturally express their full humanness. Metaneeds or B-values are goals or states of growth toward which self-actualizers move. Frustration of the metaneeds produces metapathology, a formless illness for which no specific cause can be identified. Metapathologies represent a thwarting of full human growth and development.

Self-actualizers constitute less than 1 percent of the population. They exhibit the following characteristics: a highly efficient perception of reality (B- or Being-cognition); an acceptance of themselves, of other people, and of nature; a spontaneity, simplicity, and naturalness; a focusing on problems rather than on self, in which the metaneeds are satisfied through dedication to work; a need for privacy and independence; a continued freshness of appreciation; mystical or peak experiences, which peakers experience more frequently than nonpeakers, though both are self-actualizing; social interest; more intense interpersonal relations; creativeness; a democratic character structure; and a resistance to enculturation.

Not everyone is self-actualizing, because self-actualization is the weakest need in the hierarchy and so is easily interfered with; some people fear their highest possibilities; self-actualization requires courage, discipline, and hard work; and too much freedom or lack of security in childhood inhibit self-actualization.

Maslow's image of human nature is optimistic, emphasizing free will, conscious choice, human uniqueness, the ability to overcome childhood experiences, and innate goodness. Personality is affected by heredity and environment. Our ultimate goal is self-actualization.

Maslow used interviews, free association, projective techniques, and biographical material to assess personality. The Personal Orientation Inventory is a self-report test to measure self-actualization. Its two major scales are Time Competence and Inner Directedness. High scores on the POI correlate positively with emotional health and adjustment, creativity, well-being following therapy, academic achievement, and autonomy. High scores correlate negatively with alcoholism, being institutionalized, neuroticism, depression, and hypochondriasis.

Industrial/organizational research provides little support for Maslow's theory, but one study did support the order of needs and demonstrated a greater concern for higher rather than lower needs.

Maslow has been criticized for using too small a sample on which to base his theory and for not making explicit his criteria for selecting his self-actualizing subjects. His descriptions of their characteristics may have been influenced by his own moral values. Further, his research methods are weak and his definitions of key terms are inconsistent and ambiguous.

Glossary

deficit needs   The lower needs; failure to satisfy these needs produces a deficit in the body.

growth needs   The higher needs; these needs are less necessary for survival but involve instead the realization and fulfillment of one's potentialities.

hierarchy of needs   An arrangement of innate needs from strongest to weakest that activates and directs behavior; includes the physiological, safety, belonging and love, esteem, and self-actualization needs.

Jonah complex   The fear that maximizing one's potential will bring about a situation with which one will be unable to cope.

metamotivation   The motivation of self-actualizers; involves the maximizing of one's potential rather than the striving for a particular object needed to correct a deficit.

peak experiences   Moments of intense ecstasy, not unlike deep religious or mystical experiences, during which the self is transcended.

self-actualization   The fullest development of the self.

Review questions

1. What criticisms have humanistic psychologists made of behaviorism and psychoanalysis?
2. Describe the hierarchy of needs. How can each need be satisfied?
3. What are some of the differences between higher needs and lower needs?
4. At what age do we develop the needs to know and to understand? Which of these needs is the stronger?
5. Discuss the characteristics of the self-actualizing person.
6. Describe the motivation of self-actualizing persons.
7. What is a peak experience? Are peak experiences necessary for self-actualization?
8. List four factors that may explain why less than 1 percent of the population satisfies the self-actualization need.
9. What does recent correlational research reveal about the relationship between self-actualization and certain personality characteristics?
10. How does Maslow's image of human nature differ from Freud's image of human nature?

Suggested reading

Goble, F. G. *The third force: The psychology of Abraham Maslow.* New York: Grossman, 1970.

Hall, M. H. A conversation with Abraham H. Maslow. *Psychology Today*, July 1968, pp. 35–37, 54–57.

Lowry, R. J. *A. H. Maslow: An intellectual portrait.* Monterey, CA: Brooks/Cole, 1973.

Lowry, R. J., Ed. *The journals of Abraham Maslow.* Monterey, CA: Brooks/Cole, 1979.

Maddi, S. R. & Costa, P. T. *Humanism in personology: Allport, Maslow, and Murray.* Chicago: Aldine-Atherton, 1972.

Maslow, A. H. *Toward a psychology of being*, 2nd ed. New York: Van Nostrand Reinhold, 1968.

Maslow, A. H. *Motivation and personality*, 2nd ed. New York: Harper & Row, 1970.

Maslow, A. H. *The farther reaches of human nature.* New York: Viking, 1971.

PART 6

The Cognitive
Approach

If you look up the word *cognition* in a dictionary, you will find that it means the act or process of *knowing*. The cognitive approach to personality focuses on the ways in which people know their environment and themselves—how they perceive, evaluate, learn, think, make decisions, and solve problems. This is the most rational or truly psychological approach to personality because it focuses exclusively on conscious mental activities.

It may seem, however, that this exclusive interest in the mind or mental processes neglects some of the ideas dealt with by other approaches. For example, we do not find in the cognitive approach needs, drives, or emotions discussed as separate activities of the personality. Instead, they are considered to be parts of the personality that are controlled, like all the other parts, by cognitive processes.

Other approaches to personality also deal with cognitive processes. The contemporary developments in psychoanalysis, and the work of Erikson, which accord a greater autonomy and importance to the ego, are in effect recognizing the importance of cognitive functions. So too are the humanistic theorists, who deal in part with how we perceive our world and our experiences. Theorists such as Murray and Allport treat the concept of reasoning, and Adler spoke of the creative self, which results from one's perception or interpretation of experience. Some theorists who take a behavioral approach to personality also invoke cognitive processes (see Part 7).

The difference between all these other theorists and the cognitive approach to personality represented here by the work of George Kelly is that Kelly attempts to define and understand *all* aspects of personality in terms of cognitive processes. These acts or processes of knowing are seen not as an element of the personality but rather as the entire personality.

CHAPTER 13

George Kelly

The life of Kelly (1905–1967)
Personal constructs: Ways of anticipating and interpreting life events
  The fundamental postulate
  Similarities among repeated events
  Individual differences in interpreting events
  Relationships among constructs
  Dichotomies among constructs
  Freedom of choice
  The range of applicability
  Exposure to new experiences
  Adapting to new experiences
  Competition among constructs
  Similarities among people in interpreting events
  Interpersonal relationships
Kelly's image of human nature
Assessment in Kelly's theory
  The Role Construct Repertory Test
Research in Kelly's theory
  Cognitive styles
A final commentary
Summary
Glossary
Review questions
Suggested reading

Each individual man formulates in his own way constructs through which he views the world of events.

GEORGE KELLY

Kelly's personal construct approach to personality is not only one of the more recent theories to be proposed but also one of the more original. Each of the theories discussed in this book has distinctive features and characteristic positions that set it apart from other theories. There are certain similarities among the earlier theorists as well, however—a focus on the conscious or the unconscious, for example, or on motivating forces that push the individual (as with instincts) or pull him or her (as in a drive toward self-actualization).

Kelly's theory shares virtually nothing with the other approaches. He warned us that we will not find in it many of the familiar terms and concepts commonly found in personality theories. Having warned us, he then proceeds to shock us by pointing out how many of these terms are missing in his approach: unconscious, ego, need, drive, stimulus, response, reinforcement, and—most amazing of all—motivation and emotion. How can one hope to understand the human personality without considering motivation and emotion?

The opening quotation provides some clue to how Kelly proposed to do that. All people, he said, are able to create and shape cognitive constructs about their own environment; that is, individuals interpret all the physical and social objects in their world to form a pattern. On the basis of this pattern, people make predictions about objects, other people, and themselves and use the predictions to guide them in their actions. Thus, to understand individuals, one must understand their patterns—the way in which they personally construct their world. Therefore, it is the individual's interpretation of events, rather than the events themselves, that is of importance.

Kelly derived his theory of personality from his experience in working with troubled individuals, as is the case with most of our theorists. For several reasons, however—the kind of client with whom he dealt, his own scientific training, and his lack of a Freudian or other analytic bias—he interpreted this clinical experience in a vastly different manner.

The model of human nature that Kelly developed from his clinical work is unlike that of any other theorist in psychology: he viewed people as, in a sense, scientists. That is, he believed that people function in the same way that scientists do. "What do scientists do?" Kelly asked. They construct theories and hypotheses and then test them against their form of reality, using experiments in the laboratory. If the theory is supported by the experiments, it is retained. If it is not supported, it is rejected or modified in some way and then retested.

This is, in essence, the way the psychologist who studies personality proceeds. Yet, Kelly noted, psychologists do not ascribe the same intellectual and rational facility to their subjects or patients that they do to themselves. "Why not?" Kelly asked. It is as if psychologists have two theories about human nature—one that applies to themselves and the way they look at the world and another that applies to the people they study. They see those they study as incapable of functioning in rational terms and instead motivated by all manner of drives and subject to control by unconscious forces. The individual is believed to function on a purely emotional level, with few if any rational processes involved—quite unlike the way the psychologist functions.

Are psychologists superior beings? No, they are really no different from the people they study. What works for one works for the other, Kelly said; what explains one explains the other. Both are concerned with predicting and controlling the events in their lives, which they are capable of doing on a rational basis.

Individuals, like scientists, construct their own theories, their own *personal constructs*, by which they are able to predict and exercise some control over events in their environment. The way to understand the individual, then, is through an examination of his or her personal constructs.

In the light of the emphases we have seen with other personality theories, it is not surprising that a theory that stresses human rationality instead of emotionality, and self-interpretations of experience instead of universal and instinctive drives, does not enjoy overwhelming popularity among traditional personality theorists. However, former students of Kelly actively pursue and defend this unique and provocative view of human functioning, "a genuine new departure and a spirited contribution to the psychology of personality" (Bruner, 1956, pp. 356–357).

The life of Kelly (1905–1967)

There is little information available on the childhood and youth of George Kelly, so it is not possible to speculate on early experiences that may have influenced his theory of personality.

He was born on a farm in Kansas. An only child, he received a great deal of attention and affection from his parents, who were devoutly religious and firmly committed to helping the needy and the sick. His father had been trained as a Presbyterian minister but worked as a clergyman only sporadically. His parents worked hard on the farm and were fundamentalist in their religious beliefs and opposed to frivolous entertainments such as dancing and card playing.

In 1909, when Kelly was 4 years old, the family traveled by covered wagon to Colorado to try farming there, but before long they returned to Kansas. Kelly's early education was irregular and conducted as much by his parents as by teachers. By the time he was 13, he was attending a high school in Wichita, and he seldom lived at home again.

In 1926, he received a B.A. in physics and mathematics from Park College. His future was uncertain, since his interests were shifting from engineering and science to problems of a social nature. He worked briefly as an engineer and then switched to education, teaching at a labor college in Minneapolis, then working as an instructor for the American Banking Association, and even offering a course in citizenship to immigrants. During this time, he received a master's degree in educational sociology from the University of Kansas.

In 1928, he taught at a junior college in Iowa, where he also coached students in drama. Until this time his career had exhibited no firm direction toward psychology, but his professional training took a different turn in 1929, when he was awarded a fellowship at the University of Edinburgh in Scotland. In a year there he earned a bachelor of education degree (credit having been given for his previous academic experience) and developed a strong interest in psychology.

He undertook doctoral studies at the State University of Iowa, receiving a Ph.D. in 1931. His academic career began at Fort Hays Kansas State College, in the midst of the severe economic recession of the 1930s. There was not much opportunity to work in physiological psychology, the area that most interested him at the time, and so he changed to clinical psychology, for which there was a need.

He developed a clinical-psychology service, both for the public school system and for the students at his college. He formed traveling clinics, which went from school to school and which gave him the opportunity to try out new approaches to clinical practice. He began this work in the absence of a theoretical bias. That is, he was not already committed to a single approach to therapy or to one view of the nature of personality. Unlike so many personality theorists, he had not been psychoanalyzed as part of his training. As a result, he felt free to experiment with existing methods as well as with new ones of his own design.

It was during his 13-year stay at Fort Hays Kansas State College that he developed his own approach. He offered the view that people can, on a rational and intellectual level, formulate their own personal constructs about their world, which they use to predict and control events.

It is important to understand the kind of clinical experiences Kelly was exposed to, for they influenced the nature of his theory. For the most part, the people he treated were not severely mentally disturbed. They were not institutionalized psychotics or neurotics who sought the services of a psychologist because they were having emotional difficulties. His counseling work was done with college and public school students referred for counseling by their teachers.

Unlike the seriously maladjusted patients in a psychiatric ward or a psychoanalyst's office, Kelly's clients were perhaps more capable of functioning, or at least of expressing their problems, in rational and intellectual terms—the terms in which most functioning occurs in an academic setting. In the classroom, for example, one is taught to intellectualize—to discuss rationally the material being dealt with. Perhaps this intellectual context and attitude carried over from the classroom to the counseling situation, for it too took place in an academic setting. It is possible that, had circumstances placed Kelly during his formative professional years at work in the severely disturbed ward of a mental institution, his theory would not have leaned so heavily on rational and intellectual abilities.

World War II interrupted Kelly's academic career, and he joined the Navy as a psychologist in the Bureau of Medicine and Surgery in Washington, D.C. When the war ended, in 1945, Kelly joined the faculty of the University of Maryland, where he stayed for a year before moving to Ohio State University. He spent 19 years there, during which time he refined his theory of personality and, with the help of his students, conducted research on various aspects of it. One of his colleagues at Ohio State was Julian Rotter, whose cognitive-based personality theory is discussed in Chapter 16.

Also during those years, he lectured at several universities in North and South

America. In 1960, he traveled around the world, speaking throughout Europe and the Soviet Union on the ways that his construct theory might be applied to resolving international problems. In 1965, he accepted an appointment to an endowed chair at Brandeis University, but he died shortly thereafter.

Kelly was a major force in developing the profession of clinical psychology, which was growing rapidly during the years after World War II. He held several honored positions in the field, among them the presidencies of the Clinical and Consulting Divisions of the American Psychological Association and of the American Board of Examiners in Professional Psychology.

Personal constructs: Ways of anticipating and interpreting life events

Kelly proposed that a person looks upon and organizes his or her world in the same way that a scientist does—by making various hypotheses about the world and testing them against the reality of his or her own experience. People observe all the events in their world—the facts or data of their experience—and interpret them. This interpreting or *construing* of experience represents the individual's own unique view of these events, a pattern within which he or she fits or places them. Kelly wrote: "Man looks at his world through transparent patterns of templets which he creates and then attempts to fit over the realities of which the world is composed" (Kelly, 1955, pp. 8–9).

As a perhaps overly simplified example, we might compare these patterns or templets to sunglasses that provide a particular tint or coloring to everything the wearer sees. One person's glasses may have a bluish tint, another's a greenish tint. Each person can look at the identical scene and yet perceive it in a different way, as a function of the tint that frames and biases his or her view. So it is with the hypotheses, patterns, or templets each of us constructs. We each see the world through our own special lens. And it is this special view, this unique pattern created by each individual, that defines the word *construct* as Kelly used it. A **construct** is a person's way of looking at the events in his or her world, a way of explaining or interpreting that world.

Each person advances a hypothesis that a particular construct he or she holds will fit over the realities of some event in his or her world. Like a scientist, the person then proceeds to test this hypothesis by acting in accordance with it in relation to the event. For example, take the case of a student who is in danger of failing a course and is trying to influence her professor to give her a passing grade. On the basis of observing the professor for most of the semester, the student concludes that the professor acts in a very authoritarian and superior manner in the classroom and seems to have an inflated picture of himself and his importance.

From this observation, the student forms the hypothesis (the construct) that if she behaves in a manner that plays up to the professor's exaggerated sense of self-importance, the teacher will respond favorably. The student now tests this hypothesis against reality. She goes to the library and reads an article the professor has written. Then she asks the professor questions about it, praises the professor's insight, comments on the importance of the area in which he is working, and asks when the next article will be published.

If the professor gives the student a passing grade at the end of the semester, then the hypothesis is confirmed. The construct is a useful one and can be called into play again if the student takes another course with the same professor. If the student fails the course, then she must construct a new hypothesis for dealing with that professor in a later course or with other professors who seem similar in nature.

We develop many constructs over the course of our lives—one to deal with every kind of situation or event or person with whom we come in contact. We are always increasing the repertoire of constructs as we meet new people and events. Further, existing constructs may need to be refined, modified, or elaborated on because people and events change over time.

Not only do we form a large number of constructs but, throughout our lives, alternative constructions must always remain available to us. There is nothing absolute or final about any construct, because none can be created that will predict or anticipate every eventuality. Revision, to a greater or lesser extent, is always necessary, and the individual must have alternative constructions to turn to. Otherwise— if constructs were fixed and rigid—the person would, as Kelly stated, "paint himself into a corner."

He firmly believed that this need not happen: "No one needs to be completely hemmed in by circumstances; no one needs to be the victim of his biography" (Kelly, 1955, p. 15). People are not dictated to by the constructs they have developed for use. Kelly's notion of **constructive alternativism** holds that we are free to revise or replace our constructs. However, while they are always capable of being changed, the change must be judicious and based on the facts of experience. Inappropriate constructs can do more harm than good. Kelly noted that the alternative hypotheses chosen must represent improvements.

Kelly's theory of constructs and how they work is presented in a straightforward fashion, organized into one fundamental postulate and 11 corollaries.

The fundamental postulate

The fundamental postulate in Kelly's **theory of personal constructs** is as follows: "A person's processes are psychologically channelized by the ways in which he anticipates events."

By using the word *processes*, Kelly made it clear that he was not suggesting the existence of any kind of inert substance, such as mental energy, in his view of humanity. Rather, the person is seen as a flowing, moving process. The psychological processes are directed (channelized) by the constructs, by the way in which the person construes his or her world. While always subject to change, there is nevertheless a degree of stability in the way a person behaves, because he or she operates through a network of channels. Channels can change, of course, but they are structured, and changes ordinarily occur within the limits or range imposed by this structure.

Another key word in the postulate is *anticipates*. The whole notion of constructs is anticipatory in nature in that a person uses them to predict (anticipate) the future, so that he or she has some idea of what will happen as the result of behaving in one way or another.

The 11 corollaries in Kelly's system both evolve from and build upon the fundamental postulate (Kelly, 1955, pp. 46–95).

Similarities among repeated events

1. *Construction Corollary*: "A person anticipates events by construing their replications."

Kelly believed that no event or experience in a person's life is ever reproduced exactly as it occurred before. Even though an event is repeated, it will not be precisely the same the second time it is experienced. If you listen to the same recording today that you heard yesterday, the experience that you have can differ. Your mood may not be the same, and during the passage of one day you were exposed to diverse experiences that may have influenced you in a variety of ways.

However, even though repeated events are not experienced identically, there will be recurrent features. Certain aspects of the repeated experience will be similar to those found in its earlier occurrences. On the basis of these continuing themes, a person is able to make predictions—to set up anticipations—about how an event will be experienced in the future. The predictions are based on the notion that future events, while not duplicates of past events, are nevertheless going to be at least partial repeats of past events. Certain themes of the past will appear again in the future. Constructs are formulated on the basis of these recurring themes.

Individual differences in interpreting events

2. *Individuality Corollary*: "Persons differ from each other in their construction of events."

With this corollary, Kelly introduced the notion of individual differences into his system. He pointed out that people differ from one another in how they perceive or interpret an event. As the result of construing events in different ways, people formulate quite different constructs. Constructs, then, do not so much reflect the objective reality of the event as they constitute the interpretation the person places on the event.

However, in spite of these individual differences in constructs, Kelly believed, there are recurrent characteristics of constructs common to all persons. In other words, no matter how individual the interpretation of an event may be, there is some degree of sharing of experiences. It is possible to find some common ground among people's construed experiences, particularly when the people have similar cultural and group norms, values, and mores.

Nevertheless, remember that the corollary is labeled *individuality*. Kelly's main emphasis remains on the uniqueness of each person's constructs.

People differ from one another in how they perceive or interpret the same event.

Relationships among constructs

3. *Organization Corollary*: "Each person characteristically evolves, for his convenience in anticipating events, a construction system embracing ordinal relationships between constructs."

What Kelly is suggesting here is that a person tends to organize his or her individual constructs into a system or pattern of constructs according to his or her own view of the relationships (both similarities and contrasts) among them. Because of this organization of the constructs, two people who have highly similar individual constructs may yet differ markedly from each other because the constructs are ordered in different ways.

By using the phrase *ordinal relationships between constructs*, Kelly proposed that constructs are organized in a hierarchical fashion, with some subordinate to others. That is, one construct can include one or more others. The construct *good*, for example, may include among its subordinates the constructs *intelligent, moral*, and *efficient*. The construct *moral* could, in turn, include other subordinate concepts. Also, the construct *good* could be subordinate to yet another construct.

These relationships, while usually longer lasting than the individual constructs, can nevertheless change; they are not rigid. For example, if a person feels that he or she has been harmed in some way by people more intelligent than himself or herself, that individual may switch the construct *intelligent* from a subordinate place under the construct *good* to a place under the construct *bad*. As with individual constructs, the test for a construction system is its predictive efficiency. If a system no longer provides a valid prediction of future events, it will be modified or discarded.

Dichotomies among constructs

4. *Dichotomy Corollary*: "A person's construction system is composed of a finite number of dichotomous constructs."

All constructs, in Kelly's view, are bipolar or dichotomous. This dichotomous nature is necessary if future events are to be correctly anticipated. Just as it is necessary to note similarities among events or people, dissimilarities must also be noted. It is not enough, according to Kelly, to have a construct about a friend that notes his or her characteristic of honesty. One must also note the opposite of that construct (dishonesty) to show how the honest friend differs from people who are dishonest. If such a contrast did not exist—for example, if all people were honest—then forming the construct of honesty about a person would serve no predictive purpose. One friend can be predicted to be honest in future relations only in contrast to someone else who can be predicted to be dishonest.

The personal construct, then, would be *honest–dishonest*. Friends A and B may be construed as honest, in contrast to Friend C who is construed as dishonest. Of course, the same three people could also be construed in other terms. Friends A and C may be construed as helpful, Friend B as not helpful. The view—the construct—is always in terms of a dichotomy, a pair of qualities.

Freedom of choice

5. *Choice Corollary*: "A person chooses for himself that alternative in a dichotomized construct through which he anticipates the greater possibility for extension and definition of his system."

The notion that an individual has choice is a theme that runs through all of Kelly's writings. According to the *Dichotomy Corollary*, each construct has two opposing poles. For any particular situation, a person must choose which of the alternatives will work best—that is, which will best help predict future events. Ordinarily, and ideally, the person will choose the alternative that provides the best opportunity for anticipating future events.

However, there is some latitude (or choice) involved in deciding between the alternatives, and that choice is between *security* and *adventure*. To give a modest example, suppose a student must decide which of two courses to take next semester. One course is easy because it is very much like one the student is now completing and is taught by a professor who gives high grades for very little work. There is virtually no risk involved, but perhaps not much reward either; the student knows the professor is dull, and the similar course that he is now finishing has not taught him much he didn't already know. There is no risk or gamble involved in taking the new course—it is the secure choice. The student can make a highly accurate prediction about the outcome of this choice.

The other course he can choose is filled with unknowns: the professor is new but rumored to be tough, and the content is not like anything the student has studied. However, the material to be covered seems to be interesting and would expose the student to a new field that he would like to know more about. Here there is a risk or gamble. The student cannot make a fully accurate prediction about the outcome of his choice. However, the potential reward and satisfaction could be much higher than with the other course. This is the more adventurous choice.

The student must choose between the low-risk, minimal-reward secure choice and the high-risk, high-reward adventurous choice. The first has a high predictive efficiency; the second has a much lower predictive efficiency. Kelly believed that we face such choices all our lives—choices between *definition* and *extension* of the personal construct system. The secure choice—that which closely resembles past choices—further defines the individual's construct system by repeating similar experiences and events. The more adventurous choice leads to an extension of the construct system by introducing new experiences and events into it.

Kelly felt that a tendency to take the secure, no-risk alternative may explain why some people persist in behaving in the wrong way. Why, for example, does a person continue to behave in a hostile fashion toward others—even when rebuffed for it—instead of being friendly and open? Kelly answered that such a person is simply making the secure, low-risk choice by behaving in that way. For whatever reasons, the person has come to know what to expect, to be able to predict how others will react when he or she is hostile. (Remember that choices are made in terms of how best to anticipate the future, not necessarily in terms of what is best for the individual.)

If such a person were to choose to behave in a friendly and nonhostile fashion, he or she would not be able to anticipate the future as well, not knowing what to expect. The rewards might be greater, but so is the uncertainty. And the individual, like the scientist, does his or her best to predict future events with a high degree of certainty.

The range of applicability

6. *Range Corollary*: "A construct is convenient for the anticipation of a finite range of events only."

This corollary is largely self-explanatory. Very few, if any, personal constructs are appropriate or relevant for all situations. Kelly offered the example of the construct *tall versus short*. It obviously has a limited **range of convenience**; it is simply not relevant to everything. It can be useful with respect to buildings, trees, or people, but it is of no value in describing a pizza or the weather.

Some constructs can be applied to many situations or people, while others can be applied in an extremely narrow and limited way, perhaps only to one person or situation. What is appropriate or relevant for a construct—what is within its range of convenience—is a matter of individual choice. Let us take the construct *trust versus suspicion*, for example. One person applies it to all people with whom she has contact, another finds it relevant for only some people, and a third person does not find it appropriate for people at all. The last may apply it to his pet dog but not to people. In understanding an individual, Kelly noted, it is just as important to know what is excluded from the range of convenience of a construct as to know what is included.

Exposure to new experiences

7. *Experience Corollary*: "A person's construction system varies as he successively construes the replications of events."

We have seen that each construct is like a hypothesis, in that it is generated on the basis of past experience to predict or anticipate future experiences. Each hypothesis is tested against reality by determining how well it predicted a future event. Most people are continually exposed to new events, and so the process of testing the fit of a construct (seeing how well it predicted the event) is going on much of the time.

If a construct has not been a valid predictor, it must be reformulated or replaced in the light of the new experiences. Events and experiences must be reconstrued as a person's world broadens and varies. Constructs that worked at age 16, for example, may be harmful at age 40. In the years between 16 and 40, then, the individual must constantly reinterpret the nature of his or her experiences. In other words, learning is taking place, as a result of which one's construction system undergoes continuous revision.

Construct systems cannot remain fixed, unless a person lives a life involving no change, no new experiences. In that case, constructs would not have to change, for such a person would have no new events to anticipate. But those whose lives involve meeting new people and facing new situations must reconstrue these experiences and alter their constructs accordingly.

Adapting to new experiences

8. *Modulation Corollary*: "The variation in a person's construction system is limited by the permeability of the constructs within whose range of convenience the variants lie."

Before attempting to explain this corollary, we must define one of its key terms, **permeability**. To permeate means to penetrate or pass through something, and that is the sense in which Kelly used the term. A construct that is capable of being permeated (is permeable) is one that will allow entirely new elements to be admitted into its range of convenience. Such a construct is thus open to new experiences and events.

Therefore, how thoroughly a person's construction system may be changed, adjusted, or modulated as a function of new experiences and new learning depends on how open or permeable the constructs are. An impermeable or concrete construct is not capable of being revised or replaced, no matter what new experiences are available to it. For example, if a person holds the impermeable construct that all black people are of inferior intelligence, he or she will not change that belief, regardless of how many highly intelligent blacks he or she meets. The construct is closed tightly against the intrusion of any new experiences, and the person is closed to new learning.

Competition among constructs

9. *Fragmentation Corollary*: "A person may successively employ a variety of construction subsystems which are inferentially incompatible with each other."

At first glance, this corollary may appear to be a bit strange. How can individual constructs that are incompatible with one another exist within the pattern of an overall construction system? It would seem that all constructs would have to be consistent with one another.

Yet it must be remembered that ordinarily a construction system is in a continual state of change in the light of new experiences. However, even though it is changing within the framework of an overall pattern or design, new constructs do not necessarily derive from or grow out of old ones. Even when they do, the new construct may not be compatible with the old. In one situation, two constructs may be compatible or consistent, but in a changed situation (even one involving a minor change) the same constructs may be inconsistent.

For example, you meet a person for the first time and immediately like him. He is also a psychology major and his interests in the field are the same as yours. His views and attitudes in that area coincide with yours. He thus fits with your construct of friend—someone to be liked and respected. The next day you meet him again, this time at a political meeting, and you are disappointed to find him expressing views opposite to your own. He now fits a different construct for you—that of extreme conservatism—and this places him in the category of enemy. However, this inconsistency is at a subordinate level. The larger, superordinate construct—liberals are friends, conservatives are enemies, for example—remains undisturbed. A person can tolerate a number of subordinate inconsistencies without discarding or modifying the overall construct.

Similarities among people in interpreting events

10. *Commonality Corollary*: "To the extent that one person employs a construction of experience which is similar to that employed by another, his psychological processes are similar to those of the other person."

With this corollary (and the *Sociality Corollary* below), Kelly extended his theory of personal constructs into the area of interpersonal relations. As we saw with the *Individuality Corollary*, people differ from one another in the ways in which they construe events, and unique constructs develop as a result. However, just as people differ because of differences in ways of construing, so they can be similar to one another because of similarities in construing. If two people or 20 million people construe an experience in a similar way, their psychological processes will be highly similar. They will not be identical in their psychological makeup, but they will share certain characteristics and processes.

Consider a large group of people who have in common cultural norms, mores, and ideals. Their anticipations and expectations of one another will be similar, and they will construe their experiences in like ways. Therefore, people in the same culture may behave in the same manner even though they were exposed to entirely different specific events.

Interpersonal relationships

11. *Sociality Corollary*: "To the extent that one person construes the construction processes of another, he may play a role in a social process involving the other person."

As we have just seen, people in the same culture will tend to construe events in the same, or at least similar, ways. While this makes for a commonality among people, it does not by itself bring about constructive interpersonal relationships among them. In order for that to take place, it is not enough that one person construe experiences in the same way as another. The person must also construe the other's constructions. In other words, he or she must have an understanding of how the other person thinks and thus be able to anticipate how that person will predict events.

Construing the constructions of others is a task in which we are constantly engaged. Kelly gave the example of driving down a highway. We literally stake our lives on our anticipations of what other drivers will do. It is, Kelly stated, "an amazing example of people predicting each other's behavior through subsuming each other's perception of a situation."

Only when we can anticipate, with at least a reasonable degree of accuracy, what other drivers, friends, wives, husbands, or professors will do, can we adjust ourselves to them. While we are anticipating and adjusting to others, they are doing the same with regard to us. In this mutual adjustment we each come to assume a certain role with respect to every other person. We play one role with a close friend, another with a lover, another with a police officer. Each role is a behavior pattern that evolves from our understanding of the way in which the other person construes events. In a sense, we put ourselves into that person's constructs.

Kelly's image of human nature

Kelly's theory of personality presents us with an optimistic, even flattering image of human nature. More than any other theorist, Kelly treated people as rational beings. We are capable not only of forming our own constructs, through which we view the world, but also of formulating our own unique approach to reality. "Man is the author of his destiny," not its victim.

Such a view endows us with free will—the ability to choose the path our own life will take. More important, we are able to change paths; we are always capable of changing our outlook and forming new constructs, with their related anticipations. A person is not bound to a path chosen in childhood, adolescence, or at any age. No single stage of life is more important than any other. We change and revise our constructs throughout our lifetime. The direction is clearly toward the future because our constructs are formulated in terms of predictions. Humanity, Kelly argued, lives in anticipation; our lives are governed by what we predict for the future and where we think our choices will lead us.

Thus, Kelly does not consider events of the past to be capable of totally deter-

mining present behavior. We are not victims of our biographies, he said—not prisoners of harsh toilet training, early sex experiences, or parental rejection. However,
while the actual events of the past do not enslave us, we can be influenced by our
interpretation of those events. But such interpretations result from the free and rational choices of the individual, in Kelly's view.

We are prisoners neither of biological instincts nor of unconscious influences.
We are not pushed and prodded by any such determinants. As we saw earlier, Kelly
invoked none of the usual motivating forces—incentives, needs, drives—not even
the concept of motivation. There is no type of energy force that motivates us. It is
not needed because we are already motivated—that is, in motion—for the simple
reason that we are alive. Life itself is movement, and Kelly saw no need to invoke
any other explanation. We do not have to be pushed or pulled by needs or drives,
for we are "delivered fresh into the psychological world alive and struggling."

Kelly did not explicitly state a position on the nature–nurture issue. Although
he did not discuss the role of heredity in personality, he noted that we are not
shaped by our environment. We form our constructs on the basis of how we interpret the environment, not in terms of what it does to us. He did not posit any ultimate and necessary goal of life, but it can be suggested that our goal is the definition of the set of constructs that best enables us to predict events.

Kelly took a moderate position on the question of uniqueness. His commonality corollary states that persons in the same culture will develop a number of
similar constructs. The individuality corollary, however, stresses the uniqueness of
many of a person's constructs, and hence of the person himself or herself.

Assessment in Kelly's theory

Kelly's theory of personal constructs evolved from his clinical experience with public school and college students. These students, while no doubt troubled, were still
capable of functioning in an academic setting; they were not locked away in a mental institution. Also, as noted, they were in a situation that values rational functioning and logical discussion of issues. Not surprisingly, then, Kelly's main method of
assessment took advantage of these characteristics.

His primary technique was a straightforward interview. "If you don't know
what is going on in a person's mind," Kelly said, "ask him; he may tell you!" (Kelly,
1958, p. 330). Adopting what he called the *credulous attitude*, Kelly noted that one
should accept what the client says at face value, for this is a way of determining what
constructs he or she is using. However, the client may deliberately lie and distort
his or her version of events. Kelly's major point is that what the client says must be
respected, even if not fully believed.

Another technique used to assess a person's view of the world was to have the
person write a self-characterization sketch. His standard instructions to a client are
as follows. "I want you to write a character sketch of [the client's name], just as if he
were the principal character in a play. Write it as it might be written by a friend who
knew him very *intimately* and very *sympathetically*, perhaps better than anyone

ever really could know him. Be sure to write it in the third person. . . . Start out by saying, '[the client's name] is . . .'" (Kelly, 1955, p. 323). Kelly found this a useful technique for learning how a person perceives himself or herself and his or her relations with others.

The Role Construct Repertory Test

After having developed the notion of personal constructs more fully, Kelly devised a test to uncover the constructs by which a person construes important people in his or her life. It is called the Role Construct Repertory Test, perhaps better known under its abbreviated title, REP Test. First, the client is asked to write the names of people who have performed each of a number of significant roles in his or her life. For instance, the client is asked who played the role of mother, father, spouse, closest friend of the same sex, or person most pitied or most attractive. Kelly's role title list is shown in Table 13.1.

The client is then asked to sort the listed people. Given three of the names at a time, he or she is asked to select the two who are most alike and to tell how they differ from the third person. For example, the client may be given the names of the threatening person, pitied person, and attractive person. He or she describes how two of them are similar in some aspect of their behavior or character and how they differ from the third.

This information is usually presented on a matrix known as a *repertory grid*, a

---

TABLE 13.1   Role title list from the Role Construct Repertory Test

1. A teacher you liked.
2. A teacher you disliked.
3. Your wife/husband or present boyfriend/girlfriend.
4. An employer, supervisor, or officer under whom you worked or served and whom you found hard to get along with.
5. An employer, supervisor, or officer under whom you worked or served and whom you liked.
6. Your mother or the person who has played the part of a mother in your life.
7. Your father or the person who has played the part of a father in your life.
8. Your brother nearest your age or the person who has been most like a brother.
9. Your sister nearest your age or the person who has been most like a sister.
10. A person with whom you have worked who was easy to get along with.
11. A person with whom you have worked who was hard to understand.
12. A neighbor with whom you get along well.
13. A neighbor whom you find hard to understand.
14. A boy you got along well with when you were in high school.
15. A girl you got along well with when you were in high school.
16. A boy you did not like when you were in high school.
17. A girl you did not like when you were in high school.
18. A person of your own sex whom you would enjoy having as a companion on a trip.
19. A person of your own sex whom you would dislike having as a companion on a trip.
20. A person with whom you have been closely associated recently who appears to dislike you.
21. The person whom you would most like to be of help to or whom you feel most sorry for.
22. The most intelligent person whom you know personally.
23. The most successful person whom you know personally.
24. The most interesting person whom you know personally.

Source: G. A. Kelly, *The Psychology of Personal Constructs*, vol. 1 (New York: Norton, 1955), pp. 221–222.

CONSTRUCTS

SORT NO.	EMERGENT POLE	IMPLICIT POLE
1	Don't believe in God	Very religious
2	Same sort of education	Complete different education
3	Not athletic	Athletic
4	Not girls	A boy
5	Parents	Ideas different
6	Understand me better	Don't understand at all
7	Teach the right thing	Teach the wrong thing
8	Achieved a lot	Hasn't achieved a lot
9	Higher education	No education
10	Don't like other people	Like other people
11	More religious	Not religious
12	Believe in higher education	Not believing in too much education
13	More sociable	Not sociable
14	Boy girls	Not girls
15	Boy girls	Not girls
16	Both have high morals	Low morals
17	Think alike	Think differently
18	Same eye	Different eyes
19	Believe the same about me	Believe differently about me
20	Both friends	Not friends
21	More understanding	Less understanding
22	Both appreciate music	Don't understand music

Row elements (with SORT NO.):

- Ethical person — 19
- Happy person — 18
- Successful person — 17
- Boss — 16
- Rejected teacher — 15
- Accepted teacher — 14
- Attractive person — 13
- Threatening person — 12
- Pitied person — 11
- Rejecting person — 10
- Ex-pal — 9
- Pal — 8
- Ex-boyfriend/girlfriend — 7
- Spouse — 6
- Sister — 5
- Brother — 4
- Father — 3
- Mother — 2
- Self — 1

FIGURE 13.1 A grid for the Role Construct Repertory Test
Source: G. A. Kelly, The Psychology of Personal Constructs, vol. 1 (New York: Norton, 1955), p. 270.

sample of which is shown in Figure 13.1. For each row, the person must consider the three people indicated by circles in each row. For each group of three, the person must find a word or phrase that describes two of them. That word—for example, "cheerful"—is written in the Emergent Pole column, and an X is placed in the circles of the two people who share that characteristic. The opposite word—for example, "sad"—is written in the Implicit Pole column. This word describes the third person being evaluated in each row.

The person then places a check mark in the squares of anyone else in the repertory grid who can be described by the construct in the Emergent Pole column. In our example, this would mean everyone else who could be described as cheerful. This procedure is repeated line by line until all the rows of the grid have been completed.

The basic assumption underlying the use of this test is that people always construe events in dichotomies. By forcing the person into repeated judgments of like–unlike or similar–dissimilar, Kelly was able to uncover the dichotomies that are important in the person's life. There are several variations in the administration of the REP Test, but its rationale and conclusions remain the same: a person construes the world in dichotomies that, when revealed, show the pattern of his or her personal constructs.

There are no objective scoring techniques for the REP Test. Therefore, its interpretation depends entirely on the skill and training of the psychologist administering it. It must be remembered, however, that despite the word *test* in its title, it was not intended to be a standardized, objective self-report inventory. Kelly designed it as a means of assessing a person's constructs and as a necessary stage in therapy, to induce the person to begin revealing the constructs by which he or she views the world and the people in it.

Research in Kelly's theory

Little research has been conducted on Kelly's theory as a whole or on any of its specific aspects. The REP Test, however, has been the subject of research, some of it devoted to its reliability and validity.

It has been shown that an individual's constructs as assessed by the REP Test are stable over time. A group of subjects took the test twice. The second time they were instructed not to use the same people in the role figures that they had used the first time. Although the people differed, the constructs revealed by the subjects remained the same (Fjeld & Landfield, 1961; Landfield, 1971).

The evidence for the validity of the REP Test is less clear and conclusive. Although research has shown that a variety of interpretations of test performance can yield similar conclusions about a person, and that the test can validly measure personality changes resulting from group therapy, the test's validity remains highly dependent on the skill of the psychologist interpreting it (Adams-Webber, 1970; Bonarius, 1976).

Other studies have been conducted using the REP Test to investigate different variables. One study dealt with how an individual's construct system is organized in terms of its complexity and how it changes as the individual develops. The results showed that the system becomes increasingly differentiated and integrated as a function of development and is able to process more information by being able to function in more abstract terms (Crockett, 1982).

Another study suggested that friendships may depend on a similarity of personal constructs (Duck & Spencer, 1972). A group of college students took the REP Test during their first week at the university, when they were newly acquainted with one another, and again six months later, when friendships had formed. The data showed that the similarity in constructs or attitudes found among close friends did not develop during the course of the relationships but rather had existed prior to the formation of the friendships. Thus, we may seek as friends persons whose constructs are similar to our own.

The REP Test has been used to study the thought disorders of schizophrenics, who have inconsistent and poorly interrelated constructs compared with normal persons, neurotics, depressives, and those suffering organic brain damage (Bannister & Fransella, 1966). Schizophrenics were also found to be unstable and inconsistent in their construing of other people, compared with normal subjects. Their construing of objects, however, was stable and consistent, suggesting that their thought disorders are specific and apply only to interpersonal construing, rather than general and applying to all construing (Bannister & Salmon, 1966).

Cognitive styles

One outgrowth of research on Kelly's personal constructs relates to *cognitive styles*, differences in how we perceive or construe the objects and persons in our environment. One example of differences in cognitive styles is reflected in the work of Herman Witkin on field-dependent and field-independent people. We shall discuss this in Chapter 17 as a limited-domain approach to personality.

Other research on cognitive styles deriving more directly from the REP Test has focused on **cognitive complexity**. A person's degree of cognitive complexity can be determined from the pattern of Xs on his or her repertory grid. A pattern that is the same or highly similar for each construct indicates that the person is incapable of perceiving differences in the ways in which he or she construes other people. This style is known as **cognitive simplicity**. A highly differentiated pattern of Xs indicates the ability to discriminate in the process of construing others, the style called cognitive complexity.

Differences between people possessing these two cognitive styles have been demonstrated. For example, persons high in cognitive complexity are better able to make predictions about the behavior of others. They can more readily recognize differences between themselves and others, are more empathetic, and can deal better with inconsistent information in construing others than can persons high in cognitive simplicity (Bieri, 1955; Crockett, 1982; Mayo & Crockett, 1964).

In terms of Kelly's theory, cognitive complexity is the more desirable and useful cognitive style. According to Kelly, a primary goal in developing construct systems is to reduce uncertainty by being able to predict what other people will do and what our interactions with them will be. Persons possessing cognitive complexity will be more successful at these crucial tasks than those who possess cognitive simplicity.

Cognitive style is thus an important dimension of personality, and several researchers have attempted to determine its origins. We mentioned that cognitive complexity increases as a function of development. In general, then, we would expect adults to possess a greater degree of cognitive complexity than children.

Simply growing older, however, does not provide the complete explanation, because many adults still possess cognitive simplicity. Much depends on the level of complexity the person experiences in childhood. Adults high in cognitive complexity were found to have been exposed in childhood to more diverse cultures. Their parents were less authoritarian and more likely to grant them autonomy than were the parents of adults high in cognitive simplicity (Sechrest & Jackson, 1961).

A final commentary

It was mentioned in the introduction to this chapter that Kelly developed a unique theory of personality and that his work is neither a derivative of nor an elaboration on other theories. It emerges from his own interpretation—his own construct—of the data provided from his clinical experience. It is a highly personal view, and the originality of its construction parallels its message—that every individual is capable of developing his or her own view of life. With no other personality theory do we see such a correspondence—in fact, a duplication—between the way the theorist works and the way his theory explains how human beings function.

Despite its distinctive flavor, or perhaps because of it, Kelly's theory of personal constructs has not gained wide acceptance, either in academic psychology or in the clinic. In the survey of the relative importance of 286 psychologists, Kelly ranked in 103rd place overall and in last place among the theorists covered in this book (Gilgen, 1982). The theory has generated little research, but there is a growing group of followers carrying on Kelly's work, especially in England and in Europe. Perhaps it is too extremely different from the concepts and theories that those who work in the area of personality are used to dealing with. Whether in research or practice, psychologists who are concerned with personality expect to think in terms of such familiar concepts as motivation and emotion, unconscious influences, drives, needs, and the like. These familiar concepts—the ones we all learn about, beginning with our very first course in psychology—are not part of Kelly's theory.

Perhaps another reason for Kelly's general lack of acceptance by psychology has to do with the fact that he published little, relative to other personality theorists. Most of his time and effort were devoted to clinical work and the training of students. In all, he published only about a dozen articles and two books. Further, the style of Kelly's writing is scholarly and academic in tone, clearly not intended for general public consumption or for the psychologist who might be looking for human passion and drama highlighted by interesting and illustrative case histories. This was not the style of the man or his theory.

A third reason for his less-than-overwhelming acceptance has to do with criticisms directed against the system itself. Many psychologists take issue with a system that omits one of their major conceptual tools—that is, some device or principle that attempts to explain human motivation. As noted above, the omission of such familiar weapons from psychology's arsenal is seen by many as a serious flaw.

An equally important and related point of criticism involves Kelly's concentration on the intellectual and rational aspects of human functioning, to the exclusion of the emotional aspects. Where, the critics ask, are the passions—loves, hates, fears, and dreams? Kelly's image of us rationally constructing our present and future, forming hypotheses, and making predictions does not square with the everyday experiences of many psychologists, who face the heights and depths of human passion with so many of their clients. Kelly's rational human being seems to many people to be an ideal, existing only in the abstract and decidedly not in reality.

It must be noted in Kelly's defense that although he did not deal with the emotional side of life explicitly, he did so implicitly. Emotions are considered in his system, but they are believed to be constructs no different in their formation from other constructs. Also, Kelly argued that just because his system was a rational one did not mean that it could not be applied to the nonrational.

It has been said that Freud's view of human beings derived from his exposure to middle-class, Viennese, neurotic patients, which gave him a distorted and unrepresentative view of people. Kelly's view, critics charge, was equally distorted and unrepresentative, limited as it was to midwestern students, adolescents very much involved in the process of trying to construct their individual worlds.

There are a number of questions left unanswered in Kelly's theory. Each person is able to construe events and experiences in his or her own unique way, but how does one person construe a particular event in one way while another person construes the identical event in an entirely different way? What mechanism or process accounts for this difference?

A person is constantly making choices toward definition or extension of his or her construct system. What determines whether, and under what conditions, a person will opt for security or for adventure—will choose the safer or the riskier step forward?

Without belaboring the point, we can simply say that Kelly's view, like the other systems discussed, contains gaps, uncertainties, and unanswered questions. Kelly recognized these limitations and made no pretense of setting forth a finished and final theory of personality. Just as an individual's constructs are constantly changing in the light of new experiences, so too the personal construct theory was seen as subject to constant change. "At best it is an ad interim theory," Kelly wrote; we must consider the theory to be "expendable in the light of tomorrow's outlooks and discoveries." Even in the years since Kelly's death, his theory has not been finished. Some of the students he so thoroughly trained have continued to refine and develop the theory and to train a new generation of students who may take it further.

Kelly's unique contributions have been recognized with honors accorded him by his former students and by the profession. His theory, whatever the ultimate judgment of its merit, is certainly one of the most controversial to appear in a century of theorizing about the nature of the human personality. Whatever the nature of one's own personal constructs, Kelly's singular contribution cannot be ignored.

And it must be noted that, within the last ten years, personal construct psychology has been gaining in acceptance and popularity. Kelly's approach may be reaching a wider audience because of its compatibility with the growing interest in cognitive theories in all areas of psychology. As the only truly cognitive theory of personality, the personal construct theory is seen by some psychologists as "a classic that was ahead of its time" (Rorer & Widiger, 1983, p. 456). It is therefore possible that Kelly's work will assume a greater importance in the future.

Summary

Kelly's cognitive approach to personality omits most of the familiar terms and concepts of other personality theories. Instead, he explains personality in terms of cognitive constructs, which people use to make predictions about themselves and others. Kelly viewed people as scientists, constructing theories and hypotheses and testing them against reality, the same procedure used by psychologists to study personality. Our individual theories are personal constructs. Kelly's theory of personality was influenced by the kinds of patients he treated. These were public school and college students, capable of functioning in rational and intellectual terms.

The interpreting or construing of experience represents the individual's unique view of reality. A construct is a person's way of looking at the events in his or her world. We develop constructs to deal with every situation or person. Existing constructs need to be refined because people and events change over time. Thus, constructs are not absolute or final; alternative constructions must always be available. The notion of constructive alternativism holds that we are free to revise or replace our constructs.

Kelly's fundamental postulate states that a person's psychological processes are directed by the ways in which that person construes the world. Our constructs are anticipatory, in that we use them to anticipate or predict future events. Eleven corollaries derive from and build upon the fundamental postulate:

1. *Construction Corollary*: A person anticipates events by construing them in terms of their similarities with past events. Constructs are formulated on the basis of themes in our past that will reappear in the future.

2. *Individuality Corollary*: People differ in the way in which they construe events. Thus, they form different constructs when perceiving or interpreting the same event.

3. *Organization Corollary*: People organize their individual constructs into a system or pattern according to their own view of the relationships among them. They form ordinal relationships among constructs, arranging them in a hierarchy so that some are subordinate to others.

4. *Dichotomy Corollary*: All constructs are bipolar or dichotomous, so as to take account of opposites or dissimilarities among people and among events.

5. *Choice Corollary*: A person always chooses the alternative in a dichotomized construct that will lead to the greater possibility for defining and extending his or her construct system. Definition refers to the secure choice, that which repeats similar events and experiences from the past. Extension refers to the adventurous choice, which introduces new experiences and events into a person's construction system.

6. *Range Corollary*: A construct has a limited range of convenience, that is, it is not relevant or applicable to all events or situations.

7. *Experience Corollary*: A person's construction system must be continually revised in the light of new experiences. These new experiences must be reconstrued and their constructs altered accordingly.

8. *Modulation Corollary*: How thoroughly a person's construction system may be changed or modulated as a function of new experiences depends on how permeable or open his or her constructs are. Impermeable or concrete constructs are not capable of being revised, regardless of the new experiences that are available.

9. *Fragmentation Corollary*: In one situation, two constructs may be compatible or consistent, but if the situation changes, the same constructs may be inconsistent.

10. *Commonality Corollary*: If more than one person construes an experience in a similar way, their psychological processes and certain other characteristics will be similar.

11. *Sociality Corollary*: For effective interpersonal relations, a person must construe the constructions of the other person. He or she must have an understanding of how the other person thinks and thus be able to anticipate how that person will predict events.

Kelly presents a flattering and optimistic image of human nature which views people as rational beings with free will, capable of formulating their own destinies. People are not bound by constructs developed at any one stage of life, nor by past experiences, unconscious conflicts, or biological instincts. People are motivated simply by being alive. Their ultimate goal is to define a set of constructs that enables them to predict events. There is both commonality and uniqueness in a person's constructs and hence in personality.

Kelly assessed personality by adopting a credulous attitude, accepting a person's words at face value; by having the person write a self-characterization sketch, as if he or she were a character in a play; and by using the Role Construct Repertory (REP) Test.

In the REP Test, subjects record the names of people who have played significant roles in their lives. They sort the people by repeatedly selecting two out of three who are most alike and indicating how they differ from the third person in each set of comparisons. In this way, the dichotomies that are important in a person's life are uncovered, and this reveals the person's pattern of personal constructs.

Little research has been conducted on Kelly's theory, although much research has used the REP Test. It has shown that a person's constructs are stable over time, that the test can measure personality changes resulting from group therapy, and that the test's validity is highly dependent on the skill of the psychologist interpreting it.

Schizophrenics have been found to have inconsistent and poorly interrelated constructs and to be unstable in their construing of other people.

People high in cognitive complexity are better able to predict the behavior of others, can more readily recognize differences between themselves and others, are more empathetic, can deal better with inconsistent information in construing others, and have experienced greater complexity in childhood than persons high in cognitive simplicity.

Kelly's work has been criticized for omitting familiar concepts such as motivation and emotion, for concentrating on the intellectual and rational aspects of human functioning to the exclusion of the emotional aspects, and for relying on an unrepresentative sample of subjects. Although the theory does not enjoy wide acceptance, it may assume a greater importance in the future because its emphasis on cognitive factors is compatible with the growing interest in cognitive theories in all areas of psychology.

Glossary

cognitive complexity   A cognitive style or personal way of construing the environment that is related to the ability to perceive differences between oneself and others; contrasts with cognitive simplicity.

construct   An intellectual hypothesis devised and used by an individual to interpret or explain the sense of the events in his or her world; constructs are necessarily bipolar or dichotomous (e.g., tall–short, honest–dishonest).

constructive alternativism   The idea that the individual is free to revise or replace his or her constructs as needed.

permeability   The idea that con-

structs are capable of being revised and extended in light of new experiences.

personal-construct theory   Kelly's approach to personality in terms of cognitive processes; individuals are capable of interpreting the objects and events in the world and of using this personal understanding to guide their behavior and to predict the behavior of others.

range of convenience   The spectrum of events to which a construct is applicable; some constructs are relevant to only a limited number of persons or situations, whereas others are broader.

Review questions

1. How does Kelly's approach to personality differ from other approaches to personality?
2. How does Kelly define the word *construct*?

3. What is constructive alternativism?
4. What factors influence the way we anticipate events that are similar to past events?
5. Why must our constructs be dichotomous?
6. How do we choose between the two alternatives offered by a construct?
7. What is the range of convenience of a construct? What is the range of convenience for the construct cheerful-versus-sad in your own construction system?
8. What mechanism did Kelly propose to account for changes in the range of convenience of a construct?
9. How is it possible for a person to hold incompatible or inconsistent constructs?
10. What is the purpose of the Role Construct Repertory Test?
11. What does research using the REP Test show about the cognitive styles called cognitive simplicity and cognitive complexity?

Suggested reading

Bannister, D. *New perspectives in personal construct theory*. New York: Academic Press, 1977.
Kelly, G. A. *The psychology of personal constructs*. New York: Norton, 1955.
Kelly, G. A. The theory and technique of assessment. *Annual Review of Psychology*, 1958, 9, 323–352.
Maher, B., Ed. *Clinical psychology and personality: The selected papers of George Kelly*. New York: Wiley, 1969.
Sechest, L. The psychology of personal constructs: George Kelly. In J. Wepman & R. Heine, Eds., *Concepts of personality*. Chicago: Aldine, 1963.
Thompson, G. G. George Alexander Kelly (1905–1967). *Journal of General Psychology*, 1968, 79, 19–24.

PART 7

The Behavioral Approach

The behavioral approach to psychology was discussed in Chapter 1, where we considered briefly the work of the founder of behaviorism, John B. Watson. His behavioristic psychology focused solely on overt behavior, on the responses made by subjects to external stimuli. This natural-science approach to psychology, based on careful experimental research and precise quantification of both stimulus and response variables, became extremely popular in psychology in the 1920s and is still a major force in the field.

There was no room in Watson's behaviorism for conscious or unconscious forces because these cannot be seen, manipulated, or measured. Watson believed that whatever might be happening inside an organism, between the presentation of a stimulus and the elicitation of a response, has no value or use for science. Such internal processes cannot be experimented on.

Thus, we find in the traditional behavioral approach no reference to such internal entities as anxiety, drives, motives, needs, defense mechanisms, or similar processes invoked by other personality theorists. To the behaviorists, personality is nothing more than an accumulation of learned responses to stimuli, sets of overt behaviors, or habit systems. Personality, therefore, refers only to what can be objectively observed and manipulated.

The behavioral approach to personality is represented in this section by B. F. Skinner, Albert Bandura, and Julian Rotter. All have carried out their work within the behaviorist tradition, but beyond that point of commonality, their approaches to the understanding of personality differ.

Skinner's work reflects the original (now seen as radical) form of behaviorism, and follows faithfully the tradition of John B. Watson. Skinner vehemently rejects as irrelevant any alleged internal forces or processes. His sole concern is overt behavior and the external stimuli that fashion it.

Bandura and Rotter typify a modified version of behaviorism. Although they focus on overt behavior, they also invoke or allow for the operation of internal cognitive variables that mediate between the stimulus and the response. Their work, however, is no less experimental than Skinner's. They study cognitive variables with a high degree of experimental sophistication and rigor. They use human subjects and observe behavior in social rather than individual situations.

All three theorists attempt to understand the human personality through work in the laboratory rather than the clinic, though their work has also been applied successfully in the clinical setting through the popular behavior-modification techniques.

CHAPTER 14

B. F. Skinner

The life of Skinner (1904–)
Reinforcement: The basis of behavior
 Operant behavior
Schedules of reinforcement
Successive approximation: The shaping of behavior
Superstitious behavior
The self-control of behavior
Applications of operant conditioning
 The token economy
 Behavior modification in industry
 Comments on behavior modification
Skinner's image of human nature
Assessment in Skinner's theory
 Direct observation of behavior
 Self-report procedures
 Physiological measurements of behavior
Research in Skinner's theory
 The single-subject experiment
 The operant-conditioning apparatus for
  animals
 Studies of human subjects
A final commentary
Summary
Glossary
Review questions
Suggested reading

Man is a machine in the sense that he is a complex system behaving in lawful ways.

B. F. SKINNER

It may seem strange, at first glance, to find B. F. Skinner, the foremost exponent of **behaviorism**, in a book that discusses theories of personality. His position would seem to be out of place here for two reasons: (1) he does not believe psychology is ready, in the sense of having enough factual data, to theorize about anything and (2) he does not deal specifically with the topic of personality, considering it nothing more than a label for certain aspects of behavior. In view of this, it is hardly surprising that he has not offered a theory of personality that can be contrasted and compared with the ones previously discussed. Indeed, he has not offered a theory of personality at all.

Skinner's work is an attempt to account for all behavior, not just that which some theorists call personality, and to account for it in purely factual and descriptive terms. He rejects all attempts to theorize about personality: "You can't get results by sitting around and theorizing about the inner world. . . . I want to say to those people: get down to the facts" (Hall, 1967, p. 70).

Getting down to facts has been the guiding theme of all of Skinner's work, for more than a half-century. He has argued strongly that psychology must restrict itself to what it can see and what can be manipulated and measured in the laboratory. And that means an exclusive emphasis on the overt responses the subject makes, and on nothing beyond that. Simply stated, Skinner's argument is that psychology is the science of behavior—the study of what the organism does.

We have noted that this approach fits the one proposed by John B. Watson. The spirit of Watson's behaviorist revolution in psychology, which greatly influenced the young Skinner, lives on in more sophisticated and more fully developed fashion in Skinner's exclusive emphasis on behavior. Skinner's work, like Watson's before him, is the antithesis of the psychoanalytic, trait, and humanistic approaches to personality, differing not only in subject matter but in methodology and aims as well. In addition to denying that there is a separate entity or process known as personality, Skinner's approach diverges from other approaches as follows.

In their explanations of the nature of personality, most other theorists we have discussed have looked inside the organism. The causes, motives, and drives—the motivating and directing forces—originate, in their views, within the person. Other personality theorists invoke needs, whether innate or learned, such as self-actualization, superiority, safety, or security—all of which serve to direct the person from within. Whether they invoke traits, instincts, or needs, other theorists all use what Skinner calls the "inner man" approach.

Skinner's approach, in contrast, makes absolutely no reference to any presumed internal state in accounting for the behavior of the organism. After all, a basic tenet of the behaviorist position is that psychology must deal only with that which can be observed. Unconscious forces, defense mechanisms, traits, and the like cannot be seen and therefore can have no place in a scientific psychology. Skinner argues that such internal driving forces are no more real, and have no more value to science, than the old philosophical and theological concept of the soul.

The same argument is used by Skinner in relation to physiological events or processes, which again are not overtly observable and so have no relevance for science. "As far as I'm concerned," he wrote, "the inside of the organism is irrelevant either as the site of physiological processes or as the locus of mentalistic activities" (Evans, 1968, p. 22). The only aspect of human beings that is real and relevant to psychology, he argues, is overt behavior, and the only way to be able to predict and control behavior is by relating it to antecedent events in the environment. The reference is always to something external to the organism—something in the environment—as the cause of behavior. There is no need to look inside the organism for some form of inner activity. As far as Skinner is concerned, a human being is an empty organism; there is nothing inside us that can be invoked to explain our behavior scientifically.

Notice that Skinner does not say that internal processes of a physiological or mentalistic nature do not exist. In recent years, Skinner has argued that psychology must be able to explain aspects of our inner mental life, but only when they can be observed objectively. His later writings do not exclude mention of internal events. They are still excluded in his work, however, which continues to focus only on overt behavior. Until such time as cognitive variables can be manipulated and observed objectively, Skinner believes, they are of no use in predicting and controlling behavior. Not only are they irrelevant, but consideration of the mental processes by a scientific psychology might also be harmful. "The exploration of the emotional and motivational life of the mind has been described as one of the great achievements in the history of human thought, but it is possible that it has been one of the great disasters. . . . Mentalism has obscured the environmental antecedents which would have led to a much more effective analysis" (Skinner, 1974, p. 165).

A second point of difference between Skinner and the other personality theorists involves the matter of individual differences. Regardless of the variations among them, our other theorists were all concerned with some aspect of individual differences. Whether they talked in terms of traits, lifestyle, or ego and superego, most of the theorists recognized the fundamental uniqueness of the individual. Even those theorists who posited universal drives or conflicts pointed out the vast range of differences in the means of satisfying the drives or of defending oneself against the conflicts.

Skinner, in contrast, has shown very little interest in the matter of individual differences, primarily because his search has been for general laws of human behavior. He seeks unchangeable empirical statements of the relationships between stimulus events and responses. If there are differences in behavior among people, it is because the events that elicited their responses were different. The laws relating the response to a stimulus are immutable.

A third way in which Skinner diverges radically from the other theorists is in the kind of subject studied. As we have seen, some theorists used as subjects those who are emotionally disturbed. Others have insisted that only normal, average individuals be studied, while at least one (Maslow) has used only the best and the brightest individuals.

Skinner does not take the normal, the subnormal, or the supernormal as his subjects of study. But what is left if you exclude these categories? Animals. While Skinner's approach to behavior has been applied to humans with great success, the research that led to his theory of behavior was conducted with rats and pigeons.

That statement is often met with incredulity and shock. How can anything be learned about human personality by studying pigeons? The first thing to remember is that Skinner is dealing not with personality but with all behavior (of which what others call personality is but one aspect). His focus is on the responses the organism makes, not on what a patient reports of his or her childhood or how a subject says he or she feels.

Responding to stimuli is something animals can usually do as well as humans—and sometimes better. Skinner grants that human beings are vastly more complex than animals, but he also notes that the differences between them are in degree, not in kind, and that the basic processes are not very different. He believes that any science must proceed from simple to complex, the basic processes being investigated first. Thus, Skinner studies animal behavior because it is simpler.

There are additional advantages to the use of animals in laboratory study. Their genetic and experiential backgrounds can be well controlled, and they can be studied for longer periods of time and in more dangerous or uncomfortable situations than humans are usually willing to endure. Also, they do not, as a rule, become hostile to experimenters and behave in ways opposite to the ways they think the experimenter wants them to behave. Nor do they become overly cooperative and behave as they think the experimenter wants them to. (They also don't have to be paid as much as college students, the usual human subjects.) Skinner has extrapolated from his animal data to human behavior, and, as noted earlier, there has been considerable practical application of his work to humans in a variety of situations. But the basic data of Skinner's approach were derived from experiments with rats and pigeons.

Since Skinner is decidedly not a personality theorist, and since his approach to the study of people is so vastly different from the approaches described in earlier chapters of this book, it is natural to ask: What is he doing here? Why has he been included among those who attempt to understand the nature of personality?

It would be more difficult to justify his exclusion than to explain his inclusion. Skinner is simply too important a force and commands too much status in contemporary psychology to be ignored. A textbook that purports, as this one does, to bring into view the diversity of approaches available for the understanding of personality would be incomplete without consideration of Skinner, even though he avoids recognition of personality as a separate entity or structure.

Whether one agrees or disagrees with his views, there is no denying Skinner's monumental importance and influence in American psychology. In 1958, the American Psychological Association awarded him the Distinguished Scientific Contribution Award and noted that "few American psychologists have had so profound an impact on the development of psychology and on promising younger psychologists" (APA, 1958, p. 735). The magazine *Psychology Today* wrote in 1967 that "when history makes its judgment, he may well be known as the major contributor to psychology in this century" (Hall, 1967, p. 21). In 1968, the United States awarded Skinner the National Medal of Science, the highest public award for scientific contribution, and in 1971 the American Psychological Foundation presented him with its Gold Medal. In that same year he was featured on the cover of *Time* magazine. In 1982, a historian of psychology summed up Skinner's importance by noting that he is "without question the most famous American psychologist in the world" (Gilgen, 1982, p. 97).

Skinner's work has had wide practical ramifications. He invented an automatic baby-tending device and is largely responsible for the widespread use of teaching machines. He has also published a successful novel that spells out a program of behavioral control of human societies. In addition, Skinner's methodology has found its way into the clinical setting, where it is being used to treat psychotics, the mentally retarded, and autistic children. His approach to the modification of behavior (as distinct from trying to change personalities) has become popular in a variety of settings, including schools, prisons, and hospitals.

Skinner's influence is strong not only in psychology but also among the general public. In 1971, his book *Beyond Freedom and Dignity* won best-seller status, generated much publicity, and prompted Skinner's appearance on several television talk shows. The controversy surrounding his ideas is extensive and usually of a highly emotional nature.

The life of Skinner (1904–   )

Skinner views the human organism as a machine, "a complex system behaving in lawful ways" (Skinner, 1971, p. 202). He considers the causes or driving forces of behavior to have their origins in external forces. In this view, a person is a product of past reinforcements; those behaviors that have been rewarded will be repeated, and those that have not been rewarded or that have brought punishment will not be repeated. Our behavior is thus predetermined, lawful, and controlled.

A test of this approach would be to see if it fits what is known of Skinner's life. Were there events (or reinforcements) in Skinner's childhood that have determined his adult view of and approach to the study of humanity? Was Skinner's life predetermined, lawful, and controlled, as he says all human lives are? Was his character determined solely by the external environment? By his own account, the answer is yes. "I do not believe that my life shows a type of personality à la Freud, an archetypal pattern à la Jung, or a schedule of development à la Erikson. There have been a few abiding themes but they can be traced to environmental sources" (Skinner, 1983, p. 25).

Skinner was born in Susquehanna, Pennsylvania, the older of two sons; his brother died at the age of 16. His parents were hardworking people who instilled in him a strong sense of proper behavior. "I was taught to fear God, the police, and what people will think," Skinner wrote (Skinner, 1967, p. 407). His mother had strict standards of what was right and proper, and she never deviated from them. She evidenced great alarm if her son demonstrated any tendency to stray from the path she had so clearly pointed out. Her method of control (reinforcement), Skinner said, was to say "Tut-tut" and "What will people think?" (Skinner, 1967, p. 391). His grandmother made certain that young Skinner understood what hell was all about by pointing out to him the red-hot bed of coals in the parlor stove.

Skinner's father, an ambitious lawyer, longed for praise but bitterly considered himself to be a failure. He too contributed to his son's moral education, continually telling him what would happen if he turned out to be a criminal. He showed Skinner the county jail and on another occasion took him to a lecture (with slides) on life in Sing Sing (a notorious state prison in New York).

Skinner's autobiography contains a number of references to the influence on his adult behavor of the admonitions and instruction given him in childhood. Referring to his father's harping on the punishments that would befall him for breaking the law, Skinner wrote: "As a result I am afraid of the police and buy too many tickets to their annual dances" (Skinner, 1967, p. 391). He tells of visiting a cathedral as an adult and taking great pains to avoid stepping on the gravestones in the floor. As a child, he had played in a cemetery next door to his house and had been cautioned never to step on a grave—it wouldn't be right. These and other instances made it clear to him that many facets of his adult life were determined by reinforcements in childhood.

Prophetic of his later view of people as machines, Skinner as a youth spent many hours designing and constructing machines—wagons, seesaws, merry-go-rounds, slingshots, water pistols, a steam cannon (used to shoot potato and carrot plugs over neighboring houses), model airplanes, and a flotation system that separated ripe from unripe elderberries. He also worked for years on a perpetual-motion machine (which perpetually failed).

Skinner's adult interest in the study of animal behavior also seems to have derived from childhood experiences. He caught and made pets of an assortment of animals, including turtles, snakes, toads, lizards, and chipmunks. He read a great deal about animals and spent time talking with the local livery-stable owner about the behavior of horses. And at a county fair he once saw a flock of performing pigeons. They raced on the stage pulling a fire engine up to a burning building. Wearing red hats, they put a ladder against the building, and one pigeon climbed to an upper-story window and rescued another pigeon. Skinner was later to train pigeons to perform a variety of amazing feats, including playing ping-pong and guiding a missile to its target.

As a boy, Skinner liked school—so much so that he was always the first to arrive there in the morning. After he graduated from high school (in a class of eight), he went to Hamilton College in upstate New York. As he tells it, he never felt part of the student life, was poor at sports, objected to some of the college requirements (like compulsory chapel), and was disappointed by the lack of intellectual interest shown by his fellow students.

By his senior year he was in open revolt. He disrupted the college with hoaxes, including one that jammed the campus and the railroad station with swarms of people arriving to hear a lecture by Charlie Chaplin, whose appearance Skinner had falsely announced with posters he had printed and distributed all over town. He also wrote articles highly critical of the faculty and administration. His antics continued up to the last possible moment; the college president warned Skinner and his friends during commencement ceremonies that they would not graduate if they did not behave themselves.

His career plans after graduation were clear and had nothing to do with psychology. He had majored in English and was firmly committed to becoming a writer. Spurred on by favorable comment on some of his work from the eminent poet Robert Frost, Skinner built a study in the attic of his parents' home, now in Scranton, Pennsylvania, and sat down to write. What resulted, he notes, was disastrous. He read, listened to the radio, played the piano, built ship models, and considered seeing a psychiatrist.

He left Scranton for Greenwich Village, New York, and then went to Europe for a summer. Finally, he decided to give up his attempt at writing, because he had nothing important to say. He felt he still wanted to understand human behavior, so he turned from a literary investigation of it to a scientific one. While living in Greenwich Village, he read books by Ivan Pavlov and John B. Watson, which influenced him greatly. As a result, he entered graduate school at Harvard in 1928 to study psychology. Working with tremendous dedication and effort, he was able to earn his Ph.D. in three years.

Skinner remained at Harvard, with postdoctoral fellowships, until 1936, when he joined the faculty of the University of Minnesota. He stayed there until 1945, spent two years at Indiana University, and then returned to Harvard, where he works with as much enthusiasm and dedication as when he entered the field a half-century ago. He still regulates his work habits with precision, carefully recording his daily work output and his average time spent per published word (two minutes)—continuing to reflect his own definition of a person as "a complex system behaving in lawful ways."

Reinforcement: The basis of behavior

Though based on thousands of hours of well-controlled research, Skinner's approach to behavior is quite simple in its essential concept. It says, in effect, that all behavior can be controlled by its consequences—by what follows the behavior. Skinner believes that an animal or a human can be trained to perform virtually any kind of behavior by the extent and nature of the reinforcement that follows the behavior. Thus, whoever controls the reinforcement available to a person (or a group of people) is in a position to change and control the behavior of that person (or that group of people), in the same way that an experimenter can control the behavior of a laboratory rat.

Skinner's position distinguishes between two kinds of behavior: respondent and operant. **Respondent behavior**, as the name suggests, involves a response made to or *elicited* by specific and known stimuli in the environment. At the simplest level of behavior, a reflex such as the knee jerk is respondent behavior. A stimulus is applied (a tap on the knee) and the response occurs (the leg jerks forward). The behavior in this example is, of course, unlearned. We don't have to be trained (or conditioned) to make the appropriate response; it is elicited automatically and involuntarily.

At a higher level, there is respondent behavior that is learned. This learning, known as *conditioning*, involves the substitution of one stimulus for another. The concept originated with the important work of the Russian physiologist Ivan Pavlov. It was Pavlov, as you no doubt remember from other courses, who gave the concept of conditioning to psychology. Working with dogs, Pavlov found by accident that they would salivate to stimuli that were neutral—for instance, to the sound of their keeper's footsteps. Previously, the response of salivation had been elicited by only one stimulus—the presentation of food.

Intrigued by this observation, Pavlov began to study the phenomenon more systematically. For example, he would sound a bell shortly before feeding a dog. At first the dog salivated only to the food; after all, what meaning could the bell have? But after a number of pairings of the bell followed by the food, the dog began to salivate at the sound of the bell. The dog had been conditioned to respond to the bell; the response had shifted to a previously neutral stimulus.

The essential feature of this now classic experiment was the demonstration of the importance of **reinforcement**. The dogs would never learn to respond to the bell unless they were getting something for it—in this case, food. Pavlov thus formulated his first law of learning, which was that a conditioned response cannot be established in the absence of reinforcement.

Nor can an established conditioned response be maintained in the absence of reinforcement. Take a dog already conditioned to respond to the sound of the bell; every time the bell rings, the dog salivates. Now the experimenter suddenly stops presenting food after sounding the bell. The dog hears the bell and then nothing happens—no more food (no more reinforcement). With successive ringings of the bell, the dog's response decreases in frequency and intensity until finally no response is made at all. The response has been *extinguished* because reinforcement for it was no longer forthcoming.

Animals can be conditioned by reinforcing them with food for exhibiting the desired behaviors.

Operant behavior

Respondent behavior, then, depends on reinforcement and is made directly to an immediately present physical stimulus. Every response is elicited by a specific stimulus. Skinner feels that this form of conditioning is much less important than what he calls **operant behavior**. He recognizes that we are indeed conditioned to respond directly to many stimuli in our environment, but he also believes that not all of our behavior can be accounted for in this way. Both humans and animals behave in what seem like spontaneous ways; that is, the behaviors cannot be traced to specific stimuli. Such behaviors are, in Skinner's terms, *emitted* rather than elicited by a stimulus. They involve acting in ways that appear to be voluntary rather than reacting involuntarily to a stimulus to which one has been conditioned.

The nature and frequency of operant behavior will be determined and/or modified by the reinforcement that follows it. Respondent behavior has absolutely no effect on the environment. The dog's salivary response to the ringing bell does nothing to change either the bell or the reinforcement (the food) that follows it. Operant behavior, on the other hand, operates on the environment and, as a result, changes it. For example, the cries of an infant may bring attention from its mother or father, thus changing the infant's environment. The changes that are introduced into the environment serve as feedback to the behavior. If the environmental changes brought about by the behavior are reinforcing (provide some reward to the organism or eliminate some noxious stimulation), then the probability is increased that that behavior will be emitted again. If the infant's cries are reinforced with food or caressing, the infant may well emit such behavior again. If, on the other hand, the environmental changes provide no reinforcement, that behavior is less likely to recur.

Note that the reinforcement is dependent upon the kind of behavior displayed. Whether any reinforcement will follow the behavior depends on how the behavior changes the environment. The reinforcement, if there is to be any, comes after the behavior and acts to modify the behavior in the future. Perhaps this **operant conditioning** process will become less strange as we follow the progress of a rat in Skinner's well-known piece of laboratory equipment, which he prefers to call an *operant-conditioning apparatus* but which seems destined to be forever known as the *Skinner box*. "I have asked my friends not to use the expression 'Skinner box,'" he wrote (Skinner, 1983, p. 32).

We will describe the use of this apparatus in the research section of this chapter, but for now an examination of the rat's behavior in the box is more important. When a rat that has been deprived of food for a period of time is placed in the box, its behavior is initially spontaneous and random. Usually, the rat is very active, poking, sniffing, and prodding its new environment. These behaviors are emitted and not elicited; the rat is not responding to any specific environmental stimuli.

At some time during the course of this random and spontaneous activity, the rat will depress a lever or bar located on one wall of the box, which causes a food pellet to drop into a trough. Note that the rat's behavior has operated on the environment and changed it: the environment now includes a food pellet. That food pellet is a reinforcement for the behavior of depressing the bar. The rat begins to depress the bar more often. What happens? It gets more food (reinforcement) and consequently depresses the bar even more frequently. Its behavior is now under the control of the reinforcement. Its actions in the box have become considerably less random and spontaneous. The rat now spends most of its time pressing the bar (and eating).

If we put the rat back in the box the following day, we can predict with great accuracy what it will do, and we can control its actions by presenting or withholding the reinforcement (or presenting the reinforcement at different schedules or rates, as we will see later). Withholding the reinforcement—not presenting it after conditioning has taken place—serves to extinguish operant behavior in the same way that it extinguishes respondent behavior. The unreinforced behavior no longer works—it no longer brings reward—and so, after a while, it stops.

A classic example is the crying of a baby, which usually brings reinforcement in the form of attention from its parents. Thus, the baby is able to influence parental behavior. The mother or father responds (provides reinforcement) every time the infant cries. If the parents wish to stop this crying behavior, they can do so by consistently not reinforcing it. The behavior will then be extinguished because it no longer brings attention. The person who controls reinforcement thus controls behavior. Skinner said: "I had the clue from Pavlov; control your conditions and you will see order." (A popular cartoon shows one rat in a Skinner box saying to another "I really have this experimenter well conditioned. Every time I press that bar, he gives me another food pellet.")

Skinner believes that most human and animal behavior is learned in this way. An infant initially displays a great deal of random, spontaneous behavior, only some of which is reinforced by its parents. As the infant grows older, the positively reinforced behaviors (those of which the parents approve, approval being a form of reinforcement) are continued, while those of which the parents disapprove may not be continued. The concept is the same as with the rat in the Skinner box: those behaviors that work are repeated and those that don't work are not. The organism's behavior operates on the environment; the environment, in the form of reinforcement, operates in turn on the organism's behavior.

You can see how powerful reinforcement—and those who control an individual's or a society's reinforcement—is in determining behavior. "Operant conditioning," Skinner wrote, "shapes behavior as a sculptor shapes a lump of clay" (Skinner, 1953, p. 91). If the lump of clay wants or needs the reinforcer badly enough, there is virtually no limit to how it can be shaped by an experimenter with a food pellet, a puppy owner with a dog biscuit, a mother with a smile, a boss with a pat on the back, or a government with a promise.

From infancy on, we emit a great many behaviors, and those that are reinforced grow stronger and form into networks or patterns. And that is all that Skinner means when he occasionally refers to *personality*: a pattern or collection of operant behaviors, and nothing more. What others have called neurotic or abnormal behavior is, to Skinner, nothing more mysterious than the continued performance of certain behaviors that (for whatever reason) have been reinforced.

Always seeking to perfect a method of modifying and controlling behavior,

Skinner asked another question. Having demonstrated how behavior can be modified by *continuous reinforcement*—presenting a reinforcement after every response—he then asked how behavior might be modified by varying the rate at which behavior is reinforced. Actually, what led Skinner to ask this question was a practical, even mundane, matter—a matter more of expediency than of intellectual curiosity. It is worth examining the impetus for this new line of research, for it demonstrates something of the nature of science, which is often quite different from the idealized picture that textbooks present.

It all started with the food pellets used to reinforce the rat in the Skinner box. Today, such pellets are commercially available and need merely to be taken from a bag to be ready to use. In the 1930s, however, experimenters (or their luckless graduate students) had to make their own food pellets—a time-consuming and laborious procedure. In Skinner's laboratory, at that time, at least 800 pellets a day were required to keep the research going.

One Saturday afternoon, Skinner discovered that, unless he were to spend the rest of that day and evening making more pellets, the supply would be exhausted by the following Monday morning. Spending the rest of the day slaving over the pill machine was not, even for a dedicated researcher, the most attractive prospect. It was then that another choice occurred to him. Why, he asked himself, must every response be reinforced? What would happen if the rat were reinforced only one time per minute, regardless of how many responses it was making?

As a result of this line of reasoning, he and his students spent considerably less time making pills, and Skinner embarked on a program of research that has come to be considered by many psychologists as his most important contribution: the investigation of different schedules of reinforcement.

Schedules of reinforcement

It is obvious that, in everyday life outside the laboratory, behavior is not reinforced each time it occurs. A baby is not picked up by its mother every time it cries. The Little League baseball player doesn't get a home run, or even a hit, every time at bat. The bagger in a supermarket does not receive pay or a cry of "Well done!" from the boss every time he or she packs a bag. There are countless examples of behaviors that, although only intermittently reinforced, persist.

Seeing that his rats continued to press the bar at a fairly constant response rate, even when they were not being reinforced continuously, Skinner proceeded to investigate different schedules or rates of reinforcement to determine which would be most effective in controlling behavior. We will discuss four different **reinforcement schedules**: fixed interval, fixed ratio, variable interval, and variable ratio.

The *fixed-interval schedule* of reinforcement means precisely that: the reinforcement is presented at fixed intervals of time. For example, the reinforcement might be given every one minute or every three minutes. Note that the reinforcement has nothing to do with how many responses are being made. Whether the rat responds once a minute or 20 times a minute, the reinforcement still arrives only after the passage of a fixed interval of time.

There are many real-life situations that operate in accordance with this schedule of reinforcement. In your own case, if your instructor gives a midterm and a final examination, he or she is operating on a fixed-interval schedule. A job in which a salary is paid once a week or once a month also operates on the fixed-interval schedule. Under such a system, a worker is paid not by the number of items he or she produces (the number of responses made) but by the number of hours, days, or weeks that elapse.

The research results are what you would probably predict. The shorter the interval between reinforcements, the greater the frequency of the organism's response. The response rate declines as the interval between reinforcements is lengthened. How frequently the reinforcements appear also affects how quickly a response will be extinguished. The response will stop sooner if the rat has been continuously reinforced (and the reinforcement then stopped) than if it has been reinforced intermittently.

In the *fixed-ratio schedule* of reinforcement, the reinforcement is presented only after the organism has made a specified number of responses. For example, the experimenter could reinforce at every 10th or at every 20th response. In this schedule, then, unlike the fixed-interval schedule, the reinforcement depends on how frequently the animal responds, for the animal will not receive a food pellet until it emits the required number of responses. As a result, this reinforcement schedule brings about a faster rate of response than the fixed-interval one.

The higher response rate of the fixed-ratio schedule has been found to hold true in a variety of situations for rats, pigeons, and humans. In a job in which the pay is determined on a piece-rate basis, how much a worker makes depends on how much he or she produces. The more items produced, the higher the pay. Thus, the person's reinforcement depends directly upon his or her rate of responding. The same holds for a salesperson working solely on a commission basis. His or her income depends on the number of units of the product sold; the more sold, the more earned. A salesperson on a weekly salary, in contrast, will earn the same each week, whether he or she sells 5 or 50 units of the product.

It often happens in real life that reinforcement does not follow a fixed interval or fixed ratio but rather appears on a variable basis. In the *variable-interval schedule*, the reinforcement might appear after two hours one time, after an hour and 30 minutes the next time, after two hours and 15 minutes the third time, and so on, averaging approximately two hours between reinforcements. A person spending a day fishing might be rewarded (if at all) on such a variable-interval basis, the rate of reinforcement being determined by the random appearance of fish.

A *variable-ratio schedule* of reinforcement is based on an average number of responses between reinforcements, but there is great variability around that average. Skinner has found that the variable-ratio schedule is extremely effective in bringing about high and stable response rates, as those who operate gambling casinos can happily attest. Slot machines, roulette wheels, horse races, and the like pay off on this variable-ratio reinforcement schedule and, as any addicted gambler can tell you, it is an extremely effective means of controlling behavior.

The variable-ratio schedule of
reinforcement is an effective
means of controlling behavior.

What all of this research on different schedules of reinforcement means is an
increased efficiency in controlling, modifying, and shaping behavior. If you are in
charge of rats, salespeople, or assembly-line workers, or are trying to train your
dog, cat, or child, you can see how such operant conditioning techniques can be
useful in inducing the kind of behavior you would like to see. The same techniques
have also been used in the clinical setting.

Successive approximation: The shaping of behavior

In the original operant conditioning experiment, the operant behavior (pressing
the lever) is a simple kind of behavior, one that the animal would be expected to
display naturally in the course of exploring its environment. The probability of its
occurrence is high. It is obvious that both animals and humans demonstrate more
complex operant behaviors that, in the normal course of events, have a low probability of occurrence. How are these complex behaviors learned? How can an experimenter or a parent condition a pigeon or a child to perform behaviors that are not
likely to occur spontaneously?

Skinner answered this question with the technique of **shaping**, also known as
the method of *successive approximation*. He demonstrated its use by training a
pigeon in a very short time to peck at a particular spot in its cage. The probability of
the pigeon's pecking at that one spot on its own was quite low.

First, the pigeon was reinforced with food whenever it turned toward the spot.
Then reinforcement was withheld until the pigeon made some movement, no
matter how slight, toward the spot. Reinforcements were then given only for movements that brought the pigeon nearer the spot. Next, the pigeon was reinforced

only when it moved its head forward. Finally, it was reinforced only when its beak touched the spot.

This may sound like a time-consuming and laborious procedure, but Skinner found that pigeons could be conditioned in this manner in two to three minutes. You can now understand why this is called the method of successive approximation. The organism is reinforced only as its behavior comes, successively, to approximate the final behavior desired. This method is used routinely to train animals to do tricks, and it is also the way in which infants learn to speak.

Babies emit all sorts of meaningless sounds, which parents reinforce by smiling, laughing, and talking. Soon parents begin to reinforce their baby's babbling differentially, providing stronger reinforcements for the sounds that approximate words. As the process continues, parental reinforcement is increasingly restricted to the proper use and pronunciation of words.

Complex behavior, then, can be "constructed by a continual process of differential reinforcement from undifferentiated behavior, just as the sculptor shapes his figure from a lump of clay" (Skinner, 1953, pp. 92–93).

Superstitious behavior

Life is not as orderly or well controlled as events in the laboratory, and sometimes we are reinforced accidentally after we have displayed some behavior. As a result, that behavior, which in itself did not lead to or cause a reinforcement, may be repeated in a similar situation. Suppose, for example, that an aspiring actor wears a blue shirt for his first audition and gets the part. At the next audition, which also results in a job, the actor is again wearing a blue shirt. The connection between the blue shirt and getting acting roles is, of course, coincidental, but the actor may come to believe that one has caused the other, and he will never attend an audition unless he is wearing his lucky blue shirt.

Skinner calls this **superstitious behavior**. Like everything else in his system, he first demonstrated it in the laboratory. Consider the case of a hungry pigeon in an operant-conditioning apparatus being reinforced on a fixed-interval schedule of reinforcement every 15 seconds. Recall that under such a schedule, the reinforcement is given after the appropriate time interval, whether or not the pigeon has displayed the desired response.

It is likely that the pigeon will be exhibiting some behavior when the reinforcement is given. It may be turning around, raising its head, strutting, hopping on one foot, or standing still. Whatever is occurring at the moment of reinforcement will be reinforced. Skinner has found that single reinforcements are so powerful that the pigeon will display the accidentally reinforced behavior more frequently for a while, thus increasing the probability that another reinforcement will appear while the behavior is being displayed. With short intervals between reinforcements, superstitious behaviors are learned quickly.

Yet, like the actor and his blue shirt, the superstitious behavior offered by the pigeon has no functional relationship to the reinforcement. The connection is unintentional. Still, the behavior may persist throughout the life of the organism; only occasional reinforcements are required to maintain it.

The self-control of behavior

As we have seen, the basic tenet of Skinner's approach is that our behavior is caused and modified by variables external to the organism. There is nothing inside us, no process or form of internal activity, that determines our behavior. But, although external stimuli and reinforcers are the all-powerful shapers of our behavior, we can act to change them.

Skinner speaks of **self-control**. He does not mean control by some mysterious force inside us labeled the "self," but rather control of those variables that determine our behavior. If the sound of your neighbor's stereo set is interfering with your ability to concentrate on this chapter, for example, you could leave your room and go to the library to study, thereby removing yourself from an external variable that has been affecting your behavior. By avoiding some person or situation that always makes you angry, you are reducing the amount of control that person or situation has on your behavior. In similar fashion, problem drinkers can avoid the stimuli that determine their behavior by not allowing liquor to be kept in their houses.

Skinner discussed other techniques of self-control. Through *satiation*, for example, people can cure themselves of bad habits by overdoing the behavior. A smoker who wants to quit might force himself or herself to chain smoke all day, inhaling constantly, until he or she becomes disgusted by the behavior; this technique has been successful in clinical programs to eliminate smoking.

Another technique involves the use of *aversive stimulation*. Let us consider alcoholics who want to stop drinking or obese persons who want to lose weight. They could declare their intentions in the presence of friends. If their resolutions are not kept, they must face the unpleasant consequences of failing to stick to a stated course of action and the criticism of those to whom it had been announced.

Another technique of self-control is to *reinforce oneself* for displaying good or desirable behaviors. A teenager who agrees to care for a younger brother or sister might reward himself or herself by buying a new record or a pair of jeans.

It is important to remember that, to Skinner, external variables are still what shape and control our behavior, but we are sometimes able, through various means, to ameliorate the effects of these external forces.

Applications of operant conditioning

As we have seen, Skinner's approach to learning has been applied to a variety of real-world problems, including the learning of languages, the training of pets, and the acquisition of superstitious behaviors. In these situations, we apply, perhaps unwittingly, Skinner's principles for reinforcing desirable emitted behaviors and ig-

noring undesirable behaviors. In many clinical, industrial, and educational institutions, psychologists practice operant conditioning to modify behavior. This approach, called *behavior modification*, has been successfully applied in several
institutional or group settings: prisons, school classrooms, reform schools, and fac-
tories, and with groups of mentally disturbed and mentally retarded children. It has
also been used to treat a variety of individual behavior problems, including hyperactivity, bed-wetting, temper tantrums, stuttering, and constipation.

The token economy

In one example of a real-world application of Skinner's conditioning principles, an entire ward of more than 40 female psychotic patients in a state mental
institution was treated as a Skinner box (Ayllon & Azrin, 1968). All the patients were
considered beyond treatment (and hope), had been institutionalized for very long
periods of time, were generally unable to take care of themselves, and spent their
days in aimless isolation.

In this setting, the patients were offered opportunities to work at certain jobs
(jobs usually performed by paid hospital attendants) for which they would receive
tokens. These tokens could be used like money to buy extra privileges and possessions. For example, with a certain number of tokens the patients could purchase
candy, cigarettes, lipstick, gloves, newspapers, or a variety of other consumer goods.
Also, by paying tokens they could attend a movie (on the ward), take a 20-minute
walk around the hospital grounds, or get a more private room. The most expensive
privileges (those that required the greatest number of tokens—100) were a trip
into town with an escort and a private meeting with a social worker. (A private
meeting with a psychologist was only one-fifth the price of the social worker.)

Like people on the outside, the patients could buy items and privileges to improve the quality of their lives. Their tokens functioned like money, and the approach has come to be called the **token economy**. What did they have to do to
earn these tokens? What kinds of behaviors did they have to emit in order to be
reinforced? If they bathed at the time designated, brushed their teeth, made their
beds, combed their hair, and dressed properly, they earned one token for each activity. More tokens (up to ten per activity) were earned by working for short periods in the hospital kitchen or laundry, helping to clean the ward, running errands,
or helping to care for other patients (taking them for walks, for example). You
might think that these tasks are simple and low-level, and so they are. But remember that these patients were hopeless psychotics, most of whom could not even
take care of their own bodily needs, at least not before given a reinforcement for
doing so.

The system worked dramatically. Not only did the patients begin to groom
themselves and clean and improve their ward, but they also began to be busy at a
variety of jobs. They interacted much more, both with one another and with the
staff. Some degree of responsibility for patient care shifted from the staff to the patients themselves, and their sense of self-esteem and self-worth improved markedly.

The reinforcement offered in return for certain behaviors altered their overall behavior. The patients changed from dependent, incompetent, hopeless psychotics to less dependent and more responsible individuals.

A word of caution is necessary. The token economy seems to be effective only within the institution in which it is implemented. The modified behavior is unlikely to carry over to life outside the institution. Further, the program must often be continued for the behavior changes to persist. When tokens are no longer provided, patient behavior usually reverts to its original state (Kazdin & Bootzin, 1972; Repucci & Saunders, 1974). These criticisms notwithstanding, the dramatic changes in behavior that may be achieved by the application of positive reinforcement have made the token economy a widely-used approach in clinical and other institutions.

A token economy program established in an elementary school class of third- and fourth-grade students was shown to be effective in modifying socially disruptive behavior. Undesirable activities included coming late to class, being out of one's chair, being fidgety and noisy, being aggressive, touching someone else's property, not paying attention, and playing and talking out of turn. Points were awarded for desirable behaviors, and each point could be exchanged for one minute of free-play time in an activity area that offered games and arts-and-crafts materials. Significant decreases in disruptive behavior were noted, even several weeks after the point system was discontinued (O'Leary, Drabman & Kass, 1973).

Behavior modification in industry

Operant conditioning has also been applied to problems in business and industry. Organizations using behavior modification programs for their employees have reduced absenteeism, reduced tardiness, and reduced abuse of sick-leave privileges, and improved on-the-job performance and safety (Wexley & Latham, 1981). Some of the rewards or reinforcers investigated in industry are pay, job security, recognition from supervisors, job or company status, and the opportunity for personal growth on the job (Blood, 1973). Further, behavior-modification techniques have been used to teach specific job skills to disadvantaged workers and have often succeeded when more traditional training programs have failed.

Comments on behavior modification

There are two additional points of interest about behavior modification. First, no attempt is made to deal with any presumed underlying conflict, repressed trauma, or unconscious motivating force. The focus in the practical application of the behavior-modification technique is strictly on overt behavior. There was no more concern for what might be happening inside the psychotic patients, the students in the classroom, or the workers in the factory than for what might be going on inside a rat in the operant-conditioning apparatus. The concern is solely with behavior and the kind and rate of presentation of reinforcement that will change behavior.

Second, most operant-conditioning applications involve positive reinforcement and not **punishment**. The patients in the hospital study, the children in the elementary-school research, and the employees, were not punished for failing to behave in more desirable ways. Rather, they were reinforced only when their behavior did change in positive ways. Skinner feels that punishment is not very effective, in general, in changing behavior from undesirable to desirable or from abnormal to normal. Positive reinforcement applied to behaviors that are considered desirable is much more effective. (It is interesting to note that Skinner reported that he was never physically punished as a child by his father and only once by his mother; she washed out his mouth with soap and water for saying a naughty word. He did not report whether that worked to change his behavior.)

Mention should be made here of negative reinforcement, which is not the same as punishment. A **negative reinforcement** is an aversive or noxious stimulus, the removal of which is rewarding. An operant-conditioning situation can be set up, in the laboratory or in an applied setting, in which the aversive stimulus (such as a loud noise or an electric shock) will continue until the subject makes the desired response. As with positive reinforcement, the environment will change (the noxious stimulus will disappear) as a consequence of behavior. Certainly it is reinforcing to escape something odious or harmful, and thus negative reinforcement can be a powerful way of modifying behavior.

We see examples of negative reinforcement in many situations. You study for this course and attend most of the class meetings at least in part to avoid the aversive stimulus of a failing grade. A child behaves in certain ways to avoid or escape the disapproval or loss of affection of its parents. Negative reinforcement is also used in the clinical setting, where a noxious stimulus is continued when the undesirable behavior is displayed and discontinued only when the desirable behavior is displayed.

Skinner is strongly opposed to the use of noxious stimuli in trying to modify behavior, because he feels the consequences are not as firmly predictable as they are with positive reinforcement—in other words, negative reinforcement does not always work. In general, positive reinforcement is more consistently effective.

It is easy to see in the case of Skinner how research with rats and pigeons can lead to important and practical ramifications for changing or modifying what others call *personality*.

Skinner's image of human nature

Skinner's position is clear on the nature–nurture issue. Although he recognizes the existence of hereditary factors, he emphasizes the role of environment in influencing behavior. We are primarily products of learning, shaped more by external variables than by genetic factors. Therefore, it can be inferred that childhood experiences are more important than those that occur later in life; our basic behaviors are formed in childhood. This does not mean that our behavior cannot change later in life. What has been learned can be unlearned or modified, and new patterns of behavior can be acquired, presumably at any age.

It also follows from Skinner's belief that we are shaped primarily by learning that each of us is unique. Because we are molded by experiences—and we are all subject to different experiences, particularly in childhood—no two people will behave in exactly the same way.

Skinner has not addressed the problem of an ultimate and necessary goal in life. There is no reference in his system to our being pushed to overcome inferiority feelings or to reduce anxieties and conflicts, or our being pulled by a drive toward some state such as self-actualization; all such motivations assume internal, subjective concepts, which are anathema to Skinner. If there is any indication of the goal of life in Skinner's work, it is in social not individual terms. In his novel *Walden Two* and in other writings, he discussed his notion of the best society that could be designed (Skinner, 1948). He stated that the behavior of individuals must be directed toward the kind of society that has the greatest chance of survival.

There is no ambiguity concerning where Skinner stands on the issue of free will versus determinism. Humans function in the same way machines function—in lawful, orderly, predetermined fashion. As noted in the introduction, Skinner firmly rejects all notions of an inner person—an autonomous self—determining a course and choosing to act spontaneously and freely. We are operated by forces in the external world, not by forces within ourselves. Not since Freud have we met a theorist who is so completely deterministic in his viewpoint, allowing for not even the slightest hint of freedom of will and spontaneity of behavior.

From Skinner's highly technical writing to his popular novel about a utopian society based on operant conditioning principles, the message is the same: "If we are to use the methods of science in the field of human affairs, we must assume that behavior is lawful and determined. . . ." "The issue of personal freedom must not be allowed to interfere with a scientific analysis of human behavior" (Skinner, 1953, p. 6).

All aspects of human behavior are controlled from without. A person's behavior is beyond that person's control, which means that it is pointless to blame or punish people for their actions. In this view, Adolf Hitler can no more be held responsible for what he did than can a driverless car that plunged down a hill—both operate in lawful, predictable ways and are controlled only by variables outside themselves.

We are left, it seems, with a pessimistic view of ourselves as helpless and passive robots, unable to play an active role in the determination of our own behavior. Surprisingly, however, that does not represent Skinner's ultimate view. He does not see us as victims, or even as mere passive spectators, in spite of the fact that our behavior is so thoroughly controlled. "I take an optimistic view," Skinner wrote. "Man can control his future even though his behavior is wholly determined" (Evans, 1968, p. 107).

But how can this be? How can one who is totally controlled also control? Skinner deals with this apparent paradox in the following manner. It is true, he said, beyond doubt, that people are controlled by their environment—but who designs the environment? People. Skinner points out that our physical environment is, for the most part, designed and built by humans. Clothing, building, tools, vehicles—virtually everything we see, hear, and work and play with—are the result of human fabrication. So too is our social environment. Our language, customs, and mores are human products.

And we are constantly changing our environment, often to our own advantage. When we do bring about changes in the social and physical environment, we are at once controller and controlled; we design a controlling culture and are the product of the culture. The fact that we are products of a culture may somewhat limit or inhibit our freedom to change it; we will be guided, in making changes, by those characteristics in the environment that have provided positive reinforcement in the past. In changing our culture, we seek ever-greater opportunities for positive reinforcement, and in the process we can change our own behavior. We are left with the paradoxical image of person-as-machine, constantly changing the environmental conditions that guide the machine's behavior.

Assessment in Skinner's theory

How can there be any assessment of personality in a system that does not deal with personality, a system that derives its data from laboratory studies of rats and pigeons? There cannot be. Skinner never used any of the assessment techniques we have discussed for other theorists. There is no place in his work for free association, dream analysis, or projective techniques.

Although neither Skinner nor his followers have any interest in assessing personality, they often have expressed a clear, even pressing, need to assess behavior. This is particularly important with behavior-modification techniques. Specific behaviors, both desirable and undesirable, must be assessed, along with the features of the environment that serve as reinforcers and can be manipulated to change behavior. No behavior can properly be modified without such assessment.

This behavioral assessment is known as **functional analysis**, and it usually involves three aspects of behavior: (1) the frequency of the behavior, (2) the situation in which the behavior occurs, and (3) the reinforcements associated with the behavior. Unless these factors are assessed in advance, it is not possible to plan the proper course of behavior modification, much less implement it.

Consider, as an example, a functional analysis for a cigarette smoker who wants to break the smoking habit. He or she would keep an accurate record first of the number of cigarettes smoked daily and second of the situations in which they were smoked. Does smoking occur in a certain place or at a certain time? In the presence of others or alone? After meals or while driving? And third, what about the reinforcers? With the exception of so-called chain smokers, most people who smoke do so more frequently in the presence of certain stimuli. Identifying these stimuli is necessary, because modifying them should lead to a modification of behavior.

Formal programs of behavior modification use three approaches to assess behavior: direct observation, self-report, and physiological measurements.

Direct observation of behavior

Many behaviors are assessed through the method of direct observation. Usually, two or more persons conduct the observation to assure accuracy and reliability. In one case of behavior modification, a woman sought treatment for her 4-year-old son whose behavior was considered unruly (Hawkins et al., 1966). Two psychologists observed the mother and the child in their home to assess the nature and frequency of the child's undesirable behaviors, the times and places at which they occurred, and the reinforcements the child received for the behaviors.

Nine undesirable behaviors were identified, including kicking, throwing things, biting himself, and pushing his sister. The psychologists also observed that the mother was reinforcing the child by giving him toys or food every time he engaged in an undesirable behavior. Her intent was to get him to stop misbehaving, but she was, in fact, rewarding him for it. The direct observation assessment took 16 hours to complete, but without it the psychologists would not have known what specific behaviors to try to eliminate or what reinforcements the child had been receiving.

Following such comprehensive direct observations, it is not difficult to plan a behavior-modification program. In this case, the psychologists instructed the mother to give the boy attention and approval (reinforcers) only when he was behaving in positive ways, never when he displayed one of the nine observed undesirable behaviors. The precise count of the frequency of the undesirable behaviors provided a baseline against which behavior during and after the treatment could be compared.

Self-report procedures

The second approach to the assessment of behavior is the self-report technique, and there are several procedures, such as interviews and questionnaires, by which this may be carried out. The person is, in a sense, observing his or her own behavior and reporting on it to the examiner. A number of self-report questionnaires are in current use, including the Fear Survey Schedule (Geer, 1965), which assesses how much fear a person experiences in such situations as driving a car, going to the dentist, or speaking in public.

Questionnaires for assessing behavior do not differ in format from the other types of self-report inventories we have discussed in previous chapters. The distinction lies in the ways in which such inventories are interpreted, a difference described as the *sign versus sample* approach to assessment (Mischel, 1976). In the sign approach, used to assess personality, the psychologist infers the existence of character types, traits, or unconscious conflicts from the way in which the individual responds to the self-report inventory. If a person indicates that he or she is afraid of being in an elevator, for example, this might be interpreted as a sign or indirect symptom of some inner, underlying fear, motive, or conflict.

In the sample approach, used to assess behavior, the questionnaire responses are interpreted simply and directly as indicative of a sample of behavior. No attempt is made to draw inferences or conclusions about the person's character or traits. The behavior itself (the fear, in our example) and the stimulus associated with it (the elevator) are the important things. There is no concern with subjective motives, childhood experiences, or anything else that may be going on inside the person's head.

Physiological measurements of behavior

Physiological assessment, a third means of assessing behavior, involves the measurement of bodily processes such as heart rate, muscle tension, and brain waves. In this manner, it is possible to assess the effects of different stimuli on the individual. Such measures can also be used to assess the accuracy of the information obtained by the other methods of assessment. For example, a person who is too embarrassed about his or her fear of being in an elevator to reveal it in an interview or questionnaire might show a change in pulse rate or muscle tension when asked about elevators while connected to the appropriate physiological measuring apparatus.

Whatever technique of assessment is used, its purpose is to assess behavior in different stimulus situations. The focus is on the outside, not the inside—on what the person does, not on what might have motivated the person to do it. The ultimate purpose is to modify behavior, not to change personality.

Research in Skinner's theory
The single-subject experiment

We have seen that Skinner's methods of assessment are radically different from those discussed in other chapters. In addition, his research methods differ from the rest of experimental psychology in several important respects.

The usual procedure followed by non-Skinnerian experimental psychologists is to study large groups of subjects (animal or human) and statistically compare the average responses of these subjects. In contrast, Skinner chooses to study a single subject intensively. He argues that knowledge of how an average subject performs is of very little value in dealing with an individual. A science that deals with averages, he contends, provides little information in understanding the unique case.

Skinner believes that valid and replicable results can be obtained without the use of statistical analyses, so long as sufficient data are collected from a single subject under well-controlled experimental conditions. He argues that the use of a large group of subjects forces the experimenter to attend to average behavior. As a result, individual response behavior and individual differences in behavior do not appear in the data. Thus, Skinner favors the idiographic rather than the nomothetic research approach.

Skinner's single-subject experiments follow the *reversal experimental design*, which consists of three, and sometimes four, stages. The first stage involves establishing the *baseline*. The subject's behavior (the dependent variable) is observed to determine the normal rate of response before the experimental treatment is introduced.

The second stage is the *conditioning* or experimental stage, when the independent variable is introduced. If this variable affects behavior, it will produce a marked
change from the subject's baseline rate of responding.

The purpose of the third stage, the *reversal* stage, is to determine whether
some factor other than the independent variable may have been responsible for the
observed change in behavior. During this stage, the independent variable is no
longer applied. If the behavior in question returns to its baseline rate, then the researcher can conclude that the independent variable was responsible for the difference in behavior observed in the conditioning stage. If the behavior does not return to the baseline level, then some factor other than the independent variable
must have been operative.

These three stages—baseline, conditioning, and reversal—are usually sufficient for laboratory experiments. When the procedure is used for behavior modification, however, a fourth stage, the *reconditioning* stage, is added. In this stage,
the independent variable is reintroduced, assuming that it was shown to be effective in changing behavior. Without the fourth stage, the subject of the behavior-
modification program would remain in the reversal stage with his or her behavior
at its baseline level, unchanged by the treatment that had been shown to be effective. Therefore, it would be unethical to fail to reintroduce the effective treatment.

The operant-conditioning apparatus for animals

Skinner's research on animals uses the operant-conditioning apparatus (popu-
larly known as the Skinner box). The rat or pigeon to be studied is placed inside the
Skinner box. A sophisticated piece of laboratory apparatus, the Skinner box contains a variety of equipment that can be used for operant conditioning. We have
mentioned the bar or lever that a rat can depress in order to obtain reinforcement.
A model for use with pigeons contains a translucent disk mounted on one wall,
about ten inches from the floor. The disk can be illuminated from behind and is
usually red in color. When the pigeon pecks at the disk, food is delivered into
the box.

The Skinner box is well lighted, and its walls are soundproof and opaque to
eliminate all stimulation from outside the box. The only stimuli to which the animal
is exposed are those directly under the experimenter's control. More important, in
terms of the sophistication and refinement of the experimental procedure, is the
automatic, precision recording of every operant response the subject emits. The
box is wired to additional equipment so that every press of the bar or peck of
the disk is recorded and the food is delivered automatically. Once the proper reinforcement rate has been determined by the experimenter, the experiment will run
by itself, with only a periodic clicking sound as evidence that the complex system is
behaving in a lawful way.

Skinner has also introduced a precise and yet simple means of recording responses, a device called a *cumulative recorder*. Recording paper revolves sideways
on a drum at a constant speed, and a recording stylus or pen moves upward each
time a response is made. The steeper the line, the faster the animal is responding.

When the experiment is finished, a cumulative record of every response and its rate is available. This technique also indicates changes in the rate of responding.

Studies of human subjects

Thousands of experiments have been conducted by Skinner and his followers on all aspects of operant conditioning, including schedules of reinforcement, language acquisition, behavior shaping, and superstitious behavior. In addition, much research has been performed, as we noted, with human subjects in behavior-modification programs. This research is highly supportive of Skinner's position; indeed, his work has stronger empirical validation than any other theory we have discussed.

A final commentary

It is easy for people to retain an emotional neutrality about some of the theorists in this book, but it is difficult to do so in the case of B. F. Skinner. His is an extreme stance in behaviorism, just as Freud's was an extreme stance in quite the opposite direction. As radical positions, these approaches to the understanding of human personality or behavior invite a polarity of opinion, with highly emotionally charged disagreement between opponents and proponents.

Skinner's approach has been criticized on a number of points. Obviously, those persons who oppose a deterministic view of human nature must oppose Skinner. Some of the more vocal attacks against him have come from those who believe that humans are more than machines directed by external forces. These critics, notably the humanistic psychologists, object to Skinner's image of us as overgrown white rats and argue that the exclusive emphasis on overt behavior ignores those human characteristics that set us apart from rats or pigeons. People, these critics contend, are not merely empty organisms or robots, but conscious beings who can act with free will and spontaneity.

These and other critics also express concern over Skinner's belief that we can be totally controlled and manipulated, arguing that such a point of view lends support to fascist thinking—to the idea that a demagogue could mold and shape a culture in any desired direction. These critics argue that if Skinner's view of humanity were to become totally accepted, it would ease the way for a government to institute a society in which every aspect of behavior, from infancy on, would be controlled and directed.

At a more specific level, we find criticism directed at the type of subject and the simplicity of the situations studied. As noted, Skinner has made many assertions and predictions about human behavior and human societies. His writings have ranged from social and economic to religious and cultural speculations, all of which he puts forth with great confidence (even arrogance, some have said). How, it is asked, can Skinner extrapolate from a pigeon pecking at a disk in a Skinner box to a highly complex person functioning in a world consisting of a vast range of stimuli? The gap between human and pigeon, these critics charge, is too vast to permit Skinner's broad generalizations. Most of the other personality theorists discussed dealt with the whole person functioning in the real world. Even those who are more experimentally oriented, such as Raymond Cattell, have at least studied human beings. Many aspects of human behavior, it is charged, cannot be reduced meaningfully to the level at which behavior is investigated by Skinner.

In addition, criticisms have been directed against technical aspects of Skinner's research methodology and the statistical analyses he uses. It has been charged that his research approach ignores individual differences and aspects of behavior other than the rate of responding, and that it provides no information on the learning process.

For the most part, Skinner's reaction to his critics has been to ignore them. "I read a bit of it," he said, referring to a negative review of one of his books, "and saw that he missed the point, so I never read the rest. I never answer any of my critics. . . . There are better things to do with my time than clear up their misunderstandings" (Rice, 1968, p. 90).

Despite these criticisms, Skinner is undoubtedly one of the most potent forces in 20th-century psychology. American psychology in general has been shaped and influenced more by his work than by the work of any other individual. Huge quantities of supporting research have been performed by Skinner and those who follow his point of view.

In the survey dealing with the relative importance of 286 psychologists in the second half of the 20th century, Skinner is ranked as the most influential of all. In another survey dealing with the relative importance of more than 150 events and innovations in psychology, Skinner's contributions, and behavior modification, are ranked in first and second place respectively (Gilgen, 1982).

His radical behaviorist position remains strong and vital in both the laboratory and the applied setting, although it is being challenged by the more cognitive-oriented positions taken by Bandura and Rotter (Chapters 15 and 16). The Skinnerian *Journal of the Experimental Analysis of Behavior* has flourished since 1958, as has the Division for the Experimental Analysis of Behavior of the American Psychological Association. Some university psychology departments take Skinner's position as their basic orientation in training their graduate students. Behavior modification as a technique of changing behavior has gained increasing popularity, providing more empirical support for his approach.

Whether we agree or disagree with Skinner's position, its presence can be felt in many areas—from classrooms to assembly lines, from Skinner boxes to prisons and mental institutions. In Skinner's view, he has presented and refined a technique that will vastly improve human nature and the societies humans design.

Summary

Skinner believes that the course of his own life was determined by environmental sources, the reinforcements in childhood that influenced his approach to the study of behavior. He attempts to account for all behavior, not just what others call personality, and to do so in purely factual and descriptive terms. Psychology must restrict itself to overt responses if it is to be defined as the science of behavior, of what the organism does. Skinner's approach differs from those of other personality theorists in denying the existence of a separate entity known as personality and in not seeking 'the causes of behavior within the organism. Neither mentalistic nor physiological processes are overtly observable, and so they have no relevance for science. The only way to predict and control behavior is to relate it to antecedent events in the environment. Thus, the cause of behavior is always external to the organism. All behavior can be controlled by its consequences, by the reinforcement that follows the behavior.

Skinner searches for general laws of human behavior and expresses little interest in individual differences. He studies animals because they are simpler than human beings, and their basic processes are not so dissimilar. Further, animal subjects offer the opportunity to control genetic and experiential backgrounds, can be studied for longer periods of time and in more dangerous environments than humans, and do not attempt to outwit the experimenter.

Respondent behavior involves a response elicited by specific stimuli in the environment. Conditioning (respondent behavior that is learned) involves the substitution of one stimulus for another, as shown by Pavlov. The essential feature of Pavlov's work was the demonstration of the importance of reinforcement. Conditioning will not take place without reinforcement. A response will be extinguished when reinforcement is no longer presented.

Skinner believes that operant behavior is much more important than respondent behavior. Operant behavior is emitted and is determined and modified by the reinforcement that follows it. Operant behavior cannot be traced to any specific stimulus; it operates on the environment and changes it. Operant behavior was demonstrated in Skinner's operant-conditioning apparatus (Skinner box) using rats who were reinforced with food when they depressed a lever. Withholding the reinforcement extinguished the behavior. The cumulative recorder automatically records every response made in the operant-conditioning apparatus. The faster the animal responds, the steeper the line made by the pen on the revolving recording paper.

Personality, to Skinner, is nothing more than a pattern or collection of operant behaviors.

Skinner investigated four schedules of reinforcement: (1) fixed interval, in which reinforcement is presented at fixed intervals of time; (2) fixed ratio, in which reinforcement is presented after a fixed number of responses; (3) variable interval, in which reinforcement is presented at variable intervals of time; and (4) variable ratio, in which reinforcement is presented after variable numbers of responses. The fixed-ratio schedule results in higher response rates than the fixed-interval schedule. The variable-ratio schedule is effective in bringing about a high and stable response rate.

Shaping, the method of successive approximation, involves reinforcing the organism only as its behavior comes to approximate the final behavior desired. This is the way in which infants learn to speak.

Superstitious behavior results when reinforcement is presented on a fixed- or variable-interval schedule. Whatever behavior is occurring at the moment of reinforcement will be reinforced. The organism will then display that accidentally reinforced behavior more frequently, thus increasing the probability that another reinforcement will occur when the behavior is displayed.

Self-control of behavior refers to changing or avoiding certain external stimuli and reinforcers. Other techniques of self-control include satiation, overdoing the behavior; aversive stimulation, establishing unpleasant consequences for continuing the behavior; and reinforcing oneself for displaying desirable behavior.

Behavior modification applies operant conditioning to real-world problems. Desirable behaviors are positively reinforced, and undesirable behaviors are ignored. The token economy involves rewarding desirable behaviors with tokens that can be used to acquire objects or experiences of value. The token economy may be effective only within the institution in which it was implemented, and it usually has to be continued for the behavior changes to persist. The approach has been successful in hospitals, schools, and industry, and with a variety of individual behavior problems. Behavior modification deals only with overt behavior and uses positive reinforcement, not punishment.

Negative reinforcement involves the removal of an aversive or noxious stimulus. It is not as effective as positive reinforcement for changing behavior.

Skinner's image of human nature emphasizes determinism, human uniqueness, the role of the environment in influencing behavior, and the ultimate goal of designing societies that maximize our chance of survival. Although we are controlled by our environment, Skinner believes that we can control our own future by properly designing that environment.

Skinner assesses behavior, not personality. These behavioral assessments or functional analyses involve the determination of the frequency of the behavior, the situation in which the behavior occurs, and the reinforcement associated with the behavior. Three ways of assessing behavior are direct observation, self-report, and physiological measurements. Direct observation is carried out by two or more observers to assure accuracy and reliability. Self-report questionnaires used to assess behavior differ from those used to assess personality in the way in which they are interpreted (the sign versus sample approach). In the sign approach, used to assess personality, personal characteristics or traits are inferred from the person's responses. In the sample approach, used to assess behavior, the questionnaire responses are interpreted as samples of behavior; no inferences are drawn about the person's thoughts or past experiences.

Skinner's research is idiographic; it focuses on the intensive study of an individual subject. His approach, the reversal experimental design, consists of four stages: (1) baseline, establishing the normal rate of response; (2) conditioning, introducing the independent variable; (3) reversal, withholding the independent variable to determine if the behavior returns to the baseline; and (4) reconditioning, reintroducing the effective variable to reintroduce the changed behavior.

Although no system has as much empirical support as that of Skinner, it has been criticized for its deterministic view of human nature and its belief that people can be totally controlled and manipulated. Other criticisms relate to the simplicity of the experimental situations, the lack of interest in individual differences or in aspects of behavior other than the rate of responding, and the failure to consider any distinctly human characteristics that may set us apart from rats and pigeons.

Glossary

behaviorism   The approach to psychology proposed by John B. Watson that focused solely on overt behavior, that is, on responses that could be measured or observed made by the organism to external stimuli.

functional analysis   An approach to the understanding of behavior that involves an assessment of the frequency of a behavior, the situation in which it occurs, and the reinforcements associated with it.

negative reinforcement   The strengthening of a response by the removal of an aversive or noxious stimulus.

operant behavior   Behaviors emitted spontaneously or voluntarily that operate on the environment and thus change it.

operant conditioning   The procedure in which a change in the consequences of a response will affect the rate at which the response occurs.

punishment   The application of an aversive stimulus following a response in an effort to decrease the likelihood that the response will reoccur.

reinforcement   The act of strengthening a response by adding a reward, thus increasing the likelihood that the response will be repeated.

reinforcement schedules   Patterns or rates of providing and withholding reinforcers.

respondent behavior   Responses made to or elicited by specific and known stimuli in the environment.

self-control   The ability of an individual to exert control over the variables that determine his or her behavior.

shaping   An explanation for the acquisition of complex behaviors in which behaviors are reinforced only as they come successively to approximate the final desired behavior.

superstitious behavior   Persistent behavior that has only a coincidental and not a functional relationship to the reinforcement received.

token economy   A behavior modification technique in which persons receive tokens (which can be exchanged for objects of value or for privileges) for performing desirable behaviors.

Review questions

1. How does Skinner's approach differ from the other approaches discussed in this book?
2. Describe Pavlov's classical conditioning experiment with dogs. How were the conditioned responses extinguished?

3. Distinguish between respondent and operant behavior.
4. What is the role of reinforcement in modifying and controlling behavior? How does reinforcement relate to superstitious behavior?
5. Distinguish between positive reinforcement, negative reinforcement, and punishment. What is Skinner's view of their relative effectiveness in modifying behavior?
6. List the four schedules of reinforcement. Which schedule applies to the person selling computer software on commission? Which schedule applies to the child who is allowed to have an ice-cream treat only occasionally?
7. How is a complex behavior, such as learning to speak, acquired through the method of successive approximation?
8. Describe the token-economy approach to the modification of behavior.
9. How does Skinner explain his preference for studying individual subjects rather than groups of subjects? Describe the stages in a typical experiment with a human subject. Describe a typical experiment using a pigeon as the subject.
10. What is Skinner's position on the nature–nurture issue? What is his position on the issue of free will versus determinism?

Suggested reading

Evans, R. I. *B. F. Skinner: The man and his ideas*. New York: Dutton, 1969.

Ferster, C. B. & Skinner, B. F. *Schedules of reinforcement*. New York: Appleton-Century-Crofts, 1957.

Skinner, B. F. *Walden two*. New York: Macmillan, 1948.

Skinner, B. F. *Science and human behavior*. New York: Free Press, 1953.

Skinner, B. F. Autobiography. In E. G. Boring & G. Lindzey, Eds., *History of psychology in autobiography*, vol. 5. New York: Appleton-Century-Crofts, 1967.

Skinner, B. F. *Beyond freedom and dignity*. New York: Alfred A. Knopf, 1971.

Skinner, B. F. *About behaviorism*. New York: Alfred A. Knopf, 1974.

Skinner, B. F. Origins of a behaviorist. *Psychology Today*, September 1983, pp. 22–33.

Skinner, B. F. *Particulars of my life*. New York: Alfred A. Knopf, 1976; *The shaping of a behaviorist*. New York: Alfred A. Knopf, 1979; *A matter of consequences*. New York: Alfred A. Knopf, 1983. (Skinner's lengthy and detailed autobiography in three volumes.)

CHAPTER 15

Albert Bandura

The life of Bandura (1925–   )
Modeling: The basis of observational learning
　Characteristics of the models
　Characteristics of the observers
　Reward consequences of the behavior
The processes of observational learning
　Attentional processes
　Retention processes
　Motor reproduction processes
　Incentive and motivational processes
The self
　Self-reinforcement
　Self-efficacy
The developmental stages of modeling
Modifying learned behavior
　Effects on self-efficacy
　Effects on anxiety
Ethical issues in behavior modification
Bandura's image of human nature
Assessment in Bandura's theory
Research in Bandura's theory
A final commentary
Summary
Glossary
Review questions
Suggested reading

Virtually every phenomenon that occurs by direct experience can occur vicariously as well—by observing other people and the consequences for them.

ALBERT BANDURA

As a learning theorist, Bandura agrees with Skinner that behavior, in its normal as well as abnormal manifestations, is learned. With that point, however, the similarity ends. Bandura has criticized Skinner's emphasis on studying individual subjects—and mainly animals—rather than human subjects in interaction with others. Bandura's approach is a truly social kind of learning theory that investigates behavior as it is formed and modified in a social context. He argues that one cannot expect findings of experiments that involve no social interaction to be relevant to the everyday world, in which few people function in social isolation.

Skinner's approach stresses that reinforcement is a necessary condition for the acquisition, maintenance, and modification of behavior. A person's behavior changes as a result of the consequences of the behavior—the reinforcement experienced directly by the individual. While Bandura recognizes that much learning does take place as a result of such reinforcement, he also stresses that virtually all forms of behavior can be learned in the absence of directly experienced reinforcement. His approach is sometimes labeled **observational learning**, to indicate the role in learning of observing the behavior of other people. Rather than having to experience reinforcement oneself, Bandura argues, one can learn through a kind of **vicarious reinforcement**, by observing the behavior of other people and the consequences of those behaviors. This emphasis on learning by observation or example, rather than always by direct reinforcement, is the most distinctive feature of Bandura's theory.

Another distinctive feature of the observational-learning approach, relative to Skinnerian theory, has to do with its treatment of inner aspects of the person. Bandura does not completely rule out the existence of internal influencing variables (as does Skinner). He believes that cognition or thought processes are capable of influencing observational learning. A person does not automatically copy or reproduce the behavior he or she sees in other people. Rather, the individual makes a deliberate, conscious decision to behave or not to behave in the same way.

To be able to learn through example and vicarious reinforcement, one must be able to anticipate and appreciate consequences that one has only observed in others and not yet experienced oneself. Bandura assumes that a person can, in this fashion, regulate and guide his or her own behavior—by visualizing or imagining the unexperienced consequences of that behavior. There is not a direct link or coupling between stimulus and response or between behavior and reinforcement, as is the case with Skinner. There is, instead, a mediating mechanism interposed between the two, and that mechanism is the person—or, more specifically, the person's cognitive processes.

For example, Bandura argues that it is not the schedule of reinforcement itself that is so powerful in changing behavior, but rather what the person thinks or perceives that schedule to be. Similarly, an aversive or painful stimulus need not actually be applied in order to modify behavior. The person's belief that it will be applied is sufficient to get that person to change his or her behavior. Thus, there is a strong recognition in Bandura's system of self-regulation, and even self-reinforcement, which represents an inner control of behavior. This is different from Skinner's form of self-control, which is defined only in reference to external variables.

We have, then, with Bandura, a less extreme form of behaviorism, which stresses the role of observation of others as a means of learning and considers learning to be mediated by cognitive factors. We, also have a theory soundly based on rigorous laboratory research with normal human subjects in social interaction situations rather than one based on rats in cages or neurotics on couches. Bandura calls it a *sociobehavioristic* approach.

The life of Bandura (1925 –   )

Albert Bandura was born in a small town in the province of Alberta, Canada. He has written little about his childhood, making it difficult to speculate on how his approach to personality may reflect his own experiences. Bandura agrees that "the published information on my pedigree and roots is quite limited" but that his time to speculate on its connection with his theory was "even in shorter supply" (Personal communication). He was one of 20 students in a high school that had only two teachers. As a result, he and the others had to educate themselves—a process that was obviously successful because Bandura and almost all of his classmates have undertaken professional careers.

Bandura attended the University of British Columbia as an undergraduate and received his Ph.D. from the University of Iowa in 1952. He spent a year at the Wichita, Kansas, Guidance Center and then joined the faculty of Stanford University, where he has remained. In 1969, he spent a year as a Fellow of the Center for Advanced Study in the Behavioral Sciences at Stanford and has been a consultant to several government organizations, including the Veterans Administration. He has compiled an extensive record of publications, and in 1973 he was elected president of the American Psychological Association.

Bandura's early work was done in collaboration with Richard Walters (1918–1967), Bandura's first Ph.D. student at Stanford University. Walters conducted a great deal of research on various aspects of social learning theory and co-authored, with Bandura, many of the early articles and books on the theory's development.

Modeling: The basis of observational learning

The notion that learning can occur through observation or example, rather than by direct reinforcement, is the most distinctive aspect of Bandura's social-learning theory. It is important to note that Bandura does not deny the importance of direct reinforcement as a technique of influencing behavior. What he is denying is the proposition that behavior can be learned or changed *only* through direct reinforcement. Also, he argues that reinforcement is a highly inefficient way of changing behavior. It is time-consuming and potentially dangerous. The world would be extremely hazardous indeed if people needed direct reinforcement in order to learn such things as not to cross an intersection on foot against a red light at the height of rush-hour traffic. This is not the kind of situation in which one would want to try out a number of behaviors before finding the one that brings reinforcement.

Operant conditioning, in which trial-and-error behavior continues until the correct response is found, is an inefficient way of teaching skills such as swimming or driving, because the person could drown or crash before finding the sequence of behaviors that leads to positive reinforcement. Most human behavior, Bandura argues, is learned through example, either intentionally or accidentally. We learn by observing other people and modeling our behavior after theirs. Some behaviors can be learned only through the influence of models; language is perhaps the best example of this. How could a child learn to speak if he or she never had the opportunity to hear words, phrases, and sentences? If learning to speak could be accomplished by operant conditioning alone, it would mean that the infant would not be reinforced for saying words (or approximations of them) until *after* he or she had said them spontaneously, having never heard them before.

Through **modeling**, that is, observing the behavior of a model and then repeating the behavior, it is possible to acquire responses never before performed or displayed and to strengthen or weaken responses that already exist in one's repertoire of behavior. In this regard, perhaps the most famous study conducted by Bandura involved the Bobo doll, an inflated plastic figure three to four feet tall (Bandura, Ross & Ross, 1963). The subjects, preschool children, watched an adult hit and kick Bobo. The adult model shouted angrily as he attacked the doll "Sock him in the nose!" "Throw him in the air!" and so on. When the children were left alone with the doll, they modeled their behavior after the example they had just seen. When their behavior was compared with that of a control group of children who had not seen the model, it was shown to be twice as aggressive.

Would it make a difference if the model were viewed on television instead of in person? No. The intensity of the aggressive behavior was the same. The intensity of aggression was also the same when the model was a filmed cartoon character.

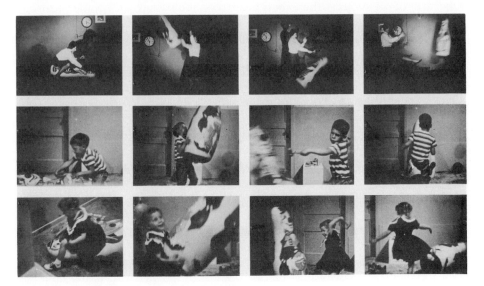

In the Bobo doll studies, children exhibited aggressive behavior after observing an aggressive model.

The effect of the model in all three forms was to elicit the same kind of behavior—behavior that was not displayed at the same intensity by other children of the same age who had not viewed the same model.

In another example of the impact of modeling on learning, Bandura compared the behavior of parents of two groups of children (Bandura & Walters, 1963). One group was made up of very aggressive children, the other of more inhibited children. According to the modeling theory, children's behavior imitates their parents' behavior. Thus, the parents of the inhibited children should be inhibited and the parents of the aggressive children should be aggressive. The study revealed this to be the case.

Other experiments have shown that an already existing form of behavior that is usually suppressed or inhibited may be performed more readily under the influence of an appropriate model (Bandura & Walters, 1963). This phenomenon, called **disinhibition** by Bandura, refers to the weakening of an inhibition through exposure to a model. There are many examples of disinhibition in everyday life. A person in a crowd (a lynch mob or a protest demonstration, for example) often performs acts that he or she would never have been able to perform if alone. A person is much more likely to violate prohibitions if he or she sees others violating them.

One experiment demonstrated that sexual responses can be disinhibited by models (Walters, Bowen & Parke, 1963). A group of male college undergraduates was shown a film that contained a series of erotic pictures of nude females and males. They were told that a spot of light that moved over the film indicated the eye movements of a previous subject, showing which parts of the pictures that subject had looked at. This represented the model. For half of the subjects, the light roamed over the bodies of the nudes, concentrating on the breasts and genitals. For the other half of the subjects, the light remained on the background of the picture, as though the subject had avoided looking at the nude bodies.

After watching this film, each subject was shown slides made from the movie sequences. By means of a special camera, the subjects' eye movements were recorded as they looked at each picture. Those subjects whose model was uninhibited (looking directly at the nude bodies) did the same thing. Those subjects whose model had avoided looking at the nudes spent significantly more time looking at the backgrounds of the pictures than at the figures.

Thus, it seems that modeling can influence not only overt behavior with respect to an object but also perceptual responses to an object. Modeling can determine not only what we do but also what we look at and what we perceive.

On the basis of his extensive research, Bandura is convinced that much of human behavior—both good and bad, normal and abnormal—is learned by imitation. From infancy on, we develop our behavioral repertoire in response to the many models society offers us. Beginning with parents as models, we learn a language and become socialized in line with the mores and customs of our culture.

The individual who deviates from the cultural norms—the delinquent, neurotic, criminal, or psychopath—has learned his or her behavior in the same way that everyone else has. The difference is that the deviant person has followed a different model—one not considered desirable by the rest of society. Bandura has been greatly concerned about the wrong models our culture provides to children, particularly the models of violent behavior that are regular fare on television, including on children's cartoon programs. He has spoken and written forcefully against these models since his research (and that of others) has clearly shown how effective they are in influencing behavior. If what we see is what we become, the distance between watching Bobo being attacked on television and then committing an act of violence ourselves is not very great.

There is no limit to the new behaviors children can acquire through modeling, including nonrational fears. A child who sees his or her father become fearful every time there is a thunderstorm or sees his or her mother become nervous every time she is around strangers will easily acquire these same fears and carry them through to adult life with no awareness of their origin. Of course, strength and courage in the face of difficulties and hope and optimism in the face of new experiences can be just as easily learned. In Skinner's system, we saw that the person who controls the reinforcers can control behavior. In Bandura's view, the person who controls the models controls behavior.

In a typical modeling experiment, the subject observes another person (the model) in the performance of some behavior or sequence of behaviors. Some time after this observation, the subject is observed, to determine if his or her behavior imitates the behavior of the model. The subject's behavior, as compared with that of a control group of subjects who did not observe the model, indicates how fully or completely modeling has occurred.

Using this kind of experiment, Bandura and his associates have investigated three factors that can influence modeling: the characteristics of the models, the attributes of the observers, and the reward consequences associated with the behavior (Bandura, 1977).

Characteristics of the models

The *characteristics of the models* will certainly affect imitation. In real life, we may be more prone to be influenced by someone who appears to be very like ourselves than by someone who differs from us in obvious and significant ways. So it is in the laboratory. For example, although children imitate the behavior of a child model in the same room, of a child in a film, and of a filmed cartoon character, the extent of the modeling decreases as the similarity between the model and the subject decreases. There is greater imitation of a live model than of a cartoon character (although in both cases the modeling behavior is significantly greater than that of control subjects).

Other characteristics of the model that may determine the extent of imitation include the model's age and sex, relative to the subject. For example, we are more likely to model our behavior after a person of the same sex than after a person of the opposite sex. An adult model might well induce more imitation in a 4-year-old than in a 16-year-old who is struggling for independence from adults. In general, however, subjects are more likely to be influenced by models their own age. Peers who seem to have solved problems similar to those faced by the subject are highly influential models.

Other important characteristics of models are status and prestige. In one study it was found that pedestrians were much more likely to cross an intersection against a red light if they saw a well-dressed person do so than if they saw a poorly dressed person do so. (In both cases, the model was the same person.) Television advertising makes effective use of high-status, high-prestige models with athletic or movie stars who claim to use a particular product.

The kind of behavior performed by the model will also influence the extent of imitation. Highly complex behaviors are not imitated as quickly or readily as simpler behaviors. Hostile and aggressive responses consistently tend to be strongly imitated, at least by children.

Characteristics of the observers

The *attributes of the observers* are also a force in determining the effectiveness of modeling. Some people, particularly those who are low in self-confidence and self-esteem, are much more likely to imitate a model's behavior than those who are high in these attributes. Also, persons who have been reinforced in the past for imitating someone's behavior—for example, a person who as a child was rewarded for behaving like her mother—are likely to be susceptible to the influence of models.

Reward consequences of the behavior

In addition, the *reward consequences associated with the behavior* may affect the power of the modeling situation. Bandura believes that these consequences are capable of overriding the other two factors. For example, a high-status model may cause a person to imitate the behavior being displayed, but if the reward consequences are not sufficient, the subject will discontinue the behavior and be less likely to be dominated by that model in the future.

The processes of observational learning

In addition to investigating the variables that influence modeling, Bandura has carefully analyzed the nature of observational learning and found it to be governed by four interrelated processes or mechanisms: attentional processes, retention processes, motor reproduction processes, and incentive and motivational processes (Bandura, 1977).

Attentional processes

Attentional processes govern observational learning by virtue of the fact that modeling will not occur unless the subject attends to the model. Merely exposing the subject to the model does not guarantee that the subject will be attentive to the relevant cues, will select the most relevant stimulus events, or will even perceive the stimulus situation accurately. It is not sufficient for the subject merely to see the model and what it is doing; the subject must attend to the model with enough perceptual accuracy to acquire the necessary information to use in imitating the model. A number of variables (including some discussed earlier) can influence how closely the subject attends to the behavior of the model. In the real world, as in the laboratory, we are more attentive and responsive to some people (and some situations) than to others.

We have mentioned such characteristics as age and sex of the model and degree of similarity between the model and the subject. These factors can determine how closely a subject will attend. It has also been found that models who appear high in competence, who are alleged to be experts, or who are celebrities command greater attention than models who lack these attributes. In general, any set of characteristics that causes a model to be perceived as more attractive increases the probability of more careful attention to the model and, consequently, the probability of imitation.

Some of the most effective models in our culture today, in terms of their ability to capture attention, are those who appear on television. So powerful are televised models, Bandura argues, that viewers attend to what they say and do in the absence of any reinforcement or other incentive. (Whether they imitate the behavior displayed depends, in part, on the reward consequences.)

Retention processes

A second mechanism in observational learning involves the *retention processes*. Unless the subject is imitating a model's behavior as that behavior is taking place, or immediately afterward, the subject must retain or remember all significant aspects of the behavior. If the subject cannot remember the behavior, he or she will not be able to imitate it five days or five minutes after observing it.

In order to retain what has been attended to, it is necessary, in some fashion, to encode and represent symbolically what has been seen. This internal process of symbolic representation is, as has been noted, a basic point of difference between the approach of Bandura and that of Skinner. The admission of cognitive processes (image formation and problem solving, for example) into his system means that Bandura recognizes certain inner aspects of the person to be operative in the development and modification of behavior. Thus, his focus is not exclusively on overt behavior, as is the case with Skinner.

Bandura proposes two internal representational systems—*imaginal* and *verbal*—as means by which the behavior of the model is retained by the subject. While observing the model, the subject forms easily retrievable images of what he or she has seen. The images are formed through a process of conditioning, so that any reference to events previously observed immediately calls forth a vivid image or picture of the physical stimuli involved, even though they are no longer present. This is a common phenomenon and accounts for your being able to see an image of the person you had a date with last week or an image of a particular place you visited last summer. We can form an image of the event or the model and then use that image as a basis for imitating the model's behavior quite some time after we actually experienced it.

The other representational system, the verbal, is similar to image formation and involves a verbal coding of something we have previously observed. During the original observation, a subject might verbally describe to himself or herself what the model is doing. These verbal descriptions (codes) can later be rehearsed internally, without an overt display of the behavior; for example, a person might talk through to himself or herself the steps in a complicated skill. In that situation, the person is silently rehearsing a sequence of behavior to be performed at a later time, and, when he or she does wish to perform the skill, the verbal code will provide cues. Together these symbolic representations—images and verbal symbols—provide the means by which we store or retain the observed events and rehearse them for later performance.

Motor reproduction processes

Translating these symbolic representations into overt behavior is what is involved in the third mechanism of observational learning, the *motor reproduction processes*. Even though a person may have carefully formed and retained symbolic representations of a model's behavior and silently rehearsed that behavior many times, he or she still may not be able to perform the behavior correctly. This is particularly applicable to highly skilled acts that require many individual component behaviors for their successful performance.

Consider the highly complex skill of driving a car. The fundamental movements involved may be learned by watching someone else drive, and the symbolic representation of the model's behavior may be repeated internally a number of times, but the translation into actual behavior will be rough and clumsy at first. Mere observation in this case is not sufficient to achieve a smooth and skillful performance of the act. Actual practice in performing the motor movements (and feedback on their correctness) is needed to refine the behavior. However, as indicated, observing and silently rehearsing some behaviors is of definite help in learning, for the person is at least able to begin to perform the necessary movements on the basis of his or her retention of what had been earlier observed. This internal rehearsal is helpful with skills such as driving, but may not be as useful with more sophisticated skills, such as playing the violin.

Incentive and motivational processes

The fourth mechanism of observational learning involves *incentive and motivational processes*. No matter how well we attend to and retain the behavior of a model, or how much ability we possess to perform that behavior, we will not perform it without sufficient incentive or motivation to do so. When sufficient incentives are available, modeling or observational learning is quickly translated into action. Proper incentive not only brings about the actual performance of the behavior, but also influences the attentional and retention processes. We do not pay as much attention to something when no incentive impels us to, and when little attention has been paid, there is little or nothing to retain.

One way in which incentive to attend, retain, and perform a certain behavior may be influenced is through the anticipation of reinforcement or punishment for so doing. The observation that the model's behavior produced some positive reward, or avoided some negative reinforcement, can be a strong incentive to attend to, retain, and later (when in a similar situation) perform that behavior. The reinforcement is thus experienced vicariously during the observation, after which the subject can anticipate that his or her performance of the same behavior will lead to the same consequences.

Bandura is careful to point out that while reinforcement can indeed facilitate learning, it is not necessary in order that learning take place. There are many factors other than the reward consequences of behavior that can determine what people will attend to. We attend to loud sounds, bright lights, interesting displays, and unusual stimuli, without receiving reinforcement for doing so.

In his experiments, Bandura has shown that children watching a model on television have imitated the model's behavior regardless of whether they had been told in advance that such imitation would lead to reinforcement. Reinforcement, therefore, can aid in modeling, but it is not vital to it. When reinforcement does occur, it can be experienced vicariously, given directly by another, or given by the self.

The self

The *self*, in Bandura's approach to personality, is not some psychic agent that determines or causes our behavior. Rather, the self is defined in terms of "cognitive structures that provide reference mechanisms" and "a set of subfunctions for the perception, evaluation, and regulation of behavior" (Bandura, 1978, p. 348). The self, therefore, is not an entity but a set of cognitive processes and structures concerned with thought and perception. Two aspects of the self are of particular importance: self-reinforcement and self-efficacy.

Self-reinforcement

Self-reinforcement, Bandura argues, can be at least as important as reinforcement administered by others, particularly for older children and adults. People often set standards of behavior or achievement for themselves in their various activities, and then reward or punish themselves for meeting, exceeding, or falling short of their own expectations. This self-administered reward may be simply a feeling of pride or satisfaction; self-administered punishment may consist of shame or guilt or depression about not having behaved the way one wanted to.

As an example of self-reinforcement, Bandura discussed the act of writing. As I write each page of this book, there is no one sitting by my side to reinforce each sentence or paragraph by telling me how good or bad it is. External reinforcement does not come until many months after the book is written, through reviews and the comments of friends and colleagues. During the writing, I reinforce myself in terms of my personal standard for acceptable work. When a chapter meets my standard, the act of writing is reinforced by a pleasing feeling of accomplishment and satisfaction. When a passage falls short of that standard, I may feel frustrated or depressed. I then must revise the work or begin again, until I feel it is good enough.

Bandura believes that most of our behavior is regulated by this continuing process of self-reinforcement. As we can see from the writing example, self-reinforcement requires some internal standard of performance, a subjective criterion or reference point against which behavior is constantly evaluated. Often, one's past behavior becomes the reference point for evaluating present behavior. This can also serve as an incentive for better performance in the future. When a certain level of achievement is reached, it may no longer challenge or motivate the person, and so the standard will be raised. Failure to achieve, however, may result in a lowering of the level to a more realistic point.

The initial set of internal standards is usually learned from the behavior of models, particularly parents and other significant people in a child's life. Once having adopted the model's standard or style of behavior, one begins to evaluate one's own behavior against that standard.

Self-efficacy

How well we meet our standards determines our sense of **self-efficacy,** the second important aspect of the self in Bandura's system. Self-efficacy refers to our sense of self-esteem and self-worth, a feeling of adequacy and efficiency in dealing with life. Bandura refers to it as our perception of our ability "to produce and to regulate events" in our lives (Bandura, 1982, p. 122). Meeting and maintaining our performance standards enhances our self-efficacy. Failure to meet and maintain those standards reduces personal efficacy.

People who set unrealistically high standards of performance—who have modeled their behavioral expectations on extraordinarily effective and successful models and who continually try to meet those standards despite persistent failure—may punish themselves severely. Such behavior can easily lead to depression, discouragement, self-disparagement, and feelings of worthlessness.

These self-produced feelings may result in a variety of undesirable behaviors. Bandura has noted that people who are low in self-efficacy may turn to alcohol, to resignation, or to a world of fantasy in which they are able to achieve at a level beyond their capacity. However it is finally expressed, low self-efficacy leads to emotional misery.

Persons low in self-efficacy feel helpless, unable to exercise any influence over the events and conditions that affect them. As a result, they believe that any effort they make is futile and worthless. Not surprisingly, they are despondent and highly anxious. When they encounter obstacles or problems, they quickly give up if their initial attempts to overcome them are ineffective. Those extremely low in self-efficacy will not even attempt to cope because of their deep conviction that nothing they do will make any difference. It is not difficult to understand why such people become "apathetic and resigned to a dreary life" (Bandura, 1982, p. 141).

Persons high in self-efficacy believe that they are capable of dealing effectively with the events in their lives. This gives them an outlook that is different from that of people who are low in self-efficacy and has a direct impact on their behavior. Because high self-efficacy persons expect success in overcoming obstacles, they will persist in their efforts much longer than those who are low in self-efficacy. They have greater confidence in their abilities and are not overwhelmed by self-doubt. They tend to persevere at tasks, and as a result often perform at a high level.

Self-efficacy can influence nearly all aspects of life. In one's choice of a career, sex differences in self-efficacy have been found to play an important role. Research has shown that men perceive themselves to be equally high in self-efficacy for both traditionally male and traditionally female occupations. Women perceive themselves as high in self-efficacy for so-called female occupations but low in self-efficacy for occupations traditionally held by males. Both men and women subjects in this research had performed at comparable levels on standardized tests of verbal and quantitative skills. Thus, they possessed the same measurable abilities. The difference lay in how they perceived their abilities, that is, their feelings about their own adequacy in dealing with the problems of a career (Betz & Hackett, 1981).

We shall see later that level of self-efficacy is also influential in therapy situations, affecting a person's expectations about whether the therapy will succeed. In turn, the more effective therapy is, the more likely it is to enhance one's level of efficacy.

Bandura believes that our judgment about our level of efficacy is based on four sources of information: performance attainment, vicarious experiences, verbal persuasion and other types of social influence, and physiological arousal (Bandura, 1982).

The most influential source of efficacy judgments is *performance attainment.* Previous success experiences at various tasks provide direct indications of our level of mastery and competence. Prior achievements demonstrate our capabilities and, in the process, strengthen our feelings of self-efficacy. Prior failures, particularly repeated failures, lower our sense of efficacy.

Vicarious experiences, seeing other people perform successfully, can also strengthen feelings of efficacy, particularly if the people being observed are judged to be similar in abilities. It follows that seeing others fail can lower self-efficacy. Effective models are, therefore, important in influencing our feelings of adequacy and competence. Such models can also demonstrate effective strategies and techniques for dealing with difficult situations.

Verbal persuasion, that is, telling people that they possess the requisite abilities to achieve what they want to achieve, can also enhance self-efficacy. This may be the most common of the four sources and the one regularly used by parents, teachers, spouses, friends, and therapists. To be effective, however, verbal persuasion must take place in a realistic context. It is pointless, for example, to tell someone who is five feet, two inches tall that he or she has the ability to play professional basketball.

A fourth source of information about self-efficacy is our level of *physiological arousal*. We often use this information—such as our level of fear or calmness in a stressful situation—as a basis for judging our ability to cope. Bandura noted that "people are more inclined to expect success when they are not beset by aversive arousal than if they are tense and viscerally agitated. In activities involving strength and stamina, people read their fatigue, aches, and pains as indicants of physical efficacy" (Bandura, 1982, p. 127).

The developmental stages of modeling

According to Bandura, modeling develops over time as a function of age and maturation level. In infancy, modeling is limited to immediate imitation. Infants have not yet developed the cognitive capacities, particularly the imaginal and verbal internal representational systems, that are needed to imitate a model's behavior some time after it has been observed. In infancy it is necessary that the modeled behavior be repeated a number of times after the infant attempts to duplicate it. The modeled behavior must be possible within the infant's level of sensorimotor development, that is, within its restricted repertoire of behaviors. At about the age of 2, children are ready to begin imitating behavior some time after it has been observed.

In addition to expanded sensorimotor and cognitive abilities, the actual behaviors people find reinforcing change with age. Infants and children are reinforced primarily by immediate physical stimuli such as food, punishment, or affection. As people grow older, physical reinforcements come to be associated with signs of approval from significant models, usually the parents, and unpleasant or punishing experiences come to be associated with signs of disapproval.

Because of these repeated associations or connections, the social reactions of approval or disapproval from others take on reinforcing characteristics and become in themselves incentives capable of guiding behavior. At the highest stage of childhood development we internalize our parents' ideal behaviors, and reinforcement as well as punishment is administered by the self. We also set our performance standards in accordance with the standards reinforced by our parents. By the time of adulthood, the significant attitudes and behaviors that make up our personality have been learned through the developmental stages of modeling.

Modifying learned behavior

Bandura had a practical goal in the development of his theory of social learning: to learn how best to modify or change behavior that is considered undesirable or abnormal. If behavior is initially learned through the principles of observational learning, it should be possible to change or relearn behavior—to eliminate undesirable acts and replace them with new ones. As we discussed in Chapter 14, Skinner uses behavior-modification techniques based on operant conditioning. Like Skinner's approach to therapy, that of Bandura focuses on external aspects of abnormality—inappropriate or destructive behaviors—in the belief that these, like all other behaviors, are learned. He does not refer to underlying unconscious conflicts that must be uncovered and then relieved. It is the behavior or symptom, rather than any presumed inner cause for a neurosis, that is the target of the social-learning approach to abnormality. In essence, Bandura believes that to treat the symptom is to treat the disorder; they are one and the same.

If modeling is the basic procedure by which we learn our behaviors originally, it should be an equally effective way of changing behavior. Modeling has been used as a device to eliminate fears and other intense emotional reactions. In one case, young children who were afraid of dogs observed a child of the same age playing with a dog. While the subjects watched from a safe distance, the model made progressively bolder movements with respect to the dog. Initially, the model petted the dog through the bars of a playpen in which the dog had been placed. Finally, the child model went inside the pen and played openly and cheerfully with the dog. The observers' fears of dogs were considerably reduced as a result of this observational learning (Bandura, Grusec & Menlove, 1967).

In a famous study with snakes, Bandura and his associates were able to eliminate an intensive fear of snakes in adult subjects (Bandura, Blanchard & Ritter, 1969). The subjects watched a film in which children, adolescents, and adults displayed progressively closer contact with a snake. At first the models handled plastic snakes, then real ones, and finally they let a large snake crawl freely over their bodies. A subject was allowed to stop the film whenever the scenes became too threatening and to move the film back to less threatening scenes. The fear of snakes was gradually overcome.

A more effective modeling procedure involved first watching a live model and then actively participating with the model, a technique known as *guided participation*. Initially, the subject watched a model who was boldly handling a snake on the opposite side of an observation window. Then the subject entered the same room with the model and observed the handling of the snake at close range. Next, wearing gloves, the subject was coaxed into touching the middle of the snake while the model held the tail and head. The subject then touched the snake without gloves and made progressively bolder approach movements.

You may be thinking that a fear of snakes is not so terrible; most of us live in cities, not in snake-infested areas. However, overcoming a fear of snakes has brought about astonishing changes in the behavior of the subjects, even those who live in places that are completely free of snakes. In addition to bolstering self-esteem and self-efficacy, getting rid of a snake phobia changes personal and work lives. One female subject was able to wear necklaces for the first time; previously, she had not been able to do so because they reminded her of snakes. A real-estate agent was able to increase his income because he was no longer afraid to visit houses in rural areas. Almost all of the persons treated by modeling therapy were freed from nightmares involving snakes.

Bandura points out that modeling, particularly when it makes use of films, offers several practical advantages in therapy. Complex behaviors can be seen as a whole, and extraneous behaviors can be edited out, so that time is spent viewing only that which is relevant to the behavior problem being treated. Second, once a film is made, it can be less expensive than the continued use of live models, since it can be repeated easily and used by many therapists simultaneously. The modeling technique, on film or live, can be used with groups of patients, circumventing the more expensive and time-consuming practice of treating people who have the same problem individually.

Effects on self-efficacy

Although this approach to behavior modification deals primarily with overt behavior, Bandura has become increasingly concerned with its beneficial effects on cognitive variables, particularly self-efficacy. In the treatment of snake phobia, for example, modeling as a technique of therapy changed not only overt behavior but also feelings and attitudes. The successfully treated person not only could handle snakes, but also no longer feared touching them, and thus came to have a higher feeling of competence or efficacy in that situation. The person's expectancies and self-perceptions had been strengthened, and he or she therefore felt more adequate and capable of dealing with an aspect of daily living that previously had been associated with low self-efficacy.

A number of research studies have been conducted on behavior and self-efficacy during and after behavior-modification therapy. The results have shown that as the subjects' self-efficacy improved during treatment they were increasingly able to deal with the object that had earlier been a strong source of fear. It was the therapeutic procedure itself that enhanced self-efficacy.

Consider, again, a snake phobia. Adult subjects who were intensely fearful of snakes had their avoidance behavior measured prior to therapy by a behavioral-avoidance test consisting of 29 tasks involving increasing closeness to and interaction with a live boa constrictor (Bandura, Adams & Beyer, 1977). The final task was to let the snake rest in the subject's lap. As you might imagine, no one got that far on the tasks before the therapy sessions began.

The subjects' self-efficacy was measured by having them rate their expectations of how far they would proceed with the 29 tasks on the behavioral-avoidance test. These expectations were rated again after treatment, but before retaking the behavioral-avoidance test. Expectations were also rated one month later.

The subjects were divided into three conditions: modeling, in which subjects observed a woman therapist engage in increasingly threatening contacts with a snake; participant modeling, in which they observed the therapist and participated in increasingly threatening contacts with the snake; and control, in which they took the behavioral-avoidance and self-efficacy tests but received no modeling therapy.

Subjects in the modeling and participant-modeling groups showed significant increases in their ratings of self-efficacy and in their approach behavior on the behavior-avoidance test, as compared with the control group. Further, the self-efficacy ratings correlated highly with actual behavior. The higher the scores on the self-efficacy ratings taken after treatment, the greater the number of tasks performed on the behavioral-avoidance test. A month later, these increases in self-efficacy and in approach behavior to the snake had even shown improvement.

There may be virtually no limit to the kinds of behaviors that can be modified through the modeling approach. Let us briefly consider two additional examples: fear of medical treatment among children, and test anxiety among college students.

Effects on anxiety

Many people have such a strong fear of dentists, doctors, and hospitals that they are unable to seek necessary medical treatment. Modeling, primarily through films, has been highly successful in eliminating these fears. In one study, children who were scheduled to go in the hospital for surgery, and who had never been in a hospital for that reason before, were divided into two groups: an experimental group, which watched a film about a young boy's experiences in the hospital, and a control group, which viewed a film about a boy taking a trip in the country (Melamed & Siegel, 1975). The boy in the hospital film was an exemplary model; despite his initial anxiety, he coped well with all medical procedures.

Anxiety in the subjects was assessed by three techniques we discussed in Chapter 14: direct observation of behavior, responses on self-report inventories, and physiological measures. These assessments were carried out on the night before the subjects underwent surgery and again three to four weeks later. The results showed that the modeling film had been effective in reducing anxiety. In addition, subjects who had seen the film demonstrated fewer behavior problems after they left the hospital than did subjects in the control group.

Anxiety about college examinations has also been treated by modeling techniques. It is such a serious problem for some students that their test performance will not accurately reflect their knowledge of the material being tested.

Based on performance on a personality test, college students were divided into two groups: those high in test anxiety and those low in test anxiety (Sarason, 1975). Some of the students viewed a film in which a woman model talked about her anxiety when taking examinations and her methods of coping with it. Another group saw a film of the same model, who talked only about her test-taking anxiety, with no mention of any coping mechanisms. A third group of subjects watched the person on film talking about her activities on campus but saying nothing about tests or test-taking.

The subjects were given a list of nonsense syllables to memorize and then were tested on their ability to recall them. The results showed that those subjects high in test anxiety had been most strongly affected by the coping model. They performed significantly better on the nonsense-syllable test than did high-anxiety subjects who had been exposed to the other two films.

Modeling has been shown to be so successful in modifying behavior that it can work even in the absence of a model. In an approach known as *covert modeling*, subjects imagine a model coping with a feared or threatening situation; they do not actually see a model. This has been used to treat snake phobias and to induce people to behave more assertively in social situations (Kazdin, 1975, 1979).

There are a great many variations, integrations, and combinations of behavior therapy techniques—too many to cover fully in a text devoted to theories of personality. The important point here is to show that very practical and successful therapeutic techniques have resulted from a conception of personality formulated in social-learning terms. Since the 1960s, hundreds of articles have been published on behavior-modification techniques. Such techniques have become increasingly popular as alternatives to psychoanalysis and to other psychotherapeutic approaches. Rather than trying to bring about changes in personality, behavior therapy tries to change the overt manifestation of personality; it tries to change behavior.

Ethical issues in behavior modification

Although the techniques of behavior change are impressive, they have drawn widespread professional and public criticism because they are alleged to be based on an inhuman and manipulative approach to human beings. Behavior modification has aroused passionate attacks in newspapers and magazines by educators, government officials, and other interested individuals because, they charge, it is sometimes used to manipulate individuals without their awareness.

Bandura has reacted sharply to these charges. It is not, he says, behavior modification that should be called inhuman. Rather, other therapeutic techniques that are not effective deserve that label. What is inhuman, he argues, is to refuse to use the most efficient technique available to help a person who is having difficulties. To do nothing for such a person, or to string him or her along for years in a doubtful program of therapy, is inhuman, not only for the individual but also for his or her family and friends and, ultimately, for all of society.

Bandura believes that the accusation of manipulative control of an individual through behavior modification is a totally false and misleading charge. For one thing, such control does not take place without the knowledge of the subject. As we have seen, Bandura has posited self-awareness and self-regulation as operative in the behavior change process. Modification of behavior does not occur, Bandura argues, unless the person is able to understand what is being reinforced. Second, Bandura suggests that it is wrong to talk about control, since it is the individuals who decide what it is about themselves they want changed. It is the client who comes to the therapist because he or she wants to eliminate a fear of snakes, a girdle fetish, or an inability to walk on a sidewalk with other people. Bandura suggests that this is analogous to going to a dentist with a toothache: the client has a problem that he or she would like to have relieved. The client–therapist relationship is therefore a contract between two consenting individuals, not a master–slave relationship.

Finally, Bandura feels that, far from manipulating or enslaving an individual, behavior modification actually increases the person's freedom. A woman who cannot leave the house, a man who can go out only if he wears a girdle, or a person who must wash his or her hands 20 times each hour is not fully free. Such people are living within the constraints imposed by their own behavior. And sometimes those constraints are very binding, allowing the person little, if any, free choice about how to behave. By removing these constraining symptoms, Bandura argues, behavior modification greatly increases the individual's true freedom and allows more opportunity for personal growth.

Bandura's image of human nature

Bandura's position is clear on the issue of free will versus determinism. Behavior is controlled both by the person, through the operation of cognitive processes, and by the environment, through external social stimulus events. He calls this view **reciprocal determinism** and notes that people are neither "powerless objects controlled by environmental forces nor free agents who can become whatever they choose. Both people and their environments are reciprocal determinants of each other" (Bandura, 1977, p. vii).

Although human behavior is influenced by external social stimuli, the individual is not considered a helpless robot with respect to outside events. Responses are not triggered automatically by external stimuli. Rather, the reactions to these stimuli are self-activated in accordance with learned anticipations. The individual is able to observe and interpret the effects of his or her own behavior and, in that way, determine which behaviors are appropriate in which situations. People are able to encode and symbolize environmental events and to anticipate that a certain behavior will bring a certain response. Thus, we choose and shape many of our behaviors in order to gain anticipated rewards or avoid anticipated pain.

Acknowledged, in this view, are self-awareness, self-reinforcement, and other forms of internal regulation of behavior. Reinforcement does not automatically change human behavior. When it does bring about a change, it does so because the individual is aware of what is being reinforced and anticipates the same reinforcement for behaving in the same way again. Thus, some degree of self-direction interacts with past and present social stimulus events. We are influenced by external forces, but we are also able to regulate and guide the extent and direction of such influences.

The introduction of the notion of inner- or self-direction of behavior (in combination with external stimuli) represents an optimistic view of human nature. Indeed, Bandura refers to himself as a devoted optimist because of his belief that individuals can, in part, create their own environments and because he believes abnormal behavior is nothing more than bad habits (Kiester & Cudhea, 1974, p. 30). Inappropriate or destructive behavior results from learning and, therefore, is amenable to change by the same techniques and principles by which it was originally acquired. If bad behavior is learned from the social environment, then good behavior can be learned just as easily.

On the nature–nurture issue, Bandura's position is also clear-cut. Most of our behavior, except for basic reflexes, is learned; genetic factors play a minor role in behavior. Bandura recognizes, however, that hereditary factors such as physical development, body type, and appearance can influence the kinds of reinforcements people receive, particularly in childhood. For example, children who are physically clumsy, small for their age, or unattractive will receive different reinforcements from children who are agile, tall, and adorable.

Bandura takes note of the importance of childhood experiences, and his view suggests that childhood learning may be more influential than learning that takes place in adulthood. Our internal performance standards, which profoundly affect our sense of self-efficacy, are established in childhood, along with our set of ideal or good behaviors. However, childhood experiences can be unlearned later in life, and new performance standards and ideal behaviors may be substituted for them. Thus, we are not captives of the reinforcing events of our early years.

Bandura has not discussed the question of uniqueness or universality of behavior. Because at least some of our behavior results from experience—and no two people have identical experiences—it may be inferred that he views each of us as unique. It may also be assumed that Bandura's ultimate and necessary goal in life is the setting of performance standards that are realistic in light of our past performance, so that our sense of self-efficacy may be maintained at a sufficient level.

Assessment in Bandura's theory

Like Skinner, Bandura focuses on behavior rather than on any inner, motivating variables that might constitute personality. As such, Bandura does not use the kinds of assessment techniques, such as free association, dream analysis, or projective techniques, preferred by other therapists we have discussed. Unlike Skinner, however, Bandura does admit the operation of certain cognitive variables, and these, as well as behavior itself, can be assessed. This is particularly true, as we have seen, in the research on and applications of behavior modification. We have already discussed examples of specific assessment techniques used in Bandura's approach.

In the modeling study involving children about to undergo surgery, the subjects were assessed by direct observation, by self-report inventories, and by physiological measures. In studies relating behavior to self-efficacy, both behavioral and cognitive variables have been assessed by precise quantitative techniques. Avoidance behavior with respect to snakes, for example, was assessed by performance on a 29-item behavioral-avoidance test. Self-efficacy was assessed by subjects' ratings of their expectations of the number of behavioral-avoidance tasks they would be able to complete. College students' test anxiety was assessed by a personality test.

Thus, assessment of both behavioral and cognitive variables is important in the social-learning approach, and self-report techniques are used widely for the assessment of cognitive variables. The primary purpose of all these assessment devices is the functional analysis of behavior and the relevant cognitive variables.

Research in Bandura's theory

Bandura favors well-controlled laboratory investigations in the rigorous tradition of experimental psychology. We have described examples of his use of experimental and control groups, as well as his precise measurement of independent and dependent variables. Unlike Skinner, who prefers the single-subject approach, Bandura studies large groups of subjects whose average performances are compared by statistical analysis. He has chosen subjects who exhibit diverse behavioral disorders such as phobias, alcoholism, fetishism, and frigidity, as well as many nonneurotic behaviors. The ages of the subjects range from preschool to adult. Bandura's social-learning theory is probably based on the broadest range of human subjects studied by any theorist we have discussed, a fact that increases the generalizability of his research findings.

Hundreds of studies have been conducted on the modeling process, providing an impressive body of empirical support. We have already offered a few examples of these studies. Bandura formulated his theory on the basis of sound research and continues to develop and apply it along the same lines.

A final commentary

The learning-theory approach to personality, as represented by Skinner, Bandura, and Rotter (Chapter 16), is seen by many research psychologists and clinicians as one of the most exciting and productive innovations in the study and treatment of personality in the 20th century. The great number of books, articles, and research studies attests to its current popularity, both as a means of studying behavior in the laboratory and as a way of changing behavior in the clinic.

Increasing numbers of psychologists are being trained in the theory and technique of observational learning, and the vigor—indeed passion—with which the adherents of this approach defend and extend the theory seems to guarantee the continued growth of interest in it.

Bandura ranked 17th among 286 psychologists in terms of his importance to American psychology and 8th among the personality theorists described in this book. These rankings may be considered high when we remember how relatively recent Bandura's work is, compared with that of the other theorists. In 1980, the American Psychological Association awarded Bandura the Distinguished Scientific Contribution Award, citing his "masterful modeling as researcher, teacher, and theoretician" (APA, 1980, p. 27). In 1984, a leading personality researcher wrote, "Social learning theory is probably the current favorite among academic personality psychologists, and a good number of clinicians would also label themselves social learning psychologists" (Pervin, 1984b, p. 434).

The social-learning approach enjoys additional advantages. First, it is highly objective and directly amenable to precise laboratory methods of investigation, making it congruent with the strong emphasis on experimental research that characterizes the mainstream of psychology in the United States. Most psychologists of an experimental persuasion reject other theoretical work in the area of personality because it posits unconscious and other internal driving forces, which cannot be manipulated or measured under laboratory conditions.

There is a great deal of empirical data to support Bandura's approach to personality. Second, observational learning and the derivative behavior modification seem directly compatible with the functional, pragmatic spirit that defines so much of American psychology. Much more readily than other approaches, observational-learning techniques can be taken from the laboratory and applied directly to problems in the real world. And there is more immediate reinforcement for the efforts of the practitioner than with more traditional approaches. The practitioner is able to see dramatic changes in a client's behavior within weeks or even days.

Critics of this approach argue that social learning, like Skinner's more extreme behaviorism, deals with only the peripheral aspects of personality—a person's overt behavior. This emphasis on overt behavior, critics suggest, misses or ignores our distinctly human aspects—conscious and unconscious motivating forces. It is perhaps analogous to a physician trying to treat a patient who complains of stomach pains by dealing only with what the patient says and does—by trying to get the patient to stop doubling over, pressing on his stomach, and saying "It hurts." What is necessary in this case, critics say, is medicine or surgery; the physician must get to the underlying source of the behavior—the afflicted internal organ. A related charge is that if only the symptom is treated and not the cause of the disorder, substitute symptoms are bound to appear, because the cause remains unaffected. This charge has not been supported by the research to date.

Other criticisms deal with Bandura's positing of cognitive variables. Radical (Skinnerian) behaviorists complain that such variables are not necessary to account for or to change behavior, and that they cannot be dealt with precisely, as can overt behavior. Other critics charge that Bandura's writings are unclear about how cognitive variables affect behavior. What, for example, are the processes by which these variables exert their influence? Still others suggest that Bandura ignores the roles of emotion and conflict in directing human behavior.

Whatever the eventual status of social-learning theory in the study of personality, there is no doubt that it is a potent force in psychology. Growing numbers of psychologists are modeling their behavior after that of Bandura and are evidently finding sufficient reinforcement for so doing.

Summary

Not enough information is available on Bandura's childhood to allow us to speculate on the relationship between his theory and his own experiences. He criticized Skinner for studying animals rather than humans in social interactions, for believing that behavior can be learned or changed only through directly experienced reinforcement, and for ignoring all cognitive variables. Bandura believes that behavior can be learned through vicarious reinforcement, that is, by observing the behavior of others and anticipating the reinforcement consequences of behaving in the same way. This emphasis on learning by observation or example is the most distinctive feature of his approach.

The mediating mechanisms between stimulus and response are the person's cognitive processes, which bring about a control of behavior through self-regulation and self-reinforcement. Directly experienced reinforcement is an inefficient, time-consuming, and potentially dangerous way of changing behavior. Operant conditioning, in which trial-and-error behavior persists until the correct response is found, is a poor way of teaching new skills. An accident could occur before the person happened upon the sequence of behaviors that would lead to positive reinforcement.

In the famous Bobo doll study, children modeled their behavior after the aggressive behavior of the model, whether the model was observed live, on television, or in a cartoon.

Disinhibition involves the weakening of an inhibition through exposure to a model. Thus, behavior that is usually suppressed or inhibited may be performed more readily under the influence of a model.

Persons who deviate from societal norms, such as neurotics or criminals, have learned such behavior by observing inappropriate models.

Three factors can influence modeling: the characteristics of the model, the attributes of the observers, and the reward consequences associated with the behavior. People are more likely to be influenced by a model who is similar to themselves in age, sex, and other personal characteristics, who has solved similar problems, and who is high in status and prestige. Simple behaviors are imitated more readily than complex behaviors. Aggressive responses tend to be strongly imitated. Some persons more likely to imitate a model's behavior have been found to rate low in self-esteem and self-confidence. Also, they have been reinforced in the past for imitating the behavior of others.

Observational learning is governed by four processes: (1) attentional processes, variables that influence how closely a subject attends to the behavior of the model; (2) retention processes, the ability to encode and represent symbolically what has been observed so as to remember it; two internal representational systems are imaginal (images of behavior) and verbal (coding what has been seen in words); (3) motor reproduction processes, translating the symbolic representations into overt behavior, which involves practice in performing the motor movements involved in the observed behavior; (4) incentive and motivational processes, indicating that behavior observed will not be performed without sufficient incentive to do so; the incentive involves anticipations of being reinforced in the way the model has been.

The self is a set of cognitive processes concerned with thought and perception. Self-reinforcement can be as important as reinforcement administered by others. It requires some internal standard of performance against which behavior is evaluated. Self-efficacy refers to the ability to control the events in one's life. Persons low in self-efficacy feel helpless and worthless and will give up quickly when they encounter obstacles. Those high in self-efficacy will persevere at tasks and often perform at a high level. Judgments of self-efficacy are based on four sources of information: (1) performance attainment, prior success experiences that demonstrate a person's capacities; (2) vicarious experiences, seeing similar people perform successfully; (3) verbal persuasion, being told that one has the requisite ability to achieve; and (4) physiological arousal, one's internal level of calmness or fear.

In infancy, modeling is limited to immediate imitation. By the age of 2, children begin to imitate behavior some time after it has been observed. Infants and children are reinforced primarily by physical stimuli. Older persons are reinforced more by approval or disapproval from others, which then becomes internalized so that reinforcement is administered by the self.

Modeling is used in behavior therapy by having models demonstrate ways of coping with feared or threatening situations. Observing the models or actively participating with them (guided participation) are effective techniques of behavior modification. Models can be observed in person or on film. In covert modeling, subjects imagine a model coping with a feared or threatening situation.

Bandura's approach to behavior modification deals primarily with overt behavior, but it is also concerned with the beneficial effects of cognitive variables, particularly self-efficacy. As a person's self-efficacy improves during treatment, he or she is increasingly able to deal with feared objects. Therapeutic procedures themselves enhance self-efficacy.

Behavior modification has been attacked on the ground that it manipulates and controls people against their will. Bandura argues, however, that because of self-awareness and self-regulation, people undergoing behavior modification understand what is being reinforced.

Behavior is controlled both by internal cognitive processes and by external stimuli, a position Bandura calls reciprocal determinism. Most behavior is learned; genetic factors play a minor role in behavior. Learning in childhood may be more influential than learning in adulthood, but adults are not victims of childhood experiences. Our ultimate goal in life is the setting of realistic performance standards so as to maintain our optimal level of self-efficacy.

Bandura assesses behavior and cognitive variables through such techniques as direct observation, self-report inventories, and physiological measures. He favors controlled laboratory investigations using large groups of subjects whose average performances are statistically analyzed. His approach has a great deal of empirical support and is quite popular in psychology today.

Criticisms relate to Bandura's focus on overt behavior to the exclusion of internal motivating forces, emotions, and conflicts; his treatment of symptoms rather than any possible internal causes; and his failure to state more clearly how cognitive variables affect behavior.

Glossary

disinhibition   The weakening of inhibitions or constraints on a behavior through observation of the behavior of a model.

modeling   A behavior-modification procedure that involves observing the behavior of others (models), then actively participating with them in performing the behavior.

observational learning   Learning new responses by observing the behavior of others.

reciprocal determinism   The position that behavior is controlled both by the individual (through the cognitive processes) and by the environment (through external social stimulus events).

self-efficacy   An individual's sense of self-esteem and self-worth.

self-reinforcement   Rewards or punishments administered by oneself for meeting, exceeding, or falling short of one's own expectations and standards.

vicarious reinforcement   Learning or strengthening a behavior by observing the behavior of other people and the consequences of their behavior, rather than experiencing the reinforcement directly oneself.

Review questions

1. What features of the observational-learning approach distinguish it from the other approaches discussed in this book?
2. What is Bandura's position on the role of reinforcement in the learning of behavior?
3. Describe a typical modeling experiment. How does modeling vary as a function of the characteristics of the models, the characteristics of the observers, and the reward consequences of the behavior?
4. Describe how modeling procedures can be used as a means of therapy to change behavior. Give two specific examples.
5. What are the four processes of observational learning? How are they related?
6. How do the types of behaviors we acquire through modeling change with age?
7. How do persons high in self-efficacy differ from persons low in self-efficacy in terms of their ability to cope with the demands of everyday life? On what sources of information do we base our judgment about our own level of efficacy?
8. What is Bandura's position on the issue of free will versus determinism? What is his position on the relative influences of heredity and environment on behavior?

Suggested reading

Bandura, A. Behavior theory and the models of man. *American Psychologist*, 1974, 29, 859–869.

Bandura, A. *Social learning theory*. Englewood Cliffs, NJ: Prentice-Hall, 1977.

Bandura, A. Self-efficacy mechanisms in human agency. *American Psychologist*, 1982, 37, 122–147.

Evans, R. I. *The making of psychology: Discussions with creative contributors*. New York: Alfred A. Knopf, 1976. (See Chapter 19, "Albert Bandura.")

Rosenthal, T. L. & Bandura, A. Psychological modeling: Theory and practice. In S. L. Garfield & A. E. Bergin, Eds., *Handbook of psychotherapy and behavior change*, 2nd ed. New York: Wiley, 1978.

Stolz, S., Wienckowski, L. & Brown, B. Behavior modification: A perspective on critical issues. *American Psychologist*, 1975, 30, 1027–1048.

Woodward, W. R. The "discovery" of social behaviorism and social learning theory, 1870–1980. *American Psychologist*, 1982, 37, 396–410.

CHAPTER 16

Julian
Rotter

The life of Rotter (1916–   )
Social-learning theory
  Behavior potential
  Expectancy
  Reinforcement value
  The psychological situation
  Freedom of movement
  The minimal goal level
The motivation of behavior
Internal versus external locus of control
Interpersonal trust
Rotter's image of human nature
Assessment in Rotter's theory
Research in Rotter's theory
A final commentary
Summary
Glossary
Review questions
Suggested reading

Behavior does not occur in a vacuum. A person is continuously reacting to aspects of his external and internal environments.

JULIAN ROTTER

Rotter, Bandura, and Skinner agree that most behavior is learned. But Rotter and Bandura disagree with Skinner's view that behavior is shaped solely by external variables. As the opening quotation indicates, Rotter looks to both the outside and the inside of the organism, to both external reinforcements and inner cognitive processes, to explain behavior. Thus, Rotter, like Bandura, is a less radical behaviorist than Skinner, and he invokes internal, subjective experiences in his approach to personality.

Rotter refers to his work as a *social-learning theory* of personality, to indicate his belief that we learn our behavior primarily through our social experiences. He is critical of Skinner's tendency to study subjects in isolation. He argues that Skinner's approach does not adequately represent learning in the real world, the milieu in which all of us function in situations of social interdependency and interaction. He also takes issue with Skinner's study of the responses of animal subjects to simple stimuli. Rotter believes that such research provides little more than a starting point for the understanding of the more complex social behavior of human beings.

In the research conducted to develop his social-learning theory, Rotter and his followers have studied only human subjects. Using a variety of techniques, Rotter has focused on normal persons, largely children and college students. His theory is grounded in the rigorous and well-controlled experimental approach to psychology that is characteristic of the behaviorist movement. Rotter's theory of personality derives directly from the laboratory and not the clinic.

Rotter deals with inner conscious processes more extensively than does Bandura. He feels that we perceive ourselves as conscious beings, able to influence our experiences and to make decisions that regulate our lives. External reinforcement plays a role in the system, but the effectiveness of the reinforcement depends on internal, cognitive factors.

Each person's behavior is influenced by several such factors. We have a subjective expectation of the outcome of our behavior in terms of the reinforcement that will follow it. We estimate the likelihood that behaving in a certain way will lead to a particular reinforcement, and we regulate our behavior accordingly. We place different values or degrees of importance on different reinforcements, judging their relative worth in various situations.

Overall, each of us functions in a unique psychological context or environment. The same reinforcement, therefore, may not have the same value for different people. We can see, then, that inner experiences are of great importance in determining the effects of external experiences.

Personality, in Rotter's view, is continually changing as a result of our constant exposure to new experiences. Yet personality also has a high degree of stability or continuity because it is influenced by our past experiences. Rotter takes what he calls a historical approach to personality: to understand a person's behavior, it is necessary to study his or her past.

Although Rotter focuses on subjective events, he does not minimize the role of external events. External reinforcing conditions give direction to our behavior because we are motivated to strive for the maximum degree of positive reinforcement and the avoidance of punishment. Thus, Rotter's approach to personality attempts to integrate two separate and important trends in personality research: reinforcement theories and cognitive theories. He describes his approach to personality in terms of "the interaction of the individual and his or her meaningful environment" (Rotter, 1982, p. 5).

The life of Rotter (1916–)

Rotter has not yet written about his childhood or adolescence, so it is difficult to assess his theory in terms of his early life experiences. He graduated from Brooklyn College in 1937 and undertook graduate work in psychology at the University of Iowa and Indiana University; he received his Ph.D. from Indiana in 1941. A major influence on Rotter during his college years was Alfred Adler. Rotter attended some of Adler's seminars and visited him at his home. Forty years later, Rotter noted that Adler had been "a strong early influence on my thinking. I was and continue to be impressed by his insights into human nature" (Rotter, 1982, p. 1).

Following service as a psychologist with the U.S. Army during World War II, Rotter accepted a position at Ohio State University, where George Kelly was director of the clinical psychology program. It is interesting that two theories that emphasize cognition should have developed at the same institution, although Kelly's work was well under way by the time Rotter arrived. At Ohio State, Rotter conducted a large amount of research on his social-learning theory and attracted a number of outstanding graduate students, who went on to establish productive careers. One of his students described that time as "the 'glory days' at Ohio State . . . what with both Rotter and Kelly right in the midst of refining their theoretical positions and writing their magnum opuses" (Sechrest, 1984, p. 228).

In 1963, Rotter went to the University of Connecticut, where today he is analyzing and refining his approach to personality.

Social-learning theory

To understand Rotter's social-learning theory, we must first describe the principles on which it is built. The four primary concepts are behavior potential, expectancy, reinforcement value, and the psychological situation. Two broader concepts will also be discussed: freedom of movement and the minimal goal level.

Behavior potential

Behavior potential refers to the likelihood that a particular behavior will occur in a given situation. That likelihood must be determined with reference to the reinforcement or set of reinforcements that may follow the behavior. There is a similarity with Skinner's views in this concept; Rotter is attempting to predict the possibility that a person will behave in a certain way in the presence of specific variables. Rotter's formulation goes beyond Skinner's in that he invokes internal, cognitive variables, in addition to environmental variables, to predict the behavior.

Rotter's concept of behavior potential is relative. He is trying to predict the likelihood of the occurrence of a specific behavior relative to the other behaviors the individual could display in that situation. What causes the individual to select one behavior instead of others? The choice is based on the person's subjective impression of the situation. Behavior potential is affected not only by what is on the outside (the stimulus events or external situation), but also by what is on the inside (the conscious selection from among available behavior alternatives in terms of our perception of the situation).

Rotter's definition of behavior differs from Skinner's. Skinner dealt only with objectively observable events. Rotter's view of behavior includes not only acts that can be directly observed, but also those that cannot be directly observed—our internal, cognitive processes. For Rotter, these processes include rationalization, repression, the consideration of alternatives, and planning, variables that more extreme behaviorists do not consider to be behavior.

These internal or implicit behaviors can be observed and measured, Rotter insists, through indirect means, such as inferring them from overt behavior. Consider the behavior of examining alternative solutions to a problem. This behavior can be inferred from observations of the behavior of subjects who are trying to complete an assigned task. If, for example, the subjects take more time to solve the problem than they needed to finish an earlier one, Rotter feels that this is evidence of the behavior of considering alternative solutions.

The objective investigation of internal, cognitive activity is difficult. Rotter admits this, but he also believes that the principles that regulate the occurrence of these implicit behaviors are no different from those that regulate overt, directly observable behaviors. And we must remember that both internal and external variables are necessary to determine behavior potential.

Expectancy

Expectancy, the second of Rotter's primary concepts, refers to an individual's belief that if he or she behaves in a certain way in a given situation, a predictable reinforcement will follow. This belief is held in terms of a probability or likelihood that the reinforcement will occur. The degree of expectancy is determined by several factors.

One factor that influences expectancy is the nature of the previous reinforcement for behaving in a given way in that situation. Has the reinforcement occurred once or a hundred times? Did it happen yesterday or a year ago? Was the person reinforced every time or only occasionally for that behavior? Thus, expectancy is affected by our reinforcement history.

Another factor that influences expectancy is the extent of **generalization** from similar (but not identical) reinforcement situations. To what degree will past sequences of behavior and reinforcement carry over to other situations? Generalized expectancies are particularly important when we face a new situation. How can we predict whether our behavior will lead to a given reinforcement if we have never been in that situation before? We can only base our expectation of the outcome on what has happened to us in the past, in similar situations.

For example, think of a person running the 100-yard dash for the first time. What is her expectancy of winning the race? According to Rotter, it cannot be based on past experience, but it can be based on the generalization from participation in other athletic events, how well she has done in, say, other races or swimming meets. When she has run the 100-yard dash several times, her expectancy of winning can be determined by, or based upon, past experience in that event. Then it is no longer necessary to generalize expectancy from similar situations.

We will discuss, later, a form of generalized expectancy—part of the personality and outlook on life—which applies to all situations we may confront. Called the *internal versus external locus of control*, this personality variable refers to our belief that reinforcing events in general are either within or beyond our control. This concept influences not only our expectancy, but also our emotional and physical well-being.

Reinforcement value

The third concept in Rotter's theory is **reinforcement value**, which refers to the degree of preference for one reinforcement over another. If a person is in a situation in which it is equally likely that one of several reinforcements can occur, how much will the person prefer one reinforcement instead of the others?

People differ in terms of what they find reinforcing. Although no doubt everyone would agree that reading this book is highly reinforcing, you would differ with your classmates about how much you prefer other activities and the reinforcements they bring. Some would select a movie, others a symphony. Some would choose football, others soccer. Each person finds reinforcements of different value in different activities.

These preferences derive from our experiences in associating past reinforcements with current ones. Out of these associations, expectancies for future reinforcements develop. Thus, there is a relationship between the concepts of expectancy and reinforcement value.

Rotter argues that this relationship is systematically independent. In other words, they are not necessarily related, but they can be shown to be related empirically because a person has acquired the relationship from past experiences. He notes that either of these variables can serve as a cue for the other, under certain conditions.

Rotter argues that this relationship is systematically independent. In other words, they are not necessarily related, but they can be shown to be related emticket. Because of this unusually high reinforcement value, most people would have a low expectancy of winning, because few people would have experienced winning something of such value. Many people, however, have won items of lower reinforcement value. Therefore, our expectancy of winning something is greater when the reinforcement value of the prize is lower. In this case, then, expectancy is influenced by reinforcement value.

The psychological situation

The **psychological situation** is the fourth basic concept of Rotter's social learning theory, and it is an important determinant of behavior. Rotter believes we are continually reacting to both our internal and external environments. Further, each of these environments constantly influences the other. It is not just to external stimuli that we respond, but to both environments. This coalition is what Rotter has termed the psychological situation. The situation is considered psychological because we react to it in terms of our perception of the external stimuli.

Rotter argues that behavior can be predicted only from knowledge of the psychological situation, and not from what some personality theorists call a *core* of personality. In the core approach, prediction of behavior is based on the assumption of constant elements of personality such as motives and traits. A person possessing a particular trait or motive is expected always to behave in a certain way, regardless of the external situation.

Rotter contends that all situations contain cues, which indicate to us (based on our past experience) an expectancy of reinforcement for behaving in a particular way. Consider, for example, a person whom a Freudian theorist might label an anal-aggressive personality. In a core or trait approach, the person would be expected to behave aggressively under all circumstances. Rotter suggests, however, that the person's behavior will vary with the situation. The person will not behave aggressively if the cues of a situation indicate that he or she will be punished severely for displaying aggression.

Rotter criticizes not only core theorists who focus solely on the internal environment but also radical behaviorists, such as Skinner, who focus only on the external environment. By ignoring the internal environment of expectancies and other cognitive variables, the radical behaviorists overlook the possibility that a stimulus can have varied effects on behavior in different situations.

For example, think of a gun collector examining a prized weapon on the wall of his den and staring at the same kind of weapon trained on him by a robber in a dark alley. The physical stimulus is the same in both cases, but the psychological situation (the perception of the stimulus) differs sharply. As a result, behavior in the two situations will differ.

Freedom of movement

Freedom of movement refers to the degree of expectancy a person has that he or she will attain a given reinforcement as a result of certain behavior. A high expectancy leads to high freedom of movement; a low expectancy brings about low freedom of movement. A person with high freedom of movement anticipates success in achieving goals, but a person with low freedom of movement with regard to important needs or goals anticipates failure or punishment.

Rotter has found that low freedom of movement (a low expectancy of success in satisfying a particular need area) is strongly related to *defensiveness*. Defensive behavior is usually followed by negative reinforcement; persons use defensive behavior because they expect more punishment from their positive efforts than from their defensive efforts.

There are several possible causes for low freedom of movement. One is simply a lack of knowledge about how to achieve a particular goal. For example, mentally retarded persons have low expectancy of achieving goals because of an inability to learn the necessary behaviors. Persons with sufficient ability may develop low freedom of movement because they have misinterpreted past situations. As children, they may have been punished by their parents and later generalize from those experiences to their present situation. As a result, they anticipate disapproval in all life situations, which they now interpret as failure. Thus, they have a low expectancy of success.

A *conflict* may result when freedom of movement is low with regard to a goal or need that has a high value. As a result of this conflict, various avoidance behaviors may be developed. The person may try to achieve goals or meet needs in a symbolic way, by retreating into a fantasy world in which there is no risk of punishment or failure. Rotter believes that most deviant or psychopathological behavior is designed to avoid the conflict between low freedom of movement and goals that are important to the person.

The minimal goal level

The second broad concept in Rotter's theory is the **minimal goal level**, which refers to the lowest level of potential reinforcement in a particular situation that will be perceived as satisfactory. Rotter conceives of reinforcements as existing on a continuum, ranging from those that are highly desirable to those that are highly undesirable. The point on this continuum at which desirable reinforcements become undesirable represents an individual's minimal goal level.

If you apply for a job, the salary you are offered could range from unusually high to disappointingly low. Somewhere within that range is the lowest level you would find satisfying. Working for a salary below that amount would not be reinforcing.

We set minimal goal levels in virtually every situation—from the grade you would find acceptable in this course to the kind of car, career, or mate you expect to have. Different people may have different minimal goal levels in the same situation. You might be satisfied with nothing less than a grade of A in this course, while your roommate might settle happily for a C. Each of you would find the attainment of your different goal levels to be equally reinforcing.

Suppose, however, that you receive a B in the course. You may experience a sense of failure, which could contribute to low freedom of movement (a low expectancy of success in future courses of this type). Your roommate would find your despondency hard to understand; because he or she expected a C, your roommate would be very satisfied with the B and would experience higher freedom of movement.

Emotional health is, obviously, influenced by where we set our minimal goal levels. The person with high minimal goal levels who does not obtain reinforcements at or above these levels has low freedom of movement. Thus, setting unrealistic minimal goal levels may be harmful.

Minimal goal levels that are too low in terms of our ability and past reinforcements may leave us with a feeling of contentment and high freedom of movement, but we would not be living up to our capacities. For example, students who are considered to be underachievers, who do not perform at levels consistent with their abilities, have set minimal goal levels that are too low.

Rotter suggests that minimal goal levels may be raised or lowered by changing reinforcement values; this may be achieved by pairing present values with higher or lower values. He discussed the case of a student for whom a grade of B is a negatively valued reinforcement. By pairing that grade with the positive reinforcement of praise, flattery, and acceptance, the grade of B can come to be a positively valued reinforcement.

The motivation of behavior

Rotter believes that all behavior has a *directional* aspect; it is directed toward some goal. The directional aspect of behavior is inferred from the effects of reinforcements and explains our ability to respond selectively to environmental cues and to display choice behavior. We are motivated to maximize our positive reinforcements in all situations.

We noted that Rotter focuses on both internal and external determinants of behavior. This is his emphasis with motivation also. When we describe external conditions, we are dealing with *goals* or *reinforcements*. When we talk about internal, cognitive conditions, we speak of *needs*. The existence of both goals and needs is inferred from the ways in which a person interacts with the environment.

According to Rotter, all of our psychological needs are *learned*. In infancy and early childhood these needs arise from the association of experiences with the reinforcement of reflexes and other unlearned behaviors, including the basic physiological needs. Early psychological needs derive from events associated with the satisfaction of such basic needs as hunger, thirst, freedom from pain, and sensory stimulation.

As children grow and develop language and cognitive skills, their psychological needs arise less from association with physiological needs and more from their relation to other acquired or learned psychological needs. Cues in the external environment become more important than internal physiological states.

Another important point in Rotter's view of motivation is that learned goals are *social* in origin; they are dependent upon other people. It is obvious that infants and children are dependent upon others, particularly parents, for their satisfactions and reinforcements. As they grow older, their reinforcements become dependent upon a broader range of people, including friends and teachers. As adults, we frequently depend on other people for the reinforcement of our needs. Because our need-satisfactions are so greatly influenced by others, such needs as love, affection, recognition, and dependency become important.

Another component of Rotter's view of motivation is **need potential**. Our behaviors, needs, and goals are interrelated and exist within functionally related systems. Within these systems, different behaviors can often lead to the same goal; this is what Rotter means by need potential, the possibility of related behaviors, all of which can lead to the same or similar reinforcements, occurring at any particular time.

The types of behaviors that can be grouped in functional systems range from overt acts to covert cognitions. These systems or categories are arranged in hierarchies, and those high on the scale can include those that stand lower. Rotter offers the example of the need potential for recognition. This is a broad category and includes lower need potentials, such as the need for recognition in psychology or the need for recognition in intercollegiate sports.

Rotter posits six categories of needs (Rotter, Chance, & Phares, 1972, pp. 31–32).

1. *Recognition-Status*
   Need to be considered competent or good in a professional, social, occupational, or play activity; need to gain social or vocational position—that is, to be more skilled or better than others.
2. *Protection-Dependency*
   Need to have another person or group of people prevent frustration or punishment, or to provide for the satisfaction of other needs.
3. *Dominance*
   Need to direct or control the actions of other people, including members of family and friends; need to have any action taken by others be the one that he or she suggests.
4. *Independence*
   Need to make own decisions and to rely on oneself, together with the need to develop skills for obtaining satisfactions directly, without the mediation of other people.
5. *Love and Affection*
   Need for acceptance and indication of liking by other individuals, in contrast to need for recognition-status, *not* concerned with social or professional positions but seeks people's warm regard.
6. *Physical Comfort*
   Learned need for physical satisfaction that has become associated with gaining security.

Rotter is careful to point out that his concept of need does not refer to any physiological or psychological condition of deprivation or arousal, the manner in which other theorists define needs. Rotter's formulation refers to the direction of behavior, which is inferred from the effects of reinforcement on behavior. This use of the word *need* assumes the inclusion of need potential, freedom of movement, and need value. Thus, needs include the earlier primary concepts of behavior potential, expectancy, and reinforcement value.

Internal versus external locus of control

A major aspect of Rotter's system is our belief about the source of control of our reinforcements. We have noted that there are individual differences in the perception of a particular event as reinforcing. Rotter's research has shown that some people believe that reinforcements are dependent on their own behavior; others think reinforcements are controlled by outside forces.

People who have the personality variable called an **internal locus of control** believe that the reinforcements they receive are a function of their own behaviors and attributes. Externally oriented people, who have an **external locus of control**, think that their receipt of reinforcement is in the hands of other people, of fate, or of luck. Whatever the nature of the external locus of control, externally oriented people are convinced that they are powerless with respect to these outside forces.

Our locus of control will have a great influence on our behavior. External locus-of-control persons, who believe that their own behavior or skills will make no difference in the reinforcements they receive, will not see the value in putting forth any effort to improve their situation. They have little belief in the possibility of controlling their own lives in the present or in the future.

Those who are internally oriented believe that they have a firm control over their own lives, and they behave accordingly. Research has shown that they perform

Externally oriented persons (left) believe they have little control over their lives. Internally oriented persons (right) may be healthier, less anxious, and more popular, believing that the rewards they receive in life depend on their own skills and behaviors.

at a higher level on laboratory tasks, are less susceptible to attempts to influence them, place a higher value on their personal skills and achievements, and are more alert to environmental cues that they can use to guide their behavior. In addition, internal locus-of-control people are more ready to take responsibility for their actions than are externally oriented people. There is also some evidence to suggest, tentatively, that internally oriented people may enjoy greater mental health (Phares, 1976). We shall note other findings in the research section.

Interpersonal trust

We have noted that internal versus external locus of control was a form of generalized expectancy. Thus, it is a relatively stable part of our personality and our outlook on life. Rotter has identified another form of generalized expectancy called **interpersonal trust**, the expectation "held by an individual that the word, promise, oral or written statement of another individual or group can be relied on" (Rotter, 1980, p. 1).

Persons high in interpersonal trust are less likely to lie, cheat, or steal, and are more likely to respect the rights of others and to give them a second chance than are persons low in interpersonal trust. They are, however, no more likely to be overly gullible or more easily fooled.

High interpersonal trust has beneficial personal consequences. Such people are much less likely to be unhappy, maladjusted, or bothered by conflicts than those who are not trusting. They are also liked more and sought out as friends more often by both people who are high and low in interpersonal trust.

We shall look at examples of research on interpersonal trust in the research section.

Rotter's image of human nature

On the issue of free will or determinism, Rotter's system seems to favor free choice and action, especially for persons who have an internal locus of control. It is clear from his emphasis on the importance of cognitive variables that Rotter believes that human beings can regulate and direct their own experiences and choose their own behaviors. People may be influenced by external variables, but they are capable of shaping the nature and extent of that influence. Externally oriented individuals do not have a sense of control over their own lives. The possibility of free will is available to them, but they feel themselves controlled by outside forces.

Rotter emphasizes that most of our behavior is learned. He gives little note to genetic factors. It is primarily nurture and not nature that guides us—experience, not inheritance.

Although Rotter views the learning experiences of childhood as being important, he does not believe that those experiences determine the ways in which we must behave for the rest of our lives. Personality is always changing and growing, not fixed in the pattern established in childhood. Early learning experiences do affect how we perceive current experiences, but we are not victims of our past. We react continuously to our internal and external environments. As these environments change, so does our perception of them.

Rotter's position on the question of uniqueness versus universality of behavior is reflected in his concept of the psychological situation. Each of us develops a unique view of the world, interpreting and reacting to external stimuli in terms of our perception of them. It follows that each of us lives and functions in a different psychological situation.

Rotter has not discussed any ultimate and necessary goal of life such as self-actualization, but he has stated forcefully that all of our behavior is goal-directed. Rather than being pulled by some ideal state to be attained, however, or pushed to escape such conditions as anxiety or inferiority feelings, we are constantly directed to achieve individual goals. We are motivated to maximize reinforcement and to minimize punishment, and we are at every moment making conscious decisions about how best to achieve these goals.

Rotter's system seems to offer an optimistic image of human nature. We are not passive victims of external events, of inheritance, or of childhood experiences. We are free to shape not only our present behavior, but our future as well.

Assessment in Rotter's theory

Rotter uses a variety of assessment techniques, including interviews; projective tests such as the Rorschach Inkblot Test, the Thematic Apperception Test, and his own Incomplete Sentences Blank; direct observations of behavior; and self-report inventories. In addition, he has designed specific techniques to assess certain of the concepts in his system.

He has taken two approaches to the measurement of reinforcement value: the ranking method and the behavioral choice method. The *ranking method* was used as follows. Verbal descriptions of 18 reinforcements—such as being praised by one's teacher for preparing a good report—were given to groups of young male subjects, who were asked to rank the statements from most reinforcing to least reinforcing. In the *behavioral choice method*, subjects actually behaved in ways so as to receive one reinforcement over another. Other ways of measuring reinforcement value have included projective techniques and rating methods.

Expectancy has been measured by Rotter and his associates through the behavioral choice method and various verbal techniques. The behavioral choice method is used in the same way as when measuring reinforcement value. When subjects choose one alternative over another, they are indicating a belief that the chosen alternative has a higher expectancy of producing reinforcement.

The other approach to measuring expectancy involves verbal techniques. Subjects were asked, for example, to predict the likelihood of achieving reinforcement in terms of different alternatives on a scale of expectancy values. In another case, subjects were graded on their performance of a task. Before receiving the grade, they were asked for their expectancies for the tasks. The hypothesis was that the grades anticipated represented the level of expectancy the subjects were most confident of receiving.

To measure need potential, it is necessary to have an indication of how frequently certain behaviors will occur. This can be accomplished by observing subjects' behaviors over a period of time. Need potential can also be assessed through the use of questionnaires, verbal choice techniques, and ranking methods, by asking subjects what they think they will do in specific situations.

Rotter also developed self-report inventories to assess the two forms of generalized expectancy: internal versus external locus of control and interpersonal trust.

The Internal versus External Locus of Control (I-E) Scale consists of 23 forced-choice alternatives. Subjects must pick one of each pair of items that best describes their belief about the nature of the world. Sample items from the I-E Scale are shown in Table 16.1. It is not difficult to determine which of each pair of alternatives represents internal or external control.

The Interpersonal Trust Scale consists of 25 items to measure trust, plus 15 filler items designed to disguise the test's purpose. Subjects indicate their degree of agreement or disagreement with each item. Sample items are shown in Table 16.2.

TABLE 16.1   Sample items from the I-E Scale

(1) a. Many of the unhappy things in people's lives are partly due to bad luck.
    b. People's misfortunes result from the mistakes they make.
(2) a. One of the major reasons why we have wars is because people don't take enough interest in politics.
    b. There will always be wars, no matter how hard people try to prevent them.
(3) a. In the long run people get the respect they deserve in this world.
    b. Unfortunately, an individual's worth often passes unrecognized no matter how hard he or she tries.
(4) a. The idea that teachers are unfair to students is nonsense.
    b. Most students don't realize the extent to which their grades are influenced by accidental happenings.
(5) a. Without the right breaks one cannot be an effective leader.
    b. Capable people who fail to become leaders have not taken advantage of their opportunities.
(6) a. No matter how hard you try some people just don't like you.
    b. People who can't get others to like them don't understand how to get along with others.

Source: J. B. Rotter, "Generalized Expectancies for Internal versus External Control of Reinforcement," *Psychological Monographs* 80 (1966):11.

TABLE 16.2   Sample items from the Interpersonal Trust Scale

(1) In dealing with strangers one is better off to be cautious until they have provided evidence that they are trustworthy.
(2) Parents usually can be relied upon to keep their promises.
(3) Parents and teachers are likely to say what they believe themselves and not just what they think is good for the child to hear.
(4) Most elected public officials are really sincere in their campaign promises.

Source: J. B. Rotter, "A New Scale for the Measurement of Interpersonal Trust," *Journal of Personality* 35 (1967):654.

Research in Rotter's theory

Rotter has primarily used the experimental and correlational research methods in testing his theory. Much of that research has focused on the I-E Scale and how it correlates with behavior and with other measures of personality.

We have noted some of the characteristics of people whose orientations are either internal or external. Additional research has been directed toward the developmental aspects of this form of generalized expectancy. Studies have shown that children become more internally oriented as they grow older (Milgram, 1971); that most college students possess an internal orientation (Rotter, 1966); and that internal control increases from late adolescence to middle age and remains at that level through old age (Ryckman & Malikiosi, 1975).

Significant racial and social-class differences have been found in performance on the I-E Scale. In general, persons in lower social classes and who are members of minority groups (with the exception of Orientals) hold an external orientation, believing that they have little or no control over the events and forces in their lives (Coleman et al., 1966). This was also shown in a study in which lower-class black children were shown to be much more externally oriented than lower- and middle-class white children or middle-class black children (Battle & Rotter, 1963). In a study of high school students, it was found that Hispanic-American and American Indian subjects were much more likely to be externally oriented than were white subjects (Graves, 1961).

Internally oriented people behave differently from externally oriented people. Internally oriented persons are more likely to gain access to more information in different situations and to learn more in those situations (Wolk & DuCette, 1974); to experience a greater sense of personal choice when choosing among alternatives (Harvey & Barnes, 1974); to be popular with their peers (Nowicki & Roundtree, 1971); and to be attracted to people they can manipulate (Silverman & Shrauger, 1970). Also, they are much less likely to have emotional problems or to become alcoholics. They experience less anxiety and fewer psychiatric symptoms (Lefcourt, 1982; Naditch, 1975; Strassberg, 1973).

Internally oriented people seem to be physically healthier than those who are externally oriented. They tend to have lower blood pressure and fewer heart attacks. When they have heart attacks, they cooperate better with the hospital staff and are likely to be released sooner than patients who are externally oriented (Strickland, 1979). Further, they are more cautious about their physical health and are more likely to wear seat belts in their automobiles, engage in exercise, and quit smoking than externally oriented people (Strickland, 1978, 1979).

In a variety of ways, then, it seems more desirable to have an internal rather than an external locus of control. But how does a person come to possess one or the other? The evidence suggests that it is learned in childhood and that a particular pattern of parental behavior is responsible for the internal orientation. Parents of children who possess an internal locus of control are highly supportive, full of praise for achievements (positive reinforcement), and consistent in their discipline.

They are not authoritarian in their attitudes. As their children grow older, these parents encourage early independence by becoming less actively involved with them (Loeb, 1975; Wichern & Nowicki, 1976).

We noted some of the research findings with regard to differences in interpersonal trust. It has also been shown that the last-born or youngest child in a family is much less trusting than the other children, that college students who express religious beliefs tend to be more trusting than those who express no such beliefs, and that a positive relationship exists between interpersonal trust and social class. The higher the social class, the higher the degree of interpersonal trust (Rotter, 1967).

A final commentary

Rotter's social-learning theory, with its emphasis on internal, subjective experiences, has attracted enthusiastic followers in American psychology. The system appeals primarily to researchers who are experimentally oriented and interested in the prominence being accorded cognitive variables in contemporary psychology. Rotter's emphasis on cognitive factors is stronger than Bandura's, and his position represents a greater departure from Skinner's radical behaviorism.

Supporters of Rotter's position argue that he offers concepts defined in precise, unambiguous terms that are amenable to testing by experimental and correlational methods. More so than Bandura, Rotter has attempted to establish the working relationship between cognitive variables and reinforcement, and he has given social-learning theory a strong motivational component.

Rotter's work is too new to have been included in the survey we have cited of the relative importance of 286 psychologists in the last half of the 20th century, but there is no denying his strong and growing influence in psychology today.

The focus on internal variables is a source of the theory's strength to some psychologists, but it is seen by others as a weakness. Critics, including some who favor the recognition of cognitive variables, have suggested that Rotter has gone too far. They contend that his position has deviated so greatly from orthodox behaviorism that it cannot be considered a behavioral approach at all. Because of the extent of Rotter's acceptance of cognitive variables, much of his methodology is seen as too subjective. We saw in the assessment section that he does use such non-experimental methods as interviews and projective techniques.

Rotter's research, however, has been as rigorous and as well controlled as his subject matter allows, and he uses objective observation of behavior wherever possible. Also, his concepts are defined with a high degree of precision, making them amenable to empirical testing. Studies of various aspects of his theory have resulted in a great deal of support. The I-E Scale has generated hundreds of research studies and is finding widespread use beyond the laboratory in clinical and educational settings. Rotter notes, "Perhaps it is in the area of personality measurement that [social-learning theory] has made its most substantial and systematic contributions" (Rotter, 1982, p. 331).

Summary

Rotter's theory has been strongly influenced by the work of Alfred Adler. Like Bandura, Rotter disagrees with Skinner's view that behavior is shaped solely by external variables. Rotter calls his work a social-learning theory to indicate his belief that we learn our behavior primarily through social experiences. He uses only normal human subjects in his experimental approach to personality and deals with conscious processes more extensively than does Bandura.

Personality is continually changing as a result of our exposure to new experiences, but it also has a high degree of stability because it is influenced by past experiences. Rotter takes a historical approach to personality, believing that it is necessary to study a person's past to understand his or her present behavior. His system integrates reinforcement theories and cognitive theories and deals with the interaction of the individual and his or her unique, meaningful environment.

The four primary concepts of social-learning theory are behavior potential, expectancy, reinforcement value, and the psychological situation. Two broader concepts are freedom of movement and the minimal goal level.

Behavior potential refers to the likelihood that a specific behavior will occur, relative to the other behaviors the individual could display in a given situation. It is affected by the stimulus events and by our conscious selection from among available behavior alternatives in terms of our perception of the situation. Behavior includes not only acts that can be observed directly, but also internal cognitive processes that cannot be observed directly but that can be inferred from overt behavior.

Expectancy refers to a person's belief that if he or she behaves in a certain way in a given situation, a predictable reinforcement will follow. The degree of expectancy is determined by the nature of the previous reinforcement for behaving in a given way in that situation, and by the extent of the generalization from similar reinforcement situations.

Reinforcement value refers to the degree of preference for one reinforcement over another. Preferences for different reinforcements derive from our experiences in associating past reinforcements with current ones, out of which develop expectancies for future reinforcements.

The psychological situation is a coalition of our internal and external environments, that is, of cognitive variables and external stimuli. Behavior can be predicted from the psychological situation and not from the motives or traits that make up what some theorists call a core of personality.

Freedom of movement refers to the degree of expectancy a person has that he or she will attain a given reinforcement as a result of certain behavior. A high expectancy leads to high freedom of movement; a low expectancy leads to low freedom of movement. Low freedom of movement is related to defensiveness. The causes of low freedom of movement include a lack of knowledge about how to achieve a particular goal and a misinterpretation of past situations. A conflict may result when freedom of movement is low with regard to a goal or need that has a high value. A conflict may lead to the development of various avoidance behaviors.

The minimal goal level refers to the lowest level of potential reinforcement in a particular situation that a person will perceive as satisfactory. Setting unrealistic minimal goal levels may be harmful to our emotional health.

Rotter believes that all behavior is directed toward some goal. We are motivated to maximize positive reinforcements. Our psychological needs are learned and are social in origin in that they depend upon other people. The concept of need potential refers to related behaviors that can lead to the same or similar reinforcements. Six categories of needs are recognition-status needs, protection-dependency needs, dominance needs, independence needs, love and affection needs, and physical comfort needs.

People who believe that reinforcements depend upon their own behavior have an internal locus of control. Those who believe that reinforcements are controlled by outside forces have an external locus of control. Externally oriented people see little value in putting forth effort to improve their situation. Internally oriented people perform at higher levels, are less susceptible to outside influences, place a higher value on their skills and achievements, and take more responsibility for their actions.

Persons high in interpersonal trust are less likely to lie, cheat, or steal; more likely to respect the rights of others; less likely to be unhappy or maladjusted; and liked more than persons low in interpersonal trust.

Rotter's image of human nature emphasizes free will, the importance of learning, the possibility that personality will change and grow, human uniqueness, and the ultimate goal of maximizing reinforcement and minimizing punishment.

Rotter uses a variety of assessment techniques, including interviews, projective tests, direct observations of behavior, and self-report inventories. To assess reinforcement value, he uses the ranking method and the behavioral choice method. Expectancy is assessed through the behavioral choice method and verbal techniques, such as asking subjects for their expectancies with regard to a particular task. Need potential is assessed by observing subject behavior over time. The Internal versus External Locus of Control (I-E) Scale and the Interpersonal Trust Scale were developed by Rotter to assess these two forms of generalized expectancy.

Research has shown that children become more internally oriented as they grow older, as do adults from adolescence to middle age. Those who are in lower social classes and who are members of minority groups (except Orientals) tend to be externally oriented.

Internally oriented people gain more access to information, feel a stronger sense of personal choice, are more popular, are more attracted to people they can manipulate, experience fewer psychiatric symptoms and less anxiety, are less likely to become alcoholics, and are physically healthier than externally oriented people.

Parents of internally oriented children are highly supportive, full of praise, consistent in their discipline, and encouraging of their children's independence as they grow older.

Last-born children are less trusting than their older siblings. College students with religious beliefs are more trusting than those with no religious beliefs. The higher the social class, the greater the interpersonal trust.

Rotter's theory is criticized for being too subjective because of what some think is an overemphasis on cognitive variables.

Glossary

behavior potential   The likelihood that a particular behavior will occur in a given situation.

expectancy   An individual's belief that if he or she behaves in a certain way in a given situation, a predictable reinforcement will follow.

freedom of movement   The degree of expectancy that a certain behavior will bring a given reinforcement; a high expectancy leads to a high freedom of movement, that is, a high expectation of success, whereas a low freedom of movement is related to a low expectation of success.

generalization   The condition in which responses made in one situation will also be made in similar reinforcement situations.

interpersonal trust   The degree of expectancy that an individual is trustworthy.

locus of control   An individual's belief about the source of control of the reinforcements he or she receives; an internal locus of control indicates a belief that one's reinforcements are brought about by one's own behavior and attitudes, while an external locus of control indicates a belief that reinforcements are in the hands of other people, of fate, or of luck, and that one is powerless with respect to these outside forces.

minimal goal level   The lowest level of potential reinforcement in a given situation that is perceived as satisfactory.

need potential   The possibility that related behaviors which lead to the same or similar reinforcements will occur at a particular time.

psychological situation   The combination of the external and internal environments that influences an individual's perception of and response to a stimulus.

reinforcement value   The basis for preferring one reinforcement over another.

Review questions

1. How does Rotter's theory of personality differ from Skinner's approach to personality? What does Rotter's theory have in common with Bandura's theory?
2. According to Rotter, what is the role of cognitive factors in personality?
3. What factors influence expectancy (our belief that if we behave in a certain way in a given situation, a predictable reinforcement will follow)?
4. What is the relationship between minimal goal levels and reinforcement values? How are we likely to respond to a minimal goal level that is set too low for our abilities?

5. Explain the difference between needs and goals. What are the six categories of needs in Rotter's theory?
6. If external locus-of-control persons were to hear on the radio that a tornado was approaching their town, would they be likely to say "Well, there's nothing I can do about it" or would they be likely to take immediate action to protect their family and property? Why?
7. What parental behaviors may foster an internal locus of control in a child?
8. What is Rotter's position on the issue of free will versus determinism? What is his position on the uniqueness of human behavior?

Suggested reading

Lefcourt, H. M. *Locus of control: Current trends in theory and research.* Hillsdale, NJ: Erlbaum, 1976.
Phares, E. J. *Locus of control in personality.* Morristown, NJ: General Learning Press, 1976.
Rotter, J. B. Interpersonal trust, trustworthiness, and gullibility. *American Psychologist,* 1980, 35, 1–7.
Rotter, J. B. *The development and applications of social learning theory: Selected papers.* New York: Praeger, 1982.

PART 8

The Limited-Domain Approach

Personality theorists, in general, have considered the achievement of comprehensiveness or completeness to be a major theoretical goal. Some theories come closer to achieving this goal than others, but more and more writers in the area of personality are concluding that no existing theory can legitimately be called comprehensive, regardless of the theorist's stated aims. Further, it has been suggested that such a goal may be unrealistic.

Some psychologists argue that few (and perhaps none) of the available theories adequately account for all aspects of personality, no matter how broadly they try to stretch their formulations. Rather, each theory is seen to operate within a *range of convenience* (to use Kelly's term); each covers only certain aspects of personality, leaving other facets relatively unexplored. For example, Erikson focuses on the developmental aspects of personality, Kelly on cognitive processes, Bandura on modeling, Cattell on traits, Murray on needs, and so on. To be sure, the range of convenience of some theories is broader than that of others, but is any theory sufficiently broad to be called comprehensive?

Because of their feeling that no theory is comprehensive—and that perhaps no theory can be—some psychologists who study personality have suggested that to achieve a fuller understanding of personality we need to develop a number of separate theories, each having a narrow range of convenience. These *limited-domain theories* would each focus on a narrow or limited aspect of personality. Restriction of the target or focus of investigation would allow the domain selected to be investigated more thoroughly, it is suggested, than occurs when the total personality is dealt with.

This kind of fragmentation in the study of personality has been taking place for some time. As one psychologist noted, "The last 25 years of personality study may be characterized as a period of construct elaboration in which a variety of single dimensions of personality . . . have been studied in depth" (Wiggins, cited in Rorer & Widiger, 1983, p. 432). Thus, the field of personality is following the example of other areas of psychology that have replaced their attempts to develop large-scale, all-encompassing theories with what have been called *miniature theories*. As researchers in other areas of psychology—such as learning and motivation—realized the impossibility of including all aspects of their subject matter in one theory, they turned to theories of limited domain and narrow range of convenience. In the field of learning, for example, we find theoretical formulations that focus on specific types of learning, such as verbal learning, conditioning, or maze learning—circumscribed areas of behavior. Theories that try to account for all aspects of learning over all situations with all types of subjects are no longer in vogue.

It is easy to see why the global-theory approach characterized the field of personality for so long. The early personality theorists—Freud, Adler, and Jung—dealt with individual patients in the clinical setting. They tried to change or cure abnormalities of behavior and were thus forced to deal with whole human beings trying to function in the real world. They attempted to treat the whole person, not just a part, not just one aspect of the personality.

The focus shifted from the whole person only when the topic of personality began to be brought out of the clinic and into the research laboratory. Experimental psychologists began to (and continue to) study one variable at a time (all other variables being controlled or held constant); thus, they focus on a limited domain. Also, their approach is characterized by the collection of large amounts of empirical data, which are derived from the investigation of how the variable relates to its antecedents and to its behavioral consequences. Therefore, limited-domain theories are characterized by a type of supporting data that is a different from those used in the clinical approach.

Limited-domain theories also place less emphasis on the therapeutic value of the theoretical formulations. Their proponents are usually not clinicians but researchers, and so their focus is more on investigating personality than on trying to change it. This does not mean, of course, that there is no therapeutic utility to these theories. It merely indicates that the theories are not developed specifically for use in the clinic, as was the case with many of our earlier theorists.

Since the study of personality and the proposing of personality theories is increasingly an experimentally oriented venture and less a clinical one, it follows that the limited-domain approach will assume greater importance in the years to come.

We will discuss three limited-domain theories: need for achievement, psychological differentiation, and temperament theory. While these are certainly not the only ones available, nor perhaps even the best ones, they do illustrate the nature and diversity of the limited-domain approach and serve as examples of what is a growing trend in personality study. Since these theories are being presented as examples of the limited-domain approach, and not as comprehensive systems of personality, they will not be discussed in as much detail as the other theories. The intent is to give the flavor of each theory. The theorists' lives and images of human nature will not be discussed, nor will assessment and research be treated in separate sections.

Arnold
Buss

Herman
Witkin

Robert
Plomin

David
McClelland

CHAPTER 17

Limited-Domain Theories

David McClelland: The need for achievement
Measuring the need for achievement
Experimental studies of the need for achievement
Behavior and the need for achievement
Culture and the need for achievement
Developing the need for achievement in adults
Developing the need for achievement in children
Age differences in the need for achievement
Sex differences in the need for achievement
Comment
Herman Witkin: Psychological differentiation
Personality and perception
Research on perceptual tasks
Psychological differentiation and personality
Stability of psychological differentiation
Comment

Arnold Buss and Robert Plomin: A temperament theory
The inherited temperaments
Studies of temperaments in twins
Assessing temperaments in adults
The nature of the temperaments
Comment
Summary
Glossary
Review questions
Suggested reading

David McClelland: The need for achievement

One of the needs Henry Murray posited was the need for achievement—the need to overcome obstacles, to excel, to live up to a high standard. Since 1947, Harvard psychologist David McClelland (1917–   ) has conducted a broad and intensive research program to investigate this need. The amount of his research (and of the additional research it has inspired) is staggering and has important theoretical as well as practical implications.

McClelland's work on **achievement motivation** provides an excellent example of how much can be learned when the domain of research is restricted to one aspect of personality. It also provides an example of the importance of the limited-domain approach to understanding the domain of the total personality. While the focus of study is narrow, the ramifications are broad. McClelland believes that concentration on a limited area is not at all narrowing. "By concentrating on one problem, on *one motive*, we have found in the course of our study that we have learned not only a lot about the achievement motive but other areas of personality as well" (McClelland et al., 1953, p. vi).

Through diligent, thorough, and imaginative research, McClelland and his associates have developed a technique with which to measure an individual's achievement motivation and have determined how behavior varies in a number of situations as a function of the level of the need for achievement. They have also uncovered sources responsible for the development of the need for achievement (or for its lack of development) in an individual.

Finally, in an exciting, far-reaching, and unusual research program, McClelland has presented an empirical account of the economic growth and decline of ancient and contemporary cultures in terms of their general level of need for achievement. As a result of this research, it is possible to predict a country's future economic growth or decline by measuring its current level of the need. He has also developed techniques for increasing the need for achievement in developing nations, with striking results. As you can see, there is nothing narrow or limited about what McClelland has been able to achieve by studying only one aspect of personality.

Measuring the need for achievement

In developing a technique for measuring achievement motivation (need achievement), McClelland was guided by certain insights of Sigmund Freud as well as by the methodological requirements of experimental psychology. From Freud he borrowed the basic approach of uncovering and measuring the motive in question through the fantasy reports of subjects. However, while Freud searched for fantasy in dreams and free association, McClelland used a specific psychological test, developed by Murray and already widely used in research: the Thematic Apperception Test (TAT). In this test, the subject is presented with a series of pictures, each of which can be interpreted in more than one way. In other words, different people see different things in the pictures presented to them. The theory behind this projective technique is that a person, in interpreting a picture, will do so in terms of his or her own needs, fears, values, or fantasies, which are projected onto the ambiguous stimulus picture.

McClelland asked groups of male college students to write brief stories about some of the TAT pictures after having been exposed to different experimental conditions (McClelland et al., 1953). For example, through the use of different test-taking instructions, weak achievement need was induced in one group and strong achievement need in another. Then the content of their stories was compared to see if the two groups differed significantly in the amount of achievement-oriented material found in their stories. The research question was: what effect does an experimentally induced state of achievement motivation have on a subject's fantasy production? If the experimental treatments worked (if the group exhorted to high achievement actually showed higher achievement in their stories than the group not so exhorted), and if these different levels of fantasy production could be detected in the TAT-produced stories, then the test could be used as a valid measure of need for achievement.

And that was precisely what happened. The stories written under the high-achievement conditions contained many more references to attaining standards of excellence and to wanting to do well or actually doing well. For example, one of the pictures showed a young man sitting at a desk with a book open in front of him. Stories from the low need-achievement group dealt with sedentary and passive activities: daydreaming, thinking, recalling past events. They contained minimal reference to doing things involving excelling, striving, or achieving. The stories told by the high need-achievement subjects involved many references to doing one's best, working instead of daydreaming, striving, and so on.

Through this initial research, McClelland concluded that TAT-produced stories can be used as a valid measure of the need to achieve, and this became the basic tool for selecting high and low need-achievement subjects for his extensive research program.

Experimental studies of the need for achievement

A large number of studies have been conducted to discover in what ways people who score high in need achievement behave differently from those who score low in this area of motivation (McClelland, 1961; McClelland et al., 1953). We will summarize these findings briefly. The findings deal with males, since males made up the primary subject group studied. We will discuss need achievement in women in a later section. High need-achievement males more often are members of the middle class and much less often of the lower or upper classes. They demonstrate a better memory than low need-achievement males for tasks uncompleted, are much more active in college and community activities, and are more likely to volunteer to serve as subjects for psychological research (including research on need achievement). In addition, they are more resistant to social pressure; that is, they are significantly less conforming than low need-achievement males.

Of potentially greater practical significance are studies comparing the performances of those with high and low need for achievement in experimentally designed work situations. In the first of these experiments, the subjects had to un-scramble the letters of a large number of scrambled words. Though both groups began the task at the same level of performance, the high achievers showed a pro-gressive improvement in their performance (Lowell, 1952). McClelland concluded that these high achievers were motivated so strongly to do the job well (to achieve) that they learned how to do it better as they continued with the task.

The high achievers worked harder and did the job better. Does it follow that persons high in achievement need perform better on any kind of task? To answer that question, other experiments were conducted, in which the task and certain conditions surrounding it were studied. In one such experiment, the task to be per-formed was highly repetitive and routine: to cross out the *E*s and *O*s in a long series of random letters. In this kind of task there is really no room for improvement; there is no way to learn to do the task better, only faster. High and low need-achievement subjects performed at the same level in this task.

In another study, high need-achievement subjects were given instructions prior to the task that eliminated all achievement significance from the work. As a result, they performed no better than low need-achievement subjects. Other stud-ies investigated the effects of extrinsic rewards (rewards other than achievement itself) for performance. In one case, subjects were told that those who performed best could leave immediately. This kind of reward held no motivation for the high achievers. They actually performed slightly worse than the low achievers.

These experiments suggest that subjects high in need for achievement do not perform better than subjects low in need for achievement unless the achievement motive itself is activated. Only when the high-need individual is challenged to excel will he do so. This point was again demonstrated in studies involving a ringtoss game in which subjects were allowed to choose how far or how close to the target they would stand. Obviously, standing very close would assure success at the task, while standing very far away would tend to assure failure. By taking either extreme position, the subject could ensure that the outcome would depend little on skill or excellence and that there would be minimal challenge to the task. Subjects low in need achievement tended to stand either very close or very far away, while subjects high in need achievement stood at distances where it was possible to demonstrate or develop skill and excellence at the task. That is, they stood neither too close (where skill was not required) nor too far away (where skill would have made little difference in the outcome). They preferred to take a moderate risk rather than no risk or an impossible risk.

From these findings, McClelland predicted that people with high achievement needs will, in their everyday activities (and particularly in their work), seek situa-tions that will allow them to satisfy these achievement needs. They will set certain achievement standards for themselves and then work hard to reach those standards.

Behavior and the need for achievement

As McClelland predicted, people with different levels of achievement motiva-tion behave in significantly different ways in their everyday lives. For example, young people high in the need to achieve are much more likely to attend college,

People who have a high need for achievement are likely to earn high grades in college and to seek challenging and responsible jobs.

to earn higher grades, and to be involved in more extracurricular activities than those low in the need to achieve (Atkinson, Lens & O'Malley, 1976; Raynor, 1970).

In business and industry, persons high in need achievement are found in higher-status jobs than those low in need achievement. In addition, high achievers work harder at their jobs and have a greater expectation of success. They choose jobs in which they will have a great deal of personal responsibility and in which success depends primarily on their own efforts. They are dissatisfied in jobs in which success depends on other people or on factors beyond their control.

Because high need achievers prefer jobs in which they have a great deal of responsibility, it would seem to follow that they prefer to be entrepreneurs, to run their own businesses. This situation would provide the optimal level of challenge and personal responsibility. In a follow-up study of college students 14 years after their need-achievement scores had been determined, it was found that 83 percent of those who had become successful entrepreneurs were high in the need to achieve. Only 21 percent of those who had become successful in nonentrepreneurial jobs were high in need achievement (McClelland, 1965).

This does not suggest that people who work for an organization are generally low in the need to achieve. Successful managers, for example, show higher need-achievement scores than unsuccessful managers. Also, a high positive correlation exists between the need-achievement scores of a company's executives and that organization's level of economic success (McClelland, 1961).

Culture and the need for achievement

If there is a strong positive correlation between a company's success and the need-achievement level of its executives, might not the same relationship hold on a larger scale? Is there a relationship between a nation's economic success and the need-achievement level of its citizens? In an ingenious and lengthy program of investigation, McClelland set out to find evidence that might link the level of need achievement among the members of a given nation's population and its level of economic growth and prosperity (McClelland, 1961). This is a rare kind of research—that designed to investigate how personality (or at least one aspect of it) may act to influence the nature of society. In the other theories discussed, we sometimes dealt with the reverse process: how society influences an individual. In other cases, we discussed the assertion that people are capable of changing society, although we saw that how that happens and which specific aspects of society the individual might influence remain unanswered questions. McClelland's research represents probably the only instance in which such questions have been empirically investigated.

The theoretical rationale for considering the possibility of a link between need for achievement and a culture's level of economic growth grew out of the work of the German sociologist Max Weber. Writing early in the century, Weber offered the suggestion that the Protestant Reformation had produced a new character orientation in Protestant countries, which in turn produced the industrial revolution and the spirit of capitalism (Weber, 1930). This orientation stressed a continuing effort to improve oneself, to progress, strive, seek, pursue—in a word, to achieve. McClelland suggested that these values of hard work and striving for excellence became the norm in Protestant cultures and were taught to each succeeding generation, as a result of which the new values became increasingly widespread. The stress on individual achievement was then manifested in ways that advanced the economic growth of the culture.

As an initial test of this proposed relationship between need achievement and economic growth, McClelland compared the average per capita consumption of electric power (a measure of level of economic development) of 12 Protestant and 13 Catholic countries. The data showed that the Protestant countries were the more economically advanced.

In a more direct study, the relationship between achievement motivation and economic growth was studied in three time periods of ancient Greek civilization—a period of growth, of climax, and of decline. If there is a causal relationship between need achievement and economic growth, then the general level of achievement motivation should have been highest during the period of growth and dropped during the climax, leading to the later decline.

But how does one measure need achievement in a culture long dead? You cannot ask individuals to write stories into which they project their need for achievement. Stories written at the time, however, can be analyzed for evidence of need-achievement themes, on the assumption that the writers reflected the values of their society. This is an indirect but clever way to assess a culture's level of achievement motivation. When these empirical measures of need achievement were compared with measures of the economic level during the three time periods, the results were as predicted. There was a high level of need achievement during the period of growth, which presumably led to the period of climax in economic development. During the climax period, the level of need achievement fell, which, it was suggested, resulted in the economic decline that followed.

Because the measures were indirect, one might question these findings had they not been strikingly confirmed in similar studies with other cultures. For example, a study of Spain during the Middle Ages and another of England from 1400 to the industrial revolution (around 1830) showed the same high level of need achievement preceding a period of heightened economic growth and a declining need achievement, he analyzed the content of children's stories found in second- to fourth-grade schoolbooks. Children's stories were chosen because they reflect the able to change the nature of that culture drastically.

To apply this idea to more contemporary cultures, McClelland undertook a complex and sophisticated investigation of more than 20 countries, comparing their economic and achievement-need levels in 1925 and in 1950. As a measure of need achievement, he analyzed the content of children's stories found in second- to fourth-grade schoolbooks. Children's stories were chosen because they reflect the motives and values a culture wants its children to learn; the stories represent the popular culture that is to be inculcated into the next generation. The morals of these stories are presented directly, "in such simple terms that even a behavioral scientist can understand them" (McClelland, 1961, p. 71).

The results showed that the higher a country's need-achievement level in 1925, the greater its rate of economic growth between 1925 and 1950. It is important to note that the need achievement came first. That is, it was not an increased level of economic development that led to an increased achievement need. Thus, examining a country's 1925 achievement need enabled McClelland to predict that country's economic level only 25 years later.

Having provided such impressive evidence of the importance of the need for achievement, McClelland turned to a related and potentially more important issue: Can the level of achievement motivation be increased in adults? Particularly in developing countries, if sufficient numbers of persons could become highly motivated to achieve, the consequences might significantly raise the economic levels of those countries.

Developing the need for achievement in adults

We have just discussed the possibility that a change in one aspect of personality can produce a meaningful change in society. In order for societal change to take place quickly, the acquisition of new motives in adulthood must be possible—and much of psychology believes that it is not. As we have seen, Freud and other theorists have argued that personality is formed and rather solidly crystallized in the very early years of life and is difficult, if not impossible, to change after that.

McClelland was encouraged in his efforts by the examples of two different groups of change agents: operant conditioners and missionaries. In operant conditioning, if you want a person to exhibit a new kind of behavior, all you have to do is arrange for that behavior to be emitted and then reinforce it. Missionaries have also changed behavior successfully, McClelland noted, through forceful programs of education and the vigorous belief that it is possible to change the behavior of adults.

Drawing on principles of learning obtained from human and animal studies, the findings of attitude-change research, and principles of psychotherapy, McClelland developed formal courses that teach achievement motivation to adult men (McClelland, 1965; McClelland & Winter, 1969). Performed in the United States, Mexico, and India, the courses were conducted with groups of 9 to 25 people. The training sessions were short but intensive, lasting up to 14 days, 12 to 18 hours a day. From the initial training sessions, McClelland derived a series of principles or guidelines, the use of which he believes can induce a change in the level of need achievement (or of any other motive).

The first objective of the training is to instill confidence in the participants that the program will work. Training techniques are more likely to be effective if the person believes that he will (and should) develop this new motive. The techniques are also more effective if the person is able to see their relevance to the real world—that is, how the person can use what he is learning. As a first step, the individual is taught to use, in a series of games, what he is learning about achievement motivation. In this way, he is able to translate theory into action. Participants are also taught to examine personal and cultural values with respect to achievement motivation and to understand how a greater level of need for achievement can work to improve both themselves and their culture. The trainees must commit themselves to a specific course of action designed to achieve definite goals in their lives, and they must record the extent of their progress in attaining those goals.

Two additional points deserve mention. First, the course leaders behaved in warm and rewarding ways and were nondirective in their relationships with the trainees. McClelland believes that motivational changes are much more likely to occur if a person feels warmly and honestly supported as well as respected by both teachers and peers. These people should reaffirm the person's belief in his ability to direct the course of his own future behavior. Second, McClelland feels that changes in motivation are more likely to occur when the training is conducted in a retreat, in which participants study and live together away from the routine of their everyday lives.

The results of these training programs show significant changes in behavior for large numbers of trainees. The behavioral index of increased achievement motivation was any activity that led to "unusual pay raises, promotions to jobs of higher entrepreneurial responsibility, increased profits, decreased costs, larger sales volumes, and the like" (McClelland & Winter, 1969, p. 79). Such behavior was evaluated for two years prior to the course and two years after it and showed significant increases in activities related to the need for achievement.

Developing the need for achievement in children

While McClelland has demonstrated that adults can be formally taught to develop a need for achievement, this is not the only way in which it can originate. No more than a few hundred people have taken McClelland's course, yet many times that number demonstrate the need for achievement. In his search for the source of need for achievement, McClelland has concentrated on the family environment—specifically, certain child-rearing practices that seem to account for the emergence of achievement motivation.

In an early study, it was demonstrated that differences in need achievement level can be detected in children as young as 5 years old and that these differences can be traced to specific attitudes held by their mothers. In another study, 8- to 10-year-old boys were divided into high and low need-achievement groups, and the mothers were interviewed about the demands and restrictions they placed on their children. Interesting differences were found between the mothers of the two groups of boys. For example, mothers of high need-achievement boys expected more self-reliant mastery (doing things on their own, taking responsibility, doing well, trying hard, and so on) than did mothers of boys with low need achievement. Mothers of the high need-achievement boys also placed fewer restrictions on their sons than did the other mothers. However, restrictions that were imposed by the high mothers were expected to be followed at an earlier age. The high need-achievement boys were encouraged to become more independent, and to do so at a younger age, than were the other boys (Winterbottom, 1958).

In another set of experiments, fathers and mothers of high and low need-achievement boys observed their children performing such tasks as building towers out of blocks, playing ringtoss, and copying patterns with blocks. During the tasks, the parents were allowed to say whatever they wished to their sons, and some interesting parent–child interactions were observed. For example, parents of high need-achievement children set higher standards of excellence than did the other parents, expecting their sons to build higher towers and to stand farther away from the peg in the ringtoss game. McClelland concluded that one way to develop a high need for achievement is to have parents who expect a high level of performance.

Another difference between the two sets of parents was in the general degree of warmth of their comments to their sons during the tasks. While exhorting their sons to do well, the high parents were pleasant, anxiety-relieving, and joking— much more so than the parents of low need achievement sons. Another finding relates to the level of authoritarian behavior of the parents. The high mothers tended to be more authoritarian (pushing or dominating the child) than the low mothers. On the other hand, the high fathers were less authoritarian than the low fathers. That finding, together with the results of other studies, led McClelland to conclude that strong rigidity or authoritarianism, particularly from the father, will tend to lower the need for achievement (Rosen & D'Andrade, 1959).

What emerges from this research is a clear picture of the parental behavior likely to produce a high need for achievement: setting realistically high standards of performance at an age when such standards can be reached, not overprotecting or indulging, not interfering with the child's efforts to achieve, and demonstrating genuine pleasure in the child's achievements.

Age differences in the need for achievement

Evidence indicates that the need to achieve declines markedly in most people after middle age, the time when the peak of one's career has usually been reached (Smith, 1970). It has been suggested, however, that this may not necessarily have a deleterious effect, because older people may define success in different terms.

They may no longer be motivated to reach the same goals they pursued when they were younger, although they may still be striving to achieve satisfaction or to experience challenges.

If an older person has achieved security and recognition in his or her work, then goals related to personal growth may replace the earlier goals of position, status, or a high income. The new goals do not require the same kind of competitive, striving behavior, but their achievement would nonetheless be considered a kind of success, albeit a different kind. Thus, the quality of achievement motivation may change with age (Maehr & Kleiber, 1981).

Sex differences in the need for achievement

McClelland initially tested for sex differences in the need to achieve by comparing men and women subjects under experimental conditions designed to arouse achievement motivation (Veroff, Wilcox & Atkinson, 1953). This experimental manipulation produced significant differences in the achievement need for men but not, or should not be, as ambitious, as desirous of achievement, as men. Fifteen years later, psychologist Matina Horner proposed that both men and women are on the need for achievement was conducted almost exclusively with male subjects.

It is important to consider the time when the study of sex differences was published. The year was 1953, a period when it was widely believed that women were not, or should not be, as ambitious, as desirous of achievement, as men. Fifteen years later, psychologist Matina Horner proposed that both men and women are motivated to achieve success, but that women also fear success; that is, they are motivated to avoid success. To succeed in a competitive world, Horner said, is something women may avoid because it would reflect so-called unfeminine characteristics (Horner, 1973).

To test her hypothesis, Horner conducted a study in which men and women college students were given the beginning of a story and asked to complete it. One of the story openings for women subjects was: "After her first term finals, Anne finds herself at the top of her medical school class. . . ." For men subjects, the statement was: "After his first term finals, John finds himself at the top of his medical school class. . . ."

Approximately two-thirds of the women subjects wrote stories that reflected a fear of success. Achieving at too high a level was seen to have negative consequences. Anne would be judged unfeminine and rejected socially because of her high grades. She would feel guilty about her success and might worry that her achievement was somehow abnormal.

The women's stories offered various solutions to the problem of Anne's success. One subject suggested that because Anne did not really want to be the best in her class, her grades would fall and she would marry the man who was then at the top of the class. Another subject wrote that because of Anne's guilt, she would have a nervous breakdown, drop out of medical school, and marry a doctor. Thus, Anne's future success was defined not by her own achievements but in terms of the achievements of the man she would marry.

The men's stories in response to the same scenario, though about John instead of Anne, exhibited highly positive feelings about success. Fewer than 10 percent indicated any fear of success or of the consequences of achieving.

To determine how a fear of success might influence behavior in an achievement situation, Horner's subjects participated in either a competitive or a noncompetitive game four days after the story test. Men and women who had scored high on the fear-of-success variable performed better in noncompetitive games than in competitive games. Those who had scored low in fear of success performed better in the competitive games (Horner, 1978).

More recent research has not consistently supported these findings on sex differences in the need to achieve. One study found that 65 percent of the women subjects were high in the fear of success, approximately the same as in the Horner study, but that 77 percent of the men subjects were also high in the fear of success. Some 30 percent of the men's stories questioned the value of success and achievement; only 15 percent of the women's stories did so. Stories for both groups of subjects contained many fewer achievement images than had been advanced by Horner's subjects (Hoffman, 1974).

The issue of fear of success in women remains unclear. Additional research suggests that it may be declining in college-age women and rising slightly in college-age men. Also, the possibility has been raised that women may display a fear of success only in jobs or careers in which they compete directly with men (Tresemer, 1977). Although some women are apparently motivated to avoid success and achievement, so too are some men, and the difference between them in this regard may not be as large today as it may have been in the past (Kaufman & Richardson, 1982).

Comment

As McClelland's work demonstrates, it is possible for a limited-domain approach to personality to have a wide domain of influence and application. In fact, some psychologists argue that McClelland's massive investigation of this one facet of personality is far more useful than most large-scale theories that attempt to account for all aspects of personality. It would be difficult not to agree that the theory of need achievement has a more solid foundation of empirical support than many of the other theories discussed. The data derive exclusively from experimental research. While other theorists speculate on the relationship between personality and environment, McClelland has empirically investigated that relationship.

His work has generated additional research within a large network of scholars. The fact that his initial research has been so widely extended is effective tribute to its importance both as a theoretical endeavor and as an applied endeavor. It provides an instructive example of how much can be accomplished when the focus of investigation is restricted to a limited domain.

Herman Witkin: Psychological differentiation

A second limited-domain approach to personality is the product of many years of research by Herman Witkin (1916–1979), long associated with the State University of New York Downstate Medical Center (New York City) as director of the psychological laboratory. At the time of his death, he held the position of distinguished research scientist at the Educational Testing Service.

Personality and perception

As the title of his first major work, *Personality Through Perception* (1954), suggests, Witkin's approach to personality is through the investigation of the relationship between an individual's personal characteristics and the way in which he or she perceives the world. As such, his work helped provoke the surge of interest in cognitive styles, such as those identified by George Kelly, that developed since the 1950s.

Specifically, Witkin's approach attempts to study the ways in which the personality may influence one's perception. This may appear to be an indirect method of studying personality, and it is, but the idea behind it has been recognized for years.

The basic idea is that a person's emotional and motivational attributes will influence his or her perception. We have already noted that this influence provides the theoretical basis for projective techniques, such as the Rorschach Inkblot Test and Murray's Thematic Apperception Test. In both cases, a subject is presented with an unstructured object and is asked to give it a structure—that is, to tell what he or she sees in it. This is a clear example of how personality influences perception; the interpretations that people give to these unstructured stimuli are a function of their own needs, fears, and values—their personality.

However, while the idea of a relationship between personality and perception has been around for quite some time, it was never investigated thoroughly and systematically until Witkin began his research, during the 1940s. The initial project took ten years to complete, which indicates the complexity of the problem and the dedication of Witkin and his associates.

To accomplish his task, Witkin had to develop a set of situations that would provide, under laboratory conditions, reliable tests of perception and that would reveal important aspects of human perceptual ability. The range of perceptual issues studied was vast: individual differences in the manner of perceiving, stability of perception over time, consistency of perception under different circumstances, perceptual changes from childhood to adulthood, and sex differences in perception. Not only were different perceptual tasks studied, but also different kinds of subjects: normals and psychotics, children and adults, males and females. Finally, the subjects' performance on different measures of personality was investigated.

Perhaps you are wondering what this has to do with personality. The focus of Witkin's research is perception, yet the title of his book, *Personality Through Perception*, gives a different impression. The analysis of the relationship between perceptual performance and personality measurements reveals personality-related individual differences in perception. To relate these two sets of data—that is, to relate personality and perception—Witkin invoked the concept of **psychological differentiation**, which has to do with the degree of complexity of the relevant structures or systems (Witkin et al., 1974).

The more highly differentiated a system is, the more heterogeneous and specialized its subsystems are. And the more heterogeneous and specialized the subsystems, the greater the number of specific functions that can be mediated by the system as a whole. Psychological differentiation refers to the extent to which the areas of psychological operation in an individual (such as feeling, perceiving, and thinking) are separate from one another and capable of functioning with a degree of specificity. In other words, the more highly differentiated a person's psychological functioning, the more capable the person is of making a specific response to a specific stimulus, instead of just a diffuse response to many stimuli. In perception, a high degree of differentiation means that a person can more readily experience and respond to individual parts of a perceptual field, instead of just to the field as a whole. The individual's perception is differentiated rather than diffuse, specific rather than general and broad.

The same reasoning applies to functioning in the sphere of personality. The highly-differentiated individual functions in a more specific and sophisticated fashion than one who is less differentiated. For example, Witkin hypothesized that subjects characterized by a low degree of differentiation will be more easily influenced by other people because they are less able to rely on their own judgments. Such a prediction proceeds from the notion of psychological differentiation in the following way. Poorly-differentiated individuals, since they respond in a diffuse fashion, are unable to separate the ideas and suggestions of others from their own. As a result, they tend to assimilate all ideas, regardless of their sources, with their own. Highly-differentiated people, on the other hand, are able to respond specifically to ideas and their sources and can thus clearly separate their own ideas from those of others.

Witkin assumed that there is a positive correlation between the level of differentiation within one sphere of behavior and the levels of differentiation within other spheres. In other words, the way you perceive will be the way you function in other areas.

We will now discuss how this linkage of perception and personality has been investigated by Witkin.

Research on perceptual tasks

Witkin's theory developed initially from his observations of subjects' behavior in a perceptual task known as the *rod-and-frame test*. The subject, seated in a darkened room, faces a luminous vertical rod surrounded by a luminous square frame. The rod has been tilted to some degree away from the true vertical position, and the surrounding frame is also tilted, sometimes in the same direction as the rod and sometimes in the opposite direction. The subject's task is to adjust the position of the rod back to the true vertical, a difficult task, considering the context in which

In the rod-and-frame test, the subject tries to bring the rod to a vertical position, overcoming the context of the surrounding frame.

it must be done. The only visual stimuli available to the subject are the rod and the frame; there are no other cues to help determine the vertical position. Thus, the frame of reference within which this perceptual task must be performed is the frame surrounding the rod. But the frame is also tilted away from the vertical, and it cannot be moved by the subject.

There are two ways of responding in this situation. Either subjects use the cues supplied by the surrounding frame of reference, or they operate independently of it. If they use the frame as a reference point, then they tilt the rod in the same direction as the frame. Thus, their perception has been determined by the surrounding visual field; they are not able to overcome its influence. Subjects who responded in this manner (on this and similar tasks) were called **field dependent** in Witkin's early work.

Those subjects who can bring the rod close to the true vertical are, in contrast, capable of functioning independently of the surrounding field. They have the ability to overcome an *embedding context*. That is, they are unaffected by misleading or irrelevant aspects of a situation (here, the surrounding frame). These subjects are able to concentrate solely on whatever provides the true basis for correct performance. In the rod-and-frame test, they are able to concentrate on the rod and its relation to their own body position. Such subjects were called **field independent**. (There seems to be a similarity between Witkin's concept of field dependence versus field independence and Rotter's personality variable of external versus internal control.)

The terms *field dependent* and *field independent* were later subsumed under the general term **psychological differentiation**, which can be represented as a continuum, ranging from full dependence on the surrounding field to full independence of that field. Witkin found a wide range of individual differences in the ability of subjects to perform perceptual tasks—differences that were later correlated with a variety of measures of personality.

Witkin used other perceptual tasks to measure a subject's ability to overcome an embedding context. One such task, the *body-adjustment test*, requires the subject to adjust his or her own body to a position of true vertical. The subject is seated in a chair that can be tilted, inside a room that can also be tilted. The subject is blindfolded while being placed in the chair and, when the blindfold is removed, finds himself or herself in a tilted position relative to the room. Chair and room tilt sometimes in the same direction and sometimes in opposite directions. It is the same conceptual arrangement as the rod-and-frame test; in a sense, the person becomes the rod that must be adjusted to the vertical position. The visual cue or frame of reference is the tilt of the room. The basic question remains: will the person perform the task independently of the visual field, or will he or she use that field (the room) as the point of reference? As with the rod-and-frame test, the results showed a wide range of individual differences in ability to perform the task.

A variation of the body-adjustment test is the *rotating-room test*, which also involves a tilting chair inside a tilting room. However, the entire room rotates on a track at almost 19 revolutions per minute. This adds the pull of gravity to the subject's frame of reference. Again, the task is to overcome the embedding context, to differentiate among the cues available.

To perform successfully in any of these experimental situations requires the ability to deal separately with the individual items in the total field. The subject, to achieve true verticality (of the body or of a rod), must disregard or ignore the tilted frame or the tilted room.

To determine whether the ability to deal with an item independently of its context or surroundings is a persistent characteristic of an individual's perception, Witkin devised a less expensive and less time-consuming measure called the Embedded Figures Test. This paper-and-pencil test is composed of 24 complex geometrical figures, samples of which are shown in Figure 17.1. Somewhere within each figure a simple figure is hidden, incorporated into the pattern of the more complex figure. The subject is first shown the complex figure and then the simple figure. When the subject is again shown the complex figure, his or her task is to find the simple figure that is embedded in it. Witkin's data show that these various tests of perception produce stable scores that are highly correlated with one another.

Thus far, we have discussed the perception side of Witkin's personality–perception relationship. To assess personality, he used the Rorschach Inkblot Test, the Thematic Apperception Test, a personality questionnaire made up of items extracted from the Minnesota Multiphasic Personality Inventory (MMPI), plus sentence-completion, figure-drawing, and word-association tests. In addition, each subject was interviewed and biographical information taken. The correlation between these personality measures and performance on the perceptual tasks was such that Witkin considered each of them to be measuring some aspect of psychological differentiation.

In the perceptual tasks, Witkin found, in general, that the visual field or surrounding frame of reference significantly influenced the subjects' performance

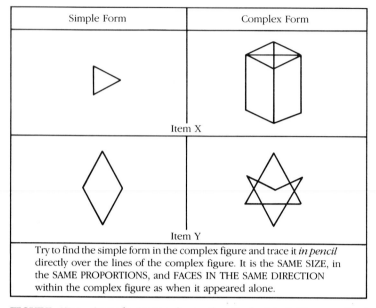

Simple Form	Complex Form
Item X	
Item Y	
Try to find the simple form in the complex figure and trace it *in pencil* directly over the lines of the complex figure. It is the SAME SIZE, in the SAME PROPORTIONS, and FACES IN THE SAME DIRECTION within the complex figure as when it appeared alone.	

FIGURE 17.1   Sample items from the Embedded Figures Test
Copyright © 1971 by Consulting Psychologists Press. Reproduced by permission.

(Witkin et al., 1954). In the rod-and-frame test, for example, subjects tended to adjust the rod in the direction in which the frame was tilted rather than to true vertical. Male subjects were considerably less influenced by the surrounding context than female subjects. The influence of the visual field was greater when the subject had to adjust the field as a whole than when he or she had to adjust only one item in the field. For example, in the body-adjustment test, the subject had much more difficulty adjusting the room to vertical than adjusting the position of his or her own body within the room. Also, adjusting the body was less influenced by the visual field than adjusting an object external to the body (the rod).

These results were from normal adult subjects; Witkin also studied children and disturbed adults. Psychotic adults made many more deviant adjustments than normal adults. Psychotics as a whole tended to score at the extremes of the psychological differentiation continuum. That is, many more psychotics than normals tended to be either highly dependent or highly independent of the visual field. Very few fell in the intermediate range. In contrast, normal subjects tended to be dependent on the visual field. Most were in the intermediate range, with very few at the extremes of very high dependence or independence.

Psychological differentiation and personality

The studies with children revealed interesting developmental changes in psychological differentiation, showing that it tends to increase with age. In one study, a group of boys and girls were studied at age 8 and later at age 13. A second group was studied at ages 10, 14, and 17. In both groups, performance on the perceptual tasks improved with age. The subjects were increasingly able to overcome the influence of the embedding context. The sex difference mentioned above with regard to adult subjects also held for children. Girls were more influenced by the visual field than were boys. Other studies have demonstrated that the rate of increase in the growth of psychological differentiation declines after the age of 25 (Schwartz & Carp, 1967).

What do these differences in perceptual functioning tell us about personality? There are a number of dimensions of personality in which those high in psychological differentiation (field independence) differ from those low in differentiation (field dependence) (Witkin, 1977; Witkin et al., 1954). In the clinical interview, poorly differentiated subjects displayed a lack of self-insight, tended to experience inferiority feelings, and were prone to repress their feelings and impulses. In the figure-drawing test, they tended to draw immature figures; highly differentiated subjects drew more mature-looking figures. In the performance on the Rorschach, poorly differentiated subjects revealed a low ability to cope with the environment and with life in general.

The way in which people interact with all aspects of their environment, including other people, seems to be influenced by their level of psychological differentiation. In their attitudes and behavior, poorly differentiated subjects tend to be passive with respect to their environment. For example, they are unable to function independently of their environment, find it difficult to initiate activity on their own, and are prone to submit to authority and be conforming. Highly differentiated subjects are more active, in that they are able to function independently of their environment, initiate, organize, and direct activities, and work to achieve mastery or control over their environment.

In their relations with other people, field-independent persons are capable of functioning more autonomously. They may even be described as impersonal and are seen by others as cold, aloof, and manipulating. Field-dependent people are described as interpersonal because they are more socially oriented. As a result of their greater dependence upon other people, field-dependent persons have more highly developed social skills, get along better with others, and are looked upon as being warm, affectionate, and considerate (Witkin & Goodenough, 1981).

The degree of differentiation also seems to be related to anxiety and to self-esteem. Poorly differentiated subjects feel inferior and tend to repress their impulses, particularly sexual and aggressive ones. In addition, they experience considerable anxiety, which they are unable to control or regulate. Allied with these feelings is a low sense of self-esteem and difficulty in accepting themselves. Those high in psychological differentiation are in better control of their impulses, have a lower level of anxiety, and have a higher sense of self-esteem. These findings, which were derived initially from the study of normal adults, were confirmed in the investigation of children and psychotics. It seems clear, then, that there is a relationship between individual differences in perceiving and individual differences in personality. Knowledge of either set of differences can be used to predict the other.

In later research, Witkin studied the Freudian concept of defense mechanisms.

On the basis of his psychological differentiation theory, he hypothesized that poorly differentiated people will tend to use more primitive (less differentiated) defense mechanisms, such as repression and denial, than well-differentiated people. The rationale is as follows.

In Freud's view, repression and denial are used in an undifferentiated or diffuse manner. They involve the repression or denial of a large area of impulses, not the isolation of a single item out of the total context, and they are also associated with the earlier stages of development. Highly differentiated people, Witkin hypothesized, will use defenses of a more intellectual or sophisticated nature, which involve the separation of the intellectual content of an impulse from its emotional content. Several studies support the hypothesis, showing the wide range of behaviors with which perceptual functioning appears to be associated—from self-esteem to interaction with others to unconscious defense mechanisms.

Our degree of psychological differentiation also influences the important choices we make in life, such as careers and spouses. These choices are made in terms of their compatibility with our individual cognitive style.

College students who are field independent tend to choose to major in engineering, mathematics, or the natural sciences, areas that demand cognitive restructuring skills and less in the way of interpersonal contact. Field-dependent students are more likely to major in such fields as social work or elementary education, where social skills may be more important than the kind of cognitive functioning required. Research has also shown that married couples with similar cognitive styles are much more satisfied with their relationship than couples who possess opposing cognitive styles (Witkin, 1977).

Stability of psychological differentiation

How stable or permanent is our degree of psychological differentiation? Witkin initially believed that our cognitive style was stable over time and highly resistant to change. In his later research, however, he found evidence to suggest that performance on perceptual tasks, such as the rod-and-frame test, could be improved through training. As a result, he suggested that a person's cognitive style was subject to much greater change over time than he had previously thought. Accordingly, he proposed a new dimension of psychological differentiation called **fixity versus mobility**. Whereas some people do possess only one cognitive style, others are capable of shifting from one mode of functioning to another, as the situation requires. Persons whose cognitive styles are more mobile can be more flexible and adaptable in their relations with other people and with objects in their environment (Witkin & Goodenough, 1981).

Witkin also raised the intriguing possibility that different cultures may be characterized by different cognitive styles. His research suggests that nomadic groups, which survive by hunting and gathering food during their travels, are field independent, whereas sedentary agricultural groups that settle in one place and farm are field dependent.

Nomadic groups operate in relative isolation in a constantly changing environment. Therefore, they need more cognitive restructuring skills and fewer interpersonal skills. Agricultural groups live in a more constant perceptual world that requires little cognitive restructuring and in larger, more cohesive communities that require both consideration and cooperation for survival.

These differences in cognitive style were found between farmers in the African nation of Sierre Leone, who were identified as field dependent, and nomadic Eskimos in Canada, who were found to be field independent. The findings also suggest that cognitive styles are learned in childhood. In training their children, nomadic groups emphasize autonomy as a requisite survival skill. Agricultural groups focus on interpersonal skills necessary for conformity and cooperation behavior (Witkin & Berry, 1975).

Comment

A prominent psychologist has commented, "Witkin's eventual place in the pantheon of eminent personality researchers is virtually assured. . . . The [field independent–field dependent] construct has few, if any, rivals for comprehensive sweep and explanatory power. One stands in awe of the sheer scope of the enterprise and the energy devoted to it over the past three decades" (Kogan, 1980, pp. 595, 597).

Witkin concluded from his research that particular modes of perceiving the world are consistently related to particular ways of adjusting to the world. The relationship between these two processes—perception and personality—seems to be one of mutual influence. On the one hand, perceptual capacities form part of the fund of resources a person uses to cope with and adjust to the world. On the other hand, a person's pattern of adjusting and coping acts to determine the nature of his or her perceptual capacities. Perception thus contributes to adjustment and at the same time reflects that adjustment. Therefore, knowledge of one process tells us something about the other process.

What does this mean for the understanding of personality? According to Witkin, it points up the necessity of considering an individual as a fully integrated system. We can understand each of the parts, he argued, only by understanding the setting or context of the whole. The reverse also holds: we cannot understand the whole without knowledge of each of the parts. Since Witkin regarded personality as the overall psychological organization of a person, personality becomes the whole or the context, of which such processes as learning, thinking, and perception are the parts. Thus, personality cannot be adequately understood without information about all of these parts. We can understand the personality of an individual only if we know his or her motivational and emotional characteristics and the ways in which he or she perceives, learns, and thinks. Personality, then, must be approached in a highly differentiated way, with proper isolation of and attention to all of its part processes. Thus, while Witkin's concept of differentiation is of limited domain with respect to approach (studying only one part—perception), it is not limited in overall aim; the goal is to develop an understanding of the whole personality.

Arnold Buss and Robert Plomin: A temperament theory

The newest theory discussed in this book is the temperament theory of personality development, presented formally in 1975 by Arnold Buss (1924–) of the University of Texas and Robert Plomin (1948–) of the University of Colorado. **Temperament** may be defined as "an individual peculiarity of physical organization by which the manner of thinking, feeling, and acting of every person is permanently affected." We usually think of temperament as a kind of natural disposition to behave in a particular way. We may say one friend has a calm temperament and another has an artistic temperament. Classifying people in this way is an easy and convenient (though not always correct) way of describing them.

The temperament approach to personality has a long history. Hippocrates, the Greek physician considered to be the father of modern medicine, believed that all behavior could be reduced to four basic temperaments. Buss and Plomin offer a contemporary temperament theory of personality grounded not on simple observation or subjective categorization of people, but on rigorous experimental research and quantitative analysis. Initially, they identified four temperaments—emotionality, activity, sociability, and impulsivity—which they believed were the building blocks of personality. Their later research prompted them to reduce the list of temperaments to three: emotionality, activity, and sociability (Buss & Plomin, 1984).

Personality is composed of various combinations of differing amounts of each of these temperaments. Out of these combinations, personality patterns, such as extraversion or introversion, are formed.

The inherited temperaments

Buss and Plomin believe that temperaments, unlike other personality characteristics, are primarily inherited. They are part of the genetic constitution with which we are equipped at birth. These inherited temperaments are broad, and they account for the range of individual differences in human behavior that allows each of us to be unique.

Buss and Plomin do not rely solely on genetic factors, however, to explain the temperamental aspects of personality. They also recognize the effects of the environment. What we inherit is not a specific degree or amount of a temperament, but rather a range of *response potential*. One person may inherit a range at the high end of a scale of responses, another at the low end, and a third person in the middle.

What determines how much or how little of the response potential of a given temperament will be realized? The social environment is the key. Thus, the temperament theory recognizes the impact of both internal genetic variables and external stimulus variables.

Buss and Plomin argue that we influence our social environment through the kind and amount of temperament we possess. The social environment, in turn, influences us because it is shaped by the temperaments of those with whom we are interacting.

The theorists offer the example of two people who differ in the temperament of sociability. One person is very sociable. She readily seeks out other people, initiates conversations, and engages in group activities. The other person is low in sociability. He avoids people, prefers solitary activities, and hesitates to get involved in conversations. Each person creates a different personal environment as a result of possessing a different level of a particular temperament.

We know from the behavioral theories that different environments produce different reinforcements, which, in turn, modify behavior. Buss and Plomin agree with this principle and look to the temperament of sociability again for an example. A person high in sociability will respond to you warmly, letting you know in several ways that meeting you is a pleasant experience. Unless you are very unsociable yourself, this warm response is reinforcing; perhaps it will cause you to seek out that person again. Meeting an unsociable person, however, may be awkward, tedious, and embarrassing, and you may choose to avoid such a person in the future.

Suggesting that personality is a product of both inherited temperament and environment, Buss and Plomin describe their approach as an interaction temperament model. However, they also point out that there are limits to how much the environment can modify temperament. "The effect of any particular environment depends in part on temperament. In the long run, even intense environmental pressure cannot *radically* alter a temperamental disposition" (Buss & Plomin, 1975, p. 4).

When the environment forces us to deviate from a natural tendency over a period of time, we come under considerable strain. We would then not be living in accordance with our dispositions. Indeed, we would be living in a way that was unnatural, an obvious source of conflict and stress.

Studies of temperaments in twins

How can we demonstrate empirically the existence of an innate temperament? The method used by Buss and Plomin was to compare monozygotic and dizygotic twins. Monozygotic (or identical) twins develop from the same fertilized ovum and have identical genetic structures. Dizygotic (or fraternal) twins develop from separate ova and so are not genetically identical. Fraternal twins are no more alike in terms of genetic structure than any set of children born to the same parents.

Using the twin-comparison method, it is assumed that the environments in which both types are raised are identical, or as nearly identical as possible. Therefore, "if the identical twins are observed to be more similar than the fraternal twins, this difference in their correlations is ascribed to the greater genetic similarity of the identical twins" (Buss & Plomin, 1975, p. 15). More simply, if identical twins are significantly more alike than fraternal twins on a particular temperament, this supports the notion that the temperament is shaped more by inheritance than by environment, because the genetic structure of the identical twins is the same.

TABLE 17.1   The EASI Temperament Survey

Emotionality
   Child gets upset easily
   Child tends to cry easily
   Child is easily frightened
   Child is easygoing or happy-go-lucky
   Child has a quick temper
Activity
   Child is always on the go
   Child likes to be off and running as soon as he wakes up in the morning
   Child cannot sit still long
   Child prefers quiet games such as block play or coloring to more active games
   Child fidgets at meals and similar occasions
Sociability
   Child likes to be with others
   Child makes friends easily
   Child tends to be shy
   Child tends to be independent
   Child prefers to play by himself rather than with others
Impulsivity
   Child tends to be impulsive
   Learning self-control is difficult for the child
   Child gets bored easily
   Child learns to resist temptation easily
   Child goes from toy to toy quickly

Source: A. H. Buss & R. Plomin, *A Temperament Theory of Personality Development* (New York: Wiley, 1975), p. 17.

Let us describe a major research study on the temperament theory. First, Buss and Plomin developed a 20-item questionnaire (the EASI Temperament Survey) with five items for each temperament (Table 17.1). The questionnaire was administered to the mothers of 139 pairs of same-sex twins. The women checked the items that best described the behavior of both of their twins. Correlations were computed for each item of the scale for the identical and the fraternal twins. The correlations were considerably higher for identical than for fraternal twins for three of the four temperaments: emotionality, activity, and sociability. This supports the notion that these temperaments have a strong genetic component. The findings for impulsivity were not as clear-cut, and it was later eliminated as a temperament. The research support for the heritability of the three remaining temperaments has increased since this early study (Buss & Plomin, 1984).

Buss and Plomin are cautious in drawing conclusions and emphasize the need for additional research. The twin investigation on the importance of the genetic component of personality dispositions illustrates but one of the five criteria established by the theorists for determining the existence of an inherited temperament. The other criteria are stability during development, presence in adults, adaptiveness, and presence in animals.

If a behavioral tendency is inherited, it should remain stable during a child's maturation and development. The tendency may fluctuate during the stresses of childhood and adolescence, but it will not—if it is a genetic component of personality—be drastically altered by environmental stimuli. Also, if a behavioral tendency is inherited and therefore remains stable in childhood, it will be present in adulthood with no significant change.

According to Darwinian theory, if a trait or characteristic is inherited, it must be adaptive. That is, it must aid the organism in functioning in its world. Buss and Plomin suggest that the temperaments of emotionality, activity, and sociability are all adaptive. They help us to cope with our physical and social environments and thus aid in our survival. Buss and Plomin recognize that other personality characteristics meet this criterion of adaptiveness. Therefore, adaptiveness is the weakest of the five criteria—necessary but not sufficient for the designation of a temperament.

Finally, if a behavioral tendency has enough adaptive value to be inherited, then it must be present not only in humans but also in other higher animals. The reasoning is that prehistoric human beings shared with animals many of the problems of everyday life, such as seeking food, mates, and shelter. As human beings evolved to higher levels, they kept at least some of those adaptive behaviors and characteristics. The theorists believe that all of the temperaments can be observed in higher animals.

Assessing temperaments in adults

Buss and Plomin have developed a self-report inventory for use with adults. Known as the EAS [Emotionality, Activity, Sociability] Temperament Survey for Adults, it measures five traits: activity; sociability; and distress, fearfulness, and anger (the components of the emotionality temperament). The test consists of the 20 statements shown in Table 17.2. Subjects respond on a scale of 1 to 5, indicating the degree to which each statement is or is not characteristic or typical of themselves.

TABLE 17.2   The EAS Temperament Survey for Adults

1. I like to be with people.
2. I usually seem to be in a hurry.
3. I am easily frightened.
4. I frequently get distressed.
5. When displeased, I let people know it right away.
6. I am something of a loner.
7. I like to keep busy all the time.
8. I am known as hotblooded and quick-tempered.
9. I often feel frustrated.
10. My life is fast-paced.
11. Everyday events make me troubled and fretful.
12. I often feel insecure.
13. There are many things that annoy me.
14. When I get scared, I panic.
15. I prefer working with others rather than alone.
16. I get emotionally upset easily.
17. I often feel as if I'm bursting with energy.
18. It takes a lot to make me mad.
19. I have fewer fears than most people my age.
20. I find people more stimulating than anything else.

Source: A. H. Buss & R. Plomin, *Temperament: Early Developing Personality Traits* (Hillsdale, NJ: Erlbaum, 1984), p. 100.

The nature of the temperaments

The *activity* temperament is concerned with one's level of energy output. We might call it a degree of vigor. We all know people who are more vigorous and active than others, and we see them display this energy in everything they do. They walk and talk fast, and appear to find it hard to remain still, even when seated. They seem to keep busy every moment and are constantly in motion.

Activity level is adaptive to both humans and animals, particularly with regard to finding food and shelter. It also meets the other four criteria for temperaments. The twin research revealed a definite inherited component to activity. It maintains at least a moderate level of stability through childhood and continues into adulthood, and its presence can be established in animals.

The second temperament, *emotionality*, refers to one's level of arousal or excitability. As noted, it consists of three components: distress, fearfulness, and anger. When we describe someone as highly emotional, we mean that he or she is easily stirred and given to emotional outbursts. Like all the temperaments, emotionality exists on a continuum. At one extreme are persons who are completely unemotional; nothing seems to arouse them. At the other extreme are persons who may explode at the slightest provocation.

Both extremes are maladaptive, because they prevent a person from responding in appropriate ways to emergency or danger situations. Further, emotionality, in Buss and Plomin's view, refers only to negative or unpleasant emotions such as distress, fearfulness, and anger, not to pleasant emotions such as happiness or love. This follows the everyday usage of the word *emotional*. We do not, as a rule, apply that label to persons who seem carefree and serene, but to those who are easily upset and likely to be angry or agitated.

An optimal degree of emotionality is adaptive in emergency situations, where one must become aroused and alert quickly to respond appropriately. Emotionality, as expressed in fear and anger, can be observed in all mammals. In humans it remains relatively stable in childhood, and there is some evidence that it persists in adulthood. These points, together with the positive results obtained in the twin research, indicate that all the criteria for the status of a temperament have been satisfied.

Sociability, the third temperament, refers to the degree of personal preference for contact and interaction with other people, a characteristic you may recognize in yourself and others. We noted the obvious differences in the temperament of sociability. Persons who are highly sociable seek out other people and prefer group activities; persons who are not sociable engage in solitary activities and avoid other people as much as possible. Data from other sources suggest that sociability is a highly persistent trait from infancy. Approximately 10 percent of all children are born with a high degree of sociability, and another 10 percent are born with a low degree of sociability (Kagan, 1984).

Sociability is an adaptive characteristic. We must interact with others to satisfy many of our needs and desires and to secure positive reinforcement. There are many activities (including most occupations) that are better accomplished socially than individually. Sociability meets the other four criteria for a temperament: the twin research showed a genetic component, higher animals display sociability, it remains stable during human development, and it persists in adulthood. According to Buss and Plomin, the empirical evidence supporting the three behavioral tendencies is strongest for the sociability temperament.

Comment

The temperament theory of Buss and Plomin is unusual and provocative, particularly in American psychology, where the behavioral and social-learning approaches have been dominant for so long. Those approaches focus on learning and experience as the primary shapers of behavior and allow for virtually no influence of genetic factors on personality. None of the other theorists discussed in this book places so great an emphasis on inheritance as do Buss and Plomin. Some theorists have posited that certain drives or needs, such as self-actualization, are innate, but none has argued that specific personality tendencies or characteristics are inherited. Further, all agree that inherited needs can be negated by strong environmental influences, particularly child-rearing practices.

Buss and Plomin's emphasis on inheritance as the primary determining force in personality seems to be out of step with the rest of the field. They recognize that environmental factors can influence the temperaments, but they suggest that such external factors cannot radically alter them. The core of their theory remains genetic. Also, the conclusion of Buss and Plomin with regard to parental influences on personality may appear difficult to accept, in light of the positions of the other personality theorists. "Child rearing," they wrote, "may not be an important influence in the development of temperament" (Buss & Plomin, 1975, p. 223).

It is important to reiterate that Buss and Plomin are putting forth a tentative theory, and they recognize that additional research is needed. Their purpose is to stimulate researchers and theorists in the field of personality to consider that the environment may not be the only influence on personality. "It is foolhardy," they suggest, "to ignore the personality dispositions that are built into each of us" (Buss & Plomin, 1975, p. 236).

Summary
The need for achievement

The need for achievement has been studied by David McClelland using the TAT. The stories subjects produce in response to the TAT pictures are interpreted and scored for achievement themes and images. The need for achievement can be manipulated and aroused in the laboratory.

High need-achievement men are more often of the middle class, have a better memory for uncompleted tasks, are more active in college and community activities, are more likely to volunteer to serve as subjects in psychological research, and are more resistant to social pressures than low need-achievement men. High need achievers work harder than low need achievers, but only on tasks in which there is room for improvement, challenge, and the opportunity to satisfy the achievement need. People high in the achievement need are more likely to attend college and to do well there. They are found in higher-status jobs in which they have a lot of personal responsibility and a greater expectation of success than low need-achievement people. High need achievers are often entrepreneurs or successful managers in organizations. A high positive correlation exists between the need-achievement scores of a company's executives and that company's economic success.

McClelland found a high positive correlation between the need-achievement level of a nation and its economic prosperity. The German sociologist Max Weber suggested that the Protestant Reformation had produced a new character orientation in Protestant countries that focused on achievement. McClelland demonstrated that Protestant countries were more economically advanced than Catholic countries. Studies of past cultures also revealed a strong positive relationship between need achievement and economic success. When the need for achievement declined among the population, the economy also declined.

Parental behavior likely to produce high need achievement in children includes setting realistically high standards of performance at an age when such standards can be reached, not overprotecting or indulging, not interfering with the child's efforts to achieve, and showing genuine pleasure in the child's achievements. High rigidity or authoritarianism, particularly in fathers, tends to lower the need for achievement.

The need to achieve declines significantly in most people after middle age. This may result from the tendency to define success in different terms at this stage of life. The achievement goals of older persons may differ from the goals they pursued when they were younger.

Matina Horner suggested that both men and women are motivated to achieve success, but that women also fear success because it reflects unfeminine characteristics. Two-thirds of her women subjects indicated a fear of the consequences of success; only 10 percent of the men subjects did so. Men and women who scored high in fear of success performed better in noncompetitive games than in competitive games. Later research has found that fear of success may be declining in college-age women and rising slightly in college-age men. Also, women may display a fear of success only in jobs in which they compete directly with men.

Psychological differentiation

Herman Witkin studied the relationship between personality and perception within the framework of the concept of psychological differentiation. This refers to the extent to which one's areas of psychological operation are separate and capable of functioning with a degree of specificity.

High psychological differentiation enables a person to make a specific response to a specific stimulus instead of a diffuse response to many stimuli. It means that a person can more readily experience and respond to individual parts of a perceptual field rather than to the field as a whole.

Witkin studied psychological differentiation using the rod-and-frame test, the body-adjustment test, the rotating-room test, and the Embedded Figures Test. Subjects respond to these tests by using the cues supplied by the surrounding frame of reference or by operating independently of it. Those who depend on the frame of reference are field dependent; they are low in psychological differentiation. Those who operate independently of the visual field, who have the ability to overcome the embedding context, are field independent; they are high in psychological differentiation.

Male subjects are less influenced by the surrounding context than female subjects. Psychotics tend to score at the extremes of the psychological differentiation continuum. Psychological differentiation tends to increase until the age of 25, at which time the rate of increase starts to decline.

Subjects low in psychological differentiation display a lack of self-insight, repress their impulses, experience inferiority feelings, have a low ability to cope with life, are passive, are prone to submit to authority, tend to be conforming, and use more primitive defense mechanisms. They have more highly developed social skills and tend to choose careers in which interpersonal skills are important.

Those high in psychological differentiation are more active and autonomous and may appear aloof to others. They tend to choose careers in engineering, mathematics, and the natural sciences.

Some people possess only one cognitive style; others are capable of shifting from one mode of functioning to another, as the situation requires.

Nomadic groups were found to be field independent; agricultural groups were found to be field dependent.

Witkin assessed personality by using the Rorschach, the TAT, objective tests, interviews, and biographical information.

Temperament theory

According to Arnold Buss and Robert Plomin, the temperaments of emotionality, activity, and sociability are largely inherited, although they can be affected by the environment. A temperamental disposition cannot be radically altered by environmental forces.

The existence of innate temperaments has been determined by comparing monozygotic (identical) twins with dizygotic (fraternal) twins. If identical twins are significantly more alike than fraternal twins on a particular temperament, then that temperament was shaped more by inheritance than by environment.

Five criteria for determining the existence of an inherited temperament are (1) genetic results of twin studies, (2) stability of the temperament during development, (3) presence of the temperament in adults, (4) presence of the temperament in animals, and (5) adaptiveness.

Temperaments can be assessed through observation of behavior and performance on the EAS Temperament Survey for Adults.

The activity temperament is concerned with one's level of energy output. The emotionality temperament is concerned with excitability and consists of distress, fearfulness, and anger. The sociability temperament refers to the degree of preference for contact and interaction with other people.

Glossary

achievement motivation   The need to achieve, to overcome obstacles, to excel, and to live up to a high standard.

field dependence versus field independence   A dimension of psychological differentiation in which field dependence represents a low degree of psychological differentiation, that is, the tendency to make general or diffuse responses to a perceptual field as a whole; field independence represents a high degree of psychological differentiation, that is, the ability to respond specifically to individual parts of a perceptual field.

fixity versus mobility   A dimension of psychological differentiation in which a more mobile cognitive style is associated with more adaptable behavior in relation to other people and situations.

psychological differentiation   The extent to which the areas of psychological functioning (such as feeling and thinking) are separate and capable of responding specifically to individual stimuli.

temperaments   Inherited dispositions to behave in a particular way; identified by Buss and Plomin as emotionality, activity, and sociability.

Review questions

1. How does McClelland's research on the need for achievement relate to the work of Sigmund Freud and Henry Murray?
2. Describe McClelland's technique for measuring the need for achievement.
3. Describe the differences between high and low achievers in terms of their college and career performance.
4. What differences have been reported between men and women in the need for achievement?
5. What parental behaviors can influence the development of the child's need for achievement?
6. Describe the relationship proposed by Witkin between personality and perception.
7. How would a highly differentiated (field independent) person probably respond to the rod-and-frame perceptual task? How is a poorly differentiated (field dependent) person likely to respond on the body-adjustment test?
8. On such personality dimensions as self-esteem, sociability, and conformity, how do highly differentiated and poorly differentiated people differ?
9. How does the concept of fixity versus mobility in cognitive style relate to psychological differentiation?

10. Describe the temperaments identified by Buss and Plomin.
11. How does the temperament theory encompass both genetic and environmental explanations for the development of the temperaments?
12. Why is research using twins as subjects helpful in demonstrating empirically the existence of an innate temperament?
13. List the five criteria used to measure the existence of a temperament. How well does each of the three temperaments meet these criteria?

Suggested reading on McClelland and the need for achievement

Evans, R. I. *The making of psychology: Discussions with creative contributors*. New York: Alfred A. Knopf, 1976. (See Chapter 12, "David McClelland.")
Kaufman, D. R. & Richardson, B. L. *Achievement and women: Challenging the assumptions*. New York: Free Press, 1982.
McClelland, D. C. *The achieving society*. New York: Free Press, 1961.
McClelland, D. C. & Winter, D. G. *Motivating economic achievement*. New York: Free Press, 1969.
Spence, J. T., Ed. *Achievement and achievement motives: Psychological and social approaches*. San Francisco: Freeman, 1983.

Suggested reading on Witkin and psychological differentiation

Witkin, H. A. *Cognitive styles in personal and cultural adaptation*. Worcester, MA: Clark University Press, 1977.
Witkin, H. A. & Goodenough, D. R. *Cognitive styles: Essence and origins; field dependence and field independence*. New York: International Universities Press, 1981.
Witkin, H. A., Dyk, R. B., Faterson, H. F., Goodenough, D. R. & Karp, S. A. *Psychological differentiation: Studies in development*. New York: Halsted Press, 1974.

Suggested reading on Buss & Plomin and temperament theory

Buss, A. H. & Plomin, R. *A temperament theory of personality development*. New York: Wiley, 1975.
Buss, A. H. & Plomin, R. *Temperament: Early developing personality traits*. Hillsdale, NJ: Erlbaum, 1984.

The Study of Personality: An Afterword

At the beginning of this book, I told you that psychology had not yet agreed on a common definition and theory of the nature of personality, or even on a single method by which to assess personality or conduct research on it. By now, I am sure you will agree that I was not exaggerating the situation or overstating the diversity of approaches to personality.

We have seen more differences than similarities, more dissension than agreement, among those who study personality. We have described 8 major types of personality theories and 18 individual approaches within those types. We have discussed psychoanalytic and neoanalytic approaches, as well as trait, developmental, humanistic, cognitive, behavioral, and limited-domain formulations. Each offers quite a different view or vision of what constitutes personality.

And we have also learned that the theorists who belong to one of these types share certain similarities that set them apart from theorists who subscribe to another type. Yet, they also differ from each other in significant ways. Skinner, Bandura, and Rotter take a behavioral approach and can be clearly distinguished from those who take a trait, humanistic, or psychoanalytic view. But they may also be distinguished from one another. A Skinnerian does not speak quite the same language as a follower of Bandura or Rotter, just as an Adlerian does not speak the same language as a follower of Jung.

To add to these differences among personality theorists, some prefer to study only a limited portion of personality, a single variable or a cluster of characteristics, instead of the totality of personality. Further, we saw that the kind and amount of research support for the various theories differs.

For those among you whose cognitive styles do not tolerate such ambiguity well, for those who need precision and definitive answers, the situation that exists in the field of personality must be difficult to accept. There is no core of common truth to embrace, no single accepted set of principles, laws, or rules to follow. Instead, there is diversity, disagreement, and difficulty. We might be tempted to label the situation as hopelessly chaotic and forget about it entirely, or switch to engineering, a field that can offer more specific answers.

Before you do anything so drastic, let me remind you of another point mentioned earlier. Any one of these personality theories may be partly correct, or all of them may be partly correct, and the final answer may involve some as-yet-unseen combination of part-truths in still another theory. We cannot deny that each theorist has offered an approach to the truth of personality which, to that theorist, seems utterly valid.

Take a moment to consider the following analogy. Let us imagine that five people, who differ in their training, orientation, purpose—and personality—set about the task of investigating a 50-acre plot of land. One of these people is a geologist. She uses sophisticated tools and equipment to probe the depths beneath the surface, looking for signs of oil and mineral deposits. Her focus is on the contents of the earth underneath the soil. She has no interest in the nature of the surface of the land. As far as she is concerned, it is nothing more than a base or platform on which her drills and rigs can stand.

The second person examining the land is an anthropologist. He, too, is interested in what lies beneath the surface. Using more primitive tools—shovels, brooms, sieves, even spoons—he carefully peels away the layers of soil in search of artifacts and residues of past cultures. From these, he will attempt to reconstruct the nature of the civilizations that once lived there. It is the history of the land that holds his interest.

The third person is a farmer, who is considering buying the land and using it to raise crops. He is interested in the surface layer of topsoil and in the topography. Is the acreage hilly or flat, full of boulders that will need to be removed or trees that will have to be felled? Will the soil support growth? Ancient cultures that once may have dwelled there or minerals that lie 100 feet below are of no concern to the farmer.

The fourth person exploring the land is a real-estate developer who is interested solely in the property's potential. What can be built on it? She sees the hills and boulders and trees differently, not as impediments but as features of the landscape that can be used to enhance the development of homes she intends to build.

The fifth person is an artist. He wanders over the field, viewing it from every angle, watching it in different light, trying to capture in oils the essence and beauty of the land as he sees it. The future of the land or its past or what lies beneath the surface are of no interest. He focuses on the present and transposes his vision of the land onto canvas.

So here are five different ways of investigating, approaching, and describing the same object. Is one way correct? Are the others wrong? No. Each approach is valid, given the training, experience, and purpose of each of our investigators.

It is true, however, that some of these approaches to the nature of the land can be verified precisely, whereas others can be verified only in less exact ways. Another geologist may replicate the first geologist's investigation. Using similar equipment, he can bore and drill near the holes left by the earlier testing and confirm the presence and concentration of the minerals. This is all highly objective and scientific, true or false, right or wrong. The rigor of the techniques helps answer the questions about the natural deposits beneath the land's surface. But these methods are of no help to the anthropologist, the farmer, the developer, or the painter. They reveal information about one aspect of the land—precisely, to be sure—but they tell us nothing about its other characteristics.

The findings of the anthropologist can be verified with less specificity. Another anthropologist viewing the same artifacts taken from the plot of land might reconstruct a somewhat different form of ancient civilization, depending on her training, skill, orientation, or beliefs. And even if the findings of the two anthropologists agreed, they would be of no use to the other people interested in the land.

Similarly, another farmer, desiring to grow a different crop, may find that the soil that will sustain potatoes will not nourish wheat. And another real-estate developer might see the land as inappropriate for housing but perfect for an industrial park. In these cases, the first investigation or assessment of the nature of the land has not been verified; different results were obtained.

Finally, consider the vision of the land painted by our artist. His creation is not a photograph capturing the objective reality of the land, but rather a subjective re-creation, what it looks like to him. Another artist will offer a different version, perhaps in watercolors or chalk. Their efforts are not amenable to objective verification, but this does not mean they are wrong or that they have nothing to tell us about the land. These are simply different approaches to the truth. For some of us, one version will appear to be the more valid; for others, another version will seem more correct.

In addition, keep in mind that none of these investigators can develop a conception that will adequately account for the totality of the land's features. Each, however, can tell us something useful (and, in some cases, verifiable) about a portion of it. Taken together, then, their findings can help us develop an understanding of what the land is like.

As with this hypothetical investigation of a plot of land, our understanding of personality depends on the questions the theorists and researchers have asked, on how they have attempted to answer them, and on their professional commitments and personal philosophies.

Are we capable of consciously guiding our lives, or are we wholly at the mercy of unconscious forces? Or are both ideas true? Are we directed solely by our childhood, motivated by past events, or are we affected (and to what degree) by more recent occurrences and by our goals and aspirations? Do human beings function like some sort of programmed computer, our behavior determined by instincts and conflicts, or can we chart the course of our own development? Is human nature determined by heredity or by learning? By both? And how much? Is our behavior merely a reaction to environmental stimuli, or do we actively influence our responses? Are we unique as individuals, or do we share broad personality patterns with other people?

These are the major questions with which personality theorists have grappled. We have seen how they have attempted to resolve these issues in different ways, but we have also seen that the riddle of the human personality has not yet been solved completely. Perhaps the continuing quest to do so constitutes one of our distinctly human characteristics. There are no simple answers, only difficult questions, and in that sense the study of personality may be a reflection of life itself.

References

Achenbach, T. & Zigler, E. Social competence and self-image disparity in psychiatric and nonpsychiatric patients. *Journal of Abnormal and Social Psychology*, 1963, *67*, 197–205.

Adams, D. *The anatomy of personality.* Garden City, NY: Doubleday, 1954.

Adams-Webber, J. R. An analysis of the discriminant validity of several repertory grid indices. *British Journal of Psychology*, 1970, *60*, 83–90.

Adler, A. Individual psychology. In C. Murchison, ed., *Psychologies of 1930.* Worcester, MA: Clark University Press, 1930.

———. *Social interest.* New York: Putnam, 1939, 1964.

———. *The practice and theory of individual psychology.* Totowa, NJ: Littlefield Adams, 1959.

Alexander, I. E. The Freud-Jung relationship—The other side of Oedipus and countertransference: Some implications for psychoanalytic theory and psychotherapy. *American Psychologist*, 1982, *37*, 1009–1018.

Allport, G. *Personality: A psychological interpretation.* New York: Holt, 1937.

———. *The use of personal documents in psychological science.* New York: Social Science Research Council, 1942.

———. *Becoming: Basic considerations for a psychology of personality.* New Haven, CT: Yale University Press, 1955.

———. *Pattern and growth in personality.* New York: Holt, 1961.

———. Traits revisited. *American Psychologist*, 1966, *21*, 1–10.

———. Autobiography. In E. G. Boring & G. Lindzey, eds., *History of psychology in autobiography*, Vol. 5. New York: Appleton-Century-Crofts, 1967.

———. *The person in psychology: Selected essays.* Boston: Beacon Press, 1968.

Allport, G., ed. *Letters from Jenny.* New York: Harcourt, Brace & World, 1965.

Allport, G. & Cantril, H. Judging personality from voice. *Journal of Social Psychology*, 1934, *5*, 37–55.

Allport, G. & Vernon, P. *Studies in expressive movement.* New York: Macmillan, 1933.

Allport, G., Vernon, P., & Lindzey, G. *A study of values*, 3rd ed. Boston: Houghton Mifflin, 1960.

American Psychological Association. Distinguished Scientific Contribution Award for 1958. *American Psychologist*, 1958, *13*, 729–738.

———. Awards for Distinguished Scientific Contributions: 1980. *American Psychologist*, 1981, *36*, 27–42.

Anastasi, A. *Psychological testing*, 5th ed. New York: Macmillan, 1982.

Annis, L. V., Tucker, G. H. & Baker, C. A. APA certification of terminal master's degree programs. *American Psychologist*, 1984, *39*, 563–566.

459

Ansbacher, H. L. Individual psychology. In R. J. Corsini, ed., *Current personality theories*. Itasca, IL: Peacock, 1977.

Aserinsky, E. & Kleitman, N. Regularly occurring periods of eye motility, and concomitant phenomena during sleep. *Science*, 1953, *118*, 273–274.

Atkinson, J. W., Lens, W. & O'Malley, P. M. Motivation and ability: Interactive psychological determinants of intellectual performance, educational achievement, and each other. In W. H. Sewell, R. H. Hanser & D. L. Featherman, eds., *Schooling and achievement in American society*. New York: Academic Press, 1976.

Atwood, G. & Tomkins, S. S. On the subjectivity of personality theory. *Journal of the History of the Behavioral Sciences*, 1976, *12*, 166–177.

Ayllon, T. & Azrin, N. *The token economy*. New York: Appleton-Century-Crofts, 1968.

Baldwin, A. L. The effect of home environment on nursery school behavior. *Child Development*, 1949, *20*, 49–61.

Bandura, A. *Social learning theory*. Englewood Cliffs, NJ: Prentice-Hall, 1977.

———. The self system in reciprocal determinism. *American Psychologist*, 1978, *33*, 344–358.

———. Self-efficacy mechanism in human agency. *American Psychologist*, 1982, *37*, 122–147.

Bandura, A. & Walters, R. *Social learning and personality development*. New York: Holt, Rinehart & Winston, 1963.

Bandura, A., Adams, N. E. & Beyer, J. Cognitive processes in mediating behavioral change. *Journal of Personality and Social Psychology*, 1977, *35*, 125–139.

Bandura, A., Blanchard, E. B. & Ritter, B. The relative efficacy of desensitization and modeling approaches for inducing behavioral, affective, and attitudinal changes. *Journal of Personality and Social Psychology*, 1969, *13*, 173–199.

Bandura, A., Grusec, J. E. & Menlove, F. L. Vicarious extinction of avoidance behavior through symbolic modeling. *Journal of Personality and Social Psychology*, 1967, *5*, 16–22.

Bandura, A., Ross, D. & Ross, S. A. Imitation of film-mediated aggressive models. *Journal of Abnormal and Social Psychology*, 1963, *66*, 3–11.

Bannister, D. Psychology as an exercise in paradox. *Bulletin of the British Psychological Society*, 1966, *19*, 21–26.

Bannister, D. & Fransella, F. A grid test of schizophrenic thought disorder. *British Journal of Social and Clinical Psychology*, 1966, *5*, 95–102.

Bannister, D. & Salmon, P. Schizophrenic thought disorder: Specific or diffuse? *British Journal of Medical Psychology*, 1966, *39*, 215–219.

Barry, H., III & Blane, H. T. Birth order of alcoholics. *Journal of Individual Psychology*, 1977, *62*, 62–79.

Battle, E. & Rotter, J. B. Children's feelings of personal control as related to social class and ethnic group. *Journal of Personality*, 1963, *31*, 482–490.

Bergin, A. E. & Strupp, H. H. *Changing frontiers in the science of psychotherapy*. New York: Aldine-Atherton, 1972.

Bettelheim, B. *Freud and man's soul*. New York: Vintage, 1984.

Betz, N. E. & Hackett, G. The relationships of career-related self-efficacy expectations to perceived career options in college women and men. *Journal of Counseling Psychology*, 1981, *28*, 399–410.

Bieri, J. Cognitive complexity-simplicity and predictive behavior. *Journal of Abnormal and Social Psychology*, 1955, *51*, 263–268.

Blood, M. R. Intergroup comparisons of introperson differences: Rewards from the job. *Personnel Psychology*, 1973, *26*, 1–9.

Bonarius, J. The interaction model of communication: Through experimental research towards existential relevance. In A. W. Landfield, ed., *Nebraska symposium on motivation*. Lincoln: University of Nebraska Press, 1976.

Boring, E. G. *A history of experimental psychology*, 2nd ed. New York: Appleton, 1950.

Bottome, P. *Alfred Adler: A biography*. New York: G. P. Putnam's Sons, 1939.

Braun, J. & Asta, P. Intercorrelations between the Personal Orientation Inventory and the Gordon Personal Inventory Scores. *Psychological Reports*, 1968, *23*, 1197–1198.

Breger, L., Hunter, I. & Lane, R. W. The effect of stress on dreams. *Psychological Issues*, 1971, 7(3, Monograph 27), 1–213.

Breland, H. M. Birth order, family configuration and verbal achievement. *Child Development*, 1974, *45*, 1011–1019.

Brome, V. *Jung: Man and myth*. New York: Atheneum, 1981.

Brown, S. R. & Hendrick, C. Introversion, extraversion and social perception. *British Journal of Social and Clinical Psychology*, 1971, *10*, 313–319.

Bruner, J. A cognitive theory of personality. *Contemporary Psychology*, 1956, *1*, 355–357.

————. *In search of mind: Essays in autobiography*. New York: Harper, 1983.

Buss, A. H. & Plomin, R. *A temperament theory of personality development*. New York: Wiley, 1975.

————. *Temperament: Early developing personality traits*. Hillsdale, NJ: Erlbaum, 1984.

Butler, J. M. & Haigh, G. V. Changes in the relationship between self-concepts and ideal concepts consequent upon client-centered counseling. In C. R. Rogers & R. F. Dymond, eds., *Psychotherapy and personality change*. Chicago: University of Chicago Press, 1954.

Carlson, R. Personology lives! *Contemporary Psychology*, 1982, *27*, 7–8.

Carlson, R. & Levy, N. Studies of Jungian typology: 1. Memory, social perception, and social action. *Journal of Personality*, 1973, *41*, 559–576.

Cattell, R. B. *Description and measurement of personality*. New York: World, 1946.

————. *Personality: A systematic theoretical and factual study*. New York: McGraw-Hill, 1950.

————. *Personality and motivation: Structure and measurement*. New York: World, 1957.

————. *The scientific analysis of personality*. Baltimore: Penguin, 1970.

————. Autobiography. In G. Lindzey, ed., *A history of psychology in autobiography*, Vol. 6. Englewood Cliffs, NJ: Prentice-Hall, 1974. (a)

————. Travels in psychological hyperspace. In T. S. Krawiec, ed., *The psychologists*, Vol. 2. New York: Oxford University Press, 1974. (b)

————. *The inheritance of personality and ability: Research methods*. New York: Academic Press, 1982.

Cattell, R. B. & Cross, K. P. Comparison of the ergic and self-sentiment structure found in dynamic traits by R- and P-techniques. *Journal of Personality*, 1952, *21*, 250–271.

Cattell, R. B. & Kline, P. *The scientific analysis of personality and motivation*. New York: Academic Press, 1977.

Cattell, R. B. & Nesselroade, J. R. Likeness and completeness theories examined by Sixteen Personality Factor measures by stably and unstably married couples. *Journal of Personality and Social Psychology*, 1967, *7*, 351–361.

Cattell, R. B., Eber, H. W. & Tatsuoka, M. M. *Handbook for the Sixteen Personality Factor Questionnaire*. Champaign, IL: Institute for Personality and Ability Testing, 1970.

Cherry, R. & Cherry, L. The Horney heresy. *New York Times Magazine*, August 26, 1973.

Chodorkoff, B. Self-perception, perceptual defense, and adjustment. *Journal of Abnormal and Social Psychology*, 1954, *49*, 508–512.

Ciacco, N. A test of Erikson's theory of ego epigenesis. *Developmental Psychology*, 1971, *4*, 306–311.

Coan, R. W. Measurable components of openness to experience. *Journal of Consulting and Clinical Psychology*, 1972, *39*, 346.

Coleman, J. S., Campbell, E. Q., Hobson, C. J., McPartland, J., Mood, A. M., Weinfeld, F. D. & York, R. L. *Equality of educational opportunity*. Washington, DC: U.S. Office of Education, 1966.

Constantinople, A. An Eriksonian measure of personality development in college students. *Developmental Psychology*, 1969, *1*, 357–372.

Coopersmith, S. *The antecedents of self-esteem*. San Francisco: W. H. Freeman, 1967.

Corsini, R. J. *Current personality theories*. Itasca, IL: Peacock, 1977.

Crandall, J. E. *Theory and measurement of social interest: Empirical tests of Alfred Adler's concept*. New York: Columbia University Press, 1981.

————. Getting Adler straight—Once more, with feeling. *Contemporary Psychology*, 1983, *28*, 424–426.

Crockett, W. H. The organization of construct systems: The organization corollary. In J. C. Mancuso & R. Adams-Webber, eds., *The construing person*. New York: Praeger, 1982.

Dement, W. C. & Kleitman, N. The relation of the eye movements during sleep to dream activity: An objective method for the study of dreaming. *Journal of Experimental Psychology*, 1957, *53*, 339–346.

Dement, W. C. & Wolpert, E. A. The relationship of eye movements, body motility, and external stimuli to dream content. *Journal of Experimental Psychology*, 1958, *55*, 543–553.

Dignan, M. Ego identity and maternal identification. *Journal of Personality and Social Psychology*, 1965, *1*, 476–483.

Duck, S. W. & Spencer, C. Personal constructs and friendship formation. *Journal of Personality and Social Psychology*, 1972, *23*, 40–45.

Edwards, A. L. *Manual for Edwards Personal Preference Schedule*. New York: Psychological Corporation, 1953.

Ellenberger, H. F. *The discovery of the unconscious: The history and evolution of dynamic psychiatry*. New York: Basic Books, 1970.

Elms, A. C. Skinner's dark year and Walden Two. *American Psychologist*, 1981, *36*, 470–479.

Endler, N. & Magnusson, D. Toward an interactional psychology of personality. *Psychological Bulletin*, 1976, *83*, 956–974.

Engler, B. *Personality theories*. Boston: Houghton Mifflin, 1979.

Epstein, S. Explorations in personality today and tomorrow: A tribute to Henry A. Murray. *American Psychologist*, 1979, *34*, 649–653.

———. A research paradigm for the study of personality and emotion. *Nebraska symposium on motivation 1982*, pp. 91–154.

Erikson, E. H. *Childhood and society*. New York: Norton, 1950.

———. *Childhood and society*, 2nd ed. New York: Norton, 1963.

———. *Young man Luther: A study in psychoanalysis and history*. New York: Norton, 1958.

———. Identity and the life cycle: Selected papers. *Psychological Issues*, 1959, *1*(Monograph 1).

———. *Childhood and society*, 2nd ed. New York: Norton, 1963.

———. *Identity: Youth and crisis*. New York: Norton, 1968.

———. *Life history and the historical moment*. New York: Norton, 1975.

Ernst, C. & Angst, J. *Birth order: Its influence on personality*. Berlin: Springer-Verlag, 1983.

Estes, S. G. Judging personality from expressive behavior. *Journal of Abnormal and Social Psychology*, 1938, *33*, 217–236.

Evans, R. I. *Dialogue with Erich Fromm*. New York: Harper & Row, 1966.

———. *B. F. Skinner: The man and his ideas*. New York: Dutton, 1968.

Exner, J. E., Jr. *The Rorschach: A comprehensive system*. New York: Wiley, 1974.

———. *The Rorschach: A comprehensive system*, Vol. 2: *Current research and advanced interpretations*. New York: Wiley, 1978.

Eysenck, H. J. *Dimensions of personality*. London: Routledge & Kegan Paul, 1947.

Eysenck, H. J. & Eysenck, J. *Eysenck Personality Inventory*. San Diego: Educational and Industrial Testing Service, 1963.

Falbo, T. Only children and interpersonal behavior: An experimental and survey study. *Journal of Applied Social Psychology*, 1978, *8*, 244–253.

Fehr, L. A. *Introduction to personality*. New York: Macmillan, 1983.

Fisher, S. & Greenberg, R. P. *The scientific credibility of Freud's theories and therapy*. New York: Basic Books, 1977.

Fjeld, S. P. & Landfield, A. W. Personal construct consistency. *Psychological Reports*, 1961, *8*, 127–129.

Fox, J., Knapp, R. & Michael, W. Assessment of self-actualization of psychiatric patients: Validity of the Personal Orientation Inventory. *Educational and Psychological Measurement*, 1968, *28*, 565–569.

Freud, S. *Outline of psychoanalysis*. London: Hogarth, 1938; New York: Norton, 1949.

———. *The origins of psycho-analysis: Letters to Wilhelm Fliess, drafts and notes: 1887–1902*. New York: Basic Books, 1954.

———. *On the history of the psycho-analytic movement*. New York: Norton, 1966.

Fromm, E. *Escape from freedom*. New York: Holt, 1941.

———. *The sane society*. New York: Holt, 1955.

———. *Beyond the chains of illusion: My encounter with Marx and Freud*. New York: Simon & Schuster, 1962.

———. *The anatomy of human destructiveness*. New York: Holt, Rinehart & Winston, 1973.

Fromm, E. & Maccoby, M. *Social character in a Mexican village*. Englewood Cliffs, NJ: Prentice-Hall, 1970.

Gatchel, R. J. & Mears, F. G. *Personality: Theory, assessment, and research*. New York: St. Martin's, 1982.

Geer, J. H. The development of a scale to measure fear. *Behavior Research and Therapy*, 1965, *3*, 45–53.

Gendlin, E. T. & Tomlinson, T. M. The process conception and its measurement. In C. R. Rogers, E. T. Gendlin, D. J. Kiesler, & C. B. Truax, eds., *The therapeutic relationship and its impact: A study of psychotherapy with schizophrenics*. Madison: University of Wisconsin Press, 1967.

Gilgen, A. R. *American psychology since World War II: A profile of the discipline*. Westport, CT: Greenwood, 1982.

Graham, W. & Balloun, J. An empirical test of Maslow's need hierarchy theory. *Journal of Humanistic Psychology*, 1973, *13*, 97–108.

Graves, T. D. *Time perspective and the deferred gratification pattern in a tri-ethnic community*. Boulder: University of Colorado Institute of Behavioral Science, 1961.

Greever, K., Tseng, M. & Friedland, B. Development of the social interest index. *Journal of Consulting and Clinical Psychology*, 1973, *41*, 454–458.

Grieser, C., Greenberg, R. & Harrison, R. H. The adaptive function of sleep: The differential effects of sleep and dreaming on recall. *Journal of Abnormal Psychology*, 1972, *80*, 280–286.

Grossack, M., Armstrong, T. & Lussieu, G. Correlates of self-actualization. *Journal of Humanistic Psychology*, 1966, *37*.

Hall, C. & Van de Castle, R. An empirical investigation of the castration complex in dreams. *Journal of Personality*, 1965, *33*, 20–29.

Hall, D. T. & Nougaim, K. E. An examination of Maslow's need hierarchy in an organizational setting. *Organizational Behavior and Human Performance*, 1968, *3*, 12–35.

Hall, E. Alfred Adler, a sketch. *Psychology Today*, 1970, *3*(9), 45, 67.

———. A conversation with Erik Erikson. *Psychology Today*, 1983, *17*(6), 22–30.

Hall, M. H. An interview with "Mr. Behaviorist" B. F. Skinner. *Psychology Today*, 1967, *1*(5), 21–23, 68–71.

———. A conversation with Henry A. Murray. *Psychology Today*, 1968, *2*(4), 56–63. (a)

———. A conversation with Abraham H. Maslow. *Psychology Today*, 1968, *2*, 35–37, 54–57. (b)

Hanewitz, W. B. Police personality: A Jungian perspective. *Crime and Delinquency*, 1978, *24*, 152–172.

Harrison, R. Thematic apperception methods. In B. B. Wolman, ed., *Handbook of clinical psychology*. New York: McGraw-Hill, 1965.

Hartmann, H. *Essays on ego psychology*. New York: International Universities Press, 1964.

Harvey, J. H. & Barnes, R. Perceived choice as a function of internal-external locus of control. *Journal of Personality*, 1974, *42*, 437–452.

Hausdorff, D. *Erich Fromm*. Boston: Twayne, 1972.

Hawkins, R. P., Peterson, R. F., Schweid, E. & Bijou, S. W. Behavior therapy in the home: Amelioration of problem parent-child relations with the parent in a therapeutic role. *Journal of Experimental Child Psychology*, 1966, *4*, 99–107.

Heidbreder, E. *Seven psychologies*. New York: Appleton, 1933.

Helson, R. & Mitchell, V. Personality. *Annual Review of Psychology*, 1978, *29*, 555–585.

Hjelle, L. Relationship of social interest to internal-external control and self-actualization in young women. *Journal of Individual Psychology*, 1975, *31*, 171–174.

Hoffman, L. W. Fear of success in males and females. *Journal of Consulting and Clinical Psychology*, 1974, *42*, 353–358.

Horner, M. S. A psychological barrier to achievement in women: The motive to avoid success. In D. C. McClelland & R. S. Steele, eds., *Human motivation*. Morristown, NJ: General Learning Press, 1973.

———. The measurement and behavioral implication of fear of success in women. In J. W. Atkinson & J. O. Raynor, eds., *Personality, motivation, and achievement*. Washington, DC: Hemisphere, 1978.

Horney, K. *The neurotic personality of our time*. New York: Norton, 1937.

———. *New ways in psychoanalysis*. New York: Norton, 1939.

———. *Self-analysis*. New York: Norton, 1942.

———. The flight from womanhood: The masculinity-complex in women as viewed by men and by women. In H. Kelman, ed., *Feminine psychology*. New York: Norton, 1967.

———. *The adolescent diaries of Karen Horney*. New York: Basic Books, 1980.

Jackson, D. N. *Personality Research Form manual*. Port Huron, MI: Research Psychologists Press, 1967.

———. Interpreter's guide to the Jackson Personality Inventory. In P. McReynolds, ed., *Advances in psychological assessment*, Vol. 4. San Francisco: Jossey-Bass, 1978.

Jaffé, A. *The myth of meaning*. New York: G. P. Putnam's Sons, 1971.

Johnson, R. C. Summing up. *Contemporary Psychology*, 1980, *25*, 299–300.

Jones, E. *The life and work of Sigmund Freud*. New York: Basic Books, 1953–1957.

Jung, C. G. *Two essays on analytical psychology*. New York: Pantheon, 1953.

———. *Memories, dreams, reflections*. New York: Vintage, 1963.

Kagan, J. *The nature of the child*. New York: Basic Books, 1984.

Katz, D. Floyd H. Allport (1890–1978). *American Psychologist*, 1979, *34*, 351.

Kaufman, D. R. & Richardson, B. L. *Achievement and women: Challenging the assumptions*. New York: Free Press, 1982.

Kaufmann, W. *Discovering the mind*, Vol. 3: *Freud versus Adler and Jung*. New York: McGraw-Hill, 1980.

Kazdin, A. E. Covert modeling, imagery assessment, and assertive behavior. *Journal of Consulting and Clinical Psychology*, 1975, *43*, 716–724.

———. Covert modeling and the reduction of avoidance behavior. In D. Upper & J. R. Cautela, eds., *Covert conditioning*. Elmsford, NY: Pergamon Press, 1979.

Kazdin, A. E. & Bootzin, R. The token economy: An evaluative review. *Journal of Applied Behavioral Analysis*, 1972, *5*, 343–372.

Kelly, G. A. *The psychology of personal constructs*, Vol. 1. New York: Norton, 1955.

———. The theory and technique of assessment. *Annual Review of Psychology*, 1958, *9*, 323–352.

Keniston, K. Remembering Erikson at Harvard. *Psychology Today*, 1983, *17*(6), 29.

Kidwell, J. The neglected birth order: Middleborns. *Journal of Marriage and the Family*, 1982, *44*, 225–235.

Kiester, E., Jr. & Cudhea, D. Albert Bandura: A very modern model. *Human Behavior*, 1974, 27–31.

Klein, M. H., Malthieu, P. L., Gendlin, E. T. & Kiesler, D. J. *The Experiencing Scale: A research and training manual*, Vol. 1. Madison: Wisconsin Psychiatric Institute, 1969.

Kleinmuntz, B. *Personality and psychological assessment*. New York: St. Martin's, 1982.

Kline, P. *Fact and fantasy in Freudian theory*. London: Methuen, 1972.

Klopfer, W. G. & Taulbee, E. S. Projective tests. *Annual Review of Psychology*, 1976, *27*, 543–568.

Knapp, R. J. Relationship of a measure of self-actualization to neuroticism and extraversion. *Journal of Consulting Psychology*, 1965, *29*, 168–172.

Kogan, N. A style of life, a life of style. *Contemporary Psychology*, 1980, *25*, 595–598.

Krug, S. E. *Clinical Analysis Questionnaire manual*. Champaign, IL: Institute for Personality and Ability Testing, 1980.

Landfield, A. W. *Personal construct systems in psychotherapy*. Chicago: Rand McNally, 1971.

Lanyon, R. I. Personality assessment. *Annual Review of Psychology*, 1984, *35*, 667–701.

Lanyon, R. I. & Goodstein, L. D. *Personality assessment*, 2nd ed. New York: Wiley, 1982.

Latané, B. & Bidwell, L. D. Sex and affiliation in college cafeterias. *Personality and Social Psychology Bulletin*, 1977, *3*, 571–574.

Lefcourt, H. J. *Locus of control: Current trends in theory and research*, 2nd ed. Hillsdale, NJ: Erlbaum, 1982.

LeMay, M. & Damm, V. The Personal Orientation Inventory as a measure of self-actualization of underachievers. *Measurement and Evaluation in Guidance*, 1968, 110–114.

Liebert, R. M. & Spiegler, M. D. *Personality: Strategies and issues*, 4th ed. Homewood, IL: Dorsey Press, 1982.

Loeb, R. C. Concomitants of boys' locus of control examined in parent-child interactions. *Developmental Psychology*, 1975, *11*, 353–358.

Loevinger, J. & Knoll, E. Personality: Stages, traits, and the self. *Annual Review of Psychology*, 1983, *34*, 195–222.

Lowell, E. L. The effect of need for achievement on learning and speed of performance. *Journal of Psychology*, 1952, *33*, 31–40.

Lowry, R. J., ed. *The journals of A. H. Maslow*, Vols. 1 & 2. Monterey, CA: Brooks/Cole, 1979.

Maccoby, M. *The gamesman*. New York: Simon & Schuster, 1976.

———. *The leader*. New York: Simon & Schuster, 1981.

Maddi, S. R. *Personality theories: A comparative analysis*, 4th ed. Homewood, IL: Dorsey Press, 1980.

Maehr, M. L. & Kleiber, D. A. The graying of achievement motivation. *American Psychologist*, 1981, *36*, 787–793.

Mahoney, J. & Hartnett, J. Self-actualization and self-ideal discrepancy. *Journal of Psychology*, 1973, *85*, 37–42.

Marcia, J. E. Development and validation of ego-identity status. *Journal of Personality and Social Psychology*, 1966, *3*, 551–558.

———. Ego identity status: Relationship to change in self-esteem, "general maladjustment" and authoritarianism. *Journal of Personality*, 1967, *35*, 118–133.

Marcia, J. E. & Friedman, M. L. Ego identity status in college women. *Journal of Personality*, 1970, *38*, 249–263.

Masling, J. M., Rabie, L. & Blondheim, S. H. Obesity, level of aspiration, and Rorschach and TAT measures of oral dependence. *Journal of Consulting Psychology*, 1967, *31*, 233–239.

Maslow, A. H. A philosophy of psychology: The need for a mature science of human nature. *Main Currents in Modern Thought*, 1957, *13*, 27–32.

———. Self-actualization and beyond. In J. F. T. Bugental, ed., *Challenges of humanistic psychology*. New York: McGraw-Hill, 1967.

———. *Toward a psychology of being*, 2nd ed. New York: Van Nostrand Reinhold, 1968.

———. Tribute to Alfred Adler. *Journal of Individual Psychology*, 1970, *26*, 13. (a)

———. *Motivation and personality*, 2nd ed. New York: Harper & Row, 1970. (b)

———. *The farther reaches of human nature*. New York: Viking, 1971.

Masson, J. M., ed. *The complete letters of Sigmund Freud to Wilhelm Fliess, 1887–1904*. Cambridge, MA: Belknap Press of Harvard University, 1985.

Mattocks, A. L. & Jew, C. Comparison of self-actualization levels and adjustment scores of incarcerated male felons. *Journal of Educational and Psychological Measurement*, 1974, *34*, 69–74.

Mayo, C. W. & Crockett, W. H. Cognitive complexity and primacy-recency effects in impression formation. *Journal of Abnormal and Social Psychology*, 1964, *68*, 335–338.

McClain, E. Further validation of the Personal Orientation Inventory: Assessment of self-actualization of school counselors. *Journal of Consulting and Clinical Psychology*, 1970, *35*, 21–22.

McClelland, D. C. *The achieving society*. New York: Free Press, 1961.

———. *N* achievement and entrepreneurship: A longitudinal study. *Journal of Personality and Social Psychology*, 1965, *1*, 389–392. (a)

———. Toward a theory of motive acquisition. *American Psychologist*, 1965, *20*, 321–333. (b)

———. The need for power and sympathetic nervous system arousal. Paper presented to the Society for Psychophysiological Research, Cincinnati, October 1979.

McClelland, D. C. & Winter, D. G. *Motivating economic achievement*. New York: Free Press, 1969.

McClelland, D. C., Atkinson, J. W., Clark, R. A. & Lowell, E. L. *The achievement motive*. New York: Appleton-Century-Crofts, 1953.

McClelland, D. C., David, W. N., Kalin, R. & Wanner, E. *The drinking man*. New York: Free Press, 1972.

McGuire, W., ed. *The Freud/Jung letters*. Princeton: Princeton University Press, 1974.

McKeachie, W. J. Psychology in America's bicentennial year. *American Psychologist*, 1976, *31*, 819–833.

Medinnus, G. & Curtis, F. The relation between maternal self-acceptance and child acceptance. *Journal of Counseling Psychology*, 1963, *27*, 542–544.

Melamed, B. G. & Siegel, L. J. Reduction of anxiety in children facing hospitalization and surgery by use of filmed modeling. *Journal of Consulting and Clinical Psychology*, 1975, *43*, 511–521.

Meng, H. & Freud, E., eds. *Psychoanalysis and faith: The letters of Sigmund Freud and Oskar Pfister*. New York: Basic Books, 1963.

Milgram, N. A. Locus of control in Negro and white children at four age levels. *Psychological Reports*, 1971, *29*, 459–465.

Miner, J. B. The validity and usefulness of theories in an emerging organizational science. *Academy of Management Review*, 1984, *9*, 296–306.

Mischel, W. Toward a cognitive social-learning reconceptualization of personality. *Psychological Review*, 1973, *80*, 252–283.

———. *Introduction to personality*. New York: Holt, Rinehart & Winston, 1976.

Morgan, C. D. & Murray, H. A. A method for investigating fantasies. *Archives of Neurology and Psychiatry*, 1935, *34*, 289–306.

Murray, H. A. *Explorations in personality*. New York: Oxford University Press, 1938.

———. What should psychologists do about psychoanalysis. *Journal of Abnormal and Social Psychology*, 1940, *35*, 150–175.

———. Some basic psychological assumptions and conceptions. *Dialectica*, 1951, *5*, 266–292.

———. Preparations for the scaffold of a comprehensive system. In S. Koch, ed., *Psychology: A study of a science*, Vol. 3. New York: McGraw-Hill, 1959.

———. Autobiography. In E. G. Boring & G. Lindzey, eds., *History of psychology in autobiography*, Vol. 5. New York: Appleton-Century-Crofts, 1967.

Naditch, M. P. Locus of control and drinking behavior in a sample of men in army basic training. *Journal of Consulting and Clinical Psychology*, 1975, *43*, 96.

Nowicki, S. & Roundtree, J. Correlates of locus of control in secondary age students. *Developmental Psychology*, 1974, *10*, 33–37.

O'Leary, K. D., Drabman, R. & Kass, R. F. Maintenance of appropriate behavior in a token program. *Journal of Abnormal Child Psychology*, 1973, *1*, 127–138.

Orgler, H. *Alfred Adler, the man and his work: Triumph over the inferiority complex*. New York: New American Library, 1963.

Orlofsky, J. L., Marcia, J. E. & Lesser, I. M. Ego identity status and the intimacy versus isolation crisis of young adulthood. *Journal of Personality and Social Psychology*, 1973, *27*, 211–219.

OSS Assessment Staff. *Assessment of men: Selection of personnel for the U.S. Office of Strategic Services*. New York: Rinehart, 1948.

Page, M. Introduction: Personality—current theory and research. *Nebraska Symposium on Motivation 1982*. Lincoln: University of Nebraska Press, 1983.

Paige, J. M. Letters from Jenny: An approach to the clinical analysis of personality structure by computer. In P. J. Stone, ed., *The general inquirer: A computer approach to content analysis*. Cambridge, MA: MIT Press, 1966.

Pervin, L. A. *Current controversies and issues in personality*, 2nd ed. New York: Wiley, 1984. (a)

———. *Personality: Theory and research*, 4th ed. New York: Wiley, 1984. (b)

Phares, E. J. *Locus of control in personality.* Morristown, NJ: General Learning Press, 1976.

Podd, M., Marcia, J. E. & Rubin, R. The effects of ego identity status and partner perception on a prisoner's dilemma game. *Journal of Social Psychology,* 1968, *82,* 117–126.

Porter, L. A. A study of perceived need satisfactions in bottom and middle management jobs. *Journal of Applied Psychology,* 1961, *45,* 1–10.

———. Job attitudes in management: II. Perceived importance of needs as a function of job level. *Journal of Applied Psychology,* 1963, *47,* 141–148.

Rabin, A. I., Aronoff, J., Barclay, A. M. & Zucker, R. A., eds. *Further explorations in personality.* New York: Wiley, 1981.

Rattner, J. *Alfred Adler.* New York: Ungar, 1983.

Raynor, J. O. Relationships between achievement-related motives, future orientation, and academic performance. *Journal of Personality and Social Psychology,* 1970, *15,* 28–33.

Reimanis, G. Psychological development, anomie, and mood. *Journal of Personality and Social Psychology,* 1974, *29,* 355–357.

Repucci, N. D. & Saunders, J. T. Social psychology of behavior modification: Problems of implementation in natural settings. *American Psychologist,* 1974, *29,* 649–660.

Rice, B. Skinner agrees he is the most important influence in psychology. *New York Times Magazine,* March 17, 1968.

Roazen, P. *Freud and his followers.* New York: Alfred A. Knopf, 1975.

Rogers, C. R. The case of Mrs. Oak: A research analysis. In C. R. Rogers & R. F. Dymond, eds., *Psychotherapy and personality change.* Chicago: University of Chicago Press, 1954.

———. *On becoming a person: A therapist's view of psychotherapy.* Boston: Houghton Mifflin, 1961.

———. Autobiography. In E. G. Boring & G. Lindzey, eds., *History of psychology in autobiography,* Vol. 5. New York: Appleton-Century-Crofts, 1967.

———. *A way of being.* Boston: Houghton Mifflin, 1980.

Rogers calls peace results "surprising." *APA Monitor,* November 1984.

Rorer, L. G. & Widiger, T. A. Personality structure and assessment. *Annual Review of Psychology,* 1983, *34,* 401–430.

Rorschach, H. *Psychodiagnostics: A diagnostic test based on perception,* trans. P. Lemkau & B. Kronenburg. Berne: Huber, 1942.

Rosen, B. C. & D'Andrade, R. G. The psychosocial origins of achievement motivation. *Sociometry,* 1959, *22,* 185–218.

Rotter, J. B. Generalized expectancies for internal versus external control of reinforcement. *Psychological Monographs,* 1966, *80,* whole no. 609.

———. A new scale for the measurement of interpersonal trust. *Journal of Personality,* 1967, *35,* 651–665.

———. Interpersonal trust, trustworthiness, and gullibility. *American Psychologist,* 1980, *35,* 1–7.

———. *The development and applications of social learning theory: Selected papers.* New York: Praeger, 1982.

Rotter, J. B., Chance, J. E. & Phares, E. J. *Applications of a social learning theory of personality.* New York: Holt, Rinehart & Winston, 1972.

Rubins, J. L. *Karen Horney: Gentle rebel of psychoanalysis.* New York: Dial Press, 1978.

Ryckman, R. M. & Malikiosi, M. X. Relationship between locus of control and chronological age. *Psychological Reports,* 1975, *36,* 655–658.

Sarason, I. G. Test anxiety and the self-disclosing coping model. *Journal of Consulting and Clinical Psychology,* 1975, *43,* 148–153.

Schachter, S. *The psychology of affiliation.* Stanford, CA: Stanford University Press, 1959.

———. Birth order, eminence, and higher education. *American Sociological Review,* 1963, *28,* 757–767.

———. Birth order and sociometric choice. *Journal of Abnormal and Social Psychology,* 1964, *68,* 453–456.

Schneider, D. J. Personal construct psychology: An international menu. *Contemporary Psychology,* 1982, *27,* 712–713.

Schultz, D. P. & Schultz, S. E. *Psychology and industry today: An introduction to industrial and organizational psychology,* 4th ed. New York: Macmillan, 1986.

Schur, M. *Freud: Living and dying.* New York: International Universities Press, 1972.

Schwartz, D. W. & Carp, S. A. Field dependence in a geriatric population. *Perceptual and Motor Skills,* 1967, *24,* 495–504.

Sechrest, L. Review of J. B. Rotter's *The development and applications of social learning theory: Selected papers. Journal of the History of the Behavioral Sciences,* 1984, *20,* 228–230.

Sechrest, L. & Jackson, D. N. Social intelligence and accuracy of interpersonal predictions. *Journal of Personality*, 1961, *29*, 169–182.

Shostrom, E. An inventory for the measurement of self-actualization. *Educational and Psychological Measurement*, 1964, *24*, 207–218.

———. *Manual for the Personal Orientation Inventory*. San Diego: Educational and Industrial Testing Service, 1974.

Shostrom, E. & Knapp, R. R. The relationship of a measure of self-actualization (POI) to a measure of pathology (MMPI) and to therapeutic growth. *American Journal of Psychotherapy*, 1966, *20*, 193–202.

Silverman, L. H. Psychoanalytic theory: "The reports of my death are greatly exaggerated." *American Psychologist*, 1976, *31*, 621–637.

Silverman, R. E. & Shrauger, J. S. Locus of control and correlates of attraction toward others. Paper presented to the Eastern Psychological Association, Atlantic City, NJ, April 1970.

Skinner, B. F. *Walden two*. New York: Macmillan, 1948.

———. *Science and human behavior*. New York: Free Press, 1953.

———. Autobiography. In E. G. Boring & G. Lindzey, eds., *A history of psychology in autobiography*, Vol. 5. New York: Appleton-Century-Crofts, 1967.

———. *Beyond freedom and dignity*. New York: Alfred A. Knopf, 1971.

———. *About behaviorism*. New York: Alfred A. Knopf, 1974.

———. Origins of a behaviorist. *Psychology Today*, September 1983, pp. 22–33.

Smith, D. Trends in counseling and psychotherapy. *American Psychologist*, 1982, *37*, 802–809.

Smith, J. Age differences in achievement motivation. *British Journal of Social and Clinical Psychology*, 1970, *9*, 175–176.

Spranger, E. *Types of men*, trans. P. J. W. Pigors. Halle: Niemeyer, 1928.

Steele, R. S. *Freud and Jung: Conflicts of interpretation*. London: Routledge & Kegan Paul, 1982.

Stephenson, W. *The study of behavior: Q-technique and its methodology*. Chicago: University of Chicago Press, 1953.

Sterba, R. F. *Reminiscences of a Viennese psychoanalyst*. Detroit: Wayne State University Press, 1982.

Stern, G. G. *Preliminary record: Activities Index—College Characteristics Index*. Syracuse: Syracuse University Psychological Research Center, 1958.

Stewart, R. A. C. Academic performance and components of self actualization. *Perceptual and Motor Skills*, 1968, *26*, 918.

Stolorow, R. D. & Atwood, G. E. *Faces in a cloud: Subjectivity in personality theory*. New York: Aronson, 1979.

Strassberg, D. S. Relationships among locus of control, anxiety and valued goal expectations. *Journal of Consulting and Clinical Psychology*, 1973, *2*, 319.

Stricker, L. J. & Ross, J. *A description and evaluation of the Myers-Briggs Type Indicator*. Princeton: Educational Testing Service, 1962.

Strickland, B. R. Internal-external expectancies and health-related behaviors. *Journal of Consulting and Clinical Psychology*, 1978, *46*, 1192–1211.

———. Internal-external expectancies and cardiovascular functioning. In L. C. Perlmutter & R. A. Monty, eds., *Choice and perceived control*. Hillsdale, NJ: Erlbaum, 1979.

Strümpfer, D. Fear and affiliation during a disaster. *Journal of Social Psychology*, 1970, *82*, 263–268.

Suinn, R., Osborne, D. & Winfree, P. The self-concept and accuracy of recall of inconsistent self-related information. *Journal of Clinical Psychology*, 1962, *18*, 473–474.

Sulloway, F. J. *Freud, biologist of the mind: Beyond the psychoanalytic legend*. New York: Basic Books, 1979.

Tresemer, D. W. *Fear of success: An intriguing set of questions*. New York: Plenum Press, 1977.

Tribich, D. & Messer, S. Psychoanalytic character type and states of authority as determiners of suggestibility. *Journal of Consulting and Clinical Psychology*, 1974, *42*, 842–848.

Turner, R. H. & Vanderlippe, R. Self-ideal consequence as an index of adjustment. *Journal of Abnormal and Social Psychology*, 1958, *57*, 202–206.

Veroff, J., Wilcox, S. & Atkinson, J. W. The achievement motive in high school and college-age women. *Journal of Abnormal and Social Psychology*, 1953, *48*, 108–119.

Walters, R. H., Bowen, N. V. & Parke, R. D. Experimentally induced disinhibition of sexual responses. Cited in A. Bandura & R. H. Walters, *Social learning and personality development*. New York: Holt, Rinehart & Winston, 1963.

Waterman, C. K., Buebel, M. E. & Waterman, A. S. Relationship between resolution of the identity crisis and outcomes of previous psychosocial crises. *Proceedings of the Annual Convention of the APA*, 1970, *5*, 467–468.

Weber, M. *The Protestant ethic and the spirit of capitalism*. New York: Scribner's, 1930.

Weisstein, N. Psychology constructs the female, or the fantasy life of the male psychologist (with some attention to the fantasies of his friends, the male biologist and the male anthropologist). In I. Cohen, ed., *Perspectives on psychology*. New York: Praeger, 1975.

Wexley, K. N. & Latham, G. P. *Developing and training human resources in organizations*. Glenview, IL: Scott, Foresman, 1981.

Whitmont, E. C. Jungian analysis today. *Psychology Today*, December 1972, pp. 63–72.

Wichern, F. & Nowicki, S., Jr. Independence training practices and locus of control orientation in children and adolescents. *Developmental Psychology*, 1976, *12*, 77.

Wilson, G. Introversion-extroversion. In T. Blass, ed., *Personality variables in social behavior*. Hillsdale, NJ: Erlbaum, 1977.

———. Introversion/extroversion. In H. London & J. E. Exner, eds., *Dimensions of personality*. New York: Wiley, 1978.

Wilson, G. D., Ausman, J. & Mathews, T. R. Conservatism and art preferences. *Journal of Personality and Social Psychology*, 1973, *25*, 286–288.

Winter, D. G. *The power motive*. New York: Free Press, 1973.

Winterbottom, M. R. The relation of need for achievement to learning experiences in independence and mastery. In J. W. Atkinson, ed., *Motives in fantasy, action, and society*. Princeton: D. Van Nostrand, 1958.

Wirt, R. D. & Lachar, D. The Personality Inventory for Children: Development and clinical applications. In P. McReynolds, ed., *Advances in psychological assessment*, Vol. 5. San Francisco: Jossey-Bass, 1981.

Witkin, H. A. *Cognitive styles in personal and cultural adaptation: Heinz Werner lecture series*, Vol. II. Worcester, MA: Clark University Press, 1977.

Witkin, H. A. & Berry, J. W. Psychological differentiation in cross-cultural perspective. *Journal of Cross-Cultural Psychology*, 1975, *6*, 4–87.

Witkin, H. A. & Goodenough, D. R. *Cognitive styles: Essence and origins*. New York: International Universities Press, 1981.

Witkin, H. A., Dyk, R. B., Faterson, H. F., Goodenough, D. R. & Karp, S. A. *Psychological differentiation: Studies in development*. New York: Halsted Press, 1974.

Witkin, H. A., Lewis, H. B., Hertzman, M., Machover, K., Meissner, P. B. & Wapner, S. *Personality through perception: An experimental and clinical study*. New York: Harper, 1954.

Wittels, F. *Sigmund Freud: His personality, his teaching, and his school*. London: Allen & Unwin, 1924.

Wolk, S. & DuCette, J. Intentional performance and incidental learning as a function of personality and task dimensions. *Journal of Personality and Social Psychology*, 1974, *29*, 91–101.

Yoe, M. R. MBTI in the workplace. *The Johns Hopkins Magazine*, February 1984.

Zaccaria, J. S. & Weir, W. R. A comparison of alcoholics and selected samples of non-alcoholics in terms of a positive concept of mental health. *Journal of Social Psychology*, 1967, *71*, 151–157.

Index

Ability traits (Cattell), 224
Achenbach, T., 290
Achievement motivation (McClelland), 173, 426–435
Activity temperament (Buss & Plomin), 444, 448
Actualization tendency (Rogers), 277–278
Adams, D., 8
Adams, N. E., 392
Adams-Webber, J. R., 339
Adler, A., 95, 100–121, 126, 129, 139–141, 146, 157, 161, 212, 299, 309
Adolescence, personality development in:
    Allport, 207
    Cattell, 231
    Erikson, 255–256
    Freud, 55–56
    Jung, 86
Adulthood, personality development in:
    Allport, 207–208
    Bandura, 390
    Cattell, 231–232
    Erikson, 256–257
    Jung, 86–88
    Maslow, 302–304
Affiliation need (Murray), 173, 183
Aggressive drive (Freud), 41
Aggressive personality (Horney), 134, 155
Alcoholism, 118, 183
Alexander, I. E., 76
Allport, F., 197
Allport, G. W., 8, 119, 161, 193–215, 223, 224, 236
Allport-Vernon-Lindzey Study of Values, 196, 211

Alpha press (Murray), 176
Anal complexes (Murray), 178
Anal personalities (Freud), 52–53, 62–63, 155
Anal stage of psychosexual development (Freud), 52–53
Analytical psychology (Jung), 74
Anastasi, A., 11, 235
Ancestral influences (Jung), 82–83
Anima/animus archetypes (Jung), 84
Animal subjects (Skinner), 351–352, 371–372
Annis, L. V., 5
Anxiety:
    Bandura, 393–394
    Cattell, 227, 229–230
    Freud, 45–50
    Horney, 130–131
    Rogers, 281–282
Archetypes (Jung), 83–85
Armstrong, T., 315
Aserinsky, E., 62
Asta, P., 315
Atkinson, J. W., 20, 429, 434
Attentional processes (Bandura), 384–385
Attitudes:
    Allport, 200
    Cattell, 228–229
    Jung, 78–81
Atwood, G. E., 24, 197
Ausman, J., 238
Authoritarianism (Fromm), 150
Automation conformity (Fromm), 151
Aversive stimulation (Skinner), 363

Ayllon, T., 364
Azrin, N., 364

Baker, C. A., 5
Baldwin, A. L., 290
Balloun, J., 316
Bandura, A., 18, 25, 373, 378–398, 403, 416
Bannister, D., 45, 340
Barnes, R., 415
Barry, H., 118
Basic anxiety (Horney), 130–131
Basic strengths (Erikson), 258–259
Battle, E., 415
Behavior modeling (Bandura), 378–398
Behavior modification:
    Bandura, 390–394
    Skinner, 364–366
Behavior potential (Rotter), 404–405
Behavioral choice method, 413
Behavioral specification equation (Cattell), 237
Behaviorism, 6, 350
Being needs (Maslow), 301
Belonging and love needs (Maslow), 300, 303
Benedict, R., 250, 299, 312
Bergin, A. E., 287
Berry, J. W., 443
Beta press (Murray), 176
Bettelheim, B., 39
Betz, N. E., 389
Beyer, J., 392
Bidwell, L. D., 183
Bieri, J., 340
Biophilious orientation (Fromm), 157
Birth order (Adler), 111–114, 118
Birth trauma (Freud), 45
Blanchard, E. B., 391
Blane, H. T., 118
Bleuler, E., 75
Blondheim, S. H., 62
Blood, M. R., 365
Body-adjustment test, 439, 440
Bonarius, J., 339
Bootzin, R., 365
Boring, E. G., 64
Bottome, P., 102
Bowen, N. V., 382
Braun, J., 315
Breger, L., 62
Breland, H. M., 118
Breuer, J., 38, 57
Briggs, K., 92
Brome, V., 91
Brown, S. R., 94
Bruner, J. S., 211, 325
Buebel, M. E., 264
Buss, A., 444–449
Butler, J. M., 289

California Psychological Inventory (CPI), 11
Cantril, H., 213

Cardinal traits (Allport), 200–201
Carlson, R., 94, 184
Carp, S. A., 441
Case study method, 15–16
Castration anxiety (Freud), 54, 62
Castration complex (Murray), 178
Catharsis (Freud), 57, 92
Cathexis:
    Freud, 41
    Murray, 176
Cattell, R. B., 21, 94, 95, 219–240, 373
Central traits (Allport), 201
Chance, J. E., 410
Character types (Fromm), 155–157, 159–160
Charcot, J., 38
Cherry, L., 126, 139, 142
Cherry, R., 126, 139, 142
Childhood, personality development in:
    Adler, 111–113
    Allport, 207
    Bandura, 390
    Cattell, 231
    Erikson, 253–255
    Freud, 52–55
    Fromm, 151–152
    Horney, 128–130
    Jung, 86
    Maslow, 302, 311
    Murray, 176–178
    Rogers, 279–282
    Rotter, 409
Chodorkoff, B., 289
Ciaccio, N., 263
Claustral complexes (Murray), 177
Client-centered therapy (*see* Person-centered therapy)
Clinical Analysis Questionnaire (CAQ), 235
Coan, R. W., 286
Cognitive complexity (Kelly), 340
Cognitive processes:
    Allport, 201–202
    Bandura, 379, 387
    Kelly, 323–343
    Rotter, 403
Cognitive simplicity (Kelly), 340
Cognitive styles:
    Kelly, 340–341
    Witkin, 442–443
Coleman, J. S., 415
Collective unconscious (Jung), 82, 83
Common traits:
    Allport, 199
    Cattell, 224
Compensation (Adler), 103
Compensation principle (Jung), 89
Complexes:
    Adler, 104–105
    Jung, 81–82
    Murray, 176–178
    (*See also* Oedipus complex)

Compliant personality (Horney), 133, 155
Conditional positive regard (Rogers), 280
Conditioned responses, 356
Conditions of worth (Rogers), 280–281
Conflict:
    Erikson, 251
    Horney, 135
    Rotter, 408
Conformity (Fromm), 151
Conscience (Freud), 44
Conscious level of personality:
    Freud, 42
    Jung, 78–81
Constantinople, A., 261, 263
Constitutional traits (Cattell), 225
Constructive alternativism (Kelly), 328
Constructs (*see* Personal constructs)
Coopersmith, S., 290
Coping behavior (Allport), 212
Correlational method, 19–22
Corsini, R. J., 24
Crandall, J. E., 116, 117, 119
Creative power of the self (Adler), 108
Crises (Erikson), 251
Crockett, W. H., 340
Cross, K. P., 238
Crystallized intelligence (Cattell), 235–236
Cudhea, D., 395
Cultural influences (*see* Social influences)
Culture Fair Intelligence Test, 236
Cumulative recorder, 371
Curtis, F., 290

Damm, V., 315
D'Andrade, R. G., 433
Death instincts (Freud), 41
Defense mechanisms (Freud), 47–50, 441–442
Defenses against anxiety:
    Horney, 130–131
    Rogers, 281–282
Defensive behavior (Rotter), 407–408
Deficit needs (Maslow), 301
Dement, W. C., 62
Depth psychology, 59–60
Destructiveness (Fromm), 150–151
Detached personality (Horney), 134–135, 155
Diffuse needs (Murray), 174
Dignan, M., 261, 263
Disinhibition (Bandura), 382
Displacement (Freud), 49
Drabman, R., 365
Dream analysis, 58–60, 62, 92, 116, 139–140, 158
Dream research, 62, 117
DuCette, J., 415
Duck, S. W., 340
Dynamic lattice (Cattell), 229
Dynamic traits (Cattell), 224

Early recollections (Adler), 115
EAS Temperament Survey for Adults, 447

EASI Temperament Survey, 446
Eber, H. W., 225
Edwards, A. L., 181
Edwards Personal Preference Schedule, 181
Effect needs (Murray), 175
Ego:
    Cattell, 231
    Erikson, 252
    Freud, 42–50
    Jung, 78–81
    Murray, 172, 177
    (*See also* Self)
Ego-ideal:
    Freud, 44
    Murray, 172
Ego identity (Erikson), 255–256, 261, 263–264
Ego-Identity Scale, 261, 263
Ego psychology, 119
Egression complex (Murray), 177
Electra complex (Freud), 54
Ellenberger, H. R., 92, 93, 117, 119
Elms, A. C., 24
Embedded Figures Test, 439
Embedding context (Witkin), 438
Emotionality temperament (Buss & Plomin), 444, 448
Engler, B., 106
Entropy principle (Jung), 78
Environmental-mold traits (Cattell), 225
Epigenetic principle of maturation (Erikson), 251
Epstein, S., 182
Equivalence principle (Jung), 77–78
Ergs (Cattell), 227–229
Erikson, E. H., 95, 212, 247–266
Erogenous zones (Freud), 50–51
Esteem needs (Maslow), 300, 303
Estes, S. G., 213
Evans, R. I., 147, 351, 367
Excitation need (Fromm), 154
Exner, J. E., 12
Expectancy (Rotter), 405–406, 413–414
Experience Inventory, 286
Experiencing Scale, 286
Experimental method, 16–19
Exploitative orientation (Fromm), 155
Expressive behavior (Allport), 212–213
External locus of control (Rotter), 406, 411–412, 414–416
Extraversion:
    Cattell, 227
    Jung, 78–80, 93–94
Eysenck, H. J., 92, 94, 315
Eysenck, J., 315

Factor analysis (Cattell), 220, 233–234, 236–238
Falbo, T., 118
Fear of success, 434–435
Fear Survey Schedule, 369
Feeling (Jung), 79–80
Fehr, L. A., 235

Feminine psychology (Horney), 136–138, 140
Fictional finalism (Adler), 107
Field dependence/independence (Witkin), 436–443
Finalism (Adler), 106
Fisher, S., 61, 140
Fixation:
    Freud, 50–51
    Murray, 177
Fixity (Witkin), 442–443
Fjeld, S. P., 339
Fliess, W., 37
Fluid intelligence (Cattell), 235–236
Focal needs (Murray), 174
Fox, J., 315
Frame of orientation need (Fromm), 154
Fransella, F., 340
Free association, 57–60, 139, 140, 158
Freedom, escaping from (Fromm), 148–151, 153–155
Freedom of movement (Rotter), 407–408
Freud, A., 39, 169, 248, 249
Freud, E., 57
Freud, S., 7, 16, 35–65, 291, 342, 426
    and Adler, 101–103, 106–108, 110, 112–114, 116
    and Allport, 194, 196
    and Erikson, 248, 249, 251, 260
    and Fromm, 146–148
    and Horney, 126, 128, 136–141
    and Jung, 74–77, 83, 85, 86, 90–95
    and Murray, 169, 171, 172, 178
Friedland, B., 117
Friedman, M. L., 264
Fromm, E., 95, 119, 127, 145–162, 212, 299
Fully functioning persons (Rogers), 274, 282–283
Functional analysis (Skinner), 368
Functional autonomy of motives (Allport), 202–205, 207

Geer, J. H., 369
Gendlin, E. T., 286
Generalized expectancy (Rotter), 405–406, 412
Genital stage of psychosexual development (Freud), 55
Gilgen, A. R., 63, 95, 119, 141, 184, 213, 239, 265, 291, 316, 341, 353, 373
Goodenough, D. R., 441, 442
Graham, W., 316
Graves, T. D., 415
Greenberg, R., 117
Greenberg, R. P., 61, 140
Greever, K., 117
Grieser, C., 117
Grossack, M., 315
Growth needs (Maslow), 301
Grusec, J. E., 391
Guilded participation (Bandura), 391

Habits (Allport), 200
Hackett, G., 389
Haigh, G. V., 289
Hall, C., 62, 140
Hall, D. T., 315
Hall, E., 120, 258, 265
Hall, M. H., 180, 298, 299, 350, 352
Hanewitz, W. B., 94
Harlow, H., 298
Harrison, R., 180
Harrison, R. H., 117
Hartmann, H., 65
Hartnett, J., 290
Harvard undergraduate assessment program (Murray), 179, 181–182
Harvey, J. H., 415
Hausdorff, D., 147
Hawkins, R. P., 369
Healthy personalities:
    Allport, 208
    Fromm, 156
    Jung, 88
    Maslow, 307–310
    Rogers, 277–278, 282–283
Heidbreder, E., 61
Helson, R., 24
Hendrick, C., 94
Heredity, research on, 230, 238, 444–447
Hierarchy of needs (Maslow), 300–317
Hjelle, L., 118
Hoarding orientation (Fromm), 155–156
Hoffman, L. W., 435
Horner, M. S., 434–435
Horney, K., 64, 119, 125–142, 146–148, 150, 155, 157, 161, 212, 299
Humanistic communitarian socialism (Fromm), 157
Humanistic psychology, 297, 317
Hunter, I., 62
Hypnosis, 38

Icarus complex (Murray), 178
Id:
    Freud, 42–45
    Murray, 171
Idealized self-image (Horney), 135–136
Identity crisis (Erikson), 248, 256 (*See also* Ego identity)
Identity need (Fromm), 154
Idiographic research, 182, 198, 212, 236, 286, 370
Impulsivity temperament (Buss & Plomin), 444
Incentive and motivational processes (Bandura), 386–387
Incomplete Sentences Blank, 413
Incongruence (Rogers), 281–282, 290
Individual psychology (Adler), 101
Individual traits (Allport), 199
Individuation:
    Fromm, 149
    Jung, 88

Infancy, personality development in:
  Bandura, 390
  Cattell, 231
  Erikson, 252–253
  Freud, 51–52
  Horney, 128–130
  Rogers, 279
  (*See also* Childhood)
Inferiority complex (Adler), 104
Inferiority feelings (Adler), 103–106
Instinctoid needs (Maslow), 297
Instincts (Freud), 39–42
Insupport complex (Murray), 177
Intelligence, 235–236
Internal locus of control (Rotter), 406, 411–412, 414–416
Internal versus External (I–E) Locus of Control Scale, 414–416
Interpersonal trust (Rotter), 412, 414
Interpersonal Trust Scale, 414
Introversion:
  Cattell, 227
  Jung, 78–81, 93–94
Intuiting (Jung), 79–81
Inventory of Psychosocial Development, 261, 263
Irrational functions (Jung), 79

Jackson, D. N., 181, 341
Jackson Personality Research Form, 181
Jaffe, A., 95
Jenny case study (Allport), 210–211
Jew, C., 315
Johnson, R. C., 223
Jonah complex (Maslow), 310–311
Jones, E., 37, 110
Jung, C. G., 24, 73–96, 117, 119, 120, 140, 141, 161, 169, 212, 234

Kagan, J., 448
Kass, R. F., 365
Kaufman, D. R., 435
Kaufmann, W., 119
Kazdin, A. E., 365, 393
Kelly, G. A., 323–343, 404, 436
Keniston, K., 248
Kidwell, J., 118
Kiester, E., 395
Kleiber, D. A., 434
Klein, M. H., 286
Kleitman, N., 62
Kline, P., 63, 235
Knapp, R., 315
Knoll, E., 36
Kogan, N., 443
Krug, S. E., 235

Lachar, D., 14
Landfield, A. W., 339
Lane, R. W., 62
Lanyon, R. I., 4, 12, 235

Latane, B., 183
Latency period (Freud), 55
Latent dream content (Freud), 58
Latent needs (Murray), 175
Latham, G. P., 365
L-data (Cattell), 233
Learning (*see* Social learning)
Lefcourt, H. J., 415
LeMay, M., 315
Lens, W., 20, 429
Lesser, I. M., 264
Letters from Jenny case study (Allport), 210–211
Levy, N., 94
Lewin, K., 250
Libido (psychic energy):
  Freud, 39–42, 51
  Jung, 77–78, 86
Life history reconstruction (Jung), 92
Life intincts (Freud), 40–41
Lifestyle (Adler), 107–109
Lindzey, G., 211
Locus of control (Rotter), 406, 411–412, 414–416
Loeb, R. C., 416
Loevinger, J., 36
Love, productive (Fromm), 152–153
Love needs (Maslow), 300, 303
Lowell, E. L., 428
Lowry, R. J., 298, 312, 314
Lussieu, G., 315

Maccoby, M., 159, 160
Maddi, S. R., 24–25
Maehr, M. L., 434
Mahoney, J., 290
Malikiosi, M. X., 415
Manifest dream content (Freud), 58
Manifest needs (Murray), 175
Marcia, J. E., 264
Marketing orientation (Fromm), 156, 160
Masling, J. M., 62
Maslow, A. H., 5, 95, 118, 119, 161, 212, 215, 296–317, 351
Masochistic strivings (Fromm), 150
Masson, J. M., 37
Mathews, T. R., 238
Mattocks, A. L., 315
Maudsley Personality Inventory, 92, 94
Mayo, C. W., 340
McClain, E., 315
McClelland, D. C., 20, 183, 426–435
McGuire, W., 76, 103
McKeachie, W. J., 26
Medinnus, G., 290
Melamed, B. G., 393
Meng, H., 57
Menlove, F. L., 391
Messer, S., 63
Metamotivation (Maslow), 305–307
Metaneeds (Maslow), 306

Metapathology (Maslow), 306–307
Mexican village study (Fromm), 159–160
Michael, W., 315
Milgram, N. A., 415
Miner, J. B., 316
Minimal goal level (Rotter), 408–409
Minnesota Multiphasic Personality Inventory
    (MMPI), 11, 12, 235, 439
Mischel, W., 369
Mitchell, V., 24
Mobility (Witkin), 442–443
Modal needs (Murray), 175
Modeling (Bandura), 378–398
Moral anxiety (Freud), 46
Morgan, C. D., 169
Motivation:
    Allport, 201–205
    Bandura, 386–387
    Cattell, 227–229
    Maslow, 300–307
    Murray, 172–176
    Rotter, 409–410
Motor reproduction processes (Bandura), 386
Mrs. Oak case study (Rogers), 288–289
Multiple abstract variance analysis, 230
Murray, H. A., 13, 20, 95, 166–185, 198, 212, 234,
    250, 313, 426, 436
Myers, I. B., 92
Myers-Briggs Type Indicator (MBTI), 92, 93

Naditch, M. P., 415
Narcissism (Fromm), 153
Necrophilious orientation (Fromm), 156
Need for achievement (McClelland), 173,
    426–435
Need potential (Rotter), 409–410, 414
Needs:
    Freud, 39–42
    Fromm, 153–155
    Horney, 131–132
    Maslow, 300–305
    Murray, 172–176
    Rotter, 409–410
Needs-hierarchy theory (Maslow), 300–317
Needs to know and understand (Maslow),
    304–305
Negative reinforcement, 366, 387
Nesselroade, J. R., 238
Neurotic anxiety (Freud), 46
Neurotic needs (Horney), 131–132
Neurotic self-image (Horney), 136
Neurotic trends (Horney), 132–135
Nomothetic research, 182, 198, 212, 236,
    370
Nondirective therapy (*see* Person-centered
    therapy)
Nonproductive orientations (Fromm), 155
Nougaim, K. E., 315
Nowicki, S., 415, 416

Object of devotion (Fromm), 155
Observational learning (Bandura), 378–398
Oedipus complex:
    Erikson, 254
    Freud, 53–54, 62
    Horney, 137–138, 140
Office of Strategic Services (OSS) assessment
    program (Murray), 169, 179–180
O'Leary, K. D., 365
O'Malley, P. M., 20, 429
Operant conditioning (Skinner), 357–359,
    363–366
Operant conditioning apparatus (Skinner),
    357–358, 371–372
Opposition principle (Jung), 77, 89
Oral complexes (Murray), 177–178
Oral personalities (Freud), 52, 62–63, 155
Oral stage of psychosexual development (Freud),
    51–52
Order of birth (Adler), 111–114, 118
Organismic valuing process (Rogers), 278
Orgler, H., 101, 102, 104
Orientations (Fromm), 155–157
Orlofsky, J. L., 264
Osborne, D., 289

Page, M., 24
Paige, J. M., 210
Parent-child interaction:
    Adler, 103–106, 108–113
    Allport, 206, 207
    Bandura, 388, 390
    Cattell, 231
    Erikson, 251–257
    Freud, 50–55
    Fromm, 151–152
    Horney, 128–130
    Rogers, 279–282
    Rotter, 409
    Skinner, 357, 362
Parke, R. D., 382
Pavlov, I., 212, 355, 356, 358
Peak experiences (Maslow), 309
Penis envy (Freud), 54, 62, 136, 140
Perceptual differentiation (Witkin), 436–443
Perfection (Adler), 106
Permeability (Kelly), 333
Perseverative functional autonomy (Allport), 203
Person-centered therapy (Rogers), 274, 285–286
Persona, 8
Persona archetype (Jung), 84
Personal constructs (Kelly), 323–343
Personal dispositions (Allport), 199
Personal-document technique, 210–211
Personal Orientation Inventory (POI), 313–315
Personal unconscious (Jung), 79, 81–82
Personality, assessment of, 9–15
    controversies about, 25–28
    definitions of, 8–9

research in, 15–22
theories of, 22–25
Personality Inventory for Children, 14–15
Personality tests, 9–15
Personology (Murray), 170
Pervin, L. A., 25, 94, 196, 212, 397
Phallic personalities (Freud), 55, 63
Phallic stage of psychosexual development
   (Freud), 53–55
Phares, E. J., 410, 412
Physiological needs:
   Freud, 39–42
   Fromm, 153
   Horney, 128
   Maslow, 300, 302
   Murray, 174
Play therapy (Erikson), 261–263
Pleasure principle (Freud), 43
Plomin, R., 444–449
Podd, M., 264
Porter, L. A., 315
Positive regard (Rogers), 279–280
Positive reinforcement (*see* Reinforcement)
Positive self-regard (Rogers), 280
Power need, 183
Preconscious (Freud), 42
Press (Murray), 176
Primary needs (Murray), 174
Primary-process thought (Freud), 43
Prince, M., 169
Proactive needs (Murray), 175
Proceedings (Murray), 182
Process needs (Murray), 175
Productive love (Fromm), 152–153
Productive orientation (Fromm), 156
Progression principle (Jung), 85
Projection (Freud), 48, 180
Projective techniques, 12–14 (*See also* Rorschach
   Inkblot Test; Thematic Apperception Test)
Propriate functional autonomy (Allport), 203
Proprium (Allport), 203, 205–206
Psyche (Jung), 77
Psychic birth (Jung), 86
Psychic energy (libido):
   Freud, 39–42, 51
   Jung, 77–78, 86
Psychic mechanisms (Fromm), 150–152
Psychoanalysis, 7, 36
Psychogenic needs (Murray), 174
Psychohistorical analysis (Erikson), 261
Psychological differentiation (Witkin), 436–443
Psychological functions (Jung), 79–81
Psychological situation (Rotter), 407
Psychological types (Jung), 80–81, 92–94
Psychosexual stages of development (Freud),
   50–56
Psychosocial stages of development (Erikson),
   251–259, 263
P technique, 237

Q-data (Cattell), 234
Q-sort (Rogers), 288–289, 315

Rabie, L., 62
Rabin, A. I., 184
Range of convenience (Kelly), 332
Rank, O., 24, 45
Ranking method, 413, 414
Rational functions (Jung), 79
Rationalization (Freud), 48–49
Rattner, J., 116
Raynor, J. O., 429
Reaction formation (Freud), 48
Reactive needs (Murray), 175
Reality principle (Freud), 43
Receptive orientation (Fromm), 155
Reciprocal determinism (Bandura), 395
Regression (Freud), 48
Regression principle (Jung), 85
Reich, W., 24
Reimanis, G., 263
Reinforcement:
   Bandura, 380–394
   Rotter, 404–413
   Skinner, 355–373
Reinforcement schedules (Skinner), 359–361
Reinforcement value (Rotter), 406, 413
Relatedness need (Fromm), 153
Reliability of tests, 10
Repertory grid (Kelly), 337–339
Repression (Freud), 47–48
Repucci, N. D., 365
Resistances (Freud), 58
Respondent behavior (Skinner), 355–356
Retention processes (Bandura), 385–386
Reversal experimental design (Skinner),
   370–371
Rice, B., 373
Richardson, B. L., 435
Ritter, B., 391
Roazen, P., 41, 57, 103
Rod-and-frame test, 437–438, 440
Rogers, C. R., 95, 212, 215, 273–292, 297
Role Construct Repertory (REP) Test, 337–340
   337–340
Rootedness need (Fromm), 154
Rorer, L. G., 343
Rorschach, H., 12
Rorschach Inkblot Test, 12, 62, 94, 159, 179, 212,
   234, 289, 313, 413, 436, 439
Rosen, B. C., 433
Ross, D., 18, 381
Ross, J., 93
Ross, S. A., 18, 381
Rotating-room test, 439
Rotter, J. B., 119, 326, 373, 397, 402–416, 438
Roundtree, J., 415
R technique, 237
Rubin, R., 264

Rubins, J. L., 127, 139
Ryckman, R. M., 415

Sadistic behavior:
  Freud, 52
  Fromm, 150
Safety needs:
  Horney, 128–130
  Maslow, 300, 302–303
Salmon, P., 340
Sarason, I. G., 393
Satiation (Skinner), 363
Saunders, J. T., 365
Schachter, S., 118, 183
Schedules of reinforcement (Skinner), 359–361
Schultz, D. P., 4
Schultz, S. E., 4
Schur, M., 39
Schwartz, D. W., 441
Sechrest, L., 341, 404
Secondary needs (Murray), 174
Secondary-process thought (Freud), 43
Secondary traits (Allport), 201
Security needs:
  Fromm, 148–151, 153–155
  Horney, 128–130
Self:
  Adler, 108
  Allport, 205–206
  Bandura, 387–390
  Jung, 78
  Rogers, 279–282
Self-actualization:
  Jung, 88
  Maslow, 300, 304–316
  Rogers, 277–278
Self-analysis (Horney), 139
Self archetype (Jung), 85
Self-concept (Rogers), 287–290
Self-control (Skinner), 363
Self-efficacy (Bandura), 388–390, 392–393
Self-esteem (Allport), 206
Self-esteem need (Maslow), 300, 303
Self-image:
  Allport, 206
  Horney, 135–136
Self orientation (Fromm), 160
Self-regard (Rogers), 280
Self-reinforcement:
  Bandura, 387–388
  Skinner, 363
Self-report inventories, 10–12
Self-sentiment (Cattell), 229
Sensing (Jung), 79–81
Sentence-completion technique, 14, 413
Sentiments (Cattell), 227–229
Serials (Murray), 182
Sex differences, in achievement motivation,
  434–435

  in play constructions, 262, 263
  in psychological differentiation, 440–441
Sex drive (Freud), 41
Sexual development (*see* Psychosexual stages of
  development)
Shadow archetype (Jung), 84–85
Shaping (Skinner), 361–362
Sheer function pleasure (Murray), 175
Shostrom, E. L., 313, 315
Shrauger, J. S., 415
Siegel, L. J., 393
Silverman, L. H., 61
Silverman, R. E., 415
Sixteen Personality Factor (16PF) Test (Cattell),
  94, 225–227, 234–236, 238
Skinner, B. F., 6, 63, 95, 212, 291, 349–373, 379,
  383, 385, 390, 396–398, 403–405, 407, 416
Skinner box, 357–358, 371–372
Smith, D., 291
Smith, J., 433
Sociability temperament (Buss & Plomin), 444,
  448–449
Social character (Fromm), 152, 159–160
Social influences:
  Adler, 107–110
  Bandura, 379–380
  Cattell, 230
  Erikson, 251–257
  Fromm, 157
  Rogers, 278
  Rotter, 403–404
Social interest:
  Adler, 109–110, 117–118
  Maslow, 309
Social Interest Index (SII), 117, 118
Social Interest Scale (SIS), 116–117
Social learning:
  Bandura, 378–398
  Rotter, 402–416
Source traits (Cattell), 225–227
Spearman, C. E., 222
Spencer, C., 340
Spranger, E., 211
Standardization of tests, 10
Steele, R. S., 25
Stephenson, W., 288
Sterba, R. F., 120
Stern, G. G., 181
Stern Activities Index, 181
Stewart, R. A. C., 315
Stolorow, R. D., 24
Strassberg, D. S., 415
Stricker, L. J., 93
Strumpfer, D., 183
Strupp, H. H., 287
Study of Values, 196, 211
Style of life (Adler), 107–109
Sublimation (Freud), 49
Subsidiation:

Cattell, 229
Murray, 175
Successive approximation (Skinner), 361–362
Suinn, R., 289
Sullivan, H. S., 127, 148
Sulloway, F. J., 16, 41
Superego:
Cattell, 231
Erikson, 254
Freud, 44–46, 54, 137, 140
Horney, 137, 140
Murray, 171–172, 177
Rogers, 280
Superiority (Adler), 106–107
Superiority complex (Adler), 105
Superstitious behavior (Skinner), 362–363
Surface traits (Cattell), 224
Symbiotic relatedness (Fromm), 152
Symptom analysis (Jung), 92
Synchronicity principle (Jung), 86
Syndromes (Cattell), 224
Syntality (Cattell), 230

Tatsuoka, M. M., 225
T-data (Cattell), 234
Temperament traits (Cattell), 224
Temperaments (Buss & Plomin), 444–449
Tension reduction:
Freud, 40
Murray, 170
Themas (Murray), 176
Thematic Apperception Test (TAT), 12–14, 159,
168, 169, 179, 180, 183, 185, 212, 234, 289,
313, 413, 426–427, 436, 439
Thinking (Jung), 79–80
Thorndike, E. L., 223
Toilet training:
Cattell, 231
Erikson, 253
Freud, 52–53
Token-economy technique, 364–365
Tomkins, S. S., 24, 197
Tomlinson, T. M., 286
Traits:
Allport, 199–201, 210–211
Cattell, 223–238
Transcendence need (Fromm), 153–154
Transcendence principle (Jung), 88
Transpersonal unconscious (Jung), 82
Tresemer, D. W., 435
Tribich, D., 63
Trust, interpersonal (Rotter), 412, 414
Tseng, M., 117
Tucker, G. H., 5
Turner, R. H., 290

Twins, 230, 445–447
Type A personality, 183

Unconditional positive regard (Rogers), 280
Unconscious level of personality:
Freud, 42
Jung, 81–83
Unique traits (Cattell), 224
Unity principle (Jung), 89
Unity-themas (Murray), 176
Urethral complex (Murray), 178

Validity of tests, 10
Value-vectors (Murray), 176
Van de Castle, R., 62, 140
Vanderlippe, R., 290
Verbal choice techniques, 413–414
Vernon, P. E., 211, 213
Veroff, J., 434
Vicarious reinforcement (Bandura), 379
Viscerogenic needs (Murray), 174

Walden Two (Skinner), 367
Walters, R. H., 380, 382
Waterman, A. S., 264
Waterman, C. K., 264
Watson, J. B., 6, 298, 350, 355
Weber, M., 430
Weir, W. R., 315
Wertheimer, M., 299, 312
Wexley, K. N., 365
Wichern, F., 416
Widiger, T. A., 343
Wilcox, S., 434
Wilson, G., 94
Wilson, G. D., 238
Winfree, P., 289
Winter, D. G., 183, 432
Winterbottom, M. R., 433
Wirt, R. D., 14
Wishes (Freud), 40
Withdrawal-destructiveness (Fromm), 152
Witkin, H. A., 340, 436–443
Wittels, F., 103
Wolk, S., 415
Wolpert, E. A., 62
Womb envy (Horney), 137
Word-association technique, 14, 91–92
Wundt, W., 5–7

Yoe, M. R., 92

Zaccaria, J. S, 315
Zigler, E., 290

Credits

This page constitutes an extension of the copyright page.